Cross-Cultural Psychology: Why Culture Matters

A Volume in
Advances in Cultural Psychology:
Constructing Human Development

Series Editor:
Jaan Valsiner

Advances in Cultural Psychology:
Constructing Human Development

Jaan Valsiner
Series Editor

Cross-Cultural Psychology: Why Culture Matters

Krum Krumov
Knud S. Larsen

≡IAP

INFORMATION AGE PUBLISHING, INC.
Charlotte, NC • www.infoagepub.com

Library of Congress Cataloging-in-Publication Data

The CIP data for this book can be found on the Library of Congress website (loc.gov).

Paperback: 978-1-62396-316-3
Hardcover: 978-1-62396-317-0
E-Book: 978-1-62396-318-7

Printed in the United States of America

CONTENTS

For the White Rose Society who lit the torch of resistance in the darkest night.

FOREWORD

Life is getting increasingly complex and the evolution of culture is both rapid and ubiquitous. For example, very recent research continues to demonstrate the improvement in IQ scores that has occurred steadily for nearly 30 years and all across the curve. These cognitive improvements specifically reflect abstract thinking and collateral changes in societies that started with the industrial revolution across large parts of the world. Although improvements in intelligence occur in components thought to be hardwired, biology cannot explain the historically rapid across the board change that must therefore reflect salient alterations in our global culture. Globalization has occurred collateral with IQ improvement and is ubiquitous in affecting nearly all cultures. Therefore many of the cultural values found in past research must be reevaluated in the present and replication work is essential for a reliable and valid cross-cultural psychology in the future.

This book reflects these varying influences and the great debates that continue between cultural and cross-cultural psychology. We favor inclusive approaches to understand both the deeper meanings of unique cultural contributions, but also what is universally found through comparative research. The great division between collectivistic societies and individualistic cultures are further examined for behavioral differences and values. The

Cross-Cultural Psychology: Why Culture Matters, pages ix–xi.
Copyright © 2013 by Information Age Publishing
All rights of reproduction in any form reserved.

research on the Big Five suggests a deep universal structure of personality upon which cultures can write unique messages. At the same time we have also allowed space for a consideration of indigenous research as we are aware of the ethnocentric bias that can be present in the transfer of Western models to more cooperative and collectivistic societies.

These basic theoretical concerns are discussed throughout the book. For example, the changing world is examined in chapter 1, especially the relationship of cross-cultural psychology to the dynamic and continuous cultural evolution in the world. In particular the reader is introduced to the salient differences between comparative cross-cultural psychology and indigenous psychology, and to the presence of culturally universal and unique values, and the potential ethnocentric bias in the research conducted by cross-cultural psychology. Chapter 2 was written with the goal of providing the logical tools essential to critical thinking in cross-cultural psychology and especially emphasizes the importance of the construct of equivalence. The origin of culture is discussed in chapter 3 where the book makes in this and succeeding chapters a strong case for the evolutionary basis of cultural development and the dual inheritance model for cultural transmission. In chapter 4 on human development the research on socialization and enculturation is evaluated along with cognitive, moral and psycho-social development. In particular we discussed that the maximizing of inclusive fitness is the basic motivation for human behavior in all its forms.

A basic and unique feature of human evolution is language and socioculture discussed in chapter 5. The existing research supports the Darwinian model for understanding phylogenetic tree-like evolution of languages and collateral sociocultural evolution. Chapter 6 is devoted to cognition believed to have derived from initial sensation and perception. The chapter evaluates the validity of cognitive styles, collectivistic and individualistic thinking, and the historical differences between Greek and Asian cognition expressed in logical and dialectical thinking processes. Emotion and human happiness are discussed in chapter 7. The biological evolutionary and universal basis of emotional life is strongly supported by the research literature although display rules may vary between cultures. The chapter argues strongly for a positive psychology of human emotion and corresponding social policies. Chapter 8 integrates the discussion on Western, Eastern and indigenous approaches to personality theory. Major theoretical approaches are discussed from the viewpoint of each theoretical orientation along with the research that supports the ubiquitous presence of the Big Five traits. The chapter also evaluates the contributions of Buddhism and Confucian thought to our understanding of personality. The related topic of the self and self-concepts are discussed in chapter 9, in particular cultural, social and cross-cultural contributions to our understanding of self-hood. The chapter highlights the discussion of the so-called "hard" and "easy" problem, and the hard problem of understanding the nature of the "knower" remains to be solved in the authors' opinions. Major theories on the development of the self are discussed. Chapter 10 discusses the cultural implications of the research on sex and gender. Although the feminist "revolution" has altered gender relationships in the Western world with some overlap in many other regions there are still salient differences in the treatment of the genders supported by the traditional versus egalitarian sex role ideology. Violence against women is paradoxically related to traditional views that devalue the role of women in society. Work is central to human life and is discussed in chapter 11. The effects of globalization and the significant research based on the Hofstede work-related values are discussed. The differences between collectivistic and individualistic cultures continue to influence work-related behavior. Finally, chapter 12 discusses the relationship between culture and health. The injustice of health disparities are directly related to socio-economic injustice. The chapter also provides a discussion on abnormal behavior as understood from both cultural and comparative approaches. From the point of view of a positive psychology well-being ought to be the first cause of both cross-cultural and cultural psychology.

As the reader can observe from these introductory remarks the book is comprehensive in coverage. The theme of evolution is supported by research in all comparative fields. The supporting biology for human cultural evolution can also be observed from collateral research. Reading this book should give the student many tools with which to understand cultural developments globally and in society.

CHAPTER 1

CROSS-CULTURAL PSYCHOLOGY IN A CHANGING WORLD

While the field of cross-cultural psychology has a moderately long history a major and rapid expansion in research has occurred over the last decades due to the opportunities derived from globalization and increased contacts between peoples of different regions and cultures. Many would agree that cultural diversity in all its ramifications is one of the largest challenges in a world that is increasingly integrated economically and in communication. Unfortunately along with increased contacts we have also observed more cultural or ethnic strife facilitated by differences in religious or ancestral myths. Together these events have increased an interest in cross-cultural psychology both from theoretical aspects but also from the perspective of practical applications. Journals devoted specifically to cross-cultural research like the Journal of Cross-cultural Psychology have been published for over several decades. Likewise the major journals of social psychology have published an increasing number of research articles focusing on cultural contributions to behavior and cross-cultural comparative research. While psychologists in the past often thought that their theories were ap-

Cross-Cultural Psychology: Why Culture Matters, pages 1–26.
Copyright © 2013 by Information Age Publishing

plicable universally, there is now a more cautious and humble recognition that behavior is mediated by cultural values.

Cross-cultural psychology is a *comparative research* approach that examines the parameters of psychological variables from varying cultural perspectives. However, whatever is learned in a field of study is framed and limited by our research methods. Without comparative or cultural analysis we would learn nothing about differences and similarities between people of varying cultures. Cross-cultural psychology is defined as a comparative discipline studying the cultural factors that influence or determine behavior. The comparative method requires the inclusion of participants from more than one cultural group and compares psychological assessments for observed similarities and differences. This definition requires an analytical ability on the part of the researcher to determine what matters in behavior from that which is trivial or insignificant. In this process we seek to establish the relationship between norms and values in behavior and how these differ in various cultural groups. Some researchers have focused on interactions between participants from different cultures and how these contacts have produced enduring or transitory traits in groups. For example the crusades brought together Christian and Muslim warriors under violent conditions, and even though this contact occurred many centuries ago the real or mythological effects of these interactions affect attitudes in the Arab world today.

1.1. BEHAVIOR AS CULTURE SPECIFIC OR UNIVERSAL

Common sense and travelling experience tell us that we have much more in common with members of even the most discrepant cultures than our differences (e.g. Schmitt, Allik, McCrae, & Benet-Martinez, 2007). We share with all peoples a common genetic heritage, and share with many cultures a more recent ancestor and a common geneographic journey. These common human factors led to deep structured *universal behavioral responses* that all peoples in the world would recognize as human such as nurturing and protecting children and cherishing the family unit. Universals refer to behavior and antecedents that are common to many and perhaps all cultures in the world (Berry, Poortinga, Segall, & Dasen, 1992). Others have found important similarities in the structure of personality in varying countries studied including the Big Five (neuroticism, extraversion, openness to experience, agreeableness, and conscientiousness (Costa, Terracciano, & McCrae, 2001; McCrae & Costa, 1997; Schmitt et al., 2007).

Berry et al advocated a global psychology that eventually would be achieved by integrating knowledge from major cultural research contributions, although they also recognized the wide variations in how these universals are displayed in behavior. Yang (2000) argued that even psychology that is developed indigenously in individual cultures (emic) will collectively serve the long-term purpose of developing a balanced global psychology.

Berry et al discussed three orientations in cross-cultural psychology. *Absolutism* is the perspective that people are essentially the same everywhere and that psychological phenomenon is not affected by culture. Basic human qualities like honesty or decency have the same connotation and culture contributes little to the underlying meaning of psychological constructs. This perspective comes from naïve cross-cultural experiences that recognize what all human beings have in common regardless of varying cultures. Therefore from the perspective of absolutism psychological testing and experimentation just requires accurate translations. On the other hand *relativism* is the perspective that all human behavior is conditioned by culture and we will never understand the deeper meanings of behavior except by evaluating the cultural context. A major motivator in *relativism* is to avoid the error of psychological ethnocentrism by trying to understand indigenous values and context. Psychological testing must therefore not only be accurate in translation but must also be made from valid conceptual comparisons. However, since meeting such criteria are never or rarely possible few cross-cultural comparisons can be made. The third perspective is *universalism* that is found somewhat midway between the other two orientations. *Universalism* contends that the basic psychological phenomenon is common to all members of the human species, but the development and manifestations of behavior are culture dependent. In the universal perspective psychological assessments must take into account the underlying cultural processes and produce culturally relevant versions. Although Berry et al defended the distinctiveness of these three conceptions others generally recognize only universalism (etic) found in cross-cultural research and absolutism (emic) rooted in indigenous approaches in studying psychological phenomenon. Berry et al argued in favor of universalism since it accepts the role of culture in producing diversity in behavior, while acknowledging the basic psychological phenomenon as common features of our human species.

1.2 THE ETIC AND EMIC APPROACHES

Some psychological attributes are common to the human heritage. We all share a genetic inheritance that has produced psychological processes common to all members of the species. However, the specific way these processes are manifested may be dependent on cultural variables. Therefore, while all humans have emotions, motivations and experience sensation and perception culture moderate how these processes are experienced. We shall learn more about what is universal in all human beings and what is culture specific in the chapters to come (Norenzayan & Heine, 2005).

According to Berry (1969) the distinction between the *emic* and *etic* approaches in cross-cultural psychology can be defined by behaviors that are either culturally specific versus those that can be observed in many cultural groups. The etic approach studies behavior by comparing varying cultures from a perspective that is outside the culture studied and with a conceptual framework that is not culturally dependent. Comparative studies are the foundation of cross-cultural psychology. The analytic conceptual structure in comparative studies is invented by the researcher based on a psychological phenomenon thought to be universal. On the other hand, the emic approach studies behavior from the perspective of the cultural values in a given culture and therefore examines only one culture in depth. The underlying psychological phenomenon in a culture is discovered in the process of emic research, and not a priori imposed by the investigator as in cross-cultural research. The subject matter is therefore only the culturally dependent traits or characteristics. The emic approach is fundamentally anthropological as the argument is made that behavior can only be understood within a cultural context by investigators conversant with that culture, therefore necessitating the in-depth involvement with informants of cultural practices and values. The researcher becomes a participant observer trying to discover cultural values, norms and customs.

From the etic perspective the communality of the human experience is sufficient to develop reasonable cross-cultural comparisons. The danger however, is ethnocentric bias since the conceptual framework underpinning the research may be based on the researchers' own culture that may be less or not relevant to the group being studied. In that sense researchers are working with what Berry called "imposed etics," although these can be progressively changed to more closely align with the culture under investigation (Ekstrand & Ekstrand, 1986).

1.3. CROSS-CULTURAL PSYCHOLOGY AND CULTURAL/ INDIGENOUS PSYCHOLOGY

Cross-cultural psychology is more than a comparative method. It is an attempt to understand human behavior within a globalized world of diverse norms and values. As a discipline it is interested in observed differences that we think of as culture-specific that in turn have cognitive or behavioral consequence. At the same time cross-cultural psychology is also sensitive to *universal* psychological phenomena by discovering and describing phenomena true for all people in all cultures. *Cross-cultural psychology is a general psychology in the context of varying cultures since it has an interest in all psychological processes including language development, cognition, emotion, child rearing, and abnormal behavior.* However, most psychological knowledge has been developed in the Western world with researchers in the US as dominant contributors. This fact indicates the importance of understanding the limits and application of this knowledge within the context of different cultural groups.

Cultural psychology, on the other hand, is emic since it seeks conceptual understanding within one culture (e.g. Segall, Dasen, Berry, & Poortinga, 1999). A major concern of cultural psychology is to examine how a particular culture is internalized and the consequences to developmental processes. From this perspective psychological outcomes are a consequence of the interaction between the individual and the culture that can only be understood by those conversant with the specific cultural values, norms and history.

Cross-cultural psychology seeks to learn if our knowledge base about human behavior is applicable to people everywhere, or if it is culturally specific. As a science it is especially important to know if psychological assessments used to create knowledge are applicable, or specific to cultural groups. Cultural diversity in research results appears to be ubiquitous at least conceptually. However, as noted, some argue that rather than developing a cross-cultural psychology that examines differences and similarities between cultures we should develop psychology within cultures. However, such a multi-cultural psychology will not be easily reducible to a single global psychology applicable in all cultures (Gergen, Gulerce, Lock, & Misra, 1996).

Indigenous psychology is largely a rebellion against the dominance of Western psychology in academic research. Western psychology developed in relatively affluent areas of the world with only minimal attention focused on what matters to the vast majority of people in the developing world. People in these struggling societies cope with significant problems of poverty, limited access to resources, disease at alarming rates, and low educational levels. These salient differences have motivated an independent force of psychologists to develop unique psychologies bounded by the context of single cultural societies (e.g. Hwang, 2012). Hwang discusses the uniqueness of filial duty as an unconditional positive duty within Confucian culture. Indigenous psychology takes the relativist point of view of cultural psychology, but as defined by indigenous researchers rather than social scientists from other cultures (Hwang & Yang, 2000).

However, since both the cross-cultural and cultural approaches seek understanding within the cultural context some feel they should be considered complementary rather than oppositional (Sinha, 1997). One approach is to see how various indigenous psychologies relate and overlap with one another. Some efforts are being made to develop culturally unique personality dimensions although there are many difficulties in comparing various indigenous theories (Kim & Berry, 1993). In the Philippines attempts have been made to develop a complete theory of psychology based on indigenous concepts (Enriquez, 1990). In support of a global theory of psychology researchers have noted significant similarities of Philippine psychological concepts with the personality theory developed in the Western world despite the independent development of each approach (Guanzon-Lapena, Church, Carlota, & Katigbak, 1998). Some believe that indigenous psychologies are a necessary step toward building universal theories of psychology.

1.4. CULTURE VERSUS ETHNICITY AND RACE

Within a multicultural society like the United States the psychological variability between ethnic groups is perceived as caused by differences rooted in culture (Shiraev & Boyd, 2001). *Ethnicity* may refer to a common cultural heritage of immigrants even in the distant past and maintained by ethnic organizations in music and dance. Ethnic identity can also be found in recent immigrants who have maintained a cultural relationship. However, ethnic group membership should not be confused with national identity since there are several or many ethnic groups in most nations today. Furthermore, the borders of ethnic groups may overlap with several nations. It is also possible to have several national groups within an ethnic category creating complexities in the concept of national identity.

Ethnicity is defined as the possession of a common cultural heritage based on geographical origin, but also possessing similar language, religion and historical traditions. Ethnicity may for many people be another word for race. However, *racial identification* provides little useful information about the cultural context. The student of cross-cultural psychology needs to know what factors link ethnicity to psychological differences between people for example as observed in emotional display, cognition or motivation. Phinney (1996) suggested that for ethnic identity to have value specific links must be established between cultural norms and values and behavior. A related issue is the relative strength of ethnic identity. If the role of ethnicity is weak in the individual it is not likely to have much influence on behavior. In turn the strength of ethnic identity probably depends on the relative acceptance of the ethnic minority within the dominant society and the route of acculturation.

A nation, on the other hand, refers to people who not only share a common origin along with history and language, but are unified as a political state and recognized as such. That might seem too narrow a definition for some peoples like the Kurds that meet all the criteria of nationhood, for example, possess a relatively independent territory in the north of Iraq, but have members of the Kurdish nationality living also in both Iran and Turkey. Likewise the Palestinian people are by all rights an autonomous nation, and would have become a national state except by the imposed refugee status and occupation.

Countries have a culture based on their salient cultural history, their type of government, and economy. If the economic base does not meet minimal living requirements it produces a constant struggle for survival that influences the development of culture and the relative authoritarianism of governments. Increasingly because of globalization we observe the creation of cultural enclaves within sovereign countries. The Hispanic community in California, and the Vietnamese community in the U.S. created after the end of the war are but two examples from many that function within cultural enclaves.

Race is also considered an important social category for identity development although the physical characteristics thought by many people to be most important are of insignificant functional use in distinguishing between people on any meaningful psychological dimension. Rushton (1995) described race as based on a combination of heritable traits, but chiefly morphological characteristics that produce varying visual impressions. It is important to remember that in all races there are overlapping traits, for example, the red hair often associated with the Irish is also present in Afghanistan, and even some Africans have red hair. The different physical appearance of race has occurred because of regional isolation and the forces of evolution, and really has little functional value except for arbitrary evaluations and categories (Brace, 2005). *Race categorization* has created considerable conceptual confusion with some researchers proposing as many as 37 different races. Although most people recognize the physical characteristics of race these morphological traits are as noted of little importance in behavior.

The most important consideration with respect to race categorization is to remember there is always more within race category variability on any genetic based trait including blood groups (and also in other physiological indicators) than differences between groups. It has been argued that race is more of a social construct than one based on biology, and developed from the natural human need to organize and categorize the world (Hirschfield, 1996). Although there is little biological differentiation on the basis of genetic and other biological distinctions, race is a powerful social construct with many very real negative consequences from prejudice and discrimination (Smedley & Smedley, 2005). It is culture that determines attitudes toward racial categories and therefore the meaning of racial constructs.

1.5. ALL GROUPS WITH A SIGNIFICANT HISTORY HAVE CULTURE

All organizations with a history have cultural values. These values are often passed by the founder defining the normative context of behavior and ethics of the organization. Organizations take a variety of forms in modern society from political parties, to religious organizations or even gangs. All lasting groups have either explicit norms that govern behavior, or implicit rules that people conform to in order to stay a member.

The differences between males and females within societies are also reinforced by varying gender cultures. Gender roles generally define what society deems to be appropriate behavior. There are large differences in gender culture between fundamentalist societies and norms found in modern liberal countries. Gender roles are impacted by the history of the larger society, and what today is considered appropriate in one society (like nude bathing) may be the subject of severe sanction in another country. In some societies women have virtually no life outside the home, whereas in others particularly in the Scandinavian countries the genders are largely treated with equality both in the workplace and in society.

The term "popular culture" is also used frequently today to connote popular music and dominant fashions or other fads. Since these preferences exist within groups of people popular culture share some common features that have psychological consequences. For example, the psychedelic culture of the past produced musical preferences and in some case drug dependency and addiction. Keep in mind that part of any definition of culture is the persistence of behavior over time. Since musical preferences and popularity of expressions in fashion and arts often change with the passage of time the cultural influence is likely to be limited.

1.6. TOWARD AN INCLUSIVE DEFINITION OF CULTURE

Culture consists of attitudes and values shared within a group that is often symbolized in explicit objects like the national flag and in music and are communicated from one generation to the next. Attitudes can take many forms from supporting political ideology to investing emotions and beliefs in religious morality norms (Larsen, 1972). Cultural values can also be manifested in the general opinions held within a society concerning a variety of objects and situations and also form the basis of attitudes toward citizens of other countries or other ethnic groups. Most groups facilitate the development of stereotypes, the generalized beliefs we have about minorities or other national groups. Culturally based values and attitudes also have behavioral components found in the customs and traditions of a society and in the roles people play in the social hierarchy. The land people live on has a great culturally symbolic meaning as we can observe in the uneven contest between the Israelis and Palestinians. Clearly the same land has great symbolic meaning to both groups (Brislin, 2000).

Berry, Poortinga, Segall, and Dasen (1992) defined culture by utilizing six broad categories. The descriptive perspective notes the major highlights of behaviors in a culture. The historical definition examines the traditions and other heritage of a people. The normative definition describes the values, norms and rules characteristic of the culture. From a psychological perspective problem solving approaches, learning and typical behaviors are discussed. All cultures can also be understood from a structural point in how society is organized. Finally, the genetic perspective examines the origin of a culture in either factual or mythological terms, or often a combination of both.

Baumeister (2005) focused on the information capabilities of a society that allows people to cope with the environment and satisfy a variety of physical and psychological needs. Culture is what allows people to live together in an organized way and provide rules and rituals establishing a sense of social solidarity. Culture is transmitted from one generation to the next, but not without alteration. The music and dance of society is what contributes to meaning and a sense of continuity. Culture encompasses more than meeting needs for survival although that is essential. Culture and the resources available determine our food consumption and the type of shelters developed. Culture also largely determines how we meet members of the opposite sex, and under what conditions we have children and provide for their protection. In some societies the issues around marriage and offspring are very strict whereas in other cultures gender relations are relaxed.

Cultures frame very complex human relationships and the behavior that is considered normal in society. Certain cultures allow people to expand their horizons thereby encouraging creativity. The development of science is a unique feature of human society, which in turn brought about exploration from the minimalist world to outer space. We are now only at the very frontiers of space knowledge and the coming decades have very exciting possibilities for the development of knowledge about the universe. None of these achievements would have been possible without the cultural contributions of mathematics and science. Improving society is a feature of human development partly a cultural product, but also the consequence of the evolution of the brain resulting in our complex cognitive abilities that enable us to learn and adapt.

It is important to remember that a person's mental life is not only the product of culture, but that people are also free to act and exercise free will in influencing society. According to Vygotsky (1930/1997) people are capable of goal directed behavior in interaction with the environment that he calls "activity." Psychological states like emotion, cognition, and motivation cannot be separated from activity. In turn human activity is determined by the socio-economic, environmental, political and other cultural conditions. However, goal directed behavior interacting with the environment is itself a process that also changes human activity. Any definition of culture must take into account the interaction between goal directed human activity and cultural conditions.

It seems obvious that children who grow up under conditions of human socio-economic desperation will develop psychological traits quite different than those who are born into safe and affluent conditions. Children who

are forced to combine economic dependency with mind numbing constric-
tions of religious or political fundamentalism will also display more conformity compared to children developing in more liberal societies. Cultures
differ in the dominant activities for survival and their subsequent human
psychology.

Obviously culture is a very complex concept that is relevant to many areas of life. The broad scope of culture makes any simplified definition of
little use (Malpass, 1993). The concept of culture also has obviously different salient meanings. A Danish definition may refer to the food traditions,
whereas in Saudi Arabia the teaching of the Koran would come to mind for
most of the inhabitants.

1.6.1. Culture is the Evolution of Human Society

Culture is the strategic response to the survival needs of society. Evolutionary psychology would argue that culture is a direct outcome of reproductive success and biological fitness (Buss, 2001). People who can adapt
to their environment through social organization are more likely to leave
offspring and ensure continuity in the future. In the course of social development people have learned to solve a variety of issues and problems
that allowed adaptation to a particular ecological context. In Greenland
the Scandinavian colony eventually died out because they did not adapt to
the harsh climate and the need to rely on the sea for food, but rather continued with their European herding practices and primitive agriculture. By
contrast the local Inuit people continued to function and adapt without in-
terruption as their food was largely available from hunting and fishing. The
culture of the native Inuit population was adaptive leading to reproductive
success and survival.

Population density affects culture in many ways. Social control is a problem in very densely populated societies like Singapore, and the response
is frequently more hierarchical and authoritarian societies. Authoritarian
cultures produce concomitant psychological functioning attributes that are
useful to survival like conformity. Modern affluent societies have an impact
on cultural values producing increased individualism. As a nation becomes
more affluent there is less of a need to rely on other members of society
thus contributing to the atomization of society. Affluence has produced
new forms of communication in computer technology that do not depend
on the physical presence of co-workers again reducing the need to rely on
others or on face to face contacts.

Culture contribute to solving many social issues and problems including
the development of leadership and group hierarchies, establishing territory
for hunting or agriculture and protecting society against cultural competi-
tors, establishing social bonds that ensure protection of children, and organizing the fight against the vicissitudes of the natural world (Buss, 2001).

Many issues salient to survival must be addressed by a cultural group including proper housing, developing an economy, organizing transportation for trade and exchanges, developing a community to ensure continuity, and forming religion or science to deal with issues that are not understood by common sense. Biological needs essential for survival became part of the habitual traditions of the group and directly impacted the social motivation in society. In short culture is produced by the interaction between biological needs and social solutions. Authoritarian structures develop more likely in societies threatened with an inability to meet biological needs as rapid and decisive responses may be required in an unforgiving ecological environment.

Sociobiology is the field that establishes links between biological determinants and human behavior. The essential claim of sociobiology contends that biological laws are the foundation of all human behavior and explain also the development of culture. The prime goal of human groups is survival and culture is a means to that end. To survive and prosper requires resources including developing adequate food resources.

Cultural values also determine decisions about potential marital partners and culture has found successful ways to protect children until they achieve independence. The foundation of sociobiology is social Darwinism. The principle of natural selection ensured that humans that are ecologically fit are more likely to survive and leave offspring than people who are less adaptive. This idea has been summarized in the concept of survival of the fittest. The cultures that produce better adjustment to the environment are more likely to have their offspring survive compared to those less fit.

Competition in sociobiology is the key to the development of society and culture by favoring those traits that are most fit and contribute to survival. Over many generations it is believed that traits that favored survival became encoded genetically and eventually became the dominant behavioral pattern in society. The culture of some societies favors individuals that show the initiative and curiosity essential for scientific progress. In other societies the harshness of the ecological environment produced authoritarian strong-men regimes, whereas in yet other cultures societies promoted survival through collectivism and cooperation. The tragedy of the 2011 Tsunami event in Japan demonstrated the ability of a collectivistic society to come together under even the most difficult conditions. Sociobiology makes the claim that significant social behavior has an evolutionary basis including such diverse manifestations as sexual preference, intelligence, cooperation and aggression.

The constant aim of human groups has been to improve survival so members of the culture may live in a better social environment with adequate food, health resources, and political democracies reflecting the will of the people. The Arab Spring showed that the dictators of the world (particularly in the Middle East) did not promote a culture that met fundamental biological needs, nor the needs for decision participation by their citizens. These cultures were not "fit" from the evolutionary perspective of sociobiology and despite military oppression did not prosper in the past or will not survive in the long run future.

1.6.2. Animal and Human Culture

Culture is a response of human groups to the environment seeking to develop solutions to problems of adaptation. Since animals and indeed all life also have to adapt to survive it can be argued that animals too have culture. The cooperation of a wolf pack in hunting or herd animals in protecting their vulnerable members are a form of culture that serves adaptive needs. Animals have also evolved hierarchies and social behaviors like grooming. In modern times we have become aware of animals that use tools like the chimpanzee employment of sticks to fish for termites (Whiten, Horner, & De Waal, 2005). Animals too have evolved solutions to adapt and meet basic requirements of survival (Boesch, 2003).

Yet there are complexities in human culture not found in the animal world. Although animals can communicate they do not possess a language that can symbolize the physical and mental worlds. The very ability to write and reduce language to symbols on paper is a unique human act. The ability to attribute intentions to other people and therefore predict their behavior appears to be another unique human trait. Human culture is constantly evolving by means of more adaptive solutions to survival. The current knowledge explosion is a manifestation of this unique human trait to improve life and seek meaning. In general human existence demonstrates an increasingly complex evolution toward more adaptive responses (Tomasello, Kruger, & Ratner, 1993). The process of human culture is toward increasing complexity and variation in the development of adaptive tools.

1.6.3. The Ecological and Sociological Context

Other researchers (e.g. Berry, Poortinga, Segall, & Dasen, 1992) have argued for a broader etiology in the development of culture. The *ecological context* is important since it places limits on what is possible, for example, the variability in the resources that help groups survive. In arid climates skills other than agriculture are needed for humans to have reproductive success. The presence and quality of food has significant influence on human development. Where food is not present in sufficient quantities there is less population density with other important ramifications for the development of society. The socio-political context that defines people's ability to participate in decisions at both the local as well as national and international level is important. Some societies have very little decision latitude and conformity is required for survival. Through generational transmissions an authoritarian ideology develops that ensures cultural survival although not without conflict.

The ecological context is vital in the development of culture. The climate and other ecological factors impact psychology of people directly. In a country where the resources are few survival demands the cooperation of all, whereas in a society with abundant resources there is less need for cooperation. Climate is also a significant factor affecting production and daily activities. When this author worked in the tropical regions of Australia he noted how slowly people moved in the street and at work. After acclimatizing a few days the reason became obvious as movement was determined by the oppressive heat and humidity. Some will argue that climate directly affects the evolution of humans (Behrensmeyer, 2006).

The sociological approach utilizes a structural analysis in understanding culture. Some theories argue that influential cultural structures exist independently of the individual and shape behavior. The norms of society developed out of the need for survival and social stability, and once in place demand obedience from all members. Cultural norms define limits of behavior and regulate society for the benefit of those who have coercive power, and at times also in the interest of all. Collectivistic societies produced a unifying morality and a strong sense of belonging. In the more individualistic society traditions are often overturned breaking down the sense of human solidarity. In extreme situations or in crisis individualism promotes the idea of "every man for himself." That notion is expressed in rational capitalist societies by the values of efficiency and achievement. While the technological revolution is an example of what a rational society can achieve, unfortunately one byproduct is abiding inequality between people. The Marxist critique contend that the ruling classes not only preserve a favored status quo, but also develop an appropriate ideology, create laws, religion and political systems that perpetuate the inequality.

1.7. RESOURCE RICH OR POOR CULTURES.

Many cultural characteristics also bear a relationship to the quantity and quality of resources available. Not only are resources essential for survival and minimal well-being, but also for progressive individual and cultural development. Some societies have great natural wealth and have managed to develop a socio-economic system that exploits it for the benefit of many. Other societies are poor in natural wealth but have developed compensations through intellectual development that ensure secure and decent living of their populations. Yet other societies are poor because their socio-political conditions prevent people from meeting basic needs. So although access to resources may be a critical variable in the development of cultural traits, the socio-political environment places limits on how the culture can respond to its particular challenges. The oil wealth of Arabia has created at least for a time artificial wealth, but the socio-economic conditions have proven dysfunctional leaving many people without decent living or participation in decision-making. Poverty of body or mind is not totally determined by access to resources, but also influenced by political power structure and conformity enforcement.

Nevertheless, poverty is linked to poor health and shorter life spans (World Health Organization, 2003). Typically the poor suffer more from harmful environments and the diseases associated with inferior health care. We know, for example, that malnutrition, a scourge of poor societies, puts individuals at lifelong disadvantages, including damage to intellectual development. The research in cross-cultural psychology reflects the consequences of the inequality brought about by the unequal access to resources (Fowers & Richardson, 1996). That the presence of resources alone does not determine social development can be observed by the poverty in Africa, a continent rich in many essential resources.

One factor of some importance is relative *collectivism* or *individualism* of society. Many authors have noted the presence of interconnectedness in Asian societies where the family and community come before the individual in importance. Even the way Asian people write their names point to this profound difference with family name listed first and the personal name second, the reverse of name listing in Western societies. Many would argue that this interconnectedness is closely linked to the achievements of Chinese and other Asian cultures (Ho, 1998).

Triandis (1996) discussed in detail the individualism-collectivism construct. He suggested it could be best understood as both a vertical and a horizontal dimension. In the vertical cultural syndrome relationships are determined from the point of view of either power or achievements. Communication in these societies is vertical because not all are equal or possess the same power. Vertical relationships include those between employers and workers, or more broadly in society between those who control coercive resources and those who have few or no means to defend themselves. However, even within totalitarian societies people also relate to each other as friends or members of a family with more benevolent and friendly attitudes. Triandis believed that societies broadly reflect these vertical dimensions. For example, totalitarian regimes are likely to emphasize the value of equality at the horizontal level (like we are all equally poor), while not allowing for freedom to act. On the other hand, Kurman and Sriram (2002) maintained that Western democracies emphasized freedom in vertical movement (anyone can become a millionaire), but not the value of equality.

According to Triandis, the population in the United States endorses vertical individualism, and is much more willing to tolerate inequality as the natural order. Living in a "just" society many U.S. citizens believe that inequality in resources is the unfortunate consequence of individual volition. On the other hand, people who live in the social democracies of Northern Europe tend to be intolerant of inequality, and set boundaries for what might be considered a decent and minimal conditions of life. They are willing to be taxed (although not without controversy) to the extent needed to maintain the basic social and ecological conditions of life. Triandis reported that the difference between the top and bottom ten percent of the population is three times higher in the United States as compared to Sweden.

1.8. CULTURAL VALUES AND DIMENSIONS

A major field of study in cross-cultural psychology is the relationship between *cultural behavior* and *cultural values*. Are cultural values human attributes common to all societies or are they particular to a culture? A heuristic area of study is the research done on work-related values by Hofstede discussed below.

1.8.1. Universal Values

Rokeach (1973) was a pioneer in investigations of values and their relationships to human behavior. His theory examined values from two perspectives values: as desirable *end states* that in turn were reached by means of *instrumental* values. Schwartz and Ross (1995) identified seven values thought to be present in all cultures. These included *embeddedness* which defines the importance that cultures place on maintaining the status quo and on behavior considered proper. Embeddedness involves avoiding actions that might disrupt harmony or the solidarity of the group and fostering respect for social institutions, for traditions, and for promoting social expectations of self-discipline. This universal value seems especially salient in Asian societies, and other traditional cultures. *Hierarchy* is a universal value describing how cultures reinforce the legitimacy of hierarchical roles in expressions of social power and the use of authority and wealth. *Mastery* is a value that encourages individuals to get ahead by self-assertion and by dominating the natural and social environments. Mastery as a universal value promotes personal ambition, risk taking, and achievement of competence.

Intellectual autonomy describes the magnitude of cultural support for cognitive independence and the ability of individuals to pursue individually based self-direction. This value seems essential to scientific curiosity and to creative efforts. *Affective autonomy* is a hedonistic value that describes the degree to which cultures support the effort of people to have positive experiences, to find pleasure and excitement in life. *Egalitarianism* measures the extent to which cultures support the common welfare by means of equality and social justice. Egalitarian societies support honesty in dealing with others, social responsibility and individual freedom. Finally, the seventh universal value *harmony* values the ecological environment by supporting the protection of the environment, and by promoting beauty and unity with nature.

Recent research (Schmitt, Allik, McCrae, & Benet-Martinez, 2007) has demonstrated a ubiquitous personality structure that support universal values and traits. A five-dimensional personality structure was discovered confirming previous research on a broad cross-cultural scale. This universal personality model was related in a predictable way to traits like self-esteem, sexuality and national personality profiles. Some regional variation retains an important role for cultural variation. That argument is also supported by the homogeneity in trait expression between neighboring countries sharing a cultural history. On the other hand, trait heterogeneity is larger in European and North American countries. As we shall see strong arguments have also been presented in favor of indigenous psychology building on unique cultural values, for example, Chinese cultural research on Confucian relationism (Hwang, 2012; Hwang, Kim, & Kou-Shu, 2006).

Some researchers (e.g., Sterelny, 2012) would argue that moral thought is variable cross-culturally. Although common moral thought and values govern behavior profound normative differences exist between the cultures studied. These differences are not just in reflective morality based on cognitive processes, but also in moral disgust that has changed in a variety of behaviors in recent years. While moral development is robust since we are biologically adapted for moral thought our developmental environment plays a key role through creating perceptual sensitivity.

1.8.2. Cultural Value Dimensions

Hofstede (2001) examined work related values that were used to describe various societies around the world. The research constitutes one of the most cited studies in both organizational and cross-cultural psychology. Hofstede based his conclusions on data from 72 countries and 117000 employees of a multinational organization that eventually generated five work-related values used to differentiate various societies. The value dimension of *individualism-collectivism* in turn has dominated much of the research in recent years (Gelfand, Erez, & Aycan, 2007). This research will be discussed further in chapter 11 on cultural values and organizational and social behavior.

Some cultures, particularly those in Asia, encourage collectivism where members place their own needs after the interest of the group, family and nation. The loyalty toward the ingroup is thought to be an exchange for the group caring for the individual. For example, in Japan employees in the past could expect lifetime employment in exchange for their loyalty and commitment. People who inhabit collectivistic cultures are thought more likely to conform. In individualistic societies people seek fulfillment away from the workplace as members claim the right to enjoy life. Individual decisions are seen as superior to collective decision making. Since harmony is valued in collectivistic societies individuals are more likely to go along with family and group demands and seek to preserve their interpersonal relations. Triandis (1995) outlined the main attributes of *individualism and collectivism.* In particular the self is construed differently in the two types of culture. The personal self in individualistic societies emphasize the primacy of personal development and achievement. Based on capitalist economics individualistic societies favor exchanges in social interaction rather than the development of supportive communal relationships. On the other hand, broad social norms tend to govern behavior in collectivistic cultures.

The disaster of the tsunami and all that followed showed the collectivistic spirit of Japanese culture (Beech-Akaushi, 2011). The young were quoted as saying "we, the young generation, will unite and work hard to get over this tragedy" (p. 44). The world view of the Japanese is that everyone wanted to share the pain, and therefore we saw little anti-social chaos and minimal looting in the aftermath. It is also thought that the rigid adherence to regulations and rules undoubtedly saved lives, as the collectivistic minded Japanese responded to the tsunami warning and earth quake alerts.

Power distance is another value discovered in Hofstede's research. This construct refers to hierarchical social relationships based on power and status. In general the concept of power distance refers to people's willingness to accept the unequal distribution of power. High power distance cultures can also be described as authoritarian and hierarchal and people are expected to conform and obey. On the other hand, in egalitarian cultures people view each other as at least moral equals, and will find ways to object to injustice. Recent events in the Arab world show that even people in hierarchical societies eventually are fed up and rebel. Only outright tyranny enforced by the willingness to kill can keep these societies from eventually developing more democratic forms of governance. The inequality between people in high power culture societies is arbitrary although front loaded with custom and tradition. The descriptive value of the power inequality concept may therefore be limited to certain social development and historical times.

Uncertainty avoidance is also a value dimension from Hofstede's work that describes the degree to which people feel threatened by the unknown or ambiguous conditions of life. The uncertainty of life is ubiquitous and in response to those conditions people seek security in many ways often by dogmatic interpretations of ideology or religion. However, even the most rigid model must confront changing social realities or are swept aside by their inability to satisfy human needs. Some cultures meet uncertainty by reinforcing rituals that produce a feeling of continuity over generations. Otherwise society may also enforce strict codes of conduct that makes life predictable, and develop rules that determine appropriate conduct. Rituals of greetings were probably developed to reduce uncertainty like the use of handshakes or bowing when meeting strangers or even those who are more intimate. The military hand salute developed out of the desire to show by an open hand that no hostile intent was present. Cultures vary in the degree to which they are comfortable with uncertainty often resulting in obedience behavior and conformity to political and religious institutions. However, seeking such an ersatz safety often prevents the uncertainty that is needed to nurture innovation. Progress in society is less likely without the encouragement of creativity that produces solutions to uncertainty in science and motivates other achievements. For example, entrepreneurship was related to both high individualism and low uncertainty avoidance in a nine country study (McGrath, MacMillan, Yang, & Tsai, 1992). Expressions of emotions are more tightly controlled in cultures that are uncertainty avoidant, and these cultures have less tolerance for discrepant ideas and people.

Hofstede called the fourth value dimension *masculinity-femininity.* Over the course of history men have displayed more dominance and assertiveness than women. The biological differences between the genders brought about an ubiquitous role for women as more nurturing and men being the traditional bread winners. Although sex roles have changed drastically over the past decades, they are a source of constant adjustment and conflict in many cultures. The masculinity-femininity dimension reflects the extent to which cultures continue to emphasize the traditional sex differences in everyday life and also in the work place. Some countries display few gender differences where both genders can now be employed in jobs traditionally dominated by one or the other. Societies that value masculinity emphasize recognition and achievement, and women in these societies are less accepted in higher paying jobs or those requiring strong efforts to qualify.

In more recent research Hofstede and Bond (1984) added a fifth dimension called **the *long-term versus short-term outlook.*** Essentially this value dimension measures the degree to which cultures are willing to delay gratification of various social needs. Some cultures demand immediate satisfaction, and consequently produce a rapid turnover in products. Other societies are more patient, and focus more on building relationships for the long term rather than emphasizing short-term profits. These long-term cultures are more likely to encourage delay in gratification of multiple social, emotional and material needs.

1.8.3. The Social Axioms of Leung and Bond

Leung, Bond, Reimel de Carrasquel, Munoz, Hernandez, Murakami, Yamaguchi, Bierbrauer and Singelis (2002) found evidence for the universal existence of five *social axioms* at the individual level from studies of 41 cultural groups. Social axioms are general beliefs we have of ourselves, about the spiritual world, and about our social and cultural context. In contrast to values axioms are assertions we make between concepts that are used to guide daily living. For example, one assertion is that the meaning of life is found through religious worship. Further work done by Bond, Leung, Au, Tong, Reimel de Carrasquel, Murakami, et al. (2004) demonstrated the cultural level validity of two axioms. *Dynamic externality* is the attempt by people to outwardly, through beliefs in fate or the Supreme Being, make sense of external forces and their consequences. This axiom helps people's psychological mobilization against the tragic problems of life and to deal with environmental difficulties. Cultures that score high on this dimension also tend to be high on conservatism, hierarchy, and collectivism. Societies high on dynamic externality also tend to have less freedom and fewer human rights while aspiring for security and better material resources. *Societal cynicism* is a form of pessimism and apprehension about the conditions of the world. Beliefs associated with this dimension are, for example, that life produces malignant outcomes, and that individuals are subject to selfish and powerful others, groups or institutions. These two cultural values and outlooks on the world overlap to some degree and are not completely independent dimensions (Schwartz, 2004). Also, although guides to behavior these psychological dimensions do not always predict behavior, as peoples beliefs do not conform to behavior all the time (Matsumoto, 2006a).

1.9. ENCULTURATION, CULTURE, AND PSYCHOLOGICAL OUTCOMES

The infant being born into a culture has no cultural attributes. Culture is a learned phenomenon obtained through a process of enculturation where the family is the primary socializing agent. However, other social institutions also play a role as the child grows and develops including the educational system, and other religious, cultural or social organizations. Culture is the communal response to the major external ecological factors confronting the individual. The climate in Africa and Greenland are sufficiently extreme that they have consequences for human development as well as for social institutions keeping in mind that the culture developed out of the need to survive. Social factors also affect child development and reinforce culture for adults as well. All humans also possess a genetic heritage that affects adaptability in various ways through, for example, perceptual response variation. None of these developmental factors are static, but they constantly interact with one another. The world is in a period of great transition for most cultures of the world, and the Internet and new means of communications may turn out to be stronger forces in enculturation than more traditional cultural factors.

Enculturation gradually shapes the individual so cultural world views are internalized and not challenged by most members of cultural groups. Since social pressure is unpleasant most members of society learn early to adapt to these views or experience the penalty of sanctions. Over a period of time culturally congenial attitudes and values are internalized as the "only true way." In turn these attributes are expressed in beliefs about the world and social institutions. On a societal level these forces find expression in social norms and also in behavior.

Globalization has produced new cultural dynamics' in cross-cultural psychology. Some have argued for the need to not only study traditionally accepted cultural categories, but also to understand the increasing contacts within multi-cultural societies and resulting multi-cultural identities (Hermans & Kempen, 1998). Many researchers are working under the illusion of ahistorical cultural development as if societies are static and remain the same for all time. However, what we have observed in the last decades are new combinations of cultures, new arenas of culture, and people possessing multi-cultural identities. Cultures are constantly adapting and changing in response to the realities of the world and to changing power relationships. Some of our cultural information is derived from travel and migration and more and more from the ubiquitous use of computers. Therefore cultural identity is also increasingly dynamic reflecting many sources of influence including those of popular music and scientific development.

Even the most isolated societies can only keep these influences under control to a limited degree. Despite conformity pressures people will chose what and who to believe on questions of personal or social development. The outcome is more heterogeneous cultures encouraging tolerance for the discrepant (Giddens, 2000). It is now quite common for people growing up in European and North American countries to have bi-cultural identities, and even multi-cultural attachments. The typical migrant may bring along the culture of the previous society, may adapt to the culture of the new homeland, and may also be influenced by global culture. These facts require a cross-cultural psychology that has the ability to adapt to these changes and makes obvious the need to replicate previous findings as these may be tenuous with changing times.

1.10. UNDERSTANDING CROSS-CULTURAL PSYCHOLOGY IN A CHANGING WORLD

Cross-cultural psychology has made scientific contributions in understanding human behavior as influenced by the cultural context. In cross-cultural psychology the variability but also the similarities of human behavior is of interest, as influenced by cultural factors, by common genetic inheritance, and by the similarity of human problems in the struggle for survival. Since cross-cultural psychology is a scientific enterprise we are interested in the systematic comparisons between populations under varying cultural situations in order to infer cause and affect relationships for important psychological dimensions. Underlying the interest in the variability in human cultural behavior is the finding that different cultural experiences with childrearing, cultural norms, and socio-economic institutions produce individuals that differ in predictable ways. In the final analysis cross-cultural psychology seeks to understand how culture affects the psychological life of individual human beings (Cole, 1996).

The above definition requires a more specific articulation of what constitutes culture as the term is used in many non-scientific ways. We can speak of people of high social economic standing as having "culture" which may simply mean they have the money to enjoy the good life and fine wine. Culture is also used to describe what is popular in society such as current fads in fashion or music. However, influential these ideas may be they are just a temporary phenomenon—here today but gone tomorrow.

Some researchers have used cross-national as synonymous for cross-cultural, however, cross-national studies can be carried out between culturally related groups like the Danes and the Dutch, and may tell us more about recent socio-economic changes and dynamics than lasting culture (Frijda & Jahoda, 1966). On the other hand, recent years have seen more studies on ethnic groups within nations. These groups seem justified for inclusion in cross-cultural studies as they often maintain particular cultural values over long time periods, and their adjustment to the dominant society is of obvious importance and utility.

Cross-cultural psychology is interested in inferring cause and effect relationships between cultural factors and subsequent behavior. Ultimately the objective is to develop a discipline where cultural variations are seen as antecedents to differences in human behavior by comparing cultural groups on salient psychological dimensions. In the process we become aware of what cultural experiences like language are salient and how these variables may be related to mental life and cognitive processes.

One important distinction is between the concepts of cultural and cross-cultural psychology (Berry, 2000; Poortinga, 1997). *In cultural (indigenous) psychology an individual culture is studied at some depth in order to observe the relationship between cultural determinants and behavior. On the other hand, the cross-cultural (comparative) discipline seeks to study both the similarities and salient differences in psychological behavior and cognition between cultures.* Research suggests that comparative differences occur because of socio-cultural factors, but also as noted from variability in ecological variables like climate, as well as biological factors. In both the cultural and cross-cultural domains we must remain conscious of the effects of rapid socio-economic and scientific change as cultural variables also respond to these forces.

1.11. THE MAJOR OBJECTIVES OF CROSS-CULTURAL PSYCHOLOGY

An important objective in the study of ethnic, cultural and national groups is to determine the validity of salient results and theories. To what extent are commonly accepted Western psychological theories actually *transferable* to other societies and cultures? Dawson (1971) suggested that the importance of cross-cultural research lies in the ability to evaluate the broader universal validity of psychological theories. More recently Segall, Dasen, Berry and Poortinga (1999) suggested that we should not consider any psychological principles as transferable in the absence of valid cross-cultural assessments.

Berry and Dasen (1974) outlined the major objectives for cross-cultural psychology. The first was called the "transport and test" goal where researchers ascertain whether established theories and research findings are valid in other cultural settings. The ultimate goal is to establish universal theories valid for all human beings. However, to reach such universal goals we have to start with what we know in our own culture and then test the validity of these research conclusions in the cross-cultural context. In that process it is also necessary to evaluate what is unique, and in particular the psychological variability and cultural specificity not apparent from our own cultural experience. If we cannot replicate common psychological research findings from our own society what are the reasons? For example, in human development adolescents typically go through a turbulent period known as "storm und drang." An important question could be posed whether adolescents in all societies go through a similar developmental process and whether there are unique cultural variations? The final goal of cross-cultural psychology is to integrate what is universal and that which is culturally specific into a more broadly based universal psychology transferable to all cultures. However, whether it is possible to develop universal laws of human behavior is a conclusion that not all investigators accept (Boesch, 1996).

1.12. THE ETHNOCENTRISM OF PSYCHOLOGY.

Ethnocentrism is ubiquitous in the world. It affects preferential judgments of every kind including evaluations of religion, ideology, and culture. Children already at a very young age have preferences for their own cultural symbols, and view the world through the lenses of their internalized cultural values. Since ethnocentrism is at best a simplification it leads to many errors of judgment. Evaluating all important perspectives from that of one's own culture distorts the truth about other people, and does not take into account the full complexity of other cultures and societies. Unfortunately, ethnocentrism must necessarily also affect cross-cultural psychology. The very choice of what we study is based on the knowledge developed in our own culture, and most cross-cultural research choices seek to expand that knowledge into other groups and societies. Indigenous psychology would argue that topics not studied in the dominant Western based cross-cultural psychology are salient in other cultures. The psychological assessments we make are often based on concepts and instruments that have culturally specific meaning, and can only be translated at the risk of introducing concepts of little or no importance to other cultures. It requires careful translation as well as some evidence of cultural relevance before cross-cultural researchers can validly apply psychological assessments from one culture to another. Likewise the development of psychological theories in general is universally based on Western thought and data. Research based on Western theories applied in other cultures may contain ethnocentric bias and error.

However, these biases can be reduced by following careful procedures, and by inclusion of diverse cultures in the data base. Scientists are not immune from cultural bias and must be on alert for ethnocentric distortion in translation and conceptual development. Replication is needed to establish the validity of any psychological construct, and since times are changing psychological models must respond to these ubiquitous developments. Only over the long run through careful replication work can we be assured of a valid and reliable cross-cultural discipline. In recent decades some researchers have sought to develop a psychology from non-Western approaches. Although only modest research has been completed the development of indigenous psychological models may gather steam in the future (Sinha, 1997). We will discuss this approach in later chapters.

SUMMARY

This chapter provides an overview of the major concepts and issues in cross-cultural psychology. Recent social developments have produced cultural diversity and multi-cultural societies that in turn have expanded an interest in comparative psychology. Cross-cultural psychology is a comparative approach that examines the parameters of general psychological variables in the cultural context. As humans we have much in common based on a similar genetic heritage that is also the basis of universal human traits. Evidence points to the presence of common structures in personality.

The perspective of absolutism argues that people are the same everywhere and therefore there is no need for comparative studies. From that point of view researchers need only ensure accurate translations when studying behavior in various cultures. Relativity is the opposite viewpoint that all human behavior is conditioned by the cultural context and therefore psychological assessments must be based on valid conceptual foundations that are unique to a culture. The outlook found between these extreme points of view is called universalism, essentially arguing that although basic psychological phenomenon is common to all human beings, the development of these and manifestations of behavior are culturally determined.

The concepts of emic and etic describe the difference between universal and culturally specific behavior perspectives.

Cross-cultural and cultural psychology reflects these different perspectives. Cross-cultural psychology utilizes the comparative approach in trying to understand human behavior in a globalized world with still diverse values and norms. We define cross-cultural psychology as general psychology in the comparative cultural context since the subject area includes major topics of interest in psychology. The aim is to develop a science applicable to all cultures in the world. Cultural psychology, on the other hand, is more anthropological as it seeks to understand in depth behavior within a given single culture. Some researchers argue that cultural psychology should be the precursor to the development of an eventual multicultural single psychology valid for all cultures.

Several concepts are used to denote culture with somewhat varying meanings. Cultural ethnicity is not the same as nationality since many different ethnic groups can exist within a single nation. Race as commonly understood refers primarily to visual morphological traits that play no role in human behavior, but because race is a social construct it plays a role in discrimination. A more accurate accounting of race would require the determination of gene frequency distributions. It is important to remember that there are always more within group variability compared to differences between racial or other social categories on any psychological dimension.

However, all groups with a history have culture defining normative behaviors, ethics and values. Genders are also believed to have attributes that meet the test of cultural significance, especially defining what is considered appropriate gender-related behavior. In popular terms culture may also refer to passing fads and fashion and while these may have psychological consequences they generally have no lasting effect.

An inclusive definition of culture requires a consideration of individual influences that mediate the social and ecological context. Cultures consist of attitudes and values expressed in ideology and religion as well as in the socio-economic system. Culture is what allows people to live together in an organized fashion and establishes the parameters of complex human relationships. Cultural products are an outcome of norms that either encourages or discourages creativity and invention. While mental life is one of the products of culture it is well to remember that human beings have volition and are motivated by goal directed behavior. In all cases individual volition interacts with culture.

Culture is the result of social evolution and the direct outcome of reproductive success. In the past cultures allowed people to survive by developing social hierarchies, by protecting its members, and by helping people master the natural world. Sociobiology is the field that links biology to culture as the means to survival in varying ecological contexts. Natural selection ensures that those who are "fit" are more likely to survive than individuals that are less adaptive. As a result genetically based traits that favor survival are encoded in genes and passed from one generation to the next.

Animals can also be defined as having culture since some species cooperate in order to survive as they adapt to the environment. Still the complexities that characterize human culture are not found in the animal world. Humans possess language that permits mental symbolization and the attribution of intentions not present among animals. An inclusive definition of culture must take into account the ecological context of society. The ecological conditions place limits on what members of a culture can do to ensure reproductive success. Climate pressures and the quantity and quality of nutrition contribute to the cultural framework that is developed and may also directly affect the evolution of human beings. In the final analysis it is the interaction between people and the environment that produces culture.

Cultural characteristics develop from the human relationship to quantity and quality of resources. The presence of ample resources alone does not guarantee positive cultural development as that is also dependent on socio-economic conditions. Nevertheless poverty is linked to poor health and shorter life spans. Relative collectivism and individualism are factors of importance in cultivating behavioral responses in people. For example, people living in the US endorse vertical individualism and the ideology of a "just" society. Hence they are more tolerant of inequality compared to people living in the social democracies in Europe.

Cultural dimensions and values have a relationship to human behavior. Some values are universal and thought present in all societies. Hofstede's value dimensions have been used to describe societies throughout the world. Axioms are general beliefs that guide behavior. In contrast with values axioms are assertions that link concepts like the presumed relationship between religion and meaning in life.

Culture is learned through the process of enculturation and the family is the primary source of socialization, but other social institutions also play a role. Culture is the response to the major external factors that confront members of groups in the quest for survival. It is well to bear in mind that the aforementioned etiological factors interact and at the same time the world is going through a period of great socio-economic change that affects even the most isolated peoples in the world. Globalization has also produced new arenas for studying the effects of culture in the development of new multicultural societies. Cultural identity is increasingly dynamic.

The major objective of cross-cultural psychology is to examine whether established psychological theories are transportable to other cultures. An important aim is to determine the broader validity of psychological theories from a more universal perspective, but also to establish behaviors that is culturally unique and specific. Ethnocentrism also affects cross-cultural psychology as the very choice of what we study is based on the researcher's culturally based concepts. Currently research seeks to transport culturally bounded and primarily Western knowledge into other cultures. However, bias can be reduced by following careful procedures and replicating studies over the long run.

CHAPTER 2

RESEARCH APPROACHES AND CRITICAL THINKING IN CROSS-CULTURAL PSYCHOLOGY

The findings of cross-cultural psychology are delimited by the reliability and validity of the research methods used. Since cross-cultural psychology is by far the most complex of the psychological disciplines the student and researcher must develop a critical eye when evaluating research data and results. Furthermore cross-cultural research can be conducted at several levels increasing the possibility that the results contain bias in either the design of the research protocol or in the analysis by the researcher. Therefore, the serious student should consider all possible alternative explanations for the reported outcomes. This chapter will outline the means by which we might evaluate results in both qualitative and quantitative research.

We noted in chapter 1 that there are disagreement as to whether comparative studies can produce valid results given the varying confounding influences and the difficulty of selecting representative sampling. The levels of research refer to both individually based studies based on surveys, interviewing, but also ecological population level variables creating complexity in theoretical analysis. Great care must be employed in evaluating the

Cross-Cultural Psychology: Why Culture Matters, pages 27–51.
Copyright © 2013 by Information Age Publishing

relevance of any conclusions in cross-cultural psychology that has derived from research at different levels of analysis.

In cross-cultural psychology we must constantly ask whether the results we obtain from different cultures are interpreted correctly and meet the criterion of equivalence. Since the researcher is not immune to cultural bias and ethnocentric interpretations how can we guard against conclusions that in fact are not valid?

2.1. CULTURAL BIAS AND CRITERION OF EQUIVALENCE

The most significant issue in cross-cultural research is the *equivalence* of comparative research concepts and methodology. Are the concepts employed in comparative research and the research methodology used equivalent in each culture? If the conceptual foundation and research methods are not similar it is not possible to draw comparative conclusions. The lack of equivalence will inevitably produce bias in the results and interpretations. Therefore a significant precursor to valid methodology is creating studies that meet the test of equivalence.

2.1.1. The Issue of Language Equivalence

By its very nature cross-cultural research is often conducted with respondents who speak different languages. The first issue in comparative research therefore is to evaluate the equivalence of translations of the original research protocol. Whether the researcher employs surveys, attitude scales or interview protocols, linguistic equivalence is the first and most important condition of valid research. The development of research instruments should initially utilize multi-lingual participants (Van de Vijver & Hambleton, 1996). However, what happens in reality most frequently is that the research protocol is developed in the investigators culture and then translated into the language of those cultural groups selected for comparison. The first step in creating linguistic equivalence is to ask a committee of bi-lingual experts to collectively evaluate the research instrument. They will be asked to indicate their opinions as to whether the individual items or statements belong to the research domain selected. The experts will be asked to look for items that do not validly reflect cultural experience and whether a participating cultural group has a unique language context that affects the item responses. Language constructs that are culturally specific, and for which there is no equivalence in other cultures, would introduce bias. The committee of bilingual experts works toward a consensus about the appropriateness of the language used in the research protocol.

The second method used since the 1970s is called *back translation* (Brislin, 1970, 1993). *The researchers have the research document translated into the other languages of interest, after which independent participants translate it back into the original language.* If the retranslation is semantically equivalent to the original language protocol the researcher can have confidence in language equivalence. In other words a satisfactory criterion is met when the independent back translation produces more or less the original language used. The back translation procedure requires the participation of experts that are fluent in the languages employed. If the original form is found not to be translatable, the researcher must return to the drawing boards and use a different alternative language in the protocol. Since many participants in cross-cultural research are bi-lingual and often use English as a second language, researchers have to be cognizant of the possibility that responses are influenced by the participant's stereotypes of the culture of the particular language (Bond, 1983).

2.1.2. Psychometric Equivalence

The research instruments must also be developed in a manner that ensures measurement equivalence. A fundamental issue in evaluating *psychometric equivalence* is the degree to which the instruments used in the cultures participating in the research measure the same construct. If equivalence is attained the researcher should expect the same or similar order of preferences as measured by the use of response categories and the same order of item difficulty. Further, a criterion of equivalence is met when similar correlation patterns between items occur in comparisons between cultures. However, even where we have followed a valid translation procedure there is no way of knowing a priori if the language chosen in the research protocol has the same meaning in different societies (Poortinga, 1989). If the protocol means different things it is not possible to make valid comparisons.

Underlying all measurement concerns are the concepts of reliability and validity. Reliability is assessed by several methods, but refers essentially to whether the instrument elicits consistent responses internally or over time. Internal reliability is determined by intercorrelations that measure the degree to which items belong together. Significant intercorrelations are expected where measures have structural equivalence. Validity, on the other hand, asks the question of whether the research instrument measures what it purports to measure.

An important consideration is equivalence in the theoretical framework used or in the constructs being employed in the study. Comparability is impossible when the theoretical framework is not the same in comparison studies for example when the constructs measured mean different things depending on interpretation. Typically respondents in Western Europe or North America are guided by rationality in responding to psychological assessments. Responses of Western participants are mainly influenced by an educational system that reinforces rationality and rewards logical thinking. Other cultures may reward intuitive thinking processes and that difference makes comparisons of cultures difficult. Different thinking processes between cultures may result in measuring an aspect of the culture that confounds the variable of interest and makes analysis guarded.

Van de Vijver and Leung (1997a,b) suggested several types of linguistic equivalence. One approach asks whether the instrument measures the same underlying construct in the cultures examined. For example is the concept of intelligence the same in the comparative cultures, or does it depend on cultural uniqueness factors not measured? However, as noted above, a test of structural equivalence is found if the pattern of intercorrelations is the same or similar across cultures.

The underlying response structure in comparative studies can also be examined by means of factor analysis. A factor analysis with varimax rotation will allow the researcher to determine the level of factorial agreement. Factor analysis group survey items together based on item intercorrelations, and the factors are thought to represent different independent concepts. If the same group of items emerge in different cultural samples that is taken as evidence of structural similarity or structural equivalence. The similarity of the factor loadings is accepted as evidence of psychometric equivalence. Statistical techniques to further assist in evaluating psychometric equivalence include regression analysis that reports the amount of variance contributed by each variable to the construct. In the analysis of variance procedure it is also possible to examine for interaction between items and cultural effects, and where none are present that result is evidence of equivalence.

2.1.3. Selecting Equivalent Samples in Cross-Cultural Psychology

The selection of *comparative and representative samples is difficult in cross-cultural research because of the complexity of the variables studied and for the practical reasons that random samples are less accessible.* Literacy rates and educational levels vary between societies and that heterogeneity may become a confounding factor in the response patterns of the participants. Further, the influence from travel and contacts that are by-products of a globalized world make it nearly impossible to obtain pure culturally influenced responses in today's world.

For practical reasons culture refers in many cross-cultural studies to the country of origin of the respondents. In effect cross-national studies often replace cross-cultural research. This imprecise definition defeats equivalence since as we noted in chapter 1 different ethnic groups and cultures can co-exist within a nation. In any event in cross-national studies care should be taken not to assume national homogeneity as even countries with intact traditions and stable socio-economic systems may in fact be very heterogeneous in ethnicity. The obvious solution is to obtain matched samples from the cultures studied. However, when matching for one variable that very psychometric control often causes mismatching on other salient factors. For example, being Black in South Africa does not mean the same as being Black in London since these matched samples may differ on variety of socio-economic variables and matching for race would not produce equivalence.

The sample selected represents a larger population. To ensure that outcome researchers have in the past examined issues related to appropriate sample selection. Probably in most cases samples are chosen for convenience, typically by the availability of university students in many societies. Convenience sampling has often been criticized as being unrepresentative of the population for the obvious reasons of the higher level of education and socio-economic standing of university students (Wintre, North, & Sugar, 2001). However, whether university samples are useful in comparative research is really an empirical issue to be investigated by comparing university students and representative samples (Ellsworth & Gonzales, 2003) and not dismissed without evidence. Pernice, Van der Veer, Ommundsen and Larsen (2008) demonstrated that university students could be successfully utilized in both concept development and scale construction in an attitude toward immigrants study in New Zealand. Students in this study based their attitudes on the same criteria as the general population supporting the effect of shared cultural and political systems in both student and population samples.

Another type of sampling is called systematic since samples are selected based on some theory. Perhaps the objective is to study the effect of membership in religious organizations, and samples are drawn with proper controls from particular religious groups in different cultures. Another study may investigate the treatment of homosexuals in different cultures and select accordingly. The underlying theory might be the effect of religious dogmatism as related to tolerance.

In random sampling an effort is made to obtain representative sampling of the population studied. Random sampling is representative, and the results obtained are assumed to represent the population studied with little error. In random samples each individual has an equal and independent chance of being selected, and if the sample size is large enough the results are reliable and the population characteristics are represented with relatively little error (Offermann & Hellman, 1997). In general the larger the number of participants the less the sample will vary from the population characteristics (Heiman, 1996). The ideal in cross-cultural sampling is to utilize the random selection of participants. As noted that is often difficult or impossible, and convenience samples are frequently used. Although convenience sampling may not produce bias in the development of assessment instruments, the researcher must be cautious in generalizing the results of the study to the overall population of the culture.

Several sampling decisions have to be made when comparing cross-cultural groups. The primary decision is what cultural groups should be compared. That conclusion might in turn be based on some theory that predicts differences on the variables of interest. Secondly, all cultures have subsets of groups that vary on important dimensions. Therefore a second consideration is what sub groups should be included. Finally, the issue of how to select individual respondents must be considered.

Finally, in cross-cultural research the interest is not just to achieve representative samples, but also in ensuring equivalent samples. In practice this requires control for equivalence on demographic factors including socio-economic status, occupation, religion or ideology, age and sex. For example, it would not be useful to compare a university sample from the United States with a sample drawn from Aboriginal fringe dwellers in Australia, since among many differences there would be obviously confounding educational and socio-economic effects. Demographic factors must therefore be controlled when comparing across cultures. However, even controlling for demographic variables may not provide proper comparative controls since, for example, being old in Japan or Europe may be very different experiences.

2.2. NONEQUIVALENCE IN CROSS-CULTURAL RESEARCH

Most researchers do what is possible to conduct comparative research with equivalent samples. However, the very nature of cross-cultural research makes that a difficult goal to achieve. Often investigators are left with what they believe are good approximations of construct and methodological equivalence. It is probably not possible given the influence of culture specific factors to ever create perfect methodological equivalence in the selection of relevant constructs and in data collection in all comparative cultures. Poortinga (1989) recognized this dilemma and suggested several approaches for dealing with nonequivalent data. Cross-cultural studies will in reality be interpreted and published even when comparisons are made with nonequivalent data. However, Poortinga suggest that the researcher can take steps to reduce nonequivalence by identifying and analyzing the research elements that are equivalent separately from those that do not meet criteria. In research employing attitude scales we have statistical methods to identify nonequivalent items and remove these from analysis (Ommundsen, Hak, Morch, Larsen, & Van der Veer, 2002; Ommundsen & Larsen, 1997, 1999; Ommundsen, Van der Veer, Van Le, Krumov, & Larsen, 2007).

Another way of looking at the nonequivalence issue is to examine it as important information about the cultures investigated. What are the reasons for the nonequivalence and what does that tell us about psychology in these societies? Cultural differences may be informed by equivalent data, but also by why some data is not equivalent. Many hypotheses for further research can be developed from these methodological issues and problems.

2.3. LEVELS OF INFERENCE

Berry, Poortinga, Segall and Dasen (1992) suggested the presence of three *levels of inferences* in cross-cultural psychology. An example of low level inferences occurs when the researcher constructs direct samples of content from the domain of interest and from such sample tests makes inferences about the domain studied. The use of scales measuring attitudes toward various groups like immigrants or intergroup relations involving contacts between national or ethnic groups are examples of low level inferences (Van der Veer, Ommundsen, Larsen, Van Le, Krumov, Pernice, & Romans, 2004). Through scaling procedures the researcher selects a representative sample of attitude statements that reflect the domain of the attitude in question. If the selection of scale items is representative comparisons to the domain of the attitude are considered valid. Here as elsewhere one must take precautions that the statements selected do not contain information that is culturally unique and relevant only to some respondents and not others. Likewise the methods used must also be clearly understood and equivalent cross-culturally.

Medium level inferences according to Berry et al refer to generalization from domains that are not directly observable including cognitive abilities or personality traits that are nevertheless manifested in predictable behaviors. Here the objective is not to obtain representative samples of the domain of study, but rather to capture the *essence* of the psychological trait. At this medium level of inference it is difficult to assume without ambiguity whether the domains studied are in fact comparable across cultures. Is the authoritarianism observed in Saudi Arabia equivalent to that observed in the United States? There are probably many differences confounded by other variables like religiosity that makes direct comparisons difficult. Some personality traits may be culturally specific and that makes comparative inferences difficult.

High level inferences refer to domains not easily specified, and that cannot be measured by standard measurement procedures. At this level of inference it is doubtful if measurements can capture the domain of interest. Observed differences are explained post hoc after the exploratory research is completed and without solid empirical evidence. Examples cited by Berry et al include the use of high level concepts like intelligence or adaptation. Since adaptability is required in all cultural environments how it is possible to state with any confidence that one culture is better adapted than another? These types of assertions go beyond what the data will support and tend to be unclear and not easily operationalized with valid comparative methodology.

2.4. STUDIES OF CULTURAL LEVEL ECOLOGICAL AVERAGES

In chapter 1 we discussed Hofstede's work-related values, Schwartz's value orientations, as well as the contributions of Leung and Bond on social axioms. These studies are examples *of ecological level research since the data collected is averaged for each culture allowing comparisons for such values as individualism and collectivism.* Typically studies in cross-cultural psychology are based on the responses of individuals. Comparisons of samples based on individual responses may yield significant differences, but how do we know what is responsible for these results? For example, differences in aggression levels between cultures may or may not be the consequence of cultural variables as aggression can also be attributed to social frustration.

Ecological level average statistics reveal the underlying psychological dimensions responsible for culturally related behavior and offer a better reference point to understand the results of individual based studies. The work-related values of Hofstede provided the researcher with a theoretical framework to develop relevant contextual and personality traits to be examined in comparative studies, and to help explain the results. Triandis, Bontempo, Villareal, Asai, and Lucca (1988) utilized other culturally based averages when they correlated the incidence of heart attacks with the value of individualism. Matsumoto and Fletcher (1996) correlated Hofstede's dimensions to the occurrence rates of various diseases, and the work-related values provided a theoretical explanation for varying incidence of illness occurrence. Other psychological constructs have also been investigated using cultural averages including personality traits (McCrae, Terracciano, Khoury, Nansubuga, Knezevic, Djuric Jocic et al., 2005). In addition to cultural dimensions other ecological level factors may also influence cultural specific variables, for example, the place of culture in relation to geopolitical issues and the political and economic system. Climatic differences may also contribute to differences linked to culture. According to Andersen (1999) climatic conditions determine the degree of intimacy between the members of a culture. He suggests that cultures located in warmer countries are "high-contact," while those located in countries with cooler climate are "low-contact." Cross-cultural psychology could benefit from more integrated studies seeking to relate cultural average data to theories and specific aspects of culture.

2.5. WHAT IS MEASURED IN CROSS-CULTURAL RESEARCH?

Research in cross-cultural psychology typically seeks to ascertain differences between populations on psychological assessments. How do scores of different cultural groups compare on survey responses to the measures of the variables of interest? However, the psychological world is just one aspect of the influences of culture. Any survey will contain only a small sampling of all the relevant information of interest and may not include other salient domains due to inadequate knowledge by the investigator. A broader concern is to examine differences in the natural world or the ecological context that influence culture. This refers to the more or less permanent features of a culture that create the context for individual behavior and can include as noted climate and other aspects of the natural world as well as the socio-economic system. The norms developed in society are thought the outcome of the ecological context.

In addition there are other factors that are cultural in nature including child rearing practices of society and customary behavior. The attitudes of the individual are the result of habitual and normatively acceptable cognition and behavior. Is culture or climate responsible for observed differences in innovation and efficiency? Often these ecological issues are not evaluated, but nevertheless may play a role. Research confined to psychological assessment only examines a narrow band of the entire context that influences behavior in cross-cultural psychology. Some think that the addition of qualitative approaches that examine behavior in the natural world helps expand the relevant information and more validly represent the overall context.

Cross-cultural research explains differences in psychological assessments of attributes by explaining the variability in terms of *context variables* like religious values that dominate the society. For example, attitudes of authoritarianism expressed in sentiments toward established institutions are explained by virtue of a culture's ubiquitous religious values. Individual psychological assessments are measured by individual responses to surveys or scales, but the *explanation* is at the context level. Some attempts have been made to differentiate the effects of context variables from psychological assessments (Poortinga & Van de Vijver, 1987). There are many possibilities for error when one level of assessment is used to explain the outcomes at another level. Individual responses may not always be correctly explained by population level context variables. For example, relative poverty might be logically thought to explain the role of education in society and individual achievement. Nevertheless in Cuba, a relatively poor country, there are very high levels of educational achievement as well as high levels of health care.

One study (Iwata & Higuchi, 2000) reported that Japanese expressed higher rates of trait anxiety. The explanation offered by the researchers was that this difference occurred because of the collectivistic society in Japan where individual well-being is secondary to the well-being of the group. However, none of these factors were actually measured in the study including controlling for level of collectivism. To make valid cross-cultural comparisons requires the measurement of some aspects of the culture examined. Relevant studies need to examine more specific aspects of culture thought responsible for behavioral differences. Culture is just an overall label, and in comparative work we need to study specific aspects of the culture thought relevant to the behavior in question.

Attempts have been made to examine at the *individual level* variables like individualism-collectivism thought to profoundly affect behavior. Triandis (1994, 1995) was influenced by Hofstede's early work on work-related values that revealed the presence of cultures dominated by values of individualism or collectivism (Hofstede, 1980). These variables were later measured at the individual level through the construction of scales. Hui (1988) developed a scale that measured the respondent's relative individualism-collectivism tendencies as related to significant social relationships including family, friends and co-workers. Matsumoto, Weissman, Preston, Brown and Kupperbusch (1997) measured tendencies influenced by the context in interpersonal situations. The context was defined as a cultural syndrome including beliefs, attitudes and behaviors as supported by fundamental values (Triandis, 1996). Others (Singelis, Triandis, Bhawuk, & Gelfand, 1995) developed a revised concept of individualism-collectivism identifying both vertical and horizontal components. In horizontal individualism members are equal and autonomous. In vertical individualist societies (like the United States) individuals are considered autonomous but unequal. In horizontal collectivism members are perceived as participants of ingroups and equal. In vertical collectivism individuals are described in terms of status and hierarchical relations.

2.6. BIAS IN PSYCHOLOGICAL ASSESSMENTS

Bias can be a factor in the construction of psychological assessments. In some cases a few survey items may be poorly worded or inadequately translated introducing error in interpretation by the respondent. However, item error can usually by eliminated by statistical means (Van de Vijver & Leung, 1997b). Item analysis procedures are based on an internal assessment of measurement bias. Eliminating poor or biased statements however, do not provide solutions to the broader problem when the entire method is inadequate. If error affects the entire survey the problems in the methodology require an examination of alternative approaches. However, a more frequent bias issue is problems with the concept being measured. When concepts are not well articulated in the methods used there are errors that follow from different interpretation by the respondents. The multiple words for snow in Inuit language makes the conceptual context in that culture different compared to participants living in the tropics. To avoid bias respondents in the cultures examined should have the same probability of responses given similar familiarity (Shepard, Camilli, & Averill, 1981).

Van de Vijver and Poortinga (1997) outlined three types of bias in psychological assessments. The difference in familiarity of concepts and constructs were discussed above and might be caused by a lack of overlap in definitions of the construct measured. Lack of familiarity could also be caused by poor sampling of the relevant construct variables. Another methodological problem is bias introduced by issues affected by social desirability. The pursuit of individual enhancement is prominent in individualistic cultures, whereas group enhancement is more characteristic of collectivistic cultures (Lalwani, Shavitt, & Johnson, 2006). Respondents from individualistic cultures engage in self-deceptive self-enhancement, whereas respondents from collectivistic cultures are more concerned with impression management in society. Both forms of deception bias the results of cultural differences. However, it is possible to statistically control items affected by social desirability. On the other hand, it is more likely that response sets play a role when respondents are unfamiliar with the construct measured. Response biases may also vary by culture producing a systematic response tendency to survey items or attitude scales. Consequently it is unclear whether comparative differences are the result of a cultural response bias or if they measure some actual difference in the trait. Bias in interpretation of items can also hamper direct comparisons producing differential meaning of the words measured. Response sets also affects survey results. Some respondents prefer to systematically acquiesce with often conflicting viewpoints or respond with the extreme response categories.

The acquiescence response bias is the general tendency to agree with a statement regardless of the actual content being measured. Other respondents may use primarily extreme ends of a scale independent of content of the statement. Since the responses may be dominated by these systematic tendencies we know less about the response to the content of the variable being measured. Responses to surveys are also affected by people's tendency to make implicit comparisons to the opinions of the reference groups to which they belong. Responses therefore are less personal and reflect rather the dominant opinions in reference groups. For example, Japanese respondents in evaluating themselves often self-rank higher on individualism compared to their Japanese reference group. That inflates their judgment of their actual individualism (Van Herk, Poortinga, & Verhallen, 2004). The major problem with these reference group biases is that participants will respond not with their own assessments, but what they think meet social approval or what they think is the dominant opinion.

Bias may also ensue from the researchers own cultural blinds. Those who organize and carry out cross-cultural studies do so from their own theoretical perspectives confounded by implicit cultural bias. Like all other people researchers see what they need to see and what they are prepared to observe. Preconceptions may influence not only the choice of what to study, but also the methods compatible to the researcher, and the inferences made from the results. Matsumoto and his collaborators noted, for example, that studies of emotion differences between Japanese and Americans often infer that the Japanese suppress their emotions. However, the results actually show that the difference is not so much Japanese suppression of emotion as the American respondents exaggerating theirs. In other words, most researchers are dependent on their own cultural perspective when evaluating the results of research (Matsumoto & Ekman, 1989; Matsumoto, Kasri, & Kooken, 1999).

2.7. INFERENCES FROM STATISTICAL TESTS ON CROSS-CULTURAL COMPARISONS

In all fields of psychology, including cross-cultural research, inferences are drawn from statistical methods like analysis of variance. These techniques allow us to determine that the differences between cultural groups are statistically significant, and have not occurred by chance. However, the fact that an observed difference does not occur by chance often leads to the unwarranted assumption that the difference is important and meaningful. Tests of mean differences do not provide estimates of the degree of difference, nor the amount of variance that is accounted for by the variables. In most cases, even when there are large and meaningful differences, the within group variance is probably greater than the between group observation.

Another faulty assumption is the idea that because there are statistically significant differences between cultural groups that most members of groups represented in the study differ in the direction indicated by the mean values. However, even with large mean differences a considerable overlap between groups is possible in the variable studied. It is important to evaluate the degree to which differences are meaningful and not just statistically significant. A test for the amount of variance accounted for by the research variables is possible with correlational techniques, and other effect size statistics (Matsumoto, Grissom, & Dinnel, 2001). Scholars in Western societies in particular value the search for significant differences consistent with individualistic culture, and less often look for similarities between cultural groups as not nearly as interesting. One outcome of the "difference obsession" is the focus on statistical tests of significance, even when differences are small and not meaningful.

2.8. EXPERIMENTAL VERSUS CORRELATIONAL STUDIES

Most studies in cross-cultural psychology are correlational in nature not properly allowing the researcher to make cause and affect inferences. For example, comparisons between cultural groups cannot be called experimental since they contain really correlational information. However, *the research reported in the literature often treat observed differences as cause and effect relationships, when a third variable or other factors may be responsible for the results.* To use a simple example, suppose differences are found between two cultures on the rate and quality of innovation. Judging the results as cause and effect might lead to the conclusion that one culture is better at innovating. However, it may be that essential nutrition in childhood is missing in one culture impairing intellectual development, or perhaps there are climatic or other factors that play a role independent of any overall generalization summarized in "culture."

Strictly speaking cause and effect conclusions are only justified in experimental studies where control and experimental groups receive equivalent treatments. That is very difficult to achieve in most cross-cultural comparative studies. In discussing the results of correlational studies it is well to remember that these studies are exploratory in nature and do not directly examine cause and effect. However, correlational studies are useful in exploring relationships and may allow us to develop further hypotheses about the domain of interest. Over time and through replication work we may get to understand more about what it is in the culture that produced the initial correlation. Matsumoto and Yoo (2006) suggested that attributing reasons for cultural differences without specific evidence from experimental work contribute to cultural attribution errors. For example, the multiple studies in individualism and collectivism have often been used to draw inferences about specific societies in the Western world and Asia. However, unless these constructs are actually operationalized and measured and found present in the samples surveyed, and unless it can be shown that these constructs are responsible for the observed differences then the attributed difference is not verified.

2.9. QUALITATIVE AND QUANTITATIVE RESEARCH IN CROSS-CULTURAL PSYCHOLOGY

Qualitative research is dominant in cross-cultural anthropology. Social scientists trained in this tradition often have contempt for the research of *quantitative* psychologists feeling that they distort social reality and glimpse only small portions of relevant information in a culture. The attempt to build psychology up as a quantitative science probably derived from the widespread disbelief and reaction to speculative psychological analysis found in psychoanalysis and other subjective approaches. Behaviorism that followed, however, seemed unsatisfactory because it did not explain much of what went on subjectively, and largely established relationships between stimuli and responses. In reaction to these concerns subjective methods came into play in cultural psychology. *Qualitative methods are employed more in studies of singular cultures whereas quantitative methods are used more in the comparative approaches of cross-cultural psychology.* However, even in comparative approaches culturally specific qualities are not easily understood by using quantitative methods. It seems desirable to use both approaches to gradually understand that which is similar between cultures, and also that which is specific to each society.

Qualitative research emphasizes that cultural reality is socially constructed and to understand that reality requires a relationship between researcher and the culture studied (Denzin & Lincoln, 2000). Specifically the relationship in question is often between the researcher and trusted informants that are conversant with cultural values and normative behavior. From the qualitative perspective the research objective is to gradually build a complete holistic picture of the culture that provides the foundation for psychological regularities (Hwang, 2012). This objective requires that research is more broadly conducted in the natural environment, and cannot consist of paper and pencil instruments.

Qualitative methods in psychology include unstructured interviews where the researcher seeks to understand some general aspect of culture by starting conversations on topics of interest allowing the informant to respond in an open fashion and without structured constraints. Observations in the natural setting is an alternative approach that allows the coding of the observed behavior related to specific events like marriage ceremonies or the birth of a child. However, it should be stressed that spontaneous observation is of little utility. Although observation from a qualitative perspective occurs in the natural environment, the behavior of interest should focus on identifiable behaviors that can be measured at least by frequency of occurrence in order to evaluate its significance and salience. Observation requires a great deal of patience as it follows no specific time rule, and requires a willingness by the culturally identified individuals to tolerate being watched. However, the technique is most effective when the researcher becomes a participant observer, and gets included in the society observed. Interviews can also be recorded and subsequently coded for frequency of responses. When the culture has written traditions it is also possible to evaluate texts. The insight that the researcher possesses about the culture is of great importance in qualitative research, and if not present creates obvious validity problems. Theory development using qualitative research is an inductive process where the researcher gradually builds abstractions based on multiple sources (Charmaz, 1995; Silverman, 1993).

Content analysis is another qualitative approach. Typically the investigator gathers relevant documents and summarizes the manifest and latent content of the writing. A variety of written or performed material can prove useful including taped conversations, media programs, newspaper articles and books. The initial task of the researcher after studying the material is to establish coding categories. For example, if hostility is of interest the researcher may establish what words are associated with the concept and then count the frequency in a given communication. Next the investigator tries to interpret what the frequencies mean in the cultural context. The presence or the frequency of reference to the issue can provide important information about a cultural context that later can be investigated by means of hypothesis testing studies. However, there are situations when for legal or moral reasons subjects do not want to provide written material in which case the interview may be a more useful methodological strategy (Shiraev & Sobel, 2006).

From the perspective of qualitative research quantitative results are often seen as distortions of the underlying reality. However, there is no reason why both approaches cannot be employed as they are not antagonistic, but rather complementary. Qualitative research can be used in the initial exploratory stages to obtain familiarity with the context or explore for key determinants. Quantitative methods can build on this initial conceptual development and be used for comparative studies. The argument by qualitative researchers is that the complexity of cultural behavior can never be fully understood using quantitative means, but rather by first understanding the important contextual variables. In qualitative research the scientist seeks to understand the values of a culture not from a priori conceptions as seen from the outside, but in the terms of the conceptions existing in the culture. An obvious danger of quantitative research is that the constructs examined are developed from the framework of the culture of the researcher. The very objects of study and methods used in such comparative approaches can create bias in the data and interpretations.

The differences between qualitative and quantitative approaches are related to the historical divisions between emic and etic conceptions of research. From the emic approach research should only be conducted within a culture and researchers examine one culture at a time. The structural relationships discovered in the process and any criteria used to evaluate findings are developed from these internal characteristics. On the other hand, the etic approach seeks to understand cultural behavior from outside the cultural system studied and engages in comparative studies. In etic research the methodological structure employed is developed by the researcher, and evaluative criteria are based on the assumption of the universality of psychological phenomenon (Berry, 1969).

In practice both methods are employed in cross-cultural psychology. Segall, Dasen, Berry and Poortinga (1999) suggested that researchers start with an "imposed etic" by applying constructs developed outside the culture. As knowledge develops from the culturally comparative studies the researcher becomes more sensitive to the similarities with other cultures and also the culturally specific ones. Eventually, researchers may discover that the traits examined have universal features, and that other aspects are culture specific (Berry, 1969).

During this writer's work with the Aborigines in Australia a combination of these methods were used to understand fringe dwellers behavior, attitudes of whites toward Aborigines, discrimination, and alcohol related behaviors (Larsen, 1977, 1978a, 1978b, 1981). These studies were based first on subjective qualitative approaches, and then followed by more quantitative analysis. For example, to understand the domain of whites' attitudes toward aborigines the researcher first informally engaged patrons in conversation about Aborigines in a variety of natural settings like hotels and bars to collect statements that could represent the attitude universe. These were then edited and subsequently used in unidimensional scaling approaches.

2.10. QUANTITATIVE COMPARATIVE CROSS-CULTURAL RESEARCH

The major quantitative methods in cross-cultural psychology are those based on interviews and surveys, and experiments that allow hypothesis testing. Surveys are the most frequently used methods. However, innovative researchers have sought to develop other approaches including the quasiexperiment.

2.10.1. Surveys

Cross-cultural psychology employs research methods common to most areas of psychology in the process of developing an objective quantitative field of study. The most common method used is testing for psychological differences utilizing established psychological instruments in two or more cultures (Van de Vijver & Leung, 1997a). Issues of equivalence as noted above remain an important concern to ensure valid comparisons. The surveys employed can be open-ended where the researcher asks the respondents for opinions or attitudes on particular subjects or issues. In open-ended surveys responses are not structured as participants can provide whatever responses seem correct. The researcher can tabulate the frequency of response categories as an index of response patterns, but in practice open-ended questions are more difficult to interpret. Multiple choice tests or multiple response category surveys are used more frequently and easier to quantify. Structured response categories, however, are also problematic as not all cultures have experiences with paper and pencil formats, nor familiarity with the topic investigated. Since the respondent must provide an answer the results can be quite meaningless when the subject matter is not understood. However, pretesting of surveys with the target population can eliminate some of these concerns.

Surveys can also be conducted by way of interviews. Since the interviewer is present with the survey participant he/she can respond and provide any necessary clarifications. In interviews careful watch must be kept to provide standardized questions, and prevent bias by not reinforcing certain responses nonverbally or otherwise. Today surveys can also take the form of telephone canvassing or by utilizing the Internet. Telephone or Internet surveying are typically easy to conduct and low in cost. However, bias in sampling becomes a major problem as typically respondents who participate are also those that are motivated because of pre-existing attitudes at opposing ends of the attitude continuum. As a result survey participation might be narrowed to those who have a special interest in the subject. There are also socio-economic biases in distance surveying since in some countries the possession of a telephone reflect higher wealth and status. A greater problem is the social desirability factor since some issues are sensitive and responses are confounded by the desire for social approval. Respondents concerned about social desirability will provide normative responses or seek to please the researcher by providing socially acceptable answers.

The results of cross-cultural psychology presented in published journals derive from multiple researchers and utilizes alternative methodologies in measuring similar or overlapping constructs. How to get a summary view of what is significant in these studies is difficult since research in psychology is approached from many perspectives, and with varying methodology. When different researchers are studying the same construct how can we create some summary judgment about the relationships found? Meta-analysis is a statistical method that permits researchers to analyze the many studies that are completed on a particular subject and provide an overall integration of the results. Since many studies are included the researcher can have some confidence in the summary statistic. However, we must keep in mind that only studies that are published come to the attention of the researcher, and hence meta-analysis has a bias toward studies that show "significant" differences. This analysis of previous analyses also often represents varied methodology and utilizes constructs not all conceptually the same. The resulting heterogeneity may produce overall results that are less reliable and valid.

2.10.2. Experiments

Experiments utilized in cross-cultural comparison studies are not true experiments. Experimental research tries to establish cause and effect relationships by assigning participants randomly to experimental and control groups and then compare for significance of mean differences. However, researchers cannot create cultural experimental groups that correspond to treatment in classical experiments, and random assignments are difficult to achieve. Nevertheless experimental procedures play a role in cross-cultural comparative studies (Van de Vijver & Leung, 1997a). It is, for example, possible to design studies that test for the effects of cultural contextual variables when cultural populations with these characteristics are selected in advance and specific hypotheses are investigated. Whether the results can be generalized depends on whether the findings in one culture can also be found in other cultures. Replication in other cultural contexts is seen as evidence for the validity of the theory that drives the research, for the instruments used, and for the presence of universal psychological characteristics.

It is difficult to apply the experimental paradigm in the cross-cultural comparative contexts. In other fields the researcher typically controls the experimental treatments administered to randomly assigned groups. However, in real life research in cultures the experimenter must be satisfied with groups that are intact, and believed to vary from each other on culturally contextual variables. Since already existing groups cannot meet the criteria of randomness they are not representative groups, although the results may be useful and interesting. Likewise is it impossible in most cases to control the treatment administered to intact groups. Any effect that is believed to derive from culturally contextual factors is made post hoc after the completion of research, and based on ethnographic or cultural value information like the results of Hofstede's work-related values.

Some studies have sought to examine cultural differences by priming the mindsets of the participants. For example, Trafimov, Triandis, and Goto (1991) manipulated the individualistic versus collectivistic orientation by priming the mental conceptions of the experimental subjects. The American and Chinese participants were asked to think about the ways they were different from friends and family in one experimental condition, and asked to write what they had in common with friends and family in the second condition. Presumably these manipulations caused the mindset of the subjects to think in either individualistic or collectivistic ways. Results showed that Americans produced more individualistic responses compared to the Chinese respondents as would be expected from the theory on collectivism-individualism as advocated by Hofstede. Further the results showed that the priming as an experimental manipulation worked since those who were primed to think in individualistic terms generated more personal responses, and those primed to think collectivistic produced more group-oriented responses. Other researchers have found similar results (Gardner, Gabriel, & Lee, 1999).

Other culturally relevant studies were carried out by Yamagishi (1986, 1988) who manipulated the sanctioning system for cooperation and relative trust of the experimental participants. In the first experiment Yamagishi found that those who were more trusting in Japan did indeed cooperate more. In the second experiment comparing Japanese with American participants Yamagishi found that high trusting American respondents cooperated more in the experiment than low-trusting respondents. However, when the sanctions were in place there were no differences between the two cultural groups. Yamagishi concluded that the greater cooperative behavior observed in Japan is due to the sanctioning system in place supporting cooperation, and when Americans are placed in similar situations they behave in the same way.

2.11 THE PROBLEMS OF VALIDITY

The *dogmatic* preference for qualitative or quantitative methods is based on controversial arguments over the validity of results and subsequent interpretation. Validity is no small matter since the objective of all research is to demonstrate a real as opposed to a fantasized interpretation of cultural behavior. The issues of validity are best answered through the utilization of methods that combine all available approaches, that demonstrate conceptual clarity, and that ensures replication of the studies over time. The results of either cultural or cross-cultural research are always approximations toward validity as no method can yield a complete picture valid for all time (Cook & Campbell, 1979).

Qualitative research poses unique problems in establishing validity. Experiments are not easily created or conducted for situations where the investigator is trying to understand underlying customs and rules of the culture. Likewise standardized surveys or scales are difficult to construct at this basic level of investigations. Further the emic approach generally is focused on individual development in interaction with cultural norms and rules. These gradual psychological processes are not easily investigated using quantitative methods that assume the measurement of stable or static qualities. To capture the developmental changes some have argued for the use of video recordings (Greenfield, 1997).

One form of qualitative validity is called interpretive and aims at establishing communication clarity between the researcher and the cultural group observed (Maxwell, 1992). Ecological validity is the extent to which data is collected consistent with the cultural context. Greenfield believes that is accomplished when studying behavior in the natural context. However, the major problem with validity in the qualitative approach is the inability of other researchers to verify (replicate) the results since selection of what to study as well as interpretations are the results of the subjective qualities of the researcher.

Experiments in cultural and cross-cultural research cannot control the experimental conditions, especially in the administration of "treatments" to an experimental group that can be properly compared to the behavior of a control group (Van de Vijver & Leung, 1997a, 1997b). However, there are ways to establish relative validity for differences between cultural groups. If cultural samples are selected for established ethnographic conditions rather than for convenience the differences between groups become more plausible. However, since any interpretation comes after the completion of the experiment the possibility for incorrect interpretations remains a significant vulnerability. Still when differences are compared based on established theory where the group-related variables are treated as independent variables the possibility for erroneous interpretation is reduced (Malpass, 1977). When the sample is chosen on the basis of the presence of these group-related variables validity is implicit in the methodology. Various statistical techniques can also be employed to remove error as discussed earlier, for example, by means of regression analysis that allows for a comparison of the contribution of various concepts to the overall behavior in question.

To address validity the inclusion of separate and independent measures of the relationships being examined are also important. That would also include conducting separate testing at different points in time, but also replication work. The latter would establish the reliability of results that is a necessary precondition for validity. Along the same line different types of measurements should be encouraged. For example, the use of surveys in conjunction with experimental work can give us some evidence of convergent validity. Likewise if the results from comparative studies are what would be predicted from other research and underlining theory, that, too, would indicate validity. In other words, validity is confirmed when the results are as expected from the theoretical perspective. Finally, meta-analysis is also another approach to convergent validity.

2.12. A CRITICAL LOOK AT THE FINDINGS FROM CROSS-CULTURAL COMPARISONS

Fundamentally cross-cultural psychology exists to contribute to the meaning of cultural differences. Since respondents in any culture evaluate psychological stimuli from the framing of their own cultural values it is essential to know how such bias affects the results. For example, Peng, Nisbett ,and Wong (1997) noted that respondents in cultural groups pay primary attention to their own cultures in evaluating their beliefs and values. This dominant presence may actually result in an underestimate of the role of underlying cultural values since these are seen as part of daily life and less noteworthy. In evaluating the self as being high or low on collectivism the respondent uses as reference the internalized stereotype of his/her own culture for comparison purposes (Heine, Lehman, Peng, & Greenholtz, 2002).

At the same time globalization and associated *values of modernity* call into question many of the value based research results. The cultural dichotomies of individualism-collectivism may be inaccurate or a stereotypic simplification particularly in the face of the knowledge explosion and new communication methodology available almost ubiquitously worldwide (Hermans

& Kempen, 1998). Even in the most remote dogmatic societies there are individual variances that cannot be measured by ecological level variables. Collectivism is related to conformity, yet we see many societies described as collectivistic where people are willing to risk all to be free. Freedom may prove a variable of universal value that trumps stereotypic secondary cultural values.

There is in all cross-cultural comparisons a bias in selection of the topic studied as derived from the cultural frame of the investigator. Further, the studies that are reported are those achieving statistical significance. That scientific procedure in turn may also produce bias since the non-reported studies of not statistically significant results may be a better representation of the cultural reality. In summarizing research in a given field we are also more likely to attend to interesting or extreme results that do not necessarily represent valid reality in particular if based on small and non-representative samples.

It is necessary to consider the method of sample selection and the validity of the method employed in cross-cultural studies. In the case of comparative studies that require cross-cultural validity in the methodology employed. Remember also that any study regardless of relevance to the populations studied represent only a fragment of the universe of psychological traits in a given culture and a portion of the cultural context. Cross-cultural research offers us a window into the psychological reality in varying cultures, but never the complete picture. We cannot know for sure what aspect of culture create the differences observed although different cultural groups may vary on the issue studied. Cultural average (ecological) studies provide some understanding of cultural dimensions related to psychological variables and it is possible to relate means of psychological variables to cultural dimensions. More informative, however, is where specific aspects of culture can be related in a measurable way to psychological variables. However, even with these studies a researcher cannot be certain that there may not be other aspects of culture not measured that might also explain the behavior studied or for that matter the direction of the causal influence.

2.13. SKEPTICAL THINKING IS THE PATH TO AN IMPROVED CROSS-CULTURAL PSYCHOLOGY.

So many aspects of human thinking are influenced by cognitive processes seeking easy solutions. Cross-cultural psychology is complex and difficult and requires students and researchers willing to cultivate a *skeptical mind*. The many problems of bias discussed above is partly the consequence of looking for simplistic answers to the most complex science of all that of understanding human behavior in the cultural context. At the foundation of many biases in cross-cultural psychology is the inability of the researcher to observe his/her own evaluative biases in how research is conducted and carried out. After completion of the research there are also many possibilities for bias in interpretation. Although we are trained to think analytically, and look for differences even when these are minimal, we should be skeptical about generalizations. Most findings apply to specific circumstances and time. An obvious evaluation question is to ask what other factors may explain our findings. This is especially salient when cultural variables are inferred and not measured directly.

Although we may find differences in comparative studies it is well to remember that the participating groups are heterogeneous along pertinent dimensions. Therefore any conclusions pertain only to the average responses required by statistical techniques that do not take into account this within group variability. Although a society may be low on average education, it still may have an educated class that has a strong influence on developments within the cultural group. A random sampling of such a society would deemphasize other problems like whether the participants were required to attain a certain educational level to understand the survey questions or research protocol.

As we can see the complexity of cross-cultural research creates many issues that undermine the validity of research results. The obvious problems of linguistic equivalence can be disposed with little difficulty using proper translation procedures. Other problems like equivalence in understanding the experimental constructs the same way in different cultures present more difficult issues in comparative research. Validity ultimately involves the correct interpretation of the results. A pertinent issue related to validity is the extent to which we have sampled issues that are truly salient in the cultures investigated. Issues significant in the society of the investigator are not necessarily salient in other cultures? Cultural comparative studies must be approached from a variety of angles including the use of alternate methods, samples, and procedures, and the researcher must recognize the continual need for replication.

SUMMARY

The value of cross-cultural psychology depends on the reliability and validity of the research. It is well to keep in mind that the complexity of the discipline offers many opportunities to bias the results. The most significant issue in comparative research is equivalence along several criteria whether the research protocol is based on surveys, attitude scales, interviewing, experiments under cultural conditions, or qualitative studies. Linguistic equivalence is possible by following proper procedures including establishing initially a bi-lingual committee to work toward a consensus about the use of language meaning in the research protocol. The back-translation procedure further ensures that the same meaning is conveyed to the groups surveyed. Psychometric equivalence seeks evidence to ensure that the same construct is measured in comparative research. Criteria are established by comparing whether the same preference order in response categories and item difficulty is found in the groups surveyed. The structure of the psychological assessment can also be established by means of item analysis. An important equivalence issue is whether the comparative research is based on the same theoretical framework in the cultures that are compared. The psychometric structure can also be examined by means of factor analysis and other statistical techniques.

Comparing equivalent samples is essential to cross-cultural research. This is not easily achieved as factors not known about the culture may affect responses such as dissimilar education and literacy. In that regard we must remember that cross-national samples do not have the same meaning as cross-cultural samples as one nation may contain many cultural groups. Heterogeneity in cultural values confounds many national comparative studies. Matched samples create other ambiguities since they may create mismatching on other salient variables. Convenience sampling is not random, but may be useful in developing measurement instruments. Sampling that is based on theoretical considerations is called systematic when such samples are drawn with proper demographic controls. However, random sampling is the only approach considered representative of the population studied and if large enough represents the cultural group with little error. Equivalent samples can also be built using similar demographic variables. Non-equivalence is, however, ubiquitous in cultural and cross-cultural studies that utilize approximations to construct methodological equivalence. In survey research equivalence can be promoted post hoc by identifying non-equivalent items and eliminating these from the analysis.

Cross-cultural studies are complex as they require different levels of inferences. Low level inference is possible when the researcher constructs item samples directly from the domain of interest as occurs in the building of attitude scales utilizing statements from the universe of all possible items. Medium level inferences are not directly observed but believed to be determining factors of behavior. Factors considered medium level include personality traits where the aim of the assessment is to capture the essence of the domain. The ambiguities that occur at this level call into question whether the construct measured is in fact comparable across cultures. High level inferences concern more complex domains not easily specified, and which are not easily captured by measurement techniques. At this level inferences are typically made post hoc without empirical evidence such as occur in evaluations of research on constructs like adaptation or intelligence.

Useful cross-cultural studies have been carried out at the ecological level reporting average statistics that point to underlying dimensions responsible for culturally related behaviors. For example, studies that report on the presence of individualism in a culture have been related to the rate of heart disease. However, cross-cultural comparative research seeks to ascertain differences on psychological assessments. We must however remember there is more to culture than the psychological world and survey results in any event measure only a small sampling of the domain of interest. Not measured are differences in the natural world, the ecological context, or childrearing procedures, that all have the potential to significantly influence behavior. Examining specific cultural context may explain differences in psychological attributes, and psychological survey results are often explained at the contextual level. There are, however, problems in interpretation when results at one level are explained by inference to another level. A step forward is to measure specific aspects of culture through the construction of scales and surveys.

The possibility of bias exists in any psychological assessment. Survey or scale items may be poorly constructed or inadequately translated. Such item error can usually be corrected by statistical testing. However, if the entire methodology is problematic the only solution is to return to the drawing board and select alternative research approaches. Bias in psychological assessments may occur due to differences in respondents familiarity with the construct measured, due to poor sampling of the concepts, and due to the influence of social desirability. Research has also demonstrated differences between individual versus group enhancement in varying cultures that also might bias the respondents answers. Response sets also influence responses in cross-cultural comparative studies, and the cultural blinds of the researcher produce implicit bias in construct and methodological selection.

All disciplines in psychology are interested in establishing cause and effect relationships. However, the special problems of cross-cultural psychology make that objective difficult. Most studies in cross-cultural psychology are correlational as it is impossible to assign cultural respondents randomly to experimental treatment. However, even in correlational research the constructs must be operationalized and measured or inferences about culture cannot be made.

Researchers in the field have often taken antagonistic positions about the value of qualitative versus quantitative research. Qualitative research is often employed for in-depth studies of a single culture, but in the context of cross-cultural research can be seen as exploratory and hypothesis generating for use in quantitative studies. The argument in favor of qualitative studies is that cultural reality is socially constructed and therefore only a relationship between the researcher and the culture (represented by informants) can assess that reality. Typically, qualitative research is associated with behavior in the natural world, and best carried out when the observer works in a participant-observer relationship. Theory development in qualitative research is based on an inductive process utilizing multiple sources.

However, both approaches are not antagonistic, but rather complementary despite contentions centered on the validity of the results produced.

Quantitative methods include surveys that test for psychological differences between cultures on established psychological assessments. Surveys can be open-ended but questions with fixed categories are easier to quantify. Interviews that use standardized questions can also be useful if the researcher is careful in not reinforcing certain responses. Although telephone and Internet surveys are easy to conduct the researcher must be careful to avoid bias derived from differences in socio-economic status measured by access to these means of communication. Meta-analysis creates a summary statistic and an overall integration of the results. However, bias may be introduced as the focus is only on statistically significant studies ignoring perhaps the larger pool of insignificant results.

It is also possible to design studies that test for the effect of cultural context variables where cultural populations are selected in advance as known to have characteristics of the domain of interest. Replications in other cultures of these results can be seen as evidence of validity as well as the presence of universal psychological characteristics. In one study the mindsets of the participants were primed for individualistic or collectivistic responses with predictable results.

All cross-cultural research deals with the issue of validity. The best answer to these concerns is to utilize all available approaches, demonstrate conceptual clarity, and replicate studies over time and cultural contexts. A critical look at the field cautions that the researcher's cultural frame may introduce bias in selection of domain and methodology. Also respondents are more sensitive to their own cultural frames and that may produce biases in responses. At the same time globalization and new means of communications call into question the permanence of any cultural values. Finally, the reporting of only statistical significant findings may introduce bias as summaries like those found in meta-analysis do not take into account the possible broader pool of insignificant results. Further any study represents only a fragment of the relevant psychological domain or the cultural context of interest. Consequently skeptical thinking is required in order to improve validity since cross-cultural psychology is both difficult and complex.

CHAPTER 3

THE ORIGIN OF CULTURE

Cultural Transformation and Sociocultural Evolution

To understand where culture comes from would help answer many of the perplexing questions of humanity. Understanding the origin of culture would help illuminate the development of religious and political thought, and anecdotally help us understand the origin of life itself. Most people find themselves in the midst of cultural structures, and accept unconsciously that reality without an evaluation of from hence it came. However, if we understood the origin of culture along with genetically based deep genealogy (geneography) we would recognize the common roots of all mankind. Genetic and cultural science might help remove some of the barriers and enmity derived from the ethnocentric evaluations of cultural values. Evolutionary psychology argues that social achievements and motivations are functions of adaptations that promote reproductive success (Buss, 2001). What matters therefore are how well people adapt to their contextual environment. Humanity has had many problems to solve over the past 30000 plus years in adapting to meet the biological needs for food and shelter, overcoming natural barriers, raising children and passing on cultural in-

Cross-Cultural Psychology: Why Culture Matters, pages 53–80.
Copyright © 2013 by Information Age Publishing

formation. In response to these demands cultures have developed cultural values as well as religious and political hierarchies.

Culture is produced by the complex interactions of biological imperatives with the solutions produced and transmitted as information to succeeding generations. All humans are born with biological needs that motivate behavior including those related to safety, good health and reproduction. Regardless of the ideological abstractions developed by cultures all groups must in the end find ways of dealing with these universal biological demands (Malinowski, 1960). The comparative evidence from animal culture shows that many species form social groups, use tools, and engage in communication in response to their biological needs for survival. Nevertheless, only humans have the unique ability to learn *natural languages,* and also employ *symbolic representations* that allow for complex cognition (Premack, 2004). Only the human species can speculate on the intent of others and form causal beliefs or attributions for the behavior of those with whom we interact. Likewise evaluation of morality appears to be based on the human ability to think and engage in higher forms of social cognition. Finally, a unique human trait is the ability to see functional relationships and continue to improve the conditions for survival. Improvement is not a linear development in cultural evolution, as different religious and political systems are tried and discarded in the course of human history. At times the constructs contained in these social systems do not respond to objective conditions causing a revolution as social groups seek more effective ways to deal with human cultural and biological needs.

The meaning of human culture is found in the *unique informational systems* that allow each group to meet basic needs for survival and well-being and that are transmitted by means of natural or symbolic language to succeeding generations (Baumeister, 2005). Culture answers many questions related to the meaning of life that are reflected in culturally developed religious world views and political ideology. The end goals of surviving and human well-being is served by the social systems that have evolved, in some cases over generations, in other cases more rapidly as new information systems have come on line. Complex systems of social interactions are a product of culture, as are the cognitive abilities required and promoted by social organization. Culture is therefore defined by the functions it provides in the pursuit of survival, in creating systems for communication and meaning, and in improving social structures for the well-being of the members of the cultural group. These cultural products did not just happen, but evolved in response to the biological imperatives that motivated our ancestors in the search for survival and well-being.

3.1. THE CASE FOR THE BIOLOGICAL FOUNDATIONS OF HUMAN CHARACTERISTICS

The research discussed below argues the case for a biological basis of human emotion and universal personality traits. These characteristics reflect the major individual components that define us as a species. Biological etiology of human traits requires an *evolutionary explanation* for human psychology. *Since cultural evolution follows a similar pattern as biological evolution both constructs are essential for a complete description of the evolution of human culture.* The emphasis in cross-cultural psychology in the past has been in describing the effects of the sociocultural environment on behavior. A complete overview, however, requires an evaluation of biological adaptation based on genetic transmissions from one generation to the next.

3.1.1. Evolution and the Mechanisms of Transmission

The essential concepts in Darwin's theory of evolution are based on trait diversity between individuals within the species studied. For many species the evolutionary strategy to survive is to have a large number of offspring as many individuals die in infancy. When a heritable trait increases the possibility of survival and reproductive success the frequency of that trait becomes magnified in succeeding generations. In evolutionary theory some traits produce a higher level of reproductive fitness. Over the eons of time in our Earth's history evolution has led to systematic genetic changes in the population described by Darwin as natural selection. The natural selection of reproductive fitness is produced by the interaction of individual and cultural groups with the physical and social environments. Most of us are familiar with evolution on a first hand basis having seen the effects of breeding programs by farmers that accelerate natural selection by selecting animals for breeding that have desirable characteristics.

Although mutations play a role in the evolution of lower species, the longer life cycles of humans preserve a stronger change effect from cultural factors including migration and choice in mating. Migration and isolation from other geographical groups can produce variations due to random occurrences also called genetic drift. Random fluctuations are of little importance in large populations, but may produce measurable long-term effects in small populations. Therefore the initial gene pool of an immigrant group may have long-term effects on the phenotypes of subsequent generations. The phenotypes of racial differences are such long lasting effects found initially in small genetic immigrant populations. Nevertheless these phenotypical gene pools for the most part refer to unimportant visible traits like skin tone. Non-random choice for sexual partners is also a factor in human evolution as these choices are governed in most societies by social rules. Daughters of the rich marry sons of the rich and in that social rule for reproductive fitness we can observe a certain amount of inbreeding and control over social resources. In some societies marriage is encouraged between close relatives reducing genetic variability. In modern societies probably the most prominent selection device is education. Since education is also related to intelligence, selection may play a role in the variability of that trait.

3.1.2, Races as a Biological and Social Construct

The phenotypic differences represented by the construct of "race" is the result of geographical isolation following human migrations, the long-term effect of aforementioned initial gene pool in immigrant groups, and the cultural emphasis on choice of mating within gene pools. *Geographic isolation* continued inbreeding especially in initially small populations responsible for some visual traits. Environmental forces also produced some selective advantages especially with skin color that people commonly associate with race. It has been argued and seems logically irrefutable, that skin color is a response to the amount and strength of sunlight in geographical regions. In the tropical areas where sunlight is especially intense a dark skin color may offer some protection and selective advantage from an evolutionary perspective. In the north where the amount of sunlight exposure is less (but needed as a source of vitamin D required for prevention of rickets), light skin conferred evolutionary advantages (Vogel & Motulsky, 1979). Today the study of deep genetic (geneographic) genealogy elicits strong support for the contention that we all came out of Africa, and that the change in skin color probably occurred as a consequence of the selective advantage of lighter skin tones in the more northern regions. In other words, people with genetic mutations for light skin were more evolutionary fit in the northern regions, and therefore left offspring that survived.

Scientific evidence supports the contention that all humans are genetically brothers and sisters and racism in stereotypic expression is incredibly disingenuous (Paabo, 2001). Although such "racial" differences are very visual, the differences in gene pools are quite small compared to the genetic overlap. Differences between population groups separated by geography are also small compared to the genetic diversity existing within established population groups. For example, although blood groups vary to a small degree across geographic regions of the world, the same groups exist everywhere. The common human genetic pool ensures that you are as well served by blood transfusions from different regions and "races" as you are in getting one from your same "race" neighbor.

Nevertheless the sad story of humanity show that "race" matters as a *social construct. As a social construct it is the beliefs of people about phenotypes that matter, and when informed by prejudice racism has proven to be a very negative force in the world.* It has played a historical role in all societies, and influenced the direction of history as in the case of slavery and all that followed. However, the human genome project of the National Geographic journal demonstrates our very common genetic heritage, and that we were only separated in relatively recent evolutionary history.

3.1.3. The Role of Adaptation

Change produced by natural selection in response to environmental pressure is called *adaptation*. Over time a population adapts to environmental demands or perishes. The Scandinavians in Greenland tried to bring a European agricultural society to a land that required adaptation to sea food and extreme weather conditions and they did not survive. The native Inuit population, on the other hand, has continued with their successful adaptation into modern times under the same harsh conditions. From the perspective of evolutionary biology adaptation is the successful adjustment of a people to environmental demands (Lewontin, 1972).

Adaptation in social science may also refer to changes that have occurred in the lifetime of people that may affect transfer of epigenetic information. Agent Orange, for example, has caused profound damage in Vietnam including epigenetic damage that has affected at least several generations (Larsen & Van Le, 2010). The Vietnamese have had to respond to this poisoning by social and medical programs unprecedented in world history.

It is important to remember that humans are not only shaped by the environment, but also interact with it. Global warming is an extreme example of human failure to adapt that may threaten other advantages acquired by natural selection. In more positive ways human population groups have contributed to the shaping of their environments through constant interaction and created niches that ensure survival and heritable culture. In today's world the environment, both social and physical, are constantly changing requiring continuous adaptation to keep up with new challenges.

3.2. THE RESEARCH SUPPORTING THE EVOLUTION OF HUMAN EMOTION

The presence of human emotions is universal and characterizes human behavior and interactions. We are not alone in possessing emotional traits as comparative research shows the presence of emotions in our primate cousins. Apes, for example, display well-defined emotional reactions including fear and anger (De Waal, 2003). Since humans and apes have shared these emotions with our primate ancestors the traits have probably evolved in response to adaptive pressures. Emotions provide context to our lives and create subjective feelings that help evaluate events or our social interaction. Depending on interpretation emotions are stimuli preparing us to take some action toward people or events. We can know when a person is emotionally affected by the tone of his/her voice or facial contractions. Facial responses can be universally identified and categorized as to specific emotions. Emotions also produce physiological changes as the affected individual react with faster heart rates and breathing in preparation to deal with flight or fight responses.

Unlike our primate cousins, however, humans have the capacity of self-reflection. For example, negative self-evaluations may produce embarrassment, shame and even guilt. With unique cognitive representations of the self as an intentional and responsible agent, humans also display morally related emotions including disgust and contempt (Haidt, 2001). Although some animals can display disgust as related to food or aversive stimuli, only humans have the capacity for interpersonal disgust as we evaluate the moral behavior of others (Gottman & Levenson, 2002). Human emotions are essentially neurophysiologic events evolved over the deep history of our species, and as discussed above are universal and represented in every society.

3.2.1. Universal Temperament and Personality Traits Are Evidence of Common Evolved History

The presence of differences in children's temperament at birth has been taken as evidence of the *heritability of personality*. Some infants are "easy" and sleep through the night, take nutrition readily, and are a pleasure to be around. Other babies are "difficult" often cry and fuss and wake repeatedly for attention throughout the night. Most parents will have observed some of these differences in their children or those of friends and family. Temperament has been defined as the dominant behavioral mode that is more or less consistent across situations (Strelau, 1998). The study of temperament has long been of interest in behavior genetics and is defined as consistent and dominant behavioral reactions across many social situations (Van der Werff, 1985). For example, we may say a person has an irritable temperament thereby describing a person's constant negative reaction to a variety of stimuli. The genetic basis for these consistencies in temperament is supported in recent research (Strelau, 1998). However, there are problems associated with heritability estimates of temperament and other human characteristics. For example, research has not located a single gene pathway link to specific personality traits. Recently more complex approaches have examined the covariance of several genes linked to behavior (Riemann & De Raad, 1998). Temperament may be the genetic component affecting the infant that explains the development of subsequent personality. Generally the environment is not seen as a significant contributor to personality differences as these individual consistencies are maintained despite varying contexts and conditions.

In recent decades research has *found solid support for the presence of universal traits of personality based on five distinct dimensions named openness, conscien-*

tiousness, extraversion, agreeableness, and neuroticism. This universal conceptual model was based on many studies that demonstrated similarities in personality dimensions within cultures, but also cross-culturally. The original research discovered five dimensions from factor analyses of trait adjectives that were used to describe the self and others (Juni, 1996). Research has established heritability estimates of personality in a fashion similar to intelligence estimates determining the proportion of the total variance of that can be attributed to genetic inheritance. Heritability estimates have been calculated for the so-called Big Five, including heritability estimates of about .50 for the extraversion-introversion dimension (Bouchard, McGue, Hur, & Horn, 1998). Other cross-cultural research found a similar constellation of traits in various societies employing other personality tests as well as trait adjectives (McCrae, Costa, del Pilar, Rolland, & Parker, 1998; Schmitt, Allik, McCrae, & Benet-Martinez, 2007).

The proportion of the total behavioral variation attributed to genetic inheritance was determined by comparing correlations between closely related persons like twins to those less closely related genetically. For example the heritability estimates for extraversion are .51 for identical twins, but only .16 for siblings, and .01 for adopted children. Heritability estimates for extraversion based on twin studies is generally around .50, whereas for the other of the Big Five traits the estimates range from .30 to .50 (Bouchard, McGue, Hur, & Horn, 1998). The low heritability estimates for adopted children suggest that the environment has very small effects on extraversion and that the consistency of personality probably is genetically determined or mediated (Plomin, DeFries, McClearn, & Rutter, 1997).

An impressive body of research has continued to support the presence of the Big Five in all societies studied (Hofstede, Kiers, De Raad, Goldberg, & Ostendorf, 1997; McCrae, 2001). The measures of the Big Five were administered in 51 cultures and subsequently subjected to factor analysis. Again the data analysis grouped the personality descriptions into the five major factors (McCrae, Terracciano, Leibovich, Schmidt, Shakespeare-Finch, Naubauer et al., 2005). In particular strong support was found for the presence of extraversion and neuroticism utilized in a graphic display of a variety of cultures being high or low on these dimensions. In another study Allik and McCrae (2004) found that the relationship in personality between cultures was a function of geographic closeness with participants more closely related in personality sharing both deep geneographic journeys as well as culture. The overall research suggests the presence of the Big Five as a universal model of personality structure.

Again we must be reminded that the research is far from conclusive since no personality trait is caused by a single gene, and it is not possible to dismiss personality-environmental interactions. Research is increasingly recognizing this complexity including the investigation of multiple genes and their interactions (Plomin & Caspi, 1998). This research is just in its infancy, but the results support an important genetic factor in behavior, and the universal basis for personality communalities independent of culture. The issue will be discussed further in chapter 8 on personality.

The universality of both human characteristics and neurophysiologic mechanisms suggest a response to evolutionary mechanisms. *The ubiquitous nature of the personality structure and optimism suggests that they have served evolutionary functions in adaptation and in problem solving, and that one might expect corresponding neurophysiologic brain structures* (MacDonald, 1998). For example, conscientiousness might be functionally advantageous by helping monitor situations that produce punishments. Conscientiousness might also help create the longer view in humans that is functional when individuals must strive for future goals even when tasks are not intrinsically rewarding. For example, students need conscientiousness in order to complete uninteresting requirements for a university degree. Consistent behaviors reflected in personality have evolved to motivate people to perform behaviors that ensure reproductive success and motivate functional outcomes.

The *Big Five* personality traits have been found in all cultures investigated (McCrae, Terracciano, Leibovich, Schmidt, Shakespeare-Finch, Naubauer et al., 2005) in studies employing a variety of measurement procedures. Again these traits tend to be stable across the lifespan suggesting little environmental influence (McCrae & Costa, 2003). Further research has shown that the relationship between parent and child has largely temporary affects (Rowe, 1994). The research on identical twins also points to a biological basis as the personalities of twins that are reared in independent environments are more similar than those of fraternal twins reared together (Bouchard & Loehlin, 2001). The persistence of personality traits have also been demonstrated over the long run in longitudinal studies pointing to hard wiring in the brain (Borkenau & Ostendorf, 1998).

3.2.2. Intelligence as a Biological and Racial Construct

The genetic contribution to intelligence is widely acknowledged. Estimates of heritability of intelligence are much larger than for other human traits. Heritability of intelligence has been established in research with estimates of around .75. The effects of the genes increase with age as the influence of family fades away around adolescence. As children age they become more independent of environmental influences and fit their intellectual activities to their genetic potential (Loehlin, Horn, & Willerman, 1989). Children as they get older score more closely to their genetic potential, and become more independent of family influences (Loehlin, Horn, & Willerman, 1989). The evidence of heritability is generally observed from twin studies where some live together and others apart. Regardless of living conditions results demonstrate that the closer the genetic relationship the more alike the IQ scores (Bouchard, Lykken, McGue, Segal, & Tellegen, 1990). The genetic component is typically estimated from differences in correlations between those who are closely related like twins compared to those that are less related or complete strangers. Comparisons have been made between identical and fraternal twins also supporting heritability. As noted the heritability estimate is .51 for identical twins (Loehlin, 1992), suggesting a significant genetic contribution to the variability of intelligence.

The construct of intelligence and its genetic component has been hotly argued over the past decades. In the past differences between races in intelligence estimates occupied much attention of researchers and the results have been used as justification to evaluate social policy (Jensen, 1985). Herrnstein and Murray (1994) argued that intelligence is the main factor predicting success in the United States, and African Americans are found at the lower end of the bell curve for intelligence. Herrnstein and others have argued that social interventions and special education will not make much difference in the intellectual achievements of Blacks since intelligence is assumed to be primarily genetic. The fixedness of intelligence in turn places limits on achievements of Blacks, Jensen, Herrnstein and Murphy argues, and social programs for these minorities are largely a waste of resources. For these researchers the evidence is clear-cut that intelligence is largely an inherited genetic capability. However, the categorization of race is quit arbitrary, particularly in the U.S. where the research was conducted. Racial categorization is typically based on self-identification of skin color that is probably the least meaningful criteria of "race" since in the U.S. the genetic heritage of most people derives from a variety of racial and ethnic backgrounds.

Other investigators have also observed that intelligence often shifts drastically under varying social and environmental conditions. Unfortunately, this *nature-nurture* debate has also become ideological as vested interests have argued that the research cited above supports the higher intelligence of some groups or "races" when compared to others. However, it should be remembered that the heritability estimates of intelligence were derived from studies of individuals to make the argument of differences between populations (Rushton, 1988). *Population differences in estimates of intelligence are impossible to ascertain since there is always an interaction effect between the genetic components and the environment.* There is no logical basis to infer from the heritability estimates of individual differences that the observed differences between populations are likewise determined by the genetic contribution as the observed differences could be the result interaction with the cultural environment. Genetic inferences for individual differences in intelligence do not allow us to assume that differences at the group or national level are based on inherent factors (Sternberg, 2004). Observed differences (whether between national or "racial" groups) can be totally attributed to environmental advantages or disadvantages.

Limitations to individual achievement based on genetics are not supported by other research. For example, improvement in diet over one generation had a profound influence on IQ scores with increases in the range from 15–20 points in Western nations (Flynn, 1987). Since we know that advantageous mutations could not occur at that rapid rate the environmental changes, including improvement in nutrition, is the more likely causal contributor. At any rate IQ scores do not appear to be stable over time therefore making populations comparisons problematic in terms of both reliability and validity. Nevertheless that the hereditary genetic component determines significant parameters of intelligence are supported by nearly all scholars (Snyderman & Rothman, 1988).

Finally, in evaluating the heritability of intelligence it is important to make a distinction between actualized genetic potential and non-actualized intelligence. *Heritability estimates are made exclusively from actualized potential and offer no information on non-actualized potential caused, for example, by adverse environmental conditions.* Measured actualized potential is a result of gene-environment interactions and is the basis of any heritability estimates. Further, there are many socio-economic differences that impact actualized potential and therefore impact scores on intelligence tests that are not controlled in studies on group differences. In fact we have no way of evaluating non-actualized intelligence. From the perspective of cross-cultural differences there is an even broader range of socio-cultural environments that are not measured by IQ tests. Finally, we need to emphasize that although group differences in intelligence is reported in research we cannot assume that these have a genetic basis. Racial and other group differences in intelligence can in fact all be accounted for by measurement problems including not utilizing constructs and terms familiar to participants in all racial groups. The heritability of intelligence issue is only important because intelligence testing has been used in the debate over social policy.

3.2.3. Behavior Genetics and Disease

Genetics make contributions to morphological and physiological traits as well as to behavior. The most obvious link between genetic heritage and phenotype (appearance) are physical characteristics. For example, identical twins have identical genetic components and also identical appearance. Since cultural influences are also powerful it is particularly difficult to ascertain the influence of genes on human behavior. Nevertheless the etiology and function of genes in certain illnesses and associated behaviors is obvious. For example, Down's syndrome is produced by genetic malfunction where instead of inheriting two number 21 chromosomes, the child inherits three.

Ongoing research has for some time linked genetic predispositions to mental disorders including depression and schizophrenia based on twin studies and other close familial relationships (Plomin, DeFries, McClearn, & Rutter, 1997). A genetic basis for these disorders is also supported by the fact that these mental disorders are universal although influenced also by cultural factors. More likely major mental illnesses are a result of an interaction between genetic factors and the environment. However, since no single gene is responsible for any behavior the gene-behavior pathway is very complex and difficult to establish. As for personality and intelligence the heritability of frequently occurring mental disorders like schizophrenia has largely been estimated from the frequency of occurrence in the patient's closely related family. The fact that these illnesses occur worldwide would also strongly suggest a genetic influence, although different environments may still influence relative frequency and severity of symptoms (Plomin, DeFries, McClearn, & Rutter, 1997).

3.2.4. Hardwired Optimism: The Driver for Cultural Development

Recent research (Sharot, 2011) has pointed toward the existence of a *universal optimism bias*. Research shows that humans are born with rose-colored glasses and more inherent optimism than justified by reality. For example, ten percent of Americans believe they will live to be 100, whereas only 0.02 percent lives to that age. Assessments of the predictions of divorce shows that zero percent of U.S. marriage applicants expect to experience divorce whereas nearly half of married partners permanently end their marriages. Many respond with pessimism to contemporary economic conditions and 70 percent believe that other families in general are less successful compared to their parents' generation. However, when it comes to evaluating their own lives 76 percent are optimistic about the future of their own families. Research also showed profound optimism about their own driving ability as compared to others with 93 percent believing they were in the top 50 percentile in driving ability. The belief that somehow the future will always be better than the past is known as the "optimism bias" and is universal. One would think the contemporary conditions of wars, natural disasters, and economic collapse would affect personal prediction in a more pessimistic direction. However, as noted above our personal optimism remains high even while our expectations for society become pessimistic.

The obvious question is why personal optimism is so ubiquitous. It seems clear that persistent optimism is functional to our survival and cultural progress. Without optimism there would be nothing to stimulate innovation, produce new ideas, or encourage a willingness to persist despite conformity pressures. If not for optimism our ancestors might never have left Africa, or produced better ways to survive. We might still have remained cave dwellers if not for the motivational spark that made it possible to seek better ways. Our cognitive ability to anticipate alternative futures has been an essential component in the journey of mankind. A positive future may well be an illusion, but optimism provides clear benefits to the present. Optimists are more likely to look after their health whereas pessimistic cancer patients died earlier than those who had hope (Furnham & Heaven, 1999).

Now there is *evidence that optimism may be hardwired into the brain as a trait selected by evolution with direct functional advantages.* That opens a new perspective that our brains are not just related to the past, but may in fact be directed toward the future as well. Sharot's research showed that the mere anticipation of the future colored even the most basic life events for the better. Could it be that optimism is the consequence of how our brains are wired? That our brains can anticipate the future has obvious survival functions as humans might better plan for contingencies and save resources for times of crisis or scarcity. Animals like squirrels and other species also have this function to anticipate winter and scarcity of food. This ability to mentally time travel is based on specific brain structures called the hippocampus. The research, however, shows that most people do not spend much time thinking about negative outcomes, but rather on how life might get better. Early research also points to the ability of the frontal cortex to communicate with subcortical regions as essential in directing our thoughts in a positive direction. Sharot (Sharot, 2011) suggests that without a neural mechanism that produces unrealistic optimism all humanity would be mildly depressed. However, on the contrary most of us find a silver lining in most events and find the positive even in negative outcomes. For example, once a decision is made we all tend to evaluate the prospects positively and expect pleasure.

Sharot suggest that optimism was selected by evolutionary processes because positive expectations are motivating and increase our odds for survival. Optimists live longer and are healthier as they behave consistent with their positive expectations. The ubiquitous nature of optimism leads to an evaluation of the possibility that this trait is linked to specific gene structures—an area of future research. While optimism is irrational we would probably not get out of bed in the morning without future positive expectations (Sharot, Guitart-Masip, Korn, Chowdhury, & Dolan, 2012; Sharot, Korn, & Dolan, 2011; Sharot, Riccardi, Raio, & Phelps, 2007).

3.3. SOCIOBIOLOGY AND EVOLUTIONARY PSYCHOLOGY

Most people are familiar with the role of genetics in changing morphological characteristics in animals. Farmers bred cows for milk production and dogs have been bred over generations to such an extent that the link to the wolf-like morphology has largely disappeared in creatures like the poodle. Recent research on genetic manipulations and induced mutations provides more evidence for the role of genes at the morphological level. There is also obvious behavior characteristics bred into animals under the broad topic of temperament. For example, bulls are bred for their aggressiveness which bullfighters anthropomorphize as "courage." The contributions of genes to both the morphology and behavior in animals are beyond dispute. Is there any reason to believe that genes should not contribute to behavior also in humans?

Studies by biologists of animal behavior offer tantalizing inferences to human social interactions. *Ethology* as a discipline has carried out field studies of animals in their natural habit that permit interesting cross-species comparisons. Varying research projects have examined territoriality, but also courtship behavior and communication in animals. Anyone who has been around dogs knows that they are territorial, and commence warning barks when any stranger invades their human defined space. Other species display similar behavior. The behavioral pattern in animals tends to be regular and predictable, and this invariance is explained by genetic control factors. However, it is within the constraints of particular ecological niches that even so-called instinctive responses occur as the behavior is also a response to stimuli in the environmental context. Human cultural groups have historically presented similar territorial and aggressive behavior as most wars have at least in part been fought over control of territories. The most intractable human conflict is over territory claimed by historical myth to belong to two different population groups as is the case of the Palestinians and the Jewish immigrant community in Palestine.

Studies from human ethology emphasize the biological basis of human behavior as significant similarities between human and animal behavior is observed (Eibl-Eibesfeldt, 1989). In recent times research has concluded that animals too have culture, although not the ability to engage in complex cognition and symbolization which is the foundation of human culture. Eibl-Eibesfeldt (1979) presented evidence that demonstrated the role of phylogenetic development at the human level. Many universal patterns of behavior are present in all cultures observed. However, there are also differences between cultures in the expression of universal behaviors. Some human rituals suggest universality, like the open hand salute used as a sign of peaceful intentions. Eibl-Eibesfeldt argues strongly for the presence of genetic components in much of human interaction and in cognition. Nevertheless there are important differences as animal behavior patterns tend to remain more fixed and invariable, and human behavior more plastic and influenced by the cultural context.

The preceding discussion has emphasized the biological predispositions essential to cultural development. The study of human ethology demonstrates our evolutionary link to other species. For example kissing is a universal sign of affection in children and is probably a phylogenetic adaptation to feeding in our evolutionary past (Eibl-Eibesfeldt, 1979, 1989). This universal response by mothers toward children probably derived from mouth to mouth feeding in early stages of evolutionary development as we can also observe this behavior in non-human primates. Although we should maintain a healthy sense of skepticism in evaluating comparative similarities of species there is a remarkable overlap between social behavior in animals and humans. Although similarities may be accidental, many behaviors are strikingly similar across species requiring at least openness toward the possibility that they are the result of similar selective evolutionary pressures that shaped behavior. These behaviors may have evolved from our phylogenetic evolution, but the source may also be cultural evolution derived from common ancestors. For example, head gestures may signal elementary responses like "no." For most of the world "no" is indicated by shaking the head horizontally leading to some conjecture of a common evolutionary origin. However, cultural influences are also at play as for example "no" in Bulgaria is indicated by up and down motion of the head, not a sideways shaking. This variance must have derived from common cultural ancestors. Eibl-Eibesfeldt suggests that genetic mechanisms are the grammar of human interaction upon which culture builds variances through socialization. However, it is well to keep in mind that the higher the organism places on the phylogenetic scale the more plastic the behavior and the greater the role of learning in adaptation.

Sociobiology seeks to explain human behavior as a response to evolutionary pressures (Wilson, 1975). *From this perspective human behavior is fundamentally motivated by the need to maximize inclusive fitness, thus leaving not only direct offspring but also supporting the productive success of close relatives.* The meaning of family closeness is produced by the evolutionary pressure to protect and ensure the reproductive success of succeeding generations. In the most extreme case Wilson argues that the humanities and social sciences can be reduced to branches of biology. The biological origin of behavior is verified if the category studied is found in nearly all or all societies. Can human culture at some level be reduced to principles of evolution?

3.3.1. Gender Differences in Mate Selection

Men and women have very different perspectives on sexual variety with men having a greater desire for multiple partners. Research has also shown that men are more jealous of promiscuity in women. *These dominating preferences are logically explained by gender based strategies for reproductive success also found among most mammals.* Since a woman can have only a limited number of children given the resources required for each she has a particular interest in the bonding of the male whether by marriage or other means. The male, on the other hand, has a large capacity for reproduction that continues for many more years compared to the female. *Reproductive success* from an evolutionary perspective is best achieved by the male through the sexual encounter with many females. Is that the explanation of the greater sexual promiscuity in males as compared to females, and the attempt to control sexual promiscuity through polygamy?

Mate selection may reflect these broader evolutionary differences between males and females. In a major study conducted in 31 countries Buss (1989) investigated the preferred characteristics in opposite sex mates (see also Buss, 1995, 2001). The gender differences discussed above found support in these studies. Females typically had a greater interest in the financial prospects of potential mates, whereas males had a greater appreciation for physical attractiveness that reflected good health and fertility. Later research found that the preferences of women and men followed these differences in reproductive strategies. While both sexes value attractive appearance that signals fertility (being youthful) *men were more interested in physical attractiveness, whereas women were more interested in providers that had financial prospects.* Support for these gender differences can also be found in a study on partner advertisements where men preferred younger women whereas women appreciated more the financial support likely in a relationship (Kenrick & Keefe, 1992). Since men are fertile for longer periods than women the male preference is seen as a sociobiological strategy to connect with younger women still capable of having children.

It is not surprising that both sexes also valued love and dependable traits along with intelligent and understanding partners. However, to summarize if mating behavior is biologically based we should observe similarities across human cultures. Human sexuality has been a special interest of sociobiologists who have observed that male dominance is ubiquitous. Men and women have different perspectives on sexuality related to their biological function (Alcock, 1984). The bonding desire by the female is an essential condition to support her offspring and ensure survival. Typically women can only look after one newborn at a time and as noted have limited potential in the number of children. Reproductive success for men, however, is linked to having many partners and thereby ensuring the survival of his genetic line. The best male strategy from a sociobiological perspective is to have as many partners as possible and therefore many offspring. Behavioral differences between cultures are just variations of the same biological themes that emphasize survival and reproductive success.

Gender differences derived from the underlying motivation for reproductive success also produce differences in the preferred age of partners (Kenrick & Keefe, 1992). As men get older they increasingly partner with younger females, again explained by the longer fertility period in older men whereas the prime of fertility for females is much younger. This age preference for younger females may be a phylogenetic strategy on the part of males to choose partners who are capable of reproduction. In discussing the evolved strategies we are not claiming any consciousness on the part of either gender, but referring to the underlying architecture of the mind that determines reproductive behavior.

Nevertheless, not all researchers on gender differences agree with *sociobiological* explanations. Eagly and Wood (1999) believe that culture is responsible for these gender patterns that are derived from women ubiquitously playing a historical role of submission. The fancy for younger women by men is explained by more hedonistic pleasure seeking than evolutionary principles in this perspective.

However, these differences in preferences are universal suggesting a biological architecture that may be adjusted by culture. Further it is well to keep in mind that even though evolutionary psychology is interested in the psychobiological foundation of behavior it does not exclude a moderating role of culture. The genetic foundations for reproductive behavior might be shaped by environments through learning and cultural heritage.

3.3.2. Are Ethnocentrism and Racism a Broader Manifestation of Inclusive Fitness for Reproductive Success?

It is a fundamental argument of evolutionary psychology that all psychological functioning has to be evaluated from its relationship to *reproductive fitness* including attitudes that lead to preferences for ingroups supported by ethnocentric or racist beliefs. The evidence for an evolutionary explanation regarding ethnocentrism has been made by Reynolds, Falger and Vine (1987). According to their research ethnocentrism reflects the underlying grammar or architecture of the human mind developed in response to evolutionary pressures. The processes that functioned to ensure reproductive success were retained during evolution, and those that were dysfunctional were discarded. Thus we are likely to have positive attitudes toward groups of people that contribute to ensuring that our genes and those related to us survive and prosper ("inclusive fitness"). *With our plastic minds we can also define inclusive fitness in varying ways using belief systems as well as ethnic considerations.* That genetics play a role in the architecture of our minds can be observed by the presence of various unlearned phobias. For example, observation of small children shows they react with avoidance to snakes, but have no hardwired fear of sticking fingers into electrical sockets- a much more recent invention in human lives.

Nazism and its various proponents argued for a perverted form of social Darwinism to justify genocide and war. Toward the end of the war Hitler had little interest in the survival of Germany since from his perspective the best elements of the German nation had already lost their lives on the battle field. Recent times have seen shocking manifestations of the willingness to kill in the name of ideology, particularly by militant Muslim ideologues. However, in case people in the West feel that civilization has made such action less likely in their countries the recent massacre in Norway is a wakeup call. The perpetrator, a native Norwegian (a man by the name of Anders Behring Breivik), exploded a bomb in front of government headquarters in downtown Oslo, and then proceeded to a nearby island where young people were enjoying summer camp and methodologically murdered close to 76 people mostly children. To all appearances he was not mentally ill producing a 1500 page statement of justification on the Internet in defense of his actions that he called atrocious but necessary. He speaks with pride of his Viking heritage and was motivated by his refusal to accept what he perceived as an increased Muslim presence in Norway.

Whereas in the past inclusive fitness might be defined by the extended family or tribe, the parameters have changed with the evolution of culture. Hitler started with defining inclusive fitness as being strictly German, then as the fortunes of war caused a reevaluation moved to pan-Germanic qualifications, and eventually in desperation to all whites who looked "Aryan." It is interesting to observe the varying parameters of inclusive fitness of modern medievalists of all persuasions that have millenarian inspirations. For Breivik the inclusiveness parameter are members of European culture.

Like Osama bin Laden, Breivik defined inclusive fitness broadly based on ideology in his case that of pan-Europeanism, whereas for the Jihadist inclusiveness is based on mediaeval interpretations of Islam. Breivik is not a racist, and does not think race is that important as his model societies are Japan and South Korea. However, like Osama Bin Laden, Breivik is focused on medieval times, and sees himself as a Christian Knight in the service of his culture. Nevertheless while his focus is on the intrusion of Islam, it is probably the broader immigrant picture that he sees as threatening the "inclusive fitness" of Norwegian society. The capital Oslo now has 28 percent of the population that is foreign born (Sandbu, Ward, & Wigglesworth, 2011). Likewise Osama Bin Laden and his cohorts dreamt of an Islamic Caliphate that existed presumably centuries ago, and perceives the threat to inclusive fitness as produced by modern societies and the progress of globalization in the Islamic world. Extremist Islamic ideologies have much in common with European totalitarian traditions, especially the idea that after terrible trials (concentration camps, war, Jihad, the Gulag, sin and chaos) we find paradisiacal deliverance. Whether religious or political the common thread is the belief that society or culture is in tension, and all it takes is a mighty blow and the walls will fall (Stephens, 2011).

3.4. CULTURE MATTERS!

The evolutionary basis of higher cognitive processes does not exclude a role for the *cultural shaping* of personality. Although the structure of personality traits may be universal, the expression may well depend on socialization and cultural emphasis (Roberts, Caspi, & Moffitt, 2003). Therefore it is necessary to make a distinction between the origin of personality as a biologically based adaptation to the environment, and the specific effects of culture that produce varying emphases and functional advantages of certain traits. Pervin (1989a, 1989b) proposed a hierarchical model with personality based behavior producing motivation that is universal at the first stage such as responding to the need for safety. These evolved personality based motive dispositions are in turn the basis for personal strivings, related to personal concerns and projects, and most basically to specific responses or action units. For example, motivation that evolved for intimacy leads a person to seek a relationship with a specific person, that desire leads to practical goals of arranging for dates and meetings or improving appearance, these practical steps in turn lead to specific actions like obtaining phone numbers and dieting.

The universality of traits does not in any way reduce the significance of either culture or individual variability that is the outcome of specific environments and individual strivings. Culture makes specific statements about the value of different dispositions. In Japanese society the cultural emphasis on courtesy or the spirit of the samurai produce different personality outcomes than the informality of relationships in the West. The development of specific characteristics and adaptations to the physical or social environment depend therefore largely on the cultural heritage as passed through generations. The very meaning of behavior is culturally dependent, and the specific actions that a person engages in, in pursuit of universal affective goals will depend on that cultural meaning.

A very interesting study on the interaction of biology with culture was reported by Caspari (2011). This study estimated the age of populations from the Paleolithic period by examining fossil teeth. The results showed that nearly everyone died very young in early human populations allowing little time for grandparents to emerge and teach fundamental cultural skills. However, adult survivorship soared late among upper Paleolithic Europeans, a finding not explained by biology. For example, even though these populations groups lived under very harsh conditions the older to young ratio increased more than double that of the middle Paleolithic humans. *Caspari argues that this was produced by the interaction of grandparents living long enough to transmit cultural knowledge, and by increasing survival rates humans were able to increase the diversity and usefulness of cultural tools and symbols.* Longevity fostered intergenerational accumulation and transfer of vital information, and the social networks that in turn contributed further to longevity. According to Caspari survivorship increased dramatically in the upper Paleolithic period as a product of cultural change and that longevity opened up the possibility for the creation of culture that defines modern humans.

3.5. SOCIO-CULTURAL EVOLUTION: A LITTLE HISTORY

Utilizing the analogy of genetic evolution to explain cultural development has occupied thinkers over the past couple of centuries. Early thinkers believed in stage theories that viewed societies as starting out in primitive conditions, and gradually over time becoming more civilized. The evolutionary theories of Comte, Spencer and Morgan developed independently from Darwin's theory of evolution, showing that the intellectual ground was prepared for theories of socio-cultural evolution. All societies exist with natural environments that define the limits of natural resources and present constraints like weather and climate conditions. Change occurs as these societies adapt to their environments by trying to develop and select cultural traits that are functional to survival and reproductive fitness. Some thinkers like Hegel argued that social development was inevitable and followed a path from primitive to civilized social structures. The definition of societies considered civilized however seemed to resemble industrialized Europe. This rigid evolutionary perspective in turn justified the development of colonial empires, and the so-called "white man's burden" to bring civilization to "primitive" peoples. Early theories of socio-cultural evolution were used to justify the political and economic domination of Europeans over other peoples.

With the industrial revolution, capitalism produced continual evolution in the means of production and social thinking that reflected these developments. All theories of change (whether Marxist, sociocultural, or social cycle) agreed that humanity had entered a fixed path of social progress. History shows that all major social events are causally tied to preceding periods and also to future happenings. For Comte, Spencer and other early thinkers, socio-cultural evolution was a scientific field of the study of social development that was influenced more and more by the theory of evolution. Societies like the biological organisms could also develop according to discernible and deterministic laws, and natural selection and inheritance played significant roles in social change. Scientists studying socioculture viewed biological evolution as an attractive model for the solution of similar problems regarding the origin of social behavior. Society evolved toward more positive stages through cognition, rationality and logic. Spencer in particular thought society was evolving toward increasing freedom for the individual.

Morgan saw social evolution as progressing from savagery through barbarism to civilization. Specifically he viewed technological progress as being the force behind social progress and change. This view was accepted by Marx and Engels since it supported their conviction that materialistic forces of technology and economy were decisive determinants in the evolution of society. In Marxism socio-cultural evolution was determined by the internal contradictions in society manifested through early stages of tribal and feudal society but ending in socialism. These thinkers all had in common the idea that societies could be described as more or less primitive or civilized, and that all societies progress through these stages in the same sequence (Wikipedia, 2011, accessed August, 3).

These theories basically described a singular path of sociocultural evolution with very sweeping assumptions about the forward movement of culture. The views represented by Spencer, and Morgan, were later largely dismissed as being speculative and not consistent with ethnographic data. Stages of evolution theories were criticized as being illusionary as the concept of primitiveness did not reflect accurately evolution or the amount of culture present in early cultures. For example non-literate societies may leave no historical records and still have evolved culture. This critical argument seems to this writer to be a little flimsy since language, particularly symbolic language, is intimately bound to sociocultural evolution. However, the criticism that social evolution has been used to justify the dominance of elites in society and the world is grounded on a more solid evidentiary basis. What is called classic socio-evolutionary theory is mostly rejected today for reasons that they were the product of ethnocentric thinking, and assumed that all cultures follow the same path on the road to civilization, and further equated civilization with material culture as found in societies benefitting from technological progress. Social Darwinism was a precursor of later racist ideas and practice and particularly became a basis for Nazi worldviews.

3.5.1. The evolution of evolutionary theories.

As in other fields of social science *modern sociocultural* theories are careful to avoid ethnocentrism that is used to make value judgment about cultures and in cross-cultural comparisons. The modern perspective is to view societies within their own historical context. Cultural evolution found in neo-evolutionist theories is now considered multi-lineal as it is determined by many complex sources. Neo-evolutionists discard the deterministic arguments of the preceding century, and suggest that sociocultural evolution is a function of probability where accidental factors as well as the will of members of society play important roles. In place of value judgment the neo-evolutionists emphasize the importance of empirical data constituting measurable information that permits a scientific investigation of sociocultural evolution and associated processes.

Some modern theories (Wilson, 1975) sought to apply biological theory in social sciences by pointing to the evolutionary mechanisms that determines such varied social behaviors like aggression, nurturance and altruism. Sociobiologists argue that humans are the products of both biological evolution, but also analogous sociocultural evolution. Each evolutionary force is distinct and based on separate selective mechanisms and forms of transmission.

3.5.2. Dual Inheritance: Approaches to Cultural Transmission

The early discussion in this chapter has focused on the genetic architecture of cultural transmission. The challenge is to provide a space for both biological and cultural factors within a single theory. Explanation of cultural transmission requires a complex mathematical model given the complexity of each form of transmission and the interaction between biology and culture. Lumsden and Wilson (1981) argued that human cultural transmission should be understood within the framework of gene-culture transmission tracing human development from the genes to the human mind to resulting culture and is a product of *gene-culture co-evolution*. Rather than accepting that human beings pursue their interests based on biological needs expressed in many arbitrary culturally acquired behaviors, Lumsden and Wilson argued for the presence of epigenetic rules that provided greater specificity for the canalization of the mind.

Cavalli-Sforza and Feldman (1981) promoted a quantitative approach to sociocultural evolution since the lateral theory of biological evolution is primarily based on the mathematics of population genetics. Recognizing that it is at best difficult to partition transmission into genetic and cultural factors they sought to understand the dynamics of change by evaluating relative frequencies of *cultural traits* within given populations. Lumsden and Wilson advocated the concept of cultgens as the basic component of inheritance. The epigenetic rules that provided direction were genetically determined peripheral sensory filters including inter-neuron coding processes, but also cognitive parameters of perception, learning and decision-making. These factors together determined whether units of culture were transmitted or some substitute. From this perspective both genetic and cultural evolution work together as culture is shaped by biological processes and over the long run biological processes change in response to cultural alterations like when societies develop a more efficient food supply.

Boyd and Richerson (1985) advocated what is known as a *dual inheritance* system. Biological and sociocultural sources of transmission tend toward abstractness and complexity when researchers use a single psychological model. *Boyd and Richerson advocated a dual inheritance model that in addition to genetic inheritance posited cultural transmission via the rules for social learning.* Specifically they argued for a role of social learning in the transmission of cultural information. What is learned during the lifetime of an individual is obviously not transmitted genetically. However, the capacity for learning may have changed with new innovations like the use of computers. Whereas genetic alterations cannot be observed in a single lifetime, during such a limited time period cultural information can be passed on to the next generation. Cultural information responding to social needs may have consequences for an entire population as can be seen in the political transformation of much of the world. Experiences that are significant can be passed on to cultural offspring, and become part of the cultural heritage, whereas genetic transmission is only possible through differential rates of reproduction of significant traits.

The basic point of departure for Richerson and Wilson for their dual inheritance model is the analogy between genetic and cultural transmission. The relationship between genes and culture presented in their view the most interesting problem for science. The evolution of cultural transmissions in humans is analogous to the evolution of our genetic system. However, genes and culture are distinct systems of inheritance in humanity, and genetic predispositions and cultural predispositions result directly from distinct sources. Richerson and Boyd applied the mathematical standards of population genetics to model the adaptive and selective nature of culture. They argued that cultural evolution exists as a separate arena and is not mechanically related to genetic evolution. Most importantly, cultural evolution is more rapid, and ultimately more influential in social development. From their perspective cultural evolution can be understood by exactly the same processes as genetic evolution since selection for fitness is the ultimate determinant. Hinde (1982), on the other hand, suggested that cultural and genetic evolution proceed independently. In summary, in sociocultural theories genetics have not been overruled by the force of culture but the contribution of genes can best be understood as the foundation that enables cultural behavior and is manifested in the reciprocal relationship between genes and culture.

The major vehicle of cultural transmission is social learning as articulated by Bandura (1977). It would be too cumbersome a task for children to learn complex social behavior by means of conditioning, and imitation is seen as a much more economic model of cultural transmission. Learning by imitation explains the cultural stability we see in culturally defined behavior patterns. Boyd and Richerson see cultural transmission to be analogous to genetic transmission of information. Although all members of a culture may be exposed to similar culture individual exposure allows for personal variants. The relative variance of the cultural repository would depend on the static or fluid nature of the culture. Very static cultures produce few variants from which to select the most adaptive. Cultural conformity is an option of selection, however, where the individual simply follows the behavior of the majority. In turn conformity reduces cultural variance in behavior within the cultural group while increasing variance between other cultural groups.

Evaluating the transmission of culture from these two perspectives seem simplistic considering the complexities of interaction. For example, Laland, Odling-Smee, and Feldman (2000) argue that species interact with the environment and in the process create niches that modify the ecological context. Hinde's (1987) theory emphasizes the importance of levels of social complexity and that at each level of social complexity culture has components not found at lower levels of analysis. Society, groups and individuals must all be considered interacting components in sociocultural evolution yet each with distinct properties. Genetic influences may not be direct and in any event genetic influence decreases in the context of culture. Campbell (1974,) promoted several levels of sociocultural transmission including genetic adaptation, learning and imitation, cultural accumulation, and the changes wrought by science. These influences are all governed by the evolutionary principles of selection of functional traits and the gradual elimination of non-adaptive components. Evidence from cross-cultural research demonstrates the complexity of cultural variation and the difficulty of tracing the interactions between genetic and learned components.

All human social groups have culture, and the essential issue addressed by this chapter is the evolutionary source of sociocultural change over time. Theories must address the origin of change and the transmission of the fundamental elements including the creation of varying social and economic systems, the development of science and religion, moral systems, and most basically the role of language. Similar to genetic evolution, natural selection played a primary role in sociocultural development as groups respond to what is adaptive in their particular environments. The theories discussed above seek to define the relationship between the genetic and cultural coevolution. However, due to the complexity of interactions there is little empirical support for the formal mathematical models based on population genetics. We are really in the early stages of the formulation of theories that adequately represent the relationships between the two forces of evolution, although the same principles of selection and adaptation may be at play a role in both types. The role of conscious reflection and creativity is fundamental to social development, and likewise the use of symbols and language evolution. These issues are largely overlooked in sociocultural evolutionary theories, although there would be no origin of cultural systems without creative innovation and no transmission of human culture without language.

3.6. THEORIES OF MODERNIZATION AND POST-INDUSTRIAL SOCIETY

Theories of modernization express the same viewpoints as those advocated in the classical sociocultural theories by defining progress as movement toward developed countries on the Western industrialized model. The basic value judgment is the proposition that Western societies are the most developed, and the rest of the world ought to be helped to achieve that stage of development. The thinking in modernization theories is uni-lineal proposing that all countries are on the same road of development, and with technological assistance developing societies will eventually reach the same level of material culture as developed industrial countries. There is some practical reality to these speculations as the developing world is indeed on a course to catch up, and in some cases like China's super trains have actually passed the developed Western world.

In modernist theories developmental stages move from traditional societies to more developed cultures if the socio-political culture permits the change required in technology and information. Modernist theories would argue that so-called Third World countries are behind the rest of the world for cultural reasons and needs the efforts of social engineering to emulate the most successful societies. The world economy reflects modernist thinking as all countries see the advantages of technological development, although many have not weighed the costs resulting from globalization.

All theories put emphasis on economic development, but also the connection between progress and democracy, ethical governance, and efficient production. Society must value innovation and personal success found through so-called "free enterprise" before modernization can take place. Individual members of society must also be encouraged to develop to provide a corps of workers and managers that value independent and rational thought and can produce long-term plans for the future.

Modernist thinkers are criticized for the same reasons as discussed for classical social evolution. The focus is seen as one-sided and the Western economic model is used exclusively in developing countries in ways that benefit only the elites. Using Western developed societies as a model is also ethnocentric and may have unforeseen negative consequences when evaluated for outcomes beyond the rewards of economic development. The ubiquitous *Great Recession* affecting economies worldwide should give pause for reflection. Further, as noted there is increasingly an acknowledgement that not all segments of the populations share equally in the benefits of economic development since economic disparity is getting larger and not smaller. The various regional trade agreements have produced new underclasses in border areas between the U.S. and Mexico, new illegal immigrants as people seek to escape poverty, and the flight of quality jobs to low wage countries. It seems a heavy price to pay for a globalized and integrated world advocated by modernist theory.

Bell (1976) defined postindustrial society by dividing social progress into three stages of pre-industrial, industrial, and post-industrial development. Societies reaching the post-industrial level are characterized by the dominance of the service sector over traditional manufacturing, and by the increasing importance of information technologies. Postindustrial societies also set aside traditional ethics and value systems in favor of technocracy and pragmatic solutions, and depend increasingly on technology. Bell also prophesized that highly educated specialists would dominate the traditional middle classes and upset the traditional social hierarchies. A megatrend expected by postindustrial thinking is what we now understand under the concepts of globalization, the World Wide Web, and the Global Village. It is thought these megatrends will weaken centralized powers as observed during the Arab Spring uprisings increasing the importance of local democracy and the power of consumers. Most critics of postindustrial society argue that the predictions and concepts are unclear and it is uncertain whether these megatrends will continue in the future. Nevertheless, we cannot argue that we are in the midst of ubiquitous change brought about in postindustrial society.

SUMMARY

This chapter addressed the research on the origin and transmission of culture. Understanding the origin of culture would respond to many perplexing issues that define us as being human including the evolution of religion, ideology, and life itself. Culture is the complex interaction of biological imperatives with cultural information and transmitted across generations. While other species possess some form of culture, humans have the unique ability to attribute intent to others and utilize symbolic representations. Culture plays a role in survival by creating systems of communication and establishing social structures to enhance the well-being of the community. Our biological foundation requires an evolutionary explanation of human psychology, and both genetic inheritance and cultural evolution must be taken into account to present a full explanation. From the evolutionary perspective when heritable traits increase the chance of survival and reproductive success their frequency in the gene pool and improved reproductive fitness also increases. The natural selection of reproductive fitness is created by the interaction of individuals and cultural groups with their physical and social environments. However, the longer life cycle of humans produces a stronger influence of cultural factors including the social decisions causing migration and the geographic isolation of human groups and the subsequent social rules for selective mate choices.

The construct "race" has both biological and social meanings. Geographic isolation, the stronger effects of the initial gene pool of the immigrant group, and cultural choices favoring ingroup members in mate choices explain the development of phenotypical race categorization. Commonly skin tone is used in defining race, although that is the least useful discriminatory tool as it is a selective evolutionary response to sunlight. Humans with genetic mutations for light skin had selective advantages in northern climates, although the current evidence is that we all arrived from a geneographic journey out of Africa. The changes produced by natural selection are called adaptation. However, it is important to remember we are not just shaped by the environment, but we also work to change it by creating niches for survival and culture.

There is now much research that supports the evolution of human motivation and characteristics. The universal presence of emotions lends support to a genetic basis or architecture of human traits. Emotions provide context to our lives and help us evaluate situations, events and social interaction. However, in contrast with other species humans have the capacity for self-reflection and have morally based emotions. Nevertheless, universal types of temperament and personality traits are evidence of our commonly evolved history. Temperament is present at birth and creates consistencies in individual responses across varying situations. Research supports the presence of universal traits of personality structured in five dimensions also called the Big Five. Heritability is determined by comparing correlations of closely related individuals with those less closely related. Heritability estimates (proportion attributed to genetic factors) is .50 for extraversion-introversion. The results are consistent across cultures presenting a universal model of personality structure that is independent of culture and therefore suggesting an evolutionary mechanism.

Intelligence is also a biological and social construct. Estimates of heritability for intelligence is higher than for the aforementioned personality structures yielding scores around .75. The effect of the heritability of intelligence increases with age as the influence of family and other environmental factors fade away. Unfortunately heritability estimates have been used in the social debate over programs intended to help disadvantaged groups. Some proponents argue that since intelligence is the major factor explaining success in society, and since it is largely determined by genes, social programs to help racial minorities who are limited by heritability are of little utility. However, these flawed arguments do not reflect the reality of the heritability of intelligence. Any population difference in intelligence test scores are impossible to validate since there is always an interaction between genes and the environment. Further, heritability estimates from individual scores cannot be used to evaluate the inherent basis of group or national differences. Further, since we only measure actualized potential, we know nothing of non-actualized potential. Also, all intelligence testing contains measurement problems that include test items not equally familiar to the members of all the cultural groups tested. However, the relationship between behavior genetics and disease is established in cases like Down's syndrome, and is also implicated in major mental illnesses like schizophrenia.

The role of heritability can also be observed in recent research on hard wired optimism. Humans appear to share a universal bias toward optimism and more optimism than justified by reality. This persistent optimism is considered essential for survival and cultural progress as it allows us to see alternative futures and thereby stimulate innovation, exploration, and the motivation of our efforts. The suggestion is strong that optimism is based on neural mechanisms that are hardwired into our brains to increase our chances for survival.

Sociobiology and evolutionary psychology have had a great impact on the discussion around cultural evolution. Most people have first-hand observation of evolution in animals, as dogs, cows and bulls have been bred for selective purposes. In animals behavior patterns appear to be under the control of genes. Ethologists have also observed many similarities between animal and universal human behavior. Sociobiologists would argue that genetic mechanisms are the grammar or architecture of the brain that explain the human communality. These mechanisms in turn interact with culture to produce the variances we observe in different societies. Sociobiology explains human behavior as a response to evolutionary pressures, and in particular the need to ensure reproductive success of those closely related to us called inclusive fitness.

Gender differences follow a pattern predicted by sociobiology. For example, men find reproductive success through a variety of partners, whereas for women pair bonding is essential to ensure the protection of children. Following the same kind of thinking females have a greater interest in the financial prospects of their male partners, whereas males seek youthful appearance suggesting fertility.

Are ethnocentrism and racism also manifestations of motivation caused by a desire for the reproductive success of near kin or inclusive fitness? The sociobiologist would argue that we must understand all psychological functioning from the perspective of reproductive fitness. Therefore attitudes toward members of ingroups and outgroups may be a special manifestation of the desire for inclusive fitness and motivated by the unconscious desire that our genes survive and prosper. Nazism was and is a perverted form of social Darwinism that emphasized inclusive fitness through genocide. The pan-European ideology of the Norwegian mass murder Breivik can be understood in the same light.

However, culture matters. The evolutionary basis of higher cognitive functioning does not exclude a role for cultural shaping of behavior or individually based motivation. The biological origin of the structure of personality still requires adaptation to specific cultural values that shape varying emphasizes. The universality of the structure of traits does not reduce the significance of culture. Culture probably provided the initial impetus that increased longevity, and that in turn allowed for further cultural improvements.

Sociocultural evolution as a field has rested on biology as a model to explain similar mechanisms in both biological evolution and in the origin of social behavior. The classical theorists made sweeping assumptions about the nature of progress and forward movement of culture. The proposed stages of sociocultural evolution have been criticized as being illusionary.

Further, social evolution was also used as a covering ideology for social dominance by elite societies in the world. Modern theories have been more careful to avoid ethnocentrism and tend to view societies as developing within their own historical contexts. Neo-evolutionism discarded the rigid determinism of the classical thinkers and emphasized instead the role of probability, free will, and accidental happenings in the evolution of society. Sociobiologists argued that humans are the product of both biological and cultural evolution.

Recent researchers have produced dual inheritance and cultural transmission models. Some based their conclusions on quantitative models similar to the mathematics of population genetics in studying the frequency of cultural traits and evidence of cultural evolution. Other researchers advocated dual transmission of genetic information and also culture by means of social learning and imitation. More complex theories followed that recognized the ability of humans to modify their environments and produce niches essential to survival and reproductive success. All these conceptions were based on evolutionary principles that viewed cultural evolution as the selection of traits functional to adaptation to both physical and cultural environments.

More recently we have seen new modernization theories of cultural transmission and of post-industrial society. In many ways these modern conceptions emphasized Western society as a model for the aspiration of developing countries. It is argued that with technological assistance all societies will eventually reach the same or similar levels of prosperity. In many ways the current world economy reflects modernist thinking as the faith in efficacy of technological change is ubiquitous. Post-industrial societies are characterized by mega-trends including globalization that fundamentally alter culture in most societies in the world. The current economic crisis in the world supports the view that evolution of society is not lineal.

CHAPTER 4

HUMAN DEVELOPMENT

Culture And Biology

A central concern in cross-cultural and cultural psychology is how people acquire behaviors that we identify as *culturally unique*. While we are interested in what is different between cultures of the world, there is also the potentially larger area of research into what we have in common. Although recent thinking point to universal psychic unity as rooted in biology supporting what is commonly called human universals, that universalism has been challenged by recent cultural and cross-cultural work. For example, cultural psychology has demonstrated that higher mental functioning is created by cultural activity and communication. Further, results from cultural neuroscience show that long term interaction with cultural settings may actually modify brain pathways and the very architecture of the brain (Kolstad, 2012). In particular acquiring culture is partly the outcome of parenting styles employed in the process of socialization. However, broader social institutions including the educational system and dominant religious or political organizations are considered important factors in producing cultural ideologies. Children also grow up with siblings and peers that have an influence on socialization. Since culture emerged out of the struggle

Cross-Cultural Psychology: Why Culture Matters, pages 81–107.

to survive, the particular environmental contexts have produced some of the cultural variability we can observe in the world today. Survival requires competencies that in turn vary with the ecological context (Kagitcibasi, 1996). To a large extent cultural learning is implicit perhaps governed by social learning and imitation, but by the time we are adults most of us have learned the cultural rules and customs and they are so integrated in our lives that few people even notice or pass judgment on habitual rituals or behaviors. Other forms of learning have also played a role in the acquisition of cultural values through reinforcement in the educational system based on operant conditioning or by the association of cultural and unconditioned stimuli that occurs in classical conditioning.

4.1. SOCIALIZATION OR ENCULTURATION?

Psychologists investigating comparative cultures make a distinction between socialization and enculturation in how cultures are transmitted from one generation to the next. Socialization as a concept has a long history in both social psychology and sociology. In particular *socialization* refers to the process of individual development that is shaped by cultural values through the deliberate teaching by culture bearers and enforcers especially the child's parents. Cultural values are learned when someone deliberately shapes the behavior of children in society. On the other hand, Herskovits (1948) used the concept of *enculturation* to define the end product of socialization. Enculturation refers to the assimilation of the components of culture considered essential in order to function adequately in a society. Enculturation describes the influence of the cultural context and the possibilities offered by that environment. In other words, enculturation describes the subjective end products manifested in behavior and represent the psychological internalization of cultural values throughout the process of development. Socialization refers more to the actual means of how children learn the rules of their societies, whereas enculturation is the end product manifested in subjective psychology. We can think of culture as the subjective psychological experience resulting from socialization, and enculturation as the resulting society that surrounds members of the culture with an inescapable context.

The processes of socialization and enculturation are not the only determinants of individual behavior. Members of a culture must also respond to the ecological environment and develop behaviors that support survival and successful adaptation. The transmission of culture is aimed at creating skills in children that support successful living. Still culture must also adapt to changing circumstances. The transmission of culture is not fixed, but is a more fluid process that prevents chaos and promotes social stability (Boyd & Richerson, 1995).

The study of child rearing practices in various cultures has a long history. For example, Whiting and Child (1953) examined child training study archives and concluded that in some ways child training is identical all over the world since parents everywhere confront similar problems. However, there are also some salient cultural differences in how child training differs between cultures. These observations are consistent with a biological perspective of all that we have in common as a species, but also a cultural comparative view based on enculturation and socialization. According to Barry, Bacon and Child (1957), and Barry, Child and Bacon (1959) six dimensions of child rearing were similar in all societies studied. These included training for obedience, responsibility, nurturance, achievement, self-reliance, and independence. Gender differences were also universally similar across cultures with girls being socialized to take on more responsibility and nurturance, and boys being encouraged to be assertive through achievement and self-reliance. However, later investigators found comparative cultural variations in socialization described as either narrow or broad (Arnett, 1995). Obedience was emphasized in the narrow transmission of a culture that required conformity as a cultural product, whereas broad transmission emphasized personal independence.

4.2. ENCULTURATION AND CHOICE

The growing child develops within a niche from which he/she learns cultural values. The major components that form the context of development are the ecological environment, the socio-political context, customs of child rearing, and the psychology that motivates parents and child care givers (Super & Harkness, 1994, 2002). These niche components interact with the child's unique genetically based temperamental traits. However, it is well to keep in mind that children are not just acted upon by the cultural environment, but are *behavioral actors* in their own right and through their choices influence family life and the broader cultural context. As Bronfenbrenner (1979) noted children are not passive recipients of cultural knowledge, but dynamically interact with the choices provided by culture. The micro-systems with the most immediate influence on development are the interaction of the child with the family, educational system, and peers. The exo-system influences development indirectly, for example, by the opportunities provided by the social standing of parents. The macro-system refers to the major normative influences that require conformity to cultural values, religion, and ideology. Nevertheless, according to Bronfenbrenner it is important to remember that members of a culture are not passive observers, but children contribute to self-development by the choices they make and through the willingness to conform or risk alternatives.

The effect of quality of life variables can be observed in studies on child development. Technological development has been practically ubiquitous in the world the last decades and has affected family life in significant ways (Berry, 1997). Differences in outcomes for family life have been found between wealthy individualistic countries compared to collectivistic countries (Georgas, Christakopoulou, Poortinga, Angleitner, Goodwin, & Charalambous, 1997). Although the search for material wealth is ubiquitous it is also associated with a decreasing frequency of helping behavior among second or third generation Mexican-American children. A salient outcome with psychological consequences is the less important role of family solidarity in the survival of children from more affluent families (Knight & Kagan, 1977).

Parents and other child caregivers generally share culturally appropriate ideas about child rearing. In a given culture parents have assimilated beliefs about the correct ways to help a child achieve developmental goals and the role of parents in creating the best learning climate. Cultural values frame the way that child caregivers express affection and love for the child and determine when the child should be fed and the appropriate time for weaning. Cultural values also create expectations about the right time to master the beginnings of speech, when the child should walk, and other developmental goals (Harkness & Super, 1995).

Differences in *child rearing ideology* were found in a study comparing Japanese with U.S. teachers (Tobin, Wu, & Davidson, 1989). For example, Japanese teachers preferred larger class rooms believing the greater number of students to constitute a more appropriate forum to teach children to get along with others. The beliefs about children's misbehavior also varied between the samples with Japanese teachers believing that misbehavior occurred when something went wrong in the relationship between child and mother, whereas U.S. teachers were more likely to attribute the cause to some inherent deficit in the child. The attribution of either individual or relationship causes is also consistent with generally recognized differences between collectivistic and individualistic cultures represented by Japan and the U.S.

LeVine (1977) suggested that early childrearing practices were created and motivated by parental goals. Initially the survival of the infant is paramount and therefore parents focus on infant health. However, at some point children in all cultures must develop self-sufficiency. Childrearing inculcates the cultural values of the broader society as mediated by parents. However, children raised in affluent cultures do not face the same struggles for survival as those raised in poverty with subsequent long-term psychological consequences. When parents have to struggle daily to put food on the table there is not much time to develop the assets and abilities of the child, and family bonding becomes a primary goal in order to create survival security. The harshness of the environment may be so extreme that mothering is directly influenced.

Frequency and length of breastfeeding also depend on the socio-economic status of society. The more advanced societies encourage the use of formula to create earlier independence between mother and child. In turn that may affect attachment and later development. Infant weakness in extremely impoverished communities is conceptualized by mothers as representing a low likelihood for survival. Hence mothers in these cultures are in some cases tentative in committing total affection for the child as the baby may be only a short-term visitor in the home. In other words, bonding is promoted when there is a chance that it will have utility in the survival of the child (Scheper-Hughes, 1992).

Parental ideology referred to as parental *ethno-theories* describes integrated beliefs about parenting (Edwards, Knoche, Aukrust, Kimru, & Kim, 2006; Harkness & Super, 2006). *The belief system about parenting determines the methods which direct the child in learning important elements of the cultural context.* Parental beliefs serve as an organizing tool in governing the daily activities of the child.

4.3. AUTHORITATIVE VERSUS AUTHORITARIAN CHILDREARING APPROACHES AND CULTURAL DIFFERENCES

Research on child rearing in the United States identified three styles of parenting (Baumrind, 1971). *Authoritative* parents provide the child with care that is firm, but also reasonable and fair. Control in authoritative child rearing is dependent on the child's maturity, and parents typically display warm and open affection for their children. Guidelines are provided by authoritative parents, but not rigidly enforced as children are given freedom to choose dependent on their level of development and responsibility. In the second style of parenting *authoritarian* parents demand obedience first and foremost and provide strict control over the child. Authoritarianism may have grown out of harsh environments where parents see their role as keeping their children out of harm's way. Baumrind's research also identified *permissiveness* as a parental style. Permissive parents allow their children to live their own lives without much interference or discipline. This style of parenting seems close to that of the uninvolved parents identified by Maccoby and Martin (1983). However, permissive parents are involved with their children and exhibit warmth in their relationships, whereas uninvolved parents are just indifferent.

The initial results from American studies supported the superiority of the authoritative style in many studies. Children who grow up with parents that use the authoritative childrearing style develop more useful traits including more positive emotions, more self-confidence and self-reliance (Karavasilis, Doyle, & Markiewicz, 2003). The authoritative parenting style prepares the child well for life resulting in children that are psychologically healthy and competent, and who live with fewer anxieties compared to children brought up by other parenting styles. By contrast children of authoritarian parents displayed more anxiety and develop cognitive styles that lack spontaneity and curiosity. The benefits for children of authoritative parents are not just confined to childhood. Studies of adolescents produced similar positive results. Adolescents with authoritative parents are more socially adept, tend to have higher self-esteem and display more creativity (Collins & Laursen, 2004; Spera, 2005). The authoritative style of parenting seems to have a positive effect on the child's sense of optimism and helps create the belief that the child lives in a well-ordered world with developmental goals that are attainable. These effects are carried over into university life where students from authoritative homes displayed less depression and greater social adaptability (Jackson, Pratt, Hunsberger, & Pancer, 2005).

For comparative psychology an important question is whether these styles are manifested in other cultures than the United States, or to what degree are they culturally specific? Are the positive outcomes of authoritative parents limited to children living in the United States? Chao (2001) argued that it is important to understand the dominant cultural values before investigating parental styles. The efficacy of parental styles may well depend on underlying values to which the child must conform. Chao argued that the role of training in Chinese culture is unique and not covered by the Baumrind's parental styles. However, in another study in China authoritarian parenting was related negatively to school adjustment, whereas children from authoritative homes fared better in overall social adjustment (Chen, Dong, & Zhou, 1997). In a multi-cultural society like the U.S. perhaps the efficacy of authoritative approaches to childrearing depends on the child's ethnic or cultural group? However, a review of more recent studies confirms the continuous advantage of authoritative approaches to childrearing that are independent of the larger cultural values associated with collectivistic or individualistic cultures (Sorkhabi, 2005). Parental warmth and acceptance of the child are important factors in positive outcomes everywhere, and authoritative parenting takes on universal value as the advantages are not limited by culture. Comparative studies have largely confirmed the advantages of authoritative versus authoritarian parenting as it produces more solidarity in families and better mental functioning (Dwairy, Achoui, Abouserie, & Farah, 2006).

4.4. CREATING THE CLIMATE OF HOME: CULTURAL AND CROSS-CULTURAL STUDIES

Parents are the principal conduits of cultural learning. Differences in social attitudes, however, reflect the broader cultural values. For example, Asian parents think effort is more important in education than ability, whereas American parents believe innate ability is responsible for success (Stevenson & Zusho, 2002). These cultural attributions for success are consistent with the cultural underpinnings of collectivistic and individualistic societies.

Differences in parental values are reflected in the parent's involvement with the school system. American parents of European background are more likely to pay attention to in-school activities and the children's teachers, whereas Asian parents are more concerned with outside events like museum and library visits as contributors to the child's education (Sy & Schulenberg, 2005). Asian parents also emphasize high expectations and explicit rules about activities that interfere with learning. Since American parents believe limits are set by ability they are less likely to emphasize high expectations and are more concerned with shoring up their child's self-esteem.

4.4.1. The Sleeping Arrangements of Childhood

The home climate is the earliest cultural influence on members of a society and the *sleeping arrangements* are thought to be very significant to the security of the child. Cultural studies demonstrate varying patterns in sleeping arrangements as parents in societies like the United States seek to create child independence from the very beginning. Mothers in the U.S. strive to have their babies sleep through the night and in a location separate from parents. The American culture is characterized by values of individualism and early independence, and separate sleeping arrangements support these values. In place of the security and warmth of parental bodies the child is often offered a soft toy or security blanket that the child carries around for several years.

Cultural studies of other societies show that independent sleeping arrangements are not ubiquitous. For example, in Sweden children often sleep with their parents through early childhood (Welles-Nystrom, 2005). This is believed by parents to provide the security essential to normal development. Likewise in Mayan cultures children often sleep with their mothers through early childhood creating bonds important to the survival of families. It is probably true that bonding through early childhood is emphasized more in societies where strong bonds are essential for survival, and sleeping arrangements have supported such collectivistic values. Socioeconomic factors may also play a role as separate sleeping facilities may not be affordable in poor families (Morelli, Rogoff, Oppenheim, & Goldsmith, 1992). In some collectivistic societies parents would be amazed at the early separation of the infant from the mother's presence during the night.

The establishment of sleeping patterns is an early concern by young parents. Super, Harkness, Van Tijen, Van der Vlugt, Fintelman, and Dijkstra (1996) found differences in regulating sleeping patterns between Dutch and American parents. Dutch parents established early regularity in sleeping patterns believing that otherwise children with inadequate sleep would be more difficult to handle. The parents in the U.S. were more likely to adopt a non-directive attitude believing that as they age children will eventually sleep properly. The child's relative alertness also varied as measured by diaries of parents. Dutch children displayed quieter arousal, whereas U.S. children were more active. Contributing to the difference was the finding that U.S. mothers spent more time talking to and touching their children. Dutch parents found it more important to organize family time for their children, whereas U.S. mothers emphasized the importance of finding special time with just the child.

Ethnic groups within a society may also practice different sleeping arrangements. The United States is a multi-cultural society, and it is not surprising that subgroups have different childrearing practices. One study demonstrated that parents sleeping with their children in early childhood are expected in the struggling communities of Appalachia (Small, 1998). Likewise in a study comparing a matched sample of white children with a sample of Latinos living in Harlem, a larger proportion of the Harlem children slept with their parents. Perhaps these studies are pointing to socio-economic differences in communities that are struggling with poverty and the acceptance of longer periods of sleeping with parents as essential for stronger bonding for survival. Sleeping arrangements reflect subliminal cultural values not articulated explicitly that still may reach into the earliest phases of life and children.

4.4.2. Attachment in Childhood

Temperament is thought to be a genetically based trait present in infancy and related to attachment (Buss & Plomin, 1984). Many mothers observe differences in child reaction to stimuli with some children temperamentally difficult and others easy. These differences may later have personality consequences as parents respond differentially dependent on the child's temperament. Cross-cultural studies suggest some important comparative attachment differences. A study of middle-class mothers in the United States were compared to a sample of mothers from Kenya. Important similarities were found in the desire of mothers to touch and hold the child. However, American mothers talked more to their infants whereas Kenyan mothers communicated more with physical touch (Berger, 1995). Perhaps differences in the mother's verbal communication have a broader effect on cognitive development required in an industrial society, and U.S. mothers reflect in their communication style a cultural evolution to provide this advantage in the U.S. sample.

An important developmental achievement in infancy is *the formation of attachment,* first to the mother and later to the broader extended family and community. The recognition of the face of the mother and members of the family are important precursors to attachment. Studies have shown that most infants form attachment to the immediate family at about age seven months, but react differentially to strangers. However, the manner that infants react in the presence of strangers appears to follow universal patterns (Gardiner, Mutter, & Kosmitzki, 1998). Some children are anxious and avoidant, others anxious and resistant, and yet others are secure and are not threatened by the presence of strangers. However, the prevalence of these types has been found to vary by cultures (Van Ijzendoorn & Kroonenberg, 1988). Secure attachment is the basis for other developmental tasks that follow.

4.4.3. Relationships with Siblings

Our relationships with brothers and/or sisters play important roles in socialization. In large families older siblings may be delegated roles as caregivers (Weisner & Gallimore, 1977). When children are close in age siblings are present along with parents for the most important events of a child's life. *The significance of family and cultural life is filtered through the eyes of siblings who struggle with similar family and cultural values.* Cultural values including interdependence are taught via sibling relationships. Our social assessment of right and wrong develop in sibling relationships whether cultivating aggression or empathy (Parke, 2004). As time moves on appropriate sex role behavior and gender relationships are learned primarily from siblings. Of all the influences in life the role of siblings is likely to be the most enduring as parents typically pass from the scene, but relationships with brothers and sisters are sustained until the end. However, the main focus of research has been on the child-parent relationship and we have only modest information on what must be the very significant influence of siblings (McHale, Crouter, & Whiteman, 2003).

4.4.4. The Influence of the Extended Family and Peers

Research on the self demonstrates the profound influence of the extended family and peers on the development of the self. Self-concept research draws on information from the fields of personality theory and social psychology (Yang & Bond, 1990). Triandis noted that aspects of the self are influenced by cultural values like individualism-collectivism. Childrearing and other interpersonal relationships are the means by which the self is formed consistent with cultural values. Kagitcibasi (1996) discussed the relational self based on a family model of material and emotional interdependence. *Societies fostering the relational self are often pre-industrial where families have to rely on one another for subsistence and survival. Individualistic Western societies are more likely to nurture a separated self where children in the extended family live lives separate and distinct from one another.* Although emotional relatedness exists in individualistic families this feeling is not extended to the rest of society or the world.

These considerations brought Markus and Kitayama (1991a) to make a distinction between the *independent and interdependent* self. They argued that the self is construed differentially in various cultures with consequences for interpersonal relationships. In the extended family and peer relationships the child first experiences the construal of the social self that becomes the model for behavior in the larger society. In collectivistic societies the self is not separate from others, but seen as interdependent and connected. On the other hand, the self is incomplete in collectivistic societies when independent from others since only in relationships is the self seen as fully functioning.

However, Matsumoto (1999) reviewed 18 studies that examined differences between Japan as a collectivistic society, and the individualistic United States on the individualism-collectivism construct. The results showed that only one study supported differences between the two countries in the direction predicted. Takano and Osaka (1999) in a review of 15 studies came to a similar conclusion calling into question the validity of the existence of individualistic and collectivistic societies. However, Kitayama, Markus, Matsumoto and Norasakkunit (1997) in other studies found evidence for the utility of the collectivistic-individualistic construct. Nevertheless, we must exercise caution in accepting results that might be more stereotypic impression management especially in a globalized world of cultural change.

Extended families are more involved in childrearing in non-European collectivistic cultures. In these societies extended families are the main source for cultural transmission. In a multi-cultural society like the United States, extended families continue to play a role transmitting expectations related to gender appropriate behavior, and emphasizing the importance of family loyalty, cooperation among family members, and duties related to childrearing (Nydell, 1998; Tolson & Wilson, 1990). Where extended families play a role children experience more frequent interaction with other family members and provide useful models for the growing child of expected duties and contributions. In polygamous extended families children are provided with mothering from several individuals, and as in other collectivistic societies the entire community takes an interest in the well-being of children and in the requirement of obedience to cultural values. In the U.S. poverty plays a role where parents utilize the extended family in support of childrearing. Since the nuclear family has lost ground in recent decades and many children are born out of wedlock grandparents and in many cases great-grandparents play a socializing role in the lives of the affected children. The grandmother is particularly important as she is often more responsive to the children of teen age mothers and is a role model for childrearing (Leadbeater & Way, 2001).

The peer group influences socialization in all societies, but probably plays distinct roles in individualistic versus collectivistic cultures. In the modern society parents are often so busy with career issues that they are unable to invest time in teaching their children cultural values. When the nuclear family cannot play that socializing role, children learn from peers the common stereotypes, norms and customs of a culture. In more industrialized societies parents have little time for family life, and children spend more time with their peers (Fugligni & Stevenson, 1995).

During the teenage years, the role of the mentor is also very important. The mentor could be a teacher, a coach, a relative, a family friend or an elder friend of the teenager. As for the teenager since this is a time for rebellion against their parents the influence of a mentor is invaluable (Dolto, 1988).

4.5. CULTURE AND THE EDUCATIONAL SYSTEM

Same aged peers make important contributions to socialization in societies with regular educational systems. While not all cultures have formal educational systems, there is little doubt that schools are major socializing agents in the vast majority of countries. The educational system in a given country inculcates children with the dominant cultural values and implicitly conveys stereotypes or attitudes, and more explicitly salient culture through music and rituals. *What is taught in the educational system is dependent on cultural values.* In the United States conservative forces prohibited for a long time the teaching of evolutionary principles, so that history shows that cultural values can determine the very educational curriculum. In individualistic societies success is seen as a consequence of achievement that is individual and relative. Hence the emphasis in the educational system on grading and ranking of students in Western societies as such presumably prepares the student for a competitive society. Although American schools have explored non-grading alternatives and cooperative learning these efforts represent decidedly minority perspectives in education.

When the child enrolls in the school system the influence of peers increases and the majority of waking hours are spent with school mates. Together the educational system and peers play dominant roles in enforcing cultural values through both positive learning events but also by sanctioning behavior that is divergent and non-conformist. The educational system reflects what society thinks is important in order to function optimally. In some societies education is not formal as elders or other experts may teach the next generation cultural competencies and social structures. As the child grows older, however, peer acceptance is very important and only few children can escape the pressures of norms and customs.

4.6. SOCIO-ECONOMIC CLIMATE

The home climate and broader socio-economic environment have primary effects on child development. Some cultural environments require the development of motor skills at an earlier age since such learning contributes to coping with harsher environments. For example, the motor skills of African infants develop several months earlier than in comparable groups of white children, and different techniques are used to encourage walking (Gardiner, Mutter, & Kosmitzki, 1998). We know that birth death rates vary by culture and country reflecting different socio-economic circumstances and different social values about medical treatment for the poor and disadvantaged. When many children die at birth or in infancy mothers and family will focus their attention on creating the optimal conditions for survival and there is little time for other developmental tasks beneficial to children. In many societies there is little possibility for parents to foster the cultural or spiritual development of children as the harshness of the socio-economic environment direct parental attention totally on day by day survival.

Although the U.S. is commonly defined as an affluent society there is relatively low social acceptance of medical treatment as a common human right, whereas the reverse is true in Cuba a relatively poor country with nevertheless equal access to quality medical science and treatment. Within the United States there are large differences in medical access by people driven by costs and socio-economic differences. These health-related differences in child care may well produce long-term consequences not only for well-being, but also for the child's sense of security and view of the world as dangerous or benign.

4.7. SOCIAL IDENTITY

The individual's social identity grows from the home climate, and interactions away from the home. Research shows that children very early begin to identify with ingroups and reference groups. School children show a clear preference for their nation's flag, and can easily identify themselves in terms of ethnic and national groups (Lawson, 1975). The cultural context is important as children from individualistic societies demonstrate more competiveness than children from other cultures (Madsen, 1971). Competitive orientations have utility where cultural values of individualism and achievement are dominant and the welfare of the group is secondary. The effect of cultural values has been confirmed in comparative studies. For example, Thailand is a country dominated by Buddhist values of non-violence and respect for others. Problems of over-control among children are more commonly reported in Thailand and are manifested by withdrawal from social interaction. On the other hand, for parents in North America disorderly behavior and violence among children are a more dominant concern (Weisz, Suwanlert, Chaiyasit, & Walter, 1987).

4.8. COMPARATIVE STUDIES IN CHILD REARING BEHAVIORS

Do attachment patterns vary by culture? Studies on collectivistic versus individualistic societies suggest that the attachment experiences of childhood vary with cultural values. For example, in Japan people are conceived as being interdependent defined by the idea of "amae." This concept refers to the tendency by the Japanese to construe the self as merging with others (Doi, 1989). Amae is encouraged by Japanese mothers and is thought to be different from the concept of dependency in Western societies which describes the child's need for attention and approval. However, the two concepts prove to be similar in the actual descriptions used (Vereijken, Riksen-Walraven, & Van Lieshout, 1997). Different labels in comparative psychology may in fact describe the same behaviors.

The impact of culture can be observed at even the neonate stage. For example Asian neonate tends to be calmer and less irritable when compared to white American neonates. After birth the response to crying varies by culture. In cultures where infants are carried around all day prolonged episodes of crying are rarely observed whereas American infants cry for much longer periods. For example Korean mothers respond much more quickly to infant crying compared to American mothers (Arnett, 2012).

Cross-cultural comparative observation studies have demonstrated further differences in the infant's home climate. A survey frequently used is the "Home Observation and Measurement of the Environment Measure" commonly called the Home Inventory. The researcher visits the home and observes the interaction between the child and parents and follows up with some questions (Bradley, Caldwell, & Corwyn, 2003; Bradley & Corwyn, 2005). In studies employing this inventory cultures vary along several dimensions. For example, while parental warmth and responsiveness is present in all the cultures studied they are not expressed the same way. In some cultures parents do not express affection physically, but rather use the voice to indicate warmth. In Western countries being responsive to a child is measured by the frequency of spontaneous and unplanned conversations with the child. In other cultures like India spontaneous conversations are less frequent since it is expected that children will respect their parents and wait for permission to speak. The comparative studies show that the home environment corresponds to the broader cultural values present in society. At the same time comparative research has also yielded significant similarities in child rearing between cultural groups as most parents' in all cultures desire their children to develop social and emotional skills, and display similar assertion in disciplining their children for infractions. *The comparative research supports the presence of differences and similarities in the home climate that implicitly teaches the child during childhood and beyond.*

The *parental ethno-theories* and goals are seen as affecting varying childrearing in Gusii mothers in Kenya compared to U.S. mothers. The cultural context of agriculture in the Kenyan sample led mothers to emphasize the protection of infants, and keeping the child physically close. In the U.S. sample mothers encouraged more social engagement and more social exchange. American mothers believe stimulation begins in the earliest moments of infancy and try to talk to their babies. By contrast Gusii mothers believe such child rearing will create a more self-centered child (LeVine, LeVine, Dixon, Richman, Leiderman, Keefer, & Brazelton, 1994). Japanese mothers are more directly responsive when babies play with them, whereas U.S. mothers reinforce babies' behavior when they play with physical objects. A significant difference between Japanese and U.S. parenting is the amount of time spent with their children. While U.S. mothers will occasionally depend on babysitters Japanese mothers will rarely leave their infants. Some believe this difference in childrearing explains the higher anxiety of Japanese children in the absence of their parents (Bornstein & Tamis-LeMonda, 1989). Consistent with the broader cultural values Japanese mothers in one study were more concerned about lack of cooperativeness and social insensitivity in their children, compared to U.S. mothers who expressed greater worry about disruptive or aggressive behavior (Olson, Kashiwagi, & Crystal, 2001).

Working class parents in the U.S. and parents in pre-industrial communities believe that children can grow up by themselves, and do not need special tutoring. Obviously children raised with differences in parental ideology will develop characteristics unique to the child rearing strategy. What is required for the child to transit to successful adulthood may also play a role in the ethnotheories of parents and in child rearing practices. In the U.S. parents believe they arc required to play a very active role in directing the development of their children (e.g. Goodnow, 1988). However, in other societies the focus is more on enjoying the parent-child relationship and allowing the child to grow up without excessive direction (Kagitcibasi, 1996).

Research on collectivism and individualism demonstrates the effect of these cultural values on parental childrearing. Collectivistic societies emphasize behavioral controls of children often making strict demands and providing sanctions for behavior that do not meet expectations (Rudy & Grusec, 2001). Parental authoritarianism is often associated with other authoritarian cultural practices derived from social instability, lower levels of education, and socio-political authoritarianism. For example, Russian adolescents see similar efforts to control behavior by both parents and teachers, and perceive that they are under more control when compared to U.S. students (Chirkov & Ryan, 2001). Comparative differences have also been found between white and Mexican-American parents, although no differences in authoritarianism were found between white and Mexican parental childrearing styles (Varela, Vernberg, Sanchez-Sosa, Riveros, Mitchell, & Mashunkashey, 2004). Obedience has great utility in societies that are struggling with survival. Children that face difficult or harsh ecological environments are likely to be raised with strict controls (Schonpflug, Silbereisen, & Schulz, 1990).

The age of mastery of various childhood skills varies by culture. Western cultures place competitive demands on the child from the very beginning reflected in expectations for early mastery. In a study of Dutch, Turkish immigrants, and Zambian mothers six types of skills were investigated. The childhood skills included physical, perceptual, cognitive, intra-individual, inter-individual, and social competencies. The expected developmental differences between cultures for physical skills across developmental stages were insignificant supporting the common biological basis of these competencies for all humans. However, for other domains like social skills the expectations by Zambian mothers were for later development compared to the other samples. Parents and other participants in a culture transmit the rules and customs of their society when rearing their children. Their specific socialization practices reflect these cultural beliefs (Segall, Dasen, Berry, & Poortinga, 1999). Once childrearing norms are established they are passed on from one generation to the next.

Childhood represents a period of continuous growth and development. Cognitive skills gradually develop to help the child cope with the complexities of the environment and social skills are developed appropriate to cultural values. Concern with the child's health causes mothers to encourage their children to eat properly and nutritiously. Although eating habits can be a way for the child to control powerful parents, it drives many mothers and fathers to distraction with worries. Worries over children's nutritional health seem, however, restricted to cultures where food is plentiful. In impoverished cultures children are just happy to fill their stomachs and are unlikely to put up a fuss over taste or texture. Eating preferences are laid down in early childhood and affect eating habits later in life

Cultural history may also encourage competitive modes at an early age. For example, Israeli mothers from European background expected earlier development of cognitive skills compared to Israeli mothers from non-European families (Ninio, 1979). Compared to U.S. mothers Japanese mothers expected earlier development of emotional control, whereas U.S. mothers by comparison expected earlier development of assertive behavior (Hess et al, 1980).

4.9. HUMAN DEVELOPMENT IS INCORPORATION OF CULTURE

Studies like the *"Wild boy of Averyon"* (Itard, 1962) call into question whether human nature exists in isolation from culture. In this early historical study Itard investigated the lack of development in a boy found in the forest of the district of Averyon in France, a boy thought to have survived in the wild without human contact. The boy was devoid of human qualities including the use of speech or recognizable emotional responses. *These and similar studies of children brought up in the wild suggest that there are no discernible human qualities developed apart from the interaction of the child with others.* Vygotsky had that right when he argued that the origin of human cognition is social interaction (Vygotsky, 1978; see also discussion by another Soviet psychologist Luria, 1976). All cultural development occurs as a result of interaction at the social level, and later represented intra-psychologically. Biological foundations are important as we shall see, however culture is what gives us human features and variations in behavior.

Human development is a function of many influences. Culture mediates between the child and the biological and environmental imperatives. Cole (1996), for example, maintained that biology does not interact directly with the ecological context but via the social environment. There is a basic distinction between the ecological context and the environment. More precisely, it is the complex interactions of biology, phylogenetic contributions, and cultural-historical factors that determine individual development. Biological influences are not directly responsible for behavior, as the impact on the child occurs through the filter of cultural values. Culture frames the social interactions that are eventually responsible for the internalization of cultural values.

Cultural values also play important roles in lifespan development (Baltes, 1997). Here biology and culture also interact dynamically. Evolutionary selection benefits derived from biology decrease in effectiveness with increasing age as the genome of older people produces more dysfunctional genes. The benefits of biological selection for fitness really have no role to play in later life, since evolutionary pressures for selection have passed with the end of the childbearing age at around 30 years. Biological decline is associated with greater demand on culture for a variety of support resources that provide culturally based functioning in the later stage of the lifespan. Lifespan development through all the stages of life is dependent on the continual interaction of genetic heritage with what culture can offer in support. Culture can help offset the lower functioning produced by aging through, for example, improving skills in reading or writing that allows the individual to continue to participate and live actively at a time in life not possible in the dawn of humankind.

4.10. STAGE THEORIES OF HUMAN DEVELOPMENT: CULTURALLY UNIQUE OR UNIVERSAL

Several prominent theorists in developmental psychology have proposed stages of development thought universal for all humans. There is evidence to support this assertion as we now have theories describing stages of cognitive, moral and psychosocial development. Nevertheless the universality is far from established as cultural ideology and the ecological context may prove more influential.

4.10.1. The Evolution of Cognition

Developmental theory has been enriched by several stage theories of human cognitive development. If these theories are validated in all societies investigated it would lend support to the presence of universal cognitive structures, and by inference point to the biological basis for development. Piaget (1963) was the most influential researcher in the field of *cognitive development*. In-depth studies of children, some his own grandchildren, led him to formulate a theory of cognitive development in four stages. Stage one is called sensorimotor where the infant learns from direct sensory engagement with the environment. This stage last from infancy to about two years. The child understands his world through sensory perceptions and motor behaviors that occur in the process of interacting with the demands of the environment. Other cognitive achievements include learning to imitate others and learning by observation. Also the child begins language acquisition at this stage an achievement significant for later communication.

Stage two from about 2 to 7 years of age is called the preoperational stage where egocentrism is supreme as children do not understand the perspectives of others. However, this stage is also fundamental to language acquisition as the child expands vocabulary and understanding. Children's thinking is dominated by conservation defined as the ability to understand that changes in appearance do not change objects volume or weight. Centration is another characteristic of cognition in stage 2 that allows the child to focus on solitary objects or problems. The child also masters irreversibility which is the ability to reverse the process of problem solving. Egocentrism that is manifested at this stage shows that children cannot yet see problems from the perspectives of others. Finally, animism is the child's fantasy that all objects have life. A doll is living and may take on aspects of personality as children at this stage do not operate by logic.

Stage three is the concrete operations stage and lasts from about 7 to 11 years of age. At this stage cognition actually increases in complexity as children are able to view problems from a variety of perspectives. Taking the perspectives of others is considered a significant cognitive achievement.

Children at this stage begin the development of more abstract thinking since they can assess more than one aspect of a problem or issue.

Finally, children learn to think abstractly in the fourth stage called formal operations. That stage lasts from about 11 years of age until the end of life. The individual operating at this stage can think logically about abstractions like notions of democracy and justice. As life progresses thinking becomes more systematic in problem solution. Formal operations is a cognitive process that allows for stage movement called assimilation where the individual fits new concepts into what is already understood, and accommodation where the individual changes his understanding by integrating concepts that do not fit the preexisting conceptual structure.

Piaget in fact believed that these stages of cognitive development were universal and each followed the preceding sequentially. Dasen (1984, 1994) found evidence for the universality of the stage sequence across cultures. However, methodological problems make valid comparisons difficult (Gardiner, Mutter, & Kosmitzki, 1998). Although Piaget valued the final stage of formal operations there is little evidence that it is a form of universal cognition as people can indeed have reproductive success in Western cultures and other societies without abstract thinking.

However, some support is present in the literature. The invariance of the stages was found in a study on school age children in several countries that showed that these children learned problem solving in the order predicted by Piaget (Shayer, Demetriou, & Perez, 1988). However, the ages that children achieved these stages varied by culture (Dasen, 1984). Some research indicated that Piaget's cognitive stages are not invariant as the children do not achieve the skills in the same order (Dasen, 1975). Finally, abstract thinking found in formal operations may be a cognitive development especially favored in societies that have benefitted from scientific development. Islamic cultures focus more on the rigid cultural transmission of faith that is less adaptable to abstract thinking required in a world of transition. Cole argued that formal operations required a Western education demonstrating the dependence of the Piagetian model of cognition on cultural values (Cole, 2006).

4.10.2. The Evolution of Moral Development

As the child develops cognitively, he/she is able to bring these skills to bear in moral judgment. Cultural values are at least partially based on how people solved problems of morality. To a large extent these values serve as a guide for behavior in social interaction. Consequently, it is not possible to understand culture without an appreciation of the underlying morality and value system.

Kohlberg (1981) proposed 6 stages of *moral development* thought invariable for all people. The preconventional stage 1 evolves out of fear of punishment framing the child's perception of what is moral. In stage 2 the child recognizes that immoral conduct has negative consequences and moral conduct positive outcomes and the child has developed the ability to make choices. In the third stage the child enters the conventional level where what is good is defined by approval from significant others, in particular the child's parents and other important persons. In stage four, obedience to law becomes dominant determining what is considered good or bad. At stage five the child enters the postconventional level where morality is determined by the protection of individual rights and by the flexibility required by varying social requirements and circumstances. Finally, at stage six the individual becomes independent of institutions and social pressure, and moral conduct is determined by universal ethical principles. Kohlberg's theory moves in stages from initial concern with punishment when the child is very young, to stages where social institutions and conformity define moral conducts, to finally individually defined moral principles. In support of Kohlberg's theory are the studies that confirm that moral development progresses with age as predicted by his stage theory (Arnett, 2012).

In a review of 45 studies conducted in 27 countries Kohlberg's theory was evaluated (Snarey, 1985). The research literature provided evidence for the universality of the first two stages, but not the following. Others have found similar results (Ma & Cheung, 1996). These research reviews call into question whether the higher stages of moral development proposed by Kohlberg are in fact universal. However, we must keep in mind that it is also at the higher stages where culture produces the greater variability. Further, we must note that Kohlberg, like other stage theorists, developed his morality concepts from studies of Western samples. It is in fact a major complaint that Kohlberg's stages seem encapsulated in Western thought, and at least the last two have primarily emerged from Western liberal societies. Postconventional thinking would not get people much traction in Saudi Arabia or other totalitarian societies, where people who display this level of morality would spend their lives contemplating their noble thoughts from prison cells or worse.

Others have found evidence for the powerful influence of *cultural axioms* that can cancel moral development (Matsumoto, 1994). Chinese culture, for example, emphasizes collectivistic moral choices as influenced by working toward consensus, obeying law, and striving for harmony. These powerful cultural values would in most cases trump any moral stage development. Nevertheless there are probably dissidents in any culture with the moral courage to operate by universal principles of ethics developed individually. Further, Kohlberg's theory has also been attacked for gender bias based since males and females view relationships in different ways affecting moral choices (Gilligan, 1982). Consequently the higher stages of moral development are not invariant, but heavily influenced by culture as one would expect when the child moves from family circles to social conformity required by prevailing cultural values. Edwards (1986) believed that comparative differences in moral stages pointed directly to differences in social organization and underlying cultural values. In particular to understand morality it is essential to examine the culture's social structure and the broader environment.

Kohlberg largely agreed with these criticisms (Kohlberg, Levine, & Hewer, 1983). However, the theory is subject to many additional criticisms. Shweder, Mahapatra and Miller (1990) argued that Kohlberg's constructs were based on individualistic cultures and offered alternative moral views rooted in natural law using the family as a model. From this collectivistic perspective morality is based on duty to others rather than on rights of individuals (Shweder, Minow, & Markus, 2002). Ma (1988) offered an alternative based on Chinese morality that requires a person to behave consistently with the morality of the majority of society.

The review by Eckensberger and Zimba (1997) addressed the criteria that must be met in order to accept Kohlberg's moral stages as universal. The first criterion is whether the moral stages are found in all cultures investigated. The answer is mainly in the affirmative as long as invariance in stage sequence is not expected. However, stage invariance is supported by the .85 correlation between age and stage suggesting the sequence of moral behavior is the same for most respondents. Do the stages appear in all the cultures examined? Here the authors found support for some of the early moral stages, but not the latter. Although research supports universal development of moral reasoning in the early stages, the differences in the later moral stages may be what really counts in intercultural relations. For example, differences in moral development and the meaning of morality are real sources of conflict today between the Islamic world and the West. Acts considered blasphemy in Pakistan and other Islamic countries are behaviors governed by free speech in the West. These same acts of "free speech" produce the death penalty or vigilante action for the "offender" in Islamic countries.

4.10.3. Evolution of Psychosocial Development

The relationship between the individual and his social environment was examined by Erickson (1950) in his theory on *psychosocial development*. Erickson believed that all human beings went through 8 developmental stages starting at birth and ending with death. At each stage the individual is faced with a developmental crisis which can have either a positive or negative resolution. A positive outcome in Erickson's stage theory results in a stronger ego as the individual is better able to adapt and consequently develop a healthy personality. The positive outcome produces individuals who have hope, will, purpose, competence, fidelity, love, care and wisdom, each the outcome of facing separate developmental crises as a person moves through life. If a person has not successfully mastered a stage it was in Erickson's theory possible to reverse the outcome through psychotherapy (Erickson, 1968).

Although some evidence has been found for the presence of these stages in other cultures (Gardiner, Mutter, & Kosmitzki, 1998) the theory is vulnerable to criticism. The main criticism is that Erickson is merely reflecting the normative culture of the West. Within Christian ethics the positive outcomes in Erickson's theory can be seen as lofty goals that permit the individual to live a complete and fearless life. This ideal is not likely replicated where people are struggling for survival. When it comes to the cross-cultural validity of the theory it should be noted that many people in both the West and in other cultures have no hope for developing "competency" or even "intimacy," goals that are valued outcomes in Erickson's theory, since survival is the daily theme of life. A Western college professor or other professional may struggle with issues of "stagnation" toward the end of professional careers, but for others less fortunate the dominant motivator is finding bread for the table. What Erickson calls "generativity" (finding new ways to make contributions in latter stages of life) never becomes a developmental issue for billions of people. People living from paycheck to paycheck who have mounting immediate problems do not have the luxury to contemplate the meaning of life in maturity or achieve wisdom and will despair from just the sheer inability to find economic security. Also despite Erickson theory there is really no struggle over "identity" in many societies since these are established at birth in cultures that define identity through obedience to ideology and social institutions. The theory has applications in societies called individualistic where individuals have some freedom to choose, but as noted even in these situations choices are limited by socio-economic circumstances.

Nevertheless that human development takes place in stages is widely accepted. That there are biological influences is very likely. However, how these stages of developmental achievement take place and when they occur is dependent on unique cultural factors. Therefore there is evidence for both universal and culturally specific behavior in these stage theories.

4.11. HUMAN DEVELOPMENT IS THE EXPRESSION OF BIOLOGY: THE PRESENCE OF UNIVERSAL VALUES

Only half of the story of cultural transmission is told in cross-cultural psychology. *The emphasis in the discipline of cross-cultural psychology is on the transfer of culture within the socio-cultural context. This bias ignores a growing body of research that points to the essential biological basis for cultural and social behavior.* The selective adaptation that has occurred over time as a result of evolution is transmitted via the genes and passed from one generation to the next (Mange & Mange, 1999). In evolution and the adaptation of humans to their environment we can understand the important story of cultural survival and the improved chances of reproductive success brought about by gene modification. Biology forms the basis of cultural transmission over the course of our evolutionary history. The key to understanding evolution is the idea that genetic material changes over time by means of natural selection.

When a heritable trait contributes to survival and therefore to successful reproduction the frequency of that trait will increase over time. If the trait contributes to greater fitness and therefore survival members of a species that do not carry the trait disappear from the evolutionary record. Natural selection is the process where the inclusion of a trait that improves fitness leads to systematic and significant changes affecting reproductive success over many generations. In modern times these changes have been associated with modification of the gene and the essential DNA sequences. Changes in genetic material called mutations are often adverse to the organism, but given sufficient time occasionally mutations may confer benefits to those that carry the modification. Other factors that affects the presence of heritable traits include selection caused by migration and isolation from the original mating population, and social rules for mating that favor or disfavor certain biological characteristics. Specified mating rules in some cases lead to inbreeding that affect the frequency of genetic components. In some societies cousins are expected to marry, whereas in other cultures such a union is viewed as incest. Although genetic contributions to behavior is thought independent of environmental factors there is increasing evidence that environmental events can at least influence the regulatory processes of these heritable factors (Gottlieb, 1998).

Natural selection will favor those individuals who possess traits that result in improved adaptation. From the perspective of evolutionary science adaptation occur through interaction with the environment. In social science adaptation refer more specifically to changes occurring within individuals as they cope with the environment. However, in some cases the environmental pressure is so significant that the impact causes changes in the surface of genes carried from one generation to the next. For example, during the war on Vietnam the U.S. military sprayed enormous amounts of Agent Orange on Vietnam. The principal component dioxin is the strongest poison known to man (Bouny, 2007), and the spraying produced 4,800,000 victims that now span three generations (Stellman, Stellman, Christian, Weber, & Tomasallo, 2003). The new field of epigenetics shows that the environment can in fact affect cellular modifications that are transmitted intergenerationally and which produces outcomes that are lasting. Although the common scientific belief in the past was that the environment could only affect the current generation, results reported by Cloud (2010) show that powerful environmental events can leave an imprint on the genetic material in both eggs and sperm and thereby short circuit evolution and pass the trait to the next generation. The change does not occur in the genetic material, but rather on the cellular material placed on top of the gene that tells the gene to switch on or off. These epigenetic changes represent the biological reactions to extreme environmental events like the poisoning by Agent Orange in Vietnam. The young discipline of epigenetics does not provide a definitive answer as to whether the genetic changes will eventually fade away in the absence of stressor, but regardless there is a cautionary tale in that our extreme disruption of the environment may produce immediate genetic consequences that formerly took many generations (Larsen & Van Le, 2010).

Human beings are not passive in the face of their environmental challenges, but are active participants in shaping the conditions that create selective success. The environment places limits on what solutions are possible, but within these parameters human beings create a variety of cultural responses. Cultural responses to environmental challenges include in the most abstract sense also religion and cultural values. Biology has long recognized the existence of behavior traits that are relatively invariable for species other than humans and coded in the genes of the organism. As science is opening the possibilities of genetic modifications including artificial mutations we are learning more about gene based behavior. Can this science also be applied to human culture?

4.12. THE EVOLUTIONARY BASIS FOR HUMAN BEHAVIOR: MAXIMIZING INCLUSIVE FITNESS

According *to sociobiological explanations all human behavior is aimed at maximizing inclusive fitness that motivates people to promote the interests of genetically related people.* The concept of inclusive fitness for the human species is not limited to offspring, but includes also maximizing the interest of other kin including nephews and nieces (Wilson, 1975). The promotion of the interest of kin is central to evolutionary reproductive success for social species like humans. Sociobiology extends the argument of genetic determinants of human behavior on a very broad scale. Wilson suggests that most of the branches of human knowledge in social sciences or humanities are reducible to the biology or sociobiology of a species.

4.13. PERSPECTIVE IN THE TRANSMISSION OF CULTURE

It is the obligation of researchers to examine both cultural as well as genetic bases in cultural transmission. The genetic underpinnings of culture are essential components in the development of cultural solutions to environmental problems. However, cultural information is transmitted by social interaction from one generation to the next. The capacity for learning is limited by our genetic inheritance, but the cultural information channels offer the possibility to pass on cultural knowledge to our offspring. Life teaches us what is useful to survival or social success, and that information is conveyed by parents and other cultural guardians. Social learning theory explains many of the differences found in comparative studies as people learn by observation and imitation. It is important to remember that members of society are not passive spectators in cultural transmission. People interact with their cultures for evolutionary benefit and create niches that serve the purpose of reproductive success (Laland, Odling-Smee, & Feldman, 2000). Members of cultural groups participate in creating niches, for example, some population groups have dominated certain professions like medicine or the sale of jewelry as these were found over time to be successful niches ensuring survival through several generations.

SUMMARY

The central concern of cross-cultural psychology is how people acquire culturally unique traits as well as communalities in behaviors across cultures. All theories of learning apply to the transmission of culture in interactions with parents, siblings, the educational system, and the ecological context. Socialization is the deliberate teaching of cultural values by parents and others whereas enculturation refers to the internalized psychological end product. In other words, socialization is the means to the encultural ends. Through the transmission of culture society passes on the skills and values thought important to survival and successful living.

There are both important similarities between cultures, but also distinct differences in childrearing as some cultures emphasize conformity and obedience and other societies promote personal independence. The ecological context, socio-political environment, customs, and psychology of caregivers provide the important niche components defining child development. However, the child is not a passive observer but actively interacts with these developmental forces and in the process affects the construal of the self. Childrearing ideology describes the dominant parental beliefs in society about the best way to raise children, and how to nurture and express warmth and affection. These and other values are inculcated in all members of a culture in the process of development. Affluent societies have more resources and time to develop unique assets of the child, whereas parents in poor societies are just struggling to stay afloat and survive.

Childrearing styles identified as authoritative and authoritarian have been found to have significant outcomes. Authoritative parents provide child care that is firm, but also reasonable and fair. The context of authoritative child rearing includes the consistent expression of warmth and affection. Authoritarian parents, on the other hand, demand obedience and practice strict control. Research has demonstrated the superiority of the authoritative style producing more positive emotions in the child more self-confidence, with long-lasting consequences.

The climate of home life is the major context in the transmission of cultural values. Differences have been observed between collectivistic and individualistic societies in the interaction of parents with the educational system. Sleeping with the mother is the earliest form of security in the home and also varies by culture. In the U.S. parents generally try to create early independence in all aspects of childrearing, and as a substitute for sleeping with the mother the child is provided with security blankets and sleep in separate quarters at the earliest moment possible. However, parents in other societies believe that keeping the child physically close provides essential security for later development. Socio-economic factors may also play a role in sleeping arrangements. Bonding has more utility in societies struggling to survive and that context may favor intimate sleeping patterns. Further, poverty may prevent the creation of additional space for separate sleeping arrangements.

The means of creating attachment in childhood varies by culture. The use of physical touch and verbal stimulation are dependent on cultural values and beliefs. Attachment is considered an important psychological achievement essential for later cultural learning. Relationships to siblings represent an early cultural influence. In fact the significant events of family and cultural life are sifted through the eyes of siblings, and cultural interdependence is taught by these relationships. How to act properly in social interaction and in gender relationships is primarily mediated by sibling relationships.

The extended family is also a source of cultural knowledge. Peers and the extended family reinforce the important cultural values in society. Material and emotional interdependence is particularly important in pre-industrial societies and in those cultures where people struggle to survive. By contrast interdependence is limited to the immediate family in Western countries and Western societies foster the separated and independent self. Although the research results are ambiguous it is thought that the self is construed differentially in collectivistic and individualistic cultures. Extended families are more involved in child rearing in collectivistic cultures. Ethnic groups in multi-cultural societies may continue to transmit the cultural expectation on gender related behavior and loyalty unique to their own group.

Culture is mediated by the country's educational system. Schools are major socializing agents in most societies in the world and serve to inculcate cultural values. In individualistic societies the educational system serves to prepare the student for a competitive future through the emphasis on grading, ranking, and competitive sports. The influence of peers on cultural learning increases in the school years. The socio-economic climate also affects development. In societies struggling for survival children learn motor skills at an earlier age compared to children from affluent communities. These motor skills are more salient to aid survival in harsh environments. Birth death rates vary by culture. Where the rates are high mothers must concentrate all their efforts on the survival of their infants and few parental resources are available to promote other assets of the child or provide enriching learning experiences. Eventually social identity grows out of the home climate and children learn early to identify with ingroups and reference groups. Children from individualistic societies also learn early the utility of competiveness for success and achievement.

Comparative studies in child rearing show that attachment experiences vary by culture as parental warmth and affection are not expressed in the same way in all cultures. In some cultures parents use physical touch to express loving feelings whereas in other cultures parents utilize their voices and intonation to express warmth. However, in all cultures parents have a desire for their children to learn emotional and social skills. Parents everywhere also use assertive behavior when disciplining their children for infractions. Parental ideology or ethnotheories play important but varying roles in different societies. These theories define play time interactions and the actual time spent with their children. Adherence to cultural values is a parental concern in all societies; however, mothers in collectivistic cultures are more concerned when the child displays a lack of cooperation, whereas American mothers are more worried about their children's disruptive behavior.

In some cultural or social groups parents have no childrearing ideology believing that their children can manage development without interference. However, in most cultures parents believe they must play an active role in raising their children. In collectivistic societies parents demand strict obedience and provide sanctions for behavior that does not meet expectations. Parental authoritarianism is related to a lack of cultural and socio-economic stability. The emphasis on competition leads Western parents to have expectations for the early development of skills.

The origin of human cognition is human interaction. In fact human "nature" does not exist in isolation from culture. Culture is the mediating variable between biological and environmental factors. Individual development is determined by the interaction of biology, phylogenetic development, and cultural variables. Culture provides the framework for the social interactions and mediates the internalization of cultural values. Culture also plays a role in lifespan development since it provides support services needed in the later stages of aging without which a person would not survive.

Stage theories in cognition, moral development and psychosocial development describe individual change in processes thought universal. Piaget's theory examines the evolution of cognition in four stages. Evidence from the comparative literature supports the universality of the early cognitive stage sequences. However, there is little evidence for the universality of "formal operations" as this type of abstract thinking probably requires a Western education. The ages at which children master the early stages also appear to vary by culture. Moral development is evaluated in Kohlberg's theory in 6 stages. Some evidence for the universality of the first two stages is supported by comparative research. However, the higher stages appear to reflect Western moral traditions. The stability of moral stages is questioned since circumstances and powerful situations may cancel any stage of moral development. Kohlberg has also been criticized for gender bias since males and females view relationships differentially. Other criticisms focus on the influence of individualistic cultures on the higher stages of moral development. Erickson believed that all human beings pass through 8 psychosocial stages starting at birth and ending with death. At each stage a crisis occurs that if solved in a positive way leads to stronger egos and better adaptability. The main criticism of psychosocial development theory is that it reflects the normative culture of the West. Psychosocial development takes a different road in societies struggling for survival, and social identity is prescribed in some societies and not the outcome of crisis. The aforementioned discussion has emphasized cultural transmission from the perspective of the socio-cultural context. The chapter concludes with a discussion of the biological underpinnings of cultural behavior. The important study of survival and cultural adaptation is based on evolutionary principles.

CHAPTER 5

THE EVOLUTION OF LANGUAGE AND SOCIO-CULTURE

Language is the most salient human attributive that co-evolved with culture. Without the innate ability to learn language it would have been impossible for our ancestors to communicate over ever larger social networks, or to solve complex problems in the ecological environment. The high level of differentiation of human language gives us the ability to convey complex information, and develop symbolic means of representation or what is called *artefactual* languages. The meaning of events around us and the natural world was symbolized on the walls of caves even in very early human cultures. Although other species communicate, they are not able to speculate about the intentions of others, but humans can not only convey their own intentions, but also attribute intentions to the behavior of others. These abilities form the foundations of human culture as informational and meaning systems that are passed from one generation to the next. Language is a *universal hardwired attribute,* but all cultures have developed their own variances and means of expressions. Examining the differences between languages helps us understand important components of cultural

Cross-Cultural Psychology: Why Culture Matters, pages 109–142.

evolutionary history. Some communications are non-verbal and cultures impart meaning also to variances of non-verbal behavior.

How languages developed is important to our understanding of the role of culture. In the world of today cultures communicate not just within, but increasingly also between cultures. Since the lexical and grammatical content may be unique to each language, there are barriers to overcome when communicating between cultures. Although we live in the age of globalization unique language attributes will continue to influence language development and culture in the foreseeable future. Language gives humans the possibility to think, and unique features of each culture may canalize our thoughts in divergent directions. Understanding the impact of culturally directed thoughts is salient in our emerging new world.

5.1. THE EVOLUTION OF SOCIOCULTURE AND LANGUAGE

The co-evolution and reciprocal nature of socio-culture and languages are accepted by all socio-linguists. Darwinian evolution of genetic traits has also been utilized as a model in sociolinguistics and the important ideas of selective adaptation have proven useful in understanding the evolution of human culture and the languages by which it is communicated. The objective conditions considered essential by Darwin for genetic evolution to occur also exist in cultural evolution. Therefore *phylogenetic* models and associated mathematics are useful in both genetic and cultural evolution. As a result of evolutionary models describing human migration, demographics, and cultural history these processes are understood better today. However, the horizontal transmission of cultural traits unique to cultural evolution creates greater complexity not easily captured by phylogenetic methods since they were first developed to understand more lineal vertical genetic evolution. Nevertheless these methods have proven of great value to researchers trying to unravel our cultural descent. Forces of cultural stability affect evolutionary trends, although the forces of globalization require new thinking on the future of cultural and language evolution. In the multiplicity of thousands of human languages we have the modern support for the evolution of languages which after all was not caused by God at the Tower of Babel.

5.2. LANGUAGE DEVELOPMENT: THE MEANING OF LANGUAGE TERMS AND EARLY SPEECH

The student of language development needs to understand a number of terms in common use by linguists. The most basic verbal element is the *lexical* or word content referring to the number and variety of words in a language. *Phonemes* are the smallest unit of sound, and *morphemes* are the most elementary meanings in a language. The grammar of a language is also called the *syntax*, and refers to the specific rules that determine how words are combined or structured. Verbal language is also about the sounds we make in speech, and phonology refers to how words should sound in a given language. *Pragmatics* is about the social context and how language is dependent on and understood within a given situation. Finally, *semantics* refers to the meaning or substance of words.

The smallest units of speech are phonemes as indicated above. Cultures produce varying emphasizes on phonemes that can cause both amusing language differences and also difficulties in pronunciation. For example l and r are not distinct in the Japanese language as it is in English. Japanese speakers cannot distinguish between la and ra, a distinction easily made by U.S. respondents (Miyawaki, Strange, Verbrugge, Liberman, Jenkins, & Fujimura, 1975). Infants are able to make phonetic distinctions before they can articulate speech. Once developed the boundaries of phonetic expression are set causing problems when later learning a second language (Goto, 1971). Infants begin to babble at about 6 months, and start forming words after one year. The lexical accumulation is followed by the learning of grammatical rules, and later learning helps the child to take the nonverbal context into account such as the pragmatic rules of taking turns in speech.

5.3. CULTURAL LANGUAGE DIFFERENCE AND LINGUISTIC RELATIVITY

Although humans have a universal hardwired ability to acquire language, variances caused by culture are noteworthy. It is by interaction with members of one's culture that language is gradually shaped by reinforcing certain sounds while ignoring or discouraging other expressions. These basic sounds gradually take on meaning and eventually produce words and vocabulary. Humans have the innate ability to produce an almost infinite set of meanings from relatively few elementary sounds, a characteristic that differentiates humans from other primates (Fitch & Hauser, 2004). Culture also determines the structure or grammar of language, and also the pragmatic rules for speech in the social context. What we know about a person's culture is largely communicated in language, and the very essence of culture and fundamental values is expressed through culturally determined speech.

Languages differ in word content and in the *cultural context* of communication. How we define relationships between ourselves and others is determined by cultural determined referents. In English we typically simplify relationships through the use of "you" for other people, whereas "I" is the word referring to ourselves. However, in other cultures this self-other referent is more complex. In Japanese what we call others depend on our mutual relationship, and in particular the relative status equity or inequity between the speakers. In Japanese if a person is of higher status the individual would refer to that individual by the role or position. Parents would say "father or mother is telling you..." or the professor would say referring to him or /herself "Professor wants you to do this...."The pragmatics of Japanese society require politeness, gender awareness, and varying degrees of familiarity. Familiarity is also part of European languages other than English, with two terms to indicate "you," one familiar and the other polite. In any event Japanese have a highly differentiated language lexical structure regarding the self-other and how the language is used depends on the social context and the existing status differential.

The cultural context is expressed in the variations of terms used to define the familiar and outgroup relationships. These words are differentiated more intimately in Japanese ingroup relationships compared to respondents in the U.S. (Gudykunst & Nishida, 1986). In one study the rules governing language use were investigated in 71 countries that used 39 languages. The principal finding supported different cultural conceptualizations of the self and others. *This finding suggests that the very meaning of the self is cultural and language determined.* Cultures also differ in the amount of self-disclosure (Chen, 1995). U.S. respondents were more self-disclosing in a variety of areas than the Japanese. The communication style carries important meanings about culture. Some languages tend to employ very direct styles whereas other cultures imbed meaning in the social context. In some cultures *the way* language is expressed is of equal or greater communicative importance compared to the content. As we can see communication between cultures is not always straight forward, especially between languages that are direct versus those that are elaborated in the social context and therefore indirect.

5.4. CULTURAL LANGUAGE AND THOUGHT

The relationship of language to thought has been debated in cross-cultural psychology for some time. Since each culture is expressed through a unique language, perhaps the lexical content and grammatical rules also affect thinking. Culture affects languages, but does the language of a culture also affect thinking processes? *The Sapir-Whorf hypothesis is a proposition that argues that variances in languages produce differences in cognition.* If true, cultures experience reality in different ways as all societies are dependent on the tools of language for perception and expression. Similar situations may be perceived differently because of variations in language structure, lexical content, and grammatical rules. Language relativity raises the issue of whether we can ever translate deeper cultural meanings accurately from one language to another. Do bilingual speakers experience different realities depending on which language they use?

The initial research compared European languages with those of Native Americans (Whorf, 1956). For example, among Hopi Indians there are no words that refer to time which is perceived as a floating continuum. The closest idea to time in Hopi expressions is expressed by differences between objective and subjective reality. For the Hopi the subjective is that which is not manifest in the present like, for example, the "future" or "desire and hope." In Hopi there are no subjective plurals, so Hopi speakers cannot indicate the number of days that pass between events, but rather would compare two events as differing in lateness.

The relationship of language to thinking processes and learning has received a great deal of attention (Levinson, 2006). The accessibility of certain complex concepts is language dependent. In turn the complexity of concepts depends on our ability to utilize a complex vocabulary. Languages in grammar form and lexical content vary profoundly producing cognitive differences between language speakers. Regier and Kay (2006) argued *that linguistic differences are causational agents of cognitive differences in members of language groups and therefore more agentic than correlational.* Although all humans are born with similar genetic constraints language learning has significant affects on our ability to think. Languages are representational systems that organize our cultural world and permit transmission of knowledge to succeeding generations.

Fishman (1960) investigated linguistic relativity at the lexical level and in the use of grammar among the Inuits . For example, Inuits have many words describing snow that is a salient component of their culture, and they can therefore differentiate its characteristics to a greater degree than people speaking English. Support for the Sapir-Whorf hypothesis was also found among Navajo speakers (Carroll & Casagrande, 1958). Research showed that because of the unique grammatical features of Navajo language that provided many words for the handling of objects Navajo children were more likely to categorize objects by shape than by color compared to English speaking children.

Another research project examined differences between Chinese and English speaking respondents (Bloom, 1981). English speakers can use counterfactual statements saying, for example: "If I were rich... I would." That statement implies that the speaker is not rich. Chinese, on the other hand, do not have counterfactual expressions, and therefore must precede the comment with an explicit statement of fact: "I am not rich, therefore …."This absence of counterfactual statements limits Chinese speakers in the use of counterfactual thinking, and according to Bloom may affect how the Chinese and English speakers think and categorize the world. However, Au (1983) found no cross-cultural differences between Chinese and English speakers, and the research literature has not definitively supported the affect of grammar on thinking. Vorster and Schuring (1989) also found no support in their study for the Sapir-Whorfian hypothesis.

The categorization of color has been used to test linguistic relativity. Color categorization permits an unambiguous testing of the Sapir-Whorfian hypotheses since it can be directly related to physical measurements. Many cultures do not have words that correspond to the basic eleven colors categorized in the English language (Berlin & Kay, 1969). However, Bornstein, Kessen, and Weiskopf (1976) showed that color categories for infants are the same as for adults supporting the primacy of perception rather than language in color perception. Their research on color perception did not lend support to linguistic relativity.

Kay and Kempton (1984), however, found that the lexical (word) content of language mattered to color categorization. They compared the thought processes of respondents speaking Tarahumara in northern Mexico with English speakers and found a comparative difference in the discrimination of color. More recent studies (Alexander, Carr, & Schwanenflugel, 1995; Gordon, 2004; Lin & Schwanenflugel, 1995; Schwanenflugel, 1991; Schwanenflugel & Rey, 1986) found support for the importance of cultural lexical knowledge in categorization processes and mathematical counting. Hoosain (1991) showed that particular elements of the Chinese language influence the relative ease of processing information.

Is it easier to discriminate and perceive subtle nuances in the real world when speakers have more words available in a language? Further, do multiple words referring to the same phenomenon make it easier to communicate in that language by describing specified nuances? Hunt and Agnoli (1991) found that the words available in a language could facilitate or inhibit the processing of certain types of information. Words available can make it easier to communicate in the language and either support or hinder thinking processes.

However, it would appear that support for the Sapir-Whorf hypothesis in comparative cross-cultural studies comes from a narrow area of research where language differences are directly relevant to perceptual or cognitive functioning. In an important review on linguistic relativity Pinker (1995) concluded that many of the studies reported above were severely flawed, noting, for example, that it is possible to think without words. Deaf children can think, and those who grow up without language invent one and engage in abstract thinking. These findings suggest that the brain is hardwired for language. Research has also supported the important role of nonverbal language and visual thinking in social cognition. Fishman (1960) concluded that lexical differences are not a strong influence on thinking, whereas grammar and pragmatics (the social context) are salient areas where language can influence cognition.

5.5. UNIVERSALS IN LANGUAGE

There is strong evidence that *language as a tool for thinking has many universal and invariant elements*. Although culture may determine to some degree our thoughts, languages do not of their own accord yield different thinking processes. The research with deaf children shows that cognitive development is to some degree independent of language (see also Eibl-Eibesfeldt, 1979). Deaf children display a language-like structure in their gestures, often using multiple gestures, compared to normal hearing children who will typically only use one gesture (Goldin-Meadow & Mylander, 1998). The structural similarities in gestures for deaf children were demonstrated in both the U.S. and China suggesting an *innate basis* for language gesture expression. Chomsky (1980) argued that humans possess a hardwired universal grammar to which all languages conform that is independent of cultural influence. When a child is born this innate organization is present in the form of a language organ analogous to other organs present for vision or hearing and is genetically based and common to all members of the species (Chomsky, 2000).

An apparent innate universal organization determines at least some aspects of word order in a language. For example, a word order placing the object first followed by the subject and then the verb does not occur in any language (Greenberg, 1978). Intonation also has universal properties (Bolinger, 1978) with emphasis indicated by a high pitch. To support this point try to listen North Korean news casters on YouTube talk about their great or dear leaders and the intonation convey the importance and reverence attributed to these more or less superhuman objects of worship. Evidence for universality in language is also supported by similar semantic meaning in all languages (Osgood, 1980). Factor analyses of adjectives were administered in surveys to respondents in varying language groups and the results showed that in all participant groups the results yielded three factors called evaluative, potency, and activity dimensions. Polarity of the positive and negative is also thought to be a basic universal characteristic of human cognition. In calculating a similarity index for 12 languages the results yielded a correlation of .67 (Osgood, 1979). Although languages are different and dependent on cultural evolution, there are cross-cultural invariant elements that also suggest our common genetic evolutionary history.

5.6. INTERCULTURAL COMMUNICATION

Culture affects the language we use, the choice of words and sentences, and our thoughts, feelings and behavior. As we have seen culture also affects our nonverbal behavior with the same gestures having different meanings in different cultural groups. Culture shapes our nonverbal behavior automatically at a cognitive level not requiring reflection. Intercultural messages are understood subjectively from the perspective of the listener. The interpretation of communication is a perceptual process influenced by ingroup values, by the emotions signaled by the nonverbal context, and by cultural stereotypes. These cultural filters are largely unconscious, but that does not minimize the impact of the cultural canalization on effective communication. Intercultural communication is especially difficult since both the encoding as well as decoding of messages is understood using different *cultural filters*, and evaluating the intent of the communicator is a judgment process influenced by our attributions rather than the content of the message (Gudykunst & Shapiro, 1996).

5.6.1. Obstacles and Uncertainty Reduction in Intercultural Communication

Obstacles that prevent clear and effective communication are present in the contact between people of different cultures. Barna (1996) has discussed several issues that distort meaningful communication. We see the world through our own eyes and therefore often think that people are like us, even when they grew up with very different ideas and values. Again because language is mediated through our own experiences, we naively assume that words have only one meaning when it may have several in the language of the other speaker. We need also to attend to nonverbal signals and understand what they mean in the culture of the communicator since misunderstandings can easily derive from differences in nonverbal meanings. All cultural groups have stereotypes of their own society and other cultures and these generalizations may prevent accurate interpretations or distort the intent of the message. There is also a tendency in all cultures to evaluate the ingroup positively and outgroups negatively and such ethnocentric attitudes are conveyed nonverbally. Finally, Barna noted that intercultural communication often produces anxiety and stress. Dysfunctional thought processes follow stress encouraging people to hang on to stereotypes even when they have proven inaccurate. Effective intercultural communication requires an awareness of these potential stumbling blocks and tolerance in seeking the common ground.

The obstacles discussed above produce uncertainty about the meaning of messages compounded by nonverbal signals that vary between cultures. Different interpretations of such nonverbal signals add another obstacle to intercultural communication producing uncertainty and potential conflict. Gudykunst and Shapiro (1996) showed that intercultural interactions were rated higher in anxiety and uncertainty. Research shows that the primary concern in the initial intercultural encounter is to reduce the uncertainty and increase the predictability of interaction outcomes (Berger & Calabrese, 1975). Gudykunst and Nishida (1986) in a study of American and Japanese respondents showed that participants tried to reduce uncertainty by indicating intent to interrogate and self-disclose, and by expressing affiliation nonverbally.

Intercultural conflict is often the result of misinterpretations of communication based on culturally laden attributions of intent to other cultural groups. As a result of miscommunication we attribute false and inaccurate motives to other cultural groups. Communicators from other cultures often conflict with our expectations and fail to conform to cultural norms. Conflict is also a natural outcome of cultural differences in the meaning of vocabularies as well as in nonverbal language. Cultural values may contribute to miscommunication as in one study Anglo-European participants communicated more individualistically, whereas East Asian students communicated in more collectivistic ways (Pekerti & Thomas, 2003).

There are both attitudinal and skill components to consider if the goal is to reduce uncertainty in intercultural communication (Gudykunst, 1993). When interacting in the cross-cultural context we need to interpret the pragmatics thoughtfully and appropriately, and in the process try to control subjective cultural factors affecting the message. To improve intercultural communication requires desire and motivation, knowledge about the target culture and skills in communication. When uncertainty is reduced it is possible to concentrate on the message and make accurate interpretations. In particular it is essential to regulate emotions and moderate ethnocentric thinking about other peoples. Conflict in intercultural communication is perhaps inevitable given different views of reality, but by moderating emotional reactions it is possible to engage in constructive communication. When emotions are regulated self-insight is possible with the collateral benefit of self-critical thinking controlling ethnocentric attributions (Matsumoto & LeRoux, 2003; Matsumoto, LeRoux, Bernhard, & Gray, 2004).

5.6.2. The Affect of Bilingualism

Is has become quite common for people to speak multiple languages with information technology bringing cultures closer and immigration creating a need for second languages (Baker & Prys, 1998). Although globalization has supported English as a world language, most people speak at least one other language fluently. Today *bilingualism* is a reality for many if not for most people, and not the exception as it was in times past and the use of multiple languages contributes to a more complex and rich linguistic knowledge. Language is symbolic of the culture that creates it, and therefore if people know two or more languages they also possess two or more mental representations of the meaning of the constructs used in language. An important issue is whether the unique cultural constructs associated with a language causes bilingual people to change their mental representation when shifting from one language to another? Hull (1987, 1990) administered the California Personality Inventory to bilinguals under language appropriate conditions. The results showed that the respondents displayed different personalities depending on which language was employed in the test. Manifestations of different personalities were thought the outcome of the respondents identifying with the stereotypes of each language culture producing trait emphasis reflecting in test differences.

Bilinguals are thought to engage in cultural code switching, moving back and forth between culturally defined meanings associated with the language spoken (Hong, Morris, Chiu, & Benet-Martinez, 2000). Even the attribution style used was dependent on the language spoken as in one study Americans made more individual attributions when primed whereas Chinese bilinguals used more culturally consistent collectivistic images (Benet-Martinez, Leu, Lee, & Morris, 2002).

Bilingualism contributes to higher intelligence when controlling for social and economic factors (Lambert & Anisfeld, 1969). *Bilingual children are advanced in creativity, the ability to think divergently, and demonstrate more cognitive complexity* (Segalowitz, 1980). The interaction of languages within the individual creates also higher sensitivity to ambiguities in sentences and a greater awareness of intonation as a clue to meaning (Mohanty, 1994). Those of you that know more than one language may also have observed that bilingualism makes the learning of other new languages easier, probably by the discernment of overlap of lexical and grammatical content (Thomas, 1988).

Bilingual people who have professional experience in more than one country are among the most desired managers and CEOs in multinational corporations. They demonstrate the ability to work in a globalized world and more easily bridge relations with peers and employees from different cultures (Muna & Zennie, 2010).

5.7. NONVERBAL COMMUNICATION AND CULTURE

Speakers utilize an array of *nonverbal signals* to convey meaning when communicating. Facial expressions, pitch, silence, gestures, interpersonal distance, body postures and touching others all communicate or emphasize aspects of the spoken word. The major part of any communication is nonverbal conveying especially important meanings about emotional states. *Nonverbal signals carry specific messages and help illustrate the meaning of the communication as well as regulating the flow of speech* (Ekman & Friesen, 1969; Gordon, 2004).

Differences in *required interpersonal space* are easily observed when travelling to various cultures in the world. Hall (1976) suggested that the need for interpersonal space depends on the relationship between the speakers which he divided into four levels from intimate (e.g. between mothers and child) to personal (within friendship or family) to social (among acquaintances) and in public arenas (among relative strangers). Cultural differences in the desire for interpersonal space have been found between Arab men who require less space when compared to American males (Watson & Graves, 1966). Likewise Latin students also required less physical space when interacting compared to European students (Forston & Larson, 1968). It would not raise an eyebrow when Arab men walk hand in hand in their culture, whereas such behavior would create very different meanings in Western societies. It is a curious irony that Americans are very informal in their verbal speech, but do not allow others to be close in interpersonal space.

Cultural differences also exist in terms of another form of nonverbal behavior—the *chronemics*. Hall defines two time systems essential for the efficient intercultural communication: monochronic and polychronic time. The monochronic time system is prevalent in the countries located in Northern Europe, and North America where time is perceived as something tangible and people speak of it as something that can be "spent," "saved," "wasted" and "lost." Time is used as a framework for organizing life through schedules in which all important life activities of individuals, except birth and death, are planned and prioritized. Typical characteristic in these cultures is putting career first and performing only one activity at a time, which require careful planning and adherence to preset schedules.

Hall argues that unlike monochronic cultures dominated by short-term relationships members of polychronic cultures (such as Hispanics and Arabs) maintain long-term relationships with wider range of people simultaneously. These relations are valued much more than time schedules and deadlines, and therefore in polychronic cultures nothing is firmly established, but flexible and constantly changing. Appointments can be changed even at the last minute in service of someone more important in the hierarchy of family, friends or partners. In these cultures monochronic time is used only when appropriate.

Gestures are also nonverbal communication that conveys a great deal of information. Efron (1941) found distinct gesture differences between Italian and Jewish immigrants that disappeared with assimilation into American culture. The presence of many gestural differences in varying cultures has been supported by research (Morris, Collett, Marsh, & O'Shaughnessy, 1980). To know these gestures is somewhat important as what may be a socially supportive gesture utilizing raised fingers in one society, may be an obscene signal in another. Societies also vary in the amount of time and in the intensity of gazing (Fehr & Exline, 1987). Gazing is connected with expression of emotions, in a love relationship it may communicate affection and concern, and in other relationships gazing can indicate aggression and dominance. Rules for gazing are articulated by cultures since aggression and loving relationships are salient to cultural stability. People from Arabic cultures are more direct in gazing and gaze longer compared to Americans. This led Watson (1970) to classify 30 countries to be contact cultures that not only facilitated physical touch, but also more gazing, touching, and required less interpersonal distance when compared to no contact societies. It is apparent that culture plays an important role in contributing to differences in the meaning of nonverbal behavior.

5.8. DARWINIAN EVOLUTION AND PHYLOGENETIC TREES OF LANGUAGE AND SOCIO-CULTURAL EVOLUTION

The model of Darwinian evolution has become increasingly influential in explaining cultural development and change. In biology researchers have for a long time estimated descent relationships by means of *phylogenetic tree-building* and by establishing network of relationships between related species. These methods have also been adapted to reconstruct cultural histories. Cultural histories are discerned from deeper signals of historical branching or division derived from the earliest phases of a cultural group's origin. *The branching of culture and the diffusion of cultural traits are the two major determinants that explain the cultural diversity we observe today.* Cultural macro-evolution refers to the historical processes that produced variability between cultures in turn created by repeated copying of cultural practices with some modification over time (Felsenstein, 2004; Mesoudi, Whiten, & Laland, 2006). Darwinian analysis has been successfully applied in several disciplines including cultural anthropology, evolutionary archeology, and is equally valid for an interpretation of historical linguistics.

The stability of cultural traits is an important theoretical area to consider in cultural evolution. Modifiability of cultural traits is essential for evolution to occur in response to selective pressures in a population. However, stability of traits occurs when these cultural factors have proven useful to social and ecological adaptation. How do cultures select certain behaviors and how do these cultural traits become stable or lead to changes in the cultural repertoire? Animal behavior evolves because genetic and behavioral traits contribute to the survival of the species (Wynne-Edwards, 1962). *Phylogenetic mathematical models have been developed that describe natural selection processes within genes in the individual but is also useful to understand cultural evolution at the group level* (Price, 1970). Group selection of a cultural trait occurs when it provides a selective advantage and therefore contributes to the evolution of cultural traits beneficial to the group.

The early development of agriculture in China several thousands of years ago produced many culturally evolutionary gains from the invention of the plow, to developing tools for grain threshing, and eventually by building canals to bring the surplus grain to market. These culturally evolutionary developments produced great advantages to the Chinese state, and created an integrated empire long before these developments occurred in Europe or elsewhere. The evolution of *cultural traits* associated with agriculture increased the competitive fitness of China compared to other cultures and led to centuries of dominance. Boyd and Richerson (2010) suggested that group selection of *genetic traits* only occurs when groups are very small and there is little chance of mating and a flow of genes between groups. In other words, group selection of genetic traits only has selective advantages for small and geographically distant groups. However, for cultural evolution the example of China shows that although cultural traits benefitting society may develop in small isolated groups with the right social structure cultural traits can be rapidly diffused over a large area.

5.8.1. Selective Group Genetic Advantages in Cultural Evolution

In rare circumstances selective genetic adaptation within a group can be a stronger culturally evolutionary force when compared to the genetic change affects produced by migration. However, even a few percentage point advantages created by a genotype change that is of selective benefit to a group could be considered an extremely significant competitive advantage over neighboring groups. Such genetic advantage could only be maintained if the incoming migration rate is very low as otherwise any beneficial change would be liquidated by the expanded gene pool. The adaptation of human groups to the lack of sunshine in the northern regions of the world and the genetic evolution of lighter skin tones is a selective genetic advantage that must be understood to have evolved in this manner. By comparison to the generally slow processes of genetic evolution the imitation of cultural traits is, on the other hand, very rapid as we saw in China and is therefore responsible for the vast amount of cultural evolution. Some researchers (e.g. Boyd & Richerson, 2010) have suggested that human cultural evolution is similar to the evolution of separate species of animals and mathematical models of phylogenetic evolution work well in explaining cultural variation as it does in understanding the development of species.

Neighboring cultural groups often compete in adaptation to similar ecological environments. The historical outcome is either the exclusion of disadvantageous groups or their assimilation into cultural groups that have evolved adaptive advantages. The power of the Western socio-economic model to influence change in other countries in modern times is a form of assimilation as countries seek inclusion in economic trade organizations and ever larger political structures. However, there are serious environmental disadvantages to long-term adaptation to the Western model as it has produced extinction of species, global warming, and endemic economic insecurity. Unlike genetic evolution that evolves vertically and requires a common ancestor, cultural evolution is driven by socio-cultural motivators that can rapidly spread horizontally. Social imitations and conformity pressures create stable models for emulation within groups and along with geographical isolation have over time produced significant differences in cultural traits between groups.

5.8.2. The Analogy of Genetic and Cultural Evolution

Boyd and Richerson argued that Darwin's model of genetic evolution is also appropriate for an analysis of cultural and language evolution. They argued that Darwin's (1859) conditions considered necessary for genetic adaptation by natural selection are also present in cultural evolution. Darwin contended that natural selection requires a struggle for existence, and heritable variations in the population so some individuals gain a selective advantage over others of the species. Boyd and Richerson noted that these conditions are met in any reproducing entity whether genetic or cultural. *The rapid cultural adaptation in human cultural groups is stabilized by socio-cultural forces (especially conformity) and produces stable differences between cultural groups that are heritable at the group level.* Adaptation continues at the group level as long as cultural groups compete so the cultural traits of successful groups will spread to the less successful.

Similar to genes, *cultural traits are units of transmission that are stabilized in societies over long periods.* Some religious beliefs have an origin going back over millennia and have evolved like other cultural traits to present day practices in thousands of religious groups. Cultural traits including religious beliefs are modifiable like genes in response to the forces of selective adaptation. For example, burning witches at the stake did not prove adaptable for the Catholic religion, and probably mass murder will not survive as an adaptable cultural trait for other dogmatic and fundamentalist groups.

However, other cultural inventions may spread quickly and horizontally through societies, especially in the new age of technology and the information revolution. Further, Mesoudi and O'Brien (2009) have argued that the distinction between genetic inheritance and cultural traits is a false dichotomy. All human behavior is biologically based and it is not possible to divide genetic and cultural determinants into separate domains. For example, language acquisition requires learning, but also the underlying biological based mental abilities that evolved from the interaction of the hardwired genetic inheritance with the environment (Nettle, 2006; O'Brien, Lyman, Mesoudi, & VanPool, 2010).

Cultural traits are analogous to genes since both serve as units of replication that can be modified by association with other cultural traits, by memory loss, or by selective personal experiences. Cultural traits like genes are replicated by humans as part of the child rearing process, and are transmitted by spoken language or imitation. O'Brien et al point out that no one has seen genes or cultural traits, but we know the latter exist through the study of artifacts and the archeological record. An evolutionary framework for understanding the development of cultural traits has been proposed also by others including VanPool and VanPool (2003) and Mesoudi and O'Brien (2009). The analogy between genetic and cultural evolution has been employed recently in explaining the heterogeneity in the rates of evolution for different linguistic traits (Pagel, Meade, & Barker, 2004). One of the insights produced by evolutionary analogies is that societies that share common cultural histories may also inherit similar social structures, a contention supported by recent research (Guglielmino, Viganotti, Hewlett, & Cavalli-Sforza, 1995).

5.9. THE TREE BRANCHING OF CULTURAL TRAITS

The application of phylogenectic methods in order to understand cultural variation has led to new insights into human migration, demography and the history of culture. *For the most part these insights have been produced by the application of phylogenetic (tree branching) methods originally developed in biology that has also proved useful to our understanding of cultural traits and data.* In genetic inheritance all members of a species including humans share a common biological history. Cultural lineages, however, vary in populations that share the same genes since cultural evolution has produced different cultural trait constellations. Genetic and cultural inheritance must therefore be treated as following separate evolutionary paths although all humans carry parallel genetic histories.

In the case of cultural evolution societies may also reach steady states where the cultural syndrome of traits remains relatively stable. The evolution of major religions have produced many enduring belief systems that although not unchallenged have remained remarkably similar for centuries. Religions have produced a multiplicity of linked beliefs systems that reflect both horizontal and vertical evolutionary processes that have become stable and rigidly adhered to through sanctions or enforcement.

The differential extinction of cultural groups through competition has reduced the variation of cultural traits in the world. To demonstrate cultural evolution requires that significant cultural differences exist between groups that in turn affect the group's relative competiveness. Groups that lose in intercultural competition are replaced by the more successful groups (Boyd & Richerson, 1990). Cultural groups that lose in competition with neighboring groups are either dispersed or assimilated into the more successful group. Members of cultural groups that assimilate are subject to the forces of social conformity or sanctions that serve to maintain cultural differences with other groups. Selection from intergroup competition is a slow process and that is supported by what we observe in the historical and archeological records. For example, there is a 5000 year time lag between the beginnings of agriculture and the next major step in cultural evolution when the first city-states emerged in the record.

5.10. LIMITATIONS OF GENETIC AND CULTURAL CO-EVOLUTIONARY THEORY: HORIZONTAL AND VERTICAL CULTURAL EVOLUTION

Researchers have advocated a dual inheritance theory that includes both genetic and cultural evolution (Cavalli-Sforza & Feldman, 1981; Richerson

& Boyd, 2005). In co-evolutionary theory genes and culture are viewed as separate but interdependent systems. Each system is based on autonomous mechanisms for transmitting information, with genes encoding for biological reproduction and learning and imitation transmitting cultural information. However, in the case of genetic evolution information can only be transmitted vertically from parents to children. *Therefore the major difference between the two types of evolution is that cultural trait information can also be transmitted horizontally between neighboring groups and in the life time of individuals* (Page, 2003).

Horizontal transmission of traits creates greater complexity in tracing cultural evolution as compared to genetic evolution. Cultural evolution also occurs more rapidly compared to biological evolution. These differences place limits on the usefulness of the comparative phylogenetic approach. Horizontal evolution occurs when two cultural groups with interdependent relationships mutually infuse cultural ideas or when the dominant group transmits cultural traits to the weaker partner. Corresponding mutations within same generation are rarely observed in genetic evolution except epigenetic changes that we noted in regard to the poisoning by Agent Orange in Vietnam or other traumatic events like the holocaust. The divergence of cultural traditions that result from population splits when cultural groups migrate ensures separate development isolated from the parent culture that can, however, be traced by phylogenetic trees. Cultural divergence patterns initially evolved when populations expanded in search of new fertile and productive land. Nevertheless Neolithic expansions in various regions still left strong signatures associated with the growth and expansion of language families (Gray & Atkinson, 2003).

Cultural transmission of traits is a primary determinant of human behavior. At some point the adoptions of these traits had adaptive functions that affected the selective fitness of cultural groups. Adaptive fitness also determined what traits were transmitted from one generation to the next. The transmissions of cultural traits that affect adaptation to ecology demonstrate the mutual interdependence between cultural and genetic evolution (Bettinger & Eerkens, 1999). The record of artifacts reveals large and complex cultural variations that could only be brought about through evolutionary change over time (Shennan, 2008). Phylogenetic comparative methods can evaluate cultural evolution vertically by using tree branching structures to demonstrate the descent of cultural traits over time. The structure of these trees can provide insights to when cultural traits diverged, and can also be used to make comparative inferences about trait evolution (Currie, Greenhill, & Mace, 2010).

As we noted cultural traits that are very adaptive may spread rapidly horizontally between cultures. The use of horses and the invention of the wheel come to mind. Fashions also move rapidly between countries in the developed parts of the world, although such horizontal transfer is produced by little effort or costs and involve primarily social conformity processes. For example, women may be exposed to two or more opposing forces of conformity in fashion decisions and the resolution is a compromise. One study (Hardy & Larsen, 1971) at a religious university showed that women responded to conflicting norms regarding dress (skirt length) by making a compromise between fashion and religious standards. Conformity to norms may also prevent adaptive change when it threatens fundamental beliefs or the entrenched power structures. However, dysfunctional beliefs create stress in a world dominated by the information revolution and will eventually be reformed or obliterated as we saw in Eastern Europe and currently in Arabia (and also in other events in world history). However, since there are significant entrenched interests in social structures new forms of social organization are not easily diffused from one culture to another (Murdock, 1949).

Cultural world views and geographic distance serve to strengthen cultural stability and coherence allowing for less horizontal transmissions of traits. These factors ensure that cultural information proceeds vertically and supports the idea that phylogenetic methods are at least to some extent suitable models (Mace & Holden, 2005). Cultures can be considered assemblages where cultural information is transmitted vertically within the cultural cluster, but communicated to other cultures horizontally producing a cultural evolution more complex than can be measured by tree-branching models. However, whether human history is phylogenetic and tree like or requires more complex evaluation is an issue still evaluated in the literature (Gray, Bryant, & Greenhill, 2010).

5.11. CULTURAL STABILITY: PROCESSES COUNTERING CULTURAL EVOLUTION

Factors that *create stability of cultural traits influence cultural evolution by ensuring that the competitive effects from neighboring cultures are minimized.* Today we live in the information age, and many of the ideas thought to create cultural stability in the past must be rewritten as the effects of globalization are better understood. However, a salient factor in cultural stability is migration that produces social stability by reducing stress in the parent culture. Whether these results are long lasting in the modern world is doubtful. Conformity mechanisms are also identified as coercive means that enforce cultural stability. Recent events, however, show that broader values of human freedom continue to encourage social and cultural change even when the price for such longing is very high. Geographical closeness influences neighboring cultures and may overcome conformity pressures to stabilize within-cultural values, at least for linguistic relationships. Imitation of successful neighbors is also motivated by dissatisfaction with the status quo.

However, under globalization short- term socio-economic advantages often encourage people to overlook the serious challenges brought on by new technology and individualistic social organization with possible long term negative consequences for changing societies and the world.

5.11.1. Migration and Cultural Stability

Cultural stability can occur as a result of *selective migrations*. Human history shows repeated efforts by people that are dissatisfied with the society of origin to migrate toward better socio-economic conditions. Migration of religious cultural groups, on the other hand, is motivated by the desire to find refuge from persecutions. These primary causes have over the last centuries produced large-scale migration to the new world of the Americas. *When a group that is dissatisfied migrates overseas the sending society is left more stable.* A similar phenomenon operated in revolutionary Cuba where the authorities permitted large-scale migration of citizens to the United States creating more social stability at home.

Migrants move from societies where their opportunities for survival or prosperity are poor, or where members of cultural groups suffer social sanction, toward other cultures that offer better economic opportunities and tolerance for their beliefs (Alba & Nee, 2003). The most frequent outcome for immigrant populations is assimilation, which promotes stability in the receiving culture. However, when migration produces cultural enclaves and conflict with the host culture social instability is the outcome. Whether migration leads to social stability in the sending culture as it has in the historical past is not easily concluded in the modern age of globalization. New research is also needed to evaluate the issues around the stability of receiving cultures exposed to large-scale immigration. Migration can be a source of a new synthesis of cultural values or produce conflict when immigrant communities do not assimilate.

5.11.2. Conformity and Geographical Mechanisms Affecting Cultural Evolution and Language Development

As noted earlier rapid horizontal cultural change is a problem for the phylogenetic model borrowed from biology. We live in the midst of an information revolution that has produced the World Wide Web, new social media, and email. These cultural forces have significantly reduced the isolation of populations previously separated by geography. We see in the so-called Arab Spring, and in population dissatisfaction elsewhere, the consequences of the transmission of new cultural values seen as instrumental to a better life in cultures that are dissatisfied with the status quo, and comparative information about how people live in other societies. Although there are cultural forces that sustain the status quo, there is also awareness among people who are dissatisfied of the new cultural values that in turn produces a desire for change and improvement. Cultural change may occur abruptly in revolutionary uprisings, or in other cases follow a gradual path of an evolutionary model.

Conformity is a ubiquitous human cultural trait that serves to inhibit change and stabilize cultural evolution in both language and other socio-culture. *Because of conformity pressures language and basic cultural traits are essentially passed unchanged to the next generation.* That language is the mediator of both cultural stability and change is demonstrated in the analysis of 277 African cultures (Guglielmino, Viganotti, Hewlett, & Cavalli-Sforza, 1995). Linguistic affiliation was the strongest predictor of variation in cultural traits. Geographical distance is associated with some cultural traits, but variations in marriage patterns and kinship are associated only with language. These fundamental cultural traits require language intimacy and evolve only in common language families.

However, while conformity may be a force for stability, geographic closeness creates the conditions for horizontal transmission and change. For example, the writing systems of the world are of recent innovation, and cultures are believed to have borrowed extensively from each other from a few original inventions (Diamond & Bellwood, 2003). Since horizontal borrowing complicates the use of phylogenetic statistical methods used to evaluate vertical cultural evolution some researchers have argued that these methods should only be used when the cultural trait is unambiguously thought to be of vertical descent (Nunn, Mulder, & Langley, 2006). However, others have demonstrated that tree-branching models are very robust producing useful results for cultural traits even at high levels of horizontal transmission (Currie, Greenhill, & Mace, 2010).

Cultural traits develop from human attempts to survive and similar traits may have evolved independently in many regions of the world. For example agricultural development does not require horizontal transmission as each cultural trait (like irrigation) may have developed locally in response to similar climate problems faced by different and even geographically distant societies. However, conformist social learning is very adaptive since it teaches the common means of survival in a society and has the additional important advantage of being approved by the majority. The underlying psychology of imitation is adaptive both in family relationships but also among members of larger cultural units. Conformist adaptive behavior is reinforcing as it produces many physical and social benefits including access to food and protection. Research employing cultural models has demonstrated the selective advantage of a conformist behavior in different social environments (Henrich & Boyd, 1998).

Conformist pressure affects cultural evolution by weeding out nonconformist traits thereby ensuring that what is common in society becomes even more common. Cultural traits including artifacts, beliefs, ideology, and especially dogmatic religion follow a process where the commonly held view becomes even more dominant. Still a dogmatic system may be in conflict with other deeply held beliefs and therefore give rise to new dissenting groups. Dissatisfaction with established religious systems gave rise to the evolution of religious beliefs and practices. However, to survive and prosper most individuals will retain the dominant beliefs of their society. If the individual grows up and is surrounded by religious believers chances are that he/she too will become a believer. On the other hand, individuals that grew up surrounded by atheistic beliefs and might well choose to imitate such non-religious perspective on life. In the United States the large majority of the population is believers and candidates for office must reaffirm their religious beliefs at every opportunity if they hope to be elected, whereas in Europe skeptical beliefs have a long history and a place in intellectual life.

Conformist behaviors are also likely to be imitated when they are supported by the sanctions of moral disapproval or punishment. Moral behaviors serve as a stabilizing force since people get into all kinds of trouble when not abiding by moral conventions. Sanctions can be severe when removing the offender from society as, for example, when women are stoned to death in Saudi Arabia or other Muslim countries for adultery. Cultural stability is also created by much less drastic means by employing the simple mechanism of disapproval, or any range of sanctions that fall between these two extremes. Conforming is adaptive because it not only ensures survival within the cultural group, but also produces social affirmation in the form of awards and recognition. When people migrate conformity plays a significant role since migrants either establish new forms of the old culture, or assimilate to the new country's moral values and beliefs. Much of current social conflict in Europe is over the refusal of new immigrant groups to conform to established cultural values and wanting to continue to conform to the expectations of the culture of origin.

5.12. SOCIAL LEARNING: IMITATING SUCCESS

There is much evidence in current world history of developing societies seeking to imitate more successful countries. *Neo-liberalism* defined by open markets and borders has been the prevailing socio-economic ideology of recent years. Developing countries have sought to emulate successful Western economies as suggested by theories of modernism and post-industrial societies. Socio-economic success is supported by norms of behavior like the so-called puritan ethic of hard work that played a role in the development of modern capitalism. Research shows that struggling societies try to imitate the successful, or what is perceived to be success (Henrich & Gil-White, 2001; Henrich & Boyd, 2002). Cultures that become aware of the success of neighbors are encouraged to develop a similar society. Johnson

(1976) pointed to the spread of Christianity during the Roman Empire as an example of the adaptive transmission of successful ideas and subsequent imitation. Romans accepted the new society formed by Christians since they demonstrated in actual behavior norms of mutual help and charity much needed during the health crises caused by epidemics in Europe. The spread of Christianity eventually led to state power the outcome of the desire of Romans to imitate the more successful within-cultural Christian group.

Imitation explains much of the current globalization effort. The benefits of one group can, especially in the information age, spread rapidly through neighboring societies. However, innovations are often transmitted without a clear understanding of underlying environmental or potential social problems accumulating in the world that contribute to ongoing economic and ecological crises. For example, the use of nuclear power has left thousands of tons of very dangerous material in unsafe storage in the United States and elsewhere without a consensus of where to securely deposit the contents. The desire to imitate neighbors has also brought about large-scale immigration of undocumented workers seeking a way out of poverty. When long-term affects of cultural imitation are taken into account imitation is not a force for cultural stability, but rather contributes to social crises the outcome of which cannot be predicted.

5.13. RELIGION, AGRICULTURE DEVELOPMENT AND CULTURAL EVOLUTION

Science is a process of self-correction and that is also true for research on sociocultural evolution. Our understanding of cultural evolution is under constant review as new evidence becomes available. The famous archaeologist V. Gordon Childe invented the term Neolithic Evolution to explain the radical change that occurred when humanity left behind foraging for food and developed agriculture. From his perspective the agricultural impetus was the most important cultural trait complex in the development of humanity next to mastery of fire. Only after the revolution of agriculture and the accumulation of surplus food did the human species begin to increase in ever larger numbers as we spread over the globe. The Neolithic Revolution was in Childe's view responsible for the advance of civilization that included the development of symbolic art and religion. In Childe's view agriculture began in the Fertile Crescent from Gaza to southern Turkey and into Iraq in the first organized state known as Sumer dating back to 4000 B.C.

However, recent research has uncovered the dawn of civilization in another remote region called Gobekli Tepe in southern Turkey. The temple complex found there dates back to 11,600 years ago, and was built by hunter gathers that were thought to live in small nomadic groups at this point in history (Mann, 2011). Childe's ideas are called into question by the fact that these people built a massive temple complex 7000 years before the temples in Egypt. The pillars of the temple are very large up to 18 feet weighing 16 tons and would require a significant development of social structure and cooperation to move and maintain long before agricultural traits had evolved. Could it be, as the excavator Klaus Schmidt (see Mann, 2011) suggests that at this point in cultural evolution people had a need to see expressions of religious awe as an explanation for changes in the natural world? From his perspective religion occurred from these deep seated human emotions and began in response to the great unknown questions and in an effort to meet spiritual needs.

In particular religion evolved when humans moved away from seeing themselves as part of the natural world, and used symbols to imagine supernatural beings in control. These supernatural beings often resembled human beings, but could be conceptualized as belonging to another realm. Then in an effort to find expressions and respond to these feelings the temples at Gobekli Tepe were built. Agriculture followed this development in the Mann paradigm as necessary support system to maintain the level of civilization required to serve the religious sites and the associated need for permanent settlement. In reality socio-cultural evolution leading to agricultural development may have occurred in many places and in different ways. Once we step away from linear thinking it is possible to imagine different tracks, where in one place agriculture came first, in others religion was an impetus to settlement. However, it is clear that there is still much to be discovered by archeologists, and as they do discover new artifacts and gifts from the past we must reset our concepts to fit changing realities.

5.14. PHYLOGENETIC EVIDENCE OF THE SOCIO-CULTURAL ORIGINS OF LANGUAGE AND OTHER CULTURAL TRAITS

As we noted phylogenetic analysis has proven a useful tool in tracing the evolution of language. Linguistic evolution is the key to understanding the journey of humanity and can be explained as the descent of linguistic traits modified over time. Through the application of the phylogenetic model it has been possible to reconstruct language related to kinship from early proto languages. Linguistic evolution has created thousands of languages and associated religious beliefs. Languages have evolved largely through geographic distance and isolation. However, the future of language evolution is in some doubt with the ubiquitous use of the English language as the world medium for communication.

5.14.1. Tracing the Evolution of Languages

Recent phylogenetic analysis borrowed from biology has largely succeeded in reconstructing meaningful lineages of cultural inheritance for several cultural domains including languages (Lipo & Madsen, 2001). *Relationships between languages show that lexical roots can be traced back to ancestral language communities across thousands of years of history* (Kitchen, Ehret, Assefa, & Mulligan, 2009). Other domains like craft technologies yielded similar phylogenetic patterns that can be recognized retrospectively as related to the origin (Buchanan & Collard, 2007; Lycett, 2009). *Reconstruction of lineages* offers useful information about the origin of cultural groups that can be considered together with geneography in understanding the dispersal of populations. Tree branch-like evidence of cultural domains is highly correlated with population histories although not perfectly so (Tehrani & Collard, 2009).

As previously noted the reason the phylogenetic approach seems a promising method for exploring cultural diversity is because of the similarities between cultural and biological evolution (see also Gray, Greenhill, & Ross, 2007; Mace & Holden, 2005). Cultural as well as linguistic evolution can be described as descent of traits with some modification. Linguistic traits are passed from one generation to the next, but can also be modified through contacts with other language groups. Anyone familiar with changes in world culture will have observed the increased utility of the English language and the inclusion of English phrases in other languages. For example, within one generation the American greeting hi (hej) replaced the perfectly fine "good day" in the Danish language, and most Danes remain unaware of this change today. In that lexical change we have an example of linguistic evolution entirely in our lifetimes. Evolutionary research shows that biological species are created by selective adaptation to environmental niches. Human populations split in an analogous manner in the search for ecological niches that provide survival and comfort. Over time these evolutionary processes evolve into differences in cultures and languages. Current research shows that linguistic data enables us to reconstruct historical relationships from these tree branch-like models (Rogers, Feldman, & Ehrlich, 2009).

Social organization as represented in marital arrangements is an essential tool in tracing the dispersal of human groups and languages (Fortunato & Jordan, 2010). *Indo-European* and *Austronesian* are two large language families traced back to Neolithic expansion. Kinship words and terminologies have been reconstructed from ancestral proto-languages using comparative linguistics, and by comparing geographical patterns in kinship language. Using the phylogenetic techniques with these language families it is possible to understand past marital arrangements. Whether the culture promoted residence with male or female kin (living near husband's or the wife's kin) corresponded to whether the pre-historical society was agricultural or pastoral (where men were typically present in daily life), or oceanic (where men were frequently absent). Through these means it was possible to conclude that Indo-European languages reflected a residence pattern with male members of the family. However, in Polynesian societies where men were frequently absent travelling the ocean a pattern of marital residence with female family was inferred. These cultural adaptations reflect concrete benefits to survival when men are present to make daily decisions or largely away fishing or using the ocean for travel. Fortunato and Jordan argue that the phylogenetic comparative method on kinship language employs rigorous statistical methods that permit the reconstruction of changes in the pattern of cultural traits and insights into evolving social organization that is not necessarily preserved in either archeological or historical records.

5.14.2. Evidence of Language Evolution

Darwin pointed to the similarities between the evolution of species and the evolution of languages (Van Wyhe, 2005). Biological evolution shares with languages the common property of heritability by transmitting essential information between generations. The analogy of biological mutations is defined in language evolution by geographic and sociolinguistic divergence which in turn explains the historical Babel of languages noted in the Bible. *Over 6000 languages have been identified globally, and cultural evolution has produced 4300 practicing religions* (Gordon, 2005). These cultural traits were at some point adaptive, but because of geographic isolation the functional value may have long been lost. However, both religion and languages are maintained by conformity and social learning. Globalization is obviously a current force in cultural evolution which has served to decrease the number of cultural traits as it has also increased biological extinction.

5.15. CULTURE AS A FUNCTION OF EVOLVING INFORMATION

Distin (2011) argues that human culture is a function of evolving information. Specifically culture is a product of heritable information, so to understand language or cultural development requires knowledge about information that is heritable and transmitted between generations. What we inherit depends on each generation receiving the appropriate information and the means to culturally interpret and implement it in cultural life. Language as well as other cultural traits consists of information that is transmitted through evolutionary development.

Jablonka and Lamb (2005) outlined four major human traits that change by evolutionary means. Humans over the course of our development and throughout history pass on genetic, epigenetic, behavioral information, and symbolic mechanisms including language. Epigenetic information includes changes in cellular decoding that interpret genetic information so different meanings can be produced from the same strand of DNA material. Epigenetic alteration occurs through interaction with the environment.

As we noted elsewhere (Larsen & Van Le, 2010) we have reported on the epigenetic changes that have occurred in the survivors of the American campaign to poison the ecology of Vietnam. Yehuda, Bierer, Schmeidler, Aferiat, Breslau and Dolan (2000), and Yehuda, Mulherin, Brand, Seckl, Marcus and Berkowitz (2005) also demonstrated epigenetic changes in holocaust survivors who carried lower cortisol levels affecting their ability to deal with stress. Recent research (Pembrey, Bygren, Kaati, Edvinsson, Northstone, Sjostrom, Golding, & Whitelaw, 2006) has also shown that a damaging prepubescent environment might influence the health of boy's sperm. The negative effects of the epigenetic changes are carried to the next generation. Other research has demonstrated ample evidence of the transmission of epigenetic transmission of epimutations in response to environmental forces (Cavalli & Paro, 1998; Xing, Shi, Le, Lee, Silver-Morse, & Li, 2007). However, there is no clear agreement on how long such environmental damage might be inherited by the following generations.

Throughout evolution humans have increased their odds of survival by creating niches that have been inherited by the following generations. This niche related behavior responded to the ecological challenges by creating improved means for adaptation. Since niche construction aids survival they are a heritable components also responding to natural selection pressures (Odling-Smee, Laland, & Feldman, 2003). Although there is no way to evaluate whether ecological evolution affects biology, it is possible to observe the evolutionary consequences on niche construction over time. Likewise behavioral changes also follow an evolutionary pathway with each generation modifying behavior according to past functionality and future expectations.

Language also is based on an inheritance mechanism (Distin, 2011) that allows each generation to pass the relevant linguistic rules and content to the next generation. The mechanisms for evolution are not biological, but rather systems of symbolic representations in language and also other symbolic systems that include music and mathematics. The mechanism for evolution is cultural and based on learning, but there are also genetic inheritance mechanisms without which language could not be learned in the first place. Humans are at birth genetically ready for language and possess an instinct for linguistic behavior. The culturally evolved linguistic inheritance mechanisms provide the impetus to the evolution of language and are all related at some point in the evolutionary past. Languages are therefore transmitted across linguistic pathways, independent from biological evolution, and importantly they change at a much faster pace. Psychology has an impact on the cultural transmission of languages since some information is easier to acquire and store and later retrieve from memory. All the forces of evolution have some interacting influences even if these are not immediately observable.

Geographical distance is thought a major factor in the diffusion and evolution of dialects and languages (Nerbonne & Heeringa, 2007). Variations in lexical (word) content have been demonstrated to be related to geographical distance. Simulation research using geographical distance as data points largely predict linguistic diffusion. The origin of the wave theory of diffusion started with the demonstration of important common linguistic features in Indo-European languages leading to the conclusion that all members of this language group shared a common origin (Schmidt, 1872). These communalities as we have seen can be represented by the tree like phylogenetic structure of languages, with diffusion also occurring between the branches of languages. Bloomfield (1933) proposed that the density of communication explained the process of diffusion as it produced greater frequency of communication. Density was operationalized as geographical distance and population size in Trudgill's model (1974). Linguistic change and evolution is promoted by contact between language groups and as noted facilitated by both the size of population and proximity. These ideas of language diffusion were inspired by the physical theory of gravity where more distant objects are thought to have less gravitational influence. Likewise linguistic innovations proceed first in large population centers and from there flow toward the periphery. However, geographical distance is thought to be the more significant force in producing language evolution (Nerbonne & Heeringa, 2007).

The divergence of single language families is represented by the branching tree structure associated with geographic distance. However, language change in the form of dialects can also be represented as overlapping waves representing the continuum of dialects within a language population. These methodological divisions correspond to and are supported by historical facts as language divergence is either explained by migration and isolation or by population expansion over continuous territory. In language splits the branches are formed by binary splits all the way back to the ancestral proto language. A language splits when the population divides by long distance migration into additional language groups and thereafter remains isolated from other groups and the ancestral source. In summary, languages evolve through population separations geographically either through migration to distant territory, or through expansion through neighboring but continuous territory.

Continuous wave evolution describes language networks showing the relationships between subgroups of language family speakers yielding a dialect continuum. This occurs when a language population moves into continuous territory and as a result maintains some degree of contact. Contacts are more likely between groups relatively close geographically and dialects will therefore largely correspond to distance. More divergence in dialects can be expected at extreme points from origin that roughly correspond to waves that cut across and overlap language dialects. A language family provides clues of the historical and linguistic record of the past and the mechanism that caused divergence in both language and also dialects.

Language evolution does not just occur by some mysterious mechanism within a language, but rather by the geographical distance caused by socio-political struggles and cultural dissatisfaction. The persecution of religious groups in Europe encouraged long distance migration into the Americas and the continuous territory of the U.S. ensured that dialects represented wave evolution of language in recent history. Research using simulation to unravel the linguistic history of Germanic languages shows that it is possible to test phylogenetic and wave models of language diffusion (Heggarty, Maguire, & McMahon, 2010). The major conclusion is that the opportunity for social contact expressed by geographical distance account for significant amounts of linguistic variation.

5.16. HOW DID LANGUAGE EVOLVE?

Linguists generally agree that humans have an innate capacity for language. However, since we all broadly share the same genetic codes, language differences can obviously not be attributed to genetic variations between language speakers. The main debate concerning the genetic origin of language is the presence of universals that appear from the analysis of many languages (Kirby, 2007). *Evolutionary linguists believe that language differences do not emerge from biology, but rather from evolution in the domain of languages.* Chomsky and others have, however, suggested that children have an innate knowledge of universal grammar that dominates any language spoken and this biological inheritance ensures that children can learn language easily with comprehension. However, Chomsky denies that language development follows a separate Darwinian selection process suggesting instead that language may have evolved from a selection process among other preexisting abilities. On the other hand, Pinker and Bloom (1990) concluded that specialization for language is apparent in the complex design of human language and the syntactic rules that emerged evolved from biological adaptation.

Most linguists think human language capacity evolved based on *important pre-adaptations* that included the ability to represent reality cognitively. Physiological change in the brain and face musculature, and especially the social nature of our species were important selective adaptations that supported language development. Most fundamentally, the origin of language comes from the inherent human instinct for cooperation. As a species we learned early in evolution to solve problems regarding the ecology and niches by cooperating with others thereby advancing socio-cognitive skills (Distin, 2011). While other primates are able to learn and cooperate only humans are capable of selective imitation based on motivation for learned behavior.

Distin notes that from the very beginning human infants display a conformity bias through which they learn arbitrary elements of human behavior, but also rational behaviors that lead to desirable goals. The human infant also appears to be born with an instinct to recognize human adults as models for imitation from whom to absorb the cultural and linguistic norms of the society. Distin argues that without an instinct for conformity language learning would not occur nor other aspects of human psychology. For example, language has important identity functions since they first of all convey social norms, but also serve to promote cultural cohesion. Language is the way by which people know their cultural group identity and therefore also serve as a means of identifying people belonging to our ingroup with whom we are more likely to cooperate compared to members of culturally competitive groups. We are less likely to cooperate with those whose language is unfamiliar, even when some of the barriers to communication are removed.

5.16.1 Contacts Between Different Language Speakers

Contacts between people speaking different languages typically lead the participants to find ways to overcome barriers to communication by means of some compromise (Winford, 2003). The need for communication compromises has been modified by the considerable borrowing from the English language as it has dominated the world in recent times as the ubiquitous medium of communication. In many cases borrowing is insignificant and amount to a few words that seem to express more precisely what the native speaker wishes to convey. Utilizing English or other dominant languages can also reflect the prestige of possessing more worldly values and is associated with status that is not conveyed by using the less dominant language.

Languages are shaped either by borrowing from other groups or by imposition of the dominant language on minorities as, for example, when English replaced native Celt languages (Van Coetsem, 2000). As we can observe in regard to the spread of the English language lexical change or vocabulary are easily changed and used in less dominant languages, however, the speaker still uses the grammar of his/her native tongue. Structural features like grammar are more resistant to change in cross-language contacts leading often to very peculiar expressions. However, in contacts where one language is clearly dominant, for example, in the context of colonialism, imposition may also affect the grammar of the recipient's language (Winford, 2005).

Those of us who have learned more than one language benefit by *metalinguistic awareness* defined as the increasing consciousness of features of our own language about which we were previously unaware. A second language also increases our ability to learn additional future new languages (Jessner, 1999). This increased language acquisition is facilitated by the common features within families of languages. For example, knowing English, German and or Danish, makes it possible for the speaker to see the considerable overlap in the Dutch language. According to Jessner, metalinguistic thinking is a higher level of cognition since we are not thinking just about what the language conveys, but rather about the language symbols themselves and the ways we are representing information in language. Contacts enable us to incorporate the information represented by seeing the common overlap, but also the distinctions between the two or more languages.

5.16.2. Artefactual Languages

Distin (2011) makes a distinction between what she calls natural languages and *artefactual representations*. Natural language evolved from the need to give immediate expression to our thoughts. The evolution of natural language enabled our ancestors to make more efficient use of their innate cooperative abilities and the representation of their beliefs. The ability to communicate had selective advantages as humans could cooperate better in hunting, gathering or in the development of agriculture. As noted above at times we expand our language knowledge by learning other languages and learn from the linguistic overlap. However, natural language is limited by the human capacity for learning and retention and is inadequate to represent all the learning of a society or culture. We must therefore look beyond natural language to other forms of representation.

Artefactual languages evolved in the course of cultural evolution to help us escape from the limitations and bias that is part of natural language use. When humans started to think about how information was represented symbolically the evolution of artefactual languages began. In artefactual languages the priority changed from immediate communication to representation. Alternative symbolic ways of representing information facilitated a more rapid cultural evolution. Artefactual languages including mathematics, music and writing evolved from the need to express complex thought not dependent on the subjectivity of the individual speaker or individual experience. Writing, an artefactual language, is the foundation of cultural development from the earliest symbols displayed in European caves, to representations on the walls of the temples in Egypt, to the use of computers at the present time. Culture's origin is completely connected to the development of symbolic representation exemplified by writing. Like natural languages artefactual languages shape our understanding of culture, and our ability to evaluate external reality. The variety of cultures and complexity of human interactions are mediated by symbolic representations that reflected the cultural demands for improved communication and effective adaptation.

Artefactual languages separate cultural information from subjectivity and language structures thus opening the possibilities for advances in science and technology. Individual cognition is limited, and can neither receive nor encode all the cultural information acquired over the centuries. Humans think not only about the content of information, but also the means used to send cultural knowledge, and this ability to think at higher metalinguistic levels has largely produced cultural evolution. We are a cooperative species and have not only the ability, but an innate desire to share what we know. Artefactual languages have the great advantage of separating the content of information from the social context. This is a fundamental attribute of humans without which we would be stuck at the level of dogmatic interpretations and believing that the universe revolves around the Earth. The ability to think outside the box is what has powered cultural evolution although dogmatic thinking is still a great inhibitor of progress. Human culture depends on the evolution of applicable information as shared by languages and also by artefactual symbolic communication. Such a representational theory of cultural evolution has explanatory power in a variety of cultural domains (Croft, 2000; Distin, 2011; Hurford, 2007; Leont'ev, 1981; Mufwene, 2001; Pinker, & Bloom, 1992).

SUMMARY

Language is central to an understanding of cultures and co-evolved with other cultural traits. Without language it was not possible for early humans to communicate to larger social networks or solve the complex problems related to ecology and the building of environmental niches. Human language is complex since we can think about the attribution of intent in others. The predisposition to language is hardwired in our brains although the particular language is a product of cultural evolution. Language and other cultural traits co-evolved over thousands of years benefitting from reciprocal contributions. Vertical evolution can be illustrated by phylogenetic trait models, but in cultural evolution horizontal transmission occur frequently between neighboring cultures creating greater complexities in tracing cultural trait development. In order to understand the developments of research in these areas it is important for students to understand the basic linguistic terms used.

Linguistic relativity refers to the influence of language on thinking processes and conceptualizations. The infant by interaction with members of his culture gradually shapes certain language sounds that eventually determine lexical content, the grammatical structure, and the pragmatic rules of the use of language in the social context. Research supports the idea that different language groups produce different conceptualizations of the self and others that are of salient importance in communication. Communication style influenced by culture carries more important meanings than the content of communications. Does the lexical content and grammar of a culture create boundaries for thinking? The Sapir-Whorf hypothesis makes this assertion, and raises the question as to whether we can ever understand deeper meanings when communicating across languages. Language is a representative system that organizes the cultural world and is heritable for following generations. Since culture determines lexical content it also influences our ability to differentiate and communicate cultural nuances. The Sapir-Whorf hypothesis receives critical support in several cultural domains where language differences have a direct impact on perceptual and cognitive functioning.

The underlying biological adaptation function of language is demonstrated by the presence of universals in linguistic research. Deaf children can communicate with gestures that are language-like and remarkably similar across countries where it has been studied. Universal function is also demonstrated by aspects of word order found in all languages. Osgood's work on meaning in the description of objects yielded similar meaning structures in all cultures. Together this research supports our common biological and/or cultural evolution in the past.

Intercultural communication creates important challenges since messages are always understood subjectively and from the perspective of the listener. Therefore interpretations are influenced by ingroup values, by the emotional signals from the nonverbal context of communication, and by cultural stereotypes. These cultural filters and attributions make the accurate interpretation of intercultural communication difficult. Obstacles present in intercultural communication include lexical content when words may have more than one meaning in one of the cultures, and nonverbal gestures that is interpreted differentially dependent on culture. These factors along with stereotyping, ethnocentric attitudes and stress often distort the reception of messages. A primary objective in intercultural communication is to reduce uncertainty. Of particular importance is the moderation of emotional reactions and control of ethnocentric thinking.

We live in a world where the majority speaks more than one language. The affect of globalization has made this trend even more efficacious. The affect of bilingualism can be seen in studies where speakers demonstrate different personality traits dependent on the language spoken. Some have described bilingualism as a cultural code switching dependent on the identification of the speaker with cultural stereotypes of the language spoken. Bilingualists benefit from their multiple language exposure that produce greater creativity, cognitive complexity, linguistic sensitivity, and increased ability to learn new languages. The relationship of nonverbal communication to culture is an important research domain. Nonverbal signals are part of any verbal communication and carry important meanings especially of emotional states. Research shows that societies vary in the interpersonal space distance required when communicating, allowing cultures to be described as either a contact or noncontact society.

The Darwinian model of evolution has taken on increased importance in explaining sociocultural and language change and development. Phylogenetic models have been used to reconstruct both cultural history and language development. From this research we can observe that the tree-like branching of culture and the diffusion of traits explain the cultural diversity we observe in the world today. In cultural evolution cultural traits gradually develop and are modified in response to selective pressures. Cultures keep traits that are important to social and ecological adaptation. For example, the evolution of cultural traits associated with agriculture in China produced many advantages, improved the competitive fitness of China and led to an integrated empire that dominated neighboring cultures.

Can cultural advantages be reflected in genetic changes? Selective genetic adaptation does occur that produces evolutionary advantages. Lighter skin color of people who live in the northern regions of the world is a selective advantage since it allows for the absorption of more vitamin D from existing sunlight. However, cultural evolution occurs much more rapidly, and is a stronger evolutionary force at this point in history. Disadvantaged cultural groups that compete for similar ecological environments are either excluded or assimilated into the more successful culture. The power of the Western socio-economic model must be seen from this perspective as developing countries are seeking inclusion in trade agreements or in political structure.

The analogy of genetic and cultural evolution is powerful since the conditions required for Darwinian evolution to occur also exist for culture namely the struggle for existence and the presence of heritable cultural trait varieties that provide differential cultural group survival advantages. Cultural stability is created by conformity processes, whereas dysfunctional traits produce stress and change. Some argue that the distinction between genetic and cultural evolution is unnecessary and false since all behavior is biological. Language requires learning, but biological templates create the necessary mechanisms for language development. Phylogenetic models have produced new insights into migration, demography and the history of culture. However, genetic and cultural evolution follows separate evolutionary paths. The extinction of cultural groups through competitive interactions has reduced the variation of cultural traits in the world, a process that has increased with globalization in recent decades. Cultural groups that loose in intercultural completion are dispersed or assimilated into the dominant culture.

Are there limitations on the genetic and cultural co-evolutionary theory? The main difference between the two evolutionary forces is that cultural traits can be transmitted horizontally between neighboring cultural groups.

Also, as we noted cultural evolution occur much more rapidly compared to adaptive genetic mutations. These facts place some limits on the usefulness of phylogenetic models. Nevertheless phylogenetic methods have proven useful in tracing the divergence of cultural traditions from branch like population splits caused by migration. In the transmission of heritable cultural traits we find the primary determinant of human behavior affecting the adaptation to ecology. Overtime there is an obvious interdependence between cultural and genetic evolution.

The selection of advantageous cultural traits creates cultural stability. Stability forces counter evolutionary pressure and create barriers for horizontal influences from neighboring cultures. However, our information age has changed these dynamics as people everywhere know how others live elsewhere, and the social media is a force for cultural evolution. Conformity mechanisms are a cultural force for stability, although dysfunctional values will always be under stress. Migration is a stabilizing factor as dissatisfied people look for new opportunities to survive or prosper and the persecuted look for escape from oppression. Migration is therefore a stabilizing factor for the sending country, but not necessarily for the receiving culture. Conformity can stabilize both language and culture for long historical periods. Conformist learning is adaptive since it ensures survival, receives approval by the majority in society, and serves stability by weeding out nonconformist traits and people. On other hand evolutionary change is encouraged when other cultures seek to emulate and imitate successful countries. For example, imitation explains the current changes associated with globalization.

The origins of cultural traits have fascinated scientists of many persuasions and produced varying theories. These perspectives often involve a "which came first the chicken or the egg" argument. An example is the debate about whether religion was a driver of agricultural development or conversely whether agricultural development encouraged the leisure and resources to entertain religious issues. The research reported shows that science is always in the process of self-correction, and our minds must always be open when new facts are discovered.

Linguistic evolution is the key to understanding the human journey and the phylogenetic methods have enabled us to reconstruct language development related to kinship going back to the earliest proto languages across thousands of years. The human journey as understood by language changes can be supplemented by new advances in genetic information that traces the human geneographic journey by means of heritable genetic markers from our common origin in Africa. Is there evidence of language evolution? The very presence of 6000 languages and 4300 established religions point to the forces of evolution in language and in sociocultural traits maintained over the ages by conformity and social learning.

Recent research suggests that human culture must be seen as a function of the transmission of information. Whether traits are heritable depends on each generation receiving the appropriate information and having the means to interpret and implement the cultural traits in life. Evolution has been observed in genetics, epigenetics, behavior, and in symbolic changes including language and other symbolic representations. Branch divisions and waves of continuity are models used to explain the divergence of languages over time. Geographic distance is seen as the major factor explaining the diffusion of languages. Migration to distant geographical areas and subsequent isolation produced new languages, whereas wave theory explains language continuity with dialect modification in adjoining geographical territory.

Language evolved from our innate capacities an assertion supported by the presence of language universals in many cultures. Theories have argued that humans are hardwired with a universal grammar applied to any language and that language is an innate biological adaptation. Human language evolution required significant pre-adaptations including the ability to think. As a cooperative species there is a conformity bias present from infancy leading us to recognize human adults as models for imitation in all areas including language.

Contacts with other language groups often create communication barriers. In initial contacts efforts are made to overcome barriers by compromise. Contacts also result in the borrowing of lexical content from other languages a demonstrated by the ubiquitous use of English words and phrases. Grammar is, however, more resistant to change except when the dominant language influence is total or under conditions of colonization. Knowledge of several languages has many beneficial advantages to knowledge expansion and understanding. Artefactual languages like writing, mathematics, and music evolved to help humans escape from the limitations of bias and subjectivity and to expand the usefulness of natural languages.

CHAPTER 6

COGNITION

Our Common Biology
and Cultural Impact

The psychological constructs that permit thinking and reflection are referred to by the term cognition. Thinking is a product of all the psychological processes that result from sensory inputs and eventually produces cultural knowledge. Our common human biology has provided universal sensory receptors referring to sensations of sight, hearing, smell, taste and touch. Perception is the process that occurs after the initial experiences of sensation in particular how sensory reactions are organized and create cultural relevant meaning. In all cultures human beings engage in *higher order mental operations* represented in language, thinking and reasoning. Problem solving and decision-making abilities emerge out of the cultural meanings produced by the social context.

6.1. CULTURE AND COGNITION.

The essence of research on cognition in cross-cultural psychology is to examine cultural differences and variations. Cognition is culture that can be manifested in material artifacts. All cultures produce in-group feelings of familiarity and people from other cultures are intuited as being fundamentally different (Kitayama & Cohen, 2007). In the past a common view was to see these cognitive differences as rooted in biology and the concept of race. Today such views are not sustainable as the phenotypical differences that we call race mean little compared to the cultural knowledge accumulated from earlier generations. We conceptually stand on the shoulders of our fathers and mothers and pass the torch of culture to our children. Culture is learned patterns of behavior reflected in daily life and practice as influenced by cultural norms and values.

Hofstede (1980) built on these ideas by describing culture as *mental programming*. Even though all humans largely have the same hardware in our computer (brain) culture creates different software programs that direct members to behave in distinct ways. The very definition of culture is rooted in the communality of shared norms, beliefs and values transmitted to each generation (Berry, Poortinga, Segall, & Dasen, 1992). The function of these common meaning systems is to enable society and the individual to adapt, to survive, and to provide an answer the existential issues of life. Cognition was developed within cultures because it enabled people to meet the demands of the environment and solve the complex problems of large groups living and surviving in a common territory.

As we learned in the preceding chapter humans evolved language and the *ability to attribute intentions* to self and others that in turn promoted selective adaptation. Intentionality develops at a very early age in humans (Warneken & Tomasello, 2006). For example, the grandson of this author learned very early to intuit the reactions of adults, and before he was corrected for misbehavior he would exhibit a broad smile and say hi! His favored past-time at 18 months was to throw rocks into the family pool, and he would energetically say "no, no," while he proceeded to smile and toss the rocks. It is the special human mental processes that created culture including the norms that direct the practice of daily life. In turn accumulated social knowledge represented by norms and cultural values are manifested in behavior and in systems of thought like ideology and religion.

The relationship between culture and cognition is based on several levels of social organization. As noted humans as a species have inherited a similar biological computer (the brain) that creates the structure and basis for all our understanding. Cognition is also influenced by evolved cultural behaviors and practices typically related to specific societies occupying defined territories. Levels of cognitive organization can only be separated at the abstract level as they are casually interdependent. Cultural cognition is what we have inherited by being born into these societies with unique social contexts. Culturally unique cognition did not appear suddenly like a revelation, but evolved over eons of time, and researchers must therefore take a developmental perspective based on biological evolution and adaptation, as well as cultural history. Further, we must also take into account the influences from individual development and the requirement to respond to the daily organization of human life in understanding cognitive processes (Vygotsky, 1930/1997).

Culture is a resource supporting individual survival and is the social glue that holds society together as a functioning unit. Cultural cognition is the understanding of accumulated behaviors transmitted over generations manifested both in individual psychology, but also in the *artifacts* created by culture that constitute resources for survival and existential meaning. The accumulated behaviors and thought patterns influence the external environment, and at the same time the material culture delimits thought processes. Human cognition produce artifacts of material culture that assist the individual and society in goal directed behaviors (Cole, 1996). Artifacts and material culture is created by human thought as we adapt and interact with the environment. Norms, beliefs and values are the mental representations typically referred to by the term *schemas* that define the roles people play and the appropriateness of behavior for various segments of society divided by gender and age.

The duality separating the material environment and cognition is not useful. For example, whatever happens in the material world has a correlate at the neurophysiological level. Luria (1976) called this a kinetic melody, a sequence of patterned movement related to the ongoing action that integrates goal directed behavior. Cognition is produced by the variety of goal related activities and the acquisition and utilization of knowledge through processes of sensation, perception, logic and dialectics, memory, language and other higher order processes. What is universal is the hardware that humans inherit that is largely independent of culture. The impact of culture is on the development of cultural products summarized by the language, tradition and ideology of a society. Whether culture can produce deficits in intellectual functioning is an issue discussed when we examined the research on intelligence. We found little credible evidence of a biological basis for deficits as defined by intelligence testing.

6.1.1. Sensation and Perception

Knowledge is developed through interaction with the material and cultural environments. As we noted the initial processes are mediated by receptor cells for the basic five senses of hearing, vision, smell, touch and taste. All sensation is initiated by some environmental stimulus that carries sufficient energy to excite the nervous system. *What we call sensation is the conversion of stimulus energy into neurophysiological processes that create a psychological experience.* You taste food from a foreign culture and the sensation may be pleasant or unpleasant dependent on individual preferences and previous sensory experience. However, not all energy that impacts our bodies is brought to our attention. For example, some wavelengths are not experienced at all. Our hearing is also limited, whereas dogs possess more acute hearing and smell. The minimum energy required to create a sensation is called the absolute threshold. However, a difference threshold is the minimum change of stimulation required to determine a change in sensation. It is believed that cognition begins with these basic sensory processes.

As we experience the sensory world we gradually build up experience as a reference point for new sensations. *Perception involves the organization of association areas* in the cortex thereby integrating previous knowledge. Without previous reference points all sensations would be experienced as new and the individual could produce no meaningful pattern from sensory input. Importantly experience creates priming effects as we expect certain feelings associated with past stimuli. Cross-cultural comparisons in the basic areas of sensation and perception show remarkable universal outcomes in various societies pointing to the similarity of the computers we have inherited (Yaroshevski, 1996).

6.1.2. Cultural Impact on Sensation and Perception

As noted our biological inheritance produces very similar sensation and perception experiences across various cultures. However, as the cultural and material environments differ between societies culture influence perception in some areas. From the outset it is important to understand that there is no one-to-one relationship between physical stimuli and sensation or perception. For example, our brain often fills in and completes sensation where receptors are missing. A case in point is the fact that most of us are not aware of the blind spot in our eyes where no receptors exist in the spot where the optic nerve projects to the brain. The deficit of sensory receptors, however, does not cause a deficit in our perception as our brain neatly cover up the lacking information and we experience perception as if we had no blind spot. However, culturally influenced experience can produce illusions, for example, the famous Mueller-Lyer optical illusion (Segall, Campbell, & Hersokowitz, 1966). Subjects asked to judge two lines of equal length are influenced by whether arrows are pointing toward the line or away with the former line perceived as longer. The most common explanation for the cultural effect on this illusionary perception is called the carpentered world theory. Most people in the developed world are accustomed to seeing objects as rectangular in shape with squared corners and not surprisingly Segall et al (1966) found that the optical illusion was stronger in industrialized societies. Further support for cultural influences on perception was found in the research by McGurk and Jahoda (1975) who found that children in different cultures had varying perceptions of spatial relationships. One explanation for cultural differences is that perceptual patterns may be associated with varying rewards that in turn produce preferences. In one study (Broota & Ganguli, 1975) Hindu and Muslim children found punitive stimuli more salient that reward stimuli, whereas children in the U.S. found reward more salient than punishment.

Culture also creates both the presence and absence of certain experiences that in turn affect our ability to perceive the world. The absence of experience has been demonstrated to be a significant factor affecting perception (Blakemore & Cooper, 1970). Cultural groups are exposed to varying environmental conditions salient to perception and experience unique socialization practices that prime perception. Children also learn that certain stimuli are important for adaptation and pay attention to these while ignoring other stimuli that are less salient. In the long run these varying experiences produce a preference for culturally based sensations and perceptions reflected for example in food or music preferences (Shiraev & Boyd, 2001).

6.2. COGNITIVE DEVELOPMENT

The duality of the mind and body has no scientific premise. In fact all data points toward the co-evolution of the brain with our complex cultural context (Richerson & Boyd, 2005). Since all developmental forces are intertwined in the course of human development it is difficult to attribute causational variance separately to biology or culture. *Without culture our fine complex brain would have no substance, but, of course, without our hardwired brain capacities there would be no culture in the first place.* Experience plays a role in the evolution of brain structures given sufficient time as humans adapt to increasingly complex social environments. In summary, culture plays a universal role in human cognition as the accumulated social inheritance is made available to the each generation and is a modifier in the ongoing interaction between the child and the material and ideological inheritance.

Cognitive development is hardwired to some extent if we accept Piaget's genetic epistemology (Piaget, 1972). As we discussed in chapter 5 on language four sequential cognitive developmental stages are proposed over the course of the child's development: The sensorimotor, pre-operational, concrete, and formal stages. At each stage the child incorporates the thought processes of the previous structures. Movement from one cognitive stage to the next occurs as a result of *assimilation* where the child incorporates new cognitive elements or *accommodation* which refers to the changes that occur as the child adapts cognition to new situations

The antecedents of cognition according to Piaget are the biological imperatives of the nervous system. However, cognition is also based on socialization influences that support the child's adaptation to society. Finally, cultural transmissions through education and social institutions that differ between cultures influence cognition in the child.

While Piaget argued for the invariance of the stages of cognitive development in all cultures there is some evidence for the universality of the sensorimotor stage, however, the review of the existing literature is complex and controversial (Segall, Dasen, Berry, & Poortinga, 1999). The stage invariance seems to run counter to what we know of cultural influences on language and other cultural processes and the current research does not fully lend support to such an inflexible stand. Our common biology would support the presence of the universal cognitive hardware and perhaps the sequence of stages, but only if understood within the context of a given culture. The rate of cognitive achievement of participants from non-western cultures has often been interpreted as a form of cognitive deficit. However, if cognitive development has a reference to the local culture there is no basis for drawing value judgment or conclusions (Cole & Scribner, 1977).

While cross-cultural research generally lends support to the presence of the stages of cognitive development research does not support the invariance in the sequence of stages. The approach of this book is to acknowledge that psychological processes are not the same everywhere, however, neither are they totally dominated by cultural variances. It is the interaction of culture with neurophysiological processes that produces cognitive development. Some researchers have revised Piaget's theory by considering both the cultural and the environmental context. These theorists look for salient structural universals in cognition while acknowledging the importance of the situational or cultural context (Case, 1992).

This has led to the consideration of both different and additional stages than those advocated by Piaget. The advantages of neo-Piagetian approaches are that cognitive invariants are independent of Western logical thinking and can be applied directly to culturally salient and valued domains including, for example, emotions and moral development (Dasen & Ribaupierre, 1987). The last mentioned authors propose that culturally relevant tasks are necessary in order to measure valid progress of stage development in naturalistic settings. Unfortunately, we have seen few studies that have taken these essential considerations into account in measuring cognitive stage development in different cultures (Fiati, 1992).

6.3. COGNITIVE STYLE AND CULTURAL VALUES

From an ethnocentric Western perspective logical, analytical and rational reasoning skills are highly valued and are assumed to be ubiquitous. If not present in other cultures the lack of reasoning skills is interpreted as a cognitive deficit. Globalization has undoubtedly promoted this perspective in nearly all modern industrial societies although not everywhere. For example, in some agrarian societies an understanding of the whole is emphasized, and collective decision-making is advanced, rather than a promotion of analytic skills (Berry, Irvine, & Hunt, 1988; Serpell, 1993). It should be obvious that psychological instruments developed to test cognitive achievements in Western societies would have little validity in agrarian cultures. Valid assessments should rather be developed based of culturally relevant values of cognition.

The emphasis on cultural values has produced collateral interest in differences in *cognitive style* between East Asian and Western students (Nisbett, 2003). Some support has been found for cultural differences in cognition as East Asian students tend to see the whole as more salient, and perceive and remember objects as being more interconnected than Western students. In a study comparing Chinese with European American students Ji, Zhang, and Nisbett (2004) found that the Chinese students organized pictorial stimuli more in relational terms using less categorical descriptions when compared to the European American participants. It seems clear from these studies that cognitive skills must be evaluated according to the criteria of a given cultural group, and not on some invariant universal basis. On the other hand as noted previously globalization may well remove the need for the study of cultural relativism over the long term.

The most basic reason for studying the relationship between culture and cognition is the belief that a given population group share common values that are persuasive in behavior and thought processes. Populations can be compared on cognitive tasks and the differences found be inferred to be the result of cultural modes of being. The rationale for such comparative studies is the belief that societies provide members with common and coherent ways of knowing that are reflected in cognition. Nisbett and Masuda (2003) compared societies thought to have evolved from Greek philosophical traditions with those of East Asian origin. Eco-cultural psychology is based on cross-cultural comparisons where differences derive from cultural values that produce consistency in behavior, motivation and explanations for behavior. In this manner psychological processes are related to the underlying socio-cultural and environmental context of these cultural groups.

These persuasive cultural ways of thinking have also been referred to in the literature as *cognitive styles*. A direct contribution of culture to cognition is the development of processors of information that lead to consistent ways of perceiving and categorizing information. Typically, cognitive styles are viewed from a bipolar perspective where the extreme ends of these poles produce distinctive ways of thinking and behaving. The most frequently researched domain is on what has been called field dependent and field independent cognition (Kitayama & Cohen, 2007).

6.3.1. Field Dependent and Independent Cognitive Style

A very influential research program based conceptualization of cognitive style produced the so-called *field dependent/independent cognitive style* (Witkin, Dyk, Patterson, Goodenough, & Karp, 1962). These cognitive styles have evolved from culture and are persuasive in determining predictable differences in a variety of psychological domains including perception, but also in attention to specific stimuli, attributions, and self-construal as interdependent or independent, and by influencing social categorization processes. Research on perception demonstrated that some subjects relied primarily on internal frames of reference whereas others consistently based their spatial orientation on external frames. From these early perceptual studies ongoing research has investigated the affect of cognitive style on cognition and social orientation. The field dependent subjects rely more on external sources of reference and tend to be more socially oriented. The field independent subjects look for reference cues within themselves and feel less drawn toward socially based behavior as a reference source for perception.

Researchers saw in this perceptual model the factors that explained important cross-cultural differences. For example, Witkin, Goodenough, and Oltman (1979) viewed bipolar cognitive style as affecting the relatively autonomous functioning of people in society. The field dependent respondents are people who accept society as it is, whereas the field independent ones more broadly analyze the eco-cultural context. Research supports the contention that the field dependent style affects a variety of psychological domains and is reliable over time and in a number of situations. In this context cognitive style refers not to the content of cognition, but rather to preferred ways of processing relevant information.

A significant amount of cross-cultural research has been completed on cognitive styles that are cognitive processors considered functional since they relate to selective adaptation (Berry, 1991). Research has established relationships between cognitive style and various ecological and cultural variables. For example, field independence is thought more salient in hunting and gathering societies compared to agricultural communities, in nomadic versus sedentary groups, where population density is low compared to high, where the family structure is nuclear compared to extended, where social stratification is loose compared to tight, where socialization produces assertive behaviors rather than compliance, where western education is high versus low, and where wage employment is high versus low (Berry, Poortinga, Segall, & Dasen, 1992). In short the field independent cognitive style typically develops in an industrialized Western society where it is functional to survival, whereas sedentary societies with rigid social structures produce relatively more field dependence. Harsh family practices in sedentary non-European cultures are supported by a stronger emphasis on adherence to authority as a reference point for cultural behaviors. To argue that people are field dependent is to say that their cognition is more heavily influenced by the cultural context in thinking about or deciding their reaction to stimuli. On the other hand, field independent people see themselves as separate from others and as living a distinct and independent existence and are therefore more autonomous in relationships with others. Berry (1976a) tested the field-independent/dependent construct in 18 subsistence societies and found support for the relationship of cognitive style to eco-cultural elements.

In summary, field dependent respondents are more attentive to external aspects of learning including the cultural contexts and the specific instructions provided. Field independent learners, on the other hand, are more autonomous in solving problems and making learning-relevant decisions. Since the U.S educational settings promote student assertiveness students that develop a field independent cognitive style were more likely to achieve in this cultural context.

6.3.2. Perception Studies and Cognitive Style

In experimental studies when an object is removed from its original context European subjects can readily identify the object as familiar whether the visual stimuli is presented isolated or with an entirely new background. On the other hand, Asians pay more attention to the total context, and have more difficulty identifying the object when the background context of perception is not familiar, and are better at identification when the object is presented in isolation (Ji, Peng, & Nisbett, 2000). Further, Nisbett, Peng, Choi, and Norenzayan (2001) found that it is difficult for European Americans to note changes in background stimuli suggesting they are less field dependent, whereas it is more difficult for Asians to note changes in objects placed in the foreground of a stimuli scene. Masuda and Nisbett (2001) noted that Asians focus more attention on interrelationships between objects and the associated contextual features consistent with interdependent Asian culture, whereas European American participants focus more attention on the important features of objects placed in the foreground. The interdependence of our neural processes and cognitive style is also manifested in the Masuda and Nisbett study where the researchers found that the eye movement of American participants focused more on objects in the foreground whereas Chinese respondents made more eye movements toward background stimuli.

Nisbett (2003) proposed that the differences in cognitive style between East Asian and Western students are rooted in the more *holistic perceptual orientation* of the former. East Asian participants in these investigations tended to display a holistic perceptual orientation where they perceive objects as interconnected. On the other hand, Western participants paid more attention to details and the singularity of differentiated objects. In another study (Ji et al., 2004) Chinese students perceived of objects in pictorial stimuli as being more relationally organized, whereas participants of European background employed categorization as boundaries for objects.

The validity of these findings is supported by studies using magnetic imaging of the brain comparing German and Chinese respondents (Nisbett, 2003). These cultural groups displayed consistent differences in areas of brain stimulation with the bilateral frontal lobes and parietal areas known as the dorsal stream being activated in initial learning by Chinese respondents. On the other hand, European American respondents activated posterior ventral regions including the fusiform gyrus and hippocampal complex. Since these areas are associated with object identification they offer evidence that differences in culture and cognitive style affects the neurological attention style in perception. The validity of field dependence and independence cognitive styles find novel support in these studies that link perceptual behavior to the underlying cerebral activity. Recent research (Cassidy, 2012) has also linked cortical activity to certain visual and cognitive styles pointing also to the importance of biological etiology or concomitants in cognitive styles. Emergence in a prolonged cultural activity may change brain patterns associated with cognitive styles supporting the importance of both biology and culture. As we live during times of globalization it is encouraging to note that field independence is promoted by intercultural contacts. When cultural groups experience acculturation through contacts with other cultures the process promotes independent thinking and a perception of cultural behavior as dimensional and relative. Acculturation contacts support a field independent cognitive style with salient impact on a person's cognitive style (Witkin & Berry, 1975). Such intercultural contact has accelerated in recent years in a globalized world economy. While contacts have diminished field dependence, there remains in the literature a strong interest in cognitive styles as defining an important difference between collectivistic and individualistic societies (Kitayama & Cohen, 2007). Styles such as field independence, engaging in reflective and divergent thinking were shown to be salient contributors to learning performance (Fan & He, 2012). Socialization also affects cognitive style in the genders where some evidence has been found for more field dependence in females in authoritarian societies (Berry, 1966). However, the women's movement is challenging authoritarian practices everywhere, and globalization will probably ensure that gender field dependent differences are only of historical interest.

6.3.3. Collectivistic and Individualistic Cognition

Collectivistic and individualistic cultures have engaged the interest of researchers for a long time. Individualistic cultures are thought to promote self-reliance and competiveness where individuals are encouraged in the pursuit of *autonomy and independence.* Collectivistic cultures, on the other hand, place a stronger emphasis and value on the interest of the group based on social norms that support higher levels of *conformity and social responsibility.* Hofstede (1980) included individualism/collectivism as a cultural value that was useful in the ranking of countries and cultural groups. Markus and Kitayama (1991b) made an important conceptual advance when they suggested that cultures identified as individualistic or collectivistic foster different kinds of self-construal called the *independent* and *interdependent* self.

Research supports the view that people living in cultures defined as promoting individualistic values like Germany and the U.S. are more field independent compared to collectivistic cultures like those found in Malaysian and Russia (Kuhnen, Hannover, Roeder, Ali Shah, Schubert, Upmeyer, & Zakaria, 2001). The cultural context may in fact limit choices for independent decision making and thereby promote a field dependent cognitive style. Is field dependence conducive to creative thinking? While creativity is promoted in entrepreneurial societies and forms of self-expression regarded as healthy and normal, in collectivistic societies behavior that seek individual distinction may be met with social disapproval (Shiraev & Sobel, 2006). Creativity is negatively impacted in societies that enforce dogmatic thinking and limit exchange of ideas. Of course, the presence of dogmatism is relative, both within cultural groups as well as between societies. In fact the disapproval of ideas is also manifested in so-called Western democratic societies as demonstrated in the persecution of communists and other unorthodox thinkers.

6.3.4. Greek Versus Asian Thinking Style

Some researchers contend that sociocultural differences are so profound that they not only create unique world views, but affect the very structure of cognitive processes (Nisbett, Peng, Choi, & Norenzayan, 2001). Cognitive differences are thought to derive from the philosophical views represented by Socrates in Greece and Confucius in China. For example, Western scholarly thought has emphasized critical thinking and skepticism in finding truthful conclusions. The Greek tradition encouraged people to be independent thinkers and to decide for themselves the correct path. Confucius, on the other hand, valued respect for educators and the pragmatic development of salient information and knowledge. Confucian modes of thinking appear to be contrary to Western thought that challenge authority whereas Asian thought urges respect for status and rank (Tweed & Lehman, 2002; Yang & Sternberg, 1997).

Nisbett and his colleagues contended that Western thought is more analytical where perception is directed toward objects and constituent categories and formal rules of logic are valued. They suggested that we can understand these norms of thinking if we understand the history of Greece as the center of trade routes and developing a herding economy that encouraged independent thinking functional to survival in that cultural context. The contribution of Greek society to Western ideas of freedom of the individual derived from these cultural experiences and context. On the other hand, Chinese society emphasized social obligations in common with other collectivistic societies. As their economy was largely based on pragmatic innovations in agriculture that required cooperation and interdependence the Chinese evolved a more authoritarian society where the role of the educator was paramount. Perceptually the Chinese created a world view of complex interacting substances, compared to the Greek perspective of a perceptual world consisting of categories.

Nisbett and his colleagues argued that it is possible to build a cognitive theory based on the history of regions that explains why perception is field dependent in case of Asians and field independent among Western respondents. The structure of the dominant thought processes grew out of efforts to solve problems in these different cultural environments and is reflected in either dialectical thinking in Asia or in the use of formal logic in the West.

6.3.5. Dialectical and Logical Thinking

Peng and Nisbett (1999) reported on cultural differences in test performance related to the cognitive styles. In the Western tradition thinking frequently involve a *logical examination of alternatives*, often opposites, and selecting a favored or correct response. For example American students are more likely to perceive different perspectives as conflicting and polarized. On the other hand, Chinese students demonstrate the more *holistic positions found in dialectical thinking* and try to unify positions and reach a consensual decision. Peng and Nisbett argued that the difference in the relative use of dialectical and logical cognition is one of several ways that Asians and people from the West differ. This position has not gone unchallenged as Chan argued that dialectical and logical thinking are not necessarily incongruent or distinct (Chan, 2000). Likewise Ho (2000) suggested that perhaps it is better to characterize Asian thinking as conciliatory rather than employing dialectical procedures, and in any event both types of thinking can be found cross-culturally.

6.3.6. Authoritarianism and Dogmatism as a Cognitive Style

Authoritarianism and dogmatism are very heuristic constructs in social psychology. These constructs can also be thought of as cognitive processors especially for people who are at the extreme end of rightwing political authoritarianism or rigid dogmatism. Authoritarian attitudes were thought to develop out of fundamental insecurities that created a worldview of intolerance (Altemeyer, 1988). Linked to social attitudes authoritarianism has predicted prejudice toward a bewildering set of victims and in particular members of minorities or outgroups. Rokeach (1973) moved from a consideration of rightwing political content to the cognitive construct of dogmatism defined as closed-mindedness and cognitive rigidity. For Rokeach dogmatism described a mind closed to new information, and the rejection of others on the basis of belief incongruence. Larsen (1970, 1971) linked authoritarianism to social judgment and demonstrated a displacement of judgments toward extremes of an attitude scale on the part of the highly dogmatic respondents. *Dogmatism can be thought of as a filter or processor that eliminates threatening and uncomfortable information and ensures stability or rigidity in the individual as well as the underlying culture.*

6.4. THE GENERAL PROCESSOR IMPLIED IN COGNITIVE STYLES VERSUS CONTEXTUALIZED COGNITION

Cole and his coworkers criticized the work on cognitive styles that essentially sought to link cognitive behavior to some hypothesized *underlying processor* (Cole, 1992, 1996). To substitute grand cognitive theories they suggested that cognitive performance should be understood through an examination of *contextual features* of the culture and specific cognitive operations. The authors received inspiration from the well-established traditions of the sociohistorical and cultural traditions that emphasized everyday behavior (Luria, 1976; Vygotsky, 1978). In particular Luria and Vygotsky noted that cognitive expertise comes from the salience of cognition to the individual and from repetition. Consequently cultural differences in cognition derive from cultural differences in *situations* to which cognitive processes are applied and not from differences in cognitive processors. In other words, the presence of some central processor in the form of an organizing cognitive style is rejected by Cole.

The work on *cognitive style represents a search for universal laws of the mind that control cognitive development. By contrast the context-specific approach tries to understand how cognitive processes that are initially context specific take on a generalizing role in people's lives over time.* Cognition from the context-specific perspective occurs within domains of activity. As the consequence of interactions within specific domains cognitive expertise is gradually developed. Research on quantitative skills and complex cognition supports the idea that thought processes are determined by the situational context and since cognition is domain specific it is not possible to generalize achievement in one domain to other contexts. More specifically, Cole's work challenged the literacy concepts of Luria that education is the signal event in human history and illiterates cannot carry out abstract cognitive operations Research results supported the idea that literacy made some limited differences in skills connected to specific contexts. The researchers concluded that there was no evidence that literacy *transformed* cognition in any major way (Scribner & Cole, 1981). Of course, Cole did not address or discuss the cultural consequences of literacy or the type of societies that evolve with or without literacy. The research addressed simply generalizing affects of literacy that was rejected by Cole and his co-workers.

6.5. COGNITIVE STYLE AND PRIMING COGNITION

However, it is not possible to dismiss the salience of cognitive style to the understanding of dominant thought processes in a culture. A great deal of research effort describes societies as relatively individualistic or collectivistic. The work by Cole and his colleagues suggests that cognitive style does not explain everything about cross-cultural differences in thinking processes, but the situational context matters. The traditional assumption about cognitive style is to argue for a direct connection between culture and cognitive processes derived from organized systems of thought that are produced by cultural values. In recent years priming studies have allowed a closer examination of these issues. Priming occurs in an experiment when the researcher prepares the respondent for the experimental task. Priming can either be conceptual by showing stimulus objects that have meaning or perceptual by showing the respondents some pictorial stimuli.

In regard to individualism as a cognitive style the respondent can be asked in what ways he/she is different from others in his/her cultural group. Collectivism can likewise be primed by asking the ways he/she is similar to members of his/her family and cultural group. It would also be possible to submit some test including pronouns and ask the respondent to circle appropriate singular (I) or collective (we or us) pronouns and note the frequency that these are selected as indicators of the influence of individualism and collectivism. When subjects are primed or prepared they are more likely to be sensitive and respond to the relevant stimuli. By priming experimentally it is possible to study cognitive variables believed important to cross-cultural differences in thinking processes. In the past cross-cultural research on cognition produced differences between cultural groups, but without being able to identify which factors were responsible. However, in priming research it is possible to operationalize and manipulate variables by presenting stimuli that appears to be unrelated. Unknown to the participant the first task in the experiment is used to prepare the mind for the remaining tasks required in the study. As noted above it is possible to prime the cultural styles known as individualism and collectivism in a variety of ways and then see if the subjects respond consistent to the prime (Oyserman & Lee, 2007).

In a salient series of studies Oyserman, Sorensen, Reber, and Chen (2009) demonstrated priming effects in several cognitive domains including memory, visual search behavior and academic preparedness test. The Asian and Western participants were primed in their native languages by asking them to circle relevant pronouns. The results showed that the effects of priming were similar regardless of cultural group (Asian or Western) and independent of the language used. The priming was powerful so once a cognitive style (e.g. individualism) has been primed it will be used even for tasks that are not relevant. In a meta-analysis Oyserman and Lee (2007) demonstrated significant and moderate effects of priming on several measures of cognition.

The results lend support to the contention *of Cole and his colleagues that thought processes are primarily determined by the situational and pragmatic context.* How people think is determined according to Oyserman by the practical requirements of the situational context. He concludes that culture rather than producing fixed immutable ways of thinking offer pragmatic requirements that in turn prime relevant cognition. Differences in cross-cultural thinking are therefore the result of the frequency by which they prime or prepare their members for particular cognitive tasks. From the Oyserman et al perspective differences between cultures in cognition is a result of mind-sets that are chronically assessable, however that are also changeable given a different context with different pragmatic imperatives. From this perspective cognitive differences between cultures are not inherent or fixed, but rather the result of how the environment elicits certain mindsets, and when the environment changes (as we observe from the influence of globalization) cognition will follow.

6.6. CROSS-CULTURAL DIFFERENCES IN COGNITION AS A FUNCTION OF PRACTICAL IMPERATIVES

The idea that societies differ in cultural practices is accepted by everyone. That these practices produce measurable differences in cognition including variable expertise in knowledge and cognitive strategies is also apparent. The contest is not really between accepting either cognitive style or cultural practices as the locus for the relationship between culture and cognition as both sources may indeed have a role to play (Cole & Packer, 2011; Greenfield, 2004; Mejia-Arauz, Rogoff, & Paradise, 2005). Studies cited above have demonstrated the presence of cultural differences in the frequencies in which participants engage in certain cultural practices connected to cognition.

Greenfield (2004) demonstrated how cognitive strategies changed as a result of historical alterations that made one type of learning (observation) obsolete and required more trial and error strategies. In his study he examined weaving practices among the Mayan culture in Mexico and the cognitive consequences of learning to weave as the community moved from a subsistence society where girls and women learned to weave the "right way" by observation of mothers and mentors, to more recent times when mothers were involved in a cash economy and weaved to sell. The study showed that in recent times learning to weave was often by self-correction and trial and error that produced more varied products. The pragmatic imperative in the cash economy was to create more products for sale that in turn created different cognitive strategies to meet the current need.

In the Mejia-Arauz et al study Mexican heritage children that came from homes of low education mothers learned as expected primarily by the cognitive strategy of observation. However, Mexican-American children from homes of mothers with higher education learned from verbal explanations producing a shift in cognitive practices that can be attributed to the mother's education. The development of cognitive skills as a result of the use of cultural artifacts was supported in a study on the utilization of abacus in Japan. Participants learned to internalize the mental representations of the beads in order to increase speed of calculations (Hatano, 1997). The interiorizing of abacus calculation occurred from the frequency of practice demonstrating how cognitive expertise derives from sociocultural repetition. Of interest mental abacus also related to changes in neural performance of the posterior superior parietal cortex specialized for spatial and motor skills (Hanakawa, Honda, Okada, Fukuyama, & Shibasaki, 2003).

Still the connection between cultural practices and cognition does not invalidate cognitive styles as an explanatory tool since cognition also evolved out of the cultural experiences of entire cultural groups and cognitive styles assisted specifically in the adaptation of people to specific sociocultural environments. Therefore, it remains valid to describe cognitive differences between cultural groups like East Asians and Western groups since cognitive style may have broad cultural and persuasive influences on thinking processes. Even where cultural practices change cognition as seen in the Hanakawa et al study such change still occurs within the salient dominant thought processes that have evolved from the history of the cultural group. We must also acknowledge that cognition and culture are interdependent. It is culture that makes cognition possible by creation of artifacts. At the same time culture would not exist except for the cognition that engages and changes the environment. Finally, we must acknowledge the role of biology, and that cultural practice produces neural changes in specific brain centers that are related to cognitive expertise.

6.7. INTELLIGENCE AND ADAPTATION: GENERAL AND CROSS-CULTURAL ASPECTS

Intelligence refers to the many intellectual capacities described by performance in analytic tasks and verbal abilities. We have in common some cognitive features with all humanity as a result of our biological inheritance. However, intelligence also refers to unique *adaptation to the ecocultural context,* and cannot be understood without a cultural framework. Some researchers have contended that group differences in intelligence should be considered inborn and hardwired. However, other significant research shows that all cognitive processes are embedded in the sociocultural context.

6.7.1. Definitions of general intelligence.

Intelligence testing grew out of Western cultural definitions that placed a high value on abstract reasoning and analytical abilities. Definitions of intelligence are therefore strongly influenced by these cultural values. *Intelligence is broadly defined as the mental abilities observed in the application of knowledge to problem solving.* In particular people of high intelligence demonstrate their capacities to adapt using rationality and reasoning in responding to environmental challenges. Intelligence is also manifested in the ability to respond to and adapt to changing personal and conditions. Keeping in mind our current economic crisis business that respond effectively to these changing circumstances may have a chance to survive. Using these definitions it is also apparent that the intelligence construct is central to any theory of cognition. However, the latter is a broader concept that includes an understanding of how people develop and apply knowledge found in processes of memory, categorization, and recognition of relevant cognitive components.

The multiplicity of intelligence components led early researchers to use factor analysis to identify both the general (first) factor, and also other variable components of intelligence (Spearman, 1927; Thurstone, 1938). In addition to a *general factor of intelligence the researchers also identified verbal comprehension, spatial abilities, speed of perception, mathematical reasoning, and word fluency.* The general factor is composed of all subcomponents mentioned above in multifactor intelligence tests. However, as intelligence testing developed out of Western values it is not surprising that abilities to reason using logical rules, and carry out mental deductive hypothesis testing are considered central components of intelligence. Thurstone (1938) identified the existence of three basic factors called verbal, mathematical and spatial intelligence. Sternberg (1997) suggested that in addition to these traditional components intelligence is also reflected in creative, analytical and practical skills whereas intelligence tests only measure the analytic component. Gardner (1983) argued that personal (social) intelligence should be evaluated. Social intelligence is reflected in a person's ability to understand the self and relate effectively to others. Further, Gardner pointed to music ability as a special form of intelligence. Research on intelligence has proceeded primarily from a psychometric perspective using intelligence tests developed in the West.

6.7.2. Nature or Nurture: What Determines Intelligence?

The question of what is responsible for a person's intelligence, *nature or nurture, is only important because it is associated with sociopolitical issues where* intelligence has been identified with phenotypical race as representative of the affect of invariable "nature." Consistent differences have been found between phenotypical races on general measures of intelligence. The direction of the differences shows that African Americans score consistently lower than Americans of European background (Jensen, 1968, 1984). The research created a storm in American psychology, not least because it was published just as Black people were finding their way forward after centuries of oppression. Jensen argued that about 80 percent of intelligence is biologically determined and fixed and that therefore compensatory programs for the underprivileged are useless and a waste of resources.

Strong support for the nature theory is found in the studies of twins reared apart compared to fraternal twins reared together (Bouchard & McGue, 1981). If intelligence has a large nature component and is biologically inherited then twins reared apart should produce very similar intelligence scores, whereas if the environment is primarily responsible then the fraternal twins raised in the same environment should yield more similarity. In fact the results showed that identical twins reared apart, had more similar scores (.82 correlation) than fraternal twins reared in the same homes. Although most researchers agree that there is a biological component in intelligence (Plomin, 1990), Jensen's application of these findings to phenotypical race is rejected by most researchers today. It would be more fruitful to examine the relationship between brain size and intelligence (Jensen & Johnson, 1994).

6.7.3. Sources of Bias in Intelligence Testing

The fact that Afro-Americans scored one standard deviation below samples of European-Americans led Jensen to conclude that significant intellectual differences existed between the two groups. A serious controversial contention occurred in psychology and the broader society when Jensen and others (Herrnstein & Murray, 1994) interpreted these differences as racial variances in intellectual capacity. However, other research has challenged Jensen's "nature" conclusions. For example, Humphreys (1985) analyzed results from a very large data bank and found that "race" only correlated .17 with intelligence, but .86 with socioeconomic status. The large correlation for socioeconomic status was attributed to the very adverse conditions associated with the lives of Black people who struggle economically that in turn affect opportunity and intelligence scores.

All the readers of this chapter will now also be aware of the large role played by the cultural context in cognition. Can we really know what component of intelligence can be attributed to nature or nurture? Hebb (1949) made a distinction between the genetic capacity associated with the brain that he called intelligence A, and intelligence B which developed in interaction with the cultural context. Vernon (1969) provided an additional distinction that he called intelligence C that was measured by a person's performance on an intelligence test. These distinctions provide us with two sources of bias in the conceptualization of the construct. First, especially in the cross-cultural context, the intelligence test employed may not adequately sample B, thereby yielding a performance that does not reflect a person's intelligence adequately. Since not all sources of test variance are controlled for in intelligence testing the lack of equivalence of test scores may be the result of cultural bias. Many variables can contribute to bias including language differences, inadequate items used to measure content, and variable motivation to respond well on the test. The results of intelligence testing then may be nothing more than an assessment of intelligence C performance on the intelligence test, not measuring either A or B. Jensen, Herrnstein and Murray who advocate in favor of racial differences in intelligence seem to confuse intelligence C (the actual measurement) as representing intelligence A (the hardwired capacity).

6.7.4. Socioeconomic Differences and Fairness

The fairness of a test is also a matter of concern. All intelligence testing assumes equivalence of knowledge in cultural groups and the verbal skills learned typically in an educational environment. However, there are wide differences in educational environments between educational systems that are rooted largely in socioeconomic differences within countries, and, of course, these differences are magnified between cultural groups. A meta-analysis of 197 separate studies examined the relationship of affluence (measured by expenditures on education) and performance on intelligence tests (Van de Vijver, 1997). The results showed a positive relationship between affluence and performance in various cultural groups. This results would suggest that intelligence performance is really primarily a result of educational differences and opportunities and not biological inheritance. For example the inductive reasoning that is embedded in intelligence tests is largely a consequence of similar educational inductive processes. The relationship between education and intelligence test results is also supported by Segall et al. (1999). It should be obvious that education as determined by socioeconomic class produces more familiarity with the content of intelligence tests and therefore higher scores.

The scores of intelligence tests are correlated positively with socioeconomic status (Neiser, Boodoo, Bouchard, Boykin, Brody, Ceci, Halpern, Loehlin, Perloff, Sternberg, & Urbina, 1996). In general results show that the higher the socioeconomic status the higher the scores on intelligence tests. Herrnstein and Murray tries to turn this relationship upside down by claiming high intelligence determine socioeconomic status. However, there is no way to determine the causal relationship from correlational studies. Since we have seen elsewhere that intelligence can be improved over a single generation the causal direction seems more likely from the contextual features of the socioeconomic environment with those who have access to educational opportunities and other resources scoring high on intelligence tests.

All these factors are intertwined. For example, the family has also been isolated as a factor affecting intelligence. It seems obvious that affluent families offer better and more stimulating experiences to a growing child having a positive influence on intellectual development. It is equally obvious that the positive stimulation is basically a socioeconomic contribution that provides the means from which middle class families can provide better opportunities, whereas poor families just struggle to survive (Shiraev, 1988). Socioeconomic factors in intelligence are a matter of no small moment in a world beset with economic crises and falling living standards.

Intelligence tests are not unbiased, but benefit certain cultural groups who are familiar with the vocabulary used. Some items used in intelligence tests may only be familiar to certain economic classes or racial groups and therefore give an unfair advantage to those with an appropriate schooling. Although in most research reports the advantage is given to Americans of European background and Asian respondents, in fact this primacy is reversed in a vocabulary test utilizing words familiar only to the Black community. The dependence of test results on the sociocultural context is shown convincingly when Black kids obtained a score of 87 out of a 100 correct responses, but the white children's mean score was 51 on the test based on Black vocabulary. The Black kids did better, because the words were relevant to the daily experience of Black youth (Hayles, 1991). Since most verbal intelligence tests contain information on knowledge generally known in the dominant culture they give advantage to those who are familiar with such information. However, this information is not available on an equivalent basis, but is to some extent specific to cultural groups. Intelligence tests may predict success, but they do not necessarily measure intelligence since that can never be divided from cultural content.

Further, if intelligence is fixed and stable as assumed by Jensen one could not expect much change over time. After all that is the argument against compensatory educational programs for the disadvantaged. However, Flynn (1987) found in his cross-national study (from fourteen countries) that increases in intelligence performance occurred in all countries. The results showed an increase in 15 IQ points over the span of a single generation suggesting the intelligence is not fixed, but rather malleable to educational improvement and may in fact largely measure educational efforts. This result is also supported by the Van de Vijver study where the author showed that the scale of differences between groups was greater in international as compared to national studies. The explanation seems straight forward that when participants are compared within a country they share similar acculturation experiences and similar education. The argument that phenotypical "race" is responsible for intelligence test differences are further undermined from studies that examine the effects of social class. In some studies the eco-cultural environment trumps "race" as poor whites living in southern (and poorer) United States scored lower than Blacks living in northern regions (Blau, 1981).

Also, the racism embedded in traditional American society produces anticipation of failure on the part of minority respondents. Related to the priming studies previously discussed, priming can also produce "stereotypic threat ," the threat perceived by minorities that others will stereotype their responses and that they therefore develop self-expectations of poor performance that affect their actual test results (Steele, 1997). For example, when Black students were asked to record their racial identification on a survey of demographic questions prior to taking an intelligence test they performed worse compared to Black students that were not primed about their race. This result suggests that broad racial prejudice in regard to intellectual performance is also internalized by minorities, preventing them from performing at their real capacity. Ogbu (1994) stated that negative testing attitudes, and feelings of hopelessness are frequently present in students from deprived communities. Their exposure to the negative stereotypes held by the majority community combined with these personal disposition factors resulted in lowering the intelligence scores of Afro-Americans and other deprived groups in the U.S. Likewise Aboriginal children typically score lower than children with European background in Australia. However, when the playing field is level and Aboriginal children live by white children (and therefore share the same eco-cultural context) their scores are very similar (Lacey, 1971).

6.7.5. Race and the Interaction Effect

Any measured performance is the outcome of the interaction of the individual and his/her environment. *This interaction affect makes it impossible to ascertain the variance that can be attributed to either genetics or the eco-cultural environment.* All the heritability estimates are therefore speculative and of limited validity. Further, race is at best an ambiguous construct as it is based on phenotypical appearance rather than meaningful biological differences. It can be argued that the social construct "race" does not refer to anything meaningful, particularly in the United States where "races" are intermixed reflecting the varied progress of humanity on our geneographical journey out of Africa. Importantly intelligence cannot be measured in a meaningful way outside the cultural framework, and the construct may in fact have no meaning except within cultural values. Cross-cultural research shows that the very meaning of intelligence varies by culture (Sternberg, 2004; Sternberg, Grigorenko, & Kidd, 2005).

The use of intelligence tests in cross-cultural work must be evaluated with skepticism. There is a history of doing such comparative work where some population groups usually get lower scores that in turn are interpreted as cognitive deficits. Unless intelligence tests serve some meaningful educational purpose it seems hard to justify their use cross-culturally. Originally intelligence tests were developed in order to help those thought unfit for traditional educational training. However, as we have seen that intelligence is not fixed, but malleable from experiences especially those associated with schooling, and it seems that the intellectual energy of conducting comparative research on intelligence testing could be better placed elsewhere. As Greenfield (1997) has noted psychological tests assume similar familiarity between respondents with content, with test taking and associated conventions that are not easily transferred from one culture to the next.

The definitive studies on the interacting effect of culture and intelligence can be observed by the so-called Flynn effect (Folger, 2012). Research shows that IQ scores have been increasing steadily since the beginning of the 20th century. The increases in IQ scores appear to be systematic, year after year, suggesting something more than biology at play. The improvements in scores are not in what psychologists call crystallized intelligence generally considered a result of knowledge derived from formal education. Most gains occur throughout the intelligence curve and are derived from subtests of the Wechsler Intelligence Scale for Children measuring *abstract reasoning* and *geometric patterns* or fluid intelligence. In other words, the improvements are in what is thought to be the hardwired capacity to solve unfamiliar problems. Since these tests are paradoxically culturally free measures of innate capacity could our modern brains have evolved at this speed? No, biological evolution could not happen in so short a time span, more likely there is something happening in the cultural environment. It would appear that our minds have evolved in interaction with the demands of modern society. Several environmental causes have been attributed for the ubiquitous improvement including better childhood nutrition, universal education, smaller families, educated mothers, and the industrial revolution that required mastery of abstract thinking. In the end the Flynn effect is explained by the continuous feedback loop between our minds and a culture dominated by technology and reflects human adaptability.

6.8. THE USE OF PSYCHOLOGICAL TESTS IN VARYING CULTURES

Other psychological tests have, however, been transferred validly for use in cross-cultural research. That seems appropriate if the test protocol meets certain criteria as we discussed in chapter 2. Does the content of the test or survey have similar meanings where tested? For example, when measuring attitudes toward undocumented immigrants cross-culturally does the psychological domain have the same meaning in the samples tested? Does illegal immigration play approximately the same or variable roles in the countries tested? Appropriate comparative conclusions can only be drawn if the domain of illegal immigration is equivalent. Psychological testing has developed several approaches including psychometric analysis to ensure structural equivalence of test items. However, the primary motivation for the development of psychological testing is practical use for educational aptitude or job placement. For that use, it is imperative that the researchers can demonstrate the valid transferability of the tests from the original to other cultures.

As also discussed in chapter 2 there is broadly a consensus that the testing procedure developed in one country can be utilized in other cultures. Equivalence of sampling of respondents and proper translation procedures are necessary considerations. For example proper cross-cultural testing would require the translation into the new language, and then a retranslation into the original language, and then again into the new language in order to ascertain the validity of the translation. Larsen and his co-workers followed these procedures and examined attitudes in a variety of societies utilizing unidimensional scaling techniques and based on comparative meanings and translation and survey procedures (Ommundsen, Hak, Morch, Larsen, & Van der Veer, 2002; Ommundsen & Larsen, 1997, 1999; Ommundsen, Van der Veer, Van Le, Krumov, & Larsen, 2007; Van der Veer, Ommundsen, Larsen, Van Le, Krumov, Pernice, & Romans, 2004).

6.9. HOW INTELLIGENCE IS VIEWED IN OTHER CULTURES

Cross-cultural research supports an expanded view of intelligence related to specific cultural values. Cross-cultural studies have traditionally not taken these conceptual differences seriously which has confounded not only the results but also interpretations of the existence of deficit functioning in other cultural groups. Cross-cultural confusion in the construct of intelligence becomes likely when we realize that many languages do not have words that correspond directly with the English word intelligence. For example, the Chinese (consistent with their collectivistic culture) associate intelligence with words that reflect their social reality including social responsibility and imitation (Keats, 1982). It seems clear that if there is no common agreement on the construct measured then Western tests applied to other cultures would yield a somewhat artificial and indeed biased picture of the meaning of intelligence in that society. Since the intelligence construct is closely related to education and the cognitive styles of the culture the tests may not provide very accurate portrayals of respondents in traditional cultural groups or in societies that are collectivistic. African cultures provide other examples of different perspectives on intelligence. For example, in one cultural group intelligence was seen as a combination of practical know-how and social skills in getting along with others. Local conceptualizations of intelligence are reviewed in Segall et al (1999).

Cultures to some extent value different cognitive traits and have alternative views on how these traits relate to success in their society. In collectivistic cultures taking tests in an effort to score high can be thought of as a form of self-enhancement where the participant seeks to differentiate him/herself from peers. However, in these societies self enhancement is perceived as arrogant since modesty and the welfare of the group are valued above individual display. *Since comparisons are particularly difficult when the samples do not share the same conceptual definitions there is a need to interpret intelligence research from the indigenous cognitive perspective.* From that point of view there is agreement on some universal aspects of cognitive functioning, but also an attempt to understand differences in cognition from the perspective of the indigenous cultural context (Berry, Irvine, & Hunt, 1988).

The major argument in favor of indigenous reinterpretations is that cross-cultural research has traditionally viewed differences between cultural groups as fixed cognitive deficits in the low scoring cultural group produced by biology and genetics. It is more consistent with what we actually know about intelligence to examine individual deficits as related to test scores. We know that the sociocultural environment unjustly deprives some people of opportunities to learn and apply knowledge because of poverty and poor health. Some cultural and ethnic groups are socially deprived and suffer from discrimination and marginalization in society impacting cognitive functioning. Focusing on these malleable differences is more realistic in terms of the meaning of intelligence, and if the socioeconomic culture can be changed that can result in improvement of cognitive life.

In the final analysis we should advocate for a definition of intelligence that is more broadly based on the cultural group experiences. From this perspective intelligence is defined by the skills and behaviors that support the individual in reaching culturally valued goals. In some cultures individual goals could include the pursuit of a career in a modern industrial society requiring high levels of cognitive functioning including logic, rational reasoning, mathematical skills and associated social skills. However, in other cultures it is more important to develop and ensure positive interpersonal relationships. The intelligent person in that culture would incorporate the social skills that permit him/her to be a successful member of the collective.

6.10. GENERAL PROCESSES IN HIGHER ORDER COGNITION AND INTELLIGENCE

General cognitive processes support higher order cognition. Although there is still much to be learned the literature points to the importance of categorization, memory, creativity, and quantitative abilities as foundations for complex and abstract thinking. Since cultures vary in eco-cultural contexts we should expect differences that correspond to these variances.

6.10.1. Categorization.

Among the cognitive processes that are building blocks in cognition and intelligence probably the most elementary is categorization. People categorize on the basis of similarity placing into categories objects that have something in common. The process of categorization is universal and has been observed in all cultures. People categorize in order to reduce the complexity of the world and provide the psychological means to react to stimuli and make appropriate decisions. Language is essentially based on categorization as the development of concepts is symbolic of communalities in our environment. We have already noted the universality of facial expressions and their common meaning across cultures. More complex verbal behaviors are also categorized as we can see in the case of stereotypes, the generalized beliefs we hold of other cultural groups and people. In fact categorization is the most elementary way we discriminate. Stereotypes attribute to an entire cultural category what we believe are common traits and is the lazy person's response to a complex multifaceted world. In fact it takes very little to categorize, particularly between ingroup and outgroup members. The mere membership in another group is sufficient to create a negative bias. The so-called minimal categorization design studies demonstrated that even groups that are nonsensical produce discriminatory categorical behavior (Doise, Csepeli, Dann, Gouge, Larsen, & Ostell, 1972).

Cross-cultural differences in categorization have been demonstrated. For example, one study showed that adult Africans tended to categorize objects on the basis of color rather than function reflecting the importance of color identification of objects in that cultural context (Suchman, 1966). Western respondents tend to categorize on the basis of shared features. For example, in pictorial stimuli of a man, a woman and child, Western respondents would place the man and woman together because they are both adults, whereas East Asians would put the child together with the adult because of their functional relationship as a family (Ji, Li-Jin, Zhang, & Nisbett, 2004). The culture provides the context for categorization and respondents classify objects together based on these cultural experiences (Wassmann & Dasen, 1994). It is the degree of familiarity with environmental objects that becomes the basis for categorization that is also largely influenced by the cultural educational system (Mishra, 1997).

6.10.2. Memory Functions

To examine cross-cultural research in memory it is necessary to discuss briefly the underlying constructs. Wagner (1993) made a distinction between two major aspects of memory referring to structural and control processes. A lot of research in memory functioning point to brain structures related to long-term and short-term memory. Most of us have had the experience of being prompted about some memory of an event that occurred long ago. Long-term memory has seemingly unlimited capacity, and a trace probably exist for all meaningful events, good or bad, that has occurred in our lives. Short-term memory, on the other hand is where we store temporary matters like telephone numbers of stores or other less significant things. Although forgetting is also a universal experience, memory in the short-term storage is forgotten more quickly, often as soon as you have acted on the information provided like when calling the store phone number for some pricing information. Baddeley (1986) suggested that short-term memory has a maximum storage of about 2 seconds, after that the memory trace must be refreshed, perhaps by repeating to yourself the phone number you intend to use. The control process in memory refers to the strategies employed in securing information and retrieving it from memory. Information that has common factors is often remembered in clusters of related facts.

Since memory storage is a hardwired recollection it tends to be similar across cultures. Even very different cultural groups tend to have similar display and patterns in immediate recall of memory (Wetherick & Deregowski, 1982). However, what is recalled depends on cultural experience and is determined by cultural values as well as socioeconomic differences that produce advantage or disadvantage for recall. Better recall occurs for subjects with which we are familiar and that is consistent with our existing knowledge (Ciborowski & Choi, 1974; Harris, Schoen, & Hensley, 1992).

Since we have so many memory aids in modern society, not least the computer, do people who depend on oral traditions have better memory recall? Some research supports this proposition, but the results are mixed (Ross & Millson, 1970). Education makes a difference since in the class room children are often asked to memorize and apply memory skills to test situations. Since memory depend on hardwiring of the brain people everywhere show the effects of aging, and memory function decrease with increasing age in all cultures investigated (Crook, Youngjohn, Larrabee & Salama, 1992). However, on the whole there does not appear strong influence of culture on structural memory. Among the control factors education seem to be a primary contributor along with urbanization (Jahoda, 1984; Wagner, 1977, 1978).

6.10.3. Mathematical Abilities

Mathematical ability is dependent on formal education as it relies on reasoning and analysis (Scribner & Cole, 1981). Formal reasoning is a cultural component and is different from the reasoning required in adaptation to cultural environments. For some researchers mathematical ability was directly an artifact of educational training, and higher order reasoning cannot occur in illiterate respondents Luria (1976). Luria suggested that reasoning is an artificial cultural product and must be learned in the context of a Westernized education. As we have seen previously that contention has been called into question. Typically Asian children have performed better than their Western counterparts (Geary, Fan, & Bow-Thomas, 1992). The explanation for the higher performance are the strong family norms for achievement that support mathematical education and the strong educational efforts made to help children develop formal mathematical skills (Van de Vijver & Willemsen, 1993).

However, despite the contention of Luria, members of a variety of illiterate cultures learn mathematical skills (Schliemann & Carraher, 2001). Illiterate farmers make very accurate estimation of volume of crops and others use a variety of devices to count and estimate. For example, string devices known as khipu were used in the ancient Inca Empire to register census data and evidence for the use of geometry to locate objects have been found among illiterate cultural groups living in the Amazon (Dehaene, Izard, Pica, & Spelke, 2006).

6.10.4. The Ultimate Pedagogical Goal: Creativity

Creativity refers to cognition that is novel and "outside the box." Cultural development for both good and bad depends in the long term on individuals who can produce new ways of exploring old problems or produce original solutions not previously thought possible. Creativity has enabled humans to take great strides in science, for example, in the exploration of space with the latest achievement the Mars landing of the vehicle "Curiosity" having occurred during the week of this writing. At the same time creativity has also enabled scientists to contribute to horrifying weapons of mass destruction. All the great thinkers of the world have had creative approaches to the issues of their day. Some researchers think of creativity in terms of personality traits, particularly individuals who are confident and acceptant of the self, and display psychological independence (Barron & Harrington, 1981).

Creative persons have consistent with personal independence the ability to *think divergently rather than relying on only the convergent cognition measured in intelligence testing.* Also consistent with personal independence is a high tolerance for ambiguity and disorder and the willingness to take risks (Sternberg & Lubart, 1996, 1999). Importantly, creative individuals have the ability to resist conformity pressures. These traits were also found in creative individuals even in highly conformist societies like the Sudan (Khaleefa, Erdos, & Ashria, 1996). The creative individual must be able to deal with and overcome many obstacles rooted in pressures from society and culture.

Research has also shown socialization practices to be important. Simonton (1987) concluded that strong parental support and stimulation encourages creativity in children. Stimulation is a necessary component that is often delimited by culture and class. For example, in one comparative study children that had socioeconomic advantages were more creative compared to children from deprived families that struggle for survival. However, even the most creative individual must operate within the boundaries of cultural norms. In one major study Shane, Venkataraman, and MacMillan (1995) results showed that the innovative strategies employed depended on the dominant cultural values. For example, using Hofstede's cultural values, the researchers found that in countries high on uncertainty avoidance creative individuals had to work through relevant organizational norms and procedures. On the other hand, in countries identified as high on power distance creative individuals sought the assistance of authorities and found they needed a broad base of support. Whether Socrates or Copernicus, creative individuals have found themselves part of cultures and social structures that had to be taken into account in order to produce creative contributions. Although creative individuals may share traits across various cultures to perform their work they have to acknowledge cultural values and work in ways approved by those who have power (Csikszentmihalyi, 1999).

SUMMARY

Differences in cognition define the very substance of what we mean by cultural differences. Cognition is culture that is learned from our daily life as influenced by social forces like cultural norms and values. Culture exerts influence through "mental programming" and serves the purpose of helping large groups living harmoniously in common territories. In other words, cultural cognition is what we inherit by being born into societies characterized by unique social contexts. Cultural cognition must be understood developmentally as a result of the accumulated behaviors and thought patterns that influence and modify the external environment. At the same time the material culture also delimits to some extent cognition. In the final analysis the impact of culture is summarized in our knowledge about language, tradition, and social ideology.

Cognition starts with sensation and perception. Sensation is the consequence of the conversion of stimulation into neurophysiological processes that create psychological experiences. Perception involves the organization of association areas of the cortex by integrating new sensations with previous knowledge. Culture influences perception in a number of ways including spatial relationships. Cultural groups are exposed to a varying environmental conditions and societies that prime members for particular cognitive processes.

Research on cognitive development supports the co-evolution of the brain with the complex human context. While cognitive development is hardwired to some extent the rate of acquisition of cognitive stages is culturally dependent on the complex interaction of biology, environment, socialization, and the transmission of cultural values through cultural institutions and education.

Research has focused a great deal of attention on the relationship of cultural values and cognitive style. From a Western perspective logical decision-making, analytical skills and reasoning abilities are highly valued. Globalization, however, requires a cautionary note on cultural differences as societies all over the world have reinforced and valued these reasoning cognitive approaches in order to deal with modern life. The relationship of cultural values to cognitive styles reveals important differences. For example, East Asian students when requested to respond to stimuli tend to perceive the whole context of the stimuli and the relationships between stimuli objects to a greater extent than Western students. Cognitive styles are typically viewed as bipolar with respondents at the extreme ends of the dimension possessing distinct ways of thinking and categorization of information.

A primary cognitive style is the so-called field dependent and field independent reference. Research on perception demonstrated that some subjects rely primarily on an internal frame of reference whereas others utilize external anchors to assist in spatial orientation. The distinction has been expanded to understand cognition and social orientation. Field dependent subjects are more socially oriented and accept society as it is, tend to be more cognitive rigid and adhere to authority. Field independent respondents, on the other hand, look for cues within themselves to process information, and tend to be more autonomous, and are located more in Western societies. Perception studies have shown that differences in cognitive style between East Asians and Western students are reliable defined by a greater emphasis on holistic perception in the former. These differences are also supported by the stimulation of different areas activated in the brain in these cultural groups.

An understanding of cognitive style grew out of the comparative research on collectivistic and individualistic societies demonstrating varying cognition. Individualistic cultures promote self-reliance and competiveness in pursuit of autonomy and independence. Collectivistic societies place a stronger emphasis on the interest of the group or collective and support higher levels of conformity and social responsibility. The two types of societies also foster different self-construal that is commonly called independent and interdependent.

Research has also pointed to the differences between Greek and Asian thinking as affecting the structure of cognitive processes. Deep sociocultural differences created different worldviews in Western and Asian societies that are thought to have originated with Socrates in Greece and Confucius in China. These ideas complement the differences between collectivistic and individualistic societies discussed above. The Western tradition emphasized critical thinking, skepticism and independence in the pursuit of truth whereas the Confucian tradition supported respect for educators and authority and the pragmatic value of information and knowledge. To understand these forms of cultural cognition we have to examine the history of each region.

Dialectical and logical thinking are also cognitive styles that are believed to have grown out of cultural experiences. For example, the Western tradition emphasizes logical examination of opposites in order to choose the correct or favored response. On the other hand, Asian and in particular the Chinese favored the more holistic positions of dialectics in order to unify ideas and form consensus decisions. In more recent times we have seen a great deal of research on authoritarianism and dogmatism as processors of cognition and cognitive style. Respondents who are extremely authoritarian and dogmatic have relatively closed minds to new information and seek thereby to eliminate threat and uncomfortable information.

The current debate is between cognitive styles as general processors of information versus the idea of contextualized cognition. As noted cognitive style refers to some hypothetically underlying processor. The sociohistorical tradition, on the other hands, suggests that cognition is the result of the salience of thinking to the individual and the repetition required by social interaction. The context specific approach tries to understand cognitive processes as initially linked to a specific social context, however, over time this initial process takes on a generalizing role in people's lives. From this perspective cognition occurs within the domain of activity as a result of interaction from which cognitive expertise gradually grows.

Recent research has demonstrating the affect of priming that supports contextual cognition. Priming of respondents occurs in an experiment when a subject is prepared, unknown to him/her self, for some experimental task. For example, a respondent may be primed for either collectivistic or individualistic cognition by asking him/her in what ways he/she is the same or different from the family or cultural group. Such priming causes the subject to be sensitive to appropriate stimuli in the actual experiment. Unknown to the participant the first task is to prepare the respondents for the remaining experimental tasks. Research shows that the affect of priming is similar regardless of cultural group and seems more powerful than the hypothesized cognitive style. The cognitive differences between cultures may therefore be summarized as the result of the frequency of priming or the cultural preparation for particular cultural tasks. Cross-cultural differences in cognition are thought to be a function of practical imperatives. In the final analysis cognitive style and cultural practice both have a role to play and must be accepted as sources for cross-cultural differences in cognition. Overall research supports cultural differences in frequencies of cultural practices related to cognition.

The chapter concludes with a discussion of intelligence, the different cultural definitions, the role of nature versus nurture, sources of bias in testing, and the role of socio-economic differences and the force of education. Research on race and interaction affects shows that it is impossible to know about the variance that can be attributed to nature versus nurture as a source of a person's intelligence. However, psychological tests can be useful and can be transferred cross-culturally with proper safeguards in comparative studies. Finally, general processors of higher order cognition is evaluated cross-culturally including the roles of categorization, memory, mathematical abilities and creativity.

CHAPTER 7

EMOTIONS AND HUMAN HAPPINESS

Universal Expressions and Cultural Values

Emotions provide meaning and color in our lives by informing us about the negative or positive stimuli that affect our well-being. We feel joy in the arrival of new life, and sadness at the life that has passed. Through the emotions we feel we know about the quality of our relationships with others. At our peak experiences in life we can feel complex emotions summarized in the word "happiness." At the same time tragedy visits all lives and corresponding emotions provide the framework for understanding these experiences. Emotions tend to be transitory, and can abruptly change or be replaced by alternate interpretations. It is generally agreed that a biological neurophysiological response platform prepares us to react to stimuli that is either benign or threatening. Our emotions consist of a syndrome of responses that in addition to our subjective feelings also include expressive facial reactions, changes in intonation of voice, the use of gestures, and physiological reactions including faster heart beats and more intense breathing. Emotions also have cognitive aspects as we think about the meaning of what

Cross-Cultural Psychology: Why Culture Matters, pages 175–203.

we feel, and behavioral reactions depending on the nature of the emotion interpreted as either positive or negative.

Although psychopaths may seem devoid of subjective feelings, and people in wartime or other crisis situation suppress inner reactions, emotions are in fact ubiquitous in our lives. Along with other psychological functions emotions evolved because they were functional to survival and helped us react and learn about situations that were benign as well as those that presented a threat to health and well-being. *Ethologists that have conducted comparative species research have found emotions among primates similar to those of humans including those of anger and fear* (De Waal, 2003). However, the fact that humans have also evolved language makes our emotions more complex and differentiated compared to our primate cousins. Furthermore, since we have unique evaluations of the self represented in our thinking processes we can reflect on our behavior. Emotions like shame or guilt are the result of self-reflections and are based on concepts of morality (Gottman & Levenson, 2002; Haidt, 2001).

In summary, any model of emotions must include antecedent stimuli that illicit the reaction. Emotions produce expressive behaviors reflected by changes in our voice or face. We also experience subjective feelings that are typically of a positive or negative valuation, and can observe corresponding physiological reactions in the autonomic and central nervous systems. We are capable of evaluating and thinking about our emotions and may therefore attribute the cause of feelings to self or others. Finally, in our behavioral reactions we may take flight from fear of the stimulus, or approach the object that we love.

From a cross-cultural perspective we need to understand the components of emotions that are invariant across all societies and therefore based on a genetic inheritance common with all humanity. However, human behavior is plastic and culture can modify both the subjective experiences of emotions and also what is considered to be appropriate behavioral expressions. The complexity of human behavior causes the discourse about emotions to be complicated and creates difficulties in cross-cultural comparisons since members of different cultural groups do not all have the same words or descriptions with which to interpret or understand emotions. Because of the language complexities discussed in chapter 5 there is always some ambiguity in all cross-cultural comparative research. However, from the consistency of research results over time emotions that are invariant across cultures can be observed along with culturally specific manifestations. The culturally invariant and the culturally specific in emotional behavior are but two sides of the same coin.

7.1. THE UNIVERSALITY OF EMOTIONS: BASIC NEUROPHYSIOLOGICAL RESPONSES

Emotions are closely connected to specific physiological reactions in the autonomic and central nervous systems. Ekman, Levenson, and Friesen (1983) found that basic emotions produce distinct and discrete signals in the autonomic system. Others have also found specific emotion related responses in the central nervous system (Davidson, Pizzagalli, Nitschke, & Kalin, 2003; Mauss, Levenson, McCarter, Wilhelm, & Gross, 2005). *Research has also demonstrated similar neurophysiological responses for the basic emotions in cross-cultural samples demonstrating their universality* (Tsai & Levenson, 1997).

Researchers in biology and neurosciences have in the past also tried to locate the locus of emotions in certain brain structures (Gazzaniga, 1995). As might be expected it is not an easy process to find the emotion pathway in specific brain locations for complex subjective feelings of anger, sadness or happiness and the biological locus of these emotions are not well understood (Cacioppo & Tassinary, 1990). Nevertheless research has demonstrated convincingly the relationship between emotions and biological processes. Darwin (1998) argued that human behavior evolved from earlier primate ancestors and emotions exists as part of our behavioral repertoire since they serve evolutionary adaptation. In particular emotions serve the function of supporting adaptive fitness by providing important information about our subjective states, our relationships to others, and the emotion stimuli.

Over the years *researchers have concluded that basic emotions (anger, fear, disgust, sadness, happiness, and surprise) are hardwired in the human brain*. Basic emotions are thought to have evolved as part of our genetic inheritance and have certain characteristics in common (Ekman, 1992; Matsumoto & Hwang, 2011). The basic emotions are identified by universally recognized signals that are also present in other primates. As noted these responses produce collateral changes in the autonomic and central nervous systems, are related to distinctive antecedent events, and demonstrate coherence in reactions. Basic emotions are rapid in onset, of brief duration, and are typically appraised automatically.

7.1.1. How we Understand the Emotion of Others: Facial Expressions

In his original research Darwin argued that humans all over the world use exactly the same facial expressions to convey emotions. According to Darwinian Theory facial expressions are a part of our biological inheritance and are adaptive by conveying important emotional information. Darwin also noted that we share with the great apes some of similar facial expressions a finding that support our common evolutionary path with other primates. Ethologists (Snowdon, 2003) have produced evidence for the universality and genetic basis of facial expressions in the primates. For example, there are many morphological similarities between primate and human expressions when evaluated in similar social contexts. Some research found that infant chimpanzee has similar facial expressions as human infants (Ueno, Ueno, & Tomonaga 2004). *Facial expressions provide a communication context to emotions thereby serving adaptive functions in intergroup and interpersonal behavior.* Ekman, (1973) however, noted that the common experiences of human infants might also provide a basis for universal human expressions and that therefore universality can only be inferred from controlled experiments. Universality, however, is supported by the research on human development. The facial musculature necessary for facial expressions is present and functional at birth (Ekman & Oster, 1979). Infants are capable of signaling their emotional states and show interest and attention (Oster, 2005). The presence of universal emotional expressions so early in development is evidence of their biological basis.

Early studies (Ekman, 1972; Izard, 1971) independently pioneered a methodology to investigate the universality of the ability to recognize facial expressions of human emotions. Ekman created a series of photographs of facial expressions thought to represent universal basic emotions recognizable in every culture. Respondents in five countries were presented and asked to provide a label for photographs that corresponded to the six common emotions of happiness, anger fear, disgust, sadness and surprise. Later (Ekman & Friesen, 1986) added contempt to the universally recognized expressions list. The results showed a very broad agreement identifying the same emotional expressions from the photographs among the judges from all cultures. Furthermore there were no significant differences in facial recognition between respondents from the different cultures. However, the respondents in these early studies all came from advanced industrialized societies leading critics to suggest that concordance in agreement might be the result of cultural diffusion in the display of emotion caused by Western movies and other media. The critics concluded that cultural diffusion and not biology contributed to the apparent universality of emotion display.

Ekman and his colleagues conducted another study (Ekman, Sorenson, & Friesen, 1969) employing similar methodology with preliterate tribes of New Guinea in an attempt to find respondents isolated from Western culture. Rather than asking for language labels that might not be available to the respondents Ekman requested that the participants tell a story illustrating the facial expression in the photographs. The results were remarkably similar to the labeling experiments as the stories were concordant with the emotions illustrated in the photographs. Cultural experience moderated responses to a small degree since recognition of emotions for children were very high around 90 percent, but lower for adults (80 percent). However, since these preliterate societies could not have experienced cultural diffusion, or at least only in very limited ways, the results were accepted as confirming the universality of emotions.

Later Ekman and his colleagues asked the tribe members to demonstrate emotions with their own facial expressions and took photographs of these responses. The facial expressions of the tribe members were then shown to American respondents who again correctly labeled the emotions displayed in the new tribal photographs supporting universality. Izard (1971) independently examined the issue of the universality of facial recognition. In general his results supported those found by Ekman and his colleagues. Further, Ekman, Friesen, O'Sullivan, Chan, Diacoyanni-Tarlatzis, Heider, Krause, LeCompte, Pitcairn, Ricci-Bitti, Scherer, Tomita, and Tzavaras (1987) in a study of ten cultures found similar universal recognition of even complex blended emotions

The aforementioned research was based on the assumption that universality can be demonstrated by common cross-cultural agreement in the labeling of or story telling about photographic stimuli. However, will people spontaneously display these basic emotions and are these reactions also universal? A study comparing responses in Japan and the U.S. (Ekman, 1972) exposed respondents to very stressful stimuli while taping their facial reactions. The results showed that the respondents from both countries showed similar facial reactions to the stressful stimuli. The universality of expression and recognition of emotions have now been documented in many research programs and is commonly accepted (Elfenbein & Ambady, 2002; Matsumoto, Keltner, Shiota, Frank, & O'Sullivan, 2008). The basic emotions are expressed very rapidly and apparently with automatic appraisal and little cognitive awareness and are thought to be the product of evolution. The social context can modify responses, but without contextual differences facial expressions are universally similar.

Further, the emotions expressed are recognized in all cultures. Matsumoto (2001) reviewed 27 research reports of facial expressions and found universal recognition of the basic emotions. The meta-analysis reported by Elfenbein and Ambady (2002) also supported the universal recognition of emotion signals produced by facial expressions. It seems indisputable that such common agreement would not be found independent of culture unless the facial expressions were in fact universal and genetically based. Further research has expanded the list of emotions that are universally recognized (Matsumoto & Ekman, 2004; Tracy & Robins, 2004). These studies together support the assertion that humans innately possess basic emotions as part of a genetically determined inheritance.

7.1.2.   The Effect of Language and Learning: Criticisms of Studies Supporting Genetically Based Facial Recognition

Birdwhistell (1970) argued that emotional expressions are learned in the process of socialization. Later Russell (1994) noted that the idea of universality was itself imprecise, and could not be completely divorced from the effects of cultural diffusion. In particular he was critical of the lack of control for language. When respondents had a free choice in terms and descriptive sentences facial recognition of emotion tends to be lower than those employing the Ekman model. According to Russell only very broad cluster of emotional terms produced similar results to those found in the original Ekman studies. The main criticism of the Ekman model is that research using photographs tells us little about facial expressions occurring naturally in social relationships and fail to take into account the social context of emotions. Russell argued that emotion categories are somewhat dependent on unique features of language, and facial emotion recognition can only be understood within broad dimensional categories similar to those found for the semantic differential by Osgood, Suci, and Tannenbaum (1957), but not by using narrow emotional labels of the basic emotions (Russell, 1991).

Izard (1994) in responding to Russell, however, noted that research on innate facial expressions is about much more than verbal descriptions, and has been observed in infants long before language had any effects. Russell's criticisms, Izard maintains, are about the universality of semantic descriptions, but not the relationship of facial expressions to biology. Further, Ekman (1994) argued that universality in recognition of emotions does not require perfect concordance in judgment, only statistically significant agreement. The matching of words to reactions that are neurocultural cannot be expected to be perfect. Later, Ekman (Ekman, 1998, 1999; Sabini & Maury, 2005) wrote that studies supporting the learned basis of facial emotional expressions were primarily anecdotal and lacked scientific credibility. Others (Haidt & Keltner, 1999) presented photographs of the basic emotions to respondents in India and the U.S. and found results that supported Ekman and his colleagues. Alternative methodologies have also been employed in studying the development of facial expressions in childhood, and other researchers have examined the similarity between human facial reactions with the expressions of nonhuman primates. Both lines of research have supported the conclusion that emotional expressions are hardwired from birth (Oster, 2005; Parr, Waller, Vick, & Bard, 2007).

Nevertheless researchers have disagreed about the source of basic emotional facial expressions, whether they are learned spontaneously through the mechanism of social learning or are automatic and dependent only on biology. Do universally recognized facial expressions occur because of similar learning processes across cultures or do they reflect biological constants. Some researchers argue that universality could result from similar social learning processes as children learn to express emotions spontaneously and automatically from watching others. From this perspective children learn to smile at happy events, because they see others doing so and experience reinforcement for context correct responses (Feldman & Russell, 1999; Fernandez-Dols & Ruiz-Belda, 1997).

7.1.3. The Definitive Answer to the Source of the Facial Expressions of Emotions: Biology is the Determinant

Whether learning has a role, or whether facial expressions of emotions are fundamentally caused by biology can be answered by a study with blind people, especially in respondents born blind who have had no opportunity to observe the expression of others. If respondents who are congenitally blind (and therefore have no possibility for visual observations and the social learning of facial emotional expressions) show similar expressions as sighted respondents such results must be accepted as evidence of their inherited nature.

Matsumoto and Willingham (2006) studied the spontaneous facial expressions of sighted athletes who won gold, silver, bronze or were fifth place winners in the judo competition at the 2004 Athens Olympic Games. The 84 athletes from 35 countries represented a very culturally diverse group and were photographed after their matches and during the medal ceremonies. The athlete's expressions were recorded immediately by using high-speed film when they knew they had won a medal (or not). The photographs were taken in a naturalistic and spontaneous field setting and recorded the athletes' expressions at what was obviously a salient emotional time. The results showed no significant differences in emotional expression between the cultures represented in the competition supporting the universality of emotional facial expressions.

In the second study (Matsumoto & Willingham, 2009) examined the facial expressions of congenitally blind and non-congenitally blind athletes who participated from 23 cultures in the 2004 Para-Olympic games in Athens. These athletes were recorded in the same way as the sighted athletes in the 2006 report. No differences in facial reactions were found between the congenital and non-congenital blind athletes, and their reaction results were therefore combined. The concordance between the sighted and blind athletes was nearly perfect with correlations for facial muscle behaviors varying from .94 for recordings made at match completion, to .98 for when the athletes received the medal, and .96 for facial expressions at the podium. *This similarity between sighted and blind spontaneous facial expressions offers definitive support that these reactions are genetically coded and not socially learned and is universal in all cultures.*

7.1.4. Universal Agreement and Cultural Emphasis in Other Emotion Constructs

Human emotions are responses of the whole person and involve various components. This consideration points to both innate components discussed above, but also to the possibility of cultural modifications in the experiencing of emotion. With our common evolutionary heritage it is easy to understand that much about emotions is similar across all cultures. At the same time cultures modify some aspects of emotion especially those components affected by cognition (Frijda, 1986, 1993, 1994; Lang, 1995). In recent research an attempt was made to distinguish different components of emotion and several cross-cultural factors have been identified (Mesquita, Frijda, & Scherer, 1997). Research has been conducted on components that elicit emotions also called antecedents. Other research has examined appraisals that are the evaluations of the antecedents. Physiological reactions as noted have also been identified in both the autonomic and central nervous systems.

7.1.4.1. Antecedents of Emotions

Research on different aspects of emotion has generally supported the universality of these related constructs. Antecedents of emotion refer to the events or themes that elicit the emotion. For example accomplishing important personal or group goals may elicit happiness. When people are frustrated from the blockage of goal attainment the emotion is often anger. Sadness occurs from the loss of a loved one or loss in something fundamental to our lives. Disgust can occur in relationships with others or from self-evaluation when we are repulsed by our own behavior or that of others. Fear occurs from specific objects or events that threaten well-being and about which we are helpless. More complex emotions like shame, contempt or surprise also have distinct elicitors that derive from self-evaluation, moral superiority, and sudden or novel stimuli.

Scherer (1997a,b) conducted a large-scale study that involved nearly 3000 participants from 37 countries. The respondents were asked how they felt when they last thought about the six basic emotions after which these subjective feelings were coded into broad antecedent categories. The results showed the same antecedent categories producing basic emotions occurred in all cultures and that culture-specific events were not required in order to code the antecedents. The researchers also found concordance in the relative frequency that antecedent events produced specific emotions. Happiness was frequently a product of relationships with other people in all cultures. Relationships also played role in anger when associated with injustice, and sadness in relationships lost due to death.

Boucher and Brandt (1981) asked respondents in Malaysia and the United States to identify the situations that produced the basic emotions. A total of 96 elicitors of emotion were collected. When U.S. participants were asked to rate the antecedents and identify the corresponding emotions they correctly identified the antecedents. This was the outcome regardless of whether the emotion situations were produced by the Malaysian or American respondents. This research was later replicated using different cultural groups (Brandt & Boucher, 1986). Informers from the U.S., Korea and Samoa were asked to write about situations that produced the basic emotions of happiness, sadness, anger, disgust and surprise. The stories that were produced subsequently had all cultural referent material removed and were then presented to the respondents. The results showed that the antecedents of emotions were similar in all three samples. However, as might be expected some cross-cultural differences remained where cultures have different cognitive interpretations of the emotion eliciting situations (Mesquita et al., 1997). For example, in some cultures aspects of the supernatural are more salient and may cause fear reactions whereas these antecedents are not present or less salient in other societies.

7.1.4.2. *Vocalization and Intonation in Emotional Expression*

People use intonation to emphasize subjective feelings and as an indication of the intensity of emotional involvement. Do intonations follow universal rules so different language speakers can still recognize emotional meaning in the language of other speakers? In one study (McCluskey, Albas, Niemi, Cuevas, & Ferrer, 1975) the researchers used a brief phrase in Dutch expressed in nine different emotional tones that included disgust, surprise, shame, joy, fear, contempt, sadness, anger, and a neutral tone. The vocal expression was used in a comparison between Dutch, Taiwanese, and Japanese respondents. In nearly all cases the various emotions were recognized at better than chance level from the intonation alone. The Dutch sample did respond at a higher level of recognition suggesting that some information loss occurred from linguistic differences between the three samples.

Other studies have yielded similar results to those found for facial recognition of emotions. In one study (Albas, McCluskey, & Albas, 1976) speech samples were collected from English and Cree language speakers that expressed emotions of happiness, sadness, love and anger. Using an electronic filter the expressions were made unintelligible semantically leaving the intonation intact. Results showed that speakers from both language groups recognized the emotions expressed, although recognition was better in their own language. These results would appear to lend some support to the universality of emotional intonation, although also a supporting role for cultural linguistic information.

7.1.4.3. *Appraisal of Emotion*

Emotions are experienced rapidly and the antecedents are more or less automatically evaluated. Frijda (1993, 1994) found similar appraisal dimensions in the cultures investigated related to change or novelty, to experiencing control or lack of control, to whether the event was pleasant or unpleasant, and what or who was responsible. A high degree of similarity across cultures suggested similar appraisal processes occurs independent of culture. The basic emotions appear to be appraised the same way, an assertion also supported in other research (Roseman, Dhawan, Rettek, Nadidu, & Thapa, 1995).

The appraisal of emotions were closely examined in the Scherer (1997a) study where the respondents were asked to think about an emotional experience connected to the basic emotions and then asked to appraise it whether the event was pleasant, frustrated goal attainment, or otherwise affected their lives. Between the basic emotions strong differences in appraisals might be expected, but within each basic emotion the appraisal patterns were very similar. Overall there is strong support for the universality of the appraisal of emotion, but also room for cultural affects based on interpretations and possibly linguistic differences.

In one study Scherer and Wallbott (1994) asked the participants to rate emotional components including feelings, physiological changes, motor reactions, and expressive behaviors that occurred when they experienced the basic emotions. The researchers observed major differences in subjective responses between the basic emotions that was not dependent on culture as there were more similarities than differences between cultural groups. The coherence in subjective responses offers strong support for universality. Coherent responses between various components including intonation and physiological responses show that they are related in meaningful ways (Matsumoto, 2006a,b).

The appraisal of emotions is linked to causality. Cultural values interact so individuals from collectivistic cultures are more likely to attribute the cause for negative emotions to themselves, whereas individualistic respondents in the U.S. are more likely to attribute causality to others. When Japanese respondents are sad they are more likely to see the source within themselves, whereas Americans attribute causality to other people for a variety of emotions including sadness, joy and shame. Japanese attribute causality to fate that promotes the acceptance that nothing can be done to improve the situation. Negative emotions for Americans (in particular fear) elicit behavior to correct or improve the situation (Matsumoto, Kudoh, Scherer, & Wallbott, 1988).

7.2. THE ROLE OF CULTURE IN EMOTIONAL REACTIONS.

As we have noted cultural and biological influences on emotions are but two sides of the same coin. All humans have an undeniable evolutionary link demonstrating our common heritage that is further supported in the separate evolution of language and socioculture. This chapter has also demonstrated a biological foundation in the universal basic emotions and its several components. As Averill (1980) stated biological and cultural theories are not really incompatible since they represent different aspects of the same emotional and behavioral phenomena. In Averill's view emotions are socially constructed transitory roles determined by what is acceptable in a given culture. From this perspective similar events may have culturally dependent meanings since the antecedents that produce emotions are interpreted by language and cognition.

Objective comparison between cultures is difficult because emotion labels that are at times not easily translated from one language to another. Some languages have a number of words for an emotional domain that is represented by a single label in the English language. Cultures that have many emotion labels can produce finer discriminations and therefore more complex emotion meanings. The presence of many emotion labels may also reflect the salience of the emotion in the culture. The people of Tahiti evidently do not have a word for sadness (Levy, 1984) so perhaps that is a less salient emotion in their culture. Labels that are important to emotional descriptions in some societies appear missing in other cultures (Russell, 1991). When labels are absent or present that difference can reflect the relative salience of the relevant emotion in the cultural discourse.

While there are some emotional labels or words missing in some societies there are also universal emotion terms present in all cultures (Wierzbicka, 1999). Overall there is support for emotion universals, but also for the influence of culture as mediated by language. For example all languages have a word for "feel" according to Wierzbicka that can be described in terms of good or bad. Likewise all cultures, as we have seen, have facial expressions that can also be linked with emotions described as good or bad. However, while the presence of universals cannot be denied, we must remember that the descriptive labels of emotions are formed through cultural discourse and may be an indicator of the cultural salience of that emotion. For Wierzbicka human emotions are not inherent, but constructed through the use of language and cognition. Markus and Kitayma (1994a) suggested that each culture has key cultural concepts and ideology used in the socialization of children that determine self-conceptions and worldviews. These central ideas affect the experiencing and display of emotions.

7.2.1. The Display of Emotions

Culture has especially a dominant effect on the display of emotions. For example, not "loosing face" is an important cultural determinant of emotional expression in Asian societies and to a lesser extent also in other cultures. "Losing face" refers to the anxiety of being evaluated negatively from some apparent breach of cultural values or self-referent expectations. Cultures have specific norms that govern the display of emotions in facial expressions. Some cultures require members to remain impassive and not reveal their true feelings and for participants to regulate their facial expressions according to the social context. In one important study (Ekman, 1973) students were shown stressful films either in isolation or in the presence of others. When the respondents watched the movie alone it produced highly similar facial expressions connected to the specific basic emotions of fear, disgust and sadness in both Japanese and American participants. However, when in the presence of others Japanese students displayed significantly fewer negative expressions compared to the U.S. participants. Americans, on the other hand, continued to display negative emotions when others were present. These results suggest that even basic universal emotional expressions are modified by cultural values and by what is considered appropriate emotional behavior in the social context. When in the presence of others Japanese respondents smiled when exposed to the stressful stimuli a response encouraged by cultural values of courtesy and by the desire not to offend the experimenter.

Ekman and Friesen (1969) suggested several ways by which cultural display rules modify emotional expression. Members of a culture may be encouraged to display more or less emotion than truly felt. People in a cultural group can also regulate emotions to the point that nothing is displayed in facial expressions. At times members of a culture may wish to conceal feelings for a variety of reasons and display a different emotion by putting on a mask. Culture also expects conformity and may in some cases encourage the display of socially appropriate but fake emotions even when members do not feel anything.

Self-report studies confirm these cultural restraints on emotional display. In one study comparing respondents in the U.S. with participants in Hungary and Poland the subjects were asked to rate appropriate expressions for the basic emotions when alone, in the company of ingroup members like family or friends, and with strangers. The results supported cultural differences in the display of emotions with the U.S. sample more open in the display of negative emotions compared to the respondents from Eastern Europe who believed it more appropriate to display positive emotions. In conclusion all cultural groups experience similar emotions, but differences in display between cultures are governed by social expectations and appropriateness.

7.2.2. Individualistic Versus Collectivistic Cultures: Display Rules in Emotion Intensity and Negativity Ratings

Although criticized by some (Matsumoto, 1999) the collectivism-individualism cultural dimension has experienced broad acceptance in cross-cultural psychology. The role of the self as related to relationships with others is especially a salient psychological component experienced differentially in the two cultural value dimensions. Saving the face of others is important in collectivistic cultures, and preserving face is achieved by suppressing or withholding negative reactions. Cultural dimensions of individualism-collectivism affect the perception of negative emotions and suppress or enhance the intensity of emotional display.

Research has supported the presence of cultural effects when raters from individualistic societies are compared in evaluating the intensity of emotions with those from collectivistic countries. Asian respondents rated emotions at lower levels of intensity compared to Western samples. Matsumoto (1992a) studied Japanese and American respondents examining their reactions to photographs displaying the basic emotions. The results showed that the Japanese respondents rated the intensity of negative emotions lower compared to American participants. The explanation is that in Japan the display of negative emotions is discouraged as they are considered disruptive of social relations. Recognition of negativity is lower when negative emotions are not customarily displayed in society. On the other hand, the U.S. respondents were more open to expressions of negativity and therefore better able to recognize these in facial photographs. Cultural dimensions especially those of collectivism-individualism, were thought responsible for differences in the perception of intensity of emotion.

In recent years the study of display rules has expanded significantly (McConatha, Lightner, & Deaner, 1994; Matsumoto, Yoo, Fontaine, Anguas-Wong, Arriola, Ataca, Bond, et al., 2008). Matsumoto et al studied 5000 respondents from 30 countries using a Display Rules Assessment Inventory. The researchers asked what the respondents would do if seven basic emotions were felt in some 42 different situations. The major results supported the idea that the close intimacy of relationships provided the safe environment that allowed people to freely express emotions regardless of culture, and such relationships were also characterized by tolerance for a variety of behaviors that were less tolerated among strangers or acquaintances.

Collectivistic cultures, however, differed from individualistic societies by encouraging members to display more positive emotions and inhibit negative expressions toward the ingroup. That finding is consistent with the emphasis on maintaining harmony as a high cultural value. Individualistic cultures, on the other hand, produced more negative emotions and members displayed fewer positive feelings toward members of the ingroup since harmony is less valued and members of these societies think it appropriate to display negative emotions. Anyone observing the discourtesies of political debate in the U.S. would find no difficulty in concurring with these display rules differences. On the other hand, collectivistic cultures encourage more negative emotions toward outgroups because, in the view of Matsumoto et al, there is a need to strengthen ingroup relations by making a clear distinction between ingroup and outgroup members.

Cultural effects on emotion display are also found in the study of ethnic groups in the U.S. Although the findings are somewhat complex the Asians participants rated the display of contempt as less appropriate than Caucasian respondents consistent with the aforementioned cultural values of harmony and courtesy in collectivistic cultures (Matsumoto, 1992b). In conclusion research supports the idea that all humans possess the same inherited emotional template of the basic emotions, but how they are exhibited depend on socialization in culturally defined display rules.

7.2.3. Personal Space and Gestures: Cultural Influences in Non-Verbal Communication

All societies define some space around the individual as personal, and only those invited to enter that area can do so without causing discomfort to the other person. Culture is a determinant of the amount of personal space required when communicating with others. Citizens of countries in Latin America, southern Europe and Arabia require less personal space and people stand very close when conversing (Hall, 1966). People from northern Europe and the U.S., on the other hand, need more personal distance and become uncomfortable when others invade uninvited the subjective personal space. The cultural reasons for these differences are not well documented, but are related perhaps to population density. When large families live together in a small physical space this environment demands close personal contact and that space requirement is habituated and translated to other relationships. Personal space varies between cultures, and within cultures depends on class differences that produce varying modes of habituation.

Emotions evolved to communicate important information (Fridlund, 1997). Gestures are forms of nonverbal communication and when used in bargaining can be considered a primitive form of language. Some gestures are universally understood, for example, the gesture "to come here" is probably understood all over the world, as is the general wave of the hand as a form of friendly greeting, and the open-handed military salute that evolved to express non-hostile intentions. However, not all gestures are uniformly used or understood. As noted in Bulgaria the head movement indicating agreement is opposite to that of other countries supporting a cultural basis for that signal. Gestures can easily become a source of confusion and misunderstanding between different cultural representatives. For example, the gesture signifying OK in the U.S. means "money" in Japan, "zero" in France, and in Russia, Brazil and Greece it is vulgar and sexually insulting (Ting-Toomey, 1999).

However, there are universal gestures like the shrug suggesting that some expressions may have an innate foundation (Argyle, 1988). Common cross-cultural gestures are also based on our shared human physiology and the need to express motion within the restriction our bodies. We should remember, however, that cultures that co-evolved can also be expected to share many symbolic gestures that derive from common cultural roots. Cultural differences in gestures are more likely discovered in the frequency of usage (Graham & Argyle, 1975). People living in countries like Italy support well established stereotypes that they gesture excitedly in conversation, whereas members of other cultures use gestures more modestly.

7.2.4. Cross-Cultural Differences in Evaluating Emotions in Other People

Although the respondents in the Ekman type model studies consistently recognized emotion in others none of the studies reported perfect agreement between cross-cultural respondents. Some studies have in fact yielded reliable cross-cultural differences in the recognition rates of different emotions. Matsumoto (1989) correlated the emotion recognition data from 15 cultures with the Hofstede cultural dimensions and found that individualism correlated significantly with the intensity ratings for fear and anger. These results support the idea that individualistic cultures are more open to negative emotions and therefore better at recognizing these compared to respondents from collectivistic cultures. Cross-cultural differences were also supported by the results of the Matsumoto (1989) study comparing Japanese with American respondents. In that study the U.S. respondents were more effective in identifying negative emotions like anger, fear and disgust, but did not differ from the Japanese in identifying positive emotions like happiness. A meta-analysis also found that emotion recognition was dependent on culture with some groups recognizing happiness better compared to other ethnic respondents (Schimmack, 1996).

Since members of all cultural groups experience emotion living with ingroup members it is not surprising to find an ingroup advantage in emotion recognition. People are somewhat better at recognizing emotions in members of their own cultural group compared to the expressions that occur among members of other groups. If these results are reliable it would suggest that culturally dependent but subtle signals are associated with emotion expression leading to better ingroup identification (Elfenbein,

Mandal, Ambady, Harizuka, & Kumar, 2004). These differences have been described as emotion dialects found in reliable differences in emotion recognition by members of specific cultures (Elfenbein & Ambady, 2002).

7.3. THE CULTURAL CONTEXT OF EMOTIONAL COMMUNICATION

Emotions are important to our happiness and well-being. Therapeutic work with disturbed or ill patients often centers on bringing a balance to their emotional life and helping them learn to accept and regulate emotions. As people we often ask about the emotional well-being of those that are close to us or people we come in contact with at work. Even the simple "how are you doing" that is so common in American vernacular is an inquiry into the emotional well-being of the person we greet. Perhaps one reason we ask is that we cannot always tell from facial expressions alone the emotional well-being of others. Moreover, the fact that such inquiries are ubiquitous strongly suggests the central role of emotions in our psychological life.

Emotions are precisely suppressed because they convey in powerful ways the psychological state of our inner that is less regulated by culture. The role of psychotherapy is focused on helping the patient to freely express important emotions, and learning how to appropriately convey this information to others in their lives. The utilization of training or counseling groups as vehicles for therapy and communication are aimed at teaching participants to express feelings appropriately and at the same time learn to listen more carefully to the emotional expressions of others. Recognizing emotions accurately is considered an important way to improve communication in industrial work groups. The underlying idea is that communication between people is disrupted unless participants feel free to convey their impressions and feelings honestly and are sensitive to the feelings of relevant others.

Culture impacts the conceptualization of emotions and the regulation and expression of emotional responses. However, although not all cultures have a word for emotion members of all societies manage to convey emotional feelings (Russell, 1991). Still as we saw in chapter 5 language places limits on our understanding by the presence or absence of words that convey finer points in conceptualization. Cross-cultural understanding may depend on the presence or absence of language to convey our emotions and thoughts. Cultures conceive of emotions and regulate the display of expressions in different ways necessitating sensitivity in cross-cultural communication. The fact that emotions are conceived differentially and are dependent on cultural values in turn shapes our behavior and our emotional life.

The varying focus on the self and relationships in individualistic and collectivistic cultures is one important cross-cultural difference. In the Western world emotions are considered self-relevant subjective experiences that tell us important information about our status and self-defined goals. Other cultures centers emotional meaning in the relationship between people. In collectivistic cultures emotions are often explained in terms of relationships to significant others in the family or work place, rather than being defined in personal subjective reactions as in individualistic societies. These cultural differences in understandings suggest that emotion conceptions are not invariant but constructed by the individual over the course of socialization

Kitayama and Markus (1994a) explained the cultural shaping of emotional life as determined in part by the ideology of society that defines what is good and moral. Ideology is sifted through the customs and norms of society and enforced by the educational system, legal principles, and norms of social interaction. The salience of the core cultural ideas is produced through experience in the home, in education, work settings, and in religious communities. These cultural influences all combine to produce habitual ways of expressing emotions with concomitants in human physiology, in the expressions of facial responses, and in our subjective feelings. Culture also impacts the specific actions related to our emotions. This comprehensive model understands emotional life by examining the collective context (including linguistic concepts) expressed in the economic and sociopolitical system. Culture also has lasting influences on emotional expression from the largely unconscious processes shaped by norms and social institutions. Nearly all societies encourage the positive emotional expressions that define cultural identity. However, people are also individuals and even in the most regimented and conformist society personal dispositions also contribute to emotional expression.

As noted the biological basis of emotions has been found everywhere and emotions tend to be produced by similar antecedent events in all cultures. *Cultures, however, determine to a large extent the way emotions are experienced through the appraisal process that is culturally dependent, and through display rules that determine how emotions may be expressed in the company of others.* Culture also affects emotional life through the presence or absence of linguistically relevant concepts. The basic emotions that are ubiquitous should be thought of as a template upon which culture write more specific meanings through socialization, norms and social institutions. The universality of the basic emotions does in no way contradict the important role of culture in defining the specific emotional experience that is culturally dependent.

7.4. TOWARD A POSITIVE PSYCHOLOGY OF EMOTION: HAPPINESS AND WELL-BEING

Recent years have seen an increased interest in building a psychology of positive human functioning (Seligman & Csikszentmihalyi, 2000). Cantril (1965) did some of the early surveys on happiness in the world, and data from these and other large-scale cross-cultural studies are now deposited in the World Database of Happiness (Veenhoven, 2011). As might be expected there is no universally accepted definition of happiness independent of culture (Harper, Guilbault, Tucker, & Austin, 2007). Nevertheless, happiness consists of both cognitive and affective components identified by the degree to which pleasure dominates in life experiences, and whether basic human needs and wants are met (Veenhoven, 2011). However, pleasure and life satisfaction (meeting the needs and wants of life) are not independent variables and both must be considered in an evaluation of overall happiness (Haller & Hadler, 2006).

Happiness is ubiquitous and experienced to some degree everywhere since we all prefer pleasure and life satisfaction. However, culture determines what is considered to be pleasant and how to satisfy needs (Kitayama & Markus, 2000). Individualistic and collectivistic cultures have different understandings of happiness. In Western cultures happiness is connected to personal achievement and reaching important personally relevant goals, whereas studies in East Asia show that happiness there is perceived to be a consequence of social harmony and positive relationships (Uchida, Norasakkunkit, & Kitayama 2004). Self-esteem lies at the core of happiness and personal well-being in the West whereas self-esteem is less salient in collectivistic societies (Diener & Diener, 1995). *Culture shapes our understanding of the very meaning of happiness whether it is to be found in social harmony or more in the self-defined well-being of the individual.*

7.4.1. Methodological Issues in Definitions of Happiness and Well-Being

The measurement of the well-being construct has presented real challenges to researchers despite the centrality of happiness in human life (Cummins & Lau, 2011). What constitutes well-being is dependent on scientific disciplines, nevertheless having sufficient money is seen as essential to well-being in economics, to good health in medicine, and to broader definitions being offered by the social sciences. Separate measures have been developed to study objective sources of well-being, as well as measuring subjective aspects. The Human Development Index (UNDP, 2007/2008) focuses on tangible variables like wealth and standards of living that define the quality of life. These objective measures, however, do not assess subjective aspects of how people feel about their lives. Furthermore, there is no one-to-one relationship between objective and subjective happiness measures since some people can subjectively feel poorly even if they score high on health or wealth. Of the two sources of happiness, the subjective is more important. A person can possess all the riches in the world, but still be depressed.

A major methodological issue is the large number of instruments developed to measure the happiness construct. The presence of so many measures in the literature reflects a lack of common agreement of what constitutes happiness or subjective well-being, and the multiple measures index quite different aspects of the construct (Diener, 2006). Latin Europeans have been assessed as less happy northern Germanic peoples (Brulé, & Veenhoven, 2012). Perhaps the words used to assess happiness have different connotations in Latin versus Germanic languages. Still an estimate 80 percent of the average happiness in nations can be attributed to objective social economic characteristics. Happiness has been used as an umbrella construct to reflect a person's level of contentment, satisfaction, fulfillment, and even joy (Zwolinski, 2011). However, in much of the literature happiness is seen as a temporary emotional state caused by positive emotional experiences. Researchers need a construct that is reliable and stable over time defined as mood happiness, however some researchers have settled on the term "subjective well-being" as a suitable construct.

Investigators have argued about the existence of a genetic basis of subjective well-being similar to that considered for the optimism bias proposed in chapter 4. From this perspective subjective well-being is seen as managed by a homeostatic system that includes dispositional aspects like the ability to adapt to challenges and positive reflections produced by selective attention. Subjective well-being is also managed through the utilization of money and the presence of close supportive relationships that shield the individual from adversity (Cummins, 2003). However, since subjective mechanisms of well-being are ubiquitous most respondents give upbeat descriptions of their lives wherever the issue has been investigated. Baring serious adverse conditions most humans possess a homeostatically protected mood dominated by personal contentment (Cummins, 2010). The positive mood is generally stable and considered by Cummins to be genetically determined.

Since all people suffer adversity what keeps the homeostasis of subjective well-being steady? Cummins and Lau (2011) argue that both internal and external buffers are in place to help the individual maintain stable positive moods. External buffers are considered the first line of defense and include as noted above the presence of close relationships and money. Psychological research has demonstrated the ubiquitous value of close personal relationships to well-being (Sarason, Sarason, & Pierce, 1990). The support we obtain from close relationships can help overcome many adverse conditions and sustain subjective well-being even in adversity. Also while money cannot buy happiness it allows the rich to be more comfortable even when suffering from negative conditions like poor health. Poor people all over the world do not have this buffer and suffer more severe consequences to well-being in adversity. Money serves as a buffer since it is also a resource for better health care or can buy useful diversions like luxuries or vacations to help escape negative reality.

To protect stable positive moods humans also possess internal buffers. Since happiness in the West is connected to achievement, internal buffers help people think differently about personal failures and minimize their impact in life. Often the real impact of suffering is buffered by these devices through religious beliefs that assure the victim of a better afterlife existence and eternal life for the loved one whose death is mourned. In these ways reality is cognitively restructured and perhaps suffering on reflection can be seen as a positive outcome. If a child died young parents might say something to the effect that he was too good for this life, and now is in a "better world."

7.4.2. Sources of Well-Being

Although money may not buy happiness there are consistent associations between the quality attained in life and happiness. Happiness is higher where members of society enjoy basic norms of well-being including social security, healthcare, political rights, and also material well-being (Ott, 2005b; Ouweneel, 2002; Ouweneel & Veenhoven, 1990; Veenhoven, 1995). Where people enjoy norms of well-being people also expect to longer lives and experience less anxiety. Norms of well-being also produce considerable differences between countries in happiness. While cultures may interpret happiness differentially dependent on language and values, material and social inequality plays a role in relative unhappiness.

In collectivistic cultures individually based happiness is less important compared to the well-being of family and society. On the other hand in the U.S. there is a bias toward self-enhancement that can cause an overestimation of happiness and self-serving achievements reported in the literature (Suh, 2000). The higher happiness scores reported by U.S. respondents are more the result of social norms supporting positive self-regard that distorts real differences in happiness scores (Argyle, 2001). Asian participants from countries that are more relationship oriented report less happiness and joy when compared to U.S. and Australian participants (Eid & Diener, 2001). The higher positive self-reports in individualistic societies compared to participants in collectivistic countries are therefore less meaningful since they reflect distortions produced by normative pressures.

7.4.3. The Trending of Happiness Scores and Economic Crises and Transitions

Studies of industrialized societies demonstrate that most people are happy (Diener & Diener, 1996). Over long periods these societies have experienced improvements in the norms of well-being, but also serious interruptions from war and other disasters. Research in less developed societies also found that the vast majority of respondents (84 percent) reported being happy. Nevertheless there is little data from poor or war ravaged countries, and whether results from these regions would report happiness at these levels is suspect. Happiness as we have seen is linked to meeting basic human needs that include basic security as well as material well-being rarely present in deprived countries.

Research has found rising levels of happiness in the world. Happiness reports indicate increasing levels over time and for most people. In studies that included 90 % of the world's population, happiness increased in 45 of the 52 countries investigated. However, most of this happiness data was collected before the Great Recession (Inglehart, Foa, Peterson, & Welzel, 2008). Within these trends there are consistent relationships between happiness and normative well-being. In countries characterized by broad economic well-being, freedom and social justice people not only live longer but also report more happiness (Veenhoven, 2005). *Other research has supported the importance of material well-being to happiness.* Stevenson and Wolfers (2008) demonstrated a clear link between economic growth and happiness. In another review Deaton (2008) found that people in richer countries reported more happiness. It seems uncontroversial that income is a significant factor in happiness, although other factors of well-being such as individual liberty and social justice are salient for personal growth and happiness. However, we live in times of socio-economic crises and whether these reports are valid over time remains to be seen. The economic insecurity of the peoples of the world may well be reflected in a downward trend in happiness not surprising given the relationship of economic well-being to happiness.

Happiness and well-being has positive consequences in other domains of life. A meta-analysis of 225 studies showed that happy people are more fortunate in love relationships. Happy people also develop significant health benefits compared to the unhappy, and do better in reaching career goals. The range of positive consequences of happiness is broad as happy people are more likely to get involved in their communities, live longer, and have better marriages (Lyubomirsky, King, & Diener, 2005).

7.4.4. The Impact of Culture on Happiness and Subjective Well-Being

It is difficult to make cross-cultural comparisons in the first instance because translations of relevant concepts are not necessarily accurate and at times difficult. Finding the equivalence of terms in cross-cultural research on happiness and well-being requires more time. However, a different but more serious problem is the culturally based response biases in research. As noted typically respondents from the collectivistic societies of East Asia respond with lower scores on measures of subjective well-being since they are influenced by modesty and culturally influenced views of what the scales represents (Lau, Cummins, & McPherson, 2005). These lower values may represent nothing more than methodological problems from different interpretations of response categories, and therefore not reflect meaningful differences between cultures.

However, happiness is understood within the framework of cultural values. The primary difference between Western cultures compared to Asian or African societies in the focus on the individual versus the group. In Western societies happiness is achieved by meeting self-relevant goals and the social recognition of personal standing. In collectivistic societies happiness is connected to the well-being of one's family or cultural group (Harper, Guilbaut, Tucker, & Austin, 2007). Happiness cannot be achieved except within the framework of these cultural givens since what is considered a source of happiness in some societies may have little or no affect in others. Oishi and Diener (2001) investigated happiness in respondents that came from European or Asian backgrounds. The participants were asked to list five goals that they desired to accomplish in the coming month. A month later the respondents were asked to rate satisfaction in goal achievement. The sample with European background reported more happiness from the achievement of independent goals, whereas in the Asian sample satisfaction and happiness increased when more interdependent goals were reached. In other words, members of Western societies achieve happiness by reaching self-relevant goals, whereas respondents from Asian cultures seek happiness by contributing to social harmony.

Cultures differ greatly in values and behavior and it is therefore logical to expect a cultural impact on subjective well-being. Life experiences are understood within the framework of cultural values, and even very similar experiences may produce different cognitive interpretations and behavioral reactions. Cultural values are often expressed through the medium of religion that is ubiquitous in the world. There are significant differences in the values espoused by religion. Some religions teach acceptance of the conditions of life, and others teach righteous struggle and holy war. Some religions demand monogamy whereas others not only approve of polygamy, but consider it the natural and approved way to live. It is therefore not surprising that religion may have a positive impact on well-being in some cultures, but a negative relationship in others (Lavric & Flere, 2008).

Cultures differ in the level of support offered to the mentally ill and physically disabled that in turn minimize or create stress affecting well-being for patients and families. In some cultures it is considered a shame to have a disabled child, and families must make efforts not to expose that shame to society. In other cultures like Western Europe and the United States society provides many valuable resources for the mentally or physically challenged, and most importantly laws and norms of equal treatment that reduces the psychological burden on the family. However, even within the U.S. there are ethnic differences in the amount of social support that white and Latino families offer for the disabled (Magana & Smith, 2006). The devotion of the extended family is stronger in Latino communities and mothers report less negative consequences from care giving for disabled family members.

Quality of life and well-being must be understood as a consequence of both objective and subjective factors. However, comparisons between cultures are difficult for the reasons discussed above. Comparisons of subjective well-being are difficult considering the interaction of cultural values and objective living standards. Nevertheless measures of subjective well-being are useful in tracking the effectiveness of social interventions in times of great change that is accelerating in the world.

Finally, there are individual factors that influence happiness within cultural frameworks. Happiness fluctuates somewhat between individuals because it is also influenced by dispositional variables and personal resources. The temperament of some people makes happiness more or less likely. Temperaments characterized by agreeableness produce more rewarding social acceptance affecting well-being (Lykken & Tellegen, 1996). Individuals also differ in the level of positive illusions that conflict with reality. Some people believe they can shape future events when these happenings are beyond the individuals' capacity to control. Some people are just poor in predicting outcomes and consequently make negative decisions affecting happiness (Haybron, 2008).

7.4.5. Creating Social Policies that Promote Well-Being

If well-being is the overarching goal of life then all relevant organizations and government institutions should develop policies that support this fundamental existential objective. Psychologists can make important contributions by assessing well-being and by trying to determine what relevant life experiences, work climate, social institutions, and educational programs promote more happy lives (Diener & Seligman, 2004). Measurement of well-being should be broad in scope and take into account not only subjective well-being, but also dimensions of social well-being. In turn psychological studies can be useful to governments whose sole reason for existence is after all to increase well-being in society. Public research can identify areas where the populations are satisfied, as well as areas that need change for optimal happiness. This research might also make the objective of well-being more relevant to policy decisions and therefore produce helpful changes in government policies.

Schimmel (2009) argued in favor of well-being assessments as a guide to government decisions and policies. The United Nations developed a measure called the Human Development Index that reflects relative poverty, wealth and social development in the world. This data was compared to the World Database of Happiness (Veenhoven, 2011). Countries were ranked according to the happiness measure that ranged from 8.2 in Denmark as the happiest country to 3.9 in Tanzania. The correlation of the two indexes demonstrated significant relationship between human development and happiness. For example, Denmark has a high ranking of 14th in the world in the Human Development Index, whereas Tanzania is 164th. These results argue for the importance of the satisfaction of human needs derived from socio-economic development and the importance of meeting these fundamental needs to well-being and happiness. However, there is not a one-to-one relationship between development and happiness as people in some countries living with underdevelopment are happier than people in more highly developed nations. Hungary is an unhappy country although it does not fare poorly in development. These results suggest the importance of subjective experiences of happiness that are to some degree independent of social development.

7.4.6. The Role of National and Local Government

Government, both local and national, can play important roles in promoting the well-being of their citizens. The economy is central to happiness as a link in meeting human needs, particularly as related to full and rewarding employment. Well-being also derives from proper balances between work and life enjoyment and governments could promote policies that reduce the working week to 20 or 30 hours, support earlier retirement, and develop an educational system that also include programs supporting well-being. In particular it is important to focus on the early years of children and facilitate parenting. The objective of social policy should be to support parenting in an effort to create happy children with paid parental leave for mothers through early childhood. Advertisement often creates false values in both children and adults promoting hedonism and immediate satisfaction and government should take action to remove these from the media. In a society created for well-being the promotion of the use of harmful products like tobacco and those directed at the manipulation of children should not have a place in the public media. Furthermore, government should seek the active participation of citizens in decision-making and in creating a society of both individual and social well-being. Social well-being in turn depends on norms of democracy and the quality of informed decisions (Ott, 2005a; Shah & Marks, 2004).

The foregoing paragraphs reflect achievable ideals for governments interested in promoting the welfare of its citizens, and a utopian society that is nevertheless possible by making happiness and well-being an explicit policy goal. This quality of government is only possible where fundamental human needs are met and where governments also promote universal values of freedom in decision making participation and expressions. The example of the Arab Spring shows that despite government terror people are motivated not only by material goals, but perhaps more importantly by opportunities for free expression and for achieving an abstract idea of liberation. Bhutan, a small country, has worked to improve the overall quality of life of its citizens and has placed well-being standards as a fundamental policy goal by suggesting that "gross national happiness" is more important than "gross national product." The effect of government intervention in Bhutan and the importance placed on well-being are reflected in a much higher ranking on happiness (Shrotryia, 2008). Although Bhutan lags behind in development indexes like the HDI, the citizens are happier than those living in more developed countries.

SUMMARY

Emotions are central to an understanding of our life experiences and provide color and meaning to communication. Although research has demonstrated the presence of emotions in other primates our linguistic and cognitive abilities makes human emotions more complex. Also we have unique self-reflections that produce self and other-related emotions which reflect moral positions. The universal presence of basic emotions points to a biological basis closely connected to signals in the autonomic and central nervous systems. Emotions evolved from primate ancestors because they served the cause of adaptation by communicating important meanings.

We understand the emotions of others through their facial expressions. The studies based on the Ekman model describes the six basic emotions and provide strong evidence for cross-cultural recognition of happiness, sadness, anger, fear, disgust and surprise. Respondents in these studies came from industrialized societies suggesting to critics that the cross-cultural concordance was a result of cultural diffusion. However, studies of respondents in pre-literate societies replicated the universal recognition of facial expressions. When investigating spontaneous responses to stressful situations these studies also produced universal agreement on the emotions expressed, a result that is now commonly accepted as genetically based.

Nevertheless these studies have been criticized by the difficulty of finding equivalent emotion labels in different cultures and the possibility that concordance in cross-cultural agreement is produced by social learning. Some researchers have also argued that emotional expressions are learned over the course of socialization, and that the universality in recognition of facial expressions cannot be divorced from cultural diffusion. The aforementioned Ekman type studies relied on photographs to display the basic emotions, but the critics ask what does that tell about expressions in real life situations? Further, it was argued that the studies do not take into account the social context, especially the varying culturally based display rules for emotion.

The defenders of the proposition that basic emotions are universal and genetically determined argue that facial recognition of emotion is an area much broader than about contentious verbal descriptions. For example, the same emotions have been found in infants long before language development. Further, perfect concordance between cultural groups is not necessary to support universality of recognition, only statistically significant cross-cultural agreement demonstrating that universality is not a chance phenomenon. Still some disagreement remain about the sources of universal recognition of emotions as to whether they can be attributed to cultural diffusion, similar cross-cultural learning processes, or to automatic responses dependent only on biology.

The definitive answer was produced by Matsumoto's and Willingham's studies of sighted and blind athletes competing at the Athens Olympic events. Although representing many different cultures there were no differences in facial expressions in the salient emotional events that resulted from the awarding of medals. The responses of the athletes were also photographed in a naturalistic setting. Results demonstrated that no differences exist in emotional facial expressions between blind and sighted athletes, or between congenital or non-congenital blind athletes. These studies provide definitive support for the contention that facial expressions of basic emotions are universal, and not dependent on cultural diffusion, but rather an adaptation that is genetically determined.

Support for universality has also been found in research on other emotion constructs. Antecedent events refer to situations that produce emotions. Large-scale studies found cross-cultural support for the contention that similar antecedents produce similar emotions in all cultural groups. However, some cross-cultural differences were observed related to different cognitive interpretations of the antecedent situations. Vocalization and intonation are also emotion constructs. Studies that controlled for linguistic meaning found cross-cultural support for the universal recognition of the emotional meanings derived from intonation. However, a small role for culture remained as some information was lost due to linguistic differences. The appraisal of emotions refers to the evaluation of the antecedent events. Results showed that similar appraisal dimensions were used in different cultural groups. Although there were differences in appraisal between the six basic emotions, within each emotion the appraisal was similar. Together these results present further evidence for the universality of experienced emotion, although with a moderating role of culture from cognitive interpretations, linguistic differences, and cultural values.

Culture and biology are but two sides of the same coin. Therefore biological and cultural theories are not incompatible since they represent but different aspects of the same phenomenon. Linguistic differences are important since the same emotion labels are not present in all societies. At the same time the presence or absence of labels may indicate something about the cultural salience of that emotion domain. Cultures socialize children in self concepts and world views that determine to some extent the experiencing and display of emotions.

Cultures have a dominant effect in formulating the display rules governing emotional expression. Society has over the course of history developed specific rules for facial and other forms of emotion expression. Asian respondents do not display emotions the same way when alone as when in the company of others. Some cultures encourage members to display less emotion than that which is truly felt, encourage control of facial expressions, or promote the use of a facial mask to distort the emotion felt. Individualistic and collectivistic cultures have different display rules for emotion intensity and negative ratings. Face is preserved by suppressing or withholding negative emotional reactions. Asian respondents also rated the intensity of negative emotions at lower levels compared to individualistic respondents. Overall, however, there is cross-cultural evidence that the intimacy of the relationship determine the display of emotions. At the same time collectivistic respondents are encouraged to display more positive emotions toward members of the ingroup and more negative emotions toward outgroup members consistent with the emphasis on ingroup social harmony.

Culture also influences the need for personal space and gestures as a form of non-verbal communication. Cultures differ in the amount of comfort zone space required when communicating with strangers. In particular Latin, southern European, and Asian countries require less personal space, perhaps a consequence of population density. Gestures are used to communicate or emphasize emotions in speech. A few gestures appear to be universal, but the cultural contexts have given meaning to most. The frequency of the use of gestures also appears culturally determined. Cultural values determine to some extent our ability to read emotions in others. Respondents from individualistic cultures are better able to read negative emotions compared to participants from collectivistic societies. Since most of us experience life within a culture there is also an ingroup advantage in recognizing emotional signals from other ingroup members.

As noted there is a cultural context to emotional communication although emotions are central to the experiencing of happiness and well-being everywhere. Therapeutic work aiming at improving mental health encourages patients to recognize and accept their emotions. In fact recognizing emotions accurately is seen as a way to improve communication in a variety of settings. Culture in particular impacts the cognitive structuring of emotional experiences, the regulation of emotional expressions, and the display rules for emotional expression.

Cross-cultural understanding of emotional communication depends on the presence of appropriate linguistic concepts. The differences between the cultural values of individualistic and collectivistic cultures produce a varying emphasis on the self and social group as a source of happiness that in turn produces habitual ways of emotion expression. Cultures also determine how emotions are experienced through the appraisal process, the enforcement of display rules, and by the presence or absence of relevant linguistic concepts and labels. In the final analysis emotions are both cultural and biological.

In recent times we have observed an increased interest in building a science of positive human functioning in psychology. Happiness has both cognitive and affective components found in the pleasure of life and the meeting of basic human needs. Happiness is ubiquitous, but individualistic and collectivistic cultures have different understandings of happiness that are consistent with cultural values. The basic cultural question is: is happiness found in self-defined well-being of the individual or in striving for social harmony.

In studying cross-cultural differences and similarities there are many methodological obstacles. Despite the centrality of happiness to human life there is little concordance in how to define and measure the construct. The Human Development Index produces a focus on tangible variables that result in a better quality of life. The second component is how people subjectively feel about their lives. The subjective component is more significant as it can overrule well-being for some who live with the best quality of life. In this chapter happiness and subjective well-being is used interchangeably, but some think happiness a more transitory term for emotion.

The chapter reviewed the case for a homeostatic theory or system designed to preserve a steady state of well-being through dispositional factors including the ability to adapt, but also cognitive abilities that allow selective attention to the positive. This homeostatic stability system is thought to have a genetic basis although the gene pathway is not understood. Homeostatic balance is maintained through external and internal buffers that help people overcome adverse conditions.

Sources of well-being include the basic material conditions of society including the presence of sufficient money. Well-being is higher when society creates norms encouraging social security, health care, political rights, and sufficient material resources. Under such favorable conditions people live longer and suffer less anxiety. Cultural values play a role since in collectivistic societies happiness is based more on the well-being of family and society whereas in individualistic cultures happiness is perceived to be more a function of self-enhancement. The lower happiness scores in collectivistic societies may be an artifact of these normative differences.

Studies show that most people are happy in both developed and developing societies. However, we have little or no data from countries ravaged by war, or in deep economic disstress. Although the trending of happiness scores have been generally upward in recent decades, it is difficult to see this trend continue with the upheavals from globalization and the Great Recession. Material conditions are essential to happiness, but other social conditions including liberty and justice norms also play a role.

Making cross-cultural comparisons about happiness is often difficult since it is a challenge to find equivalent concepts in all cultures. However, culture has an impact on happiness as understood within the framework of cultural values. Nevertheless, in each culture happiness is also dependent on dispositional factors and personal resources. For example, some individuals are born with agreeable temperaments making them a rewarding presence in social interaction, and they are therefore recipients of reciprocal affection that produces happiness. The cultivation of positive illusions might also serve as a buffer against adversity, whereas the reality oriented suffer more sorrow and anxiety. Some people just make poor predictions and suffer from consequent negative impact of decisions.

The chapter concludes with a discussion of the role of government to promote policies that produce well-being. Psychologists can make important contributions by assessing well-being and by measuring the factors that make for more happy lives. This research can and should be used by governments as a guide to policies. Countries vary widely in development related to happiness indexes. However, the role of subjective happiness is often independent of social development. Nevertheless government can play a role by promoting policies that support a better work-life balance, support well-being programs in educational systems, and in focusing on the earlier years by lending support to parenting. Finally, good quality government is only possible where fundamental human needs are met, and where universal values of democratic participation and freedom constitute fundamental norms guiding society.

CHAPTER 8

PERSONALITY THEORY

Western, Eastern and Indigenous Approaches

Personality theory has played an important role in the development of contemporary cross-cultural psychology. The personal dispositions represented by the term personality refer to enduring thinking patterns or other traits that are manifested consistently in behavior across changing situations, contexts or relationships. Some personality psychologists would argue that personality is what makes a person unique and distinct from others. However, the most important aspect of any definition is the conception of the enduring nature of personality traits that it typically remains stable across the lifespan and in different social contexts.

The personality construct has also been applied in an attempt to understand national character viewed as a syndrome of traits shared by all members of a society and providing the possibility for cross-national comparisons. Furthermore, as we observed in the last chapter advances in genetic and biological research have reliably demonstrated that some traits like temperament or intelligence are hardwired heritable traits. However, investigators in cultural psychology and anthropology believe that culture

Cross-Cultural Psychology: Why Culture Matters, pages 205–231.

plays a major role in forming culturally unique personality traits developed from the sociocultural environment and consistent cultural practices.

The dominant model of personality structure is the trait approach that examines specific qualities distinguishing the individual from other persons. For example, a person described as an affable is thought to be consistently outgoing and warm toward others regardless of changing situations. A consideration of comparative research on the Big Five personality traits discussed previously supports the conception of the universal structure of personality. Using the Big Five trait model cultures can be compared on the frequency and strength of personality structures considered universal in all cultures. The etiology of universal personality structures are linked to evolutionary forces that created genetic predispositions for behavior, but perhaps also cultures that reinforce similar learning from universal common human needs and experiences (Church & Lonner, 1998; Lonner, 1980; MacDonald, 1998).

Cultural psychologists argue that indigenous cultures have the ability to produce unique personalities consistent within a society but varying across cultures. Furthermore, the cultural psychologists would argue that since each culture produces unique personality traits it is not possible to make cross-cultural comparisons. The cultural and anthropological approach to personality would largely reject any hardwired basis for personality insisting instead on the unique within cultural forces that mold the child and adult (Kim, 2001). On the surface the cross-cultural and cultural viewpoints seem to be fundamentally opposing perspectives, but they can be reconciled. This book has argued that we need all disciplinary focuses to serve as windows into the complex reality of personality.

A discussion of personality theory typically begins with a consideration of Sigmund Freud's psychoanalytic contributions (Freud, 1961). Personality theories have been created in a dialectical process of assertion of principles or theses, protests against these conclusions about human nature as either false or lacking in comprehensiveness, and then alternative theoretical propositions. This dialectical process is pivotal to the understanding of this chapter since it describes the history of Western personality theories.

However, there are also perspectives that emerged out of the great thinkers of the East like Confucius in China and the teachings of Buddha. Both philosophical perspectives have broadly influenced thinking about what it means to be human and can also be thought of as personality theories. All personality perspectives seem to have developed from the confluence of individual experiences of the theorists and the relevant cultural and environmental milieu. Whether Freud or Buddha it was significant personal events that influenced their lives that in turn formed their thinking about personality and human development. The sociocultural environment in each case provided the conceptual framework available in building their models and the cultural values developed from historical experiences and social organization contributed significantly to their theories.

8.1. WESTERN THOUGHTS ON PERSONALITY

Personality theories in the West evolved in a way similar to the evolution of other cultural products like religion. Although thinkers about the human mind may have evaluated many important ideas over the centuries, personality theory in the West are products of just the recent centuries. Starting with Freud (1940), a medical doctor living in Vienna at the turn of the 20th century, psychoanalytic thought represented the first systematic ideas about personality. Later other neo-Freudians like Adler and Jung would differ from Freud in some essential ways and develop their own conceptions of personality. Overall, modern science has discounted many of Freud's conclusions. Nevertheless psychoanalysis was *heuristic* in inspiring and producing much research, for example, in social psychology the seminal work on the authoritarian personality. From the origin of psychoanalysis the evolution of personality theory followed a dialectical process that in turn produced the different perspectives of humanistic, behavioral, social-cognitive and personality trait perspectives (Lewis, 2008).

8.1.1. Freud's Contributions

Freud was a profound thinker, and although his theories find less scientific acceptance today, the concepts he proposed continue to influence conceptions about human personality. He started his personal medical practice by helping neurotic patients. The method he used was *free association* during which he asked his patients to speak or associate anything that came to their minds. Freud hoped thereby to produce chains of thought that would eventually reveal the patient's unconscious dynamics that he believed originated in early childhood. This process of unraveling unconscious dynamics Freud called psychoanalysis. Freud likened the human mind to an iceberg with the conscious mind only occupying a small area above the water, and the large proportion of the mind being below the water line and unconscious. Freud was also a determinist who believed that unconscious behavior is never accidental, that all that we do in life, our choice of work, our selection of mates, our career paths, all have their roots in powerful impulses of unresolved conflicts stemming from psychosexual stages of development. Few researchers today give much credence to Freud's psychosexual stage theories, but other psychoanalytic concepts have retained explanatory power.

For Freud human personality evolved out of the conflict between biologically based pleasure seeking and our efforts to restrain these impulses and make them socially acceptable. Our basic motivations for behavior grew out of the conflict between a primitive hardwired instinct of sex affirming life and creativity named the *Libidos* and the destructive and aggressive instinct for death called the *Thanatos*. Conflicts centered on components of personality, one being the *Id* considered the repository of unconscious energy seeking to satisfy basic drives based on the *pleasure principle*. For example, at birth a baby is largely motivated by the Id and demands the immediate attention of the mother with respect to basic needs like feeding. As the child develops he/she becomes conscious of the surrounding world and of the necessity to delay gratification. In colliding with social reality the child's desire to gratify the Id continues, but within the framework of the *reality principle*. The child learns to moderate the desire for immediate satisfaction replacing it with the hope of long-term pleasure and to avoid painful consequences. As a result the second component of personality structure called the *Ego* emerges from the necessity that the child faces social reality and delays the demands of the Id. The ego based on the reality principle develops through childrearing efforts of parents and later by the sociocultural environment. Parents also encourage values and morals in childrearing and the *Superego* develops out of this parent-child relationship with the child internalizing values of right and wrong. A healthy personality according to Freud is one that finds a balance between these competing demands. For example people with a weak Superego are unbalanced and might evolve into psychopaths with little regard for the welfare of others.

There is little reason to discuss Freud's psychosexual stages as they have no scientific basis and is rejected by the contemporary scientific community. However, Freud's psychoanalytic theory also produced the concept of defense mechanisms that appears to have great face validity in understanding both behavior and human interaction. Many people lose the war between the pleasure demanding Id and the conscience of the Superego and as a result experience unpleasant anxiety. To control anxiety people develop defense mechanisms that function either to reduce or redirect anxiety by distorting some aspect of reality. The most basic defense mechanism is *repression* where anxiety producing thoughts are simply banished from the mind. *Regression* is where the individual in response to anxiety returns to the behavior of a more infantile stage using conduct that was at that time successful in achieving objectives. In *reaction formation* the ego switches the unacceptable thought or impulse to the exact opposite so instead of the unacceptable schema that "I hate my parents" it becomes "I love my parents." *Projection* distorts reality by attributing the unacceptable impulses of the individual to other people. For example, a Caucasian may think Asians are deceitful in an effort to mask their own deceitful behavior. *Rationalizations* are part and parcel of most people's life as this defense mechanism seeks to reduce anxiety by proposing good reasons for behavior rather than the real reasons. *Displacement* is the diversion of unacceptable thoughts like hostile impulses toward a more psychologically acceptable target. So instead of expressing anger at parents the child might express anger toward safer targets like a pet. Finally, *sublimation* is the change of unacceptable impulses into motivations that serve socially valued objectives. It was thought by Freud to explain creative activity and other cultural achievements as a substitute for sexuality.

Psychoanalysts that followed Freud such as Adler and Jung accepted many of the basic ideas of Freud. The basic personality structure of Id, Ego, and Superego made sense to most neo-Freudians as did the importance of unconscious motivation, the significance of childhood in personality development and the roles of anxiety and defense mechanisms. However, Fromm viewed the Ego as more of a mediator between the *pleasure and reality* principles, and placed more emphasis on conscious motivation. Erikson in turn emphasized the importance of *psychosocial* stages and deemphasized the role of sexuality in human development. Heuristic research motivated by psychoanalytic concepts included the concept of unconscious motivation measured in the Thematic Apperception Test (TAT), and the Rorschach Inkblot Test. However, overall the research inspired by psychoanalysis lacked in both reliability and validity (Peterson, 1978). More importantly recent research has contradicted many of Freud's ideas and conceptions. For example, Kagan (1989) noted that despite the lower levels of sexual repression in our libertine modern society (that was thought by Freud to cause psychological disorders) the expected frequency of disorders have not diminished suggesting that other variables are at play in psychological dysfunction. *On the other hand, the ideas of unconscious motivation appear to have validity (Kihlstrom, 1990) since we are limited in the access to the information in our minds,* although now the unconscious is thought of as cognitive schemas that process stimuli and control our perceptions.

8.1.2. The Humanistic Approach to Personality

Trait psychology historically overlapped with behaviorism as a reaction to the subjective and unscientific methods articulated by psychoanalysis. Trait personality theory is also a very heuristic approach that has generated a large body of cross-cultural research to be discussed later. However, other personality theorists also grew disquiet by the apparent negative conceptualizations of Freud and his co-thinkers about human development, dysfunction and apparent lack of self-determination. The contributors to humanistic psychology were more interested in the development of a psychology of healthy people in contrast to Freud's focus on the neurotic. Maslow (1970b) and Rogers (1951) wanted to understand the human potential and from the perspective of the individual studied and rejected the unconscious motivation and abstract personality components of Freud's theory.

Maslow advocated a hierarchical theory of human motivation that explains how people strive toward although not all achieve *self-actualization*.

In his theory self-actualized people were described as sharing certain traits including a high level of self-awareness and self-acceptance. They live courageous lives and do not necessarily conform to the prevailing opinions of the day and society in which they live. Self-actualized persons tend to be problem-centered and not self-centered, are spontaneous, open and loving in their relationships with others. From the struggles of life the self-actualized person develops a compassionate attitude toward the sufferings of others, feels despair deeply at the cruelty and meanness in society, and takes personal steps to remedy what is possible to change.

Rogers, also a humanist, believed in the essential goodness of people and that we possess natural self-actualizing tendencies. For humans to grow toward fulfillment requires genuineness and a rejection of the false, acceptance of self and others, and empathy in relationships. We can nurture others in their struggle toward growth by being transparent and by our willingness to self-disclose. Further we can accept others by displaying *unconditional positive regard* despite what might be seen as failures or shortcomings in their lives. From the humanistic theory we can also nurture growth by being empathic and non-judgmental. The importance of the self-concept derives from the central role it plays in our perceptions and reactions and is central to Rogers' theory. With a positive self-concept we react to our surroundings in an affirmative way and feel happier. Although James discussed the self-concept in his seminal work (1890), it was Rogers who rescued the construct from oblivion as the pivotal center of personality and cognitive organizer in modern times (Markus & Wurf, 1987). The self-concept will be discussed later in more detail.

With a focus on the self, humanistic research has evaluated the importance of a person's self-esteem to mental health and relationships. Positive self-esteem produces many benefits creating personal happiness and health. High self-esteem is linked to positive outcomes including less likelihood of drug use, the ability to resist pressures to conform, and a determination to persist in difficult tasks. Humanistic psychology argued that a meaningful difference existed between positive self-esteem and self-righteous and prideful thinking. Positive self-esteem is not linked to attributions of others, but based on self-determined behavior (Brown, 1998). On the other hand, low self-esteem has been linked in correlational studies to a number of negative outcomes including depression and over-sensitivity to criticism (Higgins, 1987).

An overall *conclusion from humanistic theory is the affirmation of the value of the self that is very adaptive in establishing a state of personal well-being*. Even if positive thinking is illusionary it has value in supporting self-confidence and our sense of well-being, although Brown suggested that people perform best and with confidence when self-enhancement is based on modest illusions that are believable to self and others. Therefore a positive self-concept is a key to personal happiness and effective handling of social relations. The basic belief that people are good and the willingness to accept others as they are represents the fundamental values in the humanistic outlook. However, humanistic psychology has been criticized for promoting an individualism that justifies self-indulgence (Campbell, 1986). Furthermore, the idea that humans have the potential of self-actualization seems dependent on individual and social affluence in a world where most people face the ubiquitous presence of scarcity and evil represented by selfishness, greed and endless wars.

8.1.3. Social-Cognitive Interaction Theory

Kelly (1955) proposed a personal construct theory pioneering the start of cognitive theories of personality. Personality is conceived by cognitive theorists to be a complex of cognitive structures that are systematically organized and predictable. Bandura (1986) advocated a personality theory based on principles of learning and cognition. According to Bandura the environment is the critical etiological factor in personality development since we learn either by conditioning or through social learning by observation and imitation. Cognition is a vital component in personality theory since what we think about a given situation determines our behavior. However, unlike behaviorism where the focus is totally on environmental forces the social-cognitive perspective sees the critical determinant as the *interaction* of the individual with the environment. Social-cognitive theory explains the utilization of cognitive schemas to interpret a situation and how expectations of outcomes influence our actual behavior. Bandura called this process *reciprocal determinism* since we exercise some choice over aspects of the environment with which we interact and that these choices in turn shapes who we are as people.

Our interpretations are largely shaped by our personalities since we attend to *expected* stimuli based on individual reality. For example people with anxious personalities are more likely to attend to and expect threatening events (Eysenck, 1967; Eysenck, MacLeod, & Mathews, 1987). Furthermore, people also contribute to the actual creation of the expected situations by selective attention and behavior based on our personalities. For example, if we perceive our colleagues as unfriendly, we may selectively attend to this perception to the exclusion of other cues and act consistently in ways that actually encourage an unfriendly environment. According to social-cognitive interaction theory we are the shapers of our environment, but our personality is also the product or outcome of the environment in a continuous process of interaction between environmental and personality components.

In many ways people fulfill their own prophecies and expectations through preconceptions that influence interactions with the sociocultural environment. For example, students who possess a hopeful attitude are more likely to study hard and get good grades. Again the message is one of balance since unrealistic optimism may not prepare the individual for the relevant tasks and challenges. Some anxiety over possible failure might actually help motivate more effort to accomplish important goals. Moderate and realistic optimism conveys the message that achievement is possible, unrealistic optimism brings failure and reduces motivation. Students who are unrealistically optimistic may not have sufficient motivation to study properly for an exam and hence fail (Cantor & Norem, 1989; Peterson & Barrett, 1987).

8.1.4. Locus of Control

The cognitive-social perspective encouraged valuable research focused on the degree of personal control expected in interaction with our environment. Some people develop a personality where they feel they have little control in life, and that whatever happens to them is the result of fate, chance or the intervention by powerful others. People who believe the environment is all powerful and control their outcomes are said to have an *external locus of control.* Other people possess an *internal locus of control* with the opposite perspective and believe that they largely can control the outcomes of their lives through their own efforts. *There is much research that shows that the locus of control concept has practical outcomes for people. People with an internal locus of control typically fare better in life represented by higher achievement, more independence from constraints, and in having the ability to cope with stress* (Findley & Cooper, 1983; Benassi, Sweeney, & Dufour, 1988; Miller, Lefcourt, Holmes, Ware, & Saleh, 1986).

A related concept of *learned helplessness* has also generated much research. Seligman (1991) originally developed the concept from his experiments with animals, but found the construct helpful to also understand a variety of human reactions. People who have little control in their lives, for example, prisoners or those subject to powerful religious authority, often believe that there is nothing they can do that will improve their lives and they learn helplessness in the face of the all- powerful environmental forces. The outcome of learned helplessness is increased stress and lower morale, and a sense of hopelessness and depression. However, people who have not learned helplessness and who exercise opportunities for choice improve individual health and morale. Sociocultural environments like authentic democracies create subjectively a sense of control that produces greater happiness and well-being (Inglehart, 1990).

8.1.5 Cross-Cultural Research on Locus of Control and Autonomy: In Control or Being Controlled

A great deal of cross-cultural research exists on the *locus of control* concept developed by Rotter (1966). This personality trait is describes the degree to which people believe they can control the environment or reversely the extent to which they are subject to external control. The locus of control concept is based on social learning theory as the reinforcement of behavior over time create an enduring personality trait where people come to see their positive and negative life outcomes as either contingent on their own behavior (internal locus of control) or dependent on powerful forces outside individual control (external locus of control). Students with an internal locus of control believe for example that grades and other scholarly outcomes are the results of their own behavior, whereas their classmates with an external locus of control believe that chance, luck or the attitudes of the teacher are the main determinants of achievement. Not surprisingly people who have little actual power or status in their lives feel that they cannot influence outcomes and consequently develop an external locus of control. For example, more Afro-Americans possess an external locus of control compared to European Americans (Dyal, 1984) reflecting the real relationships between the actual control that people can exercise in their lives and the locus of control variable.

On the whole Americans tend to score higher on the internal locus of control variable compared to Asians reflecting the Western culture of individualism and personal responsibility (Van Haaften & Van de Vijver, 1999). Other studies have also supported the higher scores of Americans compared to other national groups (Hamid, 1994; Munro, 1979). Dyal found that European Americans had a higher internal locus of control, compared to Afro-Americans in the United States again reflecting the lack of real control by people who are impoverished and marginalized and cultural effects of learned helplessness.

Do Americans feel more in control of their lives or could that self-perception be just a manifestation of self-stereotypes and self-serving biases? The cultural values of personal independence that support an internal locus of control in the United States may be an illusionary since recent decades have shown that economically the majority of citizens in the U.S. are subject to speculators, financers and the greed of banks over which they have no control. Although socioeconomic status is a logical determinant of locus of control, research has shown that gender also create differences with females believing more strongly in an external locus of control (Smith, Dugan, & Trompenaars, 1997). The research on locus of control suggests the importance of beliefs about the environment that preceded social-cognitive interaction theories.

Some researchers have suggested that all people, regardless of culture, have fundamental psychological needs for *autonomy* although how these needs are met depends on the cultural context. As we have seen elsewhere there are basic differences between cultures in how people construe themselves with people who live in collectivistic cultures seeing themselves as more interdependent and therefore not autonomous. However, others suggest that people are autonomous whenever they can act consistent with their values regardless of whether the culture is collectivistic or individualistic (Chirkov, Ryan, Kim, & Kaplan, 2003). People internalize cultural beliefs and practices in all cultures and the perception of autonomy is universal although in many cases delusionary. However, acting consistent with personal values, even if delusionary, is related to subjective well-being (Chirkov, Ryan, & Willness, 2005).

The social-cognitive perspective stresses the viewpoint that internal dynamics do not determine all aspects of behavior, but that the powerful effects of situational pressures must be taken into account. Social-cognitive interaction theory has subsequently produced a large body of research in cognition and learning. A major criticism made of the theory is that the emphasis on the situational pressures incorrectly diminishes the importance of a person's inner traits. However, that criticism seems less credible when the theory is understood as explaining personality as the outcome of the interaction of inner traits and the environment. Genetic factors are also overlooked in social-cognitive interaction theory and we know from twin studies that many personality traits like aggression or extraversion are linked to hardwired heritage. Finally, we should remember that no personality theory contains all relevant or important ideas, and each perspective is but a window into the reality of the human psyche.

8.1.6. Personality Types and Hardwired Foundations

Scholars that recognize the importance of genetic hardwiring in the formation of personality supported with the advances in neuroscience tend to also support the presence of universal personality structures across cultures. For example, in the West the research on the so-called type A personality describes an extremely competitive behavioral pattern that probably evolved to help the individual adapt and cope with the modern competitive society (Friedman & Rosenman, 1974). Others researchers (McCrae & Costa, 1987) have used the statistical tools of factor analysis to reduce the complexity of personality traits finding common factors that define personality structure. The so-called *Big Five* personality traits are thought to be genetically determined and independent factors that describe personality structure across varying cultures.

Research has produced evidence that supports at least the partial heritability of personality traits (Plomin & Caspi, 1998). Studies of identical and fraternal twins show conclusively that personality trait similarity is based on shared genetic heritability. As noted earlier studies of the personalities of identical twins reared apart show a greater similarity in traits compared to fraternal twins reared together in the same home. Since trait similarities are reliable even when identical twins are reared apart the results strongly suggest a genetic component to some aspects of personality (Loehlin, 1992; Miller, 2012).

Traits found early in development are consistently displayed over the lifespan. Longitudinal studies have shown that children identified as shy at nine months develop elevated levels of stress hormone cortisol associated with fear (Kagan, 1989). Neuroticism is associated with a heightened activation of the autonomic nervous system involved in subjective stress (Zuckerman, 1996). On the positive side extraversion is related to higher levels of the neurotransmitter dopamine that is in turn predictive of approach related behaviors (Depue, 1995). Clearly personality cannot be understood apart from our biological inheritance. People react consistently to the varying manifestations of these traits. These reactions in turn play a significant role in how we develop as persons and how we form more complex self-identities (Malatesta, 1990).

8.1.7. The Big Five

Since genetic factors contribute to personality they are probably responsible for the stability we associate with the concept of personality. In turn reliability of personality allows us to compare personality traits between individuals within a culture and also for possible differences between cultures. The relationship of genes to personality has found support in several recent studies (Brummett, Siegler, McQuoid, Svenson, Marchuk, & Steffens, 2003). Personality traits might, like other psychological constructs, have grown out of evolutionary needs to adapt and survive. Adaptation to the environment has overlapping components in varying cultures producing universal personality traits, although as we shall see culture may also nurture specific traits. McCrae and Costa (1987) found support for the presence of what is called the *Big Five* super traits (Neuroticism, extraversion, openness, agreeableness, and conscientiousness). These traits appear universally in all cultures as determined by factor analyses of trait adjectives from surveys asking for a description of the self. Cross-cultural research based again on factor analysis of trait adjectives, but also personality inventories, found support for the presence of the Big Five in varying cultures (McCrae, Costa, del Pilar, Rolland, & Parker, 1998). In a study of 51 cultures McCrae, Terracciano, Leibovich, Schmidt, Shakespeare-Finch Neubauer et al. (2005) using a 240 item personality test found utilizing factor analysis that the survey items fell into one of the five major categories, and that some of these traits proved useful in cross-cultural comparisons. Americans, for example, are high on extraversion, and moderate on neuroticism, whereas Iranians are low on extraversion but also moderate on neuroticism.

A problem in all psychological testing is the effect of social desirability that confounds responses and interpretations. For example, respondents will often respond not with personal opinion but rather according to desirable values or norms in society. To avoid this problem Allik & McCrae (2004) asked respondents in 50 cultural groups to rate, not themselves, but someone they knew, on the 240 item scale. Again the five-factor model made an appearance from factor analysis showing that the previous results were not dependent on social desirability in enhancing the self. Of interest research showed that personalities were more similar when the cultures were geographically close, probably from sharing common cultural heritage. However, the relative strength of the traits varied between cultures (Paunonen, 2003), and recent research casts doubt on whether the five factor solution can be applied in all cultures (Xinyue, Saucier, Gao, & Liu, 2009).

Despite doubt about universality the research on the Big Five is convincing and the generalizability of the research cannot be underestimated. In the complex domain of cross-cultural psychology there are no similar comparative congruence pointing to universal traits. In a significant survey (Schmitt, Allik, McCrae & Benet-Martinez, 2007) found that the five-dimensional personality structure previously discovered was robust across all nations and regions of the world. These findings are notable since they were based an International Sexuality Description Project that included the Big Five Inventory. In turn this inventory was translated into 28 languages and administered to 17837 persons living in 56 countries. Trait levels of the Big Five related in predictable ways to self-esteem, to sociosexuality and to national personality profiles. Regional differences were meaningful. For example, results for South America and South East Asia yielded less openness scores compared to other regions perhaps based on collectivistic versus individualistic cultural values. These values may also have contributed to the greater homogeneity in Asian and African cultures as compared to Europe and the U.S where trait heterogeneity is the greatest (See also Allik & MaCrae, 2004; McCrae, 2002). Examination of the relationship of personality structures with the U.S. sample as target yielded nearly perfect (.98) congruence, and coefficients between national samples exceeded .90 except for African and Asian regions. Further, the Big Five Inventory produced reliable results for both genders across all cultures measured lending further support to the universal nature of the Big Five construct. Finally, two independent measures included in the Schmitt et all investigation yielded strong cross-cultural agreement.

Other cross-cultural researchers have argued that the Big Five personality traits do not describe very well the relatedness issues important to Asian interdependent societies. Personality dimensions described as *interpersonal relatedness* have been found in both mainland China, but also Hong Kong and in other locations (Cheung, Cheung, Leung, Ward, & Leung, 2003; Lin & Church, 2004). Other researchers have emphasized the universal importance of *authoritarianism* (Hofstede, Bond, & Luk, 1993), and the presence of particular indigenous traits in other societies (Katigbak, Church, Guanzon-Lapena, Carlota, & del Pilar, 2002).

8.1.8. The Genetic and Evolutionary Basis of Personality

The Big Five personality structure has been explained as a universal human adaptation developed in the common struggle for survival. The Big Five is seen from this functional perspective as a universal psychological mechanism important in solving problems between members of a culture and adapting to the sociocultural and physical environment. For example, the trait "conscientiousness" may help individuals in monitoring the environment and thereby avoid punishing outcomes or alternatively help the individual to persevere toward important goals in tasks that have no intrinsic reward (MacDonald, 1995, 1998). At the same time the presence of universal personality structure does not negate the importance of cultural affects. Culture can influence the mean levels of personality traits, some of the big Five traits measured high in some societies and low in others. In the final analysis it is culture that creates the specific context that shapes personality and produces the behaviors that allows individuals to reach universal affective goals like satisfying the need for intimacy (McCrae, Costa, del Pilar, Rolland, & Parker, 1998).

8.1.9. Is National Character a Psychological Reality?

Personality traits vary among individuals. The work on the Big Five traits shows that they vary also between countries and cultures while at the same time indicating little trait variance within the culture. The similarity within nations and cultures support the presence of what has been called national character. People have perceptions about the modal or average personality of people living in different countries and cultures also called national character. Research shows that national stereotypes are part of the discourse all over the world. Peabody (1985) sought to make a distinction between national stereotypes that he argued were often irrational or incorrect and national character that contained more valid descriptions of the population. In his research he found that nations differed on some traits, for example, whether members of a culture were assertive or unassertive, lending support to the concept of national character. Terracciano, Abdel-Khalek, Adam, Adamovova, Ahn and Ahn et al. (2005) asked thousands of respondents in 49 cultures to describe the "typical member" of that society. The results yielded a high agreement about perceptions of national character, yet these stereotypes *did not correlate* with the actual personality traits of members of the same cultural groups. So the question might be logically asked, why do people maintain stereotypes about themselves and others? The answer according to Terracciano, Abdel-Khalek, Adam, Adamovova,

Ahn and Ahn et al, is that stereotypes help maintain national identity and the self-worth of the national group.

8.2. EASTERN THOUGHTS ABOUT PERSONALITY

The interest in Eastern cultural thinking of Buddhism and Confucianism has emerged in recent decades partly from the struggles in developing an indigenous psychology (Hwang, 2012). In particular the argument has been made that 96 % of samples of psychological research published in the world's top journals from 2003–2007 were drawn from Western, educated, industrialized, rich and democratic societies which housed just 12 % of the world's population (p. xv). *Hwang and his co-workers have tried to encourage a scientific revolution in response to this imbalance by promoting the importance of Eastern cultural traditions and in particular Confucian relationism.* Confucian thought promoted morality and the importance of interpersonal relationships that are thought to contribute to distinctive psychological differences between people living in Asian as compared with Western societies. In particular it is argued (Hwang, Kim, & Kou-Shu, 2006) that Western psychological methods are promoted to the rest of the world from political, economic and military dominance, and that it is largely an ethnocentric construction. It is from that perspective that we must take Eastern indigenous psychology seriously in the search for a more universal psychology.

Students trained in the Western tradition may wonder why we consider the Eastern thought of Buddhism and the thoughts of Confucius important in a discussion of personality theory. However, Eastern ideas about the mind developed many centuries before Western culture produced personality theories in the West including those of Freud, Jung, Adler, Maslow and Rogers. Eastern thinking, like Western personality theory, also answers questions about what is personality, how does it develop, why do people suffer, how may delusionary responses intensify suffering, and what therapeutic approaches will minimize suffering on our path toward a mature and healthy personality? A key idea of Eastern thought is that we have power to develop our personalities by following the path that leads to ever increasing circles of relationships. Who we are is answered by our relative willingness to fulfill the roles related to these ever widening relationship circles starting with the family but progressing to ever widening responsibilities to others and society. These conceptions of human existence and how personality identity develops overlap with some of the conceptions of Western personality theory.

However, an important difference, at least between Western and Buddhist theory, is in the construal of the self or personality. In Western theories personality takes the form of a personal enduring identity. From the perspective of Buddhist thought the idea of enduring personal identity elevates or reifies the self as the locus of thoughts and behavior. The permanent self is perceived as a delusion in Buddhist philosophy and is seen as the cause of many negative and harmful behaviors. In the Western tradition the soul concept is created as an outcome of the evolution of Judeo-Christian thought, but probably has origins earlier in history as humans found it difficult to deal with the absurdity of impermanent life. Thomas Aquinas wrote about the soul, as did Descartes later, and the cultural discourse created a common assumption of the existence of the inner self without any empirical support or proof.

8.2.1. The Buddhist Tradition

Buddhism has a long history of interaction with Western psychologists and has influenced their thoughts about personality and mental health (Michalon, 2001). In particular the recent positive psychology movement has renewed an interest in Buddhism among Western scientists and therapists. Buddhist thought has had practical applications in dealing with various types of human dysfunctions. Therapists have utilized Buddhist approaches in evaluating HIV risk behaviors among drug users (Avants & Margolin, 2004) in grief counseling (Michalon, 2001), and in alleviating anxiety (Toneatto, 2002). Western therapists have also used meditative strategies (Wallace & Shapiro, 2006) to produce higher levels of consciousness and Buddhist thoughts contributed to Western thinkers like James (1890), and Maslow (1970a,b).

Buddhism is an evolved psychology and philosophy that has over time changed and assimilated ideas from a variety of cultures. Of interest is the fact that Buddha lived at about the same time as Confucius in the fifth and sixth century B.C. when Siddhartha Gautama (Buddha) left behind a life of luxury in order to understand and alleviate suffering. Central to Buddhist psychology is a search for the *middle way* as the path toward mentally healthy lives. A person living the middle way is removed from both self-indulgence and self-mortification (Wallace & Shapiro, 2006). Early in his career Buddha gave a talk known as "Setting in motion the wheel of the Dharma" in which he articulated the "Four Noble Truths" seen as the fundamental ideas of Buddhism. In a summarized form these ideas are that suffering (affliction) is real and a fact of life that we cannot escape. However, in the second truth Buddha states that from affliction feelings arise within us to aspire to find situations that are different from the present suffering. For many people escape into pleasure is seen as a solution to suffering. However, Buddha taught in the third truth that such activities or pleasurable objects do not bring lasting satisfaction although they may produce a *temporary lack of desire*. However, Buddha taught that feelings that arise within us can be controlled and contained. When we control our feelings about desire they can be the source of personal transformation.

The fourth truth is that the path that people choose can lead to self-fulfillment. The path actually consist of 8 steps that include the "right view"; "right thought";" right speech"; "right action"; " right livelihood" (doing good to others); "right effort"; right mindfulness"; and "right rapture" (the highest level of the understanding of the purpose of life). These eight paths describe how a healthy and mature person must think and act to reach the goal of enlightenment and personal development and living an authentic existence. In summary, Buddhism explains the basic existential problem of suffering and how we can react to that with attempts at either unsuccessful escape or by developing our nobility and personal maturity that places the well-being of others as a foremost ethical consideration.

We already know from the work on the interdependent and independent selves that people who live in collectivistic societies do not have self-construals of a separate or autonomous self. In Buddhism it is the ego-based self that create suffering because the byproducts are pleasure-seeking, constant fear and loneliness. Buddhism suggests that the separate self is really a delusion, and that the reality of the self is not enduring but ever changing as we move through life (Mosig, 2006). Personal identity in the Western sense seems a nonsensical notion in Buddhism, since all things including personality can only be understood in relation to other things (Sugamura, Haruki, & Koshikawa, 2007). A person exists only in the context of relationships, and everything we identify as human including speech and other aspects of culture or personality exist because of these relationships. In summary, the Buddhist perspective on personality argues that suffering is real and ubiquitous. However, by living a disciplined life and by not seeking escape in pleasure we can find fulfillment in noble service to others.

As noted above *Buddhism considers the reification of the self to be an illusion.* In the Buddhist perspective there is no soul or "little man behind the screen" in the brain that can be identified as the self or personality. Reification is the process where the mind makes sense out of mental processes by making a material object, substance or "thingness" out of cognition. In the Western tradition personality theorists like Freud reified their concepts by attributing "thingness" to personality in the holy trinity of Id, Ego and Superego. However, in Buddhism such reifications are but delusions and have a reference only in temporary memory. The individual's self-conception is also a reification and delusion. Nevertheless people conduct their lives and behavior as if they constitute separate entities in the world rather than accepting the reality that the self is a delusionary assembly of cognitive constructs put together by the mind. Cultural languages support reification of the self since personality is discussed as if it really exists. That makes it almost impossible for people to have a true intuition of the mind, personality and the self.

From the perspective of Buddhism the self as reified represents nothing real or objective. So it would seem Buddhism is essentially an atheistic philosophy and psychology since there is no soul to be saved although practitioners of Buddhism may object to this description. We would do well to keep in mind that all philosophies evolved far from their origins, and that Jesus would probably find many current Christian practices absurd. Buddha believed that not only was the teaching of an independent personal self imaginary, but also that it caused great harm to human life. It is from the reification of the self that the concepts of personal ownership derive, and along with that selfishness, conceit, egoism, hatred and pride. Not only do humans lack a soul, but so does everything else in the natural world. Nothing in the natural world can have a separate existence and the mind consist only in the form of temporary parts that are brought together by causal connections. A river is essentially a stable configuration in the mind that we may reify with a name. Nevertheless the river exists in reality as a constantly changing set of components including water and life in the water. A river can be reified and conceptualized as if it has a permanent existence, but again that is a delusion. Thus although we can apprehend the "whole" of aspects of the environment, the whole does not have a separate existence or soul and is not separate from its constituent parts.

8.2.2. The Self and Causation

Nevertheless in disregarding a separate self as unreal reification Buddhist theory is not simplistic. A person, although transitory, is composed of five components called skandhas that are labeled form, feelings, perceptions, impulses and consciousness. What constitutes a person is the temporary composition or arrangements of these components. If we remove one of these skandhas there would be no construct that we can call a person. In more definitive terms the person has no reality except in the configuration of the components. Even the skandhas have no enduring meaning or existence as each is composed of the other four skandhas. For example, we would have no conception of the form of our bodies if not for perceptions. Consciousness of others only has meaning because of the additional components of form, feelings, perceptions and occasional impulses. In summary, skandhas are interdependent in origin and function (Hanh, 1988). The fundamental teaching of Buddhism is a law of causality that everything in the universe is interconnected. Objective events or subjective experiences all have causes without which nothing exists.

Fundamentally that means that nothing exists independently or separately. Think of any object, and follow the infinitesimal connections of its history to all happenings in the universes. A flower does not exist separately, but is connected to a seed, then perhaps to a bird that carried the seed, the bird is connected to parents that laid the egg, in turn the parents are dependent on a nest, that is found in a tree, that would not have grown except for the nutrients in the soil, and so forth. In Buddhism all "things" are mere points that have infinitesimal causational extensions in the universe and can be seen as analogous to the particle-wave theory of Quantum physics (Soeng, 1991). In the self there is no little man behind the screen and no soul. A person is a temporary cognition or gestalt formed by the arrangements of the components or skandhas. This gestalt cognition is called anatta; however the permanent self is considered an illusion.

The person is still important in the Buddhist perspective once the illusion of the self is dropped and the interconnectedness of people to all elements of the universe is understood. Rather than being isolated and feeling helpless and powerless, the enlightened person in Buddhism is an interconnected part of the universe. When the boundaries between the person and all other elements disappear, the person in a process of total identification becomes the universe and experiences enlightenment (Mosig, 2006). Again, by contrast a person that perceives a wave in the ocean as separate from the ocean is experiencing a delusion. Although the gestalt of your perception tells you that the wave has substance in reality there is only transitory movement of the water, and it is only possible to separate the wave from the ocean through a delusionary abstraction. From the Buddhist perspective enlightenment is important because suffering will only disappear when we give up on the delusion of separateness of the self from the universe. When we accept the universal oneness of all the outcome is a more selfless person that has compassion and caring for everyone and for the natural world.

8.2.3. Buddhism and Consciousness

The idea of consciousness was further developed by other Buddhist scholars that followed Buddha, in particular Vasubandhu who lived in the fourth century BC. In his writings consciousness consisted of a total of eight components some of which are conscious and others unconscious. Corresponding to the fundamental sensory components of the human body there is a consciousness related to seeing, tasting, smelling, hearing and touching. The five sense consciousnesses are integrated allowing people to know, to conceive and to judge through perceptual and cognitive processing. The mind is the locus (however temporary) of complex cognition based on the information processed at the previous sensory levels. The cognition of the mind is what gives rise to the ego or subjective knower. In the process of personal awareness the mistaken and delusionary idea of a separate inner perceiver arises, that in turn deranges the other forms of consciousness and produces dysfunction and suffering (we shall discuss again the "hard" problem of the knowing self in the next chapter). In addition Buddhist thought also allow for unconsciousness as a storehouse of information derived from the other forms of consciousness (Epstein, 1995). Some have likened the unconsciousness to a living stream that flows continuously and in the process refreshes and renews itself. Unconsciousness creates all the possibilities in thinking, but by conscious efforts we allow perspectives like compassion to become more dominant. Being aware and conscious of one's thoughts and pursuing "right "thinking" is important in developing healthy mental habits and improving well-being.

8.2.4. Buddhism as a Therapeutic Approach

The basic aim of Buddhist psychology is to eliminate or ameliorate unnecessary suffering produced by the delusion of the separate self. In that respect it is very different from Western psychology that seeks to address personal dysfunctions in order to produce a more balanced and autonomous self. Whereas Western psychology contributes toward the alleviation of behavioral or psychological disorders deemed abnormal, Buddhist psychology offers ideas for normal people who suffer from the delusion of being separated from other people, the cultural context and the natural environment. The results of the delusion of the separate self are negative behaviors that become the source of unhappiness and estrangement including greed, selfishness, helplessness and existential anxiety. In Buddhism the therapeutic attempt is geared toward creating an understanding of self-based delusion and attempting to replace it with a more healthy psychological perspective of being connected to all in the universe. This interconnectedness and resulting selflessness liberates the individual from the suffering that is part of temporary human existence. The awareness of being interconnected to all produces more compassionate behavior and removes the suffering derived from feelings of impermanence since all happenings are just temporary aspects of an ever-changing reality (Wegela, 2009; Zhang, 2006). In particular meditation offers a path toward more serenity and tranquility as the person comes to perceive and accept the interconnectedness of all reality.

8.2.5. A Critical Thought

What does it matter if people's conception of the self is a reification? Behaviorally we act toward others as if the self is real and from a psychological perspective it is! If the self is an illusion so are all ideologies and religion since for most people they are reified constructs. Reified ideas create concrete identity for people in all cultures, and whether or not the concrete idea is a delusion what perhaps matters most is that people behave as if the reification is real and substantial. Ask any American, German or Vietnamese what it means to be a member of his or her national community and one will immediately elicit reifications that are central components of identity and national character. Further, from a therapeutic perspective of reducing suffering when it comes to facing the existential anxieties of a final end to life it is difficult for a Western trained mind to accept the usefulness of the Buddhist notion that individuals become selfless to such an extent that death does not matter. Therapeutically, however, there is a lot of healing in the Buddhist concept of compassion. Nevertheless no psychological or philosophical approach owns compassion as that would also be another reification and illusionary.

8.3. CONFUCIAN PERSPECTIVE ON PERSONALITY AND THE SELF

Little is known about Confucius in the Western world. Like Buddha he lived about 2500 years ago, however, he spent his life in China whereas Buddha lived in India. Later both bodies of philosophical thought spread across empires and cultures. Many who know a little about Confucian ideas would describe these as antiquated, hierarchical, feudalistic and paternalistic, although writers have in recent times sought to make Confucian thought more relevant to contemporary society (Bell, 2008; Rosemont & Ames, 2009). Confucius's thoughts are outlined in the "Analects" that contained most of the important ideas of Confucianism (Ames & Rosemont, 1998). Generally these ideas are advice on matters related to politics, social responsibility or philosophy. However arguments can also be made for the relevance of Confucian ideas to personality theory. For example, Confucianism explains basic aspects of personality, how it develops, why people suffer, behavior that will eliminate or alleviate suffering, and provide a model for what might be considered a healthy personality (Bell, 2008). In particular Confucian ideas suggested that the locus of personality development is in the family in a way analogous to Western psychology of Freud and others.

The current emphasis on a positive psychology could have taken its inspiration from the Confucius of 25 centuries ago. The ideal and healthy personality develops from a Confucian perspective when we recognize and fulfill important social roles and associated responsibilities. This thought about social responsibilities seems also to overlap with Buddhism and the concept of the interrelated self that emerged from cross-cultural studies in Asia. According to Confucius it is in fulfilling responsibilities in relationships that we reach the ideals of being human, particularly as that development occurs in families, but also within the larger community. However, Confucius sees the family as the forum for healthy human development, in contrast to Freud and others who perceive of family relationships as the locus of individual dysfunction. The outcome of Western human development produces ideally autonomous and independent persons as people achieve maturity by moving away from the family. This concept of maturity is in sharp contrast to Confucian ideas where psychological well-being is seen as a function of relationships and interdependence. In Confucianism becoming human is rooted in our relationships within our first families, but later also in our relationships with our extended families and with the community. How we evolve as persons is a direct result of our relationships according to Confucianism, and personality is fluid as we react to changes or disappearances in our relationships. For example, the relationship of a parent to a child is emotionally different from that of a grandparent to a grandchild and personality evolves accordingly.

In contrast to Western psychology that emphasizes the independent ego in Confucianism it makes no sense to see personality as autonomous since that is considered both unhealthy and dysfunctional. The self is defined by the relational roles that we fulfill and measure up to or fail to perform in a responsible way. Psychological dysfunction comes from ignoring or otherwise violating the responsibilities we have toward others in the family or community. More profoundly we can say that the self consists of our relationship roles. The healthy mature person in Confucianism does not fulfill only the narrow responsibilities of the immediate family, but also the larger community. The primary relationships, however, are identified in Confucian writings as being father-son, husband-wife, elder brother-younger brother, ruler-subject; and friend-friend (Rosemont & Ames, 2009). In the ultimate sense, however, humans are responsible for an ever widening circle of relationships that can also be conceived to exist between countries and cultures. Personality is found in responding or not responding to the demands of the roles that we intuitively feel are right and thereby to do right in our relationships.

It might have caught your attention that the principal relationships as defined by Confucius can be construed as authoritarian and hierarchical. In each of these relationships as understood by Confucius and those that followed there are individuals who are superior in the relationship and those who are inferior. For example, parent to child is manifestly hierarchical, but so are the traditional husband to wife relationship, and the elder brother to younger brother. It is a valid and principal criticism of Confucianism that is supports the authoritarian nature of human relationships. This criticism has been the basis of modern struggles against Confucianism, for example, by the Communist Party in China and elsewhere. However, as Bell (2008) notes, Confucius himself criticized the status quo of society in his day and so was not authoritarian in speaking truth to power. Also, Rosemont and Ames (2009) suggested an alternative interpretation of being "above and below," as the terms could also be defined as benefactor and beneficiary. In all it should not be surprising that philosophies growing out of societies 2500 years ago should have an authoritarian outlook. The choice for our evaluation is obvious since we can reject the hierarchical nature of relationships of Confucianism while emphasizing the importance of relationships in development and indeed in the salience of the relational personality. The saying "it takes a village" to raise a child has modern usage indicating that our responsibilities is not to only our own atomic family, but indeed to all children and families. When construed in that manner Confucius speaks an urgent message to the modern world.

8.4. CULTURE SPECIFIC PERSONALITY: AS SEEN FROM THE PERSPECTIVE OF INDIGENOUS CULTURES

There is no contradiction between perspectives discussed above that argue for a universal structure of personality and personality constructs that are developed from inside a specific culture. Within the universal structure of personality there may also be significant differences in mean values of each of the Big Five or the other traits discussed. Cultural psychologists (as opposed to cross-cultural investigators) have long rejected the idea of a universal organization of personality structure. They note that these structures have initially emerged out of American or European research and may therefore be contaminated by the research methods and ideas that are culture bound. However, the argument of this book is to also recognize the common in humanity based on our shared evolutionary history. It is not far-fetched to believe that personality has a genetic and biological basis since personality traits may have given evolutionary advantages that aided the selection and survival of those living today. The Five Factor Model described previously has been supported in the replication work using trait adjectives in many languages (De Raad, Perugini, Hrebickova, & Szarota, 1998).

Reality is always complex, and in the end there is no conflict between the culture specific and the cross-cultural universal findings of personality structure. From a mutually inclusive perspective personality is culture-specific reflecting unique cultural values and history. At the same time personality is also universal based on structures that are ubiquitous although differing in trait mean values in different societies. The cultural specific and the cross-cultural universal are not mutually exclusive, but rather complementary reflecting the reality of the contributions to personality from evolutionary adaptation, and the unique windows into psychological reality that is part of the culture-specific learning in all societies. All cultures have unique values related to tradition, to food, or religion that gives personalities a common cultural identity within a society and that differ from the personality produced by other cultures. Hwang (2012) argued for the special importance of filial duty in psychological development within Confucian societies.

For example, some researchers have argued for a three layer African personality (Sow, 1978) where the first layer is the core and spiritual center, the second layer represents psychological vitality and the third layer physiological vitality with the body serving as a frame for all three. Japanese psychology has received a lot of attention, in particular the concept of amae that describes a sweet childlike dependence thought to have grown out of mother-child relations (Doi, 1973). Since interpersonal relationships are of great salience in Japanese culture the concept of amae is relevant to all significant relationships. The Korean concept of cheung describes a central personality component of affection (Choi, Kim, & Choi, 1993). Other indigenous culturally specific traits are discussed in Church (2000). Together the work on personality supports the presence of both universal traits and cultural specific traits.

8.5. SOME EVALUATIVE COMMENTS ON CONFUCIANISM AND INDIGENOUS PSYCHOLOGY

Confucian society placed great value on "having face" derived from distinctive achievement in helping relationships and consequent social status. Chen (1988) developed a scale that measured the significance a person places on honorable experiences in life and alternatively their sensitivity to disgrace. This concern to maintain face can be easily understood within Western psychology as a form of impression formation and therefore not unique to Confucian society (Tedeschi & Riess, 1981). A unique factor in Confucian theory is the strong emphasis on filial piety that seems to have no similar comparative place in Western thought. The main difference between Confucianism and Western ideas grew out different conceptions of the origin of life. In Christianity each individual is seen as independently created by God whereas in Confucianism the individual is seen as the continuation of parents and indeed the preceding ancestors. That conception of the individual led to the idea of the "greater self" since in Confucian culture people experience shame and glory together. However, that argument must be modified by the fact that the need to preserve face is probably universal, however, manifested in different ways in varying cultures (Keil, Im, & Mahring, 2007). For example, "keeping face" is probably one way we can understand luxury consumption in both Confucian and Western societies (Qian, Razzaque, & Keng, 2007).

As we observed earlier the interest in Confucian theory and psychological concepts grew out of the dissatisfaction by non-Western psychologists with what seemed to them the domination of Western paradigms in world psychology. This assessment brought about a number of efforts to incorporate non-Western concepts and cultural factors into cultural and cross-cultural psychological research (Hwang, 2005a,b). The first wave called modernization theory was really a surrender to Western culture since it argued that the psychology in any society had to be modernized (and become more similar to U.S. and European personalities and dispositions) in order to facilitate the progress of society (Inkeles, 1966). Hofstede (1980) through his work on cultural work values later helped shift attention away from Western cultures. In the research that emerged the study on individualism and collectivism had a significant heuristic impact (Oyserman, Coon, & Kemmelmeier, 2002).

However, since the research on individualism and collectivism takes American or Europe society as reference points, how can we really understand collectivistic thinking? From these criticisms an indigenous psychology emerged in a search for non-Western psychological interpretations. The effort to create indigenous psychologies was partly motivated by the broader cultural influence of nationalism, and in particular by academic anti-colonialism (Kim, 2000).

The focus of indigenous psychologies, however, also came under criticism. For example, Triandis (2000) noted that anthropologists have used similar methods as those promoted by indigenous psychologies without producing results that significantly impacted scientific psychology. Further, the question might be asked about how many indigenous psychologies are optimal and should be developed? If every culture required a specific psychology we would not only have a confusing many, but it would represent ethnocentrism in reverse (Poortinga, 1999). Any psychology must also take into account the rapidly changing world that has produced concepts like the "global village." It is doubtful that there is any pure homogenous or distinctive culture and it could be argued that there is a broader frame of human commonness that supports a universal psychology. In fact some authors argue that the ultimate goal is to develop a more universal approach from which to understand cultural variations (Ho, 1998; Kim & Berry, 1993; Yang, 1999). That proposition suggests that regardless of cultural variation there also exist in the human mind an underlying deep universal structure that functions the same in all societies, but over time have developed into different mentalities because of the cultural environment.

SUMMARY

This chapter summarizes major approaches to theories of personality from Western conceptions to the thoughts of Eastern philosophy and the cultural psychologist's work on indigenous traits. Definitions of personality in the West refer to enduring traits that are reflected in consistent behavior across situations, context and the lifespan. The dominant contemporary personality model in Western psychology is the trait approach through which researchers can learn what distinguishes one person from another. The departure point in Western psychology is the seminal work of Sigmund Freud. Through his method of having patients "free associate" he developed a broad theory of personality that emphasized the importance of childhood development (the child is the father of the man) and the dominant role of unconscious motivation. Freud argued for the presence of two opposing instincts in human life. The Eros represented life, love and creativity, the Thanatos death, aggression and destruction. Personality structure in

Freud's theory consists of three components. The Id is based on the pleasure principle, the Ego moderates behavior in compliance with social reality and demands, and the Superego incorporates parental values in the form of individual conscience. Probably the most useful construct derived from Freud's psychoanalysis is the conceptualization of defense mechanisms that intuitively seem to match and explain great deal of human behavior. The neo-Freudians differed from Freud by emphasizing conscious motivation, the importance of social stages of development, and by deemphasizing the role of sexuality.

The contributors to humanistic psychology were more interested in the development of healthy people in contrast to Freud's work with neurotic patients. Maslow and Rogers thought and wrote about the human potential for growth and happiness. Maslow developed a theory of motivation where the peak of personal development is the self-actualized person, a concept that has greatly influenced contemporary debate and research. Traits that describe a self-actualized personality include compassion, a concept similar to that advocated in Buddhism. Rogers emphasized the essential goodness of human beings and the importance of rejecting the false in life, striving toward self-acceptance and the acceptance of others through unconditional positive regard. Humanistic psychology served a heuristic role in encouraging research on the etiology and correlates of self-esteem.

Social-cognition is an interaction theory that explains personality from the point of view of principles of learning and cognition. The critical determinant in the development of personality is found in the interaction of the person with the environment called reciprocal determinism. Bandura argued that we all exercise choices in regard to our environment, and that these choices shape our personality. In many ways we become self-fulfilling prophecies as our attitudes sensitize us to environmental variables. Social-cognition interaction theory formed the framework for research on the locus of control variable. Because of their reinforcement history some people have developed an external locus of control and come to believe that they have little or no power over environmental forces and that their behavior has no affect on outcomes. Other people believe that the outcomes of life are primarily a function of their own behavior. Learned helplessness is a related concept where people exposed to powerful forces learn that there is no relationship between their efforts and their outcomes. A great deal of cross-cultural research has emerged out social-cognition interaction theory on the locus of control and autonomy variables.

On the whole Americans are more likely to score high on beliefs in the internal locus of control compared to Asian and some other cultural groups. Research has also supported the relationship between real life conditions of control and whether people believe in an internal or external locus of control. People who come from impoverished backgrounds believe more strongly in the external locus of control thus validating the concept. Further, in related research the relative influence of individualistic versus collectivistic cultures affects the degree of autonomy people experience. However, research supports the idea that people who are able to live their values feel they are autonomous regardless of other cultural organization of life that reinforce authoritarianism.

The chapter reports on personality types and how these can be understood as a hardwired legacy from our adaptive efforts to survive. The competitive and stressed type A personality seems to be a particular contribution of modern capitalism. Research supports at least in part the genetic heritability of some personality traits and those that are discovered early in childhood have consistent affects across the lifespan. Research on the Big Five super traits support the genetic basis for personality structure as these traits appear in all cultures studied. Although the presence of the Big Five is now commonly accepted it is important to remember that culture affects the mean values of the traits within cultures. Conversely societies that are geographically closer also have a greater correspondence on the mean values of the Big Five supporting the role of culture. Criticisms suggest that the Big Five do not describe very well the interpersonal relatedness central to personality in Asia and elsewhere. Research has also demonstrated the universality of other personality traits like the relative levels of authoritarianism. Nevertheless the presence of the Big Five has been explained as a universal adaptation that developed because it gave advantages in the common human struggle for survival. The research on national character also supports the influence of culture in personality development as such self-stereotypes serve to reinforce national identity.

Eastern thought and philosophies have made important contributions to personality theory and many mind-related constructs emerged from Eastern cultures across many centuries before they occurred to people in the Western world. The major difference between Western and Eastern thought is in the construal of the self. Whereas the self is seen as an enduring aspect of personality in Western thinking, the self is viewed as a reification and delusion in the Buddhist worldview. Central to Buddhist philosophy is the concept of the middle way where the healthy person seeks to find a balance that does not lead to self-indulgence or self-mortification. Suffering in life is real and from that affliction humans search for relief often in pleasure seeking that, however, produces nothing of enduring value and only provide a temporary cessation of desire. Buddha taught that suffering and desire can be controlled and lead to a personal transformation when we choose the path leading to self-fulfillment and an authentic existence by accepting the welfare other others as a high ethical responsibility. The ego based self is an illusion that only brings suffering.

Buddhist personality theory posits components called Skandhas that are interdependent in origin and functions and are based on the consciousness that emerge from the basic sensory processes. The mind is the location of complex cognition although all these processes are temporary. Nevertheless complex cognition gives rise to the "subjective knower" that seems to be in control. The aim of Buddhism is to eliminate or reduce all unnecessary suffering by creating an understanding of the delusion of the inner self and replacing that with more healthy conceptualizations found in the interconnectedness of the person to all in the universe. When we see ourselves as connected to all in the universe we are able to empathize with the sufferings of others and develop compassion. Meditation offers a path in Buddhism that can lead to greater peace and serenity. A critical thought about the Buddhist idea of reification of the self might be: does it matter if the self is a delusion and is reified when the individual and others behave as if it is real?

Confucian philosophy also made a major contribution to our thinking about personality. As a body of thought it seeks to explain basic aspects of personality, how it develops in the family structure, why people suffer, and healthy behavior and personality. According to Confucian thinking the locus of personality development is found in the family. However, Western psychology sees maturity of personality development in the formation of independent and autonomous persons, whereas Confucianism sees a healthy personality as someone who recognizes and fulfills important roles and responsibilities of relationships. The family is the initial place of role responsibility, but as the person develops he/she must respond to ever widening circles of relationships and associated duties. The independent Ego makes no sense in Confucianism since the autonomous personality favored in the West is seen as both unhealthy and dysfunctional. Although Confucius has been criticized for supporting authoritarianism in human relationships an alternative interpretation is to view hierarchical relationships as those between benefactor and beneficent.

Collateral to the cross-cultural comparative research on personality, the cultural psychologists have found evidence for traits that are unique to a particular culture and indigenous. The overall picture revealed by personality research would support the presence of both universal personality structures that can be compared across cultures, but also culturally specific traits unique to the cultural values of particular societies.

CHAPTER 9

THE SELF

Cultural, Social and Cross-Cultural Dimensions

In chapter 8 we discussed personality theory and the contributions of Western and Eastern culture. In this chapter the discussion will evaluate the parameters of the self-concept from both cultural and cross-cultural research and perspectives. Research on the self-concept seeks to define the basic psychological question of "who am I?." Some of us have developed a positive self-concept that in turn has created an optimistic and positive expectation about the world. Other people because of their biological inheritance and/or unique social and cultural experiences have developed a darker more negative view of the self that affects their social interactions in counterproductive ways. The self serves important organizational functions in the mind as the governing center of our personality. Developing positive self-esteem helps people to persist when the going is rough, make us less likely to abuse drugs, and allows us to experience greater happiness. Low self-esteem is, on the other hand, linked to depression and other life problems.

The self-concept is an outcome of interactions between the individual and the cultural environment. The dominance of culture in forming self-hood has been a subject of research and controversial arguments. If the

Cross-Cultural Psychology: Why Culture Matters, pages 233–286.

self-concept varies by culture that conclusion must affect our appraisal of the universal trait research reported in chapter 8. If cross-cultural research lends support to the idea of cultural dependency in the self-concept can the person be described in terms of enduring traits?. However, research on the self is really an attempt to bridge the connection between personality theory and social psychology where cultural values play an important role. Cultural values can bridge that relationship, as Triandis (1989) noted that the more individualistic the culture the more a person accesses the private self for evaluative purposes and the less the collective self was salient.

Kagitcibasi (1996) developed these ideas further by observing the difference between the relational self and the separated self. *The relational self is built in the context of both material and emotional interdependence where members of the family and community rely on each other for support throughout life. On the other hand, the separated self found in Western societies emphasizes individualism in family and social relationships.* As we noted in chapter 4 on human development the model for socialization in Western societies calls for early emotional and material independence and the relationships that are found in the nuclear family. Markus and Kitayama (1991a) noted that various cultures have very different self-construal. The ideal self in Western societies is seen as separate and autonomous with the goal of independence from others. In Eastern societies the self is linked to others through the process of interdependence. The ideas of Markus and Kitayama have been found limited support in some studies (e.g. Matsumoto, 1999). The domain of the self is obviously very complex, and the dichotomies offered by cultural values too simplistic to capture the universal as well as the cultural specific contributions to self-hood. The cultural differences of interdependence and independence may simply be a matter of culturally consistent impression management motivated by the desire to have the self appear culturally congruent.

9.1. THE GRADUAL PROCESS OF SELF-AWARENESS

Self-awareness begins early in life. By about nine months of age the average child starts to differentiate the self from others (Harter, 1983). At the age of 18 months the typical child will have a developed a sense of self-awareness and can react with more emotion to pictures of themselves than to unrelated people. Gradually as our self-knowledge grows, the self takes on other attributes. If lucky our cultural environment nurture positive self-attributes leading to feelings of competence or self-efficacy. Individuals living in less stimulating cultures are not as fortunate as some societies place limits on what is possible centered in the self-concept that affects individual plans for work and development.

A biological basis for self-awareness is suggested by research in other species that demonstrates self-awareness (Gallup, 1977, 1997). In one study the experimenter initially placed a mirror in the cage of chimpanzees until it became a familiar object. Afterwards the experimenter placed an odorless red dye on the animals' ear or brow. The animals recognized that something had changed and responded with immediately touching the dyed area. Studies with dolphins and other animals demonstrate a similar pattern of self-recognition (Mitchell, 2003).

9.2. KNOWING ABOUT THE SELF

Using similar techniques with toddlers, researchers found that self-recognition is present at around age two (Lewis, 1997; Povinelli, Landau, & Perilloux, 1996). Over time the child begins to incorporate psychological attributes including more complex feelings and thoughts. This social self is based on how we are evaluated by others (Hart & Damon, 1986). As we develop more complex beliefs and feelings about the social self, we also begin to project ourselves to some degree into the future. From these initial experiences with the family, educational system, and the broader culture the social self gradually emerges.

The self-concept is the knowledge we have of ourselves, that we exist separately from others, and have our own unique properties. As part of our self-knowledge we develop a belief system that governs behavior. Do we live in a world of chaos or order? Do we believe we can accomplish important goals? Can other people be trusted? This complex web of beliefs in turn contributes to whether we approach or avoid others, impact our feelings of self-esteem, and provides a concept of what we can become in the future called a possible self. In the process of maturation children gradually place less emphasis on concrete physical descriptions of the self, as more awareness is centered on complex psychological states including thoughts, feelings, and the evaluations of others (Harter, 2003; Hart & Damon, 1986).

9.3. THE MEANING OF SELF-ESTEEM

Culture is an important dimension affecting self-esteem. In independent ego-based cultures self-esteem is connected to personal accomplishments. On the other hand, in interdependent cultures self-esteem is based more on the connectedness to others and relationships. Therefore social approval is a more significant component of overall self-esteem in the collectivistic societies. In individualistic cultures while self self-estem derive from individual accomplishments and achievement, it does not follow that accomplishments are unimportant in interdependent cultures, or that relationships are not significant in independent cultures, but rather that the cultural values are the mediators of these common factors in the self and in self-esteem. Social approval is probably of significance in all societies as it is directly related to survival and inclusion. However, self-worth reflects at least in part how the individual conform to central cultural values.

An important contribution to the self-concept is our self-evaluations or self-esteem. Self-esteem is evaluative based judgments of personal morality and whether in our own eyes we are satisfied or dissatisfied with our performance and behavior. Global self-esteem can be measured by surveys and is related to our need for approval (e.g. Larsen, 1969). The lower our self-esteem the more we have a need for affirmation and approval by others and society. High self- esteem, on the other hand, is associated with setting appropriate goals, using feedback from others to progress, and enjoying positive experiences to the fullest extent possible (Wood, Heimpel, & Michela, 2003). When experiencing rejection or frustration, those with high self-esteem will find a silver lining. High self-esteem people are adaptable and are persistent in working toward goal and have the ability when frustrated to envision alternative goals (Sommer & Baumeister, 2002). High self-esteem people will look at the past through rose-colored glasses and this selective positive memory bias may in turn support their higher self-esteem (Christensen, Wood, & Barrett, 2003).

On the other hand, people with low self-esteem not only think poorly of themselves, but the negative self-conceptions have other unfortunate consequences. Low self-esteem persons are more pessimistic about the future, tend to obsess about their negative moods, are more concerned about the opinions of others, and have higher needs for approval (Heimpel, Wood, Marshall, & Brown, 2002). Low self-esteem is also reflected in negative estimations of competence or self-efficacy and in self-loathing. On the other hand, those with positive feelings toward the self not only like themselves, but have feelings of competence (Tafarodi, Marshall, & Milne, 2003). As we shall see throughout this chapter and what follows, the cultural context matters. Members of Asian cultures, for example, are less self-enhancing in explicit ways, but enhance more in implicit ways (Koole, Dijksterhuis, & Van Knippenberg, 2001).

9.4. CULTURE AS A SOURCE OF THE SELF-CONCEPT

In chapter 1 we introduced the concept of individualistic and collectivistic cultures. It is now time to apply this cultural division to the formation of the social self. We shall see that these cultural differences created independent and interdependent selves that have applications throughout this chapter. Culture has profound effects in socialization and produces predictable differences in self-concepts. Western societies found in North America and Europe has inculcated social values significant to successful adaptation and survival in the capitalist model. The term "rugged individualism" points to a person who is first and foremost independent and was able to cope with the hazards of life in early United States. In that cultural environment each man was a king in his own house, and society was preoccupied then as now with individual self-actualization.

In Asian societies, on the other hand, we have ancient cultures that had to adapt to high levels of physical density of their large populations. Physical density is not experienced as crowding in Asia to the same degree it would be experienced in the West, because the highly developed structures of courtesy evolved to meet the need for personal space and privacy. Hall (1976) thought of independent societies, as "low-context cultures" where social roles while not unimportant mattered less. Therefore a person from independent cultures would more or less act the same regardless of the changing context of behavior or the situation. *In interdependent cultures on the other hand, the social context matters a great deal, and the individual's behavior will change dependent on the specific role played by the participant.* In interdependent cultures the behavior of the self would differ depending on role expectation and the person would behave in ways that are appropriate in interactions with parents, peers, or colleagues. As we shall see, in Western societies the bias toward independence leads to attribution errors where we underestimate the influence of the situation and attribute behavior primarily to individual traits.

In recent years social psychologists have carried out many cross-cultural studies on how motivations, emotions, and behaviors are shaped by cultural conceptions of the self (Markus & Kitayama, 1991a; Rhee, Uleman, Lee, & Roman, 1995; Triandis, 1995). From this accumulated research the cultures characterized as promoting values of self-independence are found primarily in the West. In Western societies the self is seen as autonomous, distinct and separate from other members of society. Consequently explanations for behavior are sought within the individual's personality. Not only is independence a fundamental value, but Westerners also believe that the main object of socialization is to create independent children (Kitayama, 1992). The self is therefore described as composed of individual attributes (Trafimov, Triandis, & Goto, 1991). Achievements are seen as primarily the result of individual and distinctive efforts and where family or society played at best peripheral roles.

In the interdependent cultures of Asia and in countries of the developing world the self is perceived as part of the larger social context. The self is not construed apart from other people, but rather as connected to family and larger social organizations. The willingness of people to go on suicide missions like the kamikaze pilots of Japan is related to the interdependent self-construal where country and emperor are part of the self. Western combatants may also fight with great courage, however, self-sacrifice is best elicited when there is some possibility if not probability of survival. In interdependent societies the self is completely embedded in the roles and duties of social relationships. Culture therefore determines to a large extent self-knowledge and self-esteem, as well as self-presentations and impression management. The self is connected to the attributes of others, is not seen as distinctive, but associated with family and society (Bochner, 1994). These cultural differences are thought to profoundly affect how individuals think about themselves, how they relate to others in society, and in what motivates their behavior (Markus & Kitayama, 1994b).

Studies have shown that Americans achieve primarily for personal reasons, whereas those from interdependent societies strive to achieve group goals (Iyengar & Lepper, 1999). It is the personal nature of tasks and objectives that motivates behavior in the West, whereas Asian students are motivated more by group goals. Consequently students in the West are more likely to select careers or tasks in which they have experienced previous success and which had been rewarding in the past. The career choices of Asians, on the other hand, are not based on such personal expectations or prior performance (Oishi & Diener, 2003).

These cultural differences in self-construal also affect how we organize information in memory (Woike, Gershkovich, Piorkowski, & Polo, 1999). *People in independent cultures disregard the social context in memory formation, and think of events in personal terms.* Elections in the United States are typically about the personal attributes of candidates where the social context or genuine political proposals matters little. Typically this personalized political process manipulates the indifferent electorate to disregard political programs in the search for the "right" person.

There are some researchers who feel these cultural differences in self-construal make intercultural communication very difficult (Kitayama & Markus, 1994b). Yet, at the end of the day we must remember that these cultural differences are abstractions and there are always more differences found within than between social groups. In independent cultures there are many people with interdependent self-construal, particularly among women (Cross, Bacon, & Morris, 2000; Cross & Vick, 2001). In interdependent societies, on the other hand, there are also people whose self-construal is independent. Further, migration and globalization is changing the world. For example, within United States and Europe there are many immigrants who come from cultures with interdependent self-construal. Many migrants work hard in Western societies not for individual benefit, but so they can send most of their earnings back to the home country. Globalization is also producing more converging values for example, an increasing emphasis on human rights in nearly all societies, and as that takes its course in the future we must reevaluate the cultural differences discussed above.

9.5. TOWARD THE NEW GLOBALIZED WORLD: MULTI-CULTURAL SELF-IDENTITY?

In recent decades the world has gone through great transformations as a result of globalization and intercultural contacts. How do people of different cultures develop a sense of identity becomes one of the more salient questions in cross-cultural psychology as we move forward into the 21st century (Phinney, 1999). In our emerging world the conflict that people experience is not always with other groups, but frequently within themselves and involves the acceptance of varying complementary and in some cases contradictory cultural values. As a result of commerce and global travelling many people in the world, significant minorities in many countries, have experienced exposure to more than one culture, and many speak more than one language (Padilla, 2006). One consequence is that large numbers of people now see themselves as being part of more than one culture, having a sense of identity with perhaps an original culture as well as a host society (Nguyen & Benet-Martinez, 2007). Multiculturalism can also be used to describe nations like Canada that are indeed multi-cultural with the historical British and French roots. With globalization Canada and other countries with multiple ethnic and language developments are now even more broadly multi-cultural (Fowers & Richardson, 1996). However, the label can also refer to colonial countries in which indigenous people continue to live and contribute (Burnet, 1995).

Multiculturalism is more likely to be supported and endorsed by ethnic and cultural minorities as it allows for positive contacts with both the minority and majority groups in society. In turn research shows that multiculturalism is related to better self-esteem in minorities, probably a reflection of improved coping skills and adjustment. The multi-cultural perspective permits also the continued ethnic identification and support by the minority that also contributes to adjustment to varying cultural demands and circumstances (Verkuyten, 2005, 2008). Acculturation is the process of learning about and becoming part of new cultures. In the past acculturation used to mean assimilation into the host society and loss of the previous ethnic identification. However, in recent decades a great deal of research shows this to be a simplification as acculturation is two-way and complex, and involves learning by both the minority and also majority in society (Sam & Berry, 2006). The outcome can place individuals into one of four acculturation strategies. The solutions include assimilation, but also integration where the individual identify with both cultures, separation where the individual prefer to identify only with the ethnic minority and marginalization which describe individuals not involved or identifying with either cultural perspective (Rudmin, 2003).

Anyone who has been exposed in some depth to two or more cultures knows that the cognitive cultural frame can be rapidly switched from one to the other depending on circumstances. Socio-cognitive experiments demonstrate support for the ability by multi-cultural individuals to quickly move from one perspective to another. This author is multi-lingual and has often wondered at the cognitive process that switches thinking from the current dominant language to the original language after short periods of stay in the home community. Whenever the cultural cues from the relevant culture are present the schemas from that culture becomes easily assessable (Verkuyten & Pouliasi, 2006). Again these processes are complex. However, acculturation does not proceed uniformly or apply equally to all domains that involve the individual. Some individuals may have excellent exposure leading to language acquisition, whereas their ability to affiliate may be lacking. As in all areas that involve cross-cultural experiences the outcomes are complex with many interaction effects (Zane & Mak, 2003).

9.6. CULTURAL BOUNDARIES OF SELF-ESTEEM AND SELF-ENHANCEMENT

The preoccupation with self-esteem is largely a Western self-identity phenomenon. It derives from our cultural values focusing on the individual and personal distinctions. It seems ironic that the rugged individualist valued in the West is vulnerable to feelings of low self-esteem. Westerners, however, do self-report higher levels of self-esteem as compared with interdependent peoples (Dhawan, Roseman, Naidu, Thapa, & Rettek, 1995; Markus & Kitayama, 1991a). That finding may be attributed to the greater modesty of interdependent peoples, and also the greater preoccupation with the self in Western societies. A great deal of energy is spent in Western cultures on enhancing the self, and supporting the impression management and face work of family members and acquaintances in order to enhance self-esteem. Americans and Canadians when enhancing their selves insist they have comparatively more positive qualities than others (Holmberg, Markus, Herzog, & Franks, 1997). The very nature of social interaction in the West including the effects of education, media, and socializing, encourages a preoccupation with self-esteem.

Being rewarded and praised for achievement is much more common in the West where people seek distinctiveness, whereas in interdependent cultures people are more motivated by common goals and self-improvement (Crocker & Park, 2004; Heine, 2005; Norenzayan & Heine, 2005). In Asian cultures self-criticism is common in the pursuit of social harmony and self-improvement. A student from the West invited to criticize him/herself may perceive that invitation as a threat to the self-concept and self-esteem. *Salient cultural differences between individualistic and collectivistic societies are rooted in either a preoccupation with self-esteem in the West or motivating self-improvement in interdependent societies.*

Finally, we should keep in mind that cultural differences are abstractions. Let us also emphasize again that there are more within society individual differences than is found between cultures. Furthermore societies change over time. The individualism of Western societies is a product of recent centuries and the advancement of capitalist economies (Baumeister, 1987;

Twenge, 2002). Each generation struggles with the issues related to adaptation, and in a broader sense adopt the cultural values that lead to reproductive success. Globalization has also produced common values esteemed by many people throughout the world. In the new world order people in many countries and their governments accept the values of independence promoted in the West. Overall, there is evidence that many cultures are becoming more convergent in values (Heine & Lehman, 2003).

9.7. THE SELF EMERGES OUT OF TEMPERAMENT AND HARDWIRED PERSONALITY TRAITS

As noted in the preceding chapter social scientists have identified personality traits that are universal in all cultures, although the mean values reflect cultural differences. Studies that compare identical and fraternal twins have supported the heritability of traits based on shared genes. Traits found early in development are often consistent over the life-span supporting the heritability of the structure of the self. Biological inheritance is responsible for a significant component of our behavior and therefore also our self-construal. The relationship of genes to social behavior is complex, but nevertheless an exciting new area of research that increases our understanding of the self.

Children are not truly "tabula rasa" or a blank slate when entering the world. Scientists have for some time found traits that seem to be universal in all cultures. As noted in chapter 8 personality traits typically describe cross-situational consistency and refer to the consistent way people act, think or feel despite changing circumstances (Costa & McCrae, 1988; John & Srivastava, 1999).

People use the Big Five basic traits in describing themselves, and in judging other people. The ability to describe others tends to be accurate in the sense that they match self-descriptions (Funder, 1995; John & Robins, 1993; Watson, 1989). Many psychologists believe that the Big Five traits are the basic building blocks of personality. The evidence is pointing in the direction of a biological basis since people universally use these traits in describing the self and other people (Buss, 1999).

The relationship of genetics to complex social behavior is a challenging new frontier. Social behavior is complex and both genes and the social environment play a role. Some genes require specific environments to elicit an effect so interactions matter. In a study on violence (Caspi, McClay, Moffitt, Mill, Martin, & Craig, 2002) the researchers tested for the presence of the Monoamine oxidase A gene responsible for metabolizing neurotransmitters in the brain, and for promoting smooth communication between the neurons. The absence of the gene by itself had little effect. However, when combined with abuse and maltreatment the men in the study were three times as likely to have been convicted of violent crimes by age 26. Low levels or absence of the MAOA gene combined with maltreatment developed anti-social behavior in 85 percent of the boys. The complex interaction and interdependence between our biological inheritance and the social context is clear. Many personality traits are adaptive to evolutionary requirements for selective adaptation. However, as society has also evolved many traits are no longer functional like perhaps interdependence in the new competitive global world. Being fearful and even neurotic might have been functional in the days of saber tooth tigers, but today create interpersonal problems for those who have inherited an excess of these traits today.

9.8. THE DUALITY OF THE SELF-CONCEPT: THE HARD AND EASY PROBLEM

Intuition tells us there is substance to the self. We discussed that issue in chapter 8 when we evaluated differences between cultures, and in particular Buddhist thinking. Critics of reification in psychology say that people attribute (reify) the self with a "thingness" that nevertheless is not supported by evidence. As noted in the preceding chapter Buddhists would maintain that the self is a delusion leading to many negative behaviors. However, in Western societies the independent self is promoted along with the presence of some "inner being" in control of behavior and outcomes. William James (1890) is today recognized as a founder of American Psychology. In his early writings he described the essential duality of the self-concept. The first aspect of the self-concept is composed of all the thoughts and beliefs we hold about our self, also called the "known self" or "me." The second component of the self is the "knower." The "knower" refers to the observatory function of the self, or now more commonly called self-awareness. We come to know who we are by becoming aware and thinking about ourselves.

Today the aspect of the self defined as the self-concept or "me" is gradually being understood through experimentation. The self-concept and its relationship to brain functions is what have been called the "easy" problem verified through experiments on brain functions. *The hard problem is somewhat of a mystery trying to understand what is called the "knower."* Those with religious inclinations would refer to the "knower" as the immaterial soul. The scientist does not find that construct convincing as the soul concept explains everything and in reality nothing. The soul definition is a form of nominalism that simply puts a label or name to a process, and we do not advance much in our understanding by just placing the "knower" into a category.

Why do we feel as if we have an inner self? There are many cognitive processes not accessible to conscious thought, but we possess a core of self-awareness that appears substantive to us and consistent over time. What does science have to say about the processes that give rise to the "knower or inner self"? As we shall see there are alternative interpretations of the inner self or soul as defined in Western theology. Science lend support to the Buddhist notion of the self as a delusion by describing the objective brain processes that give rise to self-awareness related to the "inner self." Freud wrote a great deal about conscious and unconscious processes. Much of our thinking is in fact accessible to our awareness. We make plans for the future, decide on what to have for dinner, save up for children's college. These self-relevant objectives and much more are conscious in the sense that they are accessible thoughts that we can think about and evaluate. Other bodily processes like the functions of the autonomic nervous system are largely unconscious. We know they are present in the body, but they are generally not available to the reasoning or planning functions of the brain.

The hard problem is trying to understand why it feels like we have a conscious process to begin with, that we are aware of a "first person" as a very subjective experience, the executive "I" or the decision maker (Pinker, 2007). The scientist finds it difficult to explain how this subjective feeling of the self arises from neural computations in the brain. Do you believe that all our joys and pain can be reduced to neurological activity in the brain? *The hard problem* is: does consciousness exist in an ethereal soul or is consciousness purely a brain function defined as the activity of the brain.

Today some cognitive neuroscientists claim that by using MRI's we can practically read people's thoughts from blood flow in the brain. Through electrical stimulation of certain areas of the brain scientists can cause hallucination such as hearing music played long ago, or experiencing childhood memories. Anti-depressants like Prozac can profoundly affect feelings and thoughts. Also supporting a brain based self is the common human experience of death and whenever the brain function ceases so far as we can see our consciousness comes to an end. No reliable reports of contacts with the dead have ever been produced. Even near death experiences where the soul purportedly departs the body only to return are probably caused by oxygen starvation of the eyes and brain. Swiss neuroscientists (Pinker, 2007) have managed to turn out-of-body experiences off and on by stimulating the part of the brain overlapping vision and bodily sensations. The fact that all observable psychological activity has a physiological concomitant lends little support for a soul construct.

Many visions or "miracles can be attributed to how the brain developed to meet survival needs. It appears, for example, that we possess a template for the recognition of faces in a variety of objects. Some years ago a woman made herself a cheese sandwich and experienced a vision, as she perceived the Virgin Mary in the brown skillet marks. She eventually sold the sandwich on eBay for $28000.00 probably to someone who wanted a vicarious vision. In another case people saw a three dimensional face on the surface of Mars after an orbiter captured images from the Cydonia region. That image ignited enthusiasm, and encouraged conspiracy theories accusing scientists or governments in the denial of life on our sister planet. All of us have had the experience of gazing into the sky and finding faces in the moving clouds. These perceptual illusions appear to be functions of three regions of the temporal lobe of the brain involved in the recognition of faces. The tendency to see faces is a result of neural architecture with obvious evolutionary advantages (Svoboda, 2007). In our distant past some faces or images should be avoided like that of the saber tooth tiger and others should be approached like that of family or other beneficent people.

The materialist brain based explanation of the "inner self" is advanced by the argument that the "knower" or "executive I" is nothing more than an illusion. In the brain based self, consciousness consists of a stream of external stimuli that compete for attention in the mind. As an evolutionary adaptation the brain developed decision-making functions to discriminate between important and non-essential input. Subsequent to decisions the brain rationalized the outcome giving us the impression that someone or some "thingness" was in charge. Information overload is the common human experience that requires the decision making function of the self. People who possessed better neural webs were the ones who survived and passed down their genes for brain functioning to the next generation. Pinker believes that the "knower" is nothing more than "executive summaries of the events and states that are most relevant to updating an understanding of the world and figuring out what to do next" (p. 65).

Damasio (2007) argues that self-awareness is a function of evolutionary biology and psychology. Initially gene networks organized themselves to evolve complex organisms with brains. Further evolution enriched the complexity of brains by developing sensory and motor maps to represent the environmental context. Eventually with more evolutionary complexity different parts of the brain developed the ability to communicate, and generate sophisticated maps of the organism interacting with the environment. From this natural knowledge and interaction the basic self emerged, and the brain's sensory-motor maps gradually changed in the course of evolution from non-conscious mental patterns to conscious mental images. Scientists are gradually developing knowledge about the neural correlates of conscious activity of the self.

Some scientists would simply call the inner experience we called the "hard problem" information processing thereby making it an "easy" problem. Others researchers would say that since there is no test that can distinguish between a well-designed robot, and a human, we should just let the problem go away as irrelevant (Dennett, 2007). Perhaps our failure to understand the hard problem is a function of the limitation of our brain. After all we have many other limitations like failing to grasp the existence of spheres greater than three dimensions. Brain limitations include also the difficulty of understanding subjectively how stimuli from the outside produce feelings on the inside.

Many fear the loss of a moral perspective if we come to believe in a unitary material self. After all if we do not have an immortal soul why worry about salvation in an unseen world to come? However, scientists would argue that believing in the materialist self would increase empathy as we are all in the same existential boat. To be aware of how temporary life and consciousness is should give poignant meaning to all existence and sympathy for all who struggle with the same reality. Keep in mind that historically (and in the present endless wars) belief in the immortal soul did not prevent believers from engaging in gross defiance of morality by committing genocide and cruelty. The crusades conquered land with great cruelty still remembered by Muslim zealots today. In the dark ages half a million women were burned at the stake by the inquisition in an attempt to save their immortal souls. The destruction of 9/11 and what followed was largely motivated by religious morality on both sides including the belief in the immortal soul and paradise. Religious ideology often provides heavenly rewards for killing and destruction. Perhaps we would all be better off believing in a fragile and temporary existence.

9.9. INTUITIVE PROBLEMS REMAIN FOR THE SELF USING THE EASY BRAIN DEFINITION

What matters to science is only the truth. It is important to remember that beliefs about the self have consequences. Beliefs in a soul that lives forever more can function to support contemporary human indifference to solve the urgent problems of this life. Is the callousness and lack of poignant appreciation for our temporary existence advanced by beliefs in as soul and a just god? Yet, the easy solution seems unsatisfactory based on intuition.

At the end of the day the hard problem remains unsolved. It seems particularly difficult to understand how deep feelings can be solely a consequence of brain activity. Some of us have experienced awe in the presence of the truly noble and good. How can one attribute these feelings as an interpretive consequence of brain activity? The sense of unspeakable joy that comes in the wake of love, the truly altruistic behavior of others resonates in our minds in ways not easily understood by the material self. The cynic can, of course, reduce altruism to "reward expectations," but the "knower" knows the difference. The feelings of grandeur in the presence of nature, the emotions experienced from certain types of music are examples of the presence of a "knower." The drumbeats of the Nazi's reflect the robotic self that resonates with martial spirit and aggression and self-aggrandizement. However, music may also cause meditation and bring to us harmony and peace. Understanding meditative feelings, altruism, and the noble as brain functions remains a hard problem.

Perhaps viewing consciousness from the perspective of brain function-ing is good science, but philosophically unsound? Science has made great progress in breaking objects into atomic and subatomic particles. Is there a bias in that perspective? Are there other routes to the factual and truth? At least we know that the whole is always more than the sum of its parts. Human attributes create questions about the "knower" as many people feel compassion towards others. Where does that come from? If we cannot find the answer in neurons firing, then is consciousness a primary principle? Is consciousness really an illusion caused by 100 billion simmering neurons? Is the locus for experiencing ideas and intentions just temporary brain ac-tivity? Do we perceive time because it is separate from us? Some parts of the self remain continuous for life, and we can recognize our basic self-components, but we are also aware of time and change. If we were caught up in time could we perceive that fact without a "knower"? These and many other self-related issues remain intriguing and fundamental problems of human existence.

There is a mysterious aspect to life that even the greatest minds cannot understand. Einstein too was in a state of awe by what he saw of a causal and ordered nature. Perhaps he was affected by the certainty of the subjective "I" when he wrote his credo: "The most beautiful emotion we can experi-ence is the mysterious. It is the fundamental emotion that stands at the cradle of all true art and science. He to whom this emotion is a stranger, who can no longer wonder and stand rapt in awe, is as good as dead, a snuffed-out candle. To sense that behind anything that can be experienced there is something that our minds cannot grasps, whose beauty and sublim-ity reaches us only indirectly: this is religiousness. In this sense, and in this sense only, I am a devoutly religious man" (Isaacson, 2007). Did Einstein address the common human limitation of our brains? Did he attribute re-ligiousness to our inability to understand what is after all natural stimuli? Or did Einstein acknowledge with certainty that the hard problem remains, and will not easily yield a solution.

9.10. THE SOCIAL SELF IS FORMED IN THE PROCESS OF SOCIALIZATION

The self consists of several components derived from socialization, cultural group membership and gender. We learn who we are by observing the re-actions of others in our interactions in the family and in cultural and edu-cational institutions. Culture is a significant modifier of the self-concept through the influence of commonly accepted values in individualistic and collectivistic societies.

The sources of the self-knowledge are primarily other people, although we can also learn by observing our own behavior, and by thinking about ourselves. We form self-attributes in the course of socialization. It is through family and other socialization agents that we learn about our level of competence, success in achieving important goals, and whether we are evaluated positively. From these socialization experiences we derive a sense of self-efficacy and self-esteem. Through socialization we acquire our standards for behavior, and we incorporate the values of our family and culture. The way we are consistently treated in early socialization forms the core of what we come to believe about ourselves that guides us throughout life.

Cooley (1902) developed a concept called the "looking glass self." From his perspective we learn about ourselves through the reactions of other people. This is called *reflected appraisals*. Those who experience constant praise come to believe they are valuable; those who experience maltreatment may think their lives are worthless. So feedback from others is a basic key to understanding the social self. The importance can be seen in a study on parental perceptions and children's self-perceptions (Felson & Reed, 1986). In general there is close similarity between parent's beliefs about children's abilities, and the children's self-concept.

Later, of course, we encounter peers and these have profound importance during adolescence (Leary, Cottrell, & Phillips, 2001). Most of us know intuitively our social standing from the preferences of our peers. The order in which children are chosen for athletic teams tells a lot about the person's perceived contribution to a team, and value to his/her peers. Whether a girl gets asked out for dates also tells her a great deal about how peers perceive her in terms of physical attractiveness and her personality. Teachers give feedback on school performance that is either encouraging or discouraging in competitive educational environments. Competitive educational experiences using the normal curve for grading student performance obviously produce losers and do not foster growth in all children. Some children will always occupy low levels of grades or fail in comparative standing in a normal curve. These early experiences contribute to whether the individual's possible self is optimistic or pessimistic. If we are encouraged in childhood and adolescence we form plans about what we can become, what contribution we can make to society, and how we can find self-fulfillment.

9.10.1. Family Socialization Creates the Framework for Possible Selves

A family has influence not only through parental guidance, but also through relationships formed with siblings. In societies with scarce resources, sibling conflict is frequent and violent. Human history bears witness to violent outcomes from the Bible story of Cain and Abel to current news stories. Even very young children engage in frequent conflict (Dunn & Munn, 1985). Birth order matters because children learn to adjust to certain niches in the family that is functional and rewarding. Older siblings

tend to be more dominant and assertive as well as more achievement oriented and conscientious (Sulloway, 1996, 2001). The larger size of older
siblings would naturally make them more dominant, and at the same time
give them a greater share of responsibility to look after the younger siblings.

On the other hand, younger siblings tend to be more open to new ideas,
and experiment with novel thoughts. In Sulloway's study of thousands of
scientists, younger siblings were more open to novelty and thinking outside
the box. On the negative side, they were also more likely to endorse pseu-
doscientific ideas like phrenology. Later born scientists possessed the consistency to make many scientific discoveries, whereas younger siblings were
risk takers traveling far away in search of novel ideas. Darwin, for example,
was the fifth sibling in his family, and developed a theory that changed
physical and social science forever. He risked a great deal in his search for
scientific data, traveling to unknown parts of the world to collect information in support of evolution, a theory that challenged the very fabric of our
religiously founded beliefs about the origin of man.

9.10.2. The Values of the Group and Our Social Self

Our social identity becomes part of our self-concept as we learn the values associated with the group membership, and its emotional significance
in our lives (Tajfel, 1981). Much work has been completed in recent decades that show that membership in even meaningless experimental groups
attaches profound significance to behavior and self-conception (e.g. Doise,
Csepeli, Dann, Gouge, Larsen, & Ostell, 1972). Since membership in nonsensical groups formed for the purpose of an experiment produced significant influence on behavior, how much more powerful is the influence of
group identity when based on memberships in real social groups? Members
of minority groups often have confusing demands made by membership
in both the minority and in coping with the larger society (Sellers, Rowley,
Chavous, Shelton, & Smith, 1997). As we have noted some minorities develop bicultural competence and identity whereas other people are assimilated into the dominant culture, and yet others are marginalized by both
societies (Phinney, 1990, 1991; Ryder, Alden, & Paulhus, 2000).

Minority status has important consequences for the self-concept and esteem. As socialization takes place, the individual often engages in self-stereotyping identifying with the attributes thought positive in the group (Biernat, Vescio, & Green, 1996). Bicultural identification seems to produce
the best results for self-esteem (Phinney, 1990, 1991). High self-esteem in
minorities is a function of strong ethnic identity combined with positive attitudes toward the mainstream culture. It stands to reason that those with
bicultural identities and competence will experience life as more rewarding, and will function more successfully in society.

9.11. THE UBIQUITOUS ROLE OF GENDER IN FORMATION OF THE SOCIAL SELF

Gender is the most obvious parameter in our self-concept. In every society males and females are treated differentially with life-long consequences. Women are more interdependent as they tend to view themselves connected to relationships as mother, daughter or wife. Their behavior therefore tends to be more influenced by the thoughts and feelings of others because relationships are construed as central to self and life (Baumeister & Sommer, 1997; Cross, Bacon, Morris, 2000; Cross & Madson 1997; Gabriel & Gardner, 1999). *Women display relational interdependence in close relationships especially within the family. On the other hand, men display relational interdependence within larger collectives such as political parties, athletic teams, or in feelings of national identity* (Brewer & Gardner, 1996). Consistent socialization processes throughout the world lead females to focus more on intimacy and to have a greater willingness to discuss emotional topics than men (Davidson & Duberman, 1982). These gender differences in self-construal appear consistent across cultures (Kashima, Siegal, Tanaka, & Kashima, 1992), and reflect the different functions of the sexes in the historical and evolutionary struggle for survival.

When women define themselves they use references to other people and relationships. For example, when asked to show photographs they are more likely to include intimate others in the photos (Clancy & Dollinger, 1993). Women spend more time thinking about their partners (Ickes, Robertson, Tooke, & Teng, 1986), are better judges of other peoples personality, and more empathetic (Bernieri, Zuckerman, Koestner, & Rosenthal, 1994; Hall, 1984). In directing their attention toward others women also demonstrate greater alertness to situational clues and the reactions of other people, whereas men focus better on internal processes such as increase in heart rate (Roberts & Pennebaker, 1995).

How does socialization encourage gender differences in self-construal? All the agents of socialization are at work. The media portray women differently from men encouraging interdependent stereotypes. The educational system forms different expectations for appropriate goals and behaviors. Parents treat girls differently than boys from the very beginning. All these socialization agents work consistently together to establish reliable gender differences (Kuebli, & Fivush, 1992). Throughout childhood girls and boys play in separate playgroups with girls playing more cooperatively, and boys engaging more in competitive games (Maccoby, 1990). In early human history these gender differences most likely evolved in response to evolutionary demands that rewarded survival to those who developed gender specific traits. As we are the most dependent of all species we are lucky for women's innate desire to love and look after defenseless infants, and their very personal interests in the survival and well-being of their babies. In the following sections we will consider two theories explaining the development of the social self.

9.12. WE DEVELOP THE SOCIAL SELF THROUGH COMPARISONS WITH OTHERS

Regardless of culture we develop a social self through comparison processes. In individualistic societies comparisons are made to assess competitive standings with peers. In collectivistic societies achievement comparisons are connected to the success of the family and social group. Festinger (1957) proposed a social comparison theory for understanding self-knowledge. He asserted that people have a drive to accurately evaluate their beliefs and opinions. Since there are no explicit physical standards for psychological constructs we learn by comparing our thoughts with those who are similar to us. This original model has been worked over a great deal since first proposed (Goethals & Darley, 1977; Suls & Wheeler, 2000; Wood, 1989). Research has shown that people compare themselves across all imaginable dimensions including emotional responses, personality traits, and objective standards like equity in salary. Any relationship that makes the self salient would evoke the comparison process, for example, the comparison of "our" marriage as compared to other couples, "our" racial group compared to other salient groups in evaluating fair treatment, and fellow students for comparing accomplishments on test questions and grades. All social comparisons contribute to relative satisfaction depending on the comparison outcomes and to our social self.

9.12.1. Downward and Upward Social Comparisons Used for Self-Enhancement or Assessing Achievement in Individualistic Cultures

We get a sense of who we are by comparisons to the accomplishments or failures of other people in similar situations? Sometimes we seek self-enhancement by comparing downward to someone not doing as well and to those less fortunate in our society or social group. By comparing ourselves to those who earn lower grades, get less salary, or are hungry, many people can at least temporarily feel better (Lockwood, 2002). *Downward comparisons are especially strategic when one has experienced failure.* By comparing downward and emphasizing one's positive qualities the damage to self-esteem is reduced (Mussweiler, Gabriel, & Bodenhausen, 2000).

At other times we are interested in improvement trying to reach a relevant and lofty goal. In that case successful others can serve as models for achievement comparisons. Most of us, perhaps all of us, would not achieve the mathematical insight of Albert Einstein. However, the aspiring scientist may be inspired by his example and seek a related self-relevant high achievement. At times upward comparisons are discouraging. When the goal is truly unreachable the comparison can result in envy and feelings of inadequacy (Patrick, Neighbors, & Knee, 2004). Anorexia and bulimia are large problems in today's society, many believe caused by the emphasis on thinness in women in the media. Nearly all models of women's clothing are super thin and in fact look unhealthy. Perhaps worse they set an unattainable standard for most other women. Women who place high value on physical appearance suffer in self-esteem from such social comparisons (Patrick et al., 2004). In summary, some comparisons can be inspirational if the goals are possible and realistic in a person's future, but discouraging and demoralizing if they involve impossible goals or dreams.

Some people also compare from a desire to bond with others in the same straits (Stapel & Koomen, 2000, 2001). How do we react to a crisis like hurricane Katrina and other natural disasters? Most of us will look to others to find the appropriate mixture of fear and courage in dealing with the situation. We also compare to similar people to enhance a sense of solidarity and common fate (Locke, 2003). When people experience common fate they compare their responses to others in order to feel the strength of the community when facing crisis situations.

Social comparisons may occur in any situation of uncertainty when we are trying to find some appropriate response (Suls & Fletcher, 1983). You find yourself invited to a formal dinner party for the first time, a situation with some anxiety. Being uncertain how to dress appropriately, you ask the host for some helpful guidelines. At the dinner party chances are that you will compare to other guests more experienced for both dress and to carry the conversation until you get your bearings.

9.12.2. A Summary of Social Comparison Research

In forming our social self we seek comparisons with similar others, and if we want to enhance the self we compare downwards, however, if we are motivated by desire for improvement we find more successful models (Blanton, Buunk, Gibbons, & Kuyper, 1999; Goethals & Darley, 1977). Sometimes we enhance the self-concept by comparing temporally with our former self (Ross & Wilson, 2002; Wilson & Ross, 2000). Most of us can find events from our earlier life that were more negative than our current situation. For example, people have fewer friends when they get older, but many believe that the quality of relationships has improved. To enhance ourselves we can compare our lives temporally over time and conclude that although the quantity of relationships has declined lifelong friendships have a higher value than those formed in our youth.

9.13. WE KNOW THE SELF THROUGH SELF-OBSERVATION

Research supports the idea that we are scientists in our own right and that we study our own behaviors for clues to the meaning of events and how we should feel. Self-perception theory proposes that in situations of ambiguity people make inferences about the meaning of the event from our own reactions. A person may feel a reaction to being at a great height, for example, in a skyscraper and infer fear or perhaps excitement as the proper label for the emotion. Experience produces familiarity and most of us know how to react in situations we have visited previously. An individual listens to a political leader and from the storehouse of memories has ready feelings about the message and the messenger. Most people have established attitudes about a variety of topics, for example, between hip-hop versus classical music and know how to react based on these schemas. At some point, however, a person may experience the novel or unfamiliar and is uncertain of how to respond. A stranger hands you a $100 bill, how should you react? Should you be happy or offended? If you react with smiles and gestures of goodwill, you may examine these reactions and conclude that you are happy. Self-perception theory (Bem, 1972) asserts that when our attitudes or feelings are ambiguous we infer their meaning by observing our own behavior as well as the situation. When we are unsure of our feelings we infer our feelings from our actions as we actually respond to the situation. You observe yourself kissing another person and from that conclude that you are in love. When a person is in a situation not previously evaluated, and feelings are somewhat of a mystery, often our objective behavior becomes a guide to explain these feelings (Andersen & Ross, 1984; Chaiken & Baldwin, 1981).

Secondly, in deciding the meaning of behavior causation is attributed to either the person or the situation. Is the situation compelling your behavior or is the "executive I" in charge? If we are in control of the situation and feel in charge we may attribute feelings and behavior to our personal dispositions. If, however, there are compelling pressures in the situation we are likely to attribute our behavior to the situation rather than to the self. Self-perception theory contends that we infer our feelings by observing our own behavior and attribute either a personal cause or a situational reason for our behavior (Albarracin & Wyer, 2000; Dolinsky, 2000).

Self-perception theory has important consequences for education and learning. For example, does learning occur because of some extrinsic reward like grades? Such extrinsic reward is likely to produce short-term learning since the student feels justified to forget the learning once the reward is achieved. All the anxiety and cramming that occur in American universities is not for any intrinsic pleasure of learning, but just to pass a course or get good grades. Some children, however, learn because of the intrinsic pleasure of mastering a subject. Students who are intrinsically motivated engage the subject matter because they find it interesting and enjoyable

(Ryan & Deci, 2000a; Senko & Harackiewicz, 2002). Self-perception theory would argue that extrinsic rewards could inhibit intrinsic motivation and destroy the pleasure of mastering the subject matter. When students come to believe that they are learning to obtain rewards it leads to an underestimation by both teacher and student of the role played by intrinsic motives (Deci, Koestner, & Ryan, 1999; Lepper, Henderlong, & Gingras, 1999). So although rewards like grades can be motivational in the short run, they may produce an external attribution for learning that overlooks and delimits the pleasure of intrinsic motivation.

It is obvious that any significant achievement occurs only where the self attributes intrinsic pleasure to the pursuit of knowledge. Students may pass courses, but little of the information learned from the reward of grade incentives will be stored in long-term memory. When the reward ceases so does the motivation to remember which is why the vast amount of information learned in lower and higher education is lost within weeks. In one study on math games children's performance was compared between a reward program and the follow-up during which no rewards were provided. The reward program did initially produce more interest and the children played more. However, those who initially had enjoyed the games lost interest during the follow-up and played less after the reward program ended (Greene, Sternberg, & Lepper, 1976). The researchers determined that it was the reward program that caused the children to like the games less. Other research (Tang & Hall, 1995) supported these conclusions and that should cause us to think about what we do to the minds of children in an obsessive grade competitive educational system.

For parents rewards can be a two-edged sword. Praise for work well done can increase the child's self-esteem and sense of self-efficacy. It can also convey something about parental expectations for future work. But it is important that the child believes that their performance is not for external rewards but for reasons that are intrinsic and enjoyable. The child must have some control in the educational process where teachers and parents can nurture intrinsic motivation by doing enjoyable learning activities (Henderlong & Lepper, 2002). Otherwise the child comes to attribute reasons for performance achievement to the reward system with resulting loss of motivation.

9.13.1. *Physiological Reactions and the Two-Factor Theory of Emotion*

When experiencing emotions the self tries to make sense of these physiological reactions by finding the most logical explanation provided by the situation. The precise same physiological reaction in the body may give rise to anger in one situational context and love in another. Schachter (1964) proposed a theory of emotion using self-perception ideas. Essentially the theory proposes that we learn to infer our emotions the same way as we learn about our self-concept by observing our own behavior. In Schachter's theory people observe their physiological internal experiences and try to make sense of these by looking for the most plausible explanation. The theory is called two-factor because we first experience the physiological reaction and then look for a reasonable cause to explain it. A now classical experiment tested this theory (Schachter & Singer, 1962). When the subject arrived for the experiment he was told he was participating in a study on the effect of a vitamin compound called Suproxin on vision. After the injection the subject was led to a waiting room to let the drug take effect. While there the subject was asked to fill out a survey containing some very insulting personal questions including one asking the subject about his mother's extramarital affairs. Another participant present, an experimental collaborator, also read the questions and angrily tossed the survey on the floor and left the room.

In fact the real purpose of the experiment was not to study vision, but to understand people's reaction to physiological arousal and the meaning attached. The participants were not given a vitamin compound but were injected with epinephrine, a hormone produced by the body that causes increased heart and breathing rates. How would you feel in a similar situation? You would have noticed the physiological change that occurred from the epinephrine. Your breathing rate would have increased and you would have felt aroused. Then the other participant reacts with anger at the survey. What is the most plausible explanation from the situation for the arousal that you feel? Since you have no information that you have been injected with epinephrine the most plausible explanation is found in the situational context of the survey and the other participant's anger. In fact that is what happened, and the participants injected with epinephrine were much angrier than the participants given a placebo.

In an extension of this work the researchers demonstrated that emotions are somewhat arbitrarily defined depending on what is the most plausible explanation found in the situational context (Schachter & Singer, 1962). For example, the emotion of anger could be aborted by offering a non-emotional explanation for the arousal. The researchers accomplished this by telling the participants that they could expect to feel aroused after being injected. When the subjects then began to feel aroused they inferred that it was the injection that caused the change and they did not react with anger. In yet another condition Schachter and Singer demonstrated that they could create a very different emotion by providing an alternate explanation for the arousal. In this condition the experimental collaborator acted as if euphoric and happy. The subjects began to feel the same way and inferred that they too were feeling happy and euphoric. In short Schachter and Singer showed that emotions are part of the self-perception process where people seek the most plausible reason for internal bodily changes.

9.13.2. Physiological Arousal Can Cause Misattribution

At times attribution for the emotional arousal is not clear. This may cause attribution to the cause most likely, but nevertheless incorrect. In other words, since people have no explicit standard to determine what causes some emotions they can misinterpret the cause (Savitsky, Medvec, Charlton, & Gilovich, 1998; Zillman, 1978). The same physiological arousal occurs in a variety of circumstances and to varying stimuli. In some situations there may be more than one source to which the arousal can be attributed. To what do we attribute the increased heartbeat, shallow breathing, and the rise in body temperature? Can another person be responsible for the physiological changes experienced? What if the situation finds you next to the other person during a parachute jump? Is the increased heartbeat then caused by the fascination with the other person or is it that you are approaching the Earth at great speed? There is no standard that will tell a person for certain to what the physiological changes can be attributed, and the possibilities of misattribution of the cause exist in all such circumstances.

In the classical study (Dutton & Aron, 1974) the researchers demonstrated the ease by which misattribution of arousal can occur. The experimenters had an attractive young woman approach males with a survey purportedly for a project for her psychology class. When they completed the survey she explained that she would be happy to explain more about the project at a later time, and she wrote her phone number on a corner, tore it off and gave it to the participant. This procedure was followed under two independent experimental conditions. In the first condition the men were approached after they had crossed a rickety 450 feet high footbridge over a river in Canada. Most of us would after the crossing experience have all the symptoms of the epinephrine injection found in the study of Schachter and Singer. People's hardwired brains prefer low and safe altitudes, and this bridge was very high and did not give the appearance of being secure. As the men were approached immediately after crossing their hearts were still racing and they experienced physiological arousal. In the second condition the men were allowed to rest for a while after crossing and calm down somewhat before the woman approached. They too were given the phone number and the opportunity to call later for more information.

What would be the predicted outcome from Schachter's two-step theory? In the first condition the men had just experienced physiological arousal and were primed to find a plausible explanation. The most plausible cause for what they felt was the crossing of the bridge, but the beautiful woman made the stronger impression. Was the arousal due to the presence of the woman? In fact the results showed that significantly more men who were approached while aroused (having just crossed the bridge) called the woman subsequently to ask for a date, whereas few did if they were approached after resting. The men misattributed the cause of their arousal from the true source, the crossing of the bridge, to the more powerful stimuli found in the lovely woman. Misattribution of arousal has also been found in other studies (Sinclair, Hoffman, Mark, Martin, & Pickering, 1994).

9.13.3. The Cognitive Interpretation Occurs First Followed by Emotion

While the previous ideas about emotion would suggest that emotion comes first and then is understood afterwards by reference to the situation an alternative interpretation would argue the reverse: that first we make sense of a situation and then we feel the emotion. Some researchers have noted that people sometimes experience emotion when there is no physiological arousal (Roseman & Smith, 2001; Russell & Barrett, 1999; Scherer, Schorr, & Johnstone, 2001). Cognitive appraisal theories explain that sometimes emotions follow cognition, after a determination of the meaning of the event or situation. For example, an event is appraised as either good or bad based on its relevance to the well-being of the self and on what is perceived as causing the event. A colleague is given a promotion, how do you interpret that event? In a professional world of zero sum game behavior when someone achieves a distinction it gives other colleagues less of a chance to advance. Consequently a person may feel envy and later anger if by the comparison process the promotion was considered unjustified. However, if the same person is already at the top of professional achievement and can advance no further he/she might feel happy for the colleague (Tesser, 1988).

The main point is that in cognitive arousal theories the emotional arousal comes after cognition, after attributing meaning and cause to the event. Arousal does not always precede the interpretation of emotion. Sometimes we feel the emotion, as we begin to fully understand the implications of what has happened and how the situation has changed. The two-step theory and cognitive appraisal theories complement each other as previous arousal is explained by the two-step theory, and interpretation followed by arousal explains emotion from the cognitive appraisal perspective.

9.14. IS INTROSPECTION TO BE BELIEVED: SELF-DECEPTION AND MORAL STANDARDS

Most people are unaware of the possibility of self-deception and therefore believe what they know about themselves from introspection to be accurate. Is it possible to learn about ourselves by "looking inside" and by examining our own thoughts and feelings? For example, you find yourself in an emergency situation where a man is drowning and immediately jump in the water to save him. Afterwards you think about the event, and come to the conclusion that the reaction was consistent with who you are, with your self-concept. Sometimes introspection can provide accurate knowledge, but at other times it can be misleading. Is introspection so obvious a source of self-knowledge that it is routine for most people? Research shows that people in fact spend little time thinking about the self (Wilson, 2002). Even when people introspect the cause for behavior may not be assessable or part of conscious cognition. In one study (Csikszentmihalyi & Figurski, 1982) the participants wore a beeper that sounded off some 7–9 times a day. Each time the beeper sounded the respondents were asked to record their thoughts and moods subsequently categorized through content analysis. From these responses about daily thinking the investigators determined that only 8 percent of all responses were about the self. Since life is about survival it is not surprising that much more thought was given to work, but nevertheless it suggests that the self is not a favorite object of contemplation.

Self-awareness theory contains the idea that people focus attention on the self in order to evaluate behavior to see whether it meets internal self-defining standards and values (Carver, 2003; Duval & Silvia, 2002). Only the psychopath would spend no time trying to evaluate the self by comparison to moral standards. Bundy, the serial killer spent the very last moments of his life trying to rationalize his behavior attributing his deeds to pornography. Of course, the opposite is also true, some people have very rigid moral systems and spend too much time in dysfunctional self-accusation and self-blame. Most of us fall in-between, and from time to time become aware of discrepancies between behavior and moral beliefs. At times such self-awareness can be very unpleasant and motivate improvement and changes in life (Fejfar & Hoyle, 2000; Mor & Winquist, 2002). When self-awareness becomes too unpleasant we seek escape. Is that the reason so many people spend a good part of their lives watching television (Moskalenko & Heine, 2002)? The popularity of soaps could be understood as a way of solving personal problems by identifying with characters outside the self. Some escape is necessary in a stressful world, however, it becomes maladaptive when fantasy substitutes for real answers to a person's life and challenges.

At times escape takes the route of alcohol or drug abuse. When people drink to excess they can at least temporarily divert attention away from the self, although the day after the alcohol abuse may bring back unpleasant anxiety. The fact that so many people worldwide are involved in drug abuse is a testimony to how unpleasant self-awareness can be (Hull, Young, & Jouriles, 1986). Religious devotion can also be a way to escape self-focus, and find forgiveness for not living up to moral standards. Like drug abuse, some religious focuses are self-destructive when the well-being of the self is totally ignored. What comes to mind are the suicide bombers who seek total escape to "paradise" in acts of self and other-destruction. Self-awareness can also be pleasant as occur when a person graduates from a university or professional school, or complete other significant achievements and feels enhanced in self-awareness (Silvia & Abele, 2002). At times self-awareness can help us avoid moral pitfalls when we are tempted to ignore moral promptings. So self-awareness can serve both positive as well as aversive roles in human psychology.

One problem with introspection is that it may not tell us the real reasons for our feelings since these may lie outside our awareness (Wilson, 2002). Introspection may not be able to access the causes of many feelings because we are simply unaware of the reasons. Most people will come up with plausible explanations, but these may in fact be untrue or incomplete.

Growing up all people have causal theories about feelings and behavior. For example, many people believe that mood is affected by the amount of sleep, whereas mood is in fact independent of preceding sleep (Niedenthal & Kitayama, 1994; Wegner, 2002). Our legal system gives women custody of children based on the common belief that they are the best custodians. Yet we know that women also commit infanticide and child abuse. Often causal theories are simplifications or simply not true, and people make incorrect judgments about behavior or actions. Influences under the screen of awareness can be the deciding factor in behavior. In one study of clothing preference people evaluated clothing of identical quality. Whereas the participants causal theories might promote the idea that choice was based on quality, the investigators showed that it was the position of the clothing on the display table that mattered. The clothing that was placed farther to the right was preferred (Nisbett & Wilson, 1977). Most people would intuitively reject that idea, but it was the causal factor in clothing selection, perhaps dictated by brain hemispheric dominance. In all, this research shows that we should use caution in accepting causes derived from introspection. People may come up with very plausible reasons, but they may be incorrect or unimportant in the final analysis.

9.15. THE SOCIAL SELF HELPS US ORGANIZE COGNITION

The social self refers to our relational identity composed in our interaction with others. Depending somewhat on culture people think of themselves as interdependent or independent and such cognitive schemas about the self help organize the world by attending to some stimuli while ignoring other aspects of our environment. Self-knowledge takes on many forms including the beliefs people have of the self, self-esteem, memories, and especially in the West distinctive attributes. Self-knowledge includes social beliefs, roles and obligations, and relational beliefs about identity as members of families and community. Furthermore self-knowledge describes personal beliefs about personality traits, abilities and other attributes (Brewer & Gardner, 1996; Deaux, Reid, Mizrahi, & Ethier, 1995).

Self-knowledge performs primarily a constricting and narrowing influence on perceptions. We construe the current situation with information from previous history thereby overlooking what might be novel. Information and experiences are made to fit preconceived ideas about the self. In general information that can be integrated into what is already known about the self, using established schemas is more easily recalled. This self-reference effect has been demonstrated in several studies (Klein & Kihlstrom, 1986; Klein & Loftus, 1988). So self-knowledge not only shapes what is likely to be remembered, but makes recall more efficient (Rogers, Kuiper, & Kirker, 1977).

9.15.1. Our Mind and Self-Schemas

What dimensions are used to think about important matters? Do people consider themselves independent? Self-schemas are defined as organized thinking about important matters that are readily available in memory. If peace as a concept was considered an important dimension in a person's mind there would be a storehouse of memories and beliefs readily available to understand the ever-growing conflicts in the world. Some beliefs might explain the causes of conflict as derived from human greed, intolerance, or the desire to control oil resources. Another schema in the person's mind might have the solution to conflict by treating everyone equitably. *For each relevant issue there is preexisting knowledge organized as schemas to help organize readily available responses.* Schemas allow us to quickly identify and recognize situations that are schema relevant (Kendzierski & Whitaker, 1997). The behavior of others is judged and according to their similarity to our own personality. One study asked the respondents to rate themselves and twenty other people. The results showed that the dimensions the respondents found important in rating themselves were also employed in rating others. The execution of Saddam Hussein was a grim affair. However, you may have noted that he went to his death with great personal courage and dignity. If you value bravery in the face of annihilation your opinion of Saddam Hussein might have changed somewhat, independent of your evaluation of his policies as a political leader. We tend to use self-knowledge in an egocentric fashion when evaluating others. If scholarship is important to you, you may apply strict standards in judging the scholastic work and ability of others (Dunning & Cohen, 1992).

It is not possible to attend to everything in the environment. People selectively attend to those situations that are most relevant to the self. Self-schemas allow us to access information quickly and respond efficiently (Markus, 1977). Self-schemas also are restrictive and prevent information from being evaluated if it is seen as inconsistent with what people already believe. Most people display self-image biases (Lewicki, 1983). Again culture may play a role. In the West the self-bias exists because the self is construed independently. Asian students, on the other hand, are more likely to say they are similar to others rather than others are similar to them. Therefore in Asian self-construal the other person becomes the standard for comparison. In one study about being the center of attention (Cohen & Gunz, 2002) the researchers showed that self-knowledge among Asian people use the perspective derived from others. In comparing Asian students with those who were native to Canada they found that Canadians were more likely to assess the situation from their own independent perspective, whereas Asians took the perspective of other persons in describing similar situations.

An important property of self-schemas is the sense of stability that they confer on the self-concept. People have a feeling that the core of the self remains the same and that we are essentially the same person over time (Caspi & Roberts, 2001). For example, children who are identified as shy as toddlers still remain shy at age 8 (Kagan, 1989), and have problems with social interaction later in life (Caspi, Elder, & Bem, 1988). Whatever people are in early life is likely to remain over time as they behave consistent and selectively to self-schemas. Consistency is true for functional and also for maladaptive behavior. People remember information that is consistent with early self-schemas and disregard disconfirming events. As people review the past, self-schemas are employed to confirm the present self-concept and we resist thinking about discrepant or novel information (Ross, 1989).

Is there a universal basis for self-schemas? Recent research on the Big Five personality model discussed several times in the book suggests an underlying personality structure that is more or less the same everywhere (Schmitt, Allik, McCrae, & Benet-Martinez, 2007). The research supports the presence of a deep psychological structure that permits us to understand one another even when surface cultural behavior is very different from the observer's point of view. At the same time cross-cultural information allows us to arrive at comparative conclusions on a variety of variables. Still even with that information there may still be unique cultural factors discovered through indigenous psychological research (Hwang, 2012; Hwang, Kim, & Kou-Shu, 2006).

9.15.2. Regulating the Self to Reach Goals and Achieve

Self-schemas tell people what and where they are currently in life, but also what they can become in the future. This conception of the possible future is a source of both motivation and planning. Possible selves are the conceptions that propel people into the future in search of goals and achievements (Markus & Nurius, 1986). Some people grow up thinking they like a particular career envisioning themselves as doctors, trade people, or mechanics. Self-schemas lead to the required training and sustain the motivation necessary to reach goals. People with a vision of the possible selves in the future work harder at accomplishing relevant tasks (Ruvolo & Markus, 1992). Self-schemas have obvious adaptive value. They allow people to quickly identify relevant situations and recall appropriate and effective behaviors from memory.

The self serves regulatory functions determining people's choices and their plans for the future (Baumeister, & Vohs, 2003; Carver & Scheier, 1981). Humans appear to be the only species capable of long-term planning. Plans for educational goals, or for family related matters like acquiring a home, require a self capable of self-regulation. In self-regulation a finite amount of energy is available to each person. If a person spends a lot of self-regulative energy during the day he/she will have less left over at night. Is that why couples have more arguments after a long hard day at work? (Baumeister & Heatherton, 1996; Vohs & Heatherton, 2000). Research shows that dieters are more likely to fail at night when they are tired. Previous smokers are more likely to take up the habit again after experiencing adversity, bulimics are more likely to binge eat after a long day of self-control. With only so much energy available self-control has limits. We all need rest periods to develop the energy necessary to achieve health related goals.

Self-regulation is determined to some extent by the culture in which people are socialized (Dhawan, Roseman, Naidu, Thapa, & Rettek, 1995). A study comparing Japanese with American college students demonstrated a cultural difference consistent with collectivistic and individualistic societies. Typically American college students perceive of themselves in terms of personal traits. The independent self-construal emphasizes traits that make the person distinct from others. Self-regulation pertaining to personal achievement would rank high as an important trait in individualistic cultures. On the other hand, Japanese students defined themselves much more in terms of social roles recognizing their relationship to family and society.

9.15.3. We Experience Stability but Also Temporary Situational Moments in the Self-Concept

People observe within themselves a sense of continuity and to some degree recognize that they are the same person as in previous years or times. However, a situation that is traumatic may demand special performances that are inconsistent with the continuous self and changes the self-concept temporarily due to these special circumstances. A stable self-concept experiences self-continuity from early memories to the present. However, some situations call for special attributes that become part of a *temporary working self-concept*. The citizen soldier may have in civilian life a stable self-concept that includes a working career and family life. However, when he goes to war that situation requires different attributes that become part of a working or temporary self. This working self-concept may involve a willingness to engage in violent behavior to guide action while in the war zone while finding these aggressive behaviors inappropriate in his stable self-concept. Sometimes behavior in the war zone permanently changes a person, and the temporary self becomes part of the stable self. Many members of the Armed Forces in the U.S. returned from the war in Vietnam with permanent scars affecting their relationships and trust in other people in their civilian life. The temporary self guides what goes in a specific situation, but may itself become part of the stable self (Ehrlinger & Dunning, 2003).

In less traumatic circumstances the working self-concept may operate on the periphery of the self, and when the individual returns to normal circumstances the stable self takes over (Nezlek & Plesko, 2001). In one study (Crocker, Sommers, & Luhtanen, 2002) the investigators evaluated applicants to graduate school. The respondents were asked to complete self-esteem measures on days when they received acceptance or rejection notices from graduate school programs. For those respondents whose self-esteem depended a great deal on scholastic achievement acceptance to programs increased self-esteem significantly, whereas rejection decreased self-esteem. In the graduate program of this author rejections and acceptances were noted on a comparative poster for all students applying for Ph.D. programs. A similar enhancement reaction occurred. Those who were accepted enhanced the self. Whose idea do you think it was? Probably those applicants who were very confident of acceptance and sought further evidence for self-enhancement in the eyes of fellow students!

9.16. OUR SELF-CONCEPT IS A SOURCE OF MOTIVATION

Why do people strive to reach goals? It is because of conceptions of both real and actual selves and individuals pursue goals in order to improve a sense of self-worth. A major function of the self-concept is its relationship to motivation (Higgins, 1999; Sedikides & Showronski, 1993). What psychological component causes people to make plans for the future? As noted possible selves refer to possibilities, what people think they can become or hope to be in the future (Cross & Markus, 1991; Markus & Nurius, 1986). The self-concept also includes social and cultural, and religious standards that people utilize in deciding about behavior. Feelings of shame or guilt are associated with these aspects of the self (Higgins, 1987, 1999). People compare their actions not only to the actual self, who they believe they are, but also to the ideal self, what they can become. The ideal self is included in all aspirations and motivations. The "ought" self also has motivating properties referring to the duties and obligations people feel toward family and society, and whether they are behaving appropriately in accordance with their responsibilities. These various aspects of the self have proven to have motivational properties both in terms of cognition as well as behavior (Shah & Higgins, 2001).

9.16.1. Actual and Ideal Selves and Motivation

When people observe discrepancies between the actual self and what they think they ought to be the result is often the experience of fear or anxiety (Boldero & Francis, 2000). Loss of self-esteem might result from the discrepancy between real and actual self-conceptions compared to the ideal or ought selves. The greater the discrepancy the more dejected the person feels (Higgins & Bargh, 1987; Moretti & Higgins, 1990). These feelings of conflicts within the self derive from what Freud called the superego, the early socialization that incorporates parental standards of morality into the self-concept. When warm and accepting parents are raising children the ideal self has a special influence on future development and aspirations since support is crucial to the formation of what is possible. Children, on the other hand, who have been raised by more rejecting parents think of behavior primarily in terms of meeting standards and avoiding rejection (Manian, Strauman, & Denney, 1998).

In one study recalling scenes of embarrassment Asians saw the situations through the eyes of other people rather than from the perspective of personal feelings (Chua, Leu, & Nisbett, 2005). People raised in individualistic cultures are more likely to look to the ideal self for guidance in regulating behavior and be motivated to reduce discrepancies between the actual and ideal selves. People who are raised in collectivistic environments pay more attention to the demands made by family and society as expressed by the "ought self" concept (Lee, Aaker, & Gardner, 2000). The route to well-being is to regulate behavior to reduce or eliminate discrepancies between these aspects of the self and the goals being pursued in life (Bianco, Higgins, & Klem, 2003).

9.16.2. The Need for a Consistent Self and Motivation

All people experience a sense of the self that is stable from childhood through the varying stages of life. Perhaps consistency in the self-concept is partially a Western cultural need as our rationalized society expects consistency in behavior in order to plan for economic and other life-sustaining activities. Without consistency, a factory could not plan a work program, without a sense of continuity in traits and abilities the individual could not plan for the future and society would be unable to educate. People need to believe that there is something within them that is consistent over time (Swann, 1983).

The motivating properties of self-consistency can be observed in a study by Swann and Read (1981). The participants were given feedback that was either consistent or inconsistent with their self-conceptions. Results showed that the students spent more time studying feedback consistent with the self-concept than inconsistent information. The need for self-affirmation can also be observed in people's selective behavior. People tend to interact only with those who confirm their self-concepts. Students who have a high estimation of their scholarly abilities will probably make friends with other students who also think they are good students and affirm their self-concept (Katz & Beach, 2000). People remember information better that confirms their self-concept (Story, 1998), and holds consistent self-beliefs as members of groups (Chen, Chen, & Shaw, 2004). This search for self-affirmation is modified by self-esteem. People who possess high self-esteem are willing to entertain both positive and negative self-affirming information. Those with low self-esteem want mainly positive self-affirming information whether accurate or not (Bernichon, Cook, & Brown, 2003).

Having an accurate self-concept has obvious adaptive value. To make plans for the future and to experience success requires a fairly accurate self-concept including realistic assessments of traits and abilities. Many of the tasks people choose are based on self-assessment of aptitudes. As discussed elsewhere all people are motivated by a desire to save face and impress others, so we are likely to pick objectives closely related to what we think we can do (Trope, 1983).

9.16.3. The Desire to Elevate Self-Esteem and Culture

Cultural values also affect self-esteem. Collectivistic and individualistic cultures produce different self-related goals to maintain or improve self-esteem. Those living in individualistic cultures experience primarily ego-based emotions. Accomplishments are a source of personal pride. People who live collectivistic cultures experiences satisfaction or frustrations based on their connectedness to others (Mesquita, 2001). Parents and their children are, for example, connected intimately in the children's scholastic achievement. Self-esteem in collectivistic cultures is likewise dependent on the interdependent form of self-construal (Crocker, Luhtanen, Blaine, & Broadnax, 1994; Diener & Diener, 1995; Yik, Bond, & Paulhus, 1998). Social approval is a primary motivator in collectivistic cultures, and a better predictor of life satisfaction for people living in these societies. In individualistic cultures life satisfaction is more a function of individual emotions (Suh, Diener, Oishi, & Triandis, 1998).

Self-esteem is a major dimension of the self-concept. Self-esteem is a global evaluative assessment people make of self-worth. Most psychologists employ simple surveys to assess self-esteem (e.g. Larsen, 1969). Individuals who have high self-esteem feel relatively good about their self-worth, those with low self-esteem feel some ambivalence, and relatively few people feel self-loathing. Trait self-esteem refers to consistent levels of self-esteem probably determined by early experiences with success or failure. Trait self-esteem is defined by self-conceptions of competence and efficacy in various areas of achievement and remains consistent over time (Block & Robins, 1993).

People also experience momentary changes in self-esteem as a result of new developments or from the impact of significant events (Heatherton & Polivy, 1991). Male self-esteem tends to increase during adolescence, whereas female self-esteem falls during the same time (Block & Robins, 1993). At various times in our lives people experience enhancing events that improves self-esteem. A large raise in salary or promotion at work may improve self-esteem. On the other hand, people can also experience failure that impact self-esteem in negative ways. When competing against contemporaries with higher levels of ability the comparison may have negative consequences for self-esteem (Brown, 1998; Marsh & Parker, 1984).

How comparisons are experienced depend on the relative centrality of the domain of achievement. Is the area of competition central to self-worth or more peripheral (Crocker & Park, 2003)? Professional achievement is central to many people's sense of self-worth. If achievement is socially appreciated and work is progressing generally in the right direction self-esteem is enhanced. Otherwise the blows of misfortune will negatively impact the self-esteem (Crocker, Sommers, & Luhtanen, 2002).

Central to a person's self-esteem is the human need to be included. There is probably no more serious punishment in society than solitary confinement. Many prisoners can endure other forms of torture and denigration, but to accept total isolation is very difficult. Some researchers assert that self-esteem is simply an index measuring relative inclusion-exclusion by others (Leary, Tambor, Terdal, & Downs, 1995). From an evolutionary perspective it is easy to understand the power of social approval. Those who obtain approval from significant others are more likely to survive and thrive. Approval seeking affects a variety of behaviors (Larsen, 1974a,b; Larsen, Martin, Ettinger, & Nelson, 1976). People who feel excluded are likely to report low self-esteem.

Changing feelings also correspond to the approval by others (Baumeister, Twenge, & Nuss, 2002). Self-esteem responds to temporary conditions of approval or disapproval. People's moods change from time to time, and the reasons why are not always clear. Temporary mood swings affect self-esteem in either positive or negative directions (Brown, 1998). Even setbacks that have very little real meaning can temporarily reduce self-esteem. For example, if your favorite athletic team loses an important game, self-esteem may decline (Hirt, Zillman, Erickson, & Kennedy, 1992). As noted self-esteem is closely related to the domains we consider most relevant to our self-concept. Most people derive self-esteem from selected human activities. For some individuals self-esteem is based on competence in scholarship or career, for others self-esteem is built on feedback from athletic prowess. Still other people think that success in family and human relationships is of greatest significance. It is really a question of what we value in life. What domains are significant to you, and have you experienced success or failure determines self-esteem?

Crocker and Wolfe (2001), and Crocker and Park (2003) have proposed a theory of self-esteem based on domains of self-worth. Self-esteem rises or falls with experiences of success or failure in key areas that are valued by the individual and cultures will vary as to what domains are considered important. Independence is a significant value in Western societies and is related to achievement of economic independence and reaching career goals. In collectivistic Asian cultures gaining the respect of others and maintaining successful relationships are more a central value. Self-worth is to some degree selected by cultural emphasis and values. Regardless of culture it is important that people do not base self-worth on just one or a few domains since failure in one area will be less salient if people have many domains of interest and achievement. Failure can be devastating for those who seek achievement in a single domain since they have no fallback position for supporting self-worth.

9.16.4. Individualistic Culture and the Obsession with Self-Enhancement

Members of Western cultures bear a special burden in life. Since self-esteem in Western societies is largely based on independent egos and achievement based distinctions, most people are motivated to enhance self-esteem (Tesser, 1988). We like to see ourselves in the most favorable light possible given the constraints of reality. According to Tesser people accomplish this vicariously by enhancing themselves through association with those who have accomplished significant goals. The pride of parents in their children's achievements and associating with people of high social status is of this type. A great deal of effort in Western societies goes into convincing others of our value by relating to those who possess status.

According to Tesser people also seek to enhance by social comparison. As we noted earlier social comparisons can be made either upward for achievement or downward to enhance self-esteem. Even in failure one can compare downward for self-enhancement. One is reminded of the academic culture in some countries where students note a university degree in their vita followed by the word "failed." Just the mere fact that a student entered a university program attributed higher status compared with those who never started!

On a more personal basis people often select friends outside their most salient domains of achievement so they can compare downward. Since these friends may perform well in other areas, the downward comparison can be in both directions: comparing for aspirations in achievement or downward comparisons for self-esteem. As a general rule people select friends they outperform in salient domains, but who are talented in other areas. Self-esteem in competitive individualistic societies is based on this fundamental desire to rank higher than someone else. In one study (Tesser, Campbell, & Smith, 1984) the researchers asked grade school children to identify their closest friends, their own most and least important domains or activities, and how good their friends were in these activities. As evidence of self-enhancing Tesser et al found that students rated their own performance as better in the salient areas, whereas they related their friends' performance as better in less self-relevant peripheral areas. In other words, the students overestimated their own performance in self-relevant areas, and underestimated their friends' performance in other domains lending support to the social comparison processes.

Self-enhancement needs are important, and perhaps of overriding importance for most people (Sedikides, 1993). They are especially important when life has struck a blow in an important domain area, for example, being refused entrance to a favorite university is very painful to the aspiring scholar. Threat or failure leads to self-enhancement efforts trying to shore up of self-esteem (Beauregard & Dunning, 1998; Krueger, 1998). Self-enhancement means that people evaluate themselves more favorably than others (Suls, Lemos, & Stewart, 2002). Our efforts at enhancing self-esteem also affect the memory process. People remember the good and positive features about themselves, and forget the negative (Sedikides & Green, 2000). People also believe they are more altruistic than others (Epley & Dunning, 2000), they think they are happier than others, and less biased (Klar & Giladi, 1999; Pronin, Lin, & Ross, 2002).

There may be times when people acknowledge that they are less than perfect. However, in their efforts to maintain self-esteem people tend to think that the negative in performance is less important than the positive (Campbell, 1986; Greve & Wentura, 2003). Not surprisingly people are less likely to falsely enhance when they can potentially be caught in little self-enhancing lies. For example, poor students are less likely to boast to their professors about previous achievements and if we are poor lovers our partners will eventually know. When the truth cannot be hidden permanently we are more likely to be modest in our self-aggrandizement (Armor & Taylor, 1998).

9.16.5. *Positive Illusions of Self-Enhancement and Stress*

From an existential perspective lying to oneself is dysfunctional as we must see and behave in accordance with how life really is and not how we wish it to be. However, in the West the exaggerated self-conceptions produced by self-enhancement can support better mental and physical health

(Taylor, Kemeny, Reede, Bower, & Grunewald, 2000). That illusions can have positive consequences runs counter to many ideas in psychology. As noted from the perspective of existential psychology self-enhancement is a form of defensive neuroticism and distorts life in the real world. Since neurotic behavior is associated with continuous anxiety and stress such false self-enhancement should be maladaptive. In one study (Taylor, Lerner, Sherman, Sage, & McDowell, 2003) students were asked for their self-assessed personal traits like intelligence and physical attractiveness as compared to their peers. Participants who rated themselves higher than their ratings by peers were considered self-enhancing. Later the participants performed tasks designed to create stress as manifested by higher heart rates and blood pressures measures. The results showed that the self-enhancing group had lower heart rates and blood pressure responses, and recovered to normal measurements more quickly compared to those that did not enhance performance. Self-enhancers also had lower cortisol levels than did the comparative group of non-enhancers. In short the self-enhancers had healthier responses, tended to be more optimistic, had feelings of personal control that all contributed to the lower cortisol levels. These experimental results support the contention that self-enhancement leads to healthier physiological and endocrine functions.

9.16.6. Self-Affirmation and Threat

All humans experience threat to the self from damage to the self-concept or the prospect of personal annihilation. When people are confronted with threats they typically shore up self-worth by reaffirming other unrelated attributes of the self. However, self-affirmation theory applies only to respondents who have high self-esteem (Aronson, Blanton, & Cooper, 1995; Koole, Smeets, van Knippenberg, & Dijksterhuis, 1999; Steele, 1988). In one study students high and low in self-esteem were led to believe they had either failed or succeeded on a test of intellectual ability. Respondents who were high in self-esteem, but who had been led to believe they had failed, exaggerated their other positive social qualities. Respondents with low self-esteem generalized their failure experience as one already consistent with the negative view they had about themselves. On the other hand, respondents with high self-esteem believe they have many other positive traits so they immediately seek to reaffirm their strengths in unrelated areas after perceived threat (Dodgson & Wood, 1998). The healthy nature of self-affirmation can be observed by the fact that the respondents felt good about themselves in the aftermath of perceived failure, and were strong enough to entertain potential negative information about the self (Sherman, Nelson, & Steele, 2000).

There is no greater threat than that of personal annihilation. Terror management theory asserts that the threat of death leads people to seek ways to minimize or manage this vulnerability (Greenberg, Porteus, Simon, Pyszczynski, & Solomon, 1995). The threat of personal annihilation is kept in control by two mechanisms. In the first case high self-esteem helps the individual to feel valued in a meaningful universe and feeling valued controls to some degree the threat of death. In the face of imminent death people have a need to reaffirm the importance of their lives, and the legacy they have created including assessments of meaningful work and personal relationships.

Secondly, a cultural world-view that provides hope for the future, or at least makes some sense of the present assists in controlling threats to mortality. Conformity to cultural expectations and values is a means by which people also control fear (Greenberg, 2012; Greenberg, Solomon, Pyszczynski, Rosenblatt, Burling, Lyon, Pinel, & Simon, 1992; Harmon-Jones, Simon, Greenberg, Pyszczynski, Solomon, & McGregor, 1997). The familiar cultural setting is soothing to most people and allows the individual to see continuity even when personal existence is ending. At the same time when confronted with the fear of death, people also seek affiliation (Wisman & Koole, 2003). We can observe that need in the increasing popularity of the hospice movement. From anecdotal experiences death threat is lowered when the patient is under the care of hospice and the individual feels less lonely or isolated through the efforts of volunteers accompanying the patient on the last journey.

When people are scared by threats to mortality they are also more likely to act with aggression toward those who challenge their world-view (McGregor et al., 1998). Hostile reactions can be observed in the anger displayed by people who are related to soldiers serving the U.S. army in Iraq or other theaters. The slogan "support the troops," the flag waving, and shrill denunciations of war opponents, emerge most likely from the perceived threat to mortality to the loved one. Leaders of nations mobilizing for war have known how to manipulate the threat of mortality in order to energize the war effort and demonize the enemy. That story continues throughout the world today.

9.16.7. False Pride, Aggressive Ideology and Self-Esteem

Endless wars and aggression are supported by the need to self-enhance after collective damage to self-esteem. The German people after the First World War were a defeated people both on the battlefield and in estimation of the international community. The Great Depression that followed World War One created economic insecurity among the Germans and a loss of faith in contemporary society. It was a perfect time for the great manipulators of history to gain power by appeals to false self-esteem and false pride. The Nazi's sought to restore self-esteem by use of in-group symbols and by finding scapegoats for social and national frustrations. Although the

Nazi's appearance on the stage of history was extreme in destruction and victimization, fundamentally they were no different from any other genocidal group. The genocide in Rwanda and Darfur were caused by similar ingroup identification and the demonization of adversaries. The concentration camp that the Palestinian people have lived in the past half a century is motivated by the similar fears that caused the victimization of the Jewish people by the Nazi's. We seem to have learned nothing from history and so repeat the crimes derived from in-group based false self-esteem.

In contemporary society the phenomenon of gang violence takes a similar path of victimization. Gang members come typically from poor and deprived environments ripe and ready for exploitation by misleaders. For many young people gang membership is compensation for all that is missing in their lives. Self-esteem in members is derived from collective gang pride emphasized by the use of symbols and colors. The Bloods (red color) and the Crips (blue color) are common criminal gangs in the U.S. Typically gang members display an elevated sense of self-worth and grandiosity not supported by achievements or good works (Wink, 1991). The fact that gang members possess false self-esteem can be observed in their sensitivity to any perceived insult or denigration. Children are shot dead in the streets of the U.S. for imagined insults to the colors of another gang, revealing the fundamentally desperate insecurity underlying enhancement and false pride.

In fact psychopaths possess the same grandiose sense of self-worth (Hare, 1993) and are responsible for a majority of violent crimes. Psychopathic criminals also have inflated views of self-worth combined with hypersensitivity to perceived threats or denigration. The murders and bullies emerging out of gang culture have no genuine self-esteem, but rather are narcissistic and arrogant individuals. Is it a coincidence that members of the White prison gang "Aryan brotherhood" use Nazi symbols? This false sense of self-esteem and pride is historically responsible for genocidal deeds whether in slavery, modern forms of terrorism, or other forms of violent behavior (Baumeister, Smart, & Boden, 1996). In fact all gangs of history, from those led by Hitler to the military fascists led by Pinochet in Chile, have in common grandiose feelings of superiority and arrogance and a deficit in real genuine self-esteem. Combined with the indifference to human suffering and lack of empathy, this leads to unimagined horrors.

9.17. THE PATH TO EXPERIENCING WELL-BEING

Feeling good and having a sense of well-being is a priority for most people regardless of culture. In traveling to other countries one can often observe the apparent sense of well-being expressed by people poor in material possessions. Yet in our modern globalized world we are taught that consumption is the road to happiness, and having money to consume produces life satisfaction. However, even in modern capitalist societies research shows that money makes little difference to a sense of well-being (Diener, Suh, Lucas, & Smith, 1999). People adjust to whatever economic and social circumstances that are present within some degree of latitude. Of course, if people live with deprivation from poverty in the form of hunger or untreated health issues well-being is impacted. Well-being is related to the quality of our life experiences (Van Boven & Gilovich, 2003). The here and now of our contemporary experiences are important to the enjoyment of life. Many people delay living in our highly competitive societies procrastinating important activities to some point in the inaccessible future. Members of individualistic societies perpetually look for the joy of the weekend, the vacation, the retirement, and eventually when all fails they look forward to a place in heaven, but in the process they do not enjoy the journey of life itself.

Realistic expectations play an important role in well-being. If expectations are too high, or if you do not have the resources necessary, frustration follows. Being able to withdraw from unrealistic goals and move in a different direction is related to satisfaction (Wrosch, Scheier, Miller, Schulz, & Carver, 2003). A sense of well-being is a result of the self manifested in personality traits and self-attributes. Some people see a glass half empty where others see the wine bottle next to the glass is still nearly full. We can focus on aspects of life that are going well for us, or we can concentrate on reliving all our failures. Important to well-being is the pursuit of goals that reflect who we are that are consistent with our basic human values.

However, those who live in poverty in third world countries may never have the same degree of freedom that we possess in advanced economies, but that in and of itself does not prevent a meaningful life. Regardless of where we live in the World we all have basic needs for self-directed lives, for autonomy, for establishing competence in mastering the social environment, and for having a supportive social network (Kang, Shaver, Sue, Min, & Jing, 2003). Being optimistic obviously matters to well-being and to maintaining positive emotions over time associated with a greater sense of feeling good (Updegraff, Gable, & Taylor, 2004).

9.17.1. The Complexity of Self-Attributes, Self-Efficacy and Well-Being

Central attributes have a significant effect on the sense of well-being. Some of us put all our achievement eggs into one or a few baskets. For students whose self-esteem is bound up with academic performance and little else, a low grade in a course of study may be devastating. Others look to achievements in a number of areas to sustain positive feelings about the self and are not defeated by failure in one domain. Students who have hobbies, special talents, wide-ranging minds, and participate in athletics have a stronger sense of well-being. As noted for respondents with complex self-concepts setbacks in any one area produce less vulnerability since they have other achievements to sustain positive feelings. On the other hand, respondents with simple self-concepts are vulnerable when experiencing setbacks, as they have little else to support their self-concept (Linville, 1985). People with simple self-conceptions feel good when successful in their defined domain, but are likely to be depressed in cases of failure (Showers & Ryff, 1996). *Self-complexity* produces a buffer for individuals with positive self-construal against the inevitable setbacks and adversity of life. However, people with negative self-views are not going to feel better by having more complex negative self-concepts, since that just provides more reasons to stay depressed.

Feelings of self-efficacy also create a sense of well-being. The lack of self-efficacy is probably the major reason that most dieters fail to stay with a program and lose weight. Many people who try to diet have little confidence that they can achieve the weight loss they want, and they behave appropriate to these expectations of failure. Others have had experiences of success in weight loss upon which to build self-efficacy. Based on past success experiences some dieters have the confidence that this approach will work again and bring down weight to a more optimal level.

Self-efficacy probably grows out of early experiences with parents and teachers. Early success leads to stable self-conceptions of efficacy in a variety of areas. Self-efficacy produces a sense of personal control giving encouragement to a person's planning for the future. Feelings of self-efficacy also help in coping with possible setbacks by self-regulating and changing behavior as necessary (Pham, Taylor, & Seeman, 2001).

Self-efficacy reduces the stress of life and produces more optimism about the future. In the long run self-efficacy produces basic approach or avoidance orientations to life. Some people develop a behavioral activation system based on positive happenings of the past. Others with negative experiences develop an inhibition system that prevents the individual from undertaking important challenges for lack of confidence (Gable, Reis, & Elliott, 2000). Researchers think of these basic approaches as stable personality traits. For example, extraversion is a behavioral activation based on social intelligence and success. On the other hand, neuroticism is an extreme example of avoidance (Carver, Sutton, & Scheier, 2000).

9.17.2. Can Positive Illusions Serve the Cause of Well-Being

Self-knowledge can affect our well-being. We need realistic self-conceptions to make good decisions and be successful. However, positive illusions about the self can be enhancing, and encourage and motivate behavior (Taylor & Brown, 1988, 1994). Many psychologists in humanistic and existential psychology (including Carl Rogers and Abraham Maslow) have encouraged us to accept life as it is and believe that self-illusions are fundamentally neurotic.

Contrary to these existential views it appears that unrealistic positive self-concepts are in fact related to well-being. Most people think that positive traits describe them better than negative dimensions showing that positive illusions are ubiquitous. When we reluctantly accept negative self-descriptions we dilute the effect on the self-concept by asserting that we share these negative attributes with many others. We can also reason that the flaws we possess are not important since we share them with many people, whereas our positive traits are distinctive aspects of our personality.

Well-adjusted people tend to have an exaggerated sense of control over their lives. Many people also believe that ritual affects the outcome of life whether in religion or the mundane. For example, on game shows in the U.S. the audience can often hear the player "command" the game to perform in the winning direction when it in fact the outcome is based on randomness. In a study on lottery tickets (Langer, 1975) the experimenter tried to buy back lottery tickets which all had the exact same probability of yielding a winning result. Those buyers who had chosen their lottery ticket based on some superstition, held out for a larger return when asked to sell the ticket prior to the drawing. On the other hand, depressed people are more accurate in their appraisals of control, but are, of course, less happy (Abramson, Metalsky, & Alloy, 1989).

Self-enhancing perceptions are adaptive (Taylor, Lerner, Sherman, Sage, & McDowell, 2003). Even if our optimism is not justified we feel better about the future based on positive illusions. Positive illusions give us feelings of control where in fact we have none. Believing in a heaven to come may be a positive illusion that nevertheless helps the believer coping with randomness and absurdity. Should we encourage people to have positive beliefs even if they are illusionary? Some research has supported the idea that optimism and false sense of control may actually help people feel better and happier (Regan, Snyder, & Kassin, 1995). Do we need a new psychology based on positive illusions since at least in some areas they are adaptive and not neurotic?

When we feel good about ourselves it has positive consequences for our social relationships. You must have noted that when you feel good about life you are more open and agreeable. Positive self-regard fosters relationships within some limits (Taylor et al., 2003). However, people will get tired of the self-promoter, and self-aggrandizement can also lead to alienation. As in the cases of most other behavior, self-enhancement is an issue of balance. Have you ever met perpetually happy people so self-enhancing that you shake your head and tell yourself "that can't be for real"?

People living in the West are likely to have unrealistic optimism about the future (Aspinwall & Brunhart, 1996; Kitayama, Markus, Matsumoto, &

Norasakkunkit, 1997; Seligman, 1991). The optimism is personalized since they believe positive events will happen to them, but not necessarily to others. Unrealistic optimism emerges out of people's egocentrism, where most people focus on their own outcomes and ignore happenings to others (Kruger, 1999; Kruger & Burrus, 2004).

Having unrealistically positive self-perceptions lead to an exaggerated sense of control over conditions of life and unrealistic optimism. Overall positive illusions improve well-being by creating positive moods, healthier social relationships, and by promoting goal directed behavior. Few of us would start any journey, even an easy one, if we did not believe the outcome would be positive. In struggling against tyranny in countries where the state holds all the power, few people would work for reform or change unless they had the positive illusions that in the near future or historically their efforts would be crowned with success.

The ego-centrism can go too far (Colvin & Block, 1994). The narcissist typically endorses extreme self-enhancement illusions. However, self-promotion turns off most people in the long run. Narcissists have the tendency to blow their own horn too long and people reject such behavior (Paulhus, 1998). Longitudinal studies have shown a further downside of positive illusions. Students who exaggerate their academic abilities eventually come up against reality and experience failure at school and loss of self-esteem (Robins & Beer, 2001; Colvin, Block, & Funder, 1995). The research suggests that not all forms of positive illusions serve the functions of well-being. It would appear that we need some positive illusions to become motivated to reach goals, but not so illusionary that we experience constant failure. A balance must be created between the positive illusions and accurate self-concepts.

9.17.3. The Role of Positive Illusions in Varying Cultures

What brings about well-being depends on the individual's relationship to the cultural values derived from individualistic or collectivistic societies. Cultures show significant differences in the endorsement of positive illusions. Westerners are more likely to embrace positive illusions when compared to Asian peoples (Heine, Lehman, Markus, & Kitayama, 1999; Kitayama, Markus, Matsumoto, & Norasakkunkit, 1997). For example, when considering academic abilities Japanese hold fewer positive illusions compared to Western students, and display less unrealistic optimism when compared to Canadian students (Heine, Kitayama, Lehman, Takata, Ide, Leung, & Matsumoto, 2001; Heine & Lehman, 1995). In a study of 42 nations Sastry and Ross (1998) found that Asians were less likely to feel they had complete control over their lives, whereas people from Western societies displayed unrealistic optimism.

So from a cultural perspective we must conclude that positive self-delusions do not automatically lead to well-being. In individualistic societies well-being is a construct closely tied to positive views of self, to control, and to optimism. In Asian societies well-being is based more on interdependent self-conceptions. The fulfillment of social roles and expectations is fundamental to self-construal in Asia, and satisfaction in these areas is more likely to bring a sense of well-being (Suh, Diener, Oishi, & Triandis, 1998).

9.18. PERFORMING IN FRONT OF OTHERS AND MANAGING THE IMPRESSION OF THE SELF

Impression management is motivated by the desire to be accepted by others. Although there may be universal aspects to managing impressions leading to social acceptance cultural variance also play a role. Conformity to cultural values that express competitive achievement in individualistic societies and concern for the social unit in collectivistic cultures seems an essential bridge to inclusion and acceptance. Have you noticed that your behavior changes depending on the person with whom you converse and with the objectives of the interaction? For example, with your parents you may act with a measure of love and social obligation, with teachers you are courteous trying to produce a favorable impression (and good outcomes), whereas with a baby you are natural and feel no need to impress. These varying responses can also be called situational conformity. Before interacting with others we have an awareness of the person, the situation and the objectives. We mold our behavior to make a correct and useful impression, especially on those who have status and power. The psychopath is perhaps the most skillful in impression management. How did Bundy, an infamous serial killer in the U.S., create enough trust in young women, so they accompanied him to his car where they were overpowered and were eventually murdered? He did it by putting his arm in a sling, and by looking helpless he appealed for help from sympathetic coeds.

In a broader way we want to be accepted by others (Baumeister & Leary, 1995). As noted previously there is psychologically nothing more painful than social exclusion. Some societies use that knowledge to torture prisoners whether at Guantanamo in Cuba, or in special penitentiaries in the US, where prisoners sit in a cage like cells for 23 hours a day with no social interaction. We can think of the death penalty as the ultimate form of social exclusion and torture that on the face is both cruel and rather unusual. As noted earlier in this chapter social exclusion is related to self-esteem. Researchers have also demonstrated that social exclusion is among the most painful and stressful conditions known to humanity (Eisenberger, Lieberman, & Williams, 2003; Twenge, Catanese, & Baumeister, 2003). We therefore spend a great deal of time in self-monitoring so that our behavior will be acceptable and we will be included by family, peers and society.

We can see by these examples that there is a significant difference between people's public and private selves. Much of the research that we have discussed in this chapter pertains to the private self, the executive "I" as decision maker or regulator of behavior and how it is influenced by the social context. We operate in a social context of no small importance, and learn early that others have power to make life better or worse. The public self is devoted to impression management, where we try to convey an image and convince others that this image is our true self. We work hard to get other people to see us the way we want to be seen (Goffman, 1959; Knowles & Sibicky, 1990; Spencer, Fein, Zanna, & Olson, 2003).

We are actors on the stage of life concerned with self-presentation and the monitoring of our behavior. Impression management is about convincing others to believe in the "face" we are presenting. We try to control what others think of us because doing so has utility in terms of material, relational, and self-relevant advantages. Goffman was probably the first to systematically examine how we construct our identities in public. He maintained that much of our public behavior is governed by claims we make in an effort to maintain a positive face. The image we want to convey Goffman called face (see also Baumeister, 1982; Brown, 1998; Leary & Kowalski, 1990).

Impression management follows a certain script we have memorized to be used whenever we interact with others. We also expect others to play their roles and to respect the identity we convey. Impression management is a mutual support society since other people depend on us to honor the claims they make. To lose face is very painful, and in Asian cultures failure in impression management can be unbearable. We want other people to respect, not the private self, but the one we present to the world. We are all actors trying to convince our audience.

In the process of impression management we can employ several strategies (Jones & Pittman, 1982). The term "brownnosing" is used to describe those who try to ingratiate themselves to gain advantage with powerful others. Ingratiation is a strategy used to make ourselves more likeable to other people that are powerful (Gordon, 1996; Vonk, 2002). However, nothing is more effective than sincerely meant praise in promoting liking relationships. On the other hand, if the praise is for ulterior motives, and most of us can feel when that occurs, the ingratiation may backfire (Kauffman & Steiner, 1968).

9.18.1. Protecting Face by Self-Handicapping

Presenting a favorable image is important in all cultures and all people seek to protect face even if it requires lowering expectations about performance. One strategy to protect face is self-handicapping. Our face is so important that we often engage in self-defeating behaviors before a test of our skills to avoid losing face. In the self-handicapping situation we set up excuses prior to performance, so if we do poorly we have an excuse that exonerates the public self (Arkin & Oleson, 1998; Thill & Curry, 2000). Students may self-handicap prior to an important exam, for example, spending the night drinking with friends provides the alibi for poor test performance and therefore does not reflect on the academic image created among fellow students. In one study (Berglas & Jones, 1978) students were offered a chance to either take a performance enhancing drug, or one that would impair test taking. The respondents were placed in one of two conditions. One group was led to believe that they were going to succeed on the test whereas the other group was led to believe that failure was likely. The participants who thought failure was likely preferred the performance-inhibiting drug even though that would result in poor test performance. From the point of view of self-handicapping, students would rather fail in an effort to support impression management, but have a good alibi for failure than take the chance for success and have no excuse if they failed.

Self-handicapping can have serious consequences for health. Condoms have proven an effective preventive of pregnancy and sexually transmitted diseases, yet from 30 to 65 percent of respondents reported that they were embarrassed when buying these health-promoting devices. Somehow buying condoms violates many people's self-presentations as perhaps non-sexual or at least not promiscuous. In this day of increasing skin cancer many people continue to sunbathe to excess in order to meet a self-presentation of beauty and ironically of health. Social approval continues to be the basic motivation for impression management (Leary & Jones, 1993).

Some self-handicapping is not so obvious to an audience. People may simply prepare ready-made excuses for poor performance. We can attribute poor performance on tests as due to test anxiety, headaches or being in a bad mood on the day of performance. In the process of self-handicapping we may also become self-fulfilling prophecies and come to believe in the excuses. Self-handicappers may become permanently poor performers and fail to establish the parameters for a successful life. It is ironic that the concerns underlying self-handicapping (which is to be liked by others for the face being conveyed) may in fact have opposite results. Most people see through the charade and do not like people that spend their time and efforts at self-handicapping rather than working (Hirt, McCrea, & Boris, 2003; McCrea & Hirt, 2011).

9.18.2. Promoting the Self by Communicating Competence or By Association

A high value is placed on competence in Western culture as it is associated with the value of individual achievement. Impression management is all about making a "good" impression (Schlenker, 1980; Schlenker & Britt, 1999; Schlenker & Pontari, 2000). However, some people use the direct route and self-promote never tiring of telling others of their many and varied accomplishments. The self-promoter is primarily interested in other people's perceptions of their competence (Jones & Pittman, 1982). The type of self-promotion depends on the norms of social interaction. For example, in athletic competition a norm of modesty prevails. Therefore it is not in good form to boast of one's own performance, but rather to attribute success to the efforts of teammates, coaches, and fans. Normative modesty works best when it is false, and the athlete actually has cause to boast. Under these conditions modesty is a strategy of positive impression management (Cialdini & De Nicholas, 1989).

Other forms of self-promotion are vicarious. We like to enjoy "the reflected glory of others." By associating with successful others we obtain positive associations that affect the opinions of our peers (Cialdini & De Nicholas, 1989). Football fans attend games or wear clothing identifying with a team in order to self-enhance. That is especially true when following a team with a winning record. Vicarious self-promotion contributes to positive impressions associated with winning and status, at least in the Western world.

9.18.3. Impression Management and Private or Public Self-Consciousness

Regardless of culture a great deal of impression management is wasted effort. The previous discussion supported a difference between a public self (known to others) and a private self (known only to the self), (Fenigstein, Scheier, & Buss, 1975). Being self-conscious in public encourages people to engage in face saving and impression management. The ironic aspect about *public self-consciousness* is that nearly everyone is conscious of his or her audience and painfully aware that others are observing them. However, since everyone including the "observers" is focused on the effect of the audience (and also being observed) a lot of face saving and impression management efforts are wasted. In public self-consciousness awareness is directed toward what others think, however, since everyone shares that attribute, the focus is as noted internally on the effects of the audience and people really do not observe others. Then why be publicly self-conscious?

There are individual differences in public self-consciousness. People with fragile egos are more concerned about what others think about them (again a wasted effort). Insecure people tend to think of themselves in terms of social popularity and approval (Fenigstein, 1984). Some people, however, possess a dimension of *private self-consciousness* and a greater awareness of internal feelings and thoughts. People with a private self tend to think of themselves more in terms of their own independent thoughts and feelings. Those with private self-consciousness care little about what others think, but they are a rare breed. Due to the long dependency period of humans beings, and the nature of the social self formed by social interactions, private self-consciousness is not only rare, but probably also affected by what others think to some degree.

Since we want to be accepted we spend energy and time on *self-monitoring* (Gangestad & Snyder, 2000). Most people want to be socially acceptable and therefore monitor behavior to see if they fit the requirements of the situation. People high in self-monitoring are the true actors on the stage of life. They are situational conformist, switching behavior like a chameleon as required from one situation to the next. Low monitors are more likely to respond to internal impulses or demands, and are less dependent on the social context. Is monitoring adaptive? In one study (Snyder, 1974) patients in a mental hospital scored low on self-monitoring. That finding suggests that to cope effectively with life requires at least some awareness of surroundings and the social demands for appropriate behavior.

9.18.4. Impression Management and Cultural Values

The social self is formed by cultural values summarized in the concept of individualistic (or independent) and collectivistic (or interdependent) cultures. In all cultures the social self emerges from social interactions and is formed by the socialization of varying social values. The fundamental difference in cultural values as noted previously is the predominant emphasis on independence in Western cultures, and interdependence in Asian and some other developing societies. The term "saving face" has been associated with Asian cultures and reflects a special sensitivity to maintaining face in these societies. To lose face is to lose identity for interdependent people. Appearance is of great importance in interdependent societies. For example, if it is important to have many wedding guests, and if one has an insufficient number of friends attending, one can rent guests in some countries (Jordan & Sullivan, 1996). If there are insufficient lamenters at a funeral one can hire professional lamenters to produce an appropriate grief display.

In Asian cultures, impression management is about measuring up to social roles and expectations whereas in the West there is a greater desire for individual enhancement (Heine & Renshaw, 2002; Sedikides, Gaertner, & Toguchi, 2003; Sedikides, Gaertner, & Vevea, 2005). In fact self-enhancement is ubiquitous in all Western societies while it is relatively uncommon in interdependent cultures. The various terms discussed in this chapter like self-consciousness and self-regulation takes on different forms depending on culture (Simon, Pantaleo, & Mummedy, 1995). Yet these cultural differences in impression management must be taken with a grain of salt. Culture may account for certain amounts of the behavioral variance, but societies are changing as the world is becoming more convergent. At the same time if we want to improve intercultural communications we must have some awareness of cultural values.

SUMMARY

The self-concept emerges from the interaction between the individual and the surrounding cultural environment. It is useful to think of research on the self as a bridge between personality theory and social psychology where the route to understanding the self must draw from all wells of knowledge. This means that rather than utilizing opposing dichotomies as research strategies we must recognize the self as both a cultural construct derived from unique cultural values, but also with cross-cultural universal components. Since so much research on the self is not reported within either the cultural or cross-cultural comparative framework it is necessary for the reader to determine what is applicable to a given culture.

This chapter discussed several dimensions of the social self, self-knowledge and self-esteem. Self-awareness starts at an early age, perhaps as early as nine months, and certainly by age two the child recognizes the self as distinct. Over time we accumulate knowledge about the self from experiences with family, school, and culture. As our interactions become more complex, a belief system about the self emerges, and along with that an understanding of our more complex attributes. Self-esteem is derived from our judgment of our personal morality and behavior, and satisfaction with our performance relative to ideal and ought selves. People who are low in self-esteem need constant approval and reaffirmation. High self-esteem is functional in setting achievement goals and helping people persist in goal directed behaviors. Individuals with low self-esteem are more pessimistic and do not believe they have self-efficacy.

The building blocks of the self point to basic traits discussed previously as being universal. The research literature supports the heritability of personality traits. We use these traits in judging others and ourselves. Since the aforementioned traits are understood everywhere they must have a biological evolutionary basis growing out of human needs to adapt and survive. The heritability of personality traits is supported by studies of fraternal and identical twins. Also, traits identified early in children, like shyness, tend to have lifelong consequences also suggesting a biological basis. Neuroticism is associated with subjective stress, and on the opposite side extraversion is associated with the presence of the neurotransmitter Dopamine. As we can see it is impossible to separate the self from biological inheritance. Recent research points to the complex interaction between genetic inheritance and specific environments in producing predictable behavior. Perhaps some traits like neuroticism were adaptable in early human history in the struggle for survival, but are non-adaptable now in our complex society.

Scientists and philosophers have long discussed the nature of the self. As science has progressed we understand more and more about the so-called "easy" problem that links thought to brain function. The "hard" problem is trying to understand the "knower" the subjective experience that someone is in charge, an executive "I" or decider. Why does it feel like we have a conscious process, and subjective experience that emerge from neural computations in the brain? When scientists use MRI's they can practically map thought processes in the brain and there is no convincing evidence of an ethereal soul. Is the "knower" nothing but an illusion required by the information overload in the brain, and the adaptive need to evaluate stimuli? Can the "knower" be understood solely as brain activity? Certainly believing in a soul construct has not supported moral behavior as is evidenced by all human history. However, the hard problem remains and may never be solved. All we can say with certainty is that the whole is greater than the sum of its parts.

The development of the social self is produced by the consistent reactions of socialization agents. Consistent interactions with others influence the development of self-knowledge and self-esteem. It is the consistent treatment by early socialization agents found in the family that is the basis of what we believe about ourselves and that knowledge guides our behavior for the rest of our lives. The family is central in the creation of the possible self, the self of the future. Other factors that influence the development of self-knowledge and self-esteem are birth order and group memberships. Birth order has an effect as children learn to occupy various niches in the family that are functional and rewarding. Group memberships are also a key to understanding the self because groups socialize cultural values that have motivational significance. Research has shown that even nonsensical groups may have profound effects on decisions and history support the idea that group categorization itself is responsible for much of the mayhem in the world. Minorities, for example, have to deal with special challenges as they cope with mainstream cultures. Although in general, strong ethnic identity combined with positive attitudes toward the larger society is associated with high self-esteem.

Culture is a major source of the self-concept. The main differences discussed in this chapter are the reliable findings between collectivistic and individualistic societies. For the interdependent societies of Asia and elsewhere, the social context of family and society matters greatly in the development of the self-concept. The individualistic societies of North American and Europe have more independent self-construal where the self is seen as autonomous, distinct, and separate from others. Whether we seek to achieve for personal reasons or for group goals are to some extent determined by culture. One's culture might also affect the choice of career and whether we seek to enhance the self or society. In independent societies self-esteem is ego based, whereas in interdependent cultures it is more related to family and social approval. As always we must remember that cultural differences are abstractions, that people differ within cultural models, and that the world is becoming more convergent.

Gender plays, along with family, groups and culture, a vital role in the development of the self-concept. All cultures treat males and females differentially with lifelong consequences. Women are more interdependent and connected to intimate relationships. Men are more affected by larger social groupings. Socialization through the efforts of families, society, and educational processes produce these predictable differences. Gender distinctions probably evolved early in human history in response to survival demands that required role specialization. A few theories have been discussed in this chapter.

Social comparison theory asserts that we learn about ourselves by comparing our behavior to that of others. We enhance ourselves when we compare downward, and inspire ourselves for achievement when comparing ourselves to high achieving models. At times when facing a crisis or in response to uncertainty, we compare in order to bond with other people.

Self-perception theory suggests that we derive the meaning of emotions from self-observation of our own behavior. At times, however, we meet with novel situations or the unfamiliar and do not know what we are supposed to feel. In these cases our objective behavior becomes the guide for understanding our emotions. We attribute meaning by ascribing the cause for our feelings to either the situation or to personal disposition. Self-perception theory has been applied to education, and supports the importance of intrinsic motivation in producing lasting learning. Schachter used self-perception theory in his two-factor model of emotion. He stated that people note their internal physiological reactions to stimuli and then look at the environment for a plausible cause to explain these feelings. This has been demonstrated in research that showed that emotional labels may be arbitrary and can be manipulated. For example happiness or anger can be attributed from the same physiological reactions depending on environmental factors for interpretation. Misattribution of arousal is possible as more than one source can explain what we feel. Research shows that misattribution for arousal can also easily be manipulated. Cognitive appraisal theories point out that sometimes we experience emotions after we think about and understand the situation. The meaning of the situation, the good or bad it implies for well-being brings on emotions after we have thought about these consequences.

We can also learn about the self-concept by introspection although introspection is not reliable. Most people spend little time thinking about themselves because it is at times painful especially if we are aware of shortcomings in meeting ideal or ought selves. We seek escape in drugs, excessive television viewing, or dogmatic religion that tells us all we need to know. Also, introspection may not tell us the real reasons for our feelings as we may rely on causal theories derived from society that offer plausible but false causes.

A major organizational function of the self is the constricting and narrowing of our perceptions. Research shows that the self affects memory as recall of material is more efficient if related to self-relevant schemas. Self-schemas refer to the basic dimensions we employ in cognizing about the self, it is our organized thinking about important self-relevant dimensions. Self-schemas are readily available in memory, and are fundamental organizing tools. We develop self-schemas because we cannot attend to everything, and therefore focus selectively on information considered most relevant. At the same time self-schemas restrict information by removing from awareness information that is inconsistent from that which we already believe. Self-schemas are stable over time precisely because we act consistently and selectively to new information.

A major function of self-schemas is self-regulation. We think about the future and envision a possible self, what we can become, and this motivates our planning and behavior. The self serves regulatory functions in determining plans and choices for creating the future that we expect and want. It is important to keep in mind that energy for self-regulation is finite. This fact makes us vulnerable when trying to stay on diets or refrain from taking up bad habits once discarded. The stable self provides a sense of continuity throughout the lifespan. At times we are faced with novel situations like soldiers in wartime, and develop temporary working selves to cope with demands. Sadly, these temporary working self-concepts can become a dysfunctional part of the permanent self when the behavior varies widely from the stable self and the situation is traumatic and powerful in its effects.

The self has motivational properties. Our current behavior is determined by our plans for the future and what we believe to be our possible selves. Possible selves also include religious and cultural standards, and are often associated with feelings of guilt and shame. The ideal self refers to our aspirations in life, whereas our "ought self" describes our obligations and duties. Discrepancies between ideal and ought and what is real causes anxiety, and produces for some people the motivation necessary to change. Most alcoholics feel the discrepancy eventually and many seek help.

In judging others we use our self-image bias. Whether we accept others is related to how similar others are to ourselves. Culture plays a role here as well. For example, in the individualistic West others are judged according to criteria of the independent self where the ideal self plays a primary role. In the collectivistic interdependent cultures others become standards for judgment, and the "ought self" including obligations and duties is the primary evaluative tool.

We are motivated by consistent and accurate self-conceptions. Especially feedback that is consistent with our self-conceptions is motivating. We seek primarily self-affirmation in our interactions with others and this in fact influences our choice of friends. We select those friends who will confirm our self-concepts. This selection is to some degree modified by self-esteem: Persons with high self-esteem are more likely to be receptive of both negative and positive self-confirming information than persons with low self-esteem. An accurate self-concept is adaptive since plans and success in the future depend on accurate self-assessments.

Most people are motivated to enhance a sense of self-worth. There are components of self-esteem that remain consistent as a personality trait throughout life. Momentary changes in self-esteem, however, may occur from developmental issues and as a consequence of significant events. A central issue in self-esteem is the desire to be accepted and included. Human isolation is therefore extremely painful, as penologists know. This preoccupation with approval derives from obvious social and evolutionary advantages. Our self-esteem may rise or fall with experience in domains key to the self. In turn culture determines to some extent what areas are considered salient domains. Research shows that self-esteem is more functional if based on more than one or a few domains. With many domains we can control better the inevitable setbacks that life hands us.

Preoccupation with self-esteem is primarily a Western phenomenon. It is derived from the cultural focus on independence and personal distinctions. Western respondents self-report higher levels of self-esteem compared to people living in collectivistic societies; however, that finding may be attributed to the greater modesty of interdependent peoples. Being rewarded or praised for achievement is more common in the West, whereas in interdependent cultures people are more motivated by common goals and self-improvement. Cultural distinctions in self-esteem are abstractions as again there are differences within cultures, and globalization is encouraging convergence in values.

False self-esteem is aggrandizement based on group memberships where the group operates by scapegoating and demonizing outsiders. Gang violence is caused by false aggrandizement as compensation for all that is missing in the gang member's life. Gang members display elevated but false self-esteem not justified by accomplishments or good works. Their fundamental insecurity is revealed by their sensitivity to perceived insults. Psychopathic individuals have grandiose conceptions of self-worth which compensate for the lack of genuine self-esteem.

The preoccupation with enhancement influences the way in which we associate with others. It leads to comparison between the self and the other for advantages looking downward for enhancement or enjoying the reflected glory of the achievements of those with whom we associate. Friendships are based on the need for enhancement. When we select our friends we ensure that we can compare downward in most salient domains. In Western cultures self-enhancement is of overriding importance, especially when we are threatened by failure. In general most people believe that their positive traits are more important than their negative attributes. Self-enhancement leads, in fact, to better mental health, and better physiological and endocrine functions.

When the self-concept is threatened we shore up self-worth by reaffirming other unrelated attributes of the self. For example, there is no greater threat than our mortality. We control this existential threat through the building of self-esteem. In positive assessments of self-esteem people assert that their lives are worthwhile and that they rely on a worldview that makes life meaningful. When people are threatened by mortality they are easily manipulated and provoked to aggression. Threat to world-views or to conventional society undermines the cultural meanings that control death anxiety releasing anger and aggression.

In a complex world how do we find a path to well-being? In Western societies people have been convinced that consumption is the road to follow. However, well-being is related to the quality of life, to the journey of life, and to realistic expectations. Furthermore, our personality also matters. For instance, for some people a glass is half empty, for others the glass is half full and next to a plentiful bottle. It is important to pursue self-relevant goals that reflect that which we value in life. Regardless of cultural differences we all have basic human needs for autonomy, for competence in dealing with challenges, and for a supportive social network.

Research shows that a complexity of attributes and self-efficacy is necessary for well-being. Respondents who possess more complex self-concepts are not overcome when facing a setback in a singular dimension. Self-efficacy is the feeling of "can do," that we have the necessary competence to succeed. Self-efficacy grows out of early experiences with parents and educators. Our early success reduces stress in life. Positive illusions refer to exaggerated optimism and sense of control in life. The well-adjusted often display positive illusions that can enhance, encourage, and motivate behavior. Those with positive illusions are happier and have better social relationships than the depressed that have more realistic conceptions. People in the West are especially likely to display unrealistic optimism about the future. The downside of positive illusions is that at times we must face unpleasant reality. However, positive illusions are more likely endorsed in Western societies. Well-being in interdependent cultures is more related to fulfillment of roles and social expectations.

Impression management research suggests that people are actors on the stage of life. Most people mold their behavior according to situational demands and we are chameleons according to need. Psychopaths are especially skilled at impression management. Since we all want to be accepted we work hard to convince others that our self-presentation is true. We encourage others to believe in our public face. Ingratiation is a form of impression management where we try to make ourselves more likeable to the powerful through flattery. Self-handicapping promotes face saving by engaging in self-defeating behaviors prior to performance. Sometimes people take foolish chances with health in order to preserve their face and image. Self-promotion is a more direct path of impression management. We seek to impress others of our competence, and our associations with others of status and power. It is primarily the publicly self-conscious who engage in impression management. People with private self-consciousness are concerned with their own independent thoughts and feelings. The social self emerges from social interaction in all cultures. The self-concept is therefore a consequence of cultural values. Saving face is of particular importance to Asian cultures. Central to these societies is the concern about roles and expectations, whereas people in the West are more concerned about individual enhancement.

CHAPTER 10

CULTURE, SEX AND GENDER

Many changes have occurred in the past few decades that have influenced the relationship between men and women. The developments that emerged out of the women's movement in the United States and Europe have had a profound influence on important social institutions including marriage, but also in opportunities for women in academia and athletics. While women and girls have made great progress in the Western world the dynamic changes in women' lives have also brought confusion and a higher divorce rate. Because of globalizations these social forces have to a lesser degree also influenced gender relations in other parts of the world. In this chapter we shall discuss many of the variables that result from the relationship between culture and gender including sex role stereotypes, gender related behaviors, and gender ideologies that define traditional or egalitarian relationships. The chapter will also discuss the impetus for change in gender relations, and the historical prejudice and discrimination toward women. Finally, in a changing world what are the consequences of these evolving relationships for mate selection and marriage?

Many events around the world have brought into a focus discriminatory practices toward women. This week a woman was decapitated in Saudi Arabia for supposedly practicing sorcery. It reminds us of the many thousands

---

of women, most probably mentally ill, who in medieval times were burned at the stake in Europe for practicing witchcraft. Societies around the world display significant differences in gender related attitudes and discriminatory behavior toward women. In some parts of the world societies are still practicing female genital mutilations signifying the transition of the girl from child to adult. It seems on the surface hard to justify such mutilation practices that are supposedly related to the roles that women play as wives and mothers, but one is left to wonder if these rituals are not aimed more at the control of women by men (Lightfoot-Klein, 1989).

Any consideration of gender related behavior must provide a narrative that describes the complexity of the interrelated variables that produce reliable differences between the sexes. Typically, this begins with an acknowledgement of the biological differences between the sexes as a platform for different socialization patterns that appear to be universal and similar in all cultures. Although the sexual platform (physiological differences between females and males) are the same in all cultures, the socialization practices that define gender are culturally determined. For example, it is generally acknowledged that females are socialized to be more dependent, nurturing, obedient and socially responsible. On the other hand, boys are reinforced positively for assertive behavior in an effort to promote independence and self-reliance. Gender related socialization practices do not occur in a vacuum, but are in turn related to ecological factors like the challenges presented by a subsistence economy, and the social and political context of society.

The biological platform of sex differences includes the obvious different sexual organs, but also physical differences as males are larger and the presence of sex hormone differences that encouraged a division of labor. The evolution of the division of labor in turn produced other gender related cultural practices. Culture to a large extent demanded differential child rearing for males and females, assigned the sexes to different roles in child rearing and determined gender roles in the home or as providers. These consistent living patterns over generations also produced gender based sex role ideologies and gender stereotypes thought to be typical of all members of the gender category. Gender related factors are all complex and interacting and because of globalization are also dynamic and in some parts of the world are rapidly changing.

As noted the common conception of gender derives from the anatomical differences between the sexes. The different psychological experiences of being male or female are rooted in this biological platform. While these biological distinctions are important and significant culture plays an important role in interpretation of appropriate roles and behavior (Eagly & Wood, 1999). In some societies like Saudi Arabia women cannot drive cars or travel without male family members. In other cultures such gender based limitations would seem absurd and if society would attempt to introduce such ideas they would be met with strong resistance by the generations of women who have achieved a better status in the struggles of the last century. The stereotypes and values we attribute to sex are largely culturally determined. The ubiquitous preference for male children that has produced infanticide in countries including India and China is also an expression of cultural values. In turn these cultural attributions determine to a large extent psychological traits including relative compliance, aggression or assertive behavior.

The term opposite sex is a misnomer. Both genders are in fact similar in so many ways also caused by our common human evolution. Even our physiology is similar with sexual structures carrying complementary rather than opposite functions. It is culture that has chosen to emphasize the differences and create ideologies that support gender stereotypes. These powerful, but largely unconscious processes have to a large extent determined gender self-concepts and behavior. Even how we think is a cultural artifact of gender based roles that is ubiquitous in the world. The women's movement in the United States challenged the way women were described in the literature and in education that seemed degrading and hostile. Psychology as a discipline underwent a profound change over the past decades through the participation of women who provided a balance in psychological research since previously most investigations were based on male dominated conceptions and participants. The opportunities that opened up for women produced important contributions by female psychologists to create a more gender balanced view of what it means to be human. Rather than assuming that women are small men research now reports routinely on sex and gender differences as vital components in any psychological research.

10.1. CULTURE AND GENDER

Apart from mono-sexual religious groups or cults, men and women live and work together in all cultures of the world. While physiological sexual differences between males and females are universal gender distinctions are the psychological outcomes of culturally determined sexual roles. The common activities of the two genders based on their biological differences and related to reproduction and physiology are called sex roles. The division of labor between the sexes must have emerged out of the need for survival that produced reproductive success when women attended to the needs of children and men worked as providers of shelter and food. Recently men in the United States and Europe are taking on more child caring roles, however, only women can breast feed their babies. On the other hand, gender roles are rapidly evolving and perhaps some will think changing to the point of absurdity. For example, ABC News in December 13th, 2011 reported that 5 million men in the U.S. are now "stay at home Dads" who care for children and other house duties while the wives go to work (Elliot & Francis, 2011).

The rapid social changes in some parts of the world have profoundly affected gender roles in contemporary societies. Men and women have both had to adapt to gender changes as society has created new role expectations and therefore also stereotypes. Many of these changes have justly benefitted females whose lives have historically been blighted by discrimination. In their eagerness to convince society of the reality and permanence of these changes new stereotypes of the "aggressive female" have emerged that have become mildly laughable. In some television programs in the U.S. we often see physically small women pushing around much larger males showing a masculine toughness that is not emerging clearly from the obvious physical and corresponding psychological differences. In any event when speaking of gender differences we are not speaking of biological sex, but rather of the culturally based behaviors and feelings associated with the social perceptions of gender. While we have much in common as human beings males and females also differ. However, these differences are largely culturally based constructions that have evolved over the course of the history.

10.1.1. Sex Roles, Gender Stereotypes, and Culture

The biological differences between the sexes are assuredly the basis for the evolution of the division of labor and corresponding sex roles. Sex roles are ubiquitous in all societies and define what men and women are permitted to do and how they are expected to behave. In more rigid traditional societies sex roles also define what the genders should or must do as part of daily interactions. Women are obviously the only sex to give birth and breast feed babies. Nevertheless with the advent of formula baby food, men are taking on feeding responsibilities in some societies. Having noted that exception the genders, however, because of their biological differences may be uniquely placed to perform complementary gender related tasks in child care. However, both sexes can perform many of the same home and work related tasks. Nevertheless women take on most of the obligations related to child care in many societies, and in the modern world where women also work they hold up more than "half "of the heavens to expand on the quotation of Mao.

Sex role theory might also explain ubiquitous gender differences in the expression of emotions. A comparative study of 37 cultures found the same general pattern of gender based emotional expression in both Western and non-Western societies. Typically men express more anger when aroused whereas women tended to express more fear or sadness compared to males (Fischer, Rodriquez Mosquera, van Vianen, & Manstead, 2004). These differences are consistent with the higher level of aggression expected of men and boys, whereas girls and women are expected to be more compassionate. The research also shows that females express emotions more openly than men except in the case of anger. Women seek to foster care-taking and affiliation and are therefore more likely to express feelings of love, sympathy, guilt, and happiness, whereas men do so to a lesser extent for fear of being vulnerable (Brody & Hall, 1993). Men in traditional cultures seek to restore honor when they have been shamed by aggressive or retaliatory behavior, whereas women will react to shame by submissive behavior (Abu-Lughod, 1986).

Culture encourages over time gender based stereotypes that have produced unique social roles. A common finding in Western cultures is the perception of females as weaker, more emotional and more compliant. Males, on the other hand, are typically viewed as assertive, more dominant and independent. The masculine traits produce in men a greater willingness to confront danger and seek adventure that is the basis of the human migration story. The most important study done on gender stereotypes was carried out by Williams and Best (1990a). They submitted a 300-item adjective check list to respondents in twenty-seven countries from the major regions of Europe, Africa, Asia and North and South America. The respondents were asked in a forced choice situation whether the adjective was more descriptive of males or females.

The results showed large differences in all countries surveyed in the perception of what men and women were like. However, even more importantly research supported a broad consensus between countries and cultures on gender stereotypes. Adjectives like active, adventurous and aggressive were associated with males; and affected, affectionate and anxious with females. The consensus in gender stereotypes support these concepts as universal psychological constructs present in all societies. However, some cultural differences were reported. A factor analysis found three meaningful factors labeled favorability, activity and strength. The first factor represented an overall evaluation of the two sexes. While there were no overall differences in male or female favorability in combining scores from all countries, the male stereotype was found to be more favorable in Japan and South Africa, whereas the female stereotype was more favorable in Italy and Peru. From the study it is not clear what cultural or historical factors were responsible for these favorability results. However, on the factor of action orientation males were considered significantly more active. On the third factor of strength there was again a very large mean difference with males scoring higher on the stereotype of being stronger. We can conclude that males and females are within countries attributed very different gender stereotypes and the results showed a remarkable similarity in how these gender distinctions are maintained across cultures.

The extent of the pan-cultural agreement on gender stereotypes is so large that some researchers have suggested that they are the equivalent of psychological universals accepted practically in all societies and by both sexes (Berry, Poortinga, Segall, & Dasen, 1992). Such universal stereotypes lead logically to a consideration of an evolutionary basis that originated in anatomical differences and the subsequent historical division of labor. Reproductive success demanded a division of labor, and those of our ancestors who adapted had an evolutionary advantage in survival. Over the eons of time since early human societies these stereotypes have become a part of cultural history internalized for many people.

The sharpness of the gender differentiation depends on cultural values (Hofstede, 1980). Countries that are conservative with hierarchical social structures and with lower socioeconomic development and where education is valued less for women also display more significant demarcation between the sexes. On the other hand, countries that value egalitarianism as an ideology, social harmony and less traditional sex role orientation, have lower levels of strict gender stereotypical distinctions. When rescoring the Adjective Check List according the BIG Five Model of Personality males were seen has having higher scores on all traits except agreeableness where females scored higher (Williams, Satterwhite, & Best, 1999).

These stereotypes are incorporated at a very early time and Williams and Best found gender stereotypes also present in childhood. Gender stereotypes existed in children in all cultures and were virtually similar to those found for the adult sample. The results suggest that children are inculcated at a very early time in gender stereotypes, in nursery schools, in the home and in other social institutions. Children's stories and the media also play a role in producing such broad agreement on female and male gender characteristics. The fact that there is cross-cultural agreement in children's gender stereotypes support the universal nature of these conceptions and the long evolutionary roots of gender based differences. Nevertheless the role of culture in reinforcing sex roles is supported by the research of Albert and Porter (1986) who reported that gender stereotyping become more prevalent with the increased age of children. Others researchers have emphasized the important role of the media in socializing children in gender stereotypes and with the mass media in the past often showing manifestly demeaning stereotypical images of women (Fejes, 1992). However, since the media in the U.S. and Western Europe were confronted by the women's movement the most blatant and offensive stereotypes have been removed. Of course, culture is persistent and some stereotypes still exist in the modern world.

As noted these stereotypic conceptualizations reflect a genetically based physical reality. However, culture plays a role by socializing gender-related practices that evolved over historical time into a sex role ideology that keep gender expectations rigid even when they do not make sense in the modern world. In the new globalized world of computers women can perform the same work related tasks as men. Women should not be delimited in modern times by a culturally based sex role ideology that grew out of the need for survival in the early history of humanity and the division of labor that placed females in the home. Today women are approaching equity and equality in many areas in the United States and Western Europe and, for example, in the universities women are in some cases out-competing their male counter parts. This independence in females has led to new relationships between the genders and today only half of adults in the United States get married. What the outcome is for family life is difficult to estimate in the intermediate or long-term future.

10.1.2. Gender and Families

While men and women can perform many of the same home-related tasks, women typically carry a disproportionate burden. Most of the work within the home is the province of women who do the majority of childcare, cooking and cleaning. Georgas, Berry, van de Vijver, Kagitcibasi and Poortinga, (2006) examined family functioning in thirty countries around the world. In all countries examined women carried the greater share of the home-related work. Of course, there are still many societies where the father remains the chief bread winner and works long hours outside the home. The injustice to women comes in countries where both parents work outside the home, but the mother still has to do the bulk of home maintenance. Georgas et al focused on three types of functioning performed in the home. Expressive behaviors refer to the parental support required to create a pleasant and emotionally supportive home atmosphere. Financial functioning is the role of the bread winner achieving the necessary income to look after the needs of the family. The third type of home functioning is childcare that includes the role of cooking nutritious food, encouraging children's progress in school, and also looking after their emotional needs.

Motherhood is seen as the major component of womanhood and female identity all over the world. Since many women feel their identity is expressed in motherhood women who are not mothers often feel that as a deficit or failure in their lives. Many mothers have impossible high self-standards and for these women the child's needs are always primary and come before their needs. In Western cultures the ideal of motherhood requires the mother to practice self-sacrifice and endless love (Wilson, 2007). Traditionally the emphasis of society placed the mother at home with her children, today in many countries mothers also work outside the home leading to a divided and burdensome effort.

The survey showed that fathers were primarily looked to for financial support of the family, followed next by supplying emotional support and last in providing actual childcare. Mothers, on the other hand, were primarily concerned with childcare at least in the more poor countries. However, in more affluent societies mothers were like fathers concerned with all three roles, however, motherhood and domestic responsibilities are still considered the primary function for women in the family. A recent study across 20 countries showed that men from 1965 to 2003 spent an average of only 14 minutes each day on child care. So unless women want totally dysfunctional families a great deal of domestic work and child care is left in their hands (Hook, 2006). Women are also the primary caregivers for the elderly and ill or disabled members of their families (Forseen, Carlstedt, & Mortberg, 2005). That expectation is present despite personal exhaustion and typically women fill these roles and responsibilities and put first the needs of family members who require help.

These demanding family responsibilities have negatively influenced the role women can play in economic activities producing lower wages and less opportunity for promotion and advancement. While such discrimination is not necessarily overt mothers often make less money than women who are childless. Family responsibilities may not allow mothers to work fulltime or overtime which give these women less work experience. Often women end up in lower paying jobs because these fit better with their children's needs for childcare, but also limiting their occupational choices (Sigle-Rushton & Waldfogel, 2007). One study on the status of women showed that in only five countries (out of the 127 countries surveyed) women held 50 % of managerial or legislative positions (United Nations Statistic Division, 2011).

Therefore although men and women have the same educational possibilities in much of the world today (except some places in Africa, Arabia and Asia) women are often segregated by occupation and tend to be hired for less powerful jobs and lower remuneration (Cunningham & Macan, 2007). Since the responsibilities associated with motherhood are not placed on men they tend to be preferred as employees and are perceived not only as more available but also more competent compared to women who have family responsibilities (Cuddy, Fiske, & Glick, 2004).

10.1.3. Traditional Versus Egalitarian Sex Role Ideologies

Sex role ideology refers to basic values and beliefs about how men and women should function in life. In many societies there is a basic conflict between those that believe in the traditional roles of men and women related to home and work compared to more egalitarian perspectives. Traditional gender ideology views the role of women to be that of a home maker and men as breadwinners. The traditional viewpoint also support men as the head of families and chief decision makers about all matters related to family functioning whereas the mother is considered the heart of the family being supportive and looking after the family's emotional needs. Traditional values are expressed in gender roles that sharply demarcate the differences in the function of males and females, whereas egalitarian roles deemphasize the distinction between males and females.

Young adolescents were asked in one study to describe the characteristics of the ideal man or woman, and the results revealed that the most important psychological traits were not sex typed as both genders preferred someone who was honest and kind (De Silva, Stiles, & Gibbons, 1992). At the same time there were gender based differences based on reproductive needs and evolutionary fitness where being attractive and good looking (and therefore fertile) was mentioned more often for women and good employment seen as more important for men. Another study (Gibbons, Stiles, & Shkodriani, 1991) supported the idea that girls hold less traditional views than boys probably because they have more opportunities in egalitarian relationships. At the same time adolescents from poorer and collectivistic countries were more traditional compared to adolescents from richer and more individualistic countries. Globalization and modern technology are changing traditional gender ideology even in conservative societies as television, the Internet, and modern education show alternative possibilities for girls. Religious beliefs and practices are powerful traditional forces in many cultures resisting the forces of modernity and social development.

Williams and Best (1990b) examined sex role ideology in another study among respondents in fourteen countries including representation from Europe, Asia, North America, Africa, and South America. The results showed significant differences between countries in sex role ideology partly related to socio-economic status. Countries that scored higher on the socio-economic index, that had a higher proportion of protestant Christians along with a low proportion of Muslims, had a larger proportion of women working outside the home, and who were more individualistic tended to favor egalitarian sex role ideology. The countries that scored lower on these indexes were more likely to endorse and favor traditional sex roles.

Since women are often the victims of sex role stereotyping it is not surprising that research shows males and females having differences in sex role preferences. In the Williams and Best study the sex role ideology opinions of males and females were examined in fourteen countries, examining their beliefs about how men and women should be and act in their relationships. In all countries (except two) males showed a stronger preference for the traditional sex roles and women scored higher in the direction of egalitarian relations. Since males benefit by controlling women in the traditional household there are strong male incentives in favor of the status quo. On the other hand women have become more conscious of the injustice of traditional sex role functioning and therefore favor a more egalitarian ideology.

That this remains a continuous hot topic for researchers can be seen in the number of published reports. The Larsen and Long (1988) sex role ideology scale measuring egalitarian versus traditional attitudes toward sex roles have appeared in 83 published studies and hundreds of student theses and dissertations. That result alone would indicate that the issue is far from settled in Western countries, and is a source of continuous conflict as men and women seek to find balance in a rapidly changing world that challenges traditional thinking.

10.2. GENDER STEREOTYPES AND DISCRIMINATION AGAINST WOMEN

Gender stereotypes have had many negative consequences for women. They have caused women in modern times to become obsessed with their bodies seeking to reach impossible standards of thinness with health consequences that include anorexia and bulimia. Further, violent behavior by men toward women that is found broadly throughout Western and other cultures in the world is promoted by gender stereotypes where women are seen as having no independent and valuable existence.

10.2.1. Dissatisfaction with Body Image

Many gender based stereotypes are maintained through discrimination against women and girls. The differential gender roles played by women and girls lead to an obsession with their physical bodies and attractiveness. The high standards of physical beauty created by the media produce significant and demoralizing pressures on women who compare themselves upward to beauty standards that for most are impossible to reach. Dissatisfaction with body image has motivated women to undergo millions of cosmetic surgeries in the United States every year and supports a large cosmetic industry that function to help women meet ideal cultural standards of beauty (Gangestad & Scheyd, 2005). In recent decades the preoccupation with thinness has produced anorexia and bulimia in many young women and teenagers with untold damage to women's health, reproductive ability and self-esteem. Ironically in less affluent societies thinness is associated with poverty and larger women are preferred. However, the results of globalization and ubiquitous Western media are that more women even in the developing world are buying into thinness as an ideal body type (Grogan, 2008).

Why are women dissatisfied to such a high degree with their physical appearance? There are, of course, many sources of influence that determine self-images including family, educational institutions and the media. However, the media in particular must be criticized for portraying women who are very thin as ideal. Models from the catwalks to popular magazines strive to portray extreme thinness to the point of looking anorexic and ill. The average woman in society compares herself with such socially prestigious models and is disappointed with her body image (Leahey, Crowther,

& Mickelson, 2007). As a result of globalization these extreme models of thinness are now accepted as ideal in many parts of the world.

The role of dolls for girls growing up in Western societies also reinforces unrealistic feminine physical proportions in girls. The Barbie doll is an example of how the mania for thinness is introduced to the minds of girls in early childhood.

There are many negative health consequences for women who are dissatisfied with their body image. We have already noted the relationship of body image to eating disorders such as anorexia and bulimia. At the psychological level dissatisfaction with body image lead to mental health related problems including depression and low self-esteem. These negative factors also have consequences for physical health including anemia, low blood pressure, kidney failure and heart related problems (National Institute of Mental Health, 2011). The media could help correct the negative modeling effects by ensuring that a broader range of women's body types appear in both the printed and visual media. Social learning by observing healthy models of all body types would reduce the pressure women feel to comply with the absurd challenges of super thin models.

10.2.2. Equal Work Equal Pay?

Whether women work outside the home depends somewhat on egalitarian and traditional cultural values. In Muslim countries like Saudi Arabia only few women are economically active outside the home. However, in most of the world more than half of the women contribute to family income by participating in the economy and holding jobs. However, as we have seen this generally means that these women carry both the burden of the larger share of home work and child care, and also in many cases a fulltime job. Women are still paid only a fraction of the income that men make. Here again cultural values of egalitarianism or traditions play a role. In the Scandinavian countries women experience the smallest gender gap in pay by earning 77 % of men's wages in Norway and 81 % in Sweden. By comparison women earn only 67 % of men's income in the U.S. However, that compares favorably with women's income in countries where gender roles are circumscribed by traditional religion. For example, in Yemen women earn only 30 % of men's wages (Hausmann, Tyson, & Zahidi, 2008).

It should be remembered that even in the advanced countries women are not paid equally for equal work. Some of the reasons may be women's role in home making that allows less time for outside work and therefore less experience or opportunity customarily rewarded by larger salaries. On the other hand, these gender discrepancies in pay are also likely the consequence of discrimination and a devaluation of women's work. Although women have progressed significantly in recent years, particularly in Northern Europe and North America, there are still very significant gender gaps in the rest of the world. This is especially disheartening to report since where men are absent due to death or delinquency the woman may be the sole breadwinner for the family. Discrimination in pay results in children growing up under conditions of hardship and poverty.

10.3. VIOLENCE AGAINST WOMEN: A DIRTY PAGE OF HISTORY AND CONTEMPORARY SOCIETY

Violence toward women takes many forms from husbands or lovers who are physically abusive to rape in intimate relationships or in war. As a result of norms that support male dominance women are often sexually exploited in prostitution, pornography and other forms of servitude. The struggle of feminists in the past century was to create laws and policies that support equality and equity in access to resources and power. Personal empowerment is not a free gift but the outcome of men and women working and struggling together across many decades.

10.3.1. Intimate Violence: The Ubiquitous Nature of Rape

Recent surveys show that 1 out every four females in the U.S. have been assaulted over the past year (Hayes, 2011). A study sponsored by the World Health Organization found that between 15 % to 71 % percent of the women interviewed in ten countries said they had been sexually or physically abused over their lifetimes, and between 4% and 54 % claimed the abuse had occurred over the past year (Garcia-Moreno, Jansen, Ellsberg, Heise, & Watts, 2006). The rape figures are consistent with the cross-cultural abuse statistics with one out of every five women claiming she had been raped over the course of her life time (Parrot & Cummings, 2006). It is hard to believe that this level of violence by men could occur unless there are culturally supportive values that view such behavior as permissible when directed against women. Women who are especially at risk for rape are those who live in cultures that emphasize male dominance and strict separation of the sexes and where a high degree of interpersonal violence is present (Sanday, 1981). Some researchers argue that it is the higher status attributed to men in a given culture that provide the support for intimate violence.

Rape statistics show that rapes are not isolated instances of abuse, but may occur over long periods of time by men who are acquainted with the victims and the victims are often blamed. Recent news tells about a young woman by name of Gulnaz who was raped by a cousin in Afghanistan, and then given a 12 year prison sentence. She was placed in prison with the child produced by the assault for the crime of adultery. It was put to her that the only way she could leave prison was if she would marry her rapist (Zakaria, 2011). Such cultural norms are incomprehensible to people who grow up in the West, although the rape figures in the West also show terrible and frequent violence toward women.

Women are also often the victims of rape in war, and these assaults have been used historically in male to male violence to demoralize an enemy population. During the genocide in Rwanda about 25 % of the women were raped, and in the wars in the former Yugoslavia tens of thousands of women were raped. When women are raped during war it is often used as a means of humiliating enemy soldiers and populations. During the Second World War probably millions of women were raped and exploited. When the enemy population is demonized in the discourse of hostility it provides the excuse and rationality for men to later take out the enmity on women who do not have the means to defend themselves.

One of the most disheartening forms of violence occurs in cultures where women are considered property to be controlled by men. In some societies the culture permits and encourages the murder of women who have somehow transgressed against cultural norms of propriety and thus brought "dishonor" to fathers or husbands. In some conservative male dominated societies such cultural transgressions may occur simply by the woman going out with men not approved by the male hierarchy and in more extreme cases having intimate relations with or marrying a man not approved by the family. According to the United Nations Population Fund (2000) about 5000 women are murdered each year to uphold this idea of "family honor" in countries like Pakistan, Egypt, Turkey and Israel. The tragedy of these killings are compounded by the intimate nature of the murders that are often carried out by a close relative like a brother, and the fact that the violence are often treated lightly by society with little sanction. Honor killings are the most extreme examples of intimate violence against women that grow out of cultural norms of male dominance and women as submissive.

10.3.2. Sexual Exploitation

The sexual exploitation of women is another nefarious form of gender based violence. For example, it is estimated that some 800000 women and girls are trafficked internationally every year for reasons of exploitation (U.S. Department of State, 2008). What facilitate these statistics are deeply grounded cultural norms that consider women as property of men to be used for their pleasure. The fact that women in many societies have few resources makes the practice of exploitation more probable and the women who are recruited often participate in prostitution in the false hope of making a better life for themselves and their families or under duress and false pretenses. Pornography is now ubiquitous in the world and in many cases women are subjected to humiliation and direct violence by participating in graphic sexuality. That pornography plays a strong role in shaping unhealthy images of women cannot be overlooked. The role of pornography can also desensitize men to violence toward women as participants falsely claim that women enjoy dominance and humiliation.

10.3.3. Gender Justice and the Empowerment of Women

Sexual violence has severe health consequences for women who experience emotional stress and with violence looming the constant need to be on guard. Violence directly impacts the victims causing self-blame and low self-esteem (Matud, 2005). Where violence against females is common it is difficult for women to move about in a normal way and it limits their possibilities for career development and other types of social progress. The threat of violence itself is a powerful way to control women who therefore must seek the protection of family and therefore restriction within the home. Gender based violence is not an individual or intimate matter as it grows out of cultural norms that control of women and any change in these deeply held beliefs require enforceable public policy to end abuses. An important step forward was the passing of legislation in the U.S. called Title IX that prohibited gender based discrimination in any programs funded by the federal government. This legislation opened up many possibilities for girls and women in academics and in athletics that now operate with criteria of equal funding for both genders. The achievements of women in the modern Olympic Games demonstrate the success of greater opportunities for girls and women.

Although women are traditionally stereotyped as less powerful and dominant some aspects of this attitudinal domain are changing. The American visual media have tried to create new stereotypes that take on features of the semi-comical as producers try to affect women's cultural images by having them perform as physically powerful police officers that subject men to female dominance in television roles. However, beyond such blatant and unrealistic invasion of male physical dominance women can achieve other sources of power that are more meaningful. When women achieve and use public power the negative impact that characterize women power seekers as unfeminine (often shared by both men and women) can be defused when women emphasize the communal aspects of their leadership that is motivated by altruistic concerns (Parks-Stamm, Heilman, & Hearns, 2008).

Although only a handful of governments are headed by women some regions are more culturally prepared to accept their leadership. Again in Scandinavia women in business and government have achieved near equity in leadership positions. On the other hand, in countries like Saudi Arabia or Yemen women have practically no say in public affairs or decision making. These developing cultures are dominated by male hierarchies and gender inequality is strongly supported by social norms. Cultural differences show that women must have political and cultural support to participate and function in public leadership positions. In some developing countries in Africa some objections have been overcome when women call themselves "mothers of their country" appealing to the broad cross-gender acceptance of their fundamental role in life (Anuradha, 2008).

A great deal of attention has been devoted recently to the concept of empowerment of women. In the most fundamental sense empowerment refer to women's abilities to live their own lives by choosing self-relevant goals and by making all important decisions related to their lives. Women have sought empowerment through feminist activism over the past century. Initially the struggle in the United States and Europe led women to seek the vote and fight for universal suffrage. Equity in academics and athletics in the U.S. were largely won with the passage of Title IX. As a consequence a large number of women have entered and achieved in fields that were formerly considered men's domain including science and law. In recent years the struggle to achieve pay equity for equal or equivalent work continues. That goal has not achieved complete success in the U.S. or elsewhere since the gender disparity is caused by cultural values that support inequality for women. In the final analysis gender equity depend in a large measure on law and policies that ban discrimination with penalties for violations.

10.3.4. Gender Ability Differences and the Role of Culture

Research on gender ability differences as influenced by culture has produced many interesting studies in several fields. An early area of research reflected the common gender stereotypes in the U.S. that males are superior on spatial abilities and numerical tasks. Associated with that stereotype is the further contention that females excel in verbal abilities as evidenced by verbal fluency, memory, and perceptual speed. Such gender differences if they exist could easily have developed from the pressures to survive that produced an evolutionary division of labor. Another area of research examining gender differences is the domain of social conformity. That too is based on gender stereotypes that females are more anxious and therefore more likely to conform. Finally, the third area of research reports the results of gender differences in aggression. Here the common stereotype finds some support that women are more empathetic and compassionate and therefore less willing to aggress.

10.3.5. Culture and Gender Differences in Spatial Abilities

Gender stereotypes have supported the idea that men are better at spatial and mathematical performance and women perform better at tasks associated with verbal comprehension. Early research in the U.S. supported these gender intellectual specialties as males performed better at experimental problems that required a comprehension of spatial relationships

(Maccoby & Jacklin, 1974). It was suggested that these ability differences are biologically hardwired and developed as a result of evolutionary demands that required men and women to play different roles in hunting and childcare? Division of labor required men to develop an understanding of spatial relationships in the pursuit of prey and in the building of structures to house families? How gender ability differences arose probably cannot be answered, however, the role of cultural socialization cannot be overlooked as it plays a significant role in all gender related behavior. Cultural relativity is supported by the research of Berry (1966) who found that females performed as well as males in Inuit (Eskimo) culture where spatial abilities were required of both genders to enhance survival.

Therefore gender ability differences in mastering spatial problems may be a result of cultural organization. For example, some societies are loosely organized and promote independence in socialization whereas other cultures have "tight" organization that rewards interdependence. Berry (1976b) examined spatial abilities in 17 cultures and the results showed that whether males or females did better was culturally dependent. In summary, males do better on spatial tasks in relatively tight and sedentary cultures that are based on agriculture, whereas females are equal or better in relatively loose and nomadic cultures where they play a role in hunting or gathering that require spatial skills. However, in a meta-analysis (Born, Bleichrodt, & Van Der Flier, 1987) the researchers noted that while there are no reliable sex differences in overall intelligence, there are persistent distinctions on some subtests including verbal ability where females perform better and mathematical tests where males perform better. Nevertheless, the fact that these gender abilities vary by culture suggest that these aptitudes are not hardwired, but related to the function that the genders perform in a given culture.

10.3.6. Current Research on Gender Differences in Mathematical Abilities

An analysis of six major national surveys on female and male performance on intelligence tests showed that seven times as many boys scored in the top 5 % on science tests and twice as many in the top 5 % on math tests compared to girls (Hedges & Nowell, 1995). At the same time boys were inferior to girls on reading comprehension, perceptual speed and memory. Since there were very little fluctuations in these gender differences it was believed that they were caused by biological hardwiring produced by how male and female brains evolved over evolutionary time periods. However, in recent decades social changes in the U.S. had largely achieved equality in education and in resources allocated to males and females, yet these social changes had not produced changes in gender math scores. Nevertheless, these research results that support male superiority in mathematics abilities do not address the subtle yet powerful expectations of stereotypes and sex discrimination. In the end girls and boys might both behave in ways that are consistent with cultural expectations, and in the case of mathematics and science these expectations may have little or no relationship to biology.

Recent research reported by Begley (2012) adds some further light on the nature versus nurture origin of gender differences in mathematical abilities. That research explains gender differences and concludes that women on the average are as competent as men, but there is a greater variability or spread in the boys and men's mathematical scores. In other words, while a large proportion of men do not score well on mathematics tests an equal number score very high explaining the gender difference that favor men in top science and engineering positions. The variability hypothesis would argue that there is something about how the male brain develops that explains the gender difference.

A recent study on mathematics performance in 52 cultures test the math scores in boys and girls and finds little support for the variability hypothesis. For example, in elite mathematical competitions the scores of males and females vary widely by culture. In some countries the variability scores are roughly equal, and in other societies the male scores vary widely, and in some cultures female scores vary more widely. Since scores of the genders vary by culture with no consistent pattern across cultures it seems clear the lower achievements of females in mathematics in some societies cannot be explained by a biological mechanism. To draw that conclusion would require us to argue that biology varies by culture.

It seems more reasonable to conclude that cultural factors are responsible for any gender gap. Some clues are delivered by the correlation of the Global Gender Gap (measuring gender inequality) index with the ratio of boys versus girls scoring in the top 5 % on an international mathematics competition. The results showed that the larger the gender inequality the larger the gap favoring boys. Also results showed that the ratio of boys versus girls scoring high on college entrance quantitative exams is narrowing in the U.S. and fell from 13 to 1 in the 1970s to 3 to 1 in the 1990s. What is at work is the greater equality of female participation in American education (with enforceable mandates to ensure equality) that narrow the gender ability difference and is the contribution of the feminist movement. While not completely definitive these results strongly suggest that any difference in mathematical abilities are directly a function of the equality of resources for females compared to males in any given society.

10.3.7. Gender and Conformity

The stereotype of greater female conformity was supported in a number of studies in the U.S. (Eagly & Carli, 1981). However, the overall difference was small and seemed related to situations that produced direct group pressure to which females yielded more. Since direct pressure is precisely what is meant by conformity the gender difference is not trivial (Becker, 1986; Eagly, 1987). In traditional society men were viewed as head of households making the major decisions affecting the family. In that society females played little or no role in decision making, but in the division of labor looked after children and the welfare of the household. However, these divisions of labor are in a flux given the growing emphasis on gender equality. Part of the conformity difference appears to be related to whether the domain is related to gender expertise. Results show that males conform more on issues considered female expertise like child rearing and women yield more on traditional male issues like science or politics (Sistrunk & McDavid, 1971).

Berry (1976b, 1979) using the same samples discussed above employed to investigate spatial differences also found culturally dependent differences in gender on conformity. Again females were found more conformist in cultures considered tight and less conformist in so-called looser samples. Cultures that were described as tighter (as defined above) fostered greater conformity in females since they also required greater conformity to traditional gender roles by both males and females. Therefore it is clear that the greater conformity of females is not a hardwired psychological characteristic, but rather a product of cultural organization. The role of child rearing and gender socialization are important in understanding gender differences as well as understanding why women occupy lower ranks in the social stratification of society. However, since all cultures are in flux gender-related conformity is an area of research that may well yield new outcomes and a reduction of gender differences.

10.3.8 Gender and Aggression

A common stereotype suggests that males are more aggressive, an understanding that is broadly shared in the world and by history. In fact this stereotype is present in all cultures investigated and probably for good reason (Brislin, 1993). Research supports gender differences as the vast amount of aggressive acts are committed by adolescent males (Segall, Ember, & Ember, 1997; Tedeschi & Bond, 2001). In the case of aggression there are no culturally specific differences based on types of culture (tight or loose), and both industrialized and non-industrialized countries demonstrate the same pattern with males more aggressive (Bacon, Child, & Barry, 1983; Goldstein, 1983).

Various reasons are provided for the differences in levels of aggression between genders. Male adolescents experience a rise in testosterone levels in the teen years that may explain the dominance behavior typically linked to male adolescence, and also anti-social behavior among male delinquents (Dabbs & Morris, 1990; Mazur, 1985). However, despite this apparent hardwired aggressive tendency in males culture also plays an important role. Some cultures encourage aggression and provide social learning models in the media for the expression of aggressive tendencies. For example, in the U.S. a considerable amount of time is devoted to violent crimes on television and aggressive social modeling can desensitize viewers to more readily accept violence in human interaction.

Gender differences in aggression emerge partially from different socialization experiences. For example, Barry, Josephson, Lauer, and Marshall, 1977, found a gender difference in the teaching of aggression in hundreds of cultures, but noted that this produced higher aggression in males in only a few very violent cultures. These results would suggest the importance of cultural factors in addition to hormones and the direct teaching of aggressive behavior. Some have suggested that aggression is a form of gender marking or assertion as the child begins the journey toward adulthood. In fact both genders can and do commit aggressive acts toward their partners in developed or Westernized nations (Archer, 2006). However, the magnitude of the gender distinction in aggression depends on the nature of the culture. Where cultures are more individualistic and empower women there is less female victimization. The division of labor between the genders created different expectations of what is considered appropriate gender related behavior, and solving problems through violence became an accepted pattern for males in many parts of the world. We can conclude by saying that since considerable differences exist between cultures in aggression such behavior is best understood as the outcome of the interaction of biological and cultural factors combined with individual psychological predispositions.

10.4. SEXUAL BEHAVIOR AND CULTURE

Culture determines to a large extent attitudes toward women who participate in premarital sex. Traditional and conservative cultures still view chastity as having a great value for women. Valuing virtue has caused real conflict between conservative Muslim societies and the more globalized societies in Europe and the United States. The gate keepers of Muslim culture seek to prevent what they see as corruption of modern society and Western cultural influences and subversion brought into the society through movies, television and books. Typically attitudes toward sexuality in traditional societies are connected to concepts of family honor where the woman commits serious transgressions by having intimate relations with a man not approved by the family, or by marrying a non-believer. As noted in some cases this perverted sense of honor has produced honor murders, the ultimate form of male control over female family members.

Male control in conservative cultures is also exerted in other sexually related behaviors especially in the case of female genital mutilations. When a female child reaches puberty in many societies in Africa, Middle East, Asia and other cultures she faces the practice of genital mutilation by the removal of external female organs. Often these "surgeries" are performed under very painful and unsanitary conditions. The objective is obvious, by removing genital organs society expects that women will not enjoy or participate in sex except for child bearing reasons. Sexual mutilations along with enforcement of the veil are means used to keep female sexuality under male control. Yet because the practice is connected to family honor not performing the mutilation can affect the girl's chance for making a good marriage in some societies. Even among Egyptian student nurses some 60% favored genital mutilation of their own daughters (Dandash, Refaat, & Eyada, 2001; Whitehorn, Ayonrinde, & Maingay, 2002). For people raised in more egalitarian cultures that practice seem not only to belong to a dark past, but barbaric in the suppression of natural sexual behavior of females.

It is difficult even under egalitarian conditions to obtain true estimates of gender differences in sexual behavior. Even though society has changed significantly in the Western world sexual permissiveness for females is not as acceptable as for males. That fact causes females to be less than truthful on surveys that seek information about premarital or extra marital sexual behavior. For example men typically report engaging in sexual behavior at an earlier time, more frequently and more promiscuously compared to females. Research shows that the distinctions between the genders may in reality not be as large as those reported in the literature, because females do not always give truthful answers when the behavior in question is considered embarrassing or shameful. In one study about sexual behavior the experimenters told the participants that a lie detector test would detect untruthfulness in their responses to a survey on sexuality. The responses of the women in that study closely paralleled that of the men in the lie detector condition, whereas under other conditions not including lie detection there were large male-female differences in reported sexuality (Alexander & Fisher, 2003).

10.4.1. Mate Selection

While we often focus on differences between cultures there are also many similarities in how men and women respond and behave cross-culturally. Attractiveness in women is associated with kindness, understanding, emotional health and intelligence in a variety of cultures. Women tend to get more distressed (a common reaction that occurs across all cultures) when their male partners kiss another woman. The reason for the distress is the same for women everywhere because kissing represents a higher level of emotional commitment in women than in men. Flirtation also appears to be ubiquitous in all cultures as a preliminary step in courtship and mate selection (Aune & Aune, 1994). A study of 33 countries showed similarities in the preference for characteristics of potential mates. For example, men universally prefer physical attractiveness (that signal fertility) and females value financial stability and achievements (that protect potential offspring), (Buss, 1994). However, there are also cross-cultural differences to note. For example, in some cultures same and cross-sex touching are entirely normal, whereas in other cultures they are taboo. Two Arab men walking hand in hand in their countries simply manifest a common tie or friendship, but in the U.S. such behavior would likely be considered homosexual.

Differences in sexual behavior are thought to originate in adaptive pressures from our common evolution that produced different strategies for men and women who are unconsciously motivated by the need to pass genes to the next generation. Men seek out a variety of young fertile partners whose youth and health support the impression of successful reproduction. On the other hand, women are interested in the survival of their offspring and therefore are more interested in stable and monogamous relationships with men who can support their children.

This pattern of fidelity distinctions appears universally. Furthermore, there are also gender differences in jealousy that are ubiquitous in all societies. Sexual infidelity is the result of a lover having multiple partners, whereas emotional infidelity occurs when the partner establishes strong emotional bonds with another person. Both types of infidelity bring about jealousy in both men and women, but the gender difference is pronounced in the greater jealousy produced by the woman's sexual infidelity in men, and the more powerful jealousy found in women produced by the emotional infidelity of men (Fernandez, Sierra, Zubeuidat, & Vera-Villarroel, 2006). For both genders the logical explanation is evolutionary. Sexual infidelity in women threatens a man's ability for reproductive success and carries the further possibility of using resources to support another man's offspring. Emotional infidelity in men threatens a woman's ability to secure the well-being of her children, and the possibility that the man would not to be present in the relationship to lend economic support.

Norms for sexual behavior varies across the world especially with regard to premarital sexual behavior and homosexuality (Widmer, Treas, & Newcomb, 1998). As we observed chastity is valued very highly in many non-western cultures, whereas in western European countries and North America premarital sexual behavior produces little or no negative evaluations. However, cultural variables reflecting stress and economic insecurity affect sexual behavior within marriages. Research shows that economic frustrations and having few resources are related to insecurity in romantic relationships and counter intuitively to higher birth rates. Typically, when countries become more secure economically fertility rates drop (Schmitt, Alcalay, Allensworth, Allik, Ault, & Austers, 2004).

The affluence of a society also affects the relative acceptability of homosexuality. A large-scale study carried out in 24 countries examined attitudes toward homosexuality, extramarital sex, premarital and teen sexual behavior. Results indicated that premarital sex is broadly accepted today, however, the samples showed less acceptance of extramarital and teen sex (Widmer, Treas, & Newcomb, 1998). Homosexuality was found to be more acceptable in industrialized and affluent cultures (Inglehart, 1997). Some sexual norms are universal, however, including the common taboo on incest (although the definition of incest may vary widely), and the rejection of adultery that is universally condemned. Finally, we can state with some certainty that sexual norms are changing in response to the pressures of globalization, and as the world becomes more homogeneous so will sexual behavior and norms.

10.4.2. Attractiveness and Culture

Cultural differences are documented in the consideration of attractiveness in a potential mate in some research (e.g. Wheeler & Kim, 1997). The saying "beauty is in the eye of the beholder" holds some validity as culture affects aspects of physical attractiveness. However, there is a growing body of literature that also supports the *universality* of certain physical attractiveness traits. When groups of cross-cultural judges were asked to evaluate the faces of European Americans, Asian, and Hispanic stimuli persons the results yielded very high correlations between the judges in attractiveness ratings. Judgments of attractiveness were based on similar facial characteristics in all cultures evaluating the eyes, nose, and smiles. A meta-analysis that examined the results of 1800 articles supported cross-cultural similarity in physical attractiveness ratings both within and across cultures suggesting universal standards for beauty and attractiveness (Langlois, Kalakanis, Rubenstein, Larson, Hallam, & Smoot, 2000). The similarity ratings may, however, be partially a response to the ubiquitous modeling of women in Western movies now viewed around the world, and the increased convergence of norms for a variety of behaviors and perceptions including the evaluation of physical attractiveness.

The universal norms of attractiveness appear to be related to evolutionary gender differences in the preferences for mates. For example, Buss (1994) in his comparative study of attractiveness in 37 cultures found support for interesting differences in gender preferences. In nearly all cultures as we noted above females appreciated more the financial factors in choosing mates than males did, and consistently evaluated more highly the industriousness and ambition in prospective male partners. On the other hand, for males the physical attractiveness of potential mates was more important than it was for females. Since the comparative gender agreement across cultures was so high Buss suggested a universal basis for mate preference related to different gender based evolutionary pressures experienced by males and females. On the other hand, social constructivists researchers emphasizing the affects of culture found that despite the noted gender differences there are also gender similarities in mate preference. For example, both genders appreciate honesty, kindness and a sense of humor in prospective mates (Goodwin, 1990). The emphasis on culture also explain the aforementioned cultural differences in perception of attractiveness, however, the evolutionary pressures are probably more dominant in the final analysis leading men to appreciate female beauty that signal fertility, and women to look for the financial security that ensures the future of their children in mates.

10.4.3. The Future of Love and Marriage

In all cultures men and women have developed love relationships that historically included marriage. However, changes in gender relations have occurred in the industrialized countries over the past several decades. It is now common for partners to live together without marriage in Europe and the United States as the formal endorsement of society seem less important and sexual satisfaction is offered without commitment. These attitudes have created problematic situations in creating many single parent families led by women who often struggle economically in the absence of a father figure. Finding and marrying a mate has been historically important since it helped create a support system that assisted both partners in the struggle of life.

However, attitudes toward love also vary by culture. Although love is universal it is valued differentially by culture and is complex in its many forms (Hatfield & Rapson, 1996). Actual commitment to love relationships also varies by country. In one study French and American participants rated love commitment more highly compared to Japanese respondents. A key factor in love commitment is whether society is organized individually and around the nuclear family, or is composed of extended kinship networks. Love is valued highly in individualistic cultures where there are few extended family ties, perhaps because in these societies the individual really has to rely on the love relationship and mate for economic security (Simmons, vom Kolke, & Shimizu, 1986). However, since women have found economic independence in many societies the mutual support function of marriage may have less relevance to today's relationships.

Nevertheless most people in the world still get married suggesting that there is a universal desire to make such a commitment. Almost 90 % of people in the world are in relationships described as married with supportive mutual interdependence (Schmitt, Alcalay, Allensworth, Allik, Ault, & Austers, 2004). However, there are cultural variations in the role of love in marriage. In some cultures there is pressure to have a woman marry before a certain age to be followed by having babies and building a family. In the U.S. that pressure has decreased in recent decades and women and men have delayed marriage or have opted to have children without marriage. The lack of commitment typified in these modern relationships is in stark contrast with the strict norms of Muslim countries or those societies that rely on tradition as a source of normative compliance. In some societies romantic attachment is the only reason to progress toward marriage, whereas in other cultures marriage is seen as a strategic alliance between families where love is secondary to fulfilling expectations of the extended family. Individualistic culture considers love an essential precondition for marriage. If love disappears that condition alone is seen as sufficient to justify divorce (Levine, Sato, Hashimoto, & Verma, 1995). In the traditional cultures arranged marriages are the norm a practice that goes back thousands of years. In the case of arranged marriage it is really two extended families that are getting married rather than a singular union of two people. Nevertheless because of modernization and globalization potential mates now refuse to marry in many traditional societies unless the commitment is based on self-selection and romantic love (Arnett, 2001).

The possibility of partners from different cultures falling in love and marrying has increased markedly due to globalization. These intercultural relationships face many potential conflicts since partners may have very different views about marriage and varying attitudes towards the role of love. All marriages require adjustments since even partners from the same cultural backgrounds may have different expectations. However, when in addition to these more normal within culture conflicts cultural distinctions and values must also be taken into account the marriage face additional problems. For example the expression of love is not universally the same in all cultures. Also the specific characteristics of the marriage commitment may vary by society, and how to raise children may also bring conflict (Corttrell, 1990). Especially difficult is the balance that must be achieved if one partner is raised with traditional expectations, and the other comes from an egalitarian culture. The traditional partner could view marriage as an extension of kinship groups, whereas the egalitarian partner may be content with his/her nuclear family. In a successful intercultural marriage the partners must be willing to compromise and use creative approaches that support the integration of the family unit. For example, if different holidays are celebrated a creative solution is to respect all holidays from the two cultures. Ultimately whether "love conquers all" depends on the willingness to find compromises, and the commitment of the relationship. Negotiations about potential conflicts should, of course, be discussed long before marriage with the optimistic hope that there is a solution for all problems.

SUMMARY

The past decades have produced many changes in gender relationships derived partly from the feminist activism and laws mandating gender equality in the West. These changes have had positive consequences for girls and women as they have provided more equal opportunities and better treatment in the workplace. Still sex roles remain ubiquitous in the world defining the distinct and common activities of the two genders. Gender roles reflect biological differences that emerged from the separate reproductive functions of males and females as based on our biological inheritance. A division of labor between the genders developed due to evolutionary pressures to survive. Today that division is less rigid since many women are now in the workforce, and labor does not just require physical strength. In fact men can also perform many of the household duties in two-earner families.

Sex roles are supported by gender stereotypes and largely explain differences between the sexes in emotional expression. Men typically express anger more easily, whereas women seeking harmony express more sadness or fear. The large gender differences in emotional expression are accepted by both genders as valid reflections of underlying variations in male and female psychology everywhere in the world. However, the sharpness of the distinction in sex roles depends on cultural values. Cultures that are conservative, hierarchical, with lower socio-economic development, and where women's education is not valued produce stronger demarcation between genders.

Women continue to bear the disproportionately larger burden in maintaining family life. In countries where both genders work women still do nearly all the housework. This unfairness is the result of the influence of sex roles and social expectations. Also contributing to the unfairness is the value that women place on motherhood as the main source of identity and therefore their role in childcare and domestic responsibilities. Men are still looked to for financial support. The double burden of home and work makes it difficult for women to play significant roles in the economic sector and therefore provide them with less opportunity for advancement and equity in remuneration.

Sex role identity refers to the commonly accepted values or beliefs about how men and women should behave. A basic conflict in many parts of the world is between the traditional perspective and egalitarianism that favor equal treatment of the genders. Girls are more in favor of egalitarian sex roles because of the negative consequences of traditional sex role ideology. Globalization is having an impact on how sex roles are viewed particularly in traditional societies. However, research on the Larsen-Long sex ideology scale shows that the conflict between tradition and egalitarianism is far from over even in advanced Western cultures.

Gender stereotyping is related to discrimination toward women. The stereotypes provided in the media often serve as unhealthy models causing women to be obsessed with their bodies and the state of their attractiveness. Women compare themselves upward toward a high Western standard of thinness and beauty that causes permanent dissatisfaction. In particular preoccupation with thinness is responsible for the large increase in eating disorders we now find among young women including anorexia and bulimia. There is a strong need for society to correct this problem emerging from the modeling in the visual and printed media by including women of all types as role models in magazines, movies and on television.

Another serious form of discrimination is the ubiquitous pay inequities as women are only paid a fraction of men's remuneration for equal or equivalent work. However, here again the values of egalitarianism affect outcomes as women from Northern Europe, particularly Scandinavia (and the U.S.), are approaching equity in pay and opportunities.

Violence against women is a dirty page of both history and contemporary society. The victimization of females occurs with regrettable frequency in a variety of cultures. Rape as an extreme form of violence is ubiquitous in the world and is also used as a sadistic weapon in wartime. Women are especially at risk for intimate violence in societies that emphasizes male dominance and enforces the strict separation of the sexes. The most extreme form of violence against women are honor killings in traditional societies, a form of male control of women who are seen as transgressing propriety in relations with men not approved by the family. Sexual exploitation is ubiquitous in the world using hundreds of thousands of girls and women each year. The trafficking of women to serve the sexual pleasure of men is supported by cultural norms that define women as property. Another chapter in the sexual exploitation of women is pornography that humiliates women and is also ubiquitous in nearly all societies.

The struggles of feminists against all forms of gender injustice and for positive programs to empower women have produced better conditions for girls and women in recent years. Changes in law and in the workplace that mandate equal opportunities and treatment have improved the conditions for women the past several decades in the Western world. Political power is seen as unfeminine by many people and is achieved by relatively few women. Women can, however, achieve success as leaders by emphasizing the communal and altruistic motivations of their leadership.

Research has over the years focused on various intellectual abilities of the two genders. The general stereotype about males supports the idea of their superiority in spatial and mathematical tasks. At the same time women are seen as superior in verbal fluency and comprehension. Some researchers believe these differences to be hardwired outcomes of how male and female brains develop. However, current research suggests that cultural expectations play a large role and relative superiority in any area of accomplishment depend on the type of culture. Evidence for different hardwiring abilities can also be observed in the ratio of superior male test outcomes in mathematics to female results. However, these differences have significantly decreased in the past few years as girls have had more educational opportunities.

Research has also examined gender differences across salient social behaviors. Social stereotypes supported by many early studies found that females were more conformist. However, with gender relations in a flux in many cultures and with a less rigid division of labor in society overall conformity differences appear to be small today. Males are more likely to conform in female areas of expertise, for example, in how to handle childrearing, and females more likely to yield in what is considered male areas of superiority. The main factor in cultural conformity appears again to be the traditional cultural organization. Males are consistently more aggressive in all societies investigated. Reasons for the higher aggression levels point to hormonal differences particularly in testosterone that are hardwired biologically. The ever present violence in the media also has a relationship to violence, particularly by the social learning provided in the male modeling of violence. In some societies aggressive behavior is also viewed as a form of gender marking and assertion. Women are less likely to be victims of aggression in individualistic cultures that empower girls and women. However, in many cultures violence is an accepted behavior used by males in solving problems.

An understanding of attitudes toward sexual behavior is basic to conflict within society, but also between cultures. Real differences exist within and between societies about the value of chastity, particularly for girls and women. These different sexual values are at the root of conflict between Muslim and more globalized cultures. In traditional societies sexual behavior is connected to the concepts of family honor which in the extreme case justify so-called honor murders by male relatives. Genital mutilation is another means of male control over female sexuality. To a Western observer that practice appears to be a particular brutal suppression of natural female sexuality and enforcement of male control. Actual gender differences in sexual behavior are difficult to determine as females do not always give truthful answer for reasons of embarrassment or shame.

Males and females are confronted in all societies with the issue of mate selection. Research supports the differential criteria used by the genders in finding an acceptably mate and these gender differences appear to be cross-culturally consistent. Selective adaptation and motivation to achieve successful reproduction put different pressures on males and females. Women are interested in the welfare of offspring and therefore look for stable and financially promising partners, whereas males are more likely to seek a variety of fertile and attractive women for reproductive success. Of course, the male reproductive strategy through promiscuity is circumvented by society that emphasizes monogamy or creates other forms of social pressures. The varying reproductive strategies between the genders also produce different types of jealousies in men and women. Women tend to be more threatened by emotional infidelity and men more by sexual infidelity.

Physical attraction is the stimuli by which the two genders make initial approaches to one another. Although there is some evidence for marginal differences in the criteria of attractiveness in women, the stronger result is the universality of physical attractiveness. The model for female beauty is converging along with the increasingly globalized world. The many changes in gender relationships in recent decades make the future of love and marriage uncertain. In all cultures men and women live together and the large majority has a desire for marriage. Recent decades have, however, produced many changes in gender relationships in the Western world. Many partners now live together without marriage and sexual satisfaction is not dependent on social sanction. This libertine atmosphere that co-evolved with the ability of women to control reproduction has a dark side. A very large proportion of children are now born to mothers without the assurance of fathers taking responsibility. Still the majority of people eventually marry although what constitute marriage is culturally dependent. Intercultural marriages produce special challenges because of different cultural expectations of marriage itself and childrearing. For such relationships to be successful would require patience and careful planning in order to cope with the different expectations.

CHAPTER 11

CULTURAL VALUES IN ORGANIZATIONAL AND SOCIAL BEHAVIOR

The discussion of the previous chapters has demonstrated the importance of cultural values in understanding the complexity of human behavior. Culture is the sea that surrounds human behavior and it influences all aspects of our lives although humans may not be aware of the cultural currents or the direction they carry us. Our common biological heritage provides the basis for understanding the human journey with the cultural distinctions that are discussed in cross-cultural comparative research. However, there are also unique aspects to culture, that are based on the specific cultural journey of a people that must be understood from the perspective of an in-depth study of unique cultural values. Culture is a complex phenomenon of many interrelated domains. Berry, Poortinga, Segall, and Dasen (1992) suggested that culture has meanings in six areas: in the particular cultural concepts used to describe social behaviors, to anchor a people's heritage, to outline accepted rules and norms, to helps us understand certain types of learning associated with culture, in describing the elements of society and the constituent organizations, and to make sense of common ancestry.

Cross-Cultural Psychology: Why Culture Matters, pages 315–353.

Culture grew out of peoples need to survive because it gave competitive advantages to those groups who were organized in relation to ecological and other environmental challenges thus enhancing their reproductive success (Buss, 2001).

People within society find themselves in constant economic, political, moral, legal, criminal and other social relationships. Interactions in these relationships are governed by specific rules that make up a complex dynamic entity called the cultural pattern of society. A specific cultural model characterizes a society during its historical development. On the one hand cultural values make distinctions between different societies and countries. However, through constant interaction between peoples cultural integration is also a feature of modern life. The modern world of globalization is formed by information processing and trade dominated by cultural integration and the imposition of a new global cultural model.

11.1. GLOBALIZATION AND CULTURAL VALUES.

Any definition of culture must include the concept of shared meanings (Shweder & LeVine, 1984). Culture emerged because it helped society adapt to the environment or was formed in past historical struggles for survival. A major feature of culture is its trans-historical foundation where values are passed from one generation to the next (Triandis, 1994).

Cultural values are the product of the interaction between fundamental biological requirements and the organizational solutions developed by people to address these needs. An important aspect of culture is the generational consistency and persistence in behaviors and values. Commonly held beliefs, attitudes, and values are passed from one generation to the next. Some cultural characteristics are visible and explicit like ceremonial dress or dance or the differences in comfort zones required for intimate or stranger communication. Other cultural variables are implicit like the organizing principles that support consistent behavior in society. Some cultures can be described as more similar and others are more distinct typically the result of geographic distance.

The same individual may be the product of several cultures or cultural experiences. Cross-cultural psychology must always be prepared to revise current research as the world is rapidly changing through globalization. Psychological values of tolerance and openness to experience are more broadly shared today as a result of globalization since they are functional to progress in many societies (Giddens, 2000). Among the increasing number of immigrants in the world many people develop bi-cultural identities. Others also have more than one cultural influence as they identify with the local culture, but also with the values fostered by globalization.

Ideological forces that want revolution against economic inequality and others that wish a return to a religious fundamentalism oppose globalization. The former have observed an increasing disparity between the rich and poor within or between societies. Religious fundamentalism, on the other hand, laments the passing of crucial conservative values of the old society. The followers of fundamentalism consider globalization as a source of the crisis that undermines the power of traditional authority and cultural symbols. The objective of fundamentalist movements is to return to the traditional society, and isolate it from what is considered vital threats.

11.2. SOCIAL AND ORGANIZATIONAL BEHAVIOR

Psychology is by no means immune to the affect of the dominant cultural ideology, but as a discipline reflects major social values in the focus of research and the conclusions drawn. Cultural values had a primary influence on the concepts developed and utilized in cross-cultural psychology and can distort perception and the analysis drawn from research (Larsen, 1993). Political culture is manifested through the peculiarities of specific organizations and transformed into aspects of organizational culture. Organizational culture also has its own characteristics manifested in distinct ways in various social groups, countries and regions (Krumov, 2005).

In the early development of industrial or organizational psychology the research focus examined issues in the developed economies of the world. For example, how human behavior was affected by the industrial setting, and human factors related to the management of enterprises, and how to increase corporation profits through efficiency and motivation, all became variables of interest. In the recent decades the field of organizational behavior has witnessed an incredible rate of change from the breakthrough of technology and intercultural contacts brought about by globalization. In past history the work force in Europe and the U.S. were more homogeneous allowing the initiation of organizational studies without considering the effect of cultural variables. Today, however, people find employment through multiple international or multinational organizations that operate in various parts on the world with increasingly diverse workforces. Trade pacts enacted over the past decades has brought the challenges of cross-cultural relations to the forefront for many organizations. The technological changes of the Internet, virtual conferencing, and email have created a global village of employment. Although members of organizations all work toward common goals, they do so from widely varying cultural perspectives that in turn affect the management of the workplace.

Like the broader society industrial organizations also develop culture and shared meanings. Particular organizational practices and policies often create an emotional or organizational climate that affects how people feel about their workplace and their level of motivation (Reichers & Schneider, 1990). This broad climate definition preceded the concept of organizational culture that today refers to shared information and meaning systems within an organization. Organizational culture is typically accepted by the workforce, at least by those who want to continue employment and prosper, and like the broader social culture is passed from one generation of employees to the next. Organizational culture is more than visible production procedures or the particular attitudes of the workforce. Organizations seek to inculcate meanings and values in the workplace, and often use company founders as heroic work models for employees (Deal & Kennedy, 1982).

Researchers have described several aspects of organizational culture (Van Muijen, Koopman, & De Witte, 1996). The proximate manifestations of culture like the technology employed, the rules and procedures of the workplace and the physical campus are all cultural components. However, organizational culture is most saliently reflected in the values and implicit norms present in the organization that govern employees' behavior and their relationships with other workers and society. The workplace values that govern organizations have in turn become a primary concern in cross-cultural organizational psychology.

The interest in organizational culture grew out of initial observations that some organizations performed better than others. For example, an interest was created in the management practices of Japanese organizations when they demonstrated very rapid improvements from the 1950s onward. These dramatic changes in the Japanese economy were attributed to Japanese culture, and organizations in the U.S. took note (Ouchi, 1981). Research sought to distinguish various aspects of organizational culture where excellent companies varied from those less achieving. One study examined differences between organizations in Denmark and the Netherlands (Hofstede, Neuijen, Ohayv, & Sanders, 1990). The major differences in organizational viability demonstrated the importance of demographic variables including age, education and nationality. These demographic factors were found to be more important to performance that organizational membership.

11.3. CULTURAL DIFFERENCES IN WORK-RELATED VALUES

We will now continue the discussion of the value research of Hofstede that we started in chapter 1 as related to work and organizational life. Values are broadly based constructs that support specific attitudes. As such they are stable and often change little over the lifetime of a person. Terminal values are basic goals that a person values above other objectives in life and reflect therefore both personal desires and social values. People can choose alternative ways of reaching the terminal goal referred to as instrumental values. Instrumental values are determined by issues of ethics and morality (Rokeach, 1973).

The dominant focus research in organizational psychology examines cultural differences in work values. The most influential series of studies were carried out by Hofstede (1980, 1983, 2001). In the original 1980 study

Hofstede's research involved responses of workers from 40 countries. In the most recent work Hofstede obtained responses from hundreds of thousands of employees working for a multinational corporation in 72 countries. From this data Hofstede identified four major types of work-related values that are predictive of specific differences in work-based attitudes, beliefs and behaviors. These values inform us of the basic social norms that framed work-related behaviors and affected the structure of organizations and their culture.

Hofstede and his colleagues created from the analysis eleven clusters of countries that demonstrated four ways of coping (or cultural values). Among these clusters were the Nordic, Anglo, Germanic, Near Eastern, Developing Asia, Developing Latin, Developed Latin, and Japan as an advanced economy. The four cultural approaches to solving the problems of organizational life included power distance, individualism-collectivism, uncertainty avoidance, and masculinity-femininity. For example the Anglo and Nordic samples demonstrated low values on power distance, but scored high on individualism. On the other hand, the nations less developed in Asia and Eastern Europe were high on power distance (favored hierarchical solutions), and tended to value individualism to a lesser degree. These work-related values will be discussed in detail below.

11.4. THE CULTURAL VALUES OF AUTONOMY, EGALITARIANISM, AND HARMONY

In addition to Hofstede's values other researchers have developed value concepts thought important to cross-cultural organizational behavior (Schwartz, Melech, Lehmann, Burgess, Harris, & Owens, 2001). Schwartz et al thought that cultural values reflected ways of coping with the basic cultural, climatic, and social problems of a society. What makes cultural groups different from one another organizationally is the extent to which people are either individualistic producing independent people or collectivistic creating interdependence in social relationships. Schwartz et al demonstrated from research in 40 countries the presence of varying values of conservatism versus autonomy, of hierarchy versus egalitarianism, and of mastery versus harmony. Their research could also be divided into clusters of nations. For example, East Asians were found to be high on hierarchy and conservatism, while scoring low on autonomy and egalitarianism consistent with the findings of Hofstede.

The same values can have very different connotations in various societies. For example, Mosquera, Manstead, and Fischer (2002) found that people in the Netherlands and Spain had very different conceptions of honor. In the Netherlands honor was associated with autonomy and self-related achievement, whereas in Spain honor was reflected by behavior in the family and by social interdependence.

11.5. WESTERN AND NON-WESTERN VALUES: OPPOSING PERSPECTIVES

Over many years scientists and philosophers have counter posed Western with non-western values. According to this generally accepted conception Western civilization is based on the puritan ethic of hard work, on personal achievement, on developing a consumption society, and on the importance of utilizing time efficiently. On the other hand non-western values typically reflect a reverence for tradition and the importance of authority and harmony. Differences between Western and non-western values often center on the position of the individual in society. In Western countries individualism is highly valued, whereas in non-western countries the collective is primary. The greater importance of competition in more urbanized and industrialized areas compared to more rural regions is consistent with these cross-cultural differences in values. The ego-based behavior supported by Western values is perhaps no longer adaptive since it defines social progress as continuous growth and competition in an increasingly complex world of population expansion and deteriorating environments (Clark, 1995). Increased conflict is expected in the future as ideological and fundamentalist movements oppose the values of Western capitalism (Huntington, 1993).

11.6. CULTURAL DIFFERENCES ON THE FIVE VALUES

Hofstede (1980) first identified four dimensions or cultural values as noted above and labeled power distance, uncertainty avoidance, individualism-collectivism and masculinity-femininity. The four dimensions were subsequently correlated with seven demographic, economic and geographic variables. The results showed that the power distance dimension correlated with conformity, and with higher levels of authoritarianism. Hofstede also found that employees at the lower levels of the organizational structure with little power had a negative evaluation of close supervision preferring instead a process of consultation in decision making. Geographical latitude turned out to be the strongest predictor of the power distance variable across forty countries. This variable describes geographical closeness and similarity of cultures. Others researchers saw the climatic factor rooted in geography initiating a causal chain where adaptation produced cross-cultural preferences for certain social structures and values (Van de Vliert, Kluwer, & Lynn, 2000).

11.6.1. Inequality and Power Distance

Responding to the need of modern capitalism organizations developed vertical hierarchical structures determining both power and/or status. These days we refer to the chain of command, and social hierarchy and status often serves as justification for inequality and inequity in the workplace.

Hofstede (1980, 2001) defines power distance as the extent to which society accepts power to be distributed unequally. Authoritarian and hierarchical societies with unequal power distribution are described as cultures with high power distance. In these societies inequality is perceived as legitimate and people are likely to obey managers or others in power. In egalitarian cultures people view each other as moral equals and workers and employees will object to unjust decisions by their managers (Sagiv & Schwartz, 2000; Schwartz, 1999).

Inequality along important dimensions like pay and benefits has accelerated over the past decade far beyond what is justified by role and position. Hierarchal relationships in organizations appear to be nearly universal. However, the power distance between players in organizational life varies widely in different cultures. Again power distance refers to the relative degree that cultures encourage power and status differences within a company. Organizations high on power distance between employees are also characterized by rigidity of rules and rituals that serve to reinforce the status differences. Cultures that are low on power distance emphasize rules that create more fluid relationships.

Hofstede argued that cultural differences in power distance had consequences for individual work and effort. Managers that operate in a high power distance organizational culture are empowered to act arbitrarily or in autocratic and paternalistic ways. Typically high power distance organizations encourage greater centralizations of the organization's structure producing taller structural pyramids, larger proportions of supervisory personnel, and larger pay differentials. These power distance characteristics in work organizations are seen as a natural outgrowth of the broader social culture. In particular preference for high power distance was related to the value of obedience, to conformity, and to having authoritarian attitudes. In high power distance organizations there is also a greater acceptance of managers acting in autocratic ways, employing paternalistic management styles, and employee fear of disagreeing with the boss.

In high power distance cultures people generally accept the inequality between those high or low in power and status. The extreme example may be the caste system of India that still today affects the status and position of millions of people. On the other hand, countries in Western Europe are low on power distance, and workers have the ability to participate in decision making or reach contractual agreements with employers.

11.6.2. The Major Focus of the Cultural Values of Individualism and Collectivism

Another important value found in the Hofstede studies described differences between Anglo and Nordic cultures when compared with less developed Near Eastern and Asian nations. The Anglo and Nordic group tended to be low on power distance, more egalitarian, while high on individualism and individualistic values. The second group from Near Eastern and Asian societies was influenced by the opposite traits as high on power distance but low on individualism and was described as collectivistic societies. This bipolar individualistic-collectivistic variable had great influence on cross-cultural research to the point where some called it an obsession (Gelfand, Erez, & Aycan, 2007). Individualistic societies, for example, emphasized the importance of personal time away from work and emotional independence from the workplace. Furthermore, individual decisions were viewed in individualistic cultures as superior to collective decisions, and organizations did not own individualistic respondents who claimed the right to enjoy life and the workplace.

The concept of individualism-collectivism is by far the most researched concept in cross-cultural psychology. It has also influenced research in many other fields including political psychology, in the management of the work place, and within psychological specialties like developmental, social and personality theory (Kagitcibasi, 1997). Individualism-collectivism is also considered an important variable in the work place since people living in collectivistic cultures are more likely to conform and comply with the demands of an organization. Harmony is valued in collectivistic cultures, and individual workers often go along with management demands in order to preserve interpersonal relations. In the Hofstede studies United States, Australia, Great Britain and Canada scored highest on individualism whereas Peru, Pakistan, and Venezuela had the highest scores on collectivism. Employees in individualistic cultures, Hofstede noted, make a sharp distinction between time at work and private time, and regard their time away from work as very important. Workers that are individualistic also savor challenges at work, freedom and initiative.

A greater concern for the self rather than the group is the primary attribute of an individualistic orientation. Others have sought to add a vertical dimension to the construct (Triandis & Gelfand, 1998). We learn from parents or the parent substitute we experience growing up with a vertical cultural transmission of cultural values. Cultural values can also be transmitted horizontally through interaction with peers. Horizontal transmission is the typical learning mode that last from early childhood until death. However, we also learn cultural values from other adults in our lives and from social institutions like the country's educational system.

Triandis (1995) described the governing attributes of individualism and collectivism. The self is construed differently in the two cultural value types. A personal self is envisioned in individualistic- independent self-conceptions, but as part of the collective in the collectivistic-interdependent self-construal. Consistent with self-construal the independent culture emphasize the primacy of personal goals whereas the priority of group goals is salient in interdependent societies. Typically independent cultures are based on capitalist economies that favor exchange in social interaction rather than the promotion of communal relationships. Personal attitudes govern behavior in independent societies whereas social norms have the primary affect in collective societies. Other attributes in independent cultures noted by Triandis included self-reliance, competition, hedonism, and emotional distance. On the other hand, in collective cultures key values include factors like interdependence, the importance of family, and sociability.

As mentioned above individualism-collectivism has been extensively studied and related to a range of variables. Hofstede (1980) studied the relationship between individualism and power distance and found a negative correlation ($r = -.67$). In other words, the greater the power distance, which measures hierarchical relations, the lower the level of individualism. Other analyses demonstrated that individualism and power distance loaded on the same factor, suggesting that they are located at opposite ends of the underlying continuum. These findings indicate that individualism and submission to authority and hierarchy are incompatible. Because Hofstede (1980) considered collectivism the opposite of individualism, his findings also implied that power distance and hierarchy are linked to collectivism.

Building on Hofstede's (1980) finding that individualism and social hierarchy are incompatible at the societal level, further research in seven societies (Bulgaria, Japan, New Zealand, Germany, Poland, Canada and the U.S.) examined the relationship between individualism-collectivism and orientations toward authority at the individual level (Kemmelmeier, Burnstein, Krumov, Genkova, Kanagawa, Hirshberg, Erb, Wieczorkowska, & Noels, 2003). The results demonstrated that self-ratings on the dimensions of individualism, collectivism and authoritarianism do not parallel the pattern found by Hofstede at the aggregate societal (national) level (Hofstede, 1980) or the pattern found for naïve perceptions of similarities and differences between the three concepts (Gelfand, Triandis, & Chan, 1996). This highlights the idea that individual beliefs about the relationship between value constructs like collectivism and authoritarianism may not correspond to the actual empirical relationships between these values, and that findings obtained at one level of analysis (e.g. societal or national) cannot automatically be generalized to other levels (e.g. individual).

Hwang (2012) suggest that from the perspective of organizational face theory variation along the cultural values explain some of the variance and provide perspective, but the simplification of cultural dimensions cannot explain more complicated cultural phenomenon. Others (e.g. Seidl-de-Moura, 2012) demonstrate the accumulating evidence for the diversity of cognition and behavior as culturally dependent, and even cultural values like individualism-collectivism reliably affect salient mental processes including the self-concept and motivation.

11.6.3 Seeking Security By Uncertainty Avoidance

The only thing certain about life is ubiquitous uncertainty. In trying to avoid uncertainty people seek security in many ways through religion or ideology. Sooner or later, however, dogmatic models fail in confrontation with reality. The future for industrial organizations is particularly uncertain these days as technology is constantly changing the workplace. New products come on the market only to become obsolete months later. Recent times have seen major restructuring of companies in response to the economic crisis. Millions of employees have lost their jobs, and few workers or managers have a crystal ball with which to predict the future. Needless to say uncertainty creates anxiety and confusion for both employers and employees.

Cultures have developed different ways of dealing with uncertainty. Rituals allow people to know what is expected and reduce the feelings of uncertainty in many societies. A handshake, a bow, a kiss on the cheek in the appropriate culture promotes the comfort of confirming expectation in interaction with others. Some companies have responded to uncertainty avoidance by adopting strict codes of conduct making behavior in the workplace predictable. Likewise written or unwritten rules may also exist for appropriate conduct with members of other organizations within a given company.

The uncertainty avoidance discovered in the Hofstede studies describes the degree to which various societies or cultures try to deal with anxiety about uncertainty. Cultures vary in the degree to which they feel uncomfortable with uncertainty. People who live in avoidant cultures seek some magical potion that might restore certainty, and in that quest support political and religious institutions that encourage conformity. Obedience to rituals and norms are an assurance that the world remains predictable and certain. From a negative perspective the comfort that conformity engenders may in turn discourage innovation and creativity thereby fail to improving culture and organizations. Countries that were low on uncertainty avoidance in the Hofstede study included Sweden, Denmark, and Singapore. On the other hand, Greece, Portugal, Belgium, and Japan had the highest scores.

High achievement in any society depends to some degree on innovation. One survey of 9 countries (McGrath, MacMillan, Yang, & Tsai, 1992) showed that entrepreneurship was related both to high individualism and low uncertainty avoidance. Japanese society has been in a state of flux during the rapid changes of the last decades. Despite high uncertainty avoidance Japan has adapted well to the challenges of modern competition. However, there may be other unique cultural factors at play in Japan since uncertainty avoidance is related to conformity in other studies (Frager, 1970). Gudykunst and his colleagues (Gudykunst, Gao, Nishida, Nadamitsu, & Sakai, 1992; Gudykunst, Gao, Schmidt, Nishida, Bond, Leung, Wang, & Barraclough, 1992) showed that in United States in contrast to Japan there are very few standard rules determining interaction in social situations. Nevertheless in many cultures uncertainty motivation has a significant effect on social interaction (Hofstede, 1980). Generally people living in high uncertainty avoidant cultures are more intolerant of ambiguity. Emotional expression is governed more rigidly in these cultures. Likewise there is less tolerance for ideas and for people that are different and stronger needs for group consensus and rigid rules of behavior.

11.6.4. Maintaining Gender Differences: The Masculinity-Femininity Value Dimension

In most cultures men are expected to display more dominance and assertiveness. Men are also traditionally the main bread winners, whereas women are expected to be more nurturing and caring and play out their principal roles within the family. The biological differences that brought about these ubiquitous roles are obvious. The important question is whether these gender differences also produce varying social roles. In short how do biological differences play out in the workplace? Sex roles are rapidly changing in most countries of the world. They are also a source of conflict as both genders adjust to changing expectations. Gender equity is far from established, and gender equality and equity are a struggle in progress being defined not only by changing norms but also by law. The origins of gender differences are of ubiquitous interest. If gender differences are the result of placement in the social structure then socialization as expressed through gender-related cultural norms, roles and stereotypes become all important. One important conclusion of a socialization origin of gender differences is that such an outcome can be considered changeable. On the other hand if gender differences are based on evolutionary forces then they are innate and not changeable. Since entrepreneurship is a modern phenomenon evolution cannot have made direct contributions, and therefore gender differences must be assumed to be the outcome of the forces of social structure and socialization (Pines, Lerner, & Schwartz, 2012).

In Hofstede's work a fourth dimension emerged from the data analysis that he labeled masculinity-femininity. It reflected the degree to which cultures seek to emphasize and maintain traditional differences between the sexes in social life and in the work place. Countries that scored high in maintaining masculinity and cultivating gender differences in work-related values included Japan, Austria, Venezuela, and Italy. Other countries displayed fewer gender differences and therefore more openness for both sexes being employed in a variety of jobs crossing the traditional gender lines.

The countries where sex differences play less of a role included Denmark, the Netherlands, Norway, and Sweden.

Cultures scoring high by favoring masculinity on the masculinity-femininity dimension valued leadership, independence and opportunities for self-realization through recognition and advancement. The obvious consequence for women in high scoring masculine societies are less participation in the better paying jobs or in jobs requiring high qualification. Other variables associated with high masculinity scores include stronger achievement motivation, higher job stress, less benevolence, and greater differences in valuation of the two genders employed in the same work. Countries that scored high included Japan, Germany, Britain, Mexico, and the Philippines.

11.6.5. Having the Long View or Seeking Immediate Gratification

More recently Hofstede has included a fifth cultural dimension based on his research in Asia (Hofstede & Bond, 1984). The dimension explores the differences between cultures in the willingness to delay gratification of various social needs. In Western Europe and the United States people desire immediate gratification demonstrated in the rapid turnover and the obsolescence of products. Countries found to have a short term perspective included also Poland, West Africa and Spain. The societies that had the longest view or patience were the Asian societies of China, Hong Kong, and Taiwan. These *long-term societies* were characterized as having stable but unequal social relationships where the family was the model for social organizations. Cultures with a long-term outlook focus on building relationships and position in the market rather than primarily pursuing profits, and seek to integrate organizational and family lives (Hofstede, 2001).

11.6.6. Globalization and Changing Values

The original work completed by Hofstede came from the survey responses of employees in a multinational but a single company. That allows some skepticism as to what degree the results were representative of the national cultures. More worrisome are problems in replication. For example, Ellis (1988) failed to replicate the pattern of values when comparing U.S. and German respondents as predicted by Hofstede. Not surprisingly given the dramatic socio-economic changes over the past decades values have also substantially shifted (Fernandez, Carlson, Stepina, & Nicholson, 1997). Partial replications have been reported by Hoppe (1990), and Merritt (2000).

11.7. SOCIAL INTERACTION RESEARCH REFLECTS A CULTURE THAT IS DYNAMIC AND EVER CHANGING

What we understand in cross-cultural psychology is based on the behavior and activities of people (Vygotsky, 1930/1997). We look for similarities and differences by comparing the salient activities of cultural groups. In turn activities are circumscribed and determined by the ecological and socio-economic environment of people who live in a given cultural society. That environment is also in a flux producing many social changes accompanying globalization. Significant changes in recent times include the widespread immigration that continues throughout the world. Furthermore, we live in a world that now is experiencing a significant economic crisis called by some the Great Recession. The decreasing quality of life and increasing poverty affects many aspects of culture including crime rates and life span. Vulnerable people are also more likely to listen to fundamentalism as a solution to a life that has few opportunities and produce much dissatisfaction.

Poverty and discrimination affect especially the life of cultural minorities. It is recognized by many that inequality and oppression are the main differences between minorities and majorities within cultures (Fowers & Richardson, 1996; Larsen, 1977, 1978a, 1978b, 1981). A major source of inferiority feelings is the unfair and unequal distribution of resources within a culture (Fowers & Richardson, 1996). Discriminatory access to resources creates not only differences in standard and quality of living, but produce also negative psychological consequences that entrap minorities in cycles of poverty.

Historically consequences for the individual are the foremost concern in individualistic countries, whereas in more collectivistic societies the welfare of the family and group are primary values. The interconnectedness or interdependence in society is considered a significant factor in understanding the major economic changes in China that has occurred over the past decades (Ho, 1998). To make valid inferences based on cross-cultural research it is essential to understand the basic economic as well as ideological processes in a society. Attitudes toward fairness are not static either, but change with globalization and development of society (Matsumoto, 2002). Research shows that even the perception of personal power changes over time (Larsen, 1972), and those who perceive low power for themselves in the future may well be establishing self-fulfilling prophecies.

Political changes throughout the world create more obstacles in outlining a coherent perspective on the dynamic and complex effects between culture and work relationships. The researcher must be aware of factors other than culture that can explain research results even when outcomes are validated and established. The level of national social development, ecological conditions, and economic development explain many cultural differences (Drenth, 1983). Organizational theories established in Western organizational psychology are also limited by culture, and the usefulness to other societies must be verified. Western models are not always applicable in Asian countries. Likewise the vaunted value of Japanese "control circles" has not been applicable to Western societies (Erez & Earley, 1993).

11.7.1. Universal Perceptions of Fairness, Cultural Perspectives and Globalization

Research on justice indicates that U.S. participants view fairness as a vital component in the evaluation of performance and merit in the workplace. On the other hand, East Asians like South Koreans see fairness in the remuneration processes should be more reflected by a consideration of needs of family size, seniority and education (Hundley & Kim, 1997). Yet these cultural differences are not static as perceptions of justice change over time (Morris & Leung, 2000). Not surprisingly, in Japan there is today a greater consideration for merit as a base for rewards compared to the past (Matsumoto, 2002). Industrial development and globalization are forces creating universal values of fairness. Over time cultural dynamics lag work relations, but eventually even deeply held values may change by degree.

Nevertheless there is also evidence for culture specific evaluations of fairness. Power distance plays a role in fairness evaluation as managers seen holding legitimate power in countries characterized as high in power distance have a greater ability to treat employees arbitrarily. The hierarchical characteristics of a society were also an important determinant of the perceived fairness of reward allocation as demonstrated in the meta-analysis of 14 cultures by Fischer and Smith (2003). The results showed egalitarian and horizontal societies preferred equality over equity (taking into account other relevant factors like seniority) in reward allocation. The hierarchical and power dimensions of culture were the more important determinants of perceived fairness compared to the individualism-collectivism profile of the culture. Hierarchical societies also showed a greater preference for using equity (need, seniority, status) along with merit based performance in reward allocation compared to egalitarian cultures.

Another meta-analysis showed that reward distribution on the basis of equity is preferred in collectivistic cultures, whereas equality is preferred in individualistic cultures (Sama & Papamarcos, 2000). However, contextual factors matters. Collectivistic cultures prefer equality with in-group members. However, when the person allocating the rewards is not a recipient of the reward equity is preferred across both individualistic and collectivistic cultures (Fischer & Smith, 2003). Other studies show that cultures high in power distance with significant hierarchical organizations preferred equity, whereas more egalitarian societies preferred equality as a method of distribution (Chen, Meindl, & Hunt, 1997). When judging pay fairness Chinese compared to U.S. respondents are more likely to weigh relationships and needs when making monetary decisions. These studies demonstrate that the concept of fairness in distributive judgment is dependent on cultural values.

On the other hand, procedural justice perceptions depend on power distance in many cultures (Pearce, Bigley, & Branyiczki, 1998). Procedural justice is recognized when employees feel they have been given a fair hearing. It has strong effects on job satisfaction and performance for respondents who preferred low power distance compared to those who endorsed high power distance acceptance (Lam, Schaubroeck, & Aryee, 2002). Procedural justice can mitigate low levels of distributive justice in collectivistic cultures, and both sources of justice are dependent on cultural variables (Brockner, Chen, Mannix, Leung, & Skarlicki, 2000; Fischer & Smith, 2006).

11.7.2. Coping with Acculturation as a Cultural Minority

The story of the world today is one of repeated tragedy and genocide where victims often have to flee for their lives. Understandably such refugees are not willing to return to further persecution and have to adjust to new circumstances and perhaps dissimilar cultures. Others refugees become migrants seeking a better life and try to improve their economic status, or search for new experience and adventure. In the United States there are currently over 12 million undocumented persons who have mainly arrived because their societies of origin in Mexico, Latin America or Asia did not meet their basic needs. As a result of the undocumented migration and bad economic times communities in the U.S. and Europe are struggling with negative attitudes toward immigrants based on the common perceptions of migrant infringements on jobs or social services (Krumov & Larsen, 2007, 2009; Ommundsen, Van der Veer, Van Le, Krumov, & Larsen, 2007; Van der Veer, Ommundsen, Larsen, Van Le, Krumov, Pernice, & Romans, 2004). Negative attitudes toward illegal migrants are aggravated by the current recession that has sharpened the distinctions in social relationships and increased the threat that people perceive from economic refugees. Many migrants find it stressful to cope with new cultural values and behavior producing cultural shock manifested by emotional disorders (Berry & Sam, 1997).

Acculturation refers to adjustment to a new culture. It is generally recognized that a person can identify with more than one culture, can have an appreciation for different cultural values, and indeed still behave consistent with each culture. The outcome of acculturation may take several different courses. Some migrants might continue to live according to the old cultural values, for example, in the United States and Europe there are entire enclaves of immigrants that live in ethnic communities speaking their native language, reading papers in the language of that culture, and enjoying its cultural food. It is as if they have simply migrated with their culture. Others assimilate totally to the new culture, and basically think of themselves in new ways consistent with that culture. Assimilation involves not only the acceptance of the new culture, but also to some degree a rejection of the one left behind. Some immigrants seek to integrate both cultures emphasizing the communalities of each. Sadly some migrants also become marginalized away from both original and current cultures and are like a person without a country or passport. Marginalization is characterized by a very high degree of collective and individual confusion and anxiety, a sense of alienation, loss of identity and extremely high levels of acculturative stress (Berry, 2001). Although these several reactions to acculturating to a new culture are generally accepted as present in many societies more attention should also be given to subcultures or from the interaction of several cultures (Rudmin, 2003).

11.7.3. The Permanence of Social Change

As noted above cultural identity is increasingly dynamic. To ensure validity cross-cultural psychology must reflect these ubiquitous changes and actively seek to revise what is known to make findings valid in the current context. The subject matter of cross-cultural psychology must change with the dynamic and globalized world. Globalization was created partially by new technology and the advances in communications technology and trade. However, the advantages of globalization have left uneven rewards for the poor while benefitting the elite of the world. Radical political changes in Eastern Europe have also altered these societies and their relationship with the rest of the word. Cross-cultural organizational psychology has changed its research focus to some degree in response to these monumental events (Roe, 1995).

11.7.4. Performance and Social Loafing

Social loafing is a well established variable in the social and organizational psychological literature. It generally refers to the phenomenon of group members exerting less effort on a given task when working in groups as opposed to working alone. Becoming members of a group allows for the diffusion of our work-related responsibilities and therefore decreases the pressure to perform. Social loafing is partially a consequence of increased anonymity in work groups where individual contributions become less noticeable and the employee therefore less concerned about evaluations. Social loafing refers to the tendency of people to perform less well on tasks in the presence of others when individual contributions are not evaluated (Williams, Harkins, & Karau, 2003). This variable has important implications for motivation and productivity, especially if it is considered a universal phenomenon. However, the results of cross-cultural research indicate that social loafing is more a culturally specific variable than previously thought. For example, Gabrenya, Wang and Latane (1985) demonstrated that while people in the United States manifested social loafing as part of their individualistic culture, people in China did not. In fact the Chinese respondent worked better in pairs than when working alone. Social loafing is not a universal behavior, but depends on cultural values that are, however, rapidly changing with globalization.

11.7.5. Conformity Pressures and Culture

A great deal of research has examined cultural conformity patterns across cultures. It is generally accepted that societies low on individualism create higher rates of conformity behavior. Since conformity is a response to vulnerability it is also logical that higher rates are of submission are found at lower levels of socio-economic success, as well as in hierarchical societies that reward conformity to the status quo (Shiraev & Bastrykin, 1988). To avoid isolation people will seek to understand the popular or prevalent opinion and behaviors in a culture and articulate the "politically correct" response. The effect of culture can be observed by variable evaluations in different societies. Conformity is valued more by Asian societies as compared to Europeans (Matsumoto, 1994). Conformity is not a universal value subscribed to by all cultures the same degree, but is rather determined by circumstances, values and history.

There are even differences in conformity rates between cultures that are similar such as Italians and Austrians (Cashmore & Goodnow, 1986). The famous Asch experiment also yielded varying degrees of conformity depending on national sample (Asch, 1956, 1957). Later Milgram (1961) replicated the experiment in Norway and France, and found the Norwegians more conforming. He explained the difference by pointing to the more coherent nature of Norwegian society. In a significant meta-analysis study Bond and Smith (1996) found significantly more conformity in collectivistic societies as compared to those that favor more individualism. Further Larsen and his colleagues (Larsen, 1974c, 1982, 1990; Larsen, Triplet, Brant, & Langenberg, 1979) demonstrated that conformity varied with social change. Higher conformity in the Asch experiment was found during periods of high social conformity. While conformity is ubiquitous the rate and expression are culturally specific and change over time.

11.7.6. The Paradigm of Obedience to Authority

The willingness of people to follow orders has consequences for the type of organization formed and its structure (Milgram, 1963). The average person has been shown to willingly follow the orders of apparent authority figures even when doing so violated their own personal standards and ethics. The business world today would yield many similar examples. However, in obedience research the results are also dynamic and changing. Studies that report research results some 25 to 40 years after the initial research by Milgram shows decreasing rates of obedience (Bond & Smith, 1996). It is not likely that this positive social change has occurred as a result of improved human ethics. However, Larsen and his co-workers have demonstrated the importance of social change. In fact laboratory studies on conformity corresponded very well to the conformity of the larger society (Larsen, 1974d; Larsen, Coleman, Forbes, & Johnson, 1972). Conformity was high during the so-called silent generation that lived during cold war McCarthyism. Later during the war in Vietnam students began to question authority and conformity rates were lower. Research on conformity rates is only valid for the period of study and must be modified by new research as culture and society changes.

11.7.7. Various Types of Power in Relationships

Power is a central concept to organizational psychology. Much of the empirical research on power in organizations (Cobb, 1980; Frost & Stahelski, 1988; Rahim, 1989; Rahim, Antonioni, Krumov, & Illieva, 2000; Raven & Rubin, 1968) uses as its theoretical foundation the classification of power presented by French and Raven (1959) that consist of five main types of power:

Coercive power is the power to influence based on the expectation of punishment for failure to conform. The fear of punishment is the main motivator of this power. *Reward power,* on the other hand, comes from the ability to facilitate desirable outcomes for others. This type of power depends on two factors, whether the individual seeking to influence owns a precious resource and whether someone needs this resource. According to French and Raven, reward power refers to the power to administer positive outcomes and reduce or remove those that are negative. *Legitimate power* is extended to leaders in the group or society and is related to the observation of norms. A person with this power is considered to have the right to control members who fail to observe the rules. On the other hand, if the person with legitimate power does not follow the same rules as the members of the organization he/she may lose the power. According to French and Raven, legitimate power stems from internalized values that support the right to influence by socially defined leadership and an obligation of others to accept this influence.

Referent power is based on the relative attractiveness of the person wielding power and can be observed in charismatic leaders or attractive groups. With their charisma and attractiveness referent leaders influence and members of the organization follow through a process of identification. *Expert power* is related to individuals who are believed to possess important intellectual abilities and knowledge in specific fields. Believing that these leaders possess expertise followers allow these individuals to influence and control procedures and outcomes. It is interesting to note that the first three types of power are formal and leaders with these types of influence will defend their power positions very decisively. The last two types of power are of a more informal nature.

Normally, managers have some or all of these five types of power. For leaders to be effective managers they must have certain characteristics preferred by the subordinates. Research shows that there are leadership attributes which are universally approved in managers. For example, an outstanding leader is expected to be encouraging, motivational, and cooperative (Den Hartog, House, Hanges, Ruiz-Quintanilla et al., 1999). Effective leadership depends also on the cultural context since different characteristics of leaders are effective with different managerial styles in varying cultures. Effective leadership is based not only on universal or specific personality characteristics but also by power distance discussed above. Different leadership styles are required in societies with high and low power distance. For example, in a study conducted with supervisors from the USA and Bulgaria it was found that supervisors' use of *referent power* based on interpersonal attraction and personal identification was positively related to subordinate effectiveness in the United States a country with low power distance. For Bulgaria, a country with high power distance, the supervisors' use of *legitimate power* was positively related to subordinate effectiveness (Rahim, Antonioni, Krumov, & Illieva, 2000).

People who exercise low social and personal power in their interactions are more likely to be pessimistic about their own lives, the status of their country, as well as the future of the world (Larsen, 1972). The sense of personal power may serve as a self-fulfilling prophecy, and is confounded by self-efficacy. In fact people will behave appropriately to self-expectations and hopes of the future. A sense of personal power encourages innovation in organizational life, and the lack thereof if shared broadly in the culture may prevent modernization and social development. Power is therefore both a stabilizing variable in cultural research of the status quo, as well as a dynamic factor as power relationships change with cultural developments.

How power is distributed is of interest in organizational psychology. A cross-cultural study (IDE, 1981) investigated the relationship of legislation to organizational structure and worker participation in eleven European countries. Despite the entrenchment of formal democratic government, and the legislation that endorsed worker participation, it was found that regular rank and file workers had little impact on the happenings of the workplace. One could characterize most industrial organizations of the West as fundamentally undemocratic. Being uninvolved in decision-making has many negative consequences for organizations including the employees feeling that they have no stake in organizational outcomes. The results of the study suggest that the actual empowerment of the individual is not defined by the legalistic social structure, but more negatively by the cultural acceptance of private property in which power is enshrined in the West.

Power is affected by the cultural differences between individualistic and collectivistic culture. There is a greater use and value of coercive power in individualistic countries like the United States, and more an emphasis on expert power in collectivistic countries (Rahim & Magner, 1996). It seems a contradiction that countries that value individuality should also employee more coercive strategies demonstrating a lack of integrity between values and behavior. One conclusion is that laws may change, but power is much less dynamic.

11.8. ACHIEVEMENT MOTIVATION AND MODERN SOCIETY

Achievement motivation is a major characteristic affecting the development of modern society. Seeking to achieve in organizations is not considered an intrinsic trait but is the outcome of parental and social norms (McClelland, 1958). A study of young children in the United States found them to be significantly more competitive and motivated individually as compared to Chinese children (Domino, 1992). In analyzing children's stories in 22 countries McClelland (1987) found that achievement motivation was strongly correlated to economic growth. In a very large-scale study of over 12000 participants Furnham, Kirkcaldy and Lynn (1994) also found a strong relationship between economic growth and achievement motivation. The above cited studies are correlational and therefore don't explain the causal pathway from social norms to individual achievement motivation. Is it learned achievement motivation that creates better economies? Or is it the opportunities provided by better economies that provide the hope of fulfilling the desire represented by achievement motivation? Logic would suggest a combination of both motivation and economic opportunities are essential for better economies. As noted earlier, learned helplessness is the outcome of believing that preparation and hard work will not get you anywhere. Believing there is no connection between efforts and outcomes can explain some lower levels of achievement motivation (Ogbu, 1994). In a study on the work-related values Segall, Dasen, Berry and Poortinga (1999) found that entrepreneurship is typically related to high power distance, tolerance for ambiguity in the workplace, high individualism, low uncertainty avoidance and high masculinity (McGrath, MacMillan, Yang, & Tsai, 1992).

11.8.1. Motivation and Cultural Values

Research on motivation in the workplace has leaned on the division between individualistic and collectivistic cultures as discussed by Hofstede and his collaborators. Individualism prevalent in Western Europe and the United States produces motivation related to personal goals. Successful motivation in collectivistic societies is more commonly oriented toward benefitting the family, group or society in general (Parsons & Goff, 1978).

The need for achievement is considered an important attribute of individualistic societies. Competence and self-efficacy are thought to be universal attributes (Bandura, 2002), whereas the novel factors that contribute to these motives are culture specific. Earley (1989) demonstrated the importance of personal feedback to self-efficacy in individualistic cultures. In collectivistic cultures, on the other hand, the main driver of self-efficacy is group feedback. Along a similar line personal control over the salient aspects of life is deemed essential in individualistic societies whereas collective control is more important in the collectivistic cultures. The main problem is trying to understand the meaning of these constructs since they are moderated by different languages. For example, what is considered achievement in individualistic oriented societies is enhancing the self in salient areas, whereas in cultures defined as collectivistic individual achievement is oriented toward making significant contributions to the group or society. So while intrinsic motives for autonomy and competence seem present in all cultures examined, what produces these motivators are different and culture specific (Ryan & Deci, 2000b).

Some people are motivated by the possibility of reward yet others by the desire to avoid disaster. For example, being promoted is motivating to workers with independent self-construal, whereas avoiding or preventing negative employment results are more motivating to workers with interdependent self conceptions (Heine, Kitayama, Lehman, Takata, Ide, Leung, & Matsumoto, 2001; Lockwood, Marshall, & Sadler, 2005).

In China collective achievement is considered of greater importance, and members of that society are more aware of the reactions of others to their work and achievements. Ethics in Asia view future orientation (the long view) and harmonious relationships as essential pillars of success in business enterprises (Cho & Kim, 1993). Of course, times are changing in China and elsewhere in Asia, and the dominant effects of globalization may be changing motivation toward more individualistic orientations. One study found no differences between U.S. and Chinese elementary students in achievement orientation (Xiang, Lee, & Solomon, 1997). The authors explain this result as the outcome of a very competitive educational system in China that has created a more personal focus on achievement.

In a study comparing New Zealander students with a sample from China, the Chinese students were shown to have stronger motivation toward educational achievement. The role of the family was also demonstrated as achievement was linked to parental expectations, and the fear of parental reaction to failure (Chung, Walkey, & Bemak, 1997). So it is important to remember that achievement motivation has different meanings dependent on culture and is not necessarily personal in nature. In the East Asian perspective achievement contains a strong collectivistic component.

11.8.2. Goals and Cultural Values

Work-related values also affect goal setting in various cultures, and the preferred rewards that motivate activity. Power distance was found to affect preferences for assigned versus participative goal setting (Sue-Chan & Ong, 2002). Participants in high power distance cultures demonstrated a preference for assigned goals which produced both higher commitment and performance. In general people living in collectivistic and high power distance cultures also preferred moderate and achievable goals to objectives that seemed less realizable (Kurman, 2001). Such differences are of practical importance for cross-cultural negotiation and collaboration.

Cultural differences also exist with respect to the preference for organizational rewards between cultures. For example, enhanced pay and bonuses were preferred in China and Chile as compared to American students who preferred interesting challenges and opportunities of promotion. The latter is consistent with individualistic self-construal. Furthermore in developing economies the material rewards are more salient along with greater need, and time must pass before economic outcomes are replaced or changed by motivation for individual recognition (King & Bu, 2005). Consistent with differences between collectivistic and individualistic cultures Japanese firms utilize seniority as a criteria for pay rewards and respect, whereas U.S. companies have implemented pay systems based on results and outcomes (Brown & Reich, 1997). Despite these relative differences the meaning of work goes beyond monetary rewards in all societies.

11.8.3. Work Serves Important Purposes of Finding Meaning

What is considered meaningful work varies by culture, but the importance of finding such an occupation cannot be overestimated. Meaningful work has been shown to improve both work motivation as well as performance (Roberson, 1990). The meaning of work is rooted in two primary components of *comprehension* and *purpose* (King, Hicks, Krull, & Del Gaiso, 2006; Steger, 2009; Steger, Oishi, & Kesebir, 2011). The concept of comprehension describes how well the worker abilities and interests match the requirements and reward systems of the organizations (Dawis & Lofquist, 1984). Meaningful work also contributes to workers sense of identity and the roles he/she plays in an organization. Comprehension of the work situation also depend on relationship factors, on the degree to which work matches the underlying identity self-construal, the role played in the organization, relative status, and the perceived value of the work.

Purpose, on the other hand, refers to the overall organizational mission and the degree that the constituent work harmonizes with the many required subsidiary activities toward the overriding goal. Employees can get lost in subsidiary activities and lose sight of the goal so employee morale is dependent on the overall acceptance of the purpose both for the organization, and also the individual employee (Steger & Dik, 2010).

There are organizational as well as individual benefits from meaningful work. Purpose and meaning in life found through work produce more satisfaction and happiness and employees with fewer psychological issues (Steger, Frazier, Oishi, & Kaler, 2006; Steger, Kashdan, Sullivan, & Lorentz, 2008; Steger, Kawabata, Shimai, & Otake, 2008). Work is an importance source of meaning, and for many people the major source (Baum & Stewart, 1990). Some people feel *a sense of calling* as their work reflects deeper meaning of self-identification. A sense of calling for work has been related to more confidence in management and better overall team functioning (Wrzesniewski, Dutton, & Debebe, 2003). The employee becomes a valuable participant in the organization as a sense of calling is also associated with career self-efficacy and intrinsic motivation (Duffy & Sedlacek, 2007). These factors are essential to job characteristics like job satisfaction and overall meaning of life.

Cultures to some extent determine the meaning of work. In interdependent cultures work and co-workers become part of the construal of the self. The relationships among people in collectivistic organizations are qualitatively different from individualistic societies and are based on stronger interpersonal relationships. In individualistic cultures meaning is to be found not only at work, but also separately away from the workplace. Likewise when negotiating or associating with business partners in individualistic cultures greater distinction are made between work and personal activities. In Japan it may be expected that co-workers socialize and have drinks after work, whereas colleagues from individualistic countries would perceive this requirement as an imposition. The nature of work may also be perceived in different ways. For many people in Western countries work is simply a way to support one's family and accumulate money as a form of prestige and security. In collectivistic societies, on the other hand, work may include feelings of obligation to the organization or the larger society. Hence collectivistic workers feel stronger ties to their organization, and cause fewer turnovers.

11.9. LEADERSHIP AND MAKING DECISIONS

The management of organizations is a complex topic. The major portion of research has, however, focused on two major management tasks: leadership and decision-making. A leader has dual functions first to clarify and set goals, and secondly to enhance the organizational climate for followers.

A good leader inspires others to follow. This is another way of saying that goals that are important to a leader is reached by means of relationships. Effective leaders form relationships by conveying the importance of the work, as related to the organization and its members (Goffee & Jones, 2006).

11.9.1. Culture and Leadership

As noted previously the organizational literature in the U.S. has identified two leadership styles which in the original Ohio state studies were labeled *consideration* and *initiating structure*. The styles refer to the major leadership roles of emotionally supporting employees on the one hand and providing organizational structure on the other. Although these styles have been seen in the literature as being occupied by different persons both aspects are essential for a successful leader in modern organizations. An integrated leader provides support and show concern for subordinates while also structuring the roles and tasks that are required (Wexley & Yukl, 1984). These leadership styles have been identified in other cultures as well including Japan (Misumi, 1985), and India (Sinha, 1984).

Sinha demonstrated an integrative leadership style and offered a more differentiated conception in India for what he called the "nurturant-task leader." The nurturant-task leader is active in creating goal orientation combined with high production efforts. At the same time he shows concern and care for subordinates and wants to promote their individual growth. A major characteristic of a good leader is the ability to be flexible and move from one leadership style to the next as required by the situation from directive roles at one point to more participatory involvement with employees as needed. Subordinates have respect for such a leader since he reflects authoritativeness without being authoritarian. Sinha found evidence for a superior leadership record of the *nurturant* leader. However, Khandwalla (1988) suggested more positive results for the *participatory* style.

A major study in leadership was performed by House, Hanges, Javidan, Dorfman, and Gupta (2004) called the Global Behavior Effectiveness Project. This large-scale study examined the relationship between leadership prototypes and social and organizational culture in 62 societies. Two leadership styles were found universally that of the *charismatic* leader and *team leadership*. Cultures described as high power distance displayed self-protective leadership (looking after number one), and were negatively related to charismatic and participatory leadership. The study revealed significant variations both within and between cultures in leadership styles as well as difference in style between higher and lower management (Den Hartog, House, Hanges, Ruiz-Quintanilla et al., 1999).

An important aspect of cross-cultural leadership style is the relative separation between a worker's personal life and time on the job. In Western Europe and the U.S. that distinction is clear, but in other cultures the boundaries between work and personal life are more fluid, and leaders can make demands that intervene in the worker's time after or before work. Often managers in Japan and other Asian societies will express concern for the personal lives of subordinates whereas in Western cultures that would be considered an intrusion and outside the portfolio of a manager.

Collectivistic cultures also require a more clear-cut direction in leadership utilizing manuals for instructions and frequent guidance from the manager. This need to have things made clear is related to uncertainty avoidance (Smith, Peterson, & Misumi, 1994).

11.9.2. Universal Components of Leadership and Cultural Values

Studies have found significant cross-cultural differences in leadership styles. One study, Howell, Dorfman, Hibino, Lee and Tale (1995) found cultural differences between the United States and Japan, Korea, Taiwan, & Mexico. The role of cultural values was confirmed in the study by Gerstner and Day (1994) who found that the traits of business leaders in 8 countries correlated with the cultural values of individualism, power distance and uncertainty avoidance outlined by Hofstede. Some studies indicated similarities in leadership style across cultures. Many studies (e.g. Bond & Smith, 1996) show similarity of managerial style. Clearly there are some universal aspects to leadership required in all societies as well as some culture specific traits. For example, Misumi (1985) suggested that leaders in all societies must attend to organizational maintenance as well as task performance involving managerial goals. How these goals are achieved might, however, be culturally specific. This argument would suggest that we must examine the effect of culture at more than one level involving both universal aspects but also culture specific instrumental behavior.

The influence of cultural values is also demonstrated in leadership studies (Smith, Peterson, & Schwartz, 2002). In particular, collectivism, high power distance and conservatism, were related to a dependence on vertical guidance found in the use of formal rules and the direction of superiors. Cultural values may also determine strategic considerations. In a study of executives in 20 countries Geletkanycz (1997) found that individualism, low power distance, and short-term orientation were related to the preference of sticking with the status quo. In individualistic cultures charismatic leadership is dependent on whether the leader is perceived to fit the characteristics of what might be considered a good and effective leader. On the other hand, in collectivistic societies the appraisal is less individual and leader effectiveness is evaluated more on organizational performance outcomes (Ensari & Murphy, 2003).

How leaders use power is also determined to some degree by cultural values (Rahim & Magner, 1996). Individualistic countries like the United States (contrary to democratic pretentions) use coercive power more in management, whereas in collectivistic societies organizations have greater respect for expertness. One conclusion is that in individualistic societies democracy is formal and limited to voting and law, but have little influence in the workplace except as defined by contractual agreement with unions. Participatory leadership has little meaning in liberal parliamentary democracies with negative effects for worker freedom. The repeated downturns of the economies and shipment of jobs overseas have destroyed what little power workers had in the past to participate in organizational decision making. Over the past 30 years union membership has fallen by two thirds in the United States, and according to the independent watchdog Freedom House the United States did not even make it to the list of 41 countries where workers met the qualifications of being free (Luce, 2010)

Collectivistic societies were found to strengthen the effectiveness of inspirational and transformational leadership. The outcome for employees was less turnover and more job satisfaction (Spreitzer, Perttula, & Xin, 2005; Walumbwa & Lawler, 2003). On the other hand, participatory leadership practices in low power distance countries brought better results. In collectivistic societies with high power distance paternalistic leadership had positive impact on work-related attitudes. In paternalistic leadership the leader guides the work and career of the subordinates in a fatherly way in return for respect and loyalty. The effect of leadership and the best utility of style must be evaluated within the cultural context.

In conclusion, reducing potential conflict by matching the preferred leadership style, using cooperation in solving organizational conflict, outlining cooperative goals, and matching leaders and followers in ethnicity produce more positive outcomes in cross-cultural settings. In recent years researchers have also begun to examine the ecological climate as a mediator of leadership style (Van de Vliert, 2006). In examining 61 cultures de Vliert found that autocratic leadership was less effective in rich countries with demanding or harsh climes, but more effective in poor countries where climate also presented challenges.

11.9.3. Globalization and the Challenges of Leadership Abroad

Globalization has created a generation of expatriate leadership working in foreign cultures. Managers have arrived in the U.S. from Japan, Korea and Hong Kong to participate in the management of subsidiaries. Likewise U.S. citizens have been asked to move to other countries as part of their management careers. Although stays in foreign cultures do not change personality or fundamental cultural values, some adaptation to the native culture produce better outcomes among American subsidiaries of foreign companies (Thomas & Toyne, 1995).

Many challenges face those who work abroad including the possibility that salient information important to the organization may be considered sensitive and censored. Some authorities will argue that political censorship is essential to protect the social order and ensure stability. Over time such customs are internalized and become habitual. Some societies high in power distance will justify censorship on the grounds that authorities must be respected. Other sources of censorship include restrictions on the grounds of ideology or religion and information that challenges authoritarian ideology is prohibited in certain countries. Both political ideology and religious authoritarianism justify limitation on information. In fundamentalist Muslim countries it is prohibited to write anything negative about the religion or produce caricatures of Mohammed.

Culture can easily be used as a rationale for not only censorship, but also for various forms of repression. Inhuman treatment of women is justified on the grounds of cultural requirements of the past as if decision makers have no current responsibility or guilt. Countries all over the world vary in the degree to which individuals are free to regulate their own behavior or depend on power relationships and customs. When working abroad such differences become apparent to the expatriate manager seeking to apply divergent rules of conduct (Murphy-Bernman, Levesque, & Bernman, 1996).

Adjustment to cultures abroad depends on three major components according to the meta-analysis by Bhaskar-Shrinivas, Harrison, Luk and Shaffer (2005). These include cultural adjustment, adjustment to the work situation, and adjustment to interaction with co-workers and the indigenous population. Good adjustment is the outcome of the willingness to learn important aspects of cultural values as well as self-efficacy (Palthe, 2004). Organizational factors play important roles especially support from co-workers and higher level management. The family situation also influences adjustment outcomes, in particular spousal support for the individual leader's work demands. Factors about the job found important to adjustment include low role ambiguity and conflict (Takeuchi, Tesluk, & Yun, 2002).

Personal traits are of great importance. For example, Huang, Chi and Lawler (2005) noted the role played by a person's openness to new experience. Individuals differ in their willingness to get out of routine comfort zones. Huang et al also noted the importance of personality traits like extraversion and agreeableness in assisting the individual in the adaptation process. In the long run the expatriate's mental health is a critical factor to successful adjustment. Wang and Kanungo (2004) found that mental health depended on the expatriate's social network including size, but also its cultural diversity. An approach where the expatriate manager seeks to solve relevant problems is superior to focusing on symptoms like loneliness (Stahl & Caligiuri, 2005). Satisfaction with the overseas job is improved by the importance of the work, and the relative autonomy and authority of the manager. Also helpful is similarity with past work experience (Gregersen & Black, 1996). Intellectual style is also considered important to the management of careers. In particular to ability to cope with stress and poor performance arising from incongruence of intellectual styles in manager-employee relationships and adaptation to cross-cultural experiences is guided by intellectual modes and styles (Armstrong, Van der Heijden, & Sadler-Smith, 2012).

11.9.4. The Cultural Context of Decision Making

Many important decisions are made in the group context affecting outcomes for production and rewards for employees. As noted, except for Scandinavia, the average employee has little to say in Western democracies. In Japan, however, a process of consensus building has historically involved every level of the organization. Employees even at lower levels affect decision outcomes although they have no veto power. Most industrial organizations are not democracies, but may best be described as oligarchies (Ferrante, 1992). It is the decisions by the small minority at the top of the organizational chart that decide strategic direction, with lower level management having some say on how decisions are implemented. It remains one of the historical puzzles how individualistic societies that view persons as autonomous beings (at least in the breach) have evolved such top down economic structures. The ability to coerce and impose managerial will is very high in countries described as democratic and arbitrary decision making is currently enhanced by worker fear of unemployment brought on by the Great Recession.

Japanese organizational behavior has been the subject of many studies on decision making, not least because of the early success of many Japanese corporations (Wright, 1985). The major decision-making idea in Japan is to reach consensus rather than promote a contest between opposing opinions with the conflict that follows. Organizational plans in Japan are frequently rough drafted at lower levels of the organization, and participants are then encouraged to add their ideas and concerns as the plan is circulated. As it is discussed the plan gradually moves up through the levels of management taking advantage of the experience and knowledge of a broad group of participants. It is believed that through this process not only are better decisions made, but more employees get involved, motivated, and committed to the implementation. The downside is the time consumed in the process of planning and consultation, but, on the other hand, once a decision is made implementation can be rapid (Misumi, 1984). The process of consensus building is time consuming, and the inability to respond rapidly when faced with urgent matters is a drawback. Influenced by these managerial ideas Japanese managers have the long view and try to build relationships by often prolonging discussions beyond what is expected in Western societies. Perhaps this prolonged evaluation process is one reason why people from the collectivistic cultures of East Asia are more confident in their decisions (Yates, Lee, & Shinotsuka, 1996).

Other cultures have also been the focus of decision-making studies (Berry, Poortinga, Segall, & Dasen, 1992). A study on managerial decision-making in Western Europe and the United States showed a continuum of power sharing from unilateral decisions at the top to shared participation at intermediate levels to workers having the power to make all lower level decisions (Heller & Wilpert, 1981). A major conclusion of the study was that the differences in decision making between national samples were much less than the differences produced by the demands of particular situational context. For example, the Mann, Radford, Burnett, Ford, Bond, Leung, Nakamura, Vaughan and Yang (1998) study employing a decision making survey found that students in individualistic countries expressed more decision-making confidence than those from collectivistic societies, a result opposite to that found by Yates et al. One explanation can be found in the role of greater individual humility fostered by the education system in collectivistic societies that moderate responses but not actual decision confidence.

Organizational culture is also a factor. Weatherly and Beach (1998) examined the relationship between organizational culture and decision making and found that the options considered are generally those consistent with the culture of the organization. Organizational culture also affects the endorsement and support of employees. Clearly there are several levels of cultures to be considered in understanding organizational decision-making.

11.9.5. Risk Taking in Varying Cultures: The Risky Shift and Group Think Phenomenon

An important tendency in group decision-making is the *risky shift*, called that because decisions tend to be more risky in group discussions than when individuals are acting alone. Perhaps one reason for the risky shift is the value placed on risk taking in Western cultures (Brown, 1965; Lamm, Schaude, & Trommsdorff, 1971). Other cultures may, however, value caution, for example, Gologor (1977) found no tendencies toward the risky shift in Liberia. Rather he found about as much polarization toward caution as toward more risky decisions. Having confidence in decisions may be related to the risky shifts since decision-makers expect a higher probability of positive outcomes than justified by the facts. Cultural differences in enhanced positive thinking were reported by Wright, Phillips, and Wisudha (1983). The study compared Western samples with south East Asian respondents and found that Asians were more overconfident than Western participants. Wright and Phillips (1980) described this result as caused by the tendency of the Asian sample to rely on intuitive non-probabilistic rather than probabilistic cognition. Comparing Western participants with Chinese, Weber and Hsee (2000) found that the Chinese participants were more likely to make risky investment decisions. The authors explained the result as a consequence of the Chinese possessing a social network to be relied upon in case of catastrophe. Overall there is little research evidence to support the contention by Brown that Western samples value risky decisions and results of the research vary with little consistency.

Group think is a related pattern of faulty decision making produced by pressure from others, by apparent unanimity in group opinion, by illusions of invulnerability, by "mindguarding" by those supporting the status quo, and by presumed morality and shared stereotypes (Janis, 1983). Group think produce bad decisions, not only in government, but also at the organizational level. Although some researchers have presented ideas for avoiding these consequences, one proposal is to transform these destructive conformity inducing thought patterns and replace them with the constructive idea of "*team think*" (Neck & Manz, 1994). Team think would turn negative conformity thought patterns upside down by encouraging divergent viewpoints in the group, by ensuring an open and free discussion of ideas, by recognizing the unique contribution of individual group members, and by inviting doubts about decision outcomes.

11.10. THE STRUCTURING OF TASKS AND TEAM WORK

All organizations regardless of culture are involved in defining and structuring various goal-related tasks. Organizations larger than those managed by small families have complex structures assigning work to separate offices for development, production and promotion. Organizational charts allow us to see the relationships between the various substructures from the CEO to the frontline managers. One important question for this chapter concerns the effect of culture on organizational structures.

11.10.1. Structure in Social Organizations and Culture

Lammers and Hickson (1979) assessed cultural variation and found evidence for three types of organizational structures labeled Latin, Anglo-Saxon, and Third World reflecting varying hierarchical levels and centralization. For example, the Latin type is a classical bureaucracy reflected by a highly centralized structure consisting of many intermediate levels. The more authoritarian Third World structure is located primarily in southern and Eastern Europe and encouraged central decision-making, paternalistic leadership, and few formal rules. According to Lammers and Hickson the Third World type can also be found in smaller firms in West European countries where the founder or manager personally manage the direction of the organization. The Anglo-Saxon type is more decentralized and flexible in structure and compared to the Latin organization has fewer hierarchical levels. Since this type of organizational structure is more flexible it is able to adjust to the frequently rapid change that has characterized modern development. The Anglo-Saxon type is located mainly in North-West Europe and the North America.

11.10.2. The Effectiveness of Team Work in Varying Cultures

The value of collectivism versus individualism is also related to attitudes toward team work. For example, where workers value high power distance they are more resistant to the self-management concept that is part of the team work effort (Kirkman & Shapiro, 1997). U.S. respondents do not like to be part of teams when they are individually competent but their teams are incompetent or performing poorly, whereas Chinese participants actually preferred teams under these conditions (Chen, Brockner, & Katz, 1998). Culture affects the construal of team work employing different metaphors and schemas. Schemas also vary across cultures. For example, participants from more collectivistic societies like Mexico believe that supportive socio-emotional behavior to be essential to success, whereas individuals from individualistic societies like the United States believe that high task orientation is important to team success (Sanchez-Burks, Nisbett, & Ybarra, 2000).

Recent research has evaluated the effectiveness of teams. The complexity of the jobs performed effect the organizational structure and combined with relative autonomy of employees are important for the cohesiveness of working groups in the United States (Man & Lam, 2003). On the other hand, what might seem obvious in creating strong group morale like task enrichment, in fact is shown to have negative effects on team support in organizational groups with high power distance (Drach-Zahavy, 2004).

Culture also affects the trust important to team work based on different relationships across cultures. For example, in Japan trust is related to indirect ties with other members of the organization, whereas in the United States it is based on belonging to some common category or history like graduating from the same university. The advantage of collectivistic teams is the higher level of cooperation elicited that also produces higher performance (Eby & Dobbins, 1997). On the other hand, Chen et al. (1998) demonstrated that it was the different situational context that produced trust across cultures. In collectivistic societies trust was built primarily through supportive socio-emotional factors including the sharing of goals and activities that enhanced group identity and positive feelings. In more individualistic countries trust was enhanced by instrumental factors that promoted goal interdependency and activities that enhanced personal identity.

As globalization has progressed organizations operating in several countries have found it necessary to organize multicultural teams. Multicultural teams are composed of individuals that may have different values and attitudes based on their national and cultural background. In order to work together team members must be united around a joint goal. Team members must also accept that goal attainment is valuable and useful individually as well as for the group as a whole. Effectiveness of multicultural teams is promoted from their ability to manage consensus and diversity (Argote & McGrath, 1993).

Bringing together team members from different cultures bring obvious problems of adjustment and misunderstandings. Some have argued that multicultural teams bring not only differences in cultural values, but frequently are hampered by the reliance on electronic communication and the difficulty of monitoring team development. The effectiveness of multicultural teams is influenced by lower team identification and the withholding of efforts (Shapiro et al., 2005). Since multicultural teams make cultural distinctions more salient it is not a surprise that higher levels of ethnocentrism, in-group biases, and conflict exist in such a varied context (Cramton & Hinds, 2005). The major issue is communication, and when leaders work to prevent miscommunication cross-cultural teams performed as effective as more homogenous groups (Ayoko, Hartel, & Callan, 2002). Some researchers have argued that with proper attention to communication multicultural teams may well have strategic advantages for organizational work presenting valued insights and viewpoints (Shapiro et al., 2005).

11.11. INDIVIDUALISTIC AND COLLECTIVISTIC CULTURES AND PSYCHOLOGICAL CONTRACTS

Regardless of where employed a worker has with the employer mutual expectations of outcomes and rewards. The perception of mutual obligation is not necessarily set down in contractual language, yet it is a significant factor in employee morale and performance. The existence of such *implicit contracts* has been established cross-culturally (Hui, Lee, & Rousseau, 2004; Rousseau, 1989). The concept is tied closely to the idea of fairness including distributive and procedural justice. A major difference is found between individualistic and collectivistic cultures to violations of psychological contracts. For example, employees in the U.S. take more serious the violation of intrinsic aspects of the contract like reducing the implicit autonomy of employees, whereas workers in Hong Kong resented more violations of extrinsic aspects like remuneration outcomes violated by cuts in pay. These differences are related to socio-economic development where material rewards of work are more important to workers in economies still developing. One important influence of cultural values is found in the construal of the self. Employes from more collectivistic societies have relationship psychological contracts aimed at enhancing the interdependent self, whereas individualistic employees are more concerned with independent self-improvement (Thomas, Au, & Ravlin, 2003).

These results were consistent with the level of organizational normative commitment. A meta-analysis (Meyer, Stanley, Herscovitch, & Topolnytsky, 2002) showed that stronger organizational commitment was created where organizations fulfilled the employee-employer psychological contract and provided workers with expected support. Individualistic employees were more concerned with job satisfaction and promotion whereas among collectivistic workers a positive relationship with the supervisor was considered a key factor in satisfying the psychological contract. This relational aspect in collectivistic cultures is closely related to perceived fairness. For example, in the U.S perceptions of fairness are tied to the level of performance and earned merit, whereas for collectivistic employees need is an important consideration (Morris & Leung, 2000).

Therefore in negotiating across cultures there are many subliminal factors at work. In Western cultures, for example, negotiation is about reaching a direct agreement based partly on problem solving and bargaining. Negotiators from Western countries tend to use direct language, with little use of nonverbal cues. Interdependent cultures, on the other hand, bring a larger array of issues to the table including customs, rules and expectations of psychological contracts. Since the aim of collectivistic negotiators is long-term benefit and establishing relationships there is an expectation of entertainment included in negotiation. Unknowing to the negotiating parties psychological contracts are not only part of the eventual outcome, but also part of the negotiating process itself (see Gelfand, Major, Raver, Nishii, & O'Brien, 2006; Okamoto, 1993). An awareness of these assumptions and subliminal psychological factors is essential to create viable cross-cultural relationships.

11.12. CULTURAL VALUES AND RESEARCH: MANAGERIAL ISSUES

The cultural typology that has emerged in cross-cultural psychology over the past decades can be helpful in understanding how culture impact managerial practices. Cultural studies have provided information on a variety of organizational variables including work attitudes and behavior, job satisfaction, motivation, burn-out and coping (Dubin & Galin, 1991). Culture is defined as a shared meaning system that is present at any level of analysis including individual members, groups, organizations, and nations (Schein, 1990). In homogenous societies also called "tight" cultures norms and values tend to be relatively uniform. In heterogeneous cultures there is greater variability between groups and individuals that often have different norms and values also called "loose" societies. Western cultures stress the importance of the independent self and are likely to be more loosely organized than the collectivistic societies in Asia that emphasize interdependence, common fate and harmony (Triandis, 1994).

Cultures also vary in the beliefs about the role of native ability versus social intelligence in work outcomes (Holloway, 1988). For example, Japanese culture emphasizes the importance of effort in successful outcomes, whereas Americans believe, consistent with the independent self, that ability is the key factor in success. In turn these cultural ideas are reflected in the relative importance placed on social intelligence in Japan as central to intelligent behavior. On the other hand, since ability is an individual trait U.S. and Western culture places a greater emphasis on individual factors consistent with a more individualistic outlook (Markus & Kitayama, 1991a).

Managers should understand that workers share the meaning system of both their work-place and also the broader social culture. One conclusion from research is that managerial practices successful in one culture are not necessarily persuasive in another society. For example, job enrichment strategies have motivational success in individualistic United States, but quality circles that were successful in collectivistic Japan have not had similar positive outcomes in the U.S. Trust in goal setting is also an important variable. For example, goal setting by shop stewards trusted by the rank and file were more successful in England compared to the United States (Earley, 1986). Participation in goal setting is particularly important in societies with collectivistic values and democratic participation (Erez & Earley, 1987).

Communication styles also vary between so-called *high versus low context* cultures. Some societies are context dependent using social experiences as reference points when communicating, whereas low context cultures are more likely to use abstract concepts to convey meaning. Low context (abstract) communication is more likely found in individualistic cultures, whereas high context references is used more in collectivistic societies (Gudykunst, Ting-Toomey, & Chua, 1988). One managerial consequence is that in conflict situations low context managers are more likely to use a direct confrontation style, whereas high context cultures will seek to avoid such direct encounter by the use of calculated vagueness. In the workplace managers in low context cultures are more likely to use direct criticism, but in high context societies managers will try not to hurt employee feelings (Miyahara, 1984).This research supports on the whole the importance of the cultural context in a successful managerial strategy and that positive outcomes depends on the congruence of these interventions with the cultural context (Lawler, 1986).

The integration of various theories on cognition, language, knowledge creation and leadership in organizational behavior await future development, but can eventually contribute to cross-culturally based information that will help management to better understand functioning of the organization. For example, with greater cultural sensitivity it is possible to align Chinese philosophy and thinking (that justify bureaucracy) with western concepts that advocate initiative. Sensitivity to Chinese culture would emphasize the role of the individual is rooted the relationship to groups and society. A proper fit between cultural actors require skilled organizational members and commonly accepted ways of proceeding in which multicultural teams play an essential role (Del Giudice, Carayannis, & Della Peruta, 2012). Still there is a common basis for understanding located in the deep structure of the Big Five personality model. Clear support has been found for the presence of this personality structure in all cultures that have been examined. This deep human psychological structure enhances communication across what may seem significant cultural divides (Schmitt, Allik, McCrae, & Benet-Martinez, 2007). However, at the same time researchers are also marshalling evidence for the importance of culturally unique values and variables (Hwang, 2012; Hwang, Kim, & Kou-Shu, 2006). Managers must be aware of both sources of behavior, as well as how the emerging global society is creating more homogeneity in the world.

SUMMARY

In this chapter we examined the role of cultural values and culture in social and organizational life. Culture grew out of people's need to survive and has produced many conceptual complexities. Culture is also used as an explanatory concept in several disciplines with overlapping meanings, and persists in real life as cultural values are passed from one generation to the next. However, interaction between cultures in the modern world has produced more cultural integration and the imposition of a global cultural model. Cross-cultural psychology is essentially based on comparison between groups affected by cultural factors. Cross-cultural psychology describes the complexity of behavior in various regions of the world, but it also examines culture as the antecedent in cause and effect relationships. In short we are interested in communalities, but also differences between cultural groups.

Recent decades have seen a dramatic increase of the field of cross-cultural organizational behavior. Primary reasons for this development are the technological breakthroughs and the cultural contact brought about by globalization. International and multi-national organizations have responded to globalization by employing an increasingly diverse workforce. In turn diversity has brought forward the challenges of cross-cultural relations. The Internet, virtual conferencing, and email have created a global village in organizational relationships.

Organizations also develop unique cultures producing shared meanings and create emotional climates for employees. The emotional climate of an organization affects employee morale and productivity whether positive or negative. Organizational culture is defined by both the technology used and the physical plant, but also by the organization's underlying values and implicit norms. The original interest in cross-cultural comparisons grew from the observation that some cultural organizations were more productive. Central to this research were the work related values by Hofstede on power distance, individualism-collectivism, uncertainty avoidance, masculinity-femininity, and long versus short-term orientation. The differences between Western and non-western countries typically center on the role of the individual in society, for example, whether individual achievement is valued versus reverence for tradition and authority.

The concept of power distance describes the extent to which society accepts inequality of power in relationships. Inequality has increased dramatically over the past decades in salient dimensions like pay and benefits. One practical effect is the finding that managers in high power distance cultures can act with less resistance with arbitrary, autocratic, and paternalistic ways toward employees compared to managers working in low power distance societies. By far the most researched cultural value is the individualism-collectivism construct. Employees in collectivistic societies are more likely to conform and comply with demands in the workplace. A primary attribute of individualistic societies is the greater value placed on the individual self versus the interdependent self-construal in collectivistic cultures. In general the higher the power distances in society, the lower the level of individualism.

We live in times of great economic uncertainty as modern society is characterized by economic crises, rapid change, and major restructuring. Cultures vary in tolerance of uncertainty, and avoidant societies seek to create a more predictable world by the use of rituals, norms, and the promotion of obedience. Uncertainty avoidance affects innovation in negative ways and may therefore be dysfunctional in coping with change. Research supports the idea that achievement is based on and dependent on innovation.

The concept of masculinity versus femininity has also been used as a work related value and examines how gender differences and expectations play out in the workplace. To what degree do cultures seek to maintain the traditional masculine dominance in the workplace and in social life? We still have societies in the world that do not permit women to leave home unescorted or drive a car. Masculine countries in particular value leadership, independence, and opportunities for self-realization. The long-term versus short-term orientation grew out of observation of Asian societies. People in Europe and the United States demand immediate gratification as seen in the rapid obsolescence of products. Cultures with more long-term outlooks are more patient and focus on building relationships. However, we must insert a cautious note as values have shifted in recent years. Also the research on Hofstede's work related values has experienced some problems in replication.

That culture is dynamic and ever changing can be observed in social interaction research. Recent events affecting culture include the immigration wave in Europe and the United States, and the current economic crisis. Poverty and discrimination affect cultural minorities negatively in their access to resources. The interconnectedness of relationships in Asia is considered a major factor in the dynamic changes that have occurred in that part of the world. However, everywhere political changes create constant change and flux.

The perception of justice is valued differentially in Western and Asian cultures, but these distinctions are also in flux. There is some evidence of convergence of social justice values, but also culture specific evaluation of fairness. Immigration has brought new challenges of acculturation. Migrants in search of a better life have created a crisis in human relationships. Migrants and citizens both have to adjust to cultural values and beliefs that are different or even antagonistic. However, this process is also changing as the economic crises affect the desirability of immigration versus coping with life in the home culture.

Social and political change produce dynamic changes in variables once thought stable like cultural identity. An important consequence for cross-cultural organizational psychology is to be on guard constantly and revalidate what is currently known to be valid that might be affected by these changes. A well established variable in social psychology is "social loafing" once thought stable. However, social loafing is dependent on situations that may be changing due to globalization. Social conformity is thought to be more valued in Asian societies compared to Western countries. However, research on the famous Asch experiment shows transhistorical changes that correspond roughly to those occurring elsewhere in society. Likewise obedience studies also demonstrate a change corresponding to social dynamics. Even power in relationships is changing as globalization challenge traditional societies to some degree.

A major interest of cross-cultural organizational psychology is motivation in the workplace. For example, achievement motivation is the outcome of parental and social norms as affected by culture and is correlated with economic growth and the opportunities produced. Achievement motivation is primarily the outcome of individualistic societies. In collectivistic societies the drive toward self-efficacy is group feedback. Ethics in Asia is determined by the long-term view that emphasizes harmony, but times are changing.

Work-related cultural values affect goal setting and motivate activity. Employees in high power distance cultures prefer assigned goals, whereas workers in Western societies prefer participatory goal setting. Culture also affects the preferences for organizational rewards. The meaning of work also varies by culture. Meaning is a salient variable as it improves work performance and motivation. For many people work is the major source of meaning in life. The meaningfulness of work in interdependent cultures is strongly influenced by relationships, whereas in individualistic societies meaning is to be found both in the workplace as well as in the personal time away from the job. For many employees in individualistic societies work is just a means to survive whereas in collectivistic cultures work is also considered an obligation to the community.

Leadership and decision-making are the main focus of research on the role of management. In prominent U.S. studies two leadership styles of "consideration," and" initiating structure" were identified. We would argue that an integrated leader would display leadership in both structural organization and also by concern for the employees. A related concept from India is the "nurturant leader." Large-scale cross-cultural research also identified two leadership styles labeled "charismatic" and "team leadership." These styles vary both within and also between cultures. Significant differences exist between cultures in leadership style related to cultural values. Although many studies also show similarity in leadership styles across cultures, how these styles are manifested are cultural specific. It is a concern that in the U.S. a disconnection exists between professed democratic values in decision-making and the authoritarian workplace where employees have little influence other than contractual language.

Globalization has created new challenges for leaders serving abroad. As a result of globalization there is now an entire generation of leaders who have served in foreign cultures. Those who adapt to the indigenous culture produce better outcomes for American foreign subsidiaries. Working abroad also creates challenges defined by cultural sensitivities. Censorship in high power distance cultures is also an issue. Culture as a concept can also be used as a rationalization for repression of women and minorities. Societies vary in the degree they allow individuals to regulate their own lives. Working abroad requires many adjustments to the workplace, to interaction with co-workers, and to the indigenous population. Those who adjust well are characterized by openness to new experience, and personality traits like extraversion, and having a sufficient social network for support.

As noted the average employee has little to say about decisions in the workplace in Western democracies and even less influence in high power distance cultures. In Japan one key to economic success is thought to be the emphasis on consensus building that allow for input from lower levels of management. Industrial organizations are not democracies, but rather specialized forms of oligarchies. In the U.S. most large organizations are characterized by a continuum of power sharing with unilateral decisions at the top and more shared decision-making at intermediate levels of management.

The "risky shift" and "group think" findings are relevant to group decision-making. Research shows that decisions in the group context tend to be more risky than those taken by individuals. Some have argued that the cause is the value of risk taking behavior in Western societies. However, there is little evidence to support this cultural difference. Group think is faulty decision-making produced by apparent unanimity, illusions of invulnerability and other factors. An important anti-dote to group think is "team think" that encourages divergent viewpoints.

Team work and organizational structure has received the interests of researchers in recent years. Three types of organizations have been identified including Latin, Anglo-Saxon, and Third World structures. The work related values of individualism versus collectivism significantly affect attitudes toward team work. Where high power distance is valued employees tend to be more resistant to self-management and team work. Culture also affects the construal of team work. Further the effectiveness of team work is dependent on cultural complexities, and the team's ability to manage consensus building and diversity issues.

Finally the chapter considers the importance of psychological contracts that refer to the implicit mutual expectations of employees and managers about outcomes and rewards of employment. This construct is closely tied to conceptions of fairness including distributive and procedural justice. Major differences exist between individualistic and collectivistic cultures. Employees in individualistic cultures resent the violation of intrinsic aspects of work like expected autonomy, whereas workers in collectivistic societies object more to violations of expected rewards like cuts in pay. Where organizations fulfill psychological contracts workers display more organizational commitment. On the whole individualistic employees are more concerned with job satisfaction, whereas collectivistic workers are more strongly influenced by interpersonal relationships. The expectations of psychological contracts also influence international negotiations.

CHAPTER 12

CULTURE AND HUMAN HEALTH

This chapter seeks to address the issues of health and mental disorder within the framework of cross-cultural and cultural research. Health is a fundamental issue in all human societies and is the key to well-being and happiness. World organizations are involved in health promotions through the prevention of disease programs and the creation of primary care agencies. Specialists in health care have over time come to recognize the importance of the social sciences in successful promotion of healthy practices through the use of public education and the media. Successful approaches to health care must be based on accurate cross-cultural understandings of what is universal and what is culture-bound in illness related attitudes and values. The involvement of indigenous communities is important in order to achieve successful health intervention outcomes as shown in the creation of Aboriginal Health Centers in Australia (Larsen, 1978a,b; Peat, 1997). The very conceptions of health have been altered in response to advances in social science. Health is now considered to be a positive human state of well-being that is more than the absence of disease. Health has become conceptually complex and covers all dimensions of life and the mental and social well-being also covered in the term "quality of life" (Diener, 1996; Minsel, Becker, & Korchin, 1991). Subjective well-being takes into account

Cross-Cultural Psychology: Why Culture Matters, pages 355–386.
Copyright © 2013 by Information Age Publishing
All rights of reproduction in any form reserved.

all factors required for optimal human development from a person's psychological life space and the cultural surroundings. In fact an interdisciplinary approach is essential in a campaign to reduce the health disparities so obvious in the world that are primarily related to socio-economic deficits (Anderson, 2009).

Cross-cultural psychology is making important contributions, particularly by providing an understanding of the cultural framework for both physical and mental health services (Kazarian & Evans, 1998). It is well recognized today that physical health and mental healthcare are interdependent, and must be understood within the framework of both cultural knowledge and cross-cultural comparative findings. Cross-cultural psychology has produced helpful knowledge in salient areas to better understand health-related cognition, but also in the assessments of emotional, behavioral and social aspects of life considered essential information for culturally based health practices and individual therapy. (Dasen, Berry, & Sartorius, 1988; Garland, Lau, Yeh, McCabe, Hough, & Landsverk, 2005; Helman, 2007; Purnell & Paulanka, 2008; Spector, 2004).

Cross-cultural researchers recognize the need for cultural sensitivity in delivering empirically verified treatment in a still heterogeneous world. The need for cultural and cross-cultural knowledge is supported by the large-scale differences in physical and mental health between various cultural groups (Gurung, 2010). Cultural values produce different conceptions about the nature of health and illness and indicate what treatment strategies will have optimal outcomes. Not all cultural groups are on a level playing field within or between nations and being poor are implicated in the etiology of most infectious and chronic disorders in the world. Low socio-economic status is linked consistently to elevated health related death rates and produces disadvantages from birth throughout life (Gottfried, Gottfried, Bathurst, Guerin, & Parramore, 2003).

12.1. THE INJUSTICE OF HEALTH DISPARITIES IN THE WORLD

Health disparities connected to socio-economic status occur all over the world. In the U.S., African Americans suffer especially from appalling infant mortality rates that are twice as high as European Americans. Likewise deaths from heart disease are 40% higher among African Americans compared to descendants of Europeans. Life expectancy is the most salient statistic that reflects relative health, and there is a difference of 35 years between some ethnic groups in the U.S. Nearly one in two people in the U.S. will suffer from a major mental disorder in their lifetimes, and millions of sufferers do not receive any care whatsoever, and this appalling situation exist in the richest country in the world. While mental illness strikes people in all social classes the poor are disproportionately represented. At any time about one in six people living at or below the poverty line in the U.S. suffer from a severe mental health problem. From an economic point of view inadequate mental health care cost billions of dollars to the U.S. economy each year (Murray, Kulkarni, Michaud, Tomijima, Bulzacchelli, et al., 2006; Editors, 2012).

It is not difficult to understand that people living in poverty within a country are more depressed as compared to people with more wealth and social standing (Pratt & Brody, 2008). Parallel socioeconomic disparity occurs also between poor and wealthy countries. In rich countries the well off persons have access to the latest in health care that is too costly to acquire for poor countries. For people who believe that good health and effective health care is a basic human right the socioeconomic disparity that drives health outcomes within and between countries appear a grand injustice. While the effect of socioeconomic disparity on health is supported by available statistics there are notable differences. Cuba, a relatively economically poor country, has poured a major portion of their meager resources into health care and education making both accessible to all citizens. A major result is a lower birth death rate in Cuba compared to the U.S., a much richer neighbor, and Cuban doctors serve all over the world in poor countries trying to bridge the disparity caused by poverty like, for example, in Haiti and Venezuela.

12.1.1. Socio-Economic Disparities and Well-Being

Culture is affected by the ecological environment, but at the same time culture also changes the environment in ways that affect both physical and mental health. Population increases in developing nations have created many challenges to ensure adequate nutrition for people and affects infant survival rates. The population of the world is increasing, especially in developing countries, stressing the world's resources, economic relations between rich and poor countries, and ultimately socio-economic stability. One reason for the larger fertility rate in developing nations is the inability of these societies to provide social security for people reaching old age, and the need of parents to have children provide essential psychological and material support. Cultural values play an important role as women who are socialized with traditional gender values tend to have larger families perpetuating the limited social roles of females in traditional cultures.

Population increases are not benign as they typically are also related to industrialization of society, larger cities and socioeconomic disparity between rich and poor. In terms of physical health the stress caused by industrialization produce hypertension and many associated illnesses including heart disease. Whether the result of industrialization is positive or negative appear directly related to wealth disparity. Where there is a relative equitable distribution of wealth and health related resources the outcome is better overall health and increased longevity of the population (Wilkinson,

1996). The key to better health is not the overall wealth of a nation, but the degree to which the wealth is distributed in egalitarian ways. For example, in the U.S. mortality rates vary directly between the states as a function of the inequality of income (Kaplan, Pamuk, Lynch, Cohen, & Balfour, 1996). The resource injustice is also present between nations varying in wealth, and the differences in health related expenditures differ widely between countries with the people needing services the most getting the least help (Aboud, 1998).

The economically disadvantaged whether within or between countries suffer more malnutrition. A major concern is the relationship between malnutrition and psychological functioning (Aboud, 1998). This is an issue of catastrophic impact and likely to get worse with a growing world population. Malnutrition that has very negative consequences on physical and psychological development and in developing countries a full 46 percent of the children suffer from inadequate nutrition (UNICEF, 1996). The causes for malnutrition are complex involving cultural practice, limitations of the environment, and economic and social organization. Nevertheless there is sufficient food in the world as a whole if political will and organization would permit nutrition to reach those that suffer (Barba, Guthrie, & Guthrie, 1982).

Psychologically the greatest impact of malnutrition is on cognitive development especially as the earliest years are of greatest significance for intellectual development (Engle, Black, Behrman, Cabral de Mello, Gertler, Kapirini, Martrell, & Eming Young 2007; Waber, Vuori-Christiansen, Ortiz, Clement, Christiansen, Mora, Reed, & Herrera, 1981). Children suffer a severe decline in intellectual functioning of about 10 IQ points when they need hospitalization to recover from malnutrition or suffer malnutrition that persist over a period of months in the first two years of life (Gorman, 1995). There is some evidence that even milder forms of malnutrition may affect intelligence and increase infant mortality (Bedi, 1987; Pelto, Dickin, & Engle, 1999). Not having sufficient nutrition also causes passivity in children and removes the normal intellectual stimulation that children experience through exploration activities when well nourished. Typically, malnutrition does not occur in isolation, but is present in conjunction with other adverse environmental conditions including exposure to disease, unhygienic surroundings, and substandard housing. These are the negative health-related effects of unjust economic distribution both within and also between cultures. Traditional cultures with many adverse environmental conditions and where resources are inadequate produce additional population stress by the presence of large families. It is clear that the adverse effects of malnutrition goes far beyond mere intellectual functioning as it may, for example, contribute to an acceptance of the status quo in people who lack the individual and social energy to work for change. Given the critical period of early childhood the general rule is that earlier nutrition intervention is better in the child's life. International intervention includes emergency food, but also teaching the skills that optimizes child development to the community (Pelto, Dickin, & Engle, 1999).

12.1.2. Mental Health Among Ethnic Minorities: Injustice in the United States.

Cultural genocide by European invaders produced poverty and discrimination as the outcome for Native Americans. The disruptions of the traditional economic lives of Native Americans and their forced resettlement into socio-economically dysfunctional reservations created stress, poverty and alcoholism. Compared to other ethnic groups Native Americans suffer the highest level of anxiety-based disorders (Smith, Stinson, & Dawson, 2006). The marginalization of Native American communities has translated into fundamental mental health disorders including depression (Nelson, McCoy, Stetter, & Vanderwagen, 1992). The social and economic base for a healthy life is missing from many Native American communities and that in turn produces mental ill health and destroys hope for the future (Organista, Organista, & Kurasaki, 2003).

Another group suffering from historical discrimination and cultural genocide are the African Americans brought to the U.S. as slaves centuries ago. The humiliating slave tradition and subsequent discrimination still affects Blacks psychologically with the principal socio-economic heritage of poverty and social dysfunction. Research has shown that mental disorders are significantly higher among African Americans compared to European Americans (Regier, Farmer, Rae, Myers, Kramer, Robins, George, Karno, & Locke, 1993). Again these results appear the direct outcome of poverty, inadequate physical and mental health services, and an economy that channels many young Black people into crime as the only utilitarian way to escape economic deprivation. The socio-economic disparities between European and African Americans are so high that rate differences in mental disorder cannot be unrelated. For example, when socio-economic differences are controlled in research, the mental health differences between the two groups largely disappear with African Americans suffering similar rates as whites in mental disorder. However, these socioeconomic disparities remain today and African Americans suffer disproportionately much higher rates of Schizophrenia, depression, and anti-social personality disorders (McCracken, Matthews, Tang, & Cuba, 2001). Other studies also report higher rate of bipolar disorders among African Americans (Smith et al., 2006).

Latin Americans are the fastest growing ethnic group in the U.S.. A very large base of social and cultural support exists for individuals suffering stressful events in that sub-culture. Members of some Latin groups integrate very readily into the broader society and do not suffer socio-economic deprivations. However, between Latin groups there are significant differences in health-related rates that can be attributed to varying socio-economic status, experience with discrimination from the broader community, and the cultural support available (Guarnaccia, Martinez, & Acosta, 2005). For example, to undermine Cuban society and encourage defections, the United States have treated Cuban immigrants preferentially with immediate socio-economic support and permanent residence, while discriminating against more needy groups like migrants arriving from Haiti. Cubans as a group have a relatively high socio-economic status and are less likely to report symptoms of mental disorder.

Likewise while Asian Americans have typically a strong cultural base there are significant differences between different ethnic Asian groups in socio-economic status and mental disorders. The Asian immigrant groups that suffer most from socio-economic disparities also report the higher rates of mental health related symptoms. Those living with poor socio-economic circumstances and/or have refugee status have higher rates of mental disorder (Uehara, Takeuchi, & Smukler, 1994). We can conclude that the differences in mental health between European Americans and other ethnic groups in the U.S. can primarily be attributed to unfavorable socio-economic circumstances among the minorities.

12.1.3. Migrants, Refugees and Stress: Mental Health Outcomes

We live in the times of globalization and people are moving legally and illegally in large numbers to new cultural societies. The adaptation to a new culture is stressful and creates mental health problems for many immigrants as they seek to adapt to new languages and cultural ways different from their former communities (Sam, 2000). The effect of migration on mental health is complex as some immigrant groups rate better in overall mental health than even the host population whereas members of other groups fare poorly by comparison (Berry, Phinney, Sam, & Vedder, 2006). It is thought that migrants with better mental health probably had stronger support from local ethnic communities and family structures. Further, to have the personal courage to immigrate to a foreign land takes to start with a robust personality and healthy ego. A critical factor in mental health is how well the immigrant adapts to the host culture. Immigrants who find it difficult to accept new ways are more likely to report mental disorder, than individuals who adapt well (Eschbach, Ostir, Patel, Markides, & Goodwin, 2004). Another factor is the disparity between the original culture and the new host society. The more divergent the two cultures the greater the challenge for adaptation and the greater the stress experienced by the migrant.

Because we live during times of bitter conflict there are also many refugees from violence seeking new homes abroad. Many of these refuges have experienced very traumatic conditions linked to their flights from the homeland that predisposes them to a variety of enduring mental disorders (Bhui, Craig, Mohamud, Warfa, Stansfeld, Thornicroft, Curtis, & McCrone, 2006; Marshall, Schell, Elliott, Berthold, & Chun, 2005). Of great importance to well-being is the network of support in the new host society. Refugees are faced with significant stress in starting life over, for example, by the need to build a home and otherwise live a meaningful life. Many refugees had standing and status in the old society, but arrive without a meaningful social role in the land of refuge. Problems of adaptation produce additional stress reactions that compound the original trauma and contribute to psychological disorders. However, when the refugees have the support of their ethnic group these symptoms are ameliorated and a better outcome can be expected.

12.2. THE ROLE OF CULTURE

Culture plays a major role in mental health in how behavioral symptoms are manifested, in the way mental disorders are communicated, and even whether patients will seek assistance (Eshun & Gurung, 2009). Ethnic groups experience varying stress living in a multicultural world and that in turn affects the rate of mental illness. Culture is often mediated through integrated ideologies including religion and beliefs in the supernatural world. A balanced perspective about mental illness supports the role of culture in having a moderate effect on mental health and outcomes (Draguns, 1997). In the therapeutic relationship culture plays a role in both directions as cultural values affect judgments of both patient and therapist. In fact mental health differs across cultural groups for a variety of reasons that include varying stress and cultural values. In addition diagnostic differences are created by unique cultural understandings that affect the rates of reported illness across cultures (Gurung, 2010).

Culture determines how symptoms develop and the level of psychological support for the patient faced with the challenges of mental illness. Patients carry cultural interpretations of the nature of illness and how, when and by whom treatment should be sought. The cultural understanding that mental illness is the just punishment of god may delay treatment and produce a self-fulfilling prophecy of chronic ill mental health. Culture may impact not only the conceptualization of the illness but whether treatment will be sought from scientific or superstitious sources. Mental illness that reflects broader social obsessions can also be promoted by culture. For example, eating disorders are primarily found in wealthy Western countries obsessed with thinness, whereas in food poor countries people are just happy to fill their stomachs. With globalization these obsessions may be increasing in the developing world.

Culture is a factor in the administration and providing of medical services. The Western scientific medical approach while complex is well understood. It is a model based on collection of evidence and medical experts provide treatment according to what is known about the illness. Progress for a variety of serious illnesses can be reported as with treatment based on the scientific model and the use of technology experts understand more about causes and efficacious treatments. Although many illnesses are still not understood researchers have made remarkable progress in some medical fields. However, poverty condemns entire generations when diseases like river blindness or malaria in Africa could be eliminated with preventive efforts.

Modern Western style health care is often supplemented by religion and superstition in the developing countries. These superstitious practices have no medical benefit other than that produced by placebo effects (Prasadaro, 2009). However, healing approaches like traditional Chinese medicine continue to have followers although based on ideas that are unverifiable like the presence of the bodily forces of the yin and yang. Practitioners of Chinese medicine argue that these opposing body forces must be in balance to create optimal health, and that this goal can be accomplished through diet and various plant and animal parts used in medicine. The importance of understanding culturally based health approaches is emphasized by the number of people who believe in their usefulness. Millions of Indians still believe in Ayurveda, a holistic form of medicine in which the use of herbs and plants play a major role. Some of these plants may in fact have an actual medical benefit probably found as a result of trial an error over centuries (Ding & Staudinger, 2005).

Superstitious beliefs continue to influence health decisions among many cultures including among the Native Americans who seek health care through purification rites in sweat lodges, the utilization of voodoo religion among the Caribbean people, and in health practices among Mexican-Americans and Latin people. Some superstitious belief-based treatments go beyond strictly medical issues and try to also deal with psychological and social issues that contribute the health or illness (Trotter & Chavira 1997). These folk remedies became popular over centuries as part an attempt to control health outcomes in the vast sea of what was unknown about disease. That some approaches might by trial and error produce useful medicine is not surprising, although the superstitions beliefs associated with these practices may also delay appropriate scientific medical treatment (Gurung, 2010).

12.2.1. Cultural Health Beliefs

Beliefs about the etiology of illness vary across cultures and therefore also the treatment offered. For example, Chinese and Indian patients have beliefs that mental illness is caused by psychosocial forces and they therefore prefer treatments based on psychosocial practices. By contrast in the West the focus is on the individual patient consistent with cultural values. Cultural health beliefs among members of ethnic groups continue even after migration to countries that provide Western scientific medicine (Cook, 1994). In some parts of India fate or cosmic influence are believed responsible for illness. Such superstitious cultural health beliefs largely determine what people think can be done to cure or mitigate the impact on health (Dalal, 2000; Dalal & Pande, 1999). Studies in Ethiopia (Mulatu, 2000) showed that some people believed that the cause for mental illness was supernatural spirit possession. These cultural thoughts have an obvious negative impact on the patient's beliefs about their ability to control illness. Helplessness derived from cultural health beliefs make it difficult for the patient to recover from mental illness (Thoresen, 1999).

The effect of cultural beliefs about health can be observed in a study in India (Berry, Dalal, & Pande, 1994). The villagers in the study believed that a mother should eat little food to allow room for the fetus to grow. Such faulty beliefs about nutrition resulted in fetal malnutrition and many subsequent illnesses in the undernourished infants. Responsibility for health care are also to some degree based on cultural beliefs and associated ideologies. In the U.S. it is commonly believed that people should look after themselves as is typical in individualistic cultures. In Cuba, on the other hand, a public health system looks after all patients and is not based on the ability to pay. Clearly socio-economic status in individualistic societies is the primary factor as to whether a person has access to necessary treatment (Lynch & Kaplan, 1997).

12.2.2. Problems in Cultural Definitions of Abnormality and Mental Illness

Culture impacts all aspects of mental illness. In some societies patients are reluctant to report psychological distress for reasons of stigma and potential social rejection. Cultural beliefs about mental illness in some cultures in Africa and China encourage patients to report *physical symptoms* rather than mental distress. On the other hand, in individualistic cultures patients convey more *psychological distress* consistent with cultural values (Kleinman, 1988). These differences in symptom reports have led cultural psychologists to believe that we can only understand abnormal behavior within the cultural context. Talking to spirits may be considered a hallucination in Western societies, but be considered normal for people in Eskimo tribes taking part in shamanistic ceremonies. In the U.S. there are certain Christian religions that practice "speaking in tongues" (glossolalia) that would be considered a clinical sign of delusionary beliefs or psychotic delusions, while totally normal within the religious group. To some extent what is normal or abnormal always has a cultural reference point (Marsella, 1980).

To identify the abnormal by statistical means as rare forms of behavior overlooks the obvious, that unique forms of behavior in one culture may in fact be common in others. More useful is a definition of abnormal behaviors as syndromes of activity and thinking that prevent effective functioning in the family or community. Serious psychotic illness is typically associated with an inability to function in relationships and in turn lead to other dysfunctional behaviors like homelessness. Some writers have defined abnormal behavior as being contrary to the social norms of society. However, that begs the question of what if society is "abnormal" or dysfunctional as in the case of Nazi Germany or the Khemer Rouge in Cambodia. Those who resisted these regimes were abnormally few in numbers, but must be considered human heroes of enormous ego strength and mental health.

Abnormal behavior also cannot be limited to what might be considered eccentric or unusual behaviors, but rather are normal reactions to stress and trauma. Today most textbooks provide categories of mental disorders that are commonly accepted although with cultural modifications (Sarason & Sarason, 1999). The main issues in the classification of psychopathology in cross-cultural psychology is whether the phenomenon is *universally present* in all cultures, (but variable as to the rate of illness and manifestation of symptoms) or *unique* to a specific culture. Ethnopsychiatric specialists argue that some disorders are unique to specific societies and therefore can only be understood within the context of that culture (Tseng, 2001).

The Diagnostic and Statistical Manual of Mental Disorders (DSMIV) is broadly used to identify categories of mental illness in the U.S. and in other parts of the world. A mental disorder according to the manual refers to behavioral or psychological syndromes that are clinically significant in impacting *feelings of distress* or that *impair functioning* in other significant ways. A patient may suffer pain, disability and the freedom to live as an active member of society a result of a valid mental disorder (Mirin, 2002). The DSMIV diagnostic system utilizes five domains where the first describes clinical symptoms, the second personality disorders, the third examines current medical issues relevant to the mental disorder, the fourth the psychosocial and environmental problems affecting mental disorder, and the fourth the clinician's report of the overall functioning of the patient

In the DSMIV the American Psychiatric Association defined mental illness in very comprehensive term. Mental impairment can occur from organic causes where brain functions are impaired as in the case of dementia, in Parkinson or in Alzheimer diseases. Some mental disorders like schizophrenia in its several forms are also thought to have strong organic components. Psychotic behavior can also be produced by drug use, abuse of alcohol, by excessive use of certain sedatives, and abuse of cocaine and hallucinogen inducing drugs. The DSMIV also describes affective disorders characterized by extreme swings of mood in manic and depressive phases of bipolar patients. Neurotic patients suffer from a variety of anxieties including phobias about objects that pose no actual threat, or when the patient attempt to control life through obsessive behavior, in hypochondria where the patient obsessively worries about health, and in extreme cases in anxiety producing disassociation through multiple personalities.

Other disorders also covered in the DSMIV refer to the consequences of physiological dysfunction and discusses anorexia and bulimia, insomnia and sexual dysfunction. Personality disorders refer to patients who exhibit sociopathic behavior manifested in obsessive gambling or criminal behavior, the tendency to impulsiveness, and sexual preferences for voyeurism or pedophilia. The DSMIV also covers criteria of the mentally challenged, developmental disorders like autism, and disorders derived from childhood dysfunction.

12.3. PSYCHOPATHOLOGY AS UNIVERSAL OR RELATIVIST

Culture has the potential of affecting the course and prognosis of mental disorder in several ways. The personal distress felt by a patient is largely mediated by the cultural context. For example, cultural beliefs determine how distress is experienced. In one cultural context a psychotic patient may believe he is possessed by harmful spirits, in a different cultural situation the patient accept the cause of distress as an outcome of brain dysfunctions or issues of stress. Culturally limited diagnoses determine how and by whom the symptoms of the disorder is treated whether by appeals to miraculous prayer or in a mental hospital. If mental disorder is believed to be the result of harmful spirits then "healing" can occur when the shaman succeed in driving the spirits out. However, from a Western scientific perspective such "healing" may just be temporary if the real substantial issues causing distress are not part of the treatment objectives (Castillo, 1997). Consequently, in mental illness the issue of whether the etiology is culturally specific or universally prevalent must be evaluated.

The *cultural specific* position argues that psychopathology is not manifested the same way in different cultures. From this point of view the norms of each society determine how behavior is moderated and the views about mental illness developed in one society are not applicable to other cultural groups. Culture determines what behavior is defined as abnormal since as we noted unusual behavior in one society may be common in another. In addition to differences in definitions of abnormal behavior varying cultures may produce different rates of mental disorder depending on the specific ecological environment and stress found in certain societies but not in other social groups, and from diagnostic identification that may vary with cultural values. Cultural values frame the expression of abnormality leading to a consideration of culture bound symptoms of mental illness. As noted above the belief in spirit possession is common in some societies and schizophrenia and psychotic behavior in general may be attributed to such supernatural forces in these cultural groups. The cultural specific perspective argues that using the common medical model developed in Western science is ethnocentric and forces the psychological reality of cultural majorities on minorities. The power disparity in society and more broadly between countries in the world ensure that it is the values of cultural majorities that will find acceptance (Lewis-Fernandez & Kleinman, 1994). To decide on the relative importance of the cultural specific or *universal etiology* of mental disorder require cross-culturally valid and reliable ways of measuring and diagnosing mental illness as otherwise comparative studies would have no merit.

Culturally specific researchers and clinicians would maintain that culture and abnormal behavior are totally interdependent and that mental disorder can therefore only be understood within particular cultural frameworks. Other researchers with universal perspectives would argue that there are many similarities in the manifestation of the symptoms of mental illness between cultures, and these cross-cultural similarities should be taken as support for the universality of diagnostic categories (Draguns, 1997). The universal viewpoint argues that psychopathology is largely the same both in etiology and in expression. Many mental disorders appear to have identical symptoms regardless of the culture including schizophrenia, mental retardation and autism. Even the symptoms of postpartum depression in Japan and the U.S. are similar despite distinctive differences in culture (Shimizi & Kaplan, 1987). As we have noted elsewhere in the book the truth about the cause of human behavior including mental illness is found in inclusion of both the cultural and cross-cultural perspectives and not by accepting one viewpoint as opposed to the other.

12.4. CULTURALLY SPECIFIC AND UNIVERSAL FACTORS IN MENTAL HEALTH

Substance disorders are strongly implicated in mental illness including the abuse of alcohol and illegal drugs ubiquitous in nearly all societies. Some societies have had no historical experience with alcohol including some American Indians tribes and the Aborigines of Australia, and do not metabolize alcohol in the same way as people of European descent leading to early alcohol dependence, especially when associated with desperate socio-economic circumstances (Baxter, Hinson, Wall, & McKee, 1998).

The DSMIV recognizes a number of mental illness syndromes as culturally specific patterns of aberrant behavior not connected to existing diagnostic categories in the DSMIV that we discussed above. These syndromes appear only in distinct cultures and those societies that are related culturally or geographically supporting the cultural context as a determinant of mental disorder. The symptoms of some culturally framed mental disorders do not appear to have an organic cause, but are nevertheless recognized as an aberration by a specific cultural society. Although a given mental disorder may in some cases appear to be related to a diagnostic category in the DSMIV the cultural context create local features. In some cases the disorder may lack distinct symptoms associated with the illness in the West. A culturally specific mental illness may not be recognized in DSMIV such as Kuru disorder in New Guinea, a progressive psychosis thought to be the result of protein malfunction. Some illnesses may occur in several cultural settings, but are only recognized as disorders in some cultural contexts and not in other situations. Aberrant behavior is linked in some traditional societies to superstitious beliefs in witchcraft or being in a state of trance brought on by spirit possession. These behaviors and beliefs would be taken as evidence of psychoses in Western medicine. Some mental disorders appear to be just local cultural varieties of the more common diagnostic syndromes found in the West. Nevertheless, the culturally specific interpretation is helpful by bringing culturally related beliefs in religion and superstition to the attention of the clinician and contributes to the understanding of the etiology of mental illness in some societies (Simons & Hughes, 1985).

Culturally specific disorders reflect cultural values in different parts of the world. They include Zar, a common belief in Africa of being in the possession of spirits and a disorder characterized by involuntary movements (Grisaru, Budowski, & Witztum, 1997). Ataque de nervios have been diagnosed in Latin groups and symptoms include extreme emotion manifested by trembling, crying, and shouting (Febo San Miguel, Guarnaccia, Shrout, Lewis-Fernandez, Canino, & Ramirez, 2006). Pfeiffer (1982) suggested that such culturally specific syndromes arise from culturally unique family, social and ecological sources of stress. The specific manifestation of aberrant symptoms develops out of societal expectations that encourage certain ways of responding to stress. Researchers in these areas argue that it is important to understand cultural values and beliefs in determining how to help victims of these disorders.

Anorexia nervosa is an illness diagnosed initially in Western affluent societies. The disorder produces distorted perception of body image so that even very skinny patients see themselves as fat. The fear of becoming fat produces serious and in many cases life-threatening loss of weight as the patient refuses to eat, or in the case of bulimia purges food after eating. The ideal of female beauty has varied across centuries and in different cultures. However, in the last decades the image of the super thin model has been promoted as the ideal for women in the Western world and transported overseas via the media. Since the image is impossible to reach for most women, and is in fact very unhealthy, most women fail to achieve the unreasonable weight loss required to become super thin and some become anorexic. Today along with globalization and the spread of Western models women all over the world are now bombarded with similar pressures to become and stay thin. Anorexia that once was thought culturally specific to Western countries has now been diagnosed in many other urban cultural areas (Gordon, 2001; Tareen, Hodes, & Rangel, 2005).

An overall conclusion of the research results lends support to the presence of universal symptoms in the diagnosis of some mental disorder categories including depression and schizophrenia. There is also evidence for some culturally specific syndromes shaped by cultural values and expectations. Culture and the presence or lack of social support determines the prognosis of a given disorder. Although both culturally specific as well as universal mental health diagnoses are supported in the literature, there is no way to predict the outcome of globalization on mental health. However, with globalization social structures and cultural influences are becoming more *homogenous* all over the world and that may influence how mental illness is viewed in the future (Guarnaccia & Rogler, 1999).

12.4.1. Anxiety Disorders

Many people suffer from anxiety disorders in a variety of cultures. The symptoms of anxiety emphasize feelings and perceptions of danger not necessarily related to any objective threat. A state of constant worry can produce many concomitant physiological consequences. Typically, the anxious individual also complains of fatigue and an inability to concentrate on tasks at hand. Anxiety may be related to impression formation when people desire to convey a favorable image to others. Anxiety can also be culturally context-related and dependent on the ecological and economic context of life, for example, agoraphobia is more prevalent among Africans (Chambless & Williams, 1995). In Western societies many people have anxieties related to economic survival and people who are successful economically are anxious about social accomplishments. Achievement anxieties are well understood from the cultural values of individualistic societies. The anxiety experienced by people everywhere is related to the cultural context. For example, people in collectivistic societies may be more anxious about inclusion in the family, the community and other valued associations. Nevertheless there is also strong evidence in some cases for universally similar anxiety symptoms including those caused by traumatic events (Koopman, 1997).

12.4.2. Regulation of Mood: Depression.

Disorders of mood described as melancholia or depression have been found in the literature for centuries. Significant evidence for the universality of depressive afflictions was found in a large cross-cultural comparative study (Tanaka-Matsumi & Draguns, 1997). The study found the presence of anxiety symptoms in all cultures studied with concomitant reports of lack of energy and dysphoria. However, peripheral symptoms of depression including headaches and bodily weakness were found only in some societies. Differences in the rate of depression diagnoses in a society might be an artifact of cultural stigma, and clinicians in Japan are reported to avoid the diagnostic category to spare the negative evaluations (Neary, 2000). Lack of insight produced by cultural frames may also prevent patients in some cultures from accurately reporting symptoms. For example, Chinese in one study did not recognize depression as being tied to feelings of hopelessness, lack of joy, or loss of self-esteem (Kleinman, 1986). In fact patients in some cultural groups see the reason for their depression distress in physiological symptoms, whereas patients in other societies believe that psychological factors are paramount (Ulusahin, Basoglu, & Paykel, 1994). Cultural values come into play in beliefs about the etiology of depression disorders since a psychological explanation may seem self-centered to patients in China and other collectivistic societies and somatic symptoms are therefore more acceptable (Ying, Lee, Tsai, Yeh, & Huang, 2000).

The psychopathology of depression includes subjective feelings of sadness and generally a lack of enjoyment of life. Physiological concomitants of depression include a lack of energy, loss of appetite and sleep disorders. Depression impacts the self-concept producing low self-esteem and feelings of hopelessness and helplessness that in extreme cases may predispose the patient to suicide. Countries vary widely in the rate of diagnosis of depression (Leff, 1977) with, for example 24 percent diagnosed with the disorder in Great Britain and only 4.7 percent in the U.S. It would appear that the local cultural assumption about depression, and the stress associated with the insecurity in Western individualistic societies and economies drives the diagnosis rates. Other cultures value extended family structures and that help buffer the individual from the effects of environmental stress and disappointments. Individualistic cultures with an atomistic family structure has produced societies where large numbers of adults live alone and the predisposition for depression is greater and the social support less compared to collectivistic societies (Marsella, 1980).

A World health Organization study (2012) projected that depression would be the second leading cause of disability in the world's population. Gender differences in depression are important as twice as many women as men are affected and experience depression independent of other contributing factors. The gender gap is consistently found across different cultures, racial or ethnic identification and even socio-economic differences (Weissman, Bland, Canino, Faravelli, Greenwald, Hwu, Joyce, Karam, Lee, Lellouch, Lepine, Newman, Rubin-Stiper, Wells, Wickramaratne, Wittchen,

& Yeh, 1996). For large a group of people depression becomes a lifelong companion as about 20 percent of women and ten percent of men retain depression symptoms across the lifespan (Weissman & Olfson, 1995).

Cultures affect the expression of symptoms. As noted, Chinese patients with depression are more likely to report somatic symptoms (Kleinman, 2004). On the other hand, patients in Uganda see depression in cognitive terms as a consequence of obsessive thinking rather than feeling sad or melancholic (Okello & Ekblad, 2006). Rates also appear to vary across cultures although different diagnostic procedures and assessments make cross-cultural comparisons difficult and unreliable. Cultural values play a role as depression is seen as primarily emotional in individualistic cultures. However, as we noted a self-focus is less acceptable in collectivistic societies and in these the blame is often placed on physiological problems like headaches (Arnault, Sakamoto, & Moriwaki, 2006; Marsella, Kaplan, & Suarez, 2002). This research on somatization seems incongruent and contradictory with the supposed underlying cultural values since the somatization of symptoms is actually based on Western conceptions of duality of mind and body whereas Eastern philosophy is more holistic (Lee, 2001). Rate variations in depression are also influenced by unique cultural sources of stress like constant war in the Middle East or Africa, or stress in societies that are impacted by economic crisis, or in countries trying to adjust to rapid change from globalization.

Chronic depression causes feelings of hopelessness and predisposes some patients to commit suicide. The practice of suicide is also influenced by cultural values. Japan, a high achievement oriented culture, has the highest suicide rate in the world. In other cultures like Sri Lanka high rate of suicide is linked to hopelessness from ethnic strife and war. Eastern Europe has experienced rapid change from the period of Stalinism that may have contributed to high suicide rates. Cultural values expressed in religion that condemn suicide can contribute to lower rates. In Japan, on the other hand, committing suicide is consistent with personal honor, whereas in religiously dogmatic countries of either Catholic or Islamic persuasion rates are lowered by religious objections of the clergy (Barraclough, 1988).

12.4.3. Schizophrenia

Physiological malfunctions predispose patients to suffer from some mental disorders and to dysfunction in social relationships. Schizophrenia is the most frequently occurring mental illness and has a biological basis. In a large-scale cross-cultural study (WHO, 1979) 77.5 percent of psychiatric patients were diagnosed as having schizophrenia. More recent research in the U.S. found that 1.1 percent of the population suffered from this debilitating illness (Regier, Narrow, Rae, Manderscheid, Locke, & Goodwin, 1993). Schizophrenia is recognized as an organically based mental illness found in all cultures and is the result of biochemical imbalances combined with cultural or family dynamics. In other words, schizophrenia includes a biological predisposition associated with salient environmental stress (Jablensky, Sartorius, Ernberg, Anker, Korten, Cooper, Day, & Bertelsen, 1992).

Schizophrenia is also the most frequently occurring mental disorder cross-culturally characterized by emotional flatness, a lack of insight into the conditions of life, and delusions and hallucinations (most frequently of an auditory nature) and behavioral disorganization. The distortion of reality and withdrawal from social interaction impacts the patient's ability to lead a normal functioning life. Typically, the schizophrenic patient also suffers from cognitive, perceptual and emotional disorganization (Carson, Butcher, & Coleman, 1988). As noted it is now commonly accepted that schizophrenia has an organic basis, although the behavioral manifestations may be culturally determined. Culture can have a direct impact on the rate of schizophrenia in society through the discouragement of families with a history of schizophrenia to have children. There is also evidence that culture may increase the rate of occurrence through the stress experienced by the complexity of information provided to the vulnerable, and by encouraging people to make decisions based on uncertain information (Murphy, 1976).

The impact of culture can be observed in the relatively better prognosis for patients from developing countries as compared to patients in developed and industrialized societies. The cultural values in developing countries reflect collectivistic worldviews that emphasize the mutual support found in interdependent families and cultural groups (Hopper & Wanderling, 2000). Dominant symptoms of the illness may also be influenced by culture. For example, a comparison between Japanese and European American schizophrenics showed that the Japanese were more withdrawn and passive compared to American patients an influence thought to be produced by Japanese cultural values in a hierarchical high power difference society (Sue & Morishima, 1982).

Culture may also impact the diagnostic process. Leff (1977) found that U.S. clinicians gave more diagnoses of schizophrenia and less of depression compared to psychiatrists in England. Within the U.S. cultural impact can also be observed in different rates of schizophrenia diagnosis between ethnic minorities. African American and Hispanics patients were more frequently diagnosed with schizophrenia compared to European Americans (Blow, Zeber, McCarthy, Valenstein, Gillon, & Bingham, 2004). Cultural values cannot be separated from the affect of low socio-economic status among ethnic minorities as Blacks and Hispanics suffered disproportionately from poverty, drug addictions and other stress factors that contribute to schizophrenia. A similarly based result was found for African Caribbean patients in England as compared to the white population (King, Nazroo,

Weich, McKenzie, Bhui, Karlson, Stansfeld, Tyrer, Blanchard, Lloyd, McManus, Sproston, & Erens, 2005).

In evaluating schizophrenia and other mental disorders it is important to remember that beliefs that are considered delusional in one culture are not necessarily so in other comparative cultures. Access to mental hospitals also differ between countries and may explain part of the disparity in diagnostic rates. Gender related values may also affect diagnosis. For example, schizophrenia is diagnosed more commonly in men in the Western world, but these results are reversed in China where for every three men, five women patients are diagnosed. Some have suggested that the stigma associated with the illness is higher for men, therefore leading to reluctance by psychiatrists in China to provide the diagnosis (Phillips, Yang, Li, & Li, 2004).

12.4.4. Attention Deficit Disorder

Psychiatric reports of attention deficit disorder affecting children's behavior have existed for many decades; however, the diagnosis has become more frequent in recent years. Attention deficit disorder is now recognized in many cultures (Biederman & Faraone, 2004; Biederman, Faraone, Wozniak, Mick, Kwon, Cayton, et al., 2005; Faraone, Sergeant, Gillberg, & Biederman, 2003; Livingston, 1999). Children diagnosed with the disorder have difficulty in paying sustained attention to issues or to other people and are easily distracted by new stimuli. Attention deficit children are impulsive and hyperactive and in constant motion interrupting the ongoing activities of others. Since the same diagnostic criteria for attention deficit are not used in all societies it is difficult to assess cultural differences in rates of occurrence from comparative cross-cultural studies. Boys are more frequently diagnosed with attention deficit as compared to girls a finding that is consistent in all societies. The overall diagnostic rates vary from 5.8 percent in Brazil to 14.9 percent in the United Arab Emirates (Rohde, Szobot, Polanczyk, Schmitz, Martins, & Tramontina, 2005; Bu-Haroon, Eapen, & Bener, 1999). However, these comparative rates may not be reliable as they depend on one or a few sources reporting on the behavior of children in the class room. Nevertheless, the rates reported are very high and attention deficit disorder obviously affect many thousands of children around the globe.

The cultural context is seen as the primary mediator for children developing the disorder. Western cultures create conditions that elicit attention deficit disorder with increased complexity and constantly changing stimuli derived from the use of technology and other sources. The globalization of the post-modern society brought this stimulation into societies more tranquil in past history (Timimi, 2004). Families live hyperactive lives in modern Western societies where the focus is constantly changing and the pace of complexity is increasing. Educational institutions impose more and more demands on children's achievements. Today's kids are exposed constantly to high levels of stress caused by meeting increasingly high standards. The reason that the disorder has been diagnosed more frequently in recent years can be attributed to the increasing complexity brought on by rapid social and technological change in recent decades. However, other researchers note that ADHD is found in many different cultures, and think it has an as yet not well understood neurobiological basis. This is an area of research in need of more comparative studies from different parts of the world in the future. The neural pathways that contribute to ADHD will hopefully be better clarified in the years to come. At the same time we need to better understand how the rapid pace and complexity of modern life promote the development of attention deficit in children.

12.4.5. Personality Disorders

Personality traits are reflected in enduring syndromes of behavior and cognitive or emotional experiences. Personality disorders refer to behaviors and psychological experiencing that is markedly different from the standards in a culture. The symptoms of personality disorders appear to be relatively consistent across cultures according to research in cross-cultural psychology. However, diagnosis must still be made within the norms of society, and therefore depend largely on a culture's *tolerance of inappropriate behavior*. Some cultures are very intolerant and punish individuals severely who transgress normative behavior. Collectivistic societies typically have less tolerance for violations of standards and are more likely to punish personality traits that are deviant. In particular behaviors that separate the individual from family and culture like narcissistic traits are unacceptable in collectivistic societies. On the other hand, obsessive-compulsive traits may actually be helpful to adjustment in collectivistic cultures since these traits supports adherence to strict demands for conformity to social rules and regulations. For example, in Japan the culture reinforces adherence to social discipline and the use of formal rules of interaction (Esaki, 2001). Keeping in mind the cultural context such conformity behavior while it appears compulsive is not deviant within Japanese society.

Modern individualistic societies of the West are more tolerant of personality that deviates from cultural standards. In Western societies deviant personality traits are often accepted as the manifestation of the person's unique personality and not a matter for society to be concerned about. However, deviant traits that run counter to Western values of self-regulation (like anti-social personalities) are a concern of Western as well as collectivistic societies. Research supports the idea that personality disorders can be reliably assessed in a variety of cultures (Fountoulakis, Iacovides, Ioannidou, Bascialla, Nimatoudis, Kaprinis, Janca, & Dahl, 2002; Loranger, Sartorius, Andreoli, Berger, Buchheim, Channabasavanna, Coid, Dahl, Diekstra, Ferguson, et al., 1994). In particular support is found for the presence of the antisocial personality in all cultural groups that have been assessed (Robins, Tipp, & Przybeck, 1991), although again culture may produce varying manifestations.

At the same time our cultural schemas serve as cognitive filters in evaluating behaviors. For example, plural wives might be an acceptable and common form of behavior in some traditional cultures while considered dysfunctional and oppressive in others. Expectations for gender related behaviors vary between traditional and modern societies and what is accepted as normal in one cultural setting could be considered abnormal or indicative of personality disorder in another. People all over the world have stereotypes of people from other cultures that deviate from the norms of the observer culture although the validity of these national personality types is not verified. Furthermore, it is important again to emphasize in this context that differences within a cultural group on any personality trait are always greater that differences between cultural societies (Zuckerman, 1990).

12.5. CULTURALLY SENSITIVE ASSESSMENT OF ABNORMAL BEHAVIOR

If culture has an impact on defining normal behavior within the cultural context, cultural values also have a modifying affect as the framework for abnormal behavior. Cultural factors valid in psychotherapy involve the relationship between the patient, the therapist and the cultural context of society. The cultural context must of necessity be understood since it influences both the manifestation of symptoms and how to understand the disorder from the patient's and the therapist's point of view. The recommended treatment is framed by the cultural context (Beardsley & Pedersen, 1997). In Western psychotherapy the healing relationships between therapist and patient have developed out of theoretical orientations prominent in psychology including learning theory, humanistic theory and gestalt approaches. These therapeutic approaches can be considered culturally specific to Western countries, although they may have relevance to other culturally different societies.

The importance of the cultural context of mental disorders requires us to evaluate whether the assessment and tests used in one cultural setting are applicable to another culture. To what extent can we transfer clinical assessment that will produce both reliable and valid measurements of mental disorder? It is clearly important to develop culturally sensitive testing since we have already observed that mental disorders that are universal have a somewhat different expression in various cultures. The Diagnostic and Statistical Manual has gone through a number of revisions since first published in 1952. The current edition takes into account how expressions of disorders might vary by culture. In addition the appendix contains a number of culturally specific syndromes, some of which we have discussed. Further the DSMIV now has guidelines to probe for relevant cultural variables that influence the manifestation of symptoms. In particular the specific factors are stressed that are relevant in the person's cultural context, and differences in the cultural outlook between the patient and the therapist (Kawa & Giordano, 2012).

Still many challenges remain for clinicians to define what is and what is not culturally specific in mental disorders (Paniagua, 2000). In response to the need for culturally specific guidelines Chinese specialists have created a separate Chinese Classification of Mental Disorders that has been influenced by the DSMIV, but nevertheless include issues unique to Chinese cultures, and have also eliminated other disorders in the DSMIV that are thought to be irrelevant like sibling rivalry. Since most Chinese have only one child sibling rivalry is not an issue for most families. In Africa other clinicians have developed guidelines thought more appropriate for dealing with patients in that context (Douki, Moussaoui, & Kacha, 1987). Ultimately culturally sensitive assessments depend on cross-cultural research identifying relevant variables that can provide valid guidelines for the therapist.

12.6. CROSS-CULTURAL ASSESSMENTS OF MENTAL DISORDER

The most extensive research on mental disorder has occurred in the U.S. and Europe and practitioners elsewhere transferred Western assessments of mental disorder for use in their cultures. Mental disorder assessments have been developed over time in Western countries through the use of surveys or interview protocols, or by using relevant structured tasks requiring behavioral responses from the patient. The problems associated with the transfer of psychological test from one culture to another have discussed in this book. In the case of mental disorder assessments cultural variables may affect the specific expressions of distress by the patient and the words used in the original culture may translate poorly into another language. All the usual issues encountered in developing reliable and valid instruments are equally important in the cross-cultural assessments of mental disorder. In particular the comparability of constructs that are clinically measured must be verified. In interviews the differential impact of cultural values on interviewers and client must be understood for valid diagnosis (Draguns, 1997). Since varying definitions exist for disorders like schizophrenia instruments developed in one culture may not assess the unique meanings or expressions in another society.

Sensitivity to cultural values does not mean that clinical instruments cannot be transferred for use in a variety of cultures. However, the transferred assessment should be validated in each new society where it is to be used. The Child Behavior Checklist (Achenbach, 2001) has been used in a number of countries to asses behavioral and mood related problems. Differences in levels of behavior control have been found to exist between children from collectivistic societies compared to children from individualistic cultures (Crijnen, Achenbach, & Verhulst, 1997, 1999; Kornadt & Tachibana, 1999). The cross-cultural use of assessment tools should be based on an understanding of the cultural norms for healthy development as well as the culturally specific criteria of abnormality and disorder. Researchers have suggested the importance of utilizing ideas from indigenous healing practices that might be efficaciously used in particular cultures (Lonner & Ibrahim, 1989).

At the same time the cultural values of the therapist are salient to the perception of healthy and abnormal behavior. For the therapist appropriate behavior in one culture might reflect disturbed behavior in another society as the norms vary. For example, the refusal of a woman to leave her home may be considered entirely normal in a fundamentalist Muslim society, but be seen as a sign of neurotic behavior in Western countries (Li-Repac, 1980). The cultural values of the therapist can produce diagnostic errors, particularly in multi-cultural societies, in the diagnostic process and also in interpretations of assessments. The culture of therapist and client vary frequently in multinational societies and an error in diagnostic judgment is possible unless the therapist is very sensitive to the cultural background of the patient. The best diagnostic and therapeutic results will probably be obtained when both therapist and patient have a common language and cultural value backgrounds.

Success can be reported for the transfer of assessments of psychopathology in a variety of cultures. The MMPI (Minnesota Multiphasic Personality Inventory) has been used successfully in number of cultures using standard scientific procedures of translation and back-translation to asses construct equivalence, and the use of bilingual test and retest procedures. The interpretations obtained cross-culturally were reported as equivalent to those obtained in the U.S. (Butcher, Lim, & Nezami, 1998). It has been argued that the equivalent results reported verify the *universal structure of personality* discussed previously, however, personality deviations can also be observed reflecting cultural variables. It seems again that the best solution in psychological assessment is a combination of universal testing procedures combined with measures that are culturally sensitive.

12.7. ABNORMAL BEHAVIOR AND PSYCHOTHERAPY FROM CULTURAL PERSPECTIVES

The guiding values of psychology are found in the therapeutic helping relationship and the search for scientific truth. We have observed in this chapter the importance of culture in defining what is normal and abnormal and the need for culturally sensitive approaches to assessment of mental disorder. Psychotherapy for mental illness emerged also out of Western psychologies, but can these treatment approaches be applied and be useful in other cultures? Can we incorporate cultural understandings in developing therapies that are empirically validated (Sue & Sue, 2008; Tanaka-Matsumi, 2008)? Empirically supported psychological interventions that are culturally sound have increased as another consequence of globalization (Bernal, Jimenez-Chafey, & Rodriquez, 2009). The confrontation of divergent cultural values is ubiquitous in the world. This fluid situation requires not only greater cultural sensitivity in the helping relationship, but also more training in developing culturally competent therapies and therapists (Marsella, 2009).

Many cultural groups live within the U.S., however, the Latinos is the largest ethnic minority, and among these Mexican-Americans constitute about 64 % (United States Census Bureau, 2009). Mexican American children are exposed to many social stressors that are reflected in mental ill health including high rates of depression. Not surprisingly drug use and suicide rates are also comparatively high among Mexican Americans (Grunbaum, Kann, Kinchen, Ross, Hawkins, Lowry, Harris, McManus, Chyen, & Collins, 2004). Collectively the statistics point to a significant need for more mental health resources and facilities for the Mexican American community. However, despite the greater need Mexican-American patients are more likely to receive poor quality care and less likely to participate in evidence based treatment and programs (Villalba, 2007). The negative mental health outcomes for this ethnic group suggest that "one standard fits all" mental health treatment is not supported by cross-cultural research and that accepted practices offering evidence based care may require culture specific changes to be ultimately effective with this minority group (Hall, 2001).

The unique cultural values of Mexican-Americans encourage a culturally sensitive approach to treatment. The social norms of the community place a high value on the family, is more hierarchical compared to other American ethnic groups, tend to be more traditional in the relationships between the genders and is more collectivistic (Rogler & Cooney, 1984; Shapiro & Simonsen, 1994). Further, the Mexican-American culture places great value on personal relationships that in turn motivate individuals with mental disorders to seek out family members for advice (Parra-Cardona, Cordova, Holtrop, Villarruel, & Wieling, 2008). Consequently, fewer Mexican Americans seek professional assistance for mental problems. When evaluating the reasons for mental illness, Mexican-Americans are less likely to believe in the causes described Western diagnostic categories, but look to forms of folk medicine for answers (Yeh, McCabe, Hough, Lau, Fakhry, & Garland, 2005). Mexican cultural values create syndromes of mental illness that validate *psychosomatic problems* as more central to complaints and unique diagnoses not be linked to other commonly accepted diagnostic categories (Pina & Silverman, 2004).

Globalization has produced new possibilities for delivering therapeutic services across borders and cultural boundaries. Psychotherapeutic systems are multiplying and validated in varying cultural contexts (La Roche & Christopher, 2008; Nathan & Gorman, 2006). Most psychotherapeutic treatments being offered today are based on cognitive behavioral traditions that emerged in the 1960s in Western clinical psychology (e.g. Ellis, 1962). Cognitive therapies seek to help the patient evaluate the rationality of beliefs, however that is an approach not particularly helpful if the beliefs systems of culture are irrational. On the other hand, cognitive-behavioral interventions seek to teach cognitive skills. The main emphasis in cognitive-behavioral strategies is to motivate the patient to change his/her thinking so he/she can modify his/her behavior, and the reverse is also possible when behavior is changed it can alter dysfunctional thinking processes (Hollon & Beck, 1994). As a result of globalization and information transfer new international therapeutic organizations have emerged with a transcultural reach like the World Congress of Behavioral and Cognitive Therapy. The use of these therapies is found now in the formerly very divergent cultures in Asia as well as all over Europe and North America (Qian & Wang, 2005).

Some researchers have suggested that there is still a great need for developing more *culturally sensitive psychotherapies*, particularly at local levels (Snowden & Yamada, 2005). The presence of culturally competent therapists appears to be a precondition for successful outcomes of psychotherapy in many ethnic and cultural groups. In particular a therapist needs to respect the cultural values of the client and be able to overcome biases from his or her own perspectives in the process of evaluating mental disorder since any form of therapy or counseling occur within the context of cultural values (Gerstein, Heppner, Stockton, Leung, & Aegisdottir, 2009).

Treatment is adapted to each culture in a process that takes into account the patient's cultural meanings. Culturally sensitive approaches would identify what is maladaptive and appropriate behavior within the cultural context, people traditionally provides assistance for mental disorder, and the client's expectations for outcomes (Van de Vijver & Tanaka-Matsumi, 2008). A meta-analysis of the literature (Griner & Smith, 2006) showed that cultural adaptation of psychotherapy benefitted the client regardless of which treatment approach was used. Cultural sensitivity appears to be an essential consideration in order to produce positive outcomes for the patient.

12.7.1. The Cultural Framework Matters in Psychotherapy

Psychotherapy grew out of Western intellectual traditions that began with the psychoanalytic treatment offered by Freud and his followers. The cultural background from which his theories grew limited the usefulness of psychoanalysis in other cultures. Freud's practice and subsequent thinking derived from his patients who were largely middle class Jewish neurotic women living in Vienna at the turn of the 20th century. While some aspects of psychoanalysis may indeed prove universally useful, theories based on such a limited cultural sample created problems when applying the concepts of psychoanalysis within other European cultural groups, and even more issues in transferring the therapy to the rest of the world. Since abnormality is framed within cultural values, treatment is linked to the therapist's knowledge and application of cultural understandings in treatment (Langman, 1997).

Freud's theory of personality and psychoanalytic treatment approach may have been entirely appropriate within the cultural framework of the middle class Jewish community in Vienna in the early part of last century, but not easily transferable to other cultures where distress is not considered a matter of internal dynamics. Some cultures believe that psychological distress is the result of *somatic problems* or in other cases is attributed to *living out of harmony* with nature or because the patient believes he/she is being possessed by *evil spirits*. Although many of these assumptions are superstitious, nevertheless the client's behavior is based on these beliefs that are rooted deeply in a cultural worldview. However, it seems to the rational mind that perpetuating superstition by the therapist lend the beliefs an air of authenticity. At the same time stress in the patient may increase if a therapist familiar with the cultural perspective begins treatment by attacking the veracity of the superstitions beliefs.

In collectivistic cultures the focus is on *relationships with others* whereas in psychoanalysis the focus is on *treating the individual*. A focus on the self in collectivistic societies could be considered abnormal, and obsessing about the self dysfunctional within interdependent societies. However, some aspects of all therapeutic approaches have value and are transferable within a framework of cultural sensitivity. Does that mean that therapists must buy into superstitions and irrationality of the local culture? That is an open question since therapy is about adjustment and getting along in society. However, if getting along means therapy that encourages conformity to irrational beliefs that present an ethical problem for Western trained therapists. Nevertheless, many patients are not able to confront the larger existential issues of irrational religious beliefs (Azhar & Varma, 1996). Cultural values suggest that group therapy that includes mixed genders would be a nonstarter in tradition-bound societies like Saudi Arabia.

Therapeutic approaches today are guided by a commitment to cultural awareness and recognition of the importance of multicultural sensitivity and cultural values in clinical work (Trull & Prinstein, 2013). These clinical principles were developed in response to an increasingly diverse population in many countries. The development of cultural competence is seen as essential to be an effective therapist. In turn that goal requires an avoidance of stereotyping while appreciating cultural diversity.

12.7.2. Homogeneity of Patient and Therapist

Successful outcome in helping relationships is based on cultural under-standings by the therapist. The role of the therapist is to interact with the client in a process of negotiation where the client is encouraged to outline the distressing problem or issue, the therapist seeks to explain the model of therapy to the patient, and the two components are then compared and translated into mutually acceptable definitions and plan of therapy (Klein-man, 1980). Successful outcomes therefore depends on the degree to which there is effective communication between the two parties based on *mutually shared cultural meanings* of the distress experienced by the patient (Frank & Frank, 1991). In a broader sense developing culturally effective services depend on understanding the patient's cultural history and tradi-tions as well as the important cultural value systems that support behavior.

In the therapeutic relationship the cultural values of both the patient and therapist matter. Cultural values have an impact on the diagnostic pro-cess and on subsequent treatment. It is generally accepted that matching the cultural backgrounds of patients with mental health providers is help-ful (Tanaka-Matsumi & Draguns, 1997; Tanaka-Matsumi & Higginbotham, 1989, 1994). The approach to treatment should make a good fit to the cultural perspective of the client in order to achieve maximum effective-ness (Sue & Sue, 2003). Similarity between client and therapist on relevant variables are important including *matching cultural background and ethnicity*. While ethnic similarity is less important effectiveness depends greatly on the similarities of cultural perspectives between therapist and client. Re-search shows that when a client identifies strongly with a culture the pa-tient prefers similarity with the therapist in ethnic backgrounds. In some cases there is also a preference for similarity of gender as clients may think this creates a basis for mutual understanding (Ponterotto, Alexander, & Hinkston, 1988). However, in a meta-analysis ethnic matching did not ap-pear important compared to similarity of cultural perspectives and values (Shin, Chow, Camacho-Gonsalves, Levy, Allen, & Leff, 2005).

12.7.3. Approaches Based in Indigenous Forms of Treatment

The activity of people in the course of daily living form the basis for un-derstanding the cultural factors that is important to psychological function-ing. That assertion in turn requires an understanding of *indigenous culture* for successful intervention. Indigenous psychology is usually thought of in opposition to and as a rejection of Western psychology as the dominating force in psychological theory. However, Western psychology can also be thought of as an indigenous approach within the cultural norms of Europe and North America. Researchers working within the indigenous field of psychology seek to develop theory and treatments that reflect the social and cultural realities of the local cultural group (Sinha, 1997). Western psychology when imported to India underwent adaptation to local needs. Sinha believed that the ultimate goal of psychology is to develop a universal theory, but that indigenous theories must be considered important inputs toward that final goal. For example, to understand Mexican culture it is essential to understand the values of machismo, the respect demanded and the male role in protecting women (Diaz-Guerrero, 1990).

Western psychology has been severely criticized (Enriquez, 1990) because its values are thought to perpetuate the dominance of colonial exploitation. Since Western psychology was developed in industrialized countries it is thought by indigenous psychologists to have limited value elsewhere. Over time efforts have been made to draw together research findings appropriate for different regions like Asia (Adair, Pandey, Begum, Puhan, & Vohra, 1995; Adair, Puhan, & Vohra, 1993; Azuma, 1984; Ho, 1998), Africa (Nsamenang, 1995) or Latin America (Diaz-Guerrero, 1984, 1975, 1977, 1984, 1990). On the other hand, indigenous psychology has also been criticized as a form of infinite regression to ever more local standards in establishing psychological principles. Further, it has been argued that indigenous psychology is oversensitive to differences between people and cultures, but don't pay enough attention to the *obvious similarities* between people all over the world who face many similar trials and developmental tasks in human development.

Indigenous treatment utilizing therapeutic beliefs dominant within a culture must be considered an intuitive art rather than a science. In contrast to modern Western approaches rooted in empirically verified treatment and scientific practices, indigenous treatments are often derived from religion and cultural conceptions of spirituality. In traditional societies there is a greater reliance on family as a source for help in distress and in the hope that are believed to come from the healing power of religion. There are also religious groups in the West that have similar beliefs, even to the exclusion of medical assistance, and seek to heal by prayer and consequently allow their children to die rather than permit medical intervention. Nevertheless such beliefs are contrary to rationality although people who believe deeply do not easily lose their grip on superstitious hopes (Yeh, Hunter, Madan-Bahel, Chiang, & Arora, 2004).

Yeh et al describe stress reduction techniques in Japanese culture that seeks to promote balance and relaxation in the practice of Reiki. Many indigenous treatment approaches promote health by a *holistic understanding* of distress that perceives the emotional and mental components of the person as totally interdependent. Indigenous approaches in varying cultures have in common an effort to encourage healing powers that already exist within the person, since distress is believed to have emerged from disharmony between the person and the sociocultural or natural environment.

12.7.4. Adding the Biomedical Model to Indigenous Beliefs

The idea of utilizing culturally sensitive therapeutic approaches is to help the patient from a framework that the distressed person can understand. Although Western treatment modified with a cultural emphasis has not produced an extensive literature, most approaches that combine Western and indigenous treatments provide the patient with some form of spiritual counseling. However, little is known about the success of these blended services. In collectivistic societies where interdependence in relationships is significant and salient, it seems logical that individual therapy be combined with outreach to family and community. The efficacy of community based forms of treatment for emotional illness is supported by research (Miller & Rasco, 2004). A first step is the identification of health resources within the community that promote healing and adaptation. Most importantly community based solutions seek to mobilize other members of the cultural group to provide optimal solutions to stress and emotional disorder.

Community based interventions have proven useful in the treatment of mental health issues among refuges, immigrants or ethnic minorities who do not seek help within available medical structures. In Australia medical services were underutilized by Aborigines who felt unwelcome and anxious when seeking social assistance and counseling from medical facilities in the dominant society (Larsen, 1977, 1978a, 1981). One solution was to create a *program of training of Aboriginal social workers* within the structure of the Aboriginal and Islander Medical Center in Townsville, Northern Australia. The training program was offered to a group of young practitioners that successfully combined aspects of Western psychology and treatment approaches and these services were turn offered in a location administered by the indigenous population (Larsen, 1978a,b, 1979a,b, 1980). The aforementioned program of training could be used as a model in other cultural settings since it blends Western approaches with cultural sensitivity.

Later studies have shown the validity of incorporating cultural sensitivity in delivering medical and mental health care to divergent cultures and ethnic minorities. For example, a five year study of Asian American adolescents found that mental health services targeting ethnic minorities were more likely to achieve success. These findings have also found support in the experiences of other ethnic communities in the U.S., and the results show that targeting ethnic groups encouraged more patients to seek services (Takeuchi, Sue, & Yeh, 1995). The reason that ethnic specific services are more successful than mainstream approaches is rooted in the cultural differences between these groups and the majority society. Since different attributions for mental illness is common among ethnic groups cultural sensitivity is essential to any treatment approach. As noted earlier in some ethnic groups the beliefs that physiological factors are responsible for disorder dominate thinking, whereas patients in other ethnic groups are motivated to suppress thoughts related to psychological distress. The Western based medical services are not well prepared to deal with these culturally based beliefs and the scientific model does not know how to respond to mental illness thought to be a consequence of evil spirit possession or other extra-terrestrial causes. However, employing bilingual staff sensitive to cultural values may contribute to greater use of existing health facilities (Snowden, Masland, Ma, & Ciemens, 2006).

SUMMARY

This chapter outlines a discussion of major physical health and mental health issues from the perspective of cultural and cross-cultural research. Successful treatments of mental health disorders rely on accurate under-standings of whether symptoms are considered universal or culturally spe-cific. Research supports the importance of cultural sensitivity in delivering empirically verified mental health services in a still heterogeneous world. Sadly there are great disparities in socio-economic status linked to health and provision of treatment services between ethnic and cultural groups. One salient outcome of health disparities is the lower expected lifespan for ethnic groups that are poor, or of low socioeconomic standing. The re-search clearly supports the relationship between socioeconomic status and access to services and healthy outcomes.

Developing nations have serious challenges in providing proper nutri-tion and lowering the infant mortality rate. Large families are encouraged in traditional societies as a form of social and psychological support. In ad-dition to overpopulation the world confronts many problems derived from industrialization and globalization that include hypertension and associ-ated illnesses. The economically disadvantaged often suffer more malnu-trition and when this occurs during critical stages in development it will negatively impact cognitive development and infant mortality. Poverty also brings greater exposure to negative collateral environments including un-hygienic conditions and exposure to disease. Hunger and malnutrition cre-ates passivity and lower motivation to change the status quo.

Ethnic minorities in the U.S. suffer both poverty and the consequenc-es of cultural genocide. Native Americans were not only dispossessed of their natural environment but also marginalized in ways that affect men-tal health. African Americans also suffer disproportionately from histori-cal discrimination and cultural genocide. This history along with broadly based lower socioeconomic status have resulted in significantly higher rates of mental illness including higher rates of schizophrenia, depression, and personality disorders. Other ethnic groups in the U.S. have fared better as a result of preferential treatment or cohesive group support.

Globalization and wars have motivated many people to migrate legally or illegally into other countries. The stress of living through traumatic events in home countries and problems of cultural adaptation in the new culture produce many health related problems in migrants. These issues are ameliorated when support is present from the migrants ethnic communities already established in the U.S. Cultural adaptation is the critical issue for migrants, and those that fail in adaptation typically have larger mental health issues. An additional factor in adaptation is the degree of divergence between the original culture and the host society.

Culture plays an important role in how symptoms of mental illness are manifested and whether a patient seeks assistance. In some cultures religion and beliefs in the supernatural frame a patient's understandings of mental illness. Unique cultural understandings affect the judgment of both patient and therapist and determine if relief is found in treatment based on science or by appealing to superstitious beliefs. Cultural health beliefs concerning the causes of mental illness vary between cultures as does the treatment offered. People in collectivistic societies believe in psychosocial etiology and prefer psychosocial treatment. However, superstitious thinking in traditional societies negatively impacts treatment outcomes by negating the patient's beliefs in the ability to control outcomes.

Definitions of what is abnormal behavior are a function of cultural values. Culture may impact the willingness of a patient to report symptoms of distress for fear of stigma in some societies. We can only understand mental disorder within the framework of cultural values since behaviors considered abnormal in one culture may in another society be viewed as normal activity. The Diagnostic and Statistical Manual is broadly used in the Western world and increasingly applied in culturally sensitive ways elsewhere. That fact makes it increasingly important to understand mental illness as both culturally specific and universal. The culturally specific viewpoint argues that diagnoses of mental illness and rate of occurrence are influenced by cultural values. The universal perspective believes that there is great similarity between symptoms of mental illness in various cultures and diagnostic categories are universally valid. This book argues in favor of the integration of both the culturally specific and universal perspectives.

Nevertheless some mental disorders are not connected to existing diagnostic categories of the DSMIV and are considered culturally unique. Other disorders are described in the diagnoses outlined in the DSMIV, but with local features that are culture specific. In treatment the cultural specific approach is useful since it helps the therapist to frame illness within cultural values found in religion or superstition and accepted by the patient. Anorexia nervosa was thought for many years to be culturally specific to Western industrialized societies, but from the influences of globalization is now diagnosed in many other urban cultures. In summary, there is evidence for both universal diagnostic categories but also distress that can best be understood within a specific culture. Globalization is producing more homogeneity in the world that may require rethinking about diagnoses in the future.

Anxiety is universally present in all societies, however, with rates that vary according to the stress derived from the ecological and socioeconomic environment. Among well off people in the West anxiety is commonly related to achievement challenges that reflect individualistic values whereas in collectivistic societies concern about inclusion is more frequently a source of anxiety. Considerable evidence exists for the ubiquitous presence of depression with cultural variance related to peripheral symptoms. Cultural values affect diagnostic decisions since in some societies depression may carry stigma. Cultural values also influence the attributions of the cause of depression where, for example, a self-centered explanation is less accepted in collectivistic societies.

Schizophrenia is universal and is believed to have a genetic basis interacting with environmental stress although symptom manifestation is influenced by cultural values. Patients from developing countries have a better prognosis that those living in industrialized nations due to the social support available in collectivistic societies. Ethnic minorities in the U.S have higher rates of schizophrenia that can be attributed to the stress derived from lower socioeconomic status. In evaluating symptoms it is well to remember that behavior considered abnormal in one culture is not necessarily considered such in another society. Attention deficit disorder has now been diagnosed in many cultures although the criteria are not the same everywhere making comparisons difficult. The rate is higher in boys and the disorder is attributed to the greater cultural complexity and rapid change in modern societies. Some researchers also believe it has an as yet undetermined neurological cause. Personality disorders refer to behaviors and psychological experiencing that is markedly different from social standards. Diagnoses must be made within cultural standards. Collectivistic societies typically have less tolerance for social deviance whereas Western countries see some social deviance as manifesting a person's unique personality and not as matter of great concern to society.

The ability to make culturally sensitive assessment of abnormal behavior is essential to the patient-therapist relationship and the prognosis of treatment outcomes. The understanding of mental disorder depends on cultural values as does the preferred treatment. The chapter addresses the issue of whether assessments developed in one culture can be utilized in different cultural settings. The partial answer to assessment transfer problems is the development of culturally sensitive instruments and utilizing indigenous tools. Cross-cultural assessment of mental disorder emerged out of Western psychological theories and was then transferred into other societies. Cross-cultural psychology has established testing procedures to evaluate the comparability of assessment instruments. However, it is important to recognize unique cultural meanings of what constitute healthy and abnormal behaviors.

Since culture is salient to the definition of what is normal or abnormal there is a broad need for culturally sensitive approaches in both assessment and therapy. The confrontation of cultures with varying values is a direct result of our globalized world. The creation of multicultural societies in various parts of the world and in many countries requires clinical training in culturally competent therapies. Research support the relevance of cultural modifications in existing assessment and therapeutic approaches since, for example, cultural values determine if a person in distress will seek assistance. Cognitive-behavioral therapies are being validated across cultures today. Cultural adaptation of therapy is beneficial to the client regardless of the therapeutic means employed.

Psychoanalysis that inaugurated Western therapy provided primarily a focus on internal personality dynamics. However, in collectivistic societies a self-focus might actually be considered abnormal because of the importance of relationships and society. Successful therapeutic outcomes therefore depend on the cultural competence of the therapist and ultimately on effective communication between therapist and patient based on shared cultural meanings. Cultural similarity is salient in establishing shared cultural understandings.

Researchers and practitioners that reject universal approaches seek to develop indigenous treatments. Western psychology has been criticized as unfairly dominating theory and treatment in other societies. On the other hand, indigenous theories are criticized for contributing to infinite cultural regression in psychology and for promoting ever more local cultural norms. Indigenous theories are also criticized for not paying attention to the manifest similarities in symptoms and behaviors across cultures.

The chapter ended with a discussion of community based approaches the effectiveness of which is supported by research. A pioneering program in Australia trained indigenous health workers in Western disciplines who subsequently offered their services in locations administered by the Aboriginal and Islander community. Studies that followed elsewhere validated the delivery of medical and mental health services that employ cultural sensitivity and thereby achieve greater success in health outcomes. Employing culturally competent staff in treatment centers contribute to their greater use by the indigenous population and more successful outcomes.

REFERENCES

Aboud, F. (1998). *Health psychology in global perspective.* Thousand Oaks, CA: Sage.

Abramson, L. Y., Metalsky, G. I., & Alloy, L. B. (1989). Hopelessness depression: A theory based subtype of depression. *Psychological Review, 96,* 358–372.

Abu-Lughod, L. (1986). *Veiled sentiments.* Berkeley: University of California Press.

Achenbach, T. M. (2001). *Child behavior checklist for ages 6 to 18.* Burlington: University of Vermont, research Center for Children, Youth and Families.

Adair, J. G., Pandey, J., Begum, H. A., Puhan, B. N., & Vohra, N. (1995). Indigenization and development of the discipline: Perceptions and opinions of Indian and Bangladeshi psychologists. *Journal of Cross-Cultural Psychology, 26,* 392–407.

Adair, J. G., Puhan, B. N., & Vohra, N. (1993). Indigenization of psychology: Empirical assessment of progress in Indian research. *International Journal of Psychology, 28,* 149–169.

Alba, R., & Nee, V. (2003). *Remaking the American mainstream: Assimilation and the new immigration.* Cambridge, MA: Harvard University Press.

Albarracin, D., & Wyer, R. S. (2000). The cognitive impact of past behavior: Influences on beliefs, attitudes, and future behavioral decisions. *Journal of Personality and Social Psychology, 79,* 5–22.

Albas, D.C., McCluskey, K. W., & Albas, C. A. (1976). Perception of the emotional content of speech. *Journal of Cross-Cultural Psychology, 7,* 48–490.

Cross-Cultural Psychology: Why Culture Matters, pages 387–462.
Copyright © 2013 by Information Age Publishing

Albert, A. A., & Porter, J. R. (1986). Children's gender role stereotypes: A comparison of United States and South Africa. *Journal of Cross-Cultural Psychology, 17,* 45–65.

Alcock, J. (1984). *Animal behavior: An evolutionary approach* (3rd ed.). Sunderland, MA: Sianauer Associates.

Alexander, J. M., Carr, M., & Schwanenflugel, P. J. (1995). Development of metacognition in gifted children: Direction for future research. *Developmental Review,* 15, 1–37.

Alexander, M. G., & Fischer, T. D. (2003). Truth and consequences: Using the bogus pipeline to examine sex differences in self-reported sexuality. *The Journal of Sex Research, 40,* 27–35.

Allik, J., & McCrae, R. R. (2004). Towards a geography of personality traits: Patterns of profiles across 36 cultures. *Journal of Cross-Cultural Psychology, 35,* 13–28.

Altemeyer, B. (1988). *Enemies of freedom: Understanding right-wing authoritarianism.* San Francisco: Jossey-Bass.

Ames, R. T., & Rosemont H. Jr. (1998). *The analects of Confucius: A philosophical translation.* New York: Ballantine Books.

Andersen, P. A. (1999). *Nonverbal communication: Forms and functions.* Mountain View, CA: Mayfield.

Andersen, S. M., & Ross, L. D. (1984). Self-knowledge and social inference: 1. The impact of cognitive/affective and behavioral data. *Journal of Personality and Social Psychology, 46,* 280–293.

Anderson, N. B. (2009). Health disparities: A multidimensional approach. *Communique, March,* 7–9. Retrieved from: http://issuu.com/oema/docs/march_2009_web_communique, Last access April 18, 2012.

Anuradha, C. S. (2008). Women political leadership and perception: A case study of South Asia. *International Journal of South Asian Studies, 1,* 1–8.

Archer, J. (2006). Cross-cultural differences in physical aggression between partners: A social-role analysis. *Personality and Social Psychology Review, 10*(2), 133–153.

Argote, L., & McGrath, J. E. (1993). Group processes in organisations: Continuity and change. *International Review of Industrial and Organisational Psychology, 8,* 333–389.

Argyle, M. (1988). *Bodily communications* (2nd ed.), London: Methuen.

Argyle, M. (2001). *The psychology of happiness* (2nd ed.), London: Routledge.

Arkin, R. M., & Oleson, K. C. (1998). Self-handicapping. In J. M. Darley & J. Cooper (Eds.), *Attribution and social interaction: the legacy of Edward E. Jones* (pp. 313–341). Washington, DC.: American Psychological Association.

Armor, D. A., & Taylor, S. E. (1998). Situated optimism: Specific outcome expectancies and self-regulation. In M. P. Zanna (Ed.), *Advances in experimental social psychology* (Vol. 30, pp. 309–379). New York: Academic Press.

Armstrong, S. J., Van der Heijden, B. I. J. M., & Sadler-Smith, E. (2012). Intellectual styles, management of careers, and improved work performance. In Zhang, L., Sternberg, R. J., & Rayner, S. (Eds.). *Handbook of intellectual styles: Preferences in cognition, learning, and thinking.* Springer Publishing Company, LLC.

Arnault, D., Sakamoto, S., & Moriwaki, A. (2006). Somatic and depressive symptoms in female Japanese and American students: A preliminary investigation. *Transcultural Psychiatry, 43*(2), 275–286.

Arnett, J. J. (1995). Broad and narrow socialization: The family in the context of a cultural theory. *Journal of Marriage and the Family, 57,* 617–628.

Arnett, J. J. (2001). *Adolescence and emerging adulthood: A cultural approach.* Upper Saddle River, NJ: Prentice Hall.

Arnett, J. J. (2012). *Human development : a cultural approach,* (1ˢᵗ ed.). Pearson Education, Inc.

Aronson, J., Blanton, H., & Cooper, J. (1995). From dissonance to disindentification: Selectivity in the self-affirmation process. *Journal of Personality and Social Psychology, 68,* 986–996.

Asch, S. E. (1956). Effects of group pressure upon modification and distortion of judgments. In H. Guetzkow (Ed.), *Groups, leadership, and men* (pp. 177–190). Pittsburgh, PA: Carnegie Press.

Asch, S. E. (1957). An experimental investigation of group influence. In Walter Reed Army Institute of Research, *Symposium on prevention and social psychiatry* (pp. 15–17). Washington, DC: US Government Printing Office.

Aspinwall, L. G., & Brunhart, S. M. (1996). Distinguishing optimism from denial: Optimistic beliefs predict attention to health threats. *Personality and Social Psychology Bulletin, 22,* 993–1003.

Au, T. K. (1983). Chinese and English counterfactuals: The Sapir-Whorf hypothesis revisited. *Cognition, 15,* 155–187.

Aune, R. K, & Aune, K.S. (1994). The influence of culture, gender, and relational status on appearance management. *Journal of Cross-Cultural Psychology, 25*(2), 258–272.

Avants, S. K., & Margolin, A. (2004). Development of spiritual self-schema therapy for the treatment of addictive and HIV risk behavior: A convergence of cognitive and Buddhist psychology. *Journal of Psychotherapy Integration, 14*(3), 253–289.

Averill, J. R. (1980). A constructivist view of emotion. In R. Plutchik & H. Kellerman (Eds.), *Emotion: Theory, research, and experience: Volume 1. Theories of emotion* (pp. 305–339). New York: Academic Press.

Ayoko, B. O., Hartel, C. E., & Callan, V. J. (2002). Resolving the puzzle of productive and destructive conflicts in culturally heterogeneous workgroups: A communication accommodation theory approach. *International Journal of Conflict Management, 13,* 165–195.

Azhar, M. Z., & Varma, S. L. (1996). Relationship of expressed emotion with relapse of schizophrenia patients in Kelantan. *Singapore Medical Journal, 37,* 82–85.

Azuma, H. (1984). Psychology in a non-Western culture: The Philippines. *Psychological Bulletin, 102,* 272–292.

Bacon, M., Child, I., & Barry, H. (1983). A cross-cultural study of correlates of crime. Journal of *Abnormal and Social Psychology, 66,* 291–300.

Baddeley, A. D. (1986). *Working memory.* Oxford: Oxford University Press.

Baker, C., & Prys, S. (1998). *Encyclopedia of bilingualism and bilingual education.* Clevedon: Multilingual Matters.

Baltes, P. (1997). On the incomplete architecture of human ontogeny: Selection, optimization, and compensation as foundation of developmental theory. *American Psychologist, 52,* 366–380.

Bandura, A. (1977). *Social learning theory.* Englewood Cliffs, NJ: Prentice: Hall.

Bandura, A. (1986). *Social foundations of thought and action: A social cognitive theory*. Upper Saddle River, NJ: Prentice-Hall.

Bandura, A. (2002). Social cognitive theory in cultural context. *Applied Psychology, 51*, 269–290.

Barba, C. V. C., Guthrie, H. A., & Guthrie, G. M. (1982). Dietary intervention and growth of infants and toddlers in a Philippine rural community. *Ecology of Food & Nutrition, 11*, 235–244.

Barna, L. M. (1996). Stumbling blocks in intercultural communication. In L. A. Samovar & R. E. Porter (Eds.), *Intercultural communications: A reader* (8ᵗʰ ed., pp. 370–379), Belmont, CA: Wadsworth.

Barraclough, B. (1988). International variation in the suicide rate of 15–24 year olds, *Social Psychiatry and Psychiatric Epidemiology, 23*, 75–84.

Barron, F., & Harrington, D. (1981). Creativity, intelligence, and personality. *Annual Review of Psychology, 32*, 439–476.

Barry, H., Bacon, M., & Child, I. (1957). A cross-cultural survey of some sex differences in socialization. *Journal of Abnormal and Social Psychology, 55*, 327–332.

Barry, H., Child, I., & Bacon, M. (1959). Relation of child training to subsistence economy. *American Anthropologist, 61*, 51–63.

Barry, H., Josephson, L., Lauer, E., & Marshall, C. (1977). Agents and techniques for child training: *Cross-cultural codes 6. Ethnology, 16*, 191–230.

Baum, S. K., & Stewart, R.B. (1990). Sources of meaning through the lifespan. *Psychological Report, 67*(1), 3–14.

Baumeister, R. F. (1982). A self-presentational view of social phenomena. *Psychological Bulletin, 91*, 3–26.

Baumeister, R. E. (1987). How the self became a problem: A psychological review of historical research. *Journal of Personality and Social Psychology, 52*, 163–176.

Baumeister, R. F. (2005). *The cultural animal: Human nature, meaning, and social life*. New York: Oxford University Press.

Baumeister, R. F., & Heatherton, T. F. (1996). Self-regulation failure: An overview. *Psychological Inquiry, 7*, 1–15.

Baumeister, R. F., & Leary, M. R. (1995). The need to belong: Desire for interpersonal attachments as a fundamental human motivation. *Psychological Bulletin, 117*, 497–529.

Baumeister, R. F., Smart, L., & Boden, J. M. (1996). Relation of threatened egotism to violence and aggression: The dark side to high self-esteem. *Psychological Review, 103*, 5–33.

Baumeister, R. F., & Sommer, K. L. (1997). What do men want? Gender differences and two spheres of belongingness: Comment on Cross and Madson. *Psychological Bulletin, 122*, 38–44.

Baumeister, R. E., Twenge, J. M., & Nuss, C. (2002). Effects of social exclusion on cognitive processes: Anticipated aloneness reduces intelligent thought. *Journal of Personality and Social Psychology, 83*, 817–827.

Baumeister, R. F., & Vohs, K. D. (2003). Self-regulation and the executive function of the self. In M. R. Leary & J. P. Tangney (Eds.), *Handbook of self and identity* (pp. 197–217). New York: Guildford Press.

Baumrind, D. (1971). Current patterns of parental authority. *Developmental Psychology monographs, Part 2, 4*(1), 1–103.

Baxter, B., Hinson, R. E., Wall, A., & McKee, S. A. (1998). Incorporating culture into the treatment of alcohol abuse and dependence. In S. Kazarian & D. Evans (Eds.), *Cultural clinical psychology: Theory, research and practice* (pp. 215–245). New York: Oxford University Press.

Beardsley, L., & Pedersen, P. (1997). Health and culture-centered interventions. In J. W. Berry, M. H. Segall, & C. Kagitcibasi (Eds.). *Handbook of cross-cultural psychology: Social behavior and applications* (Vol. 3, 2nd ed., pp. 413–448). Boston, MA: Allyn and Bacon.

Beauregard, K. S., & Dunning, D. (1998). Turning up the contrast: Self-enhancement motives prompt egocentric contrast effects in social judgments. *Journal of Personality and Social Psychology, 74*, 606–621.

Becker, B. J. (1986). Influence again: Another look at studies of gender differences in social influence. In J. S. Hyde & M. C. Linn (Eds.), *The psychology of gender: Advances through meta-analysis* (pp. 178–209). Baltimore: John Hopkins University Press.

Bedi, K. (1987). Lasting neuroanatomical changes following undernutrition during early life. In J. Dobbing (Ed.), *Early nutrition and later achievement* (pp. 1–36). New York: Academic Press.

Beech-Akaushi, H. (2011, March 28th). How Japan will reawaken. *Time*, 42–47.

Behrensmeyer, A. K. (2006). Climate change and human evolution. *Science, 311*, 476–478.

Begley, S. (2012). Anything boys can do … Biology may play only a minor role in the math gender gap. *Scientific American, 306*, 25. Published online: 28 December 2011. doi:10.1038/scientificamerican0112-25

Bell, D. (1976). *The coming of post-industrial society.* New York: Basic Books.

Bell, D. A. (2008). *China's new Confucianism: Politics and everyday life in a changing society.* Princeton, NJ: Princeton University Press.

Bem, D. J. (1972). Self-perception theory. In L. Berkowitz (Ed.), *Advances in experimental social psychology* (Vol. 6, pp. 1–62). New York: Academic Press.

Benassi, V. A., Sweeney, P. D., & Dufour, C. L. (1988). Is there a relation between locus of control orientation and depression? *Journal of Abnormal Psychology, 97*, 357–367.

Benet-Martinez, V., Leu, J., Lee, F., & Morris, M. (2002). Negotiating biculturalism: Cultural frame- switching in biculturals with "Oppositional" versus "Compatible" cultural identities. *Journal of Cross-Cultural Psychology, 33*, 492–516.

Berger, C., & Calabrese, R. (1975). Some explorations in initial interaction and beyond: Toward a developmental theory of interpersonal communication. *Human Communication Research, 1*, 99–112.

Berger, K. S. (1995). *The developing person through the lifespan.* New York: Worth Publishers.

Berglas, S., & Jones, E. E. (1978). Drug choice as a self-handicapping strategy in response to noncontingent success. *Journal of Personality and Social Psychology, 36*, 405–417.

Berlin, B., & Kay, P. (1969). *Basic color terms: Their universality and evolution.* Berkeley, CA: University of California Press.

Bernal, G., Jimenez-Chafey, M. L., & Rodriquez, M. M. D. (2009). Cultural adaptation of treatments: A resource for considering culture in evidence-based practice. *Professional Psychology: Research and Practice, 40,* 361–368.

Bernichon, T., Cook, K. E., & Brown, J. (2003). Seeking self-evaluative feedback: The interactive role of global self-esteem and specific self-views. *Journal of Personality and Social Psychology, 84,* 194–204.

Bernieri, F. J., Zuckerman, M., Koestner, R., & Rosenthal, R. (1994). Measuring person perception accuracy: Another look at self-other agreement. *Personality and Social Psychology Bulletin, 20,* 367–378.

Berry, J. W. (1966). Temne and Eskimo perceptual skills. *International Journal of Psychology, 1,* 207–229.

Berry, J. W. (1967). Independence and conformity in subsistence-level societies. *Journal of Personality and Social Psychology, 7,* 415–418.

Berry, J. W. (1969). On cross-cultural comparability. *International Journal of Psychology, 4,* 119–128.

Berry, J. W. (1976a). *Human ecology and cognitive style: Comparative studies in cultural and psychological adaptation.* New York: Sage/Halstead.

Berry, J. W. (1976b). Sex differences in behavior and cultural complexity. *Indian Journal of Psychology, 51,* 89–97.

Berry, J. W. (1979). A cultural ecology of social behavior. In L. Berkowitz (Ed.), *Advances in experimental social psychology* (Vol. 12, pp. 177–206). New York: Academic Press.

Berry, J. W. (1991). Cultural variations in field-dependence-independence. In S. Wapner & J. Demick (Eds.), *Field dependence-independence: Cognitive styles across the life span* (pp. 289–308). Hillsdale, NJ: Erlbaum.

Berry, J. W. (1997). Immigration, acculturation, and adaptation. *Applied Psychology: An International Review, 46*(1), 5–68.

Berry, J. W. (2000). Cross-cultural psychology: A symbiosis of cultural and comparative approaches. *Asian Journal of Social Psychology, 3,* 197–205.

Berry, J. W. (*2001*). A psychology of immigration. *Journal of Social Issues, 57*(3), 615–631.

Berry, J. W., Dalal, A., & Pande, N. (1994). *Disability attitudes, beliefs and behaviors: A cross-cultural study.* Kingston: International Centre for Community-Based Rehabilitation.

Berry, J. W., & Dasen, P. (Eds.). (1974). *Culture and cognition.* London: Methuen.

Berry, J. W., Irvine, S. H., & Hunt, E. B. (Eds.). (1988). *Indigenous cognition: Functioning in cultural context.* Dordrecht: Nijhoff.

Berry, J. W., Phinney, J., Sam, D., & Vedder, P. (2006). Immigrant Youth: Acculturation, Identity, and Adaptation. *Applied psychology& an international review, 55*(3), 303–332

Berry, J. W., Poortinga, Y. H., Segall, M.H., & Dasen, P. R. (1992). *Cross-cultural psychology: Research and applications.* New York: Cambridge University Press.

Berry, J. W., & Sam, D. (1997). Acculturation and adaptation. In M. H. Segall & C. Katitcibasi (Eds.), *Handbook of cross-cultural psychology: Social and behavioural applications* (Vol., 3, pp. 291–326). Boston: MA: Allyn and Bacon.

Bettinger, R. L., & Eerkens, J. (1999). Point typologies, cultural transmission, and the spread of bow-and-arrow technology in prehistoric Great Basin. *American Antiquities, 64*, 231–242.

Bhaskar-Shrinivas, P., Harrison, D. A., Luk, D. M., & Shaffer, M. A. (2005). Input-based and time-based models of international adjustment: Meta-analytic evidence and theoretical extensions. *Academy of Management Journal, 48*, 257–281.

Bhui, K., Craig, T., Mohamud, S., Warfa, N., Stansfeld, S.A., Thornicroft, G., Curtis, S., & McCrone, P. (2006). Mental disorders among Somali refugees: Developing cultural appropriate measures and assessing socio-cultural risk factors. *Social Psychiatry and Psychiatric Epidemiology, 41*(5), 400–408.

Bianco, A. T., Higgins, E. T., & Klem, A. (2003). How "fun/importance" fit affects performance: Relating implicit theories to instructions. *Personality and Social Psychology Bulletin, 29*, 1091–1103.

Biederman, J., & Faraone, S.V. (2004). The Massachusetts General Hospital studies of gender influences on attention-deficit/hyperactivity disorder in youth and relatives. *Psychiatric Clinics of North America, 27*, 225–232.

Biederman, J., Faraone, S. V., Wozniak, J., Mick, E., Kwon, A., Cayton, G. A., et al. (2005). Clinical correlates of bipolar disorder in a large, referred sample of children and adolescents. *Journal of Psychiatric Research, 39*(6), 611–622.

Biernat, M., Vescio, T. K., & Green, M. L. (1996). Selective self-stereotyping. *Journal of Personality and Social Psychology, 71*, 1194–1209.

Birdwhistell, R. L. (1970). *Kinesics and context.* Philadelphia, PA: University of Philadelphia Press.

Blakemore, C., & Cooper, G. (1970). Development of the brain depends on the visual environment. *Nature, 228*, 477–478.

Blanton, H., Buunk, B. P., Gibbons, F. X., & Kuyper, H. (1999). When better-than-others compare upward: Choice of comparison and comparative evaluation as independent predictors of academic performance. *Journal of Personality and Social Psychology, 76*, 420–430.

Blau, Z. S. (1981). *Black children/white children: Competence, socialization, and social structure.* New York: Free Press.

Block, J., & Robins, R. W. (1993). A longitudinal study of consistence and change in self-esteem from early adolescence to early adulthood. *Child Development, 64*, 909–923.

Bloom, A. H. (1981). *The linguistic shaping of thought: A study in the impact of language on thinking in China and the West.* Hillsdale, NJ: Erlbaum.

Bloomfield, L. (1933). *Language.* New York: Holt, Rinehart, & Winston.

Blow, F. C., Zeber, J. E., McCarthy, J. F., Valenstein, M., Gillon, L., & Bingham, C. R. (2004). Ethnicity and diagnostic patterns in veterans with psychoses. *Social Psychiatry and Epidemiology, 39*(10), 841–851.

Bochner, S. (1994). Cross-cultural differences in the self-concept: A test of Hofstede's individualism/collectivism distinction. *Journal of Cross-Cultural Psychology, 25*, 273–283.

Boesch, C. (2003). Is culture a golden barrier between human and chimpanzee? *Evolutionary Anthropology, 12*, 82–91.

Boesch, E. E. (1996). The seven flaws of cross-cultural psychology: The story of conversion. *Mind, Culture, and Activity, 3,* 2–10.

Boldero, J., & Francis, J. (2000). The relation between self-discrepancies and emotion: The moderating roles of self-guide, location relevance, and social self-domain centrality. *Journal of Personality and Social Psychology, 78,* 38–52.

Bolinger, D. (1978). Intonation across languages. In J. H. Greenberg (Ed.), *Universals of human language* (Vol., 2, pp. 471–524). Stanford, CA: Stanford University Press.

Bond, M. H. (1983). How language variation affects inter-cultural differentiation of values by Hong Kong bilinguals. *Journal of Language and Social Psychology 2*(1), 57–66.

Bond, M. H. (1996). *The handbook of Chinese Psychology.* Hong Kong: Oxford University Press.

Bond, M. H., Leung, K., Au, A. Tong, K. K.,Reimel De Carrasquel, S., Murakami, F., et al. (2004). Culture-level dimensions of social axioms and their correlates across 41 cultures. *Journal of Cross-Cultural Psychology, 35,* 548–570.

Bond, R., & Smith, P. B. (1996). Culture and conformity: A meta-analysis of studies using Asch's line judgment task. *Psychological Bulletin, 119,* 111–137.

Borkenau, P., & Ostendorf, F. (1998). The Big Five as states: How useful is the five-factor model to describe intraindividual variation over time? *Journal of research on Personality, 32*(2), 202–221.

Born, M., Bleichrodt, N., & Van der Flier, H. (1987). Cross-cultural comparison of sex-related differences on intelligence tests: A meta-analysis. *Journal of Cross-Cultural Psychology, 18,* 283–314.

Bornstein, M. H., Kessen, W. H., & Weiskopf, S. (1976). The categories of hue in infancy. *Science, 191,* 201–202.

Bornstein, M. H., & Tamis-LeMonda, C. (1989). Maternal responsiveness and cognitive development in children. In M. H. Bornstein (Ed.), *Maternal responsiveness: Characteristics and consequences.* San Francisco: Jossey-Bass.

Bouchard, T. J., & Loehlin, J. C. (2001). Genes, evolution, and personality. *Behavior Genetics, 31,* 243–273.

Bouchard, T. J., Lykken, D. T., McGue, M., Segal, N.L., & Tellegen, A. (1990). Sources of human psychological differences: The Minnesota study of twins reared apart. *Science, 250,* 223–228.

Bouchard T. J., McGue M. (1981). Familial studies of intelligence: a review. *Science, 212,* 1055–1059.

Bouchard, T. J., McGue, M., Hur, Y., & Horn, J. M. (1998). A genetic and environmental analysis of the California Psychological Inventory using adult twins reared apart and together. *European Journal of Personality, 12,* 307–320.

Boucher, J. D., & Brandt, M. E. (1981). Judgment of emotion: American and Malay antecedents. *Journal of Cross-Cultural Psychology, 12*(3), 272–283.

Bouny, A. (2007). The effects of Agent Orange and its consequences. *Global Research.* January 4th. Retrieved from: http://www.globalresearch.ca/index.php?context=va&aid=4490, Last access April 9, 2012.

Boyd, R., & Richerson, P. J. (1985). *Culture and the evolutionary process.* Chicago: The University of Chicago Press.

Boyd, R., & Richerson, P. J. (1990). Group selection among alternative evolutionary stable strategies. *Journal of Theoretical Biology, 145,* 331–342.

Boyd, R., & Richerson, P. J. (1995). Why does culture increase human adaptability? *Ethnology and Sociobiology, 16,* 125–143.

Boyd, R., & Richerson, P. J. (2010). Transmission coupling mechanisms: Cultural group selection. *Philosophical Transactions of the Royal Society, 365,* 3787–3795.

Brace, C. (2005). *"Race" is a four-letter word.* New York: Oxford University Press.

Bradley, R. H., & Corwyn, R.F. (2005). Caring for children around the world: a view from HOME. *International Journal of Behavioral Development, 29*(6), 468–478.

Bradley, R. H., Caldwell, B. M., & Corwyn, R. F. (2003). The child care HOME inventories: Assessing the quality of family child care homes. *Early Childhood Research Quarterly, 18*(3), 294–309.

Brandt, M. E., & Boucher, J. D. (1986). Concepts of depression in emotion lexicons of eight cultures. *International Journal of Intercultural Relations, 10,* 321–346.

Brewer, M. B., & Gardner, W. L. (1996). Who is this "we"? Levels of collective identity and self-representations. *Journal of Personality and Social Psychology, 71,* 83–93.

Brislin, R. (1970). Back-translation for cross-cultural research. *Journal of Cross-Cultural Psychology, 1*(3), 185–216.

Brislin, R. (1993). *Understanding culture's influence on behavior.* Fort Worth, TX: Hartcourt Brace Jovanovich.

Brislin, R. (2000). *Understanding culture's influence on behavior.* Fort Worth, TX: Harcourt.

Brockner, J., Chen, Y., Mannix, E., Leung, K., Skarlicki, D. P. (2000). Culture and procedural fairness: When the effects of what you do depend on how you do it. *Administrative Science Quarterly, 45,* 138–159.

Brody, L.R., & Hall, J. A. (1993). Gender and emotion. In M. Lewis & J. Haviland (Eds.), *Handbook of emotions* (pp. 447–460). New York: Guildford Press.

Bronfenbrenner, U. (1979). *The ecology of human development: Experiments by nature and design.* Cambridge, MA: Harvard University Press.

Broota, K. D. & Ganguli, H. C. (1975). Cultural differences in perceptual selectivity. *Journal of Social Psychology, 95,* 157–163.

Brown, C., & Reich, M. (1997). Micro-macro linkages in high-performance employment systems. *Organizational Studies, 18,* 765–781.

Brown, J. D. (1998). *The self.* New York: McGraw-Hill.

Brown, R. (1965). *Social psychology.* New York: Free Press of Glencoe.

Brulé, G., & Veenhoven, R. (2012). Why are Latin Europeans less happy? The impact of hierarchy. In Canevacci, M. (Ed.). *Polyphonic anthropology—Theoretical and empirical cross-cultural fieldwork.* Published by InTech, ISBN 978-953-51-0418-6.

Brummett, B. H., Siegler, I. C., McQuoid, D. R., Svenson, I.K., Marchuk, D. A., & Steffens, D. C. (2003). Associations among the NEO Personality Inventory Revised and the serotonin transporter gene-linked polymorphic region in elders: Effects of depression and gender. *Psychiatric Genetics, 13*(1), 13–1.

Buchanan, B., & Collard, M. (2007). Investigating the peopling of North America through cladistic analyses of Early Paleoindian projectile points. *Journal of Anthropological Archaeology, 26,* 366–393.

Bu-Haroon, A., Eapen, V., & Bener, A. (1999). The prevalence of hyperactivity symptoms in the United Arab Emirates. *Nordic Journal of Psychiatry, 53*(6), 439–442.

Burnet, J. (1995). Multiculturalism and racism in Canada. In J. Hjarno (Ed.), *Multiculturalism in the Nordic societies* (pp. 43–50). Copenhagen, Denmark: Tema-Nord.

Buss, A. H., & Plomin, R. (1984). *Temperament: Early developing personality traits.* Hillsdale, NJ: Erlbaum.

Buss, D. M. (1989). Sex differences in human mate preferences: Evolutionary hypothesis tested in 37 cultures. *Behavioral and Brain Sciences, 12,* 1–49.

Buss, D. M. (1994). *The evolution of desire: Strategies of human mating.* New York: Basic Books.

Buss, D. M. (1995). Evolutionary Psychology: A new paradigm for psychological sciences. *Psychological Inquiry, 6,* 1–30.

Buss, D. M. (1999). Human nature and individual differences: The evolution of human personality. In L. A. Pervin & O. P. John (Eds.), *Handbook of personality: Theory and research* (2nd ed., pp. 31–56). New York: Guildford Press.

Buss, D. M. (2001). Human nature and culture: An evolutionary psychological perspective. *Journal of Personality, 69,* 955–978.

Butcher, J. N., Lim, J., & Nezami, E. (1998). Objective study of abnormal personality in cross-cultural settings: The Minnesota Multiphasic Personality Inventory (MMPI-2). *Journal of Cross-Cultural Psychology, 29*(1), 189–211.

Cacioppo, J. T., & Tassinary, L. G. (1990). Inferring psychological significance from physiological signals. *American Psychologist, 45,* 16–28.

Campbell, D. T. (1974). Evolutionary epistemology. In P. A. Schilpp (Ed.), *The philosophy of Karl Popper* (pp. 413–463). La Salle, IL: Open Court Publishers.

Campbell, J. D. (1986). Similarity and uniqueness: The effects of attribute type, relevance, and individual differences in self-esteem and depression. *Journal of Personality and Social Psychology, 50,* 281–294.

Cantor, N., & Norem, J. K. (1989). Defensive pessimism and stress and coping. *Social Cognition, 7,* 92–112.

Cantril, H. (1965). *The pattern of human concern.* New Brunswick, NJ: Rutgers University Press.

Carroll, J. B., & Casagrande, J. B. (1958). The function of language classifications in behavior. In E. Maccoby, T. Newcomb, & E. L. Hartley (Eds.), *Readings in social psychology* (3rd ed., pp. 18–31). New York: Holt, Rinehart, & Winston.

Carson, R. C., Butcher, J. N., & Coleman, J. C. (1988). *Abnormal psychology and modern life* (8th ed.). Glenview, IL: Scott, Foresman.

Carver, C. S. (2003). Self-awareness. In M. R. Leary & J. P. Tangney (Eds.), *Handbook of self and identity* (pp. 179–196). New York: Guildford Press.

Carver, C. S., & Scheier, M. F. (1981). *Attention and self-regulation: A control-theory approach to human behavior.* New York: Springer-Verlag.

Carver, C. S., Sutton, S. K., & Scheier, M. F. (2000). Action, emotion, and personality: Emerging conceptual integration. *Personality and Social Psychology Bulletin, 26,* 741–751.

Case, R. (1992). *The mind's staircase: Exploring the conceptual underpinnings of children's thought and knowledge.* Hillsdale, NJ: Lawrence Erlbaum.

Cashmore, J., & Goodnow, J. (1986). Influences on Australian parents' values: Ethnicity vs sociometric status. *Journal of Cross-Cultural Psychology, 17*(4), 441–454.

Caspari, R. (2011). The evolution of grandparents. *Scientific American*, August, 45–49.

Caspi, A., Elder, G. H. Jr., & Bem, D. J. (1988). Moving away from the world: Life-course patterns of shy children. *Developmental Psychology, 24*, 824–831.

Caspi, A., McClay, J., Moffitt, T. E., Mill, J., Martin, J., & Craig, I. W. (2002). Role of genotype in the cycle of violence in maltreated children. *Science, 297*, 851–854.

Caspi, A., & Roberts, B. W. (2001). Personality development across the life course: The argument for change and continuity. *Psychological Inquiry, 12*, 49–66.

Cassidy, S. (2012). Measurement and Assessment of Intellectual Styles. In Zhang, L., Robert J. Sternberg, R. J., & Rayner, S. (Eds.), *Handbook of intellectual styles preferences in cognition, learning, and thinking.* Springer Publishing Company, LLC.

Castillo, R. J. (1997). *Culture and mental illnesses.* Pacific Grove, CA: ITP.

Cavalli, G., & Paro, R. (1998). The Drosophila Fab-7 chromosomal element conveys epigenetic inheritance during mitosis and meiosis. *Cell, 93*(4), 505–518.

Cavalli-Sforza, L. L., & Feldman, M. (1981). *Cultural transmission and evolution: A quantitative approach.* Princeton, NJ: Princeton University Press.

Chaiken, S., & Baldwin, M. W. (1981). Affective-cognitive consistency and the effect of salient behavioral information on self-perceptions of attitudes. *Journal of Personality and Social Psychology, 41*, 1–12.

Chambless, D., & Williams, K. (1995). A preliminary study of African Americans with agoraphobia: Symptom severity and outcome of treatment with in vivo exposure. *Behavior Therapy, 26*, 501–515.

Chan, S. F. (2000). Formal logic and dialectical thinking are not incongruent. *American Psychologist, 55*, 1063–1064.

Chao, R. (2001). Extending research on the consequences of parenting style for Chinese Americans and European Americans. *Child Development, 72*(6), 1832–1843.

Charmaz, K. (1995). Grounded theory. In J. A. Smith, R. Harre, & L. Van Langenhove (Eds.), *Rethinking methods in psychology* (pp. 27–49). London: Sage.

Chen, C. C. (1988). The empirical research and theoretical analysis of face in psychology. In K. S. Yang (Ed.), *The psychology of Chinese people* (pp. 7–55). Taipei: Chuliu Book Co.

Chen, C. C., Meindl, R., & Hunt, R. G. (1997). Testing the effects of vertical and horizontal collectivism: A study of reward allocation preferences in China. *Journal of Cross-cultural Psychology, 28*, 44–70.

Chen, G. M. (1995). Differences in self-disclosure patterns among Americans versus Chinese: A comparative study. *Journal of Cross-Cultural Psychology, 26*, 84–91.

Chen, S., Chen, K. Y., & Shaw, L. (2004). Self-verification motives at the collective level of self-definition. *Journal of Personality and Social Psychology, 86*, 77–94.

Chen, X., Dong, Q., & Zhou, H. (1997). Authoritative and authoritarian parenting practices and social and school performance in Chinese children. *International Journal of Behavioral Development, 21*(4), 855–873.

Chen, Y. R., Brockner, J., & Katz, T. (1998). Toward an explanation of cultural differences in ingroup favouritism: The role of individual versus collective primacy. *Journal of Personality and Social Psychology, 75*, 1490–1502.

Cheung, F. M., Cheung, S. F., Leung, K., Ward, C., & Leung, F. T. (2003). The English version of the Chinese personality assessment inventory. *Journal of Cross-Cultural Psychology, 34*, 433–452.

Chirkov, V., & Ryan, R. (2001). Parent and teacher autonomy-support in Russian and U.S. adolescents: Common effects on well-being and academic motivation. *Journal of Cross-Cultural Psychology, 32*(5), 618–635.

Chirkov, V. I., Ryan, R. M., Kim, Y., & Kaplan, U. (2003).Differentiating autonomy from individualism and independence: A self-determination theory perspective on internalization of cultural orientations and well-being. *Journal of Personality and Social Psychology, 84*, 97–110.

Chirkov, V. I., Ryan, R. M., & Willness, C. (2005). Cultural context and psychological needs in Canada and Brazil: Testing a self-determination approach to the internalization of cultural practices, identity, and well-being. *Journal of Cross-Cultural Psychology, 36*, 423–443.

Cho, Y., & Kim, Y. (1993). The cultural roots of entrepreneurial bureaucracy: The case of Korea. *Public Administrative Quarterly, 16*, 509–524.

Choi, S.-C., Kim, U., & Choi, S.-H. (1993). Indigenous analysis of collective representations: A Korean perspective. In U. Kim & J. W. Berry (Eds.), *Indigenous psychologies: Research and experience in cultural context* (pp. 193–210). Newbury Park, CA: Sage.

Chomsky, N. (1980). *Rules and representations.* Oxford, Blackwell.

Chomsky, N. (2000). *New horizons in the study of language and mind.* Cambridge: Cambridge University Press.

Christensen, T. C., Wood, J. V., & Barrett, L. F. (2003). Remembering everyday experience through the prism of self-esteem. *Personality and Social Psychology Bulletin, 29*, 51–62.

Chua, H. F., Leu, J., & Nisbett, R.E. (2005). Culture and diverging views of social events. *Personality and Social Psychology Bulletin, 31*(7), 925–934.

Chung, R. C., Walkey, F., & Bemak, F. (1997). A comparison of achievement and aspirations of New Zealand, Chinese, and European students. *Journal of Cross-Cultural Psychology, 28*(4), 481–489.

Church, A. T. (2000). Culture and personality: Toward an integrated cultural trait psychology. *Journal of Personality, 68*, 651–703.

Church, A. T., & Lonner, W. J. (Eds.). (1998). The cross-cultural perspective in the study of personality: Rationale and current research. *Journal of Cross-Cultural Psychology, 29*(1), 32–62.

Cialdini, R. B., & De Nicholas, M. E. (1989). Self-presentation by association. *Journal of Personality and Social Psychology, 55*, 591–621.

Ciborowski, T., & Choi, S. (1974). Nonstandard English and free recall: An exploratory study. *Journal of Cross-Cultural Psychology, 5*(3), 271–281.

Clancy, S. M., & Dollinger, S. J. (1993). Photographic depictions of the self: Gender and age differences in social connectedness. *Sex Roles, 15*, 145–158.

Clarke, J. I. (1995). Introduction, In J. I. Clarke & L. Tabah. (Eds.), Population environment development interaction. *Committee for International Cooperation in National Research (CICRED)* (pp. 1–10). Laxenburg, Austria.

Cloud, J. (2010, January 18). Why genes aren't destiny. *Time*, 49–53.

Cobb, A. T. (1980). The sales managers' bases of social power and influence upon the sales force. *Journal of marketing, 44*(4), 91–101.

Cohen, D., & Gunz, A. (2002). As seen by the other...: Perspectives on the self in the memories and emotional perceptions of Easterners and Westerners. *Psychological Science, 13,* 55–59.

Cole, M. (1992). Culture in development. In M. H. Bornstein & M. Lamb (Eds.), *Developmental psychology: An advanced textbook* (pp. 731–789). Hillsdale, NJ: Erlbaum.

Cole, M. (1996). *Cultural psychology: A once and future discipline.* Cambridge, MA: Belknap/Harvard.

Cole, M. (2006). Culture and cognitive development in phylogenetic, historical, and ontogenetic perspective. In W. Damon & R. M. Lerner (Gen. Eds.), *Handbook of child psychology* (6th ed.), D. Kuhn & R.S. Siegler (Vol. Eds.), *Cognition, perception, and language,* (Vol. 2, pp. 636–683). New York: Wiley.

Cole, M., & Packer, M. (2011). Culture and cognition. In Keith, K. D. (Ed.), *Cross-Cultural Psychology.* Malden, MA: Wiley-Blackwell.

Cole, M., & Scribner, S. (1977). Developmental theories applied to cross-cultural cognitive research. *Annals of the New York Academy of Science, 285,* 366–373.

Collins, W., & Laursen, B. (2004). Changing relationships, changing youth: Interpersonal contexts of adolescent development. *Journal of Early Adolescence, Special Issue: Memorial Issue: Adolescence: The Legacy of Hershel & Ellen Thornberg. 24*(1), 55–62. doi 10.1177/0272431603260882

Colvin, C. R., & Block, J. (1994). Do positive illusions foster mental health? An examination of the Taylor and Brown formulation. *Psychological Bulletin, 116,* 3–20.

Colvin, C. R., Block, J., & Funder, D. C. (1995). Overly positive self-evaluations and personality: Negative implications for mental health. *Journal of Personality and Social Psychology, 68,* 1152–1162.

Cook, P. (1994). Chronic illness beliefs and the role of social networks among Chinese, Indian, and Angloceltic Canadians. *Journal of Cross-Cultural Psychology, 25,* 452–465.

Cook, T. D., & Campbell, D. T. (1979). *Quasi-experimentation: Design and analysis issues for field settings.* Chicago, IL: Rand McNally.

Cooley, C. H. (1902). *Human nature and the social order.* New York: Charles Scribner's Sons.

Corttrell, A. B. (1990). Cross-national marriages: A review of the literature. *Journal of Comparative Family Studies, 21*(2), 151–169.

Costa, P. T., Jr., & McCrae, R. R. (1988). Personality in adulthood: A six year longitudinal study of self-reports and spouse ratings on the NEO Personality Inventory. *Journal of Personality and Social Psychology, 54,* 853–863.

Costa, P. T., Terracciano, A., & McCrae, R. R. (2001). Gender differences in personality traits across cultures: Robust and surprising findings. *Journal of Personality and Social Psychology, 81,* 322–331.

Cramton, C. D. & Hinds, P. L. (2005). Subgroup dynamics in internationally distributed teams: Ethnocentrism or cross-national learning? *Research on Organizational Behavior, 26,* 231–263.

Crijnen, A. A. M., Achenbach, T. M., & Verhulst, F. C. (1997). Comparisons of problems reported by parents of children in 12 cultures: Total problems, externalizing, and internalizing. *Journal of the American Academy of Child and Adolescent Psychiatry, 36,* 1269–1277.

Crijnen, A. A. M., Achenbach, T. M., & Verhulst, F. C. (1999). Problems reported by parents of children in multiple cultures: the child behavior checklist syndrome constructs. *American Journal of Psychiatry, 156,* 569–574.

Crocker, J., & Park, L. E. (2003). Seeking self-esteem: Construction, maintenance, and protection of self-worth. In M. R. Leary, & J. P. Tangney (Eds.), *Handbook of self and identity* (pp. 291–313). New York: Guildford Press.

Crocker, J., & Park, L. E. (2004). The costly pursuit of self-esteem. *Psychological Bulletin, 130,* 392–414.

Crocker, J., Luhtanen, R., Blaine, B., & Broadnax, S. (1994). Collective self-esteem and psychological well-being among White, Black, and Asian college students. *Personality and Social Psychology Bulletin, 20,* 503–513.

Crocker, J., Sommers, S. R., & Luhtanen, R. K. (2002). Hopes dashed and dreams fulfilled: Contingencies of self-worth and admissions to graduate school. *Personality and Social Psychology Bulletin, 28,* 1275–1286

Crocker, J., & Wolfe, C. (2001). *Contingencies of self-worth. Psychological Review, 108,* 593–623.

Croft, W. (2000). *Explaining language change: an evolutionary approach.* Harlow: Longman.

Crook, T. H., Youngjohn, J. R., Larrabee, G. J., & Salama, M. (1992). Aging and everyday memory: A cross-cultural study. *Neuropsychology, 6*(2), 123–136.

Cross, S. E., Bacon, P L., & Morris, M. L. (2000). The relational-interdependent self-construal and relationships. *Journal of Personality and Social Psychology, 78,* 791–808.

Cross, S. E., & Madson, L. (1997). Models of the self: Self-construals and gender. *Psychological Bulletin, 122,* 5–37.

Cross, S. E., & Markus, H. (1991). Possible selves across the life span. *Human Development, 34,* 230–255.

Cross, S. E., & Vick, N. V. (2001). The interdependent self-construal and social support: The case of persistence in engineering. *Personality and Social Psychology Bulletin, 27,* 820–832.

Csikszentmihalyi, M. (1999). Implications of a systems perspective for the study of creativity. In R. J. Sternberg (Ed.), *Handbook of creativity* (pp. 313–335). New York: Cambridge University Press.

Csikszentmihalyi, M., & Figurski, T. J. (1982). Self-awareness and aversive experience in everyday life. *Journal of Personality, 50,* 15–28.

Cuddy, A. J. C., Fiske, S. T., & Glick, P. (2004). When professionals become mothers, warmth doesn't cut the ice. *Journal of Social Issues, 60*(4), 701–718.

Cummins, R. A. (2003). Normative life satisfaction: Measurement issues and a homeostatic model. *Social Indicators Research, 64,* 225–256.

Cummins, R. A. (2010). Subjective well-being, homeostatically protected mood and depression: A synthesis. *Journal of Happiness Studies, 11,* 1–17.

Cummins, R. A., & Lau, A. L. D. (2011). Well-being across cultures: issues of measurement and the interpretation of data. In K. D. Keith (Ed.), *Cross-cultural psychology: Contemporary reader* (pp. 365–379). New York: Wiley/Blackwell.

Cunningham, J., & Macan, T. (2007). Effects of applicant pregnancy on hiring decisions and interview ratings. *Sex Roles, 57*, 497–508.

Currie, T. E., Greenhill, S. J. & Mace, R. (2010). Is horizontal transmission really a problem for phylogenetic comparative methods? A simulation study using continuous cultural traits. *Philosophical Transactions of the Royal Society, 365*, 3903–3912.

Dabbs, J. M., & Morris, R. (1990). Testosterone, social class and antisocial behavior in a sample of 4462 men. *Psychological Science, 1*, 209–211.

Dalal, A.K. (2000). Editorial: Indigenous health beliefs and practices. *Psychology and Developing Societies, 12*(1) 1–3.

Dalal, A., Pande, N. (1999). Cultural Beliefs and Family Care of the Children with Disability. *Psychology & Developing Societies, 3*(11), 55–75. doi:10.1177/097133369901100103

Damasio, A. (2007). The Brain: A story we tell ourselves. *Time, January 29*. Retrieved from: http://www.time.com/time/magazine/article/0,9171,1580386,00.html, Last access April 17, 2012.

Dandash, K. F., Refaat, A. H., & Eyada, M. (2001). Female genital mutilation: A descriptive study. *Journal of Sex and Marital Therapy, 27*, 453–458.

Darwin, C. (1859) *On the origin of the species by means of natural selection.* (1ˢᵗ ed.). London: John Murray.

Darwin, C. (1998). *The expression of the emotions in man and animals* (3rd ed., P. Ekman, Ed.). New York: Oxford University Press.

Dasen, P. (1975). Concrete operational development in three cultures. *Journal of Cross-Cultural Psychology, 6*, 156–172.

Dasen, P. R. (1984). The cross-cultural study of intelligence: Piaget and the Baoule. *International Journal of Psychology, 19*, 407–434.

Dasen, P. R. (1994). Culture and cognitive development from a Piagetian perspective. In. W. J. Lonner & R. Malpass (Eds.), *Psychology and culture* (pp. 141–150). Boston: Allyn and Bacon.

Dasen, P. R., Berry, J. W., & Sartorius, N. (1988). *Health and cross-cultural psychology.* Newbury Park, CA: Sage.

Dasen, P. R., & de Ribaupierre, A. (1987). Neo-Piagetian theories: Cross-cultural and differential perspectives. *International Journal of Psychology, 22*, 793–832.

Davidson, L., & Duberman, L. (1982). Friendship: Communication and interactional patterns in same-sex dyads. *Sex Roles, 8*, 809–822.

Davidson, R. J., Pizzagalli, D., Nitschke, J. B., & Kalin, N. H. (2003). Parsing the subcomponents of emotion and disorders of emotion: Perspectives from affective neuroscience. In R. J. Davidson, K. R. Scherer, & H. H. Goldsmith (Eds.), *Handbook of Affective Sciences* (pp. 8–24). New York: Oxford University Press.

Dawis, R. V., & Lofquist, L. (1984). *Psychological theory of work adjustment.* Minneapolis: University of Minnesota Press.

Dawson, J. L. M. (1971). Theory and research in cross-cultural psychology. *Bulletin of the British Psychological Society, 24*, 291–306.

Deal, T. E., & Kennedy, A. A. (1982). *Corporate culture: The rites and rituals of corporate life.* Reading, MA: Addison-Wesley.

Deaton, A. (2008). Income, aging, health and well-being around the world: Evidence from the Gallup World Poll. *Journal of Economic Perspectives, 22*(2), 53–72.

Deaux, K., Reid, A., Mizrahi, K., & Ethier, K. A. (1995). Parameters of social identity. *Journal of Personality and Social Psychology, 68,* 280–291.

Deci, E. L., Koestner, R., & Ryan, R. M. (1999). A meta-analytic review of experiments examining the effects of extrinsic rewards on intrinsic motivation. *Psychological Bulletin, 125,* 627–668.

Dehaene, S., Izard, V., Pica, P. & Spelke, E. (2006). Core knowledge of geometry in an Amazonian indigenous group. *Science, 311,* 381–384.

Del Giudice, M., Carayannis, E. G., Della Peruta, M. R. (2012). *Cross-Cultural Knowledge Management.* Springer Science+Business Media, LLC.

Den Hartog, D. N., House, R. J., Hanges, P. J., Ruiz-Quintanilla, S. A., Dorfman, P. W., & GLOBE Associates. (1999). Culture specific and cross-culturally generalizable implicit leadership theories: Are attributes of charismatic/transformational leadership universally endorsed? *Leadership Quarterly (Special Issue: Charismatic and Transformational Leadership: Taking Stock of the Present and Future (Part I), 10(2),* 219–256.

Dennett,D. (2007). The Brain: A clever robot. *Time, January 29.* Retrieved from: http://www.time.com/time/magazine/article/0,9171,1580363,00.html, Last access April 17, 2012.

Denzin, N. K., Lincoln, Y. S. (Eds.). (2000). *Handbook of qualitative research* (2nd ed.). Thousand Oaks, CA: Sage.

Depue, R. A. (1995). Neurobiological factors in personality and depression. *European Journal of Personality, 9,* 413–439.

De Raad, B., Perugini, M., Hrebickova, M., & Szarota, P. (1998). Lingua franca of personality: Taxonomies and structures based on the psycholexical approach. *Journal of Cross-Cultural Psychology, 29*(1), 212–232.

De Silva, S., Stiles, D., & Gibbons, J. (1992). Girls' identity formation in the changing social structure of Sri Lanka. *Journal of Genetic Psychology, 153*(2), 211–220.

De Waal, F. B. M. (2003). Darwin's legacy and the study of primate visual communication. In P. Ekman, J. Campos, R. J. Davidson, & F. B. M. de Waal (Eds.), *Emotions inside out: 130 years after Darwin's the expression of emotion in man and animals* (pp. 7–31). New York: New York Academy of Sciences.

Dhawan, N., Roseman, I. J., Naidu, R. K., Thapa, K., & Rettek, S. I. (1995). Self-concepts across two cultures: India and the United States. *Journal of Cross-Cultural Psychology, 26,* 606–621.

Diamond, J., & Bellwood, P. (2003). Farmers and their languages: The first expansions. *Science, 300,* 597–603.

Diaz-Guerrero, R. (1975). *Psychology of the Mexican: Culture and Personality.* Austin: University of Texas Press.

Diaz-Guerrero, R. (1977). A Mexican psychology. *American Psychologist, 32,* 934–944.

Diaz-Guerrero, R. (1984). Transference of psychological knowledge and its impact on Mexico. *International Journal of Psychology, 19,* 123–134.

Diaz-Guerrero, R. (1990), A Mexican ethnopsychology. In U. Kim & J. W. Berry (Eds.), *Indigenous psychologies: Experiences and research in cultural context* (pp. 44–55). Newbury Park, CA: Sage.

Diener, E. (1996). Subjective well-being in cross-cultural perspective. In H. Grad, A. Blanco, & J. Georgas (Eds.), *Key issues in cross-cultural psychology* (pp. 319–330). Lisse, Netherlands: Swets & Zeitlinger.

Diener, E. (2006). Guidelines for national indicators of subjective well-being and ill-being. *Journal of Happiness Studies, 7,* 397–404.

Diener, E., & Diener, M. (1995). Cross-cultural correlates of life satisfaction and self-esteem. *Journal of Personality and Social Psychology, 68,* 653–663.

Diener, E., & Diener, M. (1996). Most people are happy. *Psychological Science, 7,* 181–185.

Diener, E., & Seligman, M. E. P. (2004). Beyond money toward an economy of well-being. *Psychological Science in the Public Interest, 5,* 1–31.

Diener, E., Suh, E. M., Lucas, R. E., & Smith, H. L. (1999). Subjective well-being: Three decades of progress. *Psychological Bulletin, 125,* 276–302.

Ding, X., & Staudinger, J. L. (2005). Induction of drug metabolism by Forskolin: the role of the pregnane X receptor and the protein kinase: a signal transduction pathway. *Pharmacology, 312,* 849–856.

Distin, K. (2011). *Cultural evolution.* Cambridge: Cambridge University Press.

Dodgson, P. G., & Wood, J. V. (1998). Self-esteem and the cognitive accessibility of strengths and weaknesses after failure. *Journal of Personality and Social Psychology, 75,* 178–197.

Doi, T. (1973). *The anatomy of dependence.* Tokyo: Kodansha.

Doi, T. (1989). The concept of Amae and its psychoanalytic applications. *International Review of Psychoanalysis, 16,* 349–354.

Doise, W., Csepeli, G., Dann, D., Gouge, C., Larsen, K. S., & Ostell, A. (1972). An experimental investigation into the formation of inter-group representations. *European Journal of Social Psychology, 2,* 202–204.

Dolinsky, D. (2000). On inferring one's beliefs from one's attempts and consequences for subsequent compliance. *Journal of Personality and Social Psychology, 78,* 260–272.

Dolto, F. (1988). *La cause des adolescents,* Robert Laffont (Ed), Paris.

Domino, G. (1992). Cooperation and competition in Chinese and American children. *Journal of Cross-Cultural Psychology, 23*(4), 456–467.

Douki, S., Moussaoui, D., Kacha, F. (1987). *Handbook of psychiatry of expert Maghrebin.* Paris: Masson.

Draguns, J. G. (1997). Abnormal behavior patterns across culture: Implications for counseling and psychotherapy. *International Journal of Intercultural Relations, 21*(2), 213–248.

Drach-Zahavy, A. (2004). The proficiency trap: How to balance enriched job designs and the team's need for support. *Journal of Organizational Behavior, 25,* 979–996.

Drenth, P. J. D. (1983). Cross-cultural organizational psychology: Challenges and limitations. In S. H. Irvine & J. W. Berry (Eds.), *Human assessment and cultural factors* (pp. 563–580). New York: Plenum.

Dubin, R., and Galin, A. (1991). Attachment to work: Russians in Israel. *Work and Occupations, 18,* 172–93.

Duffy, R. D., & Sedlacek, W. (2007). The presence and search for a calling: Connections to career development. *Journal of Vocational Behavior, 70,* 590–601.

Dunn, J., & Munn, P. (1985). Becoming a family member: Family conflict and the development of social understanding in the second year. *Child Development, 56,* 480–492.

Dunning, D., & Cohen, G. L. (1992). Egocentric definitions of traits and abilities in social judgment. *Journal of Personality and Social Psychology, 63,* 341–355.

Dutton, D. G., & Aron, A. P. (1974). Some evidence for heightened sexual attraction under conditions of high anxiety. *Journal of Personality and Social Psychology, 30,* 510–517.

Duval, T. S., & Silvia, P. J. (2002). Self-awareness, probability of improvement, and the self-serving bias. *Journal of Personality and Social Psychology, 82,* 49–61.

Dwairy, M., Achoui, M., Abouserie, R., & Farah, A. (2006). Parenting styles, individuation, and mental health of Arab adolescents: A third cross-regional research study. *Journal of Cross-Cultural Psychology, 37*(3), 262–272.

Dyal, J. A. (1984). Cross-cultural research with the locus of control construct. In H. M. Lefcourt (Ed.), *Research with the locus of control construct* (Vol. 3, pp. 209–306). New York: Academic Press.

Eagly, A. H. (1987). *Sex differences in social behavior: A social role interpretation.* Hillsdale, NJ: Erlbaum.

Eagly, A. H., & Carli, L. L. (1981). Sex of researchers and sex-typed communications as determinants of sex differences in influence ability: A meta-analysis of social influence studies. *Psychological Bulletin, 90,* 1–20.

Eagly, A. H., & Wood, W. (1999). The origins of sex differences in human behavior: Evolved dispositions versus social roles. *American Psychologist, 54,* 408–423.

Earley, P. C. (1986). Supervisors and shop stewards as sources of contextual information in goal-setting: A comparison of the U.S. with England. *Journal of Applied Psychology, 71,* 111–18.

Earley, P. C. (1989). Social loafing and collectivism: A comparison of the United States and the people's Republic of China. *Administrative Science Quarterly, 34,* 565–581.

Eby, L. T., & Dobbins, G. H. (1997). Collectivistic orientation in teams: An individual and group-level analysis. *Journal of Organizational Behavior, 18,* 275–295.

Eckensberger, L. H., & Zimba, R. F. (1997). The development of moral judgment. In J. W. Berry, P. R. Dasen, & T. S. Saraswathi (Eds.), *Handbook of cross-cultural psychology: Basic processes and human development* (Vol. 2., pp. 299–338). Boston, MA: Allyn and Bacon.

Editors. (2012). Science Agenda. A neglect of mental illness. *Scientific American, 306,* 8. Retrieved from: http://www.scientificamerican.com/article.cfm?id=a-neglect-of-mental-illness, Last access April 19, 2012.

Edwards, C. P. (1986). Cross-cultural research on Kohlberg's stages: The basis for consensus. In S. Modgil & C. Modgil (Eds.), *Lawrence Kohlberg: Consensus and controversy* (pp. 419–430). London: The Falmer Press.

Edwards, C. P., Knoche, L., Aukrust, V., Kimru, A., & Kim, M. (2006). Parental ethnotheories of child development: Looking beyond independence and individualism in American belief systems. In U. Kim, K. S., Yang, & K. K. Hwang, (Eds.), *Indigenous and cultural psychology: Understanding people in the context* (pp. 141–162). New York: Springer Science and Media.

Efron, D. (1941). *Gesture and environment.* Oxford, England: King's Crown Press.

Ehrlinger, J., & Dunning, D. (2003). How chronic Self-views influence (and potentially mislead) estimates of performance. *Journal of Personality and Social Psychology, 84,* 5–17.

Eibl-Eibesfeldt, I. (1979). Human ethology: Concepts and implications for the sciences of man. *The Behavioral and Brain Sciences, 2,* 1–57.

Eibl-Eibesfeldt, I. (1989). *Human ethology.* New York: Aldine de Gruyter.

Eid, M., & Diener, E. (2001). Norms for experiencing emotions in different cultures: Inter- and intranational differences. *Journal of Personality and Social Psychology, 81,* 869–885.

Eisenberger, N. I., Lieberman, M. D., & Williams, K. D. (2003). Does rejection hurt? An fMRI study of social exclusion. *Science, 302,* 290–292.

Ekman, P. (1972). Universal and cultural differences in facial expressions of emotion. In J. R. Cole (Ed.), *Nebraska Symposium on motivation, 1971* (pp. 207–283). Lincoln: University of Nebraska Press.

Ekman, P. (1973). Cross-cultural studies of facial expressions. In P. Ekman (Ed.), *Darwin and facial expressions* (pp. 169–222). New York: Academic Press.

Ekman, P. (1992). Are there basic emotions? *Psychological Review, 99,* 550–553.

Ekman, P. (1994). Strong evidence for universals in facial expressions: A reply to Russell's mistaken critique. *Psychological Bulletin, 115,* 268–287.

Ekman, P. (1998). Universality of emotional expression? A personal history of the dispute. In Ekman, P. (Ed.). *The expression of the emotions in man and animals,* (3rd edition with introduction, afterwords, and commentaries, pp. 363–393). London: HarperCollins.

Ekman, P. (1999). Basic emotions. In T. Dalgleish & M. Power (Eds.). *Handbook of cognitions and emotions.* N.Y.: Wiley

Ekman, P., & Friesen, W. V. (1969). The repertoire of nonverbal behavior: Categories, origins, usage, and coding. *Semiotica, 1,* 49–98.

Ekman, P., & Friesen, W.V. (1986). A new pan-cultural facial expression of emotion. *Motivation and emotion, 10,* 159–168.

Ekman, P., Friesen, W.V., O'Sullivan, M., Chan, A., Diacoyanni- Tarlatzis, I, Heider, K., Krause, R., LeCompte, W.A., Pitcairn, T., Ricci-Bitti, P. E., Scherer, K.R., Tomita, M., & Tzavaras, A. (1987). Universals and cultural differences in the judgment of facial expressions of emotion. *Journal of Personality and Social Psychology, 53,* 712–717.

Ekman, P., Levenson, R. W., & Friesen, W. V. (1983). Autonomic nervous system activity distinguishes among emotions. *Science, 221,* 1208–1210.

Ekman, P., & Oster, H. (1979). Facial expressions of emotion. *Annual Review of Psychology, 30,* 527–554.

Ekman, P., Sorenson, E. R., & Friesen, W. V. (1969). Pan-cultural elements in facial display of emotion. *Science, 164,* 86–94.

Elfenbein, H. A., & Ambady, N. (2002). On the universality and cultural specificity of emotion recognition: A meta-analysis. *Psychological Bulletin, 128*(2), 205–235.

Elfenbein, H. A., Mandal, M. K., Ambady, N., Harizuka, S., & Kumar, S. (2004). Hemifacial differences in the in-group advantage in emotion recognition. *Cognition & Emotion, 18,* 613–629.

Ekstrand, L. H., & Ekstrand, G. (1986). Developing the emic-etic concepts for cross-cultural research. In L. H. Ekstrand (Ed.), *Ethnic minorities and immigrants in a cross-cultural perspective* (pp. 52–66). Lisse, Netherlands: Svets & Zeitlinger.

Elliot, J., Francis, E. (2011). I'm Not an Anomaly': More Dads Staying Home to Raise Kids. *ABC World News, December 13th.* Retrieved from: http://abcnews.go.com/US/Parenting/modern-family-dads-staying-home-raise-kids-wives/story?id=15147329#.Tuj3CJgqND2. Last access April 21, 2012.

Ellis, B. B. (1988). Hofstede's cultural dimensions and Rokeach's values: How reliable the relationship? In J. W. Ry & R. C. Annis (Eds.), *Ethnic psychology: Research and practice with immigrants, refugees, native peoples, ethnic groups and sojourners.* (pp. 266–274). Lisse, Netherlands: Svets & Zeitlinger.

Ellis, A. (1962). *Reason and emotion in psychotherapy.* Secaucus, NJ: Prentice-Hall.

Ellsworth, P. C., & Gonzalez, R. (2003). Questions, comparisons, and preparation: Methods of research in social psychology. In M. Hogg & J. Cooper (Eds.), *Sage Handbook of Social Psychology* (pp. 24–42). Thousand Oaks, CA: Sage Publications.

Enriquez, V. G. (Ed.). (1990). *Indigenous psychologies.* Quezon City: Psychology Research and Training House.

Engle, P. L., Black, M. M., Behrman, J. R., Cabral de Mello, M., Gertler, P. J., Kapirini, L., Martrell, R., & Eming Young, M. (2007). Strategies to avoid the loss of developmental potential in more than 200 million children in the developing world. *The Lancet, 369,* 229–242.

Ensari, N., & Murphy, S. E. (2003). Cross-cultural variations in leadership perceptions and attribution of charisma to the leader. *Organizational Behavior and Human Decision Processes, 92,* 52–66.

Epley, N., & Dunning, D. (2000). Feeling "holier than thou": Are self-serving assessments produced by errors in self- or social prediction? *Journal of Personality and Social Psychology, 79,* 861–875.

Epstein, M. (1995). *Thoughts without a thinker: Psychotherapy from a Buddhist perspective.* New York: Harper Collins.

Erez, M., & Earley, P. C. (1987). Comparative analysis of goal-setting strategies across cultures. *Journal of Applied Psychology, 72,* 658–65.

Erez, M., & Earley, P. C. (1993). *Culture, self-identity, and work.* New York: Oxford University Press.

Erickson, E. H. (1950). *Childhood and society.* New York: Norton.

Erickson, E. H. (1968). *Identity: Youth and crisis.* New York: Norton.

Esaki, L. (2001). Connecting the 21st century educational reforms in Japan and reflections on global culture. *Yomiuri Shimbun/Daily Yomiuri,* April 02. Retrieved from: http://www.accessmylibrary.com/article-1G1-72629878/connecting-21st-century-educational.html, Last access April 19, 2012.

Eschbach, K., Ostir, G. V., Patel, K., Markides, K. S., & Goodwin, J. S. (2004). Neighborhood context and mortality among older Mexican Americans: Is there a barrio advantage? *American Journal of Public Health, 94,* 1807–1812.

Eshun, S., & Gurung, R. A. R. (Eds.). (2009), *Culture and mental health: Sociocultural influences, theory, and practice.* Malden, MA: Wiley-Blackwell.

Eysenck, H. J. (1967). *The biological basis of personality.* Springfield, IL: Charles Thomas.

Eysenck, M. W., MacLeod, C. & Mathews, A. (1987). Cognitive functioning and anxiety. *Psychological Research, 49,* 189–195.

Fan, W., & He, Y. (2012). Academic Achievement and Intellectual Styles. In Zhang, L., Sternberg, R. J., & Rayner, S. (Eds.). *Handbook of intellectual styles preferences in cognition, learning, and thinking.* Springer Publishing Company, LLC.

Faraone, S. V., Sergeant, J., Gillberg, C., & Biederman, J. (2003). The worldwide prevalence of ADHD: Is it an American condition? *World Psychiatry, 2,* 104–113.

Febo San Miguel, V. E., Guarnaccia, P., Shrout, P. E., Lewis-Fernandez, R., Canino, G. J., Ramirez, R. R. (2006). A quantitative analysis of *ataque de nervios* in Puerto Rico: Further examination of a cultural syndrome. *Hispanic Journal of Behavioral Sciences, 28*(3), 313–330.

Fehr, B. J., & Exline, R. V. (1987). Social visual interactions: A conceptual and literature review. In A. W. Siegman & S. Feldstein (Eds.), *Nonverbal behavior and communication* (Vol. 2, pp. 225–326). Hillsdale, NJ: Erlbaum.

Fejes, F. (1992). Masculinity as fact: A review of empirical mass communication research on masculinity. In S. Craig (Ed.), *Men, masculinity, and the media* (pp. 9–22). Thousand Oaks, CA: Sage.

Fejfar, M. C., & Hoyle, R. H. (2000). Effect of private self-awareness on negative affect and self-referent attributions: A quantitative review. *Personality and Social Psychology Review, 4,* 132–142.

Feldman Barrett, L., & Russell, J. A. (1999). The structure of current affect: Controversies and emerging consensus. *Current Directions in Psychological Science, 8,* 10–14.

Felsenstein, J. (2004). *Inferring phylogenies.* Sunderland, MA: Sinauer Associates, Inc.

Felson, R. B., & Reed, M. D. (1986). Reference groups and self-appraisals of academic ability and performance. *Social Psychology Quarterly, 49,* 103–109.

Fenigstein, A. (1984). Self-consciousness and the overperception of self as target. *Journal of Personality and Social Psychology, 47,* 860–870.

Fenigstein, A., Scheier, M. F., & Buss, A. H. (1975). Public and private self-consciousness: Assessment and theory. *Journal of Consulting and Clinical, Psychology, 43,* 522–527.

Fernandez, A. M., Sierra, J. C., Zubeidat, I., & Vera-Villarroel, P. (2006). Sex differences in response to sexual and emotional infidelity among Spanish and Chilean students. *Journal of Cross-Cultural Psychology, 37*(4), 359–365.

Fernandez, D. R., Carlson, D. S., Stepina, L. P., & Nicholson, J. D. (1997). Hofstede's country classification 25 years later. *Journal of Social Psychology, 137,* 43–54.

Fernandez-Dols, J. M., & Ruiz-Belda, M. A. (1997). Spontaneous facial behavior during intense emotional episodes: Artistic truth and optical truth. In J. A. Russell & J. M. Fernandez-Dols (Eds.), *The psychology of facial expressions* (pp. 255–274). New York: Cambridge University Press.

Ferrante, J. (1992). *Sociology: A global perspective.* Belmont, CA: Wadsworth.

Festinger, L. (1957). *A theory of cognitive dissonance.* Stanford: Stanford University Press.

Fiati, T. A. (1992). Cross-cultural variation in the structure of children's thoughts. In R. Case (Ed.), *The minds staircase: Exploring the conceptual underpinnings of children's thought and knowledge* (pp. 319–342). Hillsdale, NJ: Lawrence Erlbaum.

Findley, M. J., & Cooper, H. M. (1983). Locus of control and academic achievement: A literature review. *Journal of Personality and Social Psychology, 44,* 419–427.

Fischer, A. H., Rodriquez Mosquera, P. M., van Vianen, A. E. M., & Manstead, A. (2004). Gender and culture differences in emotion. *Emotion, 4*(1), 87–94.

Fischer, R., & Smith, P. B. (2003). Reward allocation and culture: A meta-analysis. *Journal of Cross-cultural Psychology, 34,* 251–268.

Fischer, R., & Smith, P. B. (2006). Who cares about justice? The moderating effect of values on the link between organizational justice and work behaviour. *Applied Psychology International Review. 55,* 541–562.

Fishman, J. (1960). A systemization of the Whorfian hypothesis. *Behavioral Science, 5,* 323–329.

Fitch, W. T. & Hauser, M. (2004). Computational constraints on syntactic processing in a nonhuman primate. *Science, 303*(5656), 377–80.

Flynn, J. R. (1987). Massive IQ gains in 14 nations: What IQ tests really measure. *Psychological Bulletin, 101*(2), 171–191.

Folger, T. (2012, September). Can we keep getting smarter? *Scientific American,* 44–47.

Forseen, A. S. K., Carlstedt, G., & Mortberg, C. M. (2005). Compulsive sensitivity— A consequence of caring: A qualitative investigation into women carer's difficulties in limiting their labors. *Health Care for Women International, 26*(8), 652–671.

Forston, R. F., & Larson, C. U. (1968). The dynamics of space: An experimental study in proxemic behavior among Latin Americans and north Americans. *Journal of Communication, 18,* 109–116.

Fortunato, L., & Jordan, F. (2010). Your place or mine? A phylogenetic comparative analysis of marital residence in Indo-European and Austronesian societies. *Philosophical Transactions of the Royal Society B: Biological Sciences. 365,* 3913–3922.

Fountoulakis, K. N., Iacovides, A., Ioannidou, C. Bascialla,F. Nimatoudis, I., Kaprinis, G., Janca, A., & Dahl, A. (2002). Reliability and cultural applicability of the Greek version of the International Personality Disorder Examination. *BMC Psychiatry, 2,* 6. doi:10.1186/1471-244X-2-6

Fowers, B. J., & Richardson, F. C. (1996). Why is multiculturalism good? *American Psychologist, 51*(6), 609–621.

Frager, R. (1970). Conformity and anti-conformity in Japan. *Journal of Personality and Social Psychology, 15,* 203–210.

Frank, J. D., & Frank, J. B. (1991). *Persuasion and healing: A comparative study of psychotherapy* (3rd revised ed.). Baltimore, MD: John Hopkins University Press.

French, J. R. P., & Raven, B. (1959). The bases of social power. In D. Cartwright (Ed.) *Studies in social power.* Ann Arbor, MI: University of Michigan Press.

Freud, S. (1940). An outline of psychoanalysis. In J. Strachey (Ed.), *The complete psychological works: Standard edition* (Vol. 23). London: Hogarth Press.

Freud, S. (1961). *The interpretations of dreams.* New York: Science Editions.

Fridlund, A. J. (1997). The new ethology of human facial expressions. In J. A. Russell & J. N. Fernandez-Dols (Eds.), *The psychology of facial expressions* (pp. 103–129). Cambridge: Cambridge University Press.

Friedman, H. S., & Rosenman, R. H. (1974). *Type A behavior and your heart.* London: Wildwood House.

Frijda, N. H. (1986). *The emotions.* Cambridge: Cambridge University Press.

Frijda, N.H. (1993). Moods, emotion episodes, and emotions. In M. Lewis & J.M. Haviland-Jones (Eds.), *Handbook of emotions* (pp. 381–403). New York: Guilford Press.

Frijda, N. H. (1994). Varieties of affect: Emotions and episodes, moods, and sentiments. In P. Ekman & R. J. Davidson (Eds.), *The nature of emotion: Fundamental questions* (pp. 59–67). New York: Oxford University Press.

Frijda, N. H., & Jahoda, G. (1966). On the scope and methods of cross-cultural research. *International Journal of Psychology, 1,* 109–127.

Frost, D. E., & Stahelski, A. J. (1988). The systematic measurement of French and Raven's bases of social power in workgroups. *Journal of Applied Social Psychology, 18,* 375–389.

Fugligni, A., & Stevenson, H. (1995). Time-use and mathematics achievement among American, Chinese, and Japanese high school students. *Child Development, 66,* 830–842.

Funder, D. C. (1995). On the accuracy of personality judgment: A realistic approach. *Psychological Review, 102,* 652–670.

Furnham, A., & Heaven, P. (1999). *Personality and social behaviour.* Arnold, London

Furnham, A., Kirkcaldy, B., & Lynn, R. (1994). National attitudes to competiveness, money, and work among young people: First, second, and third world differences. *Human Relations, 47*(1), 119–132.

Gable, S. L., Reis, H. T., & Elliot, A. J. (2000). Behavioral activation and inhibition in everyday life. *Journal of Personality and Social Psychology, 78,* 1135–1149.

Gabrenya, W. K., Jr., Wang, Y., & Latane, B. (1985). Social loafing on an optimizing task: Cross-cultural differences among Chinese and Americans. *Journal of Cross-Cultural Psychology, 16,* 223–242.

Gabriel, S., & Gardner, W. L. (1999). Are the "his" and "hers" types of interdependence? The implications of gender differences in collective versus relational interdependence for affect, behavior, and cognition. *Journal of Personality and Social Psychology, 77,* 642–655.

Gallup, G. G. (1977). Self-recognition in primates: A comparative approach to the bi-directional properties of consciousness. *American Psychologist, 32,* 329–338.

Gallup, G. G. (1997). On the rise and fall of self-conceptions in primates. In J. G. Snodgrass & R. L. Thomson (Eds.), *The self across psychology: Self-recognition, self-awareness, and the self-concept* (Vol. 3, pp. 73–82). New York: New York Academy of Sciences Press.

Gangestad, S. W., & Scheyd, G. J. (2005). The evolution of human physical attractiveness. *Annual Review of Anthropology, 34,* 523–548.

Gangestad, S. W. & Snyder, M. (2000). Self-monitoring: Appraisals and reappraisals. *Psychological Bulletin, 126,* 530–555.

Garcia-Moreno, C., Jansen, H. A. F. M., Ellsberg, M., Heise, L., & Watts, C. H. (2006). Prevalence of intimate partner violence: Findings from WHO multi-Country study on Women's health and domestic violence. *Lancet, 368,* 1260–1269.

Gardiner, H. W., Mutter, J. D., & Kosmitzki, C. (1998). *Lives across cultures: Cross-cultural human development.* Boston, MA: Allyn & Bacon.

Gardner, H. (1983). *Frames of mind.* New York: Basic Books.

Gardner, W. L., Gabriel, S., & Lee, A. Y. (1999). "I" value freedom, but "we" value relationships: Self-construal priming mirrors cultural differences in judgment. *Psychological Science, 10,* 321–326.

Garland, A. F., Lau, A. S., Yeh, M., McCabe, K. M., Hough, R. L., & Landsverk, J. A. (2005). Racial and ethnic differences in utilization of mental health services among high-risk youths. *American Journal of Psychiatry, 162,* 1336–1343.

Gazzaniga, M. S. (1995). *The cognitive neuroscience.* Cambridge, MA: MIT Press.

Geary, D., Fan, L., & Bow-Thomas, C. (1992). Numerical cognition: Loci of ability differences comparing children from China and the United States. *Psychological Science, 3,* 180–185.

Geletkanycz, M. A. (1997). The salience of "culture's consequences": The effects of cultural values on top executive commitment to the status quo. *Strategic Management Journal, 18,* 615–634.

Gelfand, M. J., Erez, M., & Aycan, Z. (2007). Cross-cultural organizational behaviour. *Annual Review of Psychology, 58,* 479–514.

Gelfand, M. J., Major, V. S., Raver, J. L., Nishii, L. H., & O'Brien, K. (2006). Negotiating relationally: The dynamics of the relational self in negotiations. *Academy of Management Review, 31,* 427–451.

Gelfand, M., Triandis, H. C., & Chan, D. K. S. (1996). Individualism versus collectivism or versus authoritarianism? *European Journal of Social Psychology, 26,* 397–410.

Georgas, J., Berry, J. W., Van de Vijver, F., Kagitcibasi, C., & Poortinga. H. (Eds.). (2006). *Families across cultures: A 30 nation psychological study.* New York: Cambridge University Press.

Georgas, J., Christakopoulou, S., Poortinga, Y., Angleitner, A., Goodwin, R., & Charalambous, N. (1997). The relationship of family bonds to family structure and function across cultures. *Journal of Cross-Cultural Psychology, 28*(3), 303–320.

Gergen, K. J., Gulerce, A., Lock, A., & Misra, G. (1996). Psychological Science in cultural context. *American Psychologist, 51*(5), 496–503.

Gerstein, L. H., Heppner, P. P., Stockton, R., Leung, F. T. L., & Aegisdottir, S. (2009). The counseling profession in- and outside the United States. In L. H. Gerstein, P. P. Heppner, A. Aegisdottir, & A. A., Leung (Eds.), *International handbook of crops-cultural counseling. Cultural assumptions and practices worldwide* (pp. 53–67). Thousand Oaks, CA: Sage.

Gerstner, C. R., & Day, D. V. (1994).Cross-Cultural comparisons of leadership prototypes. *Leadership Quarterly, 5*(2), 121–134.

Gibbons, J., Stiles, D. A., & Shkodriani, G. M. (1991). Adolescents' attitudes toward family and gender roles: An international comparison. *Sex Roles, 25*(11/12), 625–643.

Giddens, A. (2000). *Runaway world: How globalization is reshaping our lives.* New York: Routledge.

Gilligan, C. (1982). *In a different voice: Psychological theory and women's development.* Cambridge, MA: Harvard University Press.

Goethals, G. R., & Darley, J. M. (1977). Social comparison theory: An attributional approach. In J. M. Suls & R. L. Miller (Eds.), *Social comparison processes: Theoretical and empirical perspectives* (pp. 259–278). Washington, DC: Hemisphere/ Halsted.

Goffee, R., & Jones, G. (2006). *Why should anyone be led by you?* Boston: Harvard Business School Publishing.

Goffman, E. (1959). *Presentation of self in everyday life.* Garden City, NY.: Anchor/ Doubleday.

Goldin-Meadow, S., & Mylander, C. (1998). Spontaneous sign systems created by deaf children in two cultures. *Nature, 391,* 279–281.

Goldstein, A. P. (1983). Causes, controls, and alternatives to aggression. In A. P. Goldstein & M. H. Segall (Eds.), *Aggression in global perspective* (pp. 435–474). Elmsford, NY: Pergamon.

Gologor, E. (1977). Group polarization in a non-risk culture. *Journal of Cross-Cultural Psychology, 8,* 331–346.

Goodnow, J. J. (1988). Parents' ideas, actions and feelings: Models and methods from developmental and social psychology. *Child Development, 59,* 286–320.

Goodwin, R. (1990). Sex differences among partner preferences: Are the sexes really very similar? *Sex Roles, 23*(9/10), 501–503.

Gordon, P. (2004). Numerical cognition without words: Evidence from Amazonia. *Science, 306,* 496–499.

Gordon, R. A. (1996). Impact of ingratiation on judgments and evaluations: A meta-analytic investigation. *Journal of Personality and Social Psychology, 71,* 54–70.

Gordon, R. A. (2001). Eating disorder East and West: A culture-bound syndrome unbound. In M. Nasser, M. A. Katzman, & R. A. Gordon (Eds.) *Eating disorder and cultures in transition* (pp. 1–16). New York: Brunner-Routledge.

Gordon, R. G. (2005). *Ethnologue: Languages of the world* (15th ed.). Dallas, TX: SIL International.

Gorman, K. (1995). Malnutrition and cognitive development. *Journal of Nutrition, Supplement 125,* 2239–2445.

Goto, H. (1971). Auditory perception by normal Japanese adults of sounds of "l" or "r." *Neuropsychologia, 9,* 317–323.

Gottfried, A. W., Gottfried, A. E., Bathurst, K., Guerin, D. W., & Parramore, M. M. (2003). Socioeconomic status in children's development and family environment: Infancy through adolescence. In M. H. Bornstein & R. H. Bradley (Eds.), *Socioeconomic status, parenting, and child development* (pp. 189–207). Mahwah, NJ: Lawrence Erlbaum.

Gottlieb, G. (1998). Normally occurring environmental and behavioral influences on gene activity: from central dogma to probabilistic epigenesist. *Psychological Review, 105,* 792–802.

Gottman, J. M., & Levenson, R. W. (2002). A two-factor model for predicting when a couple will divorce: Exploratory analyses using 14-year longitudinal data. *Family Process, 41*(1), 83–96.

Graham, J. A., & Argyle, M. (1975). A cross-cultural study of the communication of extraverbal meaning of gestures. *International Journal of Psychology, 10,* 57–67.

Gray, R. D., & Atkinson, D. (2003). Language-tree divergence times support the Anatolian theory of Indo-European origin. *Nature, 426*, 435–439.

Gray, R.D., Bryant, D., & Greenhill, S. J. (2010). On the shape and fabric of human history. *Philosophical Transactions of the Royal Society, B: Biological Sciences, 365,* 3923–3933.

Gray, R. D., Greenhill, S. J., & Ross, R. M. (2007). The pleasures and perils of Darwinizing culture (with phylogenies). *Biological Theory, 2*, 360–375.

Greenberg, J. H. (Ed.). (1978). *Universals of human language* (Vol. 1–4). Stanford, CA: Stanford University Press.

Greenberg, J. (2012). Terror management theory: From genesis to revelations. In P. R. Shaver, & M. Mikulincer (Eds.). *Meaning, mortality, and choice: The social psychology of existential concerns* (pp. 17–35). Washington D.C.: American Psychological Association.

Greenberg, J., Porteus, J., Simon, L., Pyszczynski, T., & Solomon, S. (1995). Evidence of a terror management function of cultural icons: The effects of mortality salience on the inappropriate use of cherished cultural symbols. *Personality and Social Psychology Bulletin, 21*, 1121–1228.

Greenberg, J., Solomon, S., Pyszczynski, T., Rosenblatt, A., Burling, J., Lyon, D., Pinel, E., & Simon, L. (1992). Assessing the terror management analysis of self-esteem: Converging evidence of an anxiety-buffering function. *Journal of Personality and Social Psychology, 63*, 913–922.

Greene, D., Sternberg, B., & Lepper, M. R. (1976). Overjustification in a token economy. *Journal of Personality and Social Psychology, 34*, 1219–1234.

Greenfield, P. M. (1997). You can't take it with you: Why ability assessments don't cross cultures. *American Psychologist, 52*, 1115–1124.

Greenfield, P. M. (2004). *Weaving generations together: Evolving creativity in the Maya of Chiapas.* Santa Fe, NM: School of American Research.

Gregersen, H. B., & Black, J. S. (1996). Multiple commitments upon repatriation: The Japanese experience. *Journal of Management, 22*, 209–229.

Greve, W., & Wentura, D. (2003). Immunizing the self: Self-concept stabilization through reality-adaptive self-definitions. *Personality and Social Psychology Bulletin, 29*, 39–50.

Griner, D., & Smith, T. B. (2006). Culturally adapted mental health interventions. A meta-analytic review. Psychotherapy: Theory, research, practice, *Training, 43*, 531–548.

Grisaru, N., Budowski, D., & Witztum, E. (1997). Possession by the "Zar" among Ethiopian immigrants to Israel: Psychopathology or culture-bound syndrome? *Psychopathology, 30*(4), 223–233.

Grogan, S. (2008). Body image: *Understanding body dissatisfaction in men, women, and children* (2nd Ed.). New York: Psychology press.

Grunbaum, J. A., Kann, L., Kinchen, S., Ross, J., Hawkins, J., Lowry, R., Harris, W. A., McManus, T., Chyen, D., & Collins, J. (2004). Youth risk behavior surveillance—United States, 2003. *Morbidity and Mortality Weekly Report CDC Surveillance Summaries, 2004, May 21, 53*(2), 1–96.

Guanzon-Lapena, Ma. M., Church, A. T., Carlota, A. J., & Katigbak, M. S. (1998). Indigenous personality measures: Philippine examples. *Journal of Cross-Cultural Psychology, 29*, 249–270.

Guarnaccia, P. J., Martinez, I., & Acosta, H. (2005). Mental health in the Hispanic immigrant community: An overview. *Journal of Immigrant and Refugee Services, 3,* 21–46.

Guarnaccia, P. J., & Rogler, L. H. (1999). Research on culture-bound syndromes: new directions. *American Journal of Psychiatry, 156*(9), 1322–1327.

Gudykunst, W. B. (1993). Toward a theory of effective interpersonal and intergroup communication: An anxiety/uncertainty management (AUM perspective). In R. L. Wiseman, J. Koester (Eds.), *International and Intercultural communication annuals: Intercultural communication competence* (Vol. 17, pp. 33–71), Newbury Park, CA: Sage.

Gudykunst, W. B., Gao, G., Nishida, T., Nadamitsu, Y. & Sakai, J. (1992). Self-monitoring in Japan and the United States. In S. Iwawaki, Y. Kashima & K. Leung (Eds.), *Innovations in Cross-Cultural Psychology: Selected Papers from the Tenth International Conference of the International Association for Cross-Cultural Psychology.* Berwyn, PA: Swets & Zeitlinger.

Gudykunst, W. B., Gao, G., Schmidt, K. L., Nishida, T., Bond, M., Leung, K., Wang, G., & Barraclough, R. A.(1992). The influence of individualism-collectivism, self-monitoring, and predicted-outcome value on communication in ingroup and outgroup relationships. *Journal of Cross-Cultural Psychology, 23,* 196–213.

Gudykunst, W. B., & Nishida, T. (1986). The influence of cultural variability on perceptions of communication behavior associated with relationship terms. *Human Communication Research, 13,* 147–166.

Gudykunst, W. B., & Shapiro, R. B. (1996). Communication in everyday interpersonal and intergroup encounters. *International Journal of Intercultural Relations, 20*(1), 19–45.

Gudykunst, W. B., Ting-Toomey, S., and Chua, E. (1988). *Culture and interpersonal communication.* Beverly Hills, CA: Sage.

Guglielmino, C. R., Viganotti, C., Hewlett, B. S., & Cavalli-Sforza, L.L. (1995). Cultural variation in Africa: Role of mechanisms of transmission and adaptation. *Proceedings of the National Academy of Sciences, USA, 92*(16), 7585–7589. doi:10.1073/pnas.92.16.7585

Gurung, R.A . R. (2010). *Health psychology: cultural approach* (2nd Ed.), San Francisco: Cengage.

Haidt, J. (2001). The emotional dog and its rational tail: A social intuitionist approach to moral judgment. *Psychological Review, 108,* 814–834.

Haidt, J., & Keltner, D. (1999). Culture and facial expressions: Open-ended methods find more expressions and a gradient of recognition. *Cognition and Emotion, 13,* 225–266.

Hall, E.T. (1966). *The hidden dimension.* New York: Doubleday.

Hall, E.T. (1976). *Beyond culture.* New York: Doubleday.

Hall, G. C. N. (2001). Psychotherapy research with ethnic minorities: Empirical, ethical, and conceptual issues. *Journal of Consulting and Clinical Psychology, 69,* 502–510.

Hall, J. A. (1984). *Nonverbal gender differences: Accuracy of communication and expressive style.* Baltimore: John Hopkins University Press.

Haller, M., & Hadler, M. (2006). How social relations and structures can produce happiness and unhappiness: An international comparative analysis. *Social Indicators Research, 75*, 169–216.

Hamid, P. N. (1994). Self-monitoring, locus of control, and social encounters of Chinese and new Zealand students. *Journal of Cross-Cultural Psychology, 25*(3), 353–368.

Hanakawa, T., Honda, M., Okada, T., Fukuyama, H., & Shibasaki, H. (2003). Neural correlates underlying mental calculation in abacus experts: A functional magnetic resonance imaging study. *Neuroimage, 19*, 296–307.

Hanh, N. (1988). *The heart of understanding.* Berkeley, CA: Parallax Press.

Hardy, K., & Larsen, K.S. (1971). Personality and selectivity factors as predictors of social conformity among college girls. *The Journal of Social Psychology, 83*, 147–148.

Hare, R. D. (1993). *Without conscience: The disturbing world of psychopaths among us.* New York: Simon & Shuster/Pocket.

Harkness, S., & Super, C. H. (1995). *Parent's cultural belief system: their origins, expressions, and consequences.* New York: Guildford Press.

Harkness, S., & Super, C. M. (2006). Themes and variations: Parental ethnotheories in Western cultures. In K. Rubin & O. Chung (Eds.), *Parenting beliefs, behaviors, and parent-child relations: A Cross-Cultural Perspective* (pp. 61–79). New York: Psychology Press.

Harmon-Jones, E., Simon, L., Greenberg, J., Pyszczynski, T., Solomon, S., & McGregor, H. (1997). Terror management theory and self-esteem: Evidence that increased self-esteem reduces mortality salience effects. *Journal of Personality and Social Psychology, 72*(1), 24–36.

Harper, F., Guilbault, M., Tucker, T., & Austin, T. (2007). Happiness as a goal of counseling: Cross-cultural implications. *International Journal of Advanced Counseling, 29*, 123–136.

Harris, R. L., Schoen, L. M., & Hensley, D.L. (1992). A cross-cultural study of story memory. *Journal of Cross-Cultural Psychology, 23*, 133–147.

Hart, D., & Damon, W. (1986). Developmental trends in self-understanding. *Social Cognition, 4*, 388–407.

Harter, S. (1983). Developmental perspectives on the self-system. In M. Hetherington (Ed.), *Handbook of child psychology: Social and personality development* (Vol. 4, pp. 275–385). New York: Wiley.

Harter, S. (2003). The development of self-representations during childhood and adolescence. In M. Leary & J. P. Tangney (Eds.), *Handbook of self and identity* (pp. 610–642). New York: Guildford Press.

Hatano, G. (1997). Commentary: Core domains of thought, innate constraints, and socio-cultural contexts. In H. M. Wellman & K. Inagaki (Eds.), *The emergence of core domains of thought: Children's reasoning about physical, psychological, and biological phenomena* (pp. 71–78). San Francisco: Jossey-Bass.

Hatfield, E., & Rapson, R. L. (1996). *Love and sex: Cross-cultural perspectives.* Boston: Allyn & Bacon.

Hausmann, R., Tyson, L. D., & Zahidi, S. (2008). The global gender gap report 2008. *World Economic Forum.*Geneva, Switzerland. Retrieved from: https://members.weforum.org/pdf/gendergap/report2008.pdf, Last access 16.04.2012

Haybron, D. (2008). The pursuit of unhappiness. In D. Haybron (Ed.), *The pursuit of unhappiness: The elusive psychology of well-being.* (pp. 225–252). Oxford University Press.

Hayes, A. (2011). *Survey: 1 in 3 women affected by partner's violent behavior.* CNN, December 15, Retrieved from: http://www.cnn.com/2011/12/15/health/violence-survey, Last access March 24, 2013.

Hayles, R. V. (1991). African-American strength: A survey of empirical findings. In R. Jones (Ed.), *Black Psychology* (3rd ed., pp. 379–400). Berkeley, CA: Cobb & Henry.

Heatherton, T. F., & Polivy, J. (1991). Development and validation of a scale for measuring state self-esteem. *Journal of Personality and Social Psychology, 60,* 895–910.

Hebb, D.O. (1949). *The organization of behavior.* New York: Wiley.

Hedges, L, & Nowell, A. (1995). Sex differences in mental test scores, variability, and numbers of high-scoring individuals. *Science, 269,* 41–45.

Heggarty, P., Maguire, W., & McMahon, A. (2010). Splits or weaves? Trees or webs? How divergence measures and network analysis can unravel language histories. *Philosophical Transactions of the Royal Society, 365,* 3829–3843.

Heiman, G. (1996). *Basic statistics for the behavioral sciences.* Boston, MA: Houghton Mifflin.

Heimpel, S. A., Wood, J. V., Marshall, M. A., & Brown, J. D. (2002). Do people with low self-esteem really want to feel better? Self-esteem differences in motivation to repair negative moods. *Journal of Personality and Social Psychology, 82,* 128–147.

Heine, S. J. (2005). Constructing good selves in Japan and North America. *In culture and social behavior: The tenth Ontario symposium* (pp. 115–143). Hillsdale, NJ.: Erlbaum.

Heine, S. J., Kitayama, S., Lehman, D.R., Takata, T., Ide, E., Leung, C., & Matsumoto, H. (2001). Divergent consequences of success and failure in Japan and North America: An investigation of self-improving motivations and malleable selves. *Journal of Personality and Social Psychology, 81,* 599–615.

Heine, S. J., & Lehman, D. R. (1995). Cultural variation in unrealistic optimism: Does the West feel more invulnerable than the East? *Journal of Personality and Social Psychology, 68,* 595–607.

Heine, S. J., & Lehman, D. R. (2003). Move the body, change the self: Acculturative effects on the self-concept. In M. Schaller & C. S. Crandall (Eds.), *Psychological foundations of culture* (pp. 305–331). Mahwah, NJ: Lawrence Erlbaum Associates.

Heine, S. J., Lehman, D. R., Markus, H. R., & Kitayama, S. (1999). Is there a universal need for positive self-regard. *Psychological Review, 106,* 766–794.

Heine, S. J., Lehman, D. R., Peng, K., & Greenholtz, J. (2002). What's wrong with cross-cultural comparisons of subjective Likert scales: The reference group effect. *Journal of Personality and Social Psychology, 82*(6), 903–918.

Heine, S. J., & Renshaw, K. (2002). Interjudge agreement, self-enhancement, and liking: Cross-cultural divergences. *Personality and Social Psychology Bulletin, 28,* 578–587.

Heller, F. A., & Wilpert, B. (1981). *Competence and power in managerial decision-making.* Chichester: Wiley.

Helman, C. (2007). *Culture, health, and illness* (5th ed.). Oxford: UK Butterworth Heinemann.

Henderlong, J., & Lepper, M. R., (2002). The effects of praise on children's intrinsic motivation: A review and synthesis. *Psychological Bulletin, 128,* 774–795.

Henrich, J., & Boyd, R. (1998). The evolution of conformist transmission and the emergence of between-group differences. *Evolutionary Human Behavior, 19,* 215–241.

Henrich, J., & Boyd, R. (2002). On modeling cognition and culture: Why cultural evolution does not require replication of representations. *Journal of Cognition and Culture, 2,* 87–112.

Henrich, J., & Gil-White, F. (2001). The evolution of prestige: Freely conferred deference as a mechanism for enhancing the benefits of cultural transmission. *Evolution and Human Behavior, 22*(3), 165–196.

Hermans, J. M., & Kempen, J. G. (1998). Moving cultures: The perilous problems of cultural dichotomies in a globalizing society. *American Psychologist, 53*(10), 1111–1120.

Herrnstein, R. J., & Murray, C. (1994). *The bell curve: Intelligence and class structure in American life.* New York: Free Press.

Herskovits, M. J. (1948). *Man and his works: The science of cultural anthropology.* New York: Knopf.

Hess, R. D., Kashiwagi, K., Azuma, H., Price, G. G., & Dickinson, W. P. (1980). Maternal expectation for mastery of developmental tasks in Japan and the United States. *International Journal of Psychology, 15,* 259–271.

Higgins, E. T. (1987). Self-discrepancy: A theory relating self and affect. *Psychological Review, 94,* 319–340.

Higgins, E. T. (1999). Self-discrepancy: A theory relating self and affect. In R. F. Baumeister (Ed.), *The Self in social psychology. Key readings in social psychology* (pp. 150–181). Philadelphia: Psychology Press.

Higgins, E. T. & Bargh, J. A. (1987). Social cognition and social perception. *Annual Review of Psychology, 38,* 369–425.

Hinde, R. A. (1982). *Ethology: Its nature ad relations to other sciences.* New York: Oxford University Press.

Hinde, R. A. (1987). *Individuals, relationships, and culture.* Cambridge: Cambridge University Press.

Hirschfield, L. A. (1996). *Race in the making: Cognition, culture, and the child's construction of human kinds.* Cambridge, MA: MIT Press.

Hirt, E. R., McCrea, S.M., & Boris, H. I. (2003). " I know you self-handicapped last exam": Gender differences in reactions to self-handicapping. *Journal of Personality and Social Psychology, 84,* 177–193.

Hirt, E. R., Zillman, D., Erickson, G. A., & Kennedy, C. (1992). Costs and benefits of allegiance: Changes in fan's self-ascribed competence after team victory versus defeat. *Journal of Personality and Social Psychology, 63,* 724–738.

Ho, D. Y. F. (1998). Indigenous psychologies: Asian perspectives. *Journal of Cross-Cultural Psychology, 29(1),* 88–103.

Ho, D. Y. F. (2000). Dialectical thinking: Neither Eastern nor Western. *American Psychologist, 55,* 1064–1065.

Hofstede, G. (1980). *Culture's consequences: International differences in work-related values.* Beverly Hills, CA: Sage.

Hofstede, G. (1983). The cultural relativity of organizational practices and theories. *Journal of International Business Studies, 14,* 75–89.

Hofstede, G. (2001). *Culture's consequences: Comparing values, behaviors, institutions, and organizations across nations* (2nd ed.). Thousand Oaks, CA: Sage.

Hofstede, G., & Bond, M. H. (1984). Hofstede's cultural dimensions: An independent validation using Rokeach's value survey. *Journal of Cross-cultural Psychology, 15*(4), 417–433.

Hofstede, G., Bond, M., & Luk, C. L. (1993). Individual perceptions of organizational cultures: A methodological treatise on levels of analysis. *Organization Studies, 14,* 483–503.

Hofstede, G., Neuijen, B., Ohayv, D. D., & Sanders. (1990). Measuring organizational cultures: A qualitative and quantitative study across twenty cases. *Academy of Management Journal: Administrative Science Quarterly, 35,* 286–316.

Hofstede, W. K. B., Kiers, H. A., De Raad, B., Goldberg, L. R., & Ostendorf, F. (1997). A comparison of Big Five structures of personality traits in Dutch, English, and German. *European Journal of Personality, 11*(1), 15–31.

Hollon, S. D., & Beck, A. T. (1994). Cognitive and cognitive behavioral therapies. In A. E. Bergin, & S. L. Garfield (Eds.), *Handbook of psychotherapy and behavior change* (4th ed., pp. 428–466). New York: Wiley.

Holloway, S. D. (1988). Concepts of ability and effort in Japan and the United States. *Review of Educational Research, 58,* 327–45.

Holmberg, D., Markus, H., Herzog, A. R., & Franks, M. (1997). *Self-making in American adults: Content, structure, and function.* Ann Arbor: University of Michigan.

Hong, Y. Y., Morris, M., & Chiu, C.-Y., & Benet-Martinez, V. (2000). Multicultural minds: A dynamic constructivist approach to culture and cognition. *American Psychologist, 55,* 709–720.

Hook, J. L. (2006). Care in context: Men's unpaid work in 20 countries, 1965–2003. *American Sociological Review, 71*(4), 639–660.

Hoosain, R. (1991). *Psycholinguistic implications for linguistic relativity: A case study of Chinese.* Hillsdale, NJ: Lawrence Erlbaum.

Hoppe, M. H. (1990). *A comparative study of country elites: International differences in work-related values and learning and their implications for management training development.* Unpublished Ph.D. thesis. Chapel Hill, University of North Carolina.

Hopper, K., & Wanderling, J. (2000). Revisiting the developed versus developing country distinction in course and outcome of schizophrenia: Results from ISoS, the WHO collaborative follow-up project. *Schizophrenia Bulletin, 26*(4), 835–846.

House R. J., Hanges, P. W., Javidan, M., Dorfman, P., & Gupta, V. (Eds.). (2004). *Culture, leadership, and organizations: The GLOBE study of 62 societies.* Thousand Oaks, CA: Sage.

Howell, J. P., Dorfman, P. W., Hibino, ,S. M., Lee, J. K., & Tale, U. (1995). *Leadership in Western and Asian countries: Communalities and differences in effective leadership processes and substitutes across cultures.* Las Cruces: New Mexico State University.

Huang, T., Chi, S., & Lawler, J. S. (2005). The relationship between expatriates' personality traits and their adjustment to international assignments. *International Journal of Human Resource Management, 16,* 1656–1670.

Hui, C. H. (1988). Measurement of individualism-collectivism. *Journal of Research in Personality, 22,* 17–36.

Hui, C., Lee, C. & Rousseau, D. M. (2004). Psychological contracts and organizational citizenship behavior in China: Investigating generalizability and instrumentality. *Journal of Applied Psychology, 89,* 311–321.

Hull, J. G., Young, R. D., & Jouriles, E. (1986). Applications of the self-awareness model of alcohol consumption: Predicting patterns of use and abuse. *Journal of Personality and Social Psychology, 51,* 790–796.

Hull, P. V. (1987). *Bilingualism: Two languages, two personalities? Resources in education, educational resources clearing house on education.* Ann Arbor: University of Michigan Press.

Hull, P. V. (1990) *Bilingualism: Two languages, two personalities?* Doctoral dissertation, University of California, Berkeley.

Humphreys, L. G. (1985). Race differences and the Spearman hypothesis. *Intelligence, 9,* 275–283.

Hundley, G., & Kim, J. (1997). National culture and the factors affecting perceptions of pay fairness in Korea and the United States. *International Journal of Organizational Analysis, 5,* 325–342.

Hunt, E. B., & Agnoli, F. (1991). The Whorfian hypothesis: A cognitive psychology perspective. *Psychological Review, 98,* 377–389.

Huntington, S. P. (1993). The clash of civilizations? *Foreign Affairs, 72*(3), 22–49.

Hurford, J. R. (2007). *The origins of meaning: Language in the light of evolution* (Vol. 1). Oxford: Oxford University Press.

Hwang, K. K. (2005a). From anticolonialism to postcolonialism: The emergence of Chinese indigenous psychology in Taiwan. *International Journal of Psychology, 40*(4), 228–238.

Hwang, K. K. (2005b). A philosophical reflection on the epistemology and methodology of indigenous psychologies. *Asian Journal of Social Psychology, 8*(1), 5–17.

Hwang, K. K. (2012). *Foundations of Chinese psychology: Confucian social relations.* Springer Science Business Media, LLC. Springer New York Dordrecht Heidelberg London.

Hwang, K. K., Kim, U., & Kou-Shu, Y. (2006). *Indigenous and Cultural Psychology.* New York: Springer.

Hwang, K. K., & Yang, C. F. (Eds.). (2000). Indigenous, cultural and cross-cultural psychologies. *Asian Journal of Social Psychology, 3,* 183–293.

Ickes, W., Robertson, E., Tooke ,W., & Teng, G. (1986). Naturalistic social cognition: Methodology, assessment, and validation. *Journal of Personality and Social Psychology, 51*(1), 66–82.

IDE (Industrial Democracy in Europe International Research Group). (1981). *Industrial democracy in Europe.* Oxford: Clarendon Press.

Inglehart, R. (1990). *Culture shift in advanced industrial society.* Princeton: Princeton University Press.

Inglehart, R. (1997). *Modernization and post modernization: Cultural, economic, and political change in 43 societies.* Princeton, NJ: Princeton University Press.

Inglehart, R., Foa, R., Peterson, C., & Welzel, C. (2008). Development, freedom, and rising happiness: A global perspective (1981–2007). *Perspectives on Psychological Science, 3,* 264–285.

Inkeles, A. (1966). The modernization of man. In M. Weiner (Ed.), *Modernization: The dynamics of growth* (pp.151–163). NY: Basic Books.

Isaacson, W. (2007, April 5). Einstein & faith. *Time.* Retrieved from: http://www.time.com/time/magazine/article/0,9171,1607298-2,00.html, Last access April 17, 2012.

Itard, J. M. G. (1962). *The wild boy of Aveyron.* New York: Appleton-Century-Crofts.

Iwata, N., & Higuchi, H. R. (2000). Responses of Japanese and American university students to the STAI items that assess the presence or absence of anxiety. *Journal of Personality Assessment, 74,* 48–62.

Iyengar, S. S., & Lepper, M. R. (1999). Rethinking the value of choice: A cultural perspective on intrinsic motivation. *Journal of Personality and Social Psychology, 76,* 349–366.

Izard, C. E. (1971). *The face of emotion.* New York: Appleton-Century-Crofts.

Izard, C. E. (1994). Innate and universal facial expressions: Evidence from developmental and cross-cultural research. *Psychological Bulletin, 115,* 188–299.

Jablensky, A., Sartorius, N., Ernberg, G., Anker, M., Korten, A., Cooper, J. E., Day, A., & Bertelsen, A. (1992). Schizophrenia: Manifestations , incidence and course in different cultures. A World Health Organization ten-country study. *Psychological Medicine, Monograph Supplement, 20,* 1–97.

Jablonka, E., & Lamb, M.J. (2005). *Evolution in four dimensions. Genetic, epigenetic, behavioral, and symbolic variation in the history of life.* Cambridge, MA: MIT Press.

Jackson, L. M., Pratt, M., W. Hunsberger, B., & Pancer, S. (2005). Optimism as a mediator of the relation between perceived parental authoritativeness and adjustment among adolescents: Finding the sunny side of the street. *Social Development, 14*(2), 273–304.

Jahoda, G. (1984). Do we need a concept of culture? *Journal of Cross-Cultural Psychology, 15,* 139–151.

Janis, I. L. (1983). *Groupthink* (2nd ed.). Boston: Houghton-Mifflin.

Jensen, A. (1968). Social class, race and genetics: Implications for education. *American Educational Research Journal, 5*(1), 1–42.

Jensen, A. (1984). The black-white differences on the K-ABC: Implications for future tests. *Journal of Special Education, 18*(3), 377–408.

Jensen, A. (1985). The nature of Black-White differences on various psychometric tests: Spearman's hypothesis. *Behavioral and Brain Sciences, 8,* 193–263.

Jensen, A., & Johnson, F. W. (1994). Race and sex differences in head size and IQ *Intelligence, 18*(3), 309–333.

Jessner, U. (1999). Metalinguistic awareness in multilinguals: Cognitive aspects of third language learning. *Language Awareness, 8*(3&4), 201–209.

Ji, L. J., Peng, K., & Nisbett, R. E. (2000). Culture, control, and perception of relationships in the environment. *Journal of Personality and Social Psychology, 78,* 943–955.

Ji, L. J., Zhang, Z., & Nisbett, R. (2004). Is it culture or is it language? Examination of language effects in cross-cultural research on categorization. *Journal of Personality and Social Psychology, 87*(1), 57–65.

John, O. P., & Robins, R. W. (1993). Determinants of interjudge agreement on personality traits: The Big Five domains, observability, evaluativeness, and the unique perspective of the self. *Journal of Personality, 61,* 521–551.

John, O. P., & Srivastava, S. (1999). The Big Five trait taxonomy: History, measurement, and theoretical perspectives. In L. A. Pervin & O. P. John (Eds.), *Handbook of personality: Theory and research* (2nd ed., pp. 102–138). New York: Guildford Press.

Johnson, P. (1976). A *history of Christianity*. London: Weidenfeld & Nicolson.

Jones, E. E., & Pittman, T. (1982). Toward a general theory of strategic self-presentation. In J. Suls (Ed.), *Psychological perspectives on the self* (Vol. 1, pp. 231–262). Hillsdale, NJ.: Erlbaum.

Jordan, M., & Sullivan, K. (1996, September 8). A matter of saving face: Japanese can rent mourners, relatives, friends, even enemies to buff image. *Washington Post,* A1, A28.

Juni, S. (1996). Review of the revised NEO Personality Inventory. In J. C. Conoley & J. C. Impara (Eds.), *12th mental measurement yearbook* (pp. 863–868). Lincoln: University of Nebraska Press.

Kagan, J. (1989). Temperamental contributions to social behavior. *American Psychologist, 44,* 668–674.

Kagitcibasi, C. (1996). *Family and human development across cultures: A view from the other side.* Hillsdale, NJ: Erlbaum.

Kagitcibasi, C. (1997). Individualism and collectivism. In J. W. Berry, M. H. Segall, & C. Kagitcibasi (Eds.), *Handbook of cross-cultural psychology: Social behaviour and applications* (2nd ed., Vol. 3, pp. 1–49). Boston, MA: Allyn & Bacon.

Kang, S. M., Shaver, P. R., Sue, S., Min, K. H., & Jing, H. (2003). Culture-specific patterns in the prediction of life satisfaction: Roles of emotion, relationship quality, and self-esteem. *Personality and Social Psychology Bulletin, 29,* 1596–1608.

Kaplan, G., Pamuk, E., Lynch, J., Cohen, R., & Balfour, J. (1996). Inequality in income and mortality in the United States. *British Medical Journal, 312,* 999–1003.

Karavasilis, L., Doyle, A., & Markiewicz, D. (2003). Associations between parenting style and attachment to mother in middle childhood and adolescence. *International Journal of Behavioral Development, 27*(2), 153–164.

Kashima, Y., Siegel, M., Tanaka, K., & Kashima, E. S. (1992). Do people believe behaviors are consistent with attitudes? Towards a cultural psychology of attribution process. *British Journal of Social Psychology, 31,* 111–124.

Katigbak, M. S., Church, A. T., Guanzon-Lapena, M. A., Carlota, A. J., & del Pilar, G. H. (2002). Are indigenous personality dimensions culture specific? Philippine inventories and the five-factor model. *Journal of Personality and Social Psychology, 82*(1), 89–101.

Katz, J., & Beach, S. R. H. (2000). Looking for love? Self-verification and self-enhancement effects on initial romantic attraction. *Personality and Social Psychology Bulletin, 26,* 1526–1539.

Kauffman, D. R., & Steiner, I. D. (1968). Conformity as an ingratiation technique. Journal of *Experimental Social Psychology, 4,* 404–414.

Kawa, S., Giordano, J. (2012). A brief historicity of the Diagnostic and Statistical Manual of Mental Disorders: Issues and implications for the future of psychiatric canon and practice. *Philosophy, Ethics, and Humanities in Medicine, 7*, 2. doi:10.1186/1747-5341-7-2.

Kay, P., & Kempton, W. (1984). What is the Sapir-Whorf hypothesis? *American Anthropologist, 86*, 65–79.

Kazarian, S., & Evans, D. (Eds.). (1998). *Cultural clinical psychology: theory, research and practice.* New York: Oxford University Press.

Keats, D. M. (1982). Cultural bases of concepts of intelli-gence: A Chinese versus Australian comparison. In P. Sukontasarp, N. Yongsiri, P. Intasuwan, N. Jotiban, & C. Suvannathat (Eds.), *Proceedings of the Second Asian Workshop on Child and Adolescent Development* (pp. 67–75). Bangkok: Burapasilpa Press.

Keil, M., Im, G. P., & Mahring, M. (2007). Reporting bad news on software projects: The effects of culturally constituted views of face-saving. *Information Systems Journal, 17*, 59–87.

Kelly, G. A. (1955). *The psychology of personal constructs* (Vols. 1 & 2). New York: Norton.

Kemmelmeier, M., Burnstein, E., Krumov, K., Genkova, P., Kanagawa, C., Hirshberg, M. S., Erb, H., Wieczorkowska, G., & Noels, K. (2003). Individualism, collectivism, and authoritarianism in seven societies. *Journal of Cross-Cultural Psychology, 34*, 304–322.

Kendzierski, D., & Whitaker, D. J. (1997). The role of self-schema in linking intentions with behavior. *Personality and Social Psychology Bulletin, 23*, 139–147.

Kenrick, D. T., & Keefe, R. C. (1992). Age preferences in mates reflect sex differences in human reproductive strategies. *Behavioral and Brain Sciences, 15*, 75–133.

Khalcefa, O. H., Erdos, G., & Ashria, I. H. (1996). Creativity in an indigenous Afro-Arab Islamic culture: The case of Sudan. *Journal of Creative Behavior, 30*(4), 268–282.

Khandwalla, P. N. (1988). Organizational effectiveness. In J. Panday (Ed.), *Psychology in India: The state of the art* (Vol. 3, pp. 97–215). New Delhi: Sage.

Kihlstrom, J. F. (1990). The psychological unconscious. In L. A. Pervin (Ed.), *Handbook of personality: Theory and research* (pp. 445–464). New York: Guildford Press.

Kim, U. (2000). Indigenous, cultural, and cross-cultural psychology: A theoretical, conceptual, and epistemological analysis. *Asian Journal of Social Psychology, 3*(3), 265–287.

Kim, U. (2001). Culture, science, and indigenous psychologies: An integrate analysis. In D. Matsumoto (Ed.), *Handbook of culture and psychology* (pp. 51–75). Oxford, UK: Oxford University Press.

Kim, U., & Berry, J. W. (Eds.). (1993). *Indigenous psychologies: Research and experience in the cultural context.* Newberry Park, CA: Sage.

King, L. A., Hicks, J. A., Krull, J. I., & Del Gaiso, A. K. (2006). Positive affect and the experience of the meaning of life. *Journal of Personality and Social Psychology, 90*, 179–196.

King, M., Nazroo, J., Weich, S., McKenzie, K., Bhui, K., Karlson, S., Stansfeld, S., Tyrer, P., Blanchard, M., Lloyd, K., McManus, S., Sproston, K., & Erens, B. (2005). Psychotic symptoms in the general population of England—A comparison of ethnic groups (The EMRIRIC study). *Social Psychiatry and Psychiatric Epidemiology, 40*(5), 375–381.

King, R. C., & Bu, N. (2005). Perceptions of the mutual obligations between employees and employers: A comparative study of new generation IT professionals in China and the United States. *International Journal of Human Resource Management, 16*, 46–64.

Kirby, S. (2007). The evolution of language. In R. Dunbar & L. Barrett (Eds.), *Oxford handbook of evolutionary psychology*. Oxford: Oxford University Press.

Kirkman, B. L., & Shapiro, D. L. (1997). The impact of cultural values on employee resistance to teams: Toward a model of globalized self-managing work team effectiveness. *Academy Management Review, 22*, 730–757.

Kitayama, S. (1992). Some thoughts on the cognitive-psychodynamic self from a cultural perspective. *Psychological Inquiry, 3*, 41–44.

Kitayama, S., & Cohen, D. (2007). *Handbook of cultural psychology*. New York: Guilford Press.

Kitayama, S., & Markus, H.R. (1994a). *Emotion and culture: Empirical studies of mutual influence*. Washington, DC: American Psychological Association.

Kitayama, S., & Markus, H. R. (1994b). Culture and the self: How cultures influence the way we view ourselves. In D. Matsumoto (Ed.), *People: Psychology from a cultural perspective* (pp. 17–37). Pacific Grove, CA: Brooks/Cole.

Kitayama, S., & Markus, H. R. (2000). The pursuit of happiness and the realization of sympathy: Cultural patterns of self, social relations, and well-being. In E. Diener, & E.M. Suh (Eds.), *Cultural and subjective well-being* (pp. 113–161). Cambridge, MA: MIT Press.

Kitayama, S., Markus, H. R., Matsumoto, H., & Norasakkunit, V. (1997). Individual and collective processes in the construction of the self: Self-enhancement in the United States and self-criticism in Japan. *Journal of Personality and Social Psychology, 72*, 1245–1267.

Kitchen, A., Ehret, C., Assefa, S., & Mulligan, C. J. (2009). Bayesian phylogenetic analysis of Semitic languages identifies an Early Bronze Age origin of Semitic in the Near East. Proceedings of the Royal Society, *Biological Sciences, 276*, 2703–2710.

Klar, Y., & Giladi, E. E. (1999). Are most people happier than their peers, or are they just happy? *Personality and Social Psychology Bulletin, 25*, 585–594.

Klein, S. B., & Kihlstrom, J. F. (1986). Elaboration, organization, and the self-reference effect in memory. *Journal of Experimental Psychology: General, 115*, 26–38.

Klein, S. B., & Loftus, J. (1988). The nature of self-referent encoding: The contributions of elaborative and organizational processes. *Journal of Personality and Social Psychology, 55*, 5–11.

Kleinman, A. M. (1980). *Patients and healers in the context of culture*. Berkeley, CA: University of California Press.

Kleinman, A. M. (1986). *Social origins of distress and disease: Depression, neurasthenia, and pain in modern China*. New Haven, CT: Yale University Press.

Kleinman, A. (1988). *Rethinking psychiatry: From cultural category to personal experience*. New York: Free Press.

Kleinman, A. M. (2004). Culture and depression. *New England Journal of Medicine, 351*, 951–953.

Knight, G., & Kagan, S. (1977). Acculturation of prosocial and competitive behaviors among second- and third-generation Mexican-American children. *Journal of Cross-Cultural Psychology, 8*(3), 273–285.

Knowles, E. S., & Sibicky, M. E. (1990). Continuity and diversity in the stream of selves: Metaphorical resolutions of William James's one-in-many-selves paradox. *Personality and Social Psychology Bulletin, 16,* 676–687.

Kohlberg, L. (1981). *The philosophy of moral development: Moral stages and the idea of justice.* San Francisco: Harper & Row.

Kohlberg, L., Levine, C., & Hewer, A. (1983). Moral stages: a current formulation, and a response to critics. In J. A. Meacham (Ed.), *Contributions to human development* (Vol. 10), New York: Kargen.

Kolstad, A. (2012) . Inter-functionality between mind, biology and culture: Some epistemological issues concerning human psychological development. In Seidl-de-Moura, M. L. (Ed.). *Human development—Different perspectives.* Published by InTech, ISBN 978-953-51-0610-4.

Koole, S. L., Smeets, K., van Knippenberg, A., & Dijksterhuis, A. (1999). The cessation of rumination through self-affirmation. *Journal of Personality and Social Psychology, 77,* 111–125.

Koole, S. L., Dijksterhuis, A, & van Knippenberg, A. (2001). What's in a name: Implicit self-esteem and the automatic self. *Journal of Personality and Social Psychology, 80,* 669–685.

Koopman, C. (1997). Political psychology as a lens for viewing traumatic events. *Political Psychology, 18*(4), 831–847.

Kornadt, H.-J., & Tachibana, Y. (1999). Early child-rearing and social motives after nine years: A cross-cultural longitudinal study. In W. J. Lonner & D. L. Dinnel (Eds.), *Merging past, present, and future in cross-cultural psychology: Selected papers from the Fourteenth International Congress of the International Association for Cross-Cultural Psychology* (pp. 429–441). Lisse, Netherlands: Swets & Zeitlinger.

Krueger, J. (1998). Enhancement bias in descriptions of self and others. *Personality and Social Psychology Bulletin, 24,* 506–516.

Kruger, J. (1999). Lake Wobegon be gone! The 'below-average effect' and the egocentric nature of comparative ability judgments. *Journal of Personality and Social Psychology, 77,* 221–232.

Kruger, J., & Burrus, J. (2004). Egocentrism and focalism in unrealistic optimism (and pessimism). *Journal of Experimental Social Psychology, 40*(3), 332–340.

Krumov, K. (2005). Political Culture. In Leonard, T. M. (Ed.), *Encyclopedia of the developing world* (Vol. 3). New York, London: Routledge Taylor & Francis Group..

Krumov, K., & Larsen, K. S. (Eds.). (2007). *Migration: Current issues and problems.* Sofia: SOFI-R.

Krumov, K., & Larsen, K. S. (Eds.). (2009). *Migration processes and globalization challenges.* Burgas: Bryag.

Kuebli, J., & Fivush, R. (1992). Gender differences in parent–child conversations about past emotions. *Sex Roles, 27, 683–698*

Kuhnen, U., Hannover, B., Roeder, U., Ali Shah, A., Schubert, B., Upmeyer, A., & Zakaria, S. (2001). Cross-cultural variations in identifying embedded figures: Comparisons from the United States, Germany, Russia, and Malaysia. *Journal of Cross-Cultural Psychology, 32*(3), 365–374.

Kurman, J. (2001). Self-regulation strategies in achievement settings: Culture and gender differences. *Journal of Cross-Cultural Psychology, 32,* 491–503.

Kurman, J., & Sriram, N. (2002). Interrelationships among vertical and horizontal collectivism, modesty, and self-enhancement. *Journal of Cross-Cultural Psychology, 33*(1), 71–87.

Lacey, P. (1971). Classificatory ability and verbal intelligence among high-contact Aboriginal and low socioeconomic white Australian children. *Journal of Cross-Cultural Psychology, 2*(1), 39–49.

Laland, K. N., Odling-Smee, J., & Feldman, M. W. (2000). Niche construction, biological evolution, and cultural change. *Behavioral and Brain Sciences, 23,* 131–175.

Lalwani, A. K., Shavitt, S., & Johnson, T. (2006). What is the relation between cultural orientation and socially desirable responding? *Journal of Personality and Social Psychology, 90*(1), 165–178.

Lam, S. S. K., Schaubroeck, J., Aryee, S. (2002).Relationship between organizational justice and employee work outcomes: A cross-national study. *Journal of Organizational Psychology, 23,* 1–18.

Lambert, W. E., & Anisfeld, E. (1969). A note on the relationship of bilingualism and intelligence. *Canadian Journal of Behavioral Sciences, 1,* 123–128.

Lamm, H., Schaude, E., & Trommsdorff, G. (1971). Risky shift as a function of group members' value of risk and need for approval. *Journal of Personality and Social Psychology, 20*(3), 430–435.

Lammers, C. J., & Hickson, D. J. (Eds.). (1979). *Organizations alike and unlike: International and inter-institutional studies in the sociology of organizations.* London: Routledge and Kegan Paul.

Lang, P. J. (1995). The emotion probe. *American Psychologist, 50,* 372–385.

Langer, E. (1975). The illusion of control. *Journal of Personality and Social Psychology, 32,* 311–328.

Langlois, J. H., Kalakanis, L., Rubenstein, A. J., Larson, A., Hallam, M., & Smoot, M. (2000). Maxims or myths of beauty? A meta-analytic and theoretical review. *Psychological Bulletin, 126,* 390–423.

Langman, P. F. (1997). White culture, Jewish culture and the origins of psychotherapy. *Psychotherapy: Theory, Research, Practice Training, 34,* 207–218.

La Roche, M., & Christopher, M. S. (2008). Culture and empirically supported treatments: On the road to a collision? *Culture and Psychology, 14,* 333–356.

Larsen, K. S. (1969). Authoritarianism, self-esteem, and insecurity. *Psychological Reports, 25,* 229–230.

Larsen, K. S. (1970). Cognitive complexity and dogmatism as determinants of displacement in social judgment. *Proceedings, 8th Annual Convention. American Psychological Association,* 377–378

Larsen, K. S. (1971). Affectivity, cognitive style, and social judgment. *Journal of Personality and Social Psychology, 19*(1), 119–123.

Larsen, K. S. (1972). Determinants of peace agreement, pessimism-optimism, and expectations of world conflict: A cross-national study. *Journal of Cross-Cultural Psychology, 3*(3), 283–292.

Larsen, K. S. (1974a) Social cost, belief incongruence and race: Experiments in choice behavior. *Journal of Social Psychology, 94,* 253–267.

Larsen, K. S. (1974b). Emotional responses to approval-seeking and personal identity frustration. *Psychological Reports, 23*, 403–405.

Larsen, K. S. (1974c). Conformity in the Asch experiment. *The Journal of Social Psychology, 94*, 303–304.

Larsen, K. S. (1974d). Situational pressure, attitudes toward Blacks, and laboratory aggression. *Social Behavior and Personality, 2*(2), 219–221.

Larsen, K. S. (1977). *Discrimination toward Aborigines and Islanders in Northern Queensland: The case of Townsville.* Canberra: Australian Government Publishing Service.

Larsen, K. S. (1978a). White attitudes towards Aborigines: A working framework. *The Australian Quarterly, 50*(4), 94–113.

Larsen, K. S. (1978b). The role of the Aboriginal Medical Services. *Australian Journal of Social Issues, 13*(4), 261–275.

Larsen, K. S. (1979a). Social crisis and Aboriginal alcohol abuse. *Australian Journal of Social Issues, 14*(2), 143–159.

Larsen, K. S. (1979b). A black community health program-perspective for training. *Australian Psychologist, 14*(1), 45–56.

Larsen, K. S. (1980). Aboriginal group identification and problem drinking. *Australian Psychologist, 15*(3), 385–392.

Larsen, K. S. (1981). White attitudes in Townsville: Authoritarianism, religiosity, and contact. *Australian Psychologist, 16*(1), 111–122.

Larsen, K. S. (1982). Cultural conditions and conformity: The Asch effect. *Bulletin of the British Psychological Society, 35*, 347.

Larsen, K. S. (1990) The Asch conformity experiment: Replication and transhistorical comparisons. *Journal of Social Behavior and Personality, 5*(4), 163–168.

Larsen, K. S. (1993). *Dialectics and ideology in psychology.* Norwood, NJ: Sage Publications.

Larsen, K. S., Coleman, D., Forbes, J., & Johnson, R. (1972). Is the subject's personality or the situation a better predictor of willingness to administer shock to a victim? *Journal of Personality and Social Psychology, 22*(3), 287–295.

Larsen, K. S., & Long, E. (1988). Attitudes toward sex roles: Traditional or egalitarian? *Sex Roles, 19*, 1–12.

Larsen, K. S., Martin, H. J., Ettinger, R. H., & Nelson, J. (1976). Approval seeking, social cost, and aggression: A scale and some dynamics. *The Journal of Psychology, 94*, 3–11.

Larsen, K. S., Triplet, J. S., Brant, W. D., & Langenberg, D. (1979). Collaborator status, subject characteristics, and conformity in the Asch experiment. *The Journal of Social Psychology, 108*, 259–263.

Larsen, K. S., & Van Le, H. (2010). Agent Orange and war related stress: Physical and psychological disorders. *Journal of Social Management, 8*(2), 73–88.

Lau, A. L. D., Cummins, R. A., & McPherson, W. (2005). An investigation into the cross-cultural equivalence of the Personal Well-being Index. *Social Indicators Research, 72*, 403–430.

Lavric, M., & Flere, S. (2008). The role of culture in the relationship between religiosity and psychological well-being. *Journal of Religion and Health, 47*(2), 164–175.

Lawler, E. E. III. (1986). *High involvement management.* San Francisco: Jossey-Bass.

Lawson, E. (1975). Flag preference as an indicator of patriotism in Israeli children. *Journal of Cross-Cultural Psychology, 6*(4), 490–497.

Leadbeater, B. J., & Way, N. (2001). *Growing up fast: Transitions to early adulthood of inner-city adolescent mothers.* Mahwah, NJ: Erlbaum.

Leahey, T. M., Crowther, J. H., & Mickelson, K. D. (2007). The frequency, nature, and effects of naturally occurring appearance-focused social comparisons. *Behavior Therapy, 38,* 132–143.

Leary, M. R., Cottrell, C. A., & Phillips, M. (2001). Deconfounding the effects of dominance and social acceptance on self-esteem. *Journal of Personality and Social Psychology, 81,* 898–909.

Leary, M. R., & Jones, J. L. (1993). The social psychology of tanning and sunscreen use: Self-presentational variables as a predictor of health risk. *Journal of Applied Social Psychology, 23,* 1390–1406.

Leary, M. R., & Kowalski, R. M. (1990). Impression management: A literature review and two-component model. *Psychological Bulletin, 107,* 34–47.

Leary, M. R., Tambor, E. S., Terdal, S. K., & Downs, D. L. (1995). Self-esteem as an interpersonal monitor: The sociometer hypothesis. *Journal of Personality and Social Psychology, 68,* 518–530.

Lee, A. Y., Aaker, J. L., & Gardner, W. L. (2000). The pleasures and pains of distinct self-construals: The role of interdependence in regulatory focus. *Journal of Personality and Social Psychology, 78,* 1122–1134.

Lee, S. (2001). From diversity to unity: The classification of mental disorder in 21st century China. *Cultural Psychiatry: International Perspectives, 24*(3), 421–431.

Leff, J. (1977). International variations in the diagnosis of psychiatric illness. *British Journal of Psychiatry, 131,* 329–338.

Leont'ev, A.N. (1981). *Problems of the development of mind.* Moscow: Progress Publishers.

Lepper, M. R., Henderlong, J., & Gingras, I. (1999). Understanding the effects of extrinsic rewards on intrinsic motivation-uses and abuses of meta-analysis: Comment on Deci, Koestner, and Ryan (1999). *Psychological Bulletin, 125,* 669–676.

Leung, K., Bond, M. H., Reimel de Carrasquel, S., Munoz, C., Hernandez, M., Murakami, F., Yamaguchi, S., Bierbrauer, G., & Singelis, T. M. (2002). Social axioms: The search for universal dimensions of general beliefs about how the world functions. *Journal of Cross-Cultural Psychology, 33*(3), 286–302.

LeVine, R. A. (1977). Child rearing as cultural adaptation. In P. H. Leiderman, S. R. Tulkin, & A. Rosenfeld (Eds.), *Culture and infancy: Variations in the human experience* (pp. 15–27). New York: Academic Press.

LeVine, R. A., LeVine, S. E., Dixon, S., Richman, A., Leiderman, P. H., Keefer, C. & Brazelton, T. B. (1994). *Child care and culture: Lessons from Africa.* Cambridge, UK: Cambridge University Press.

Levine, R., Sato, S., Hashimoto, T., & Verma, J. (1995). Love and marriage in eleven cultures. *Journal of Cross-Cultural Psychology, 26*(5), 544–571.

Levinson, S. C. (2006). Introduction: The evolution of culture in a microcosm. In S. C. Levinson & P. Jaisson (Eds.), *Evolution and culture: A Fyssen Foundation symposium.* (pp. 1–41). MA: Massachusetts Institute of Technology Press.

Levy, E. I. (1984). The emotions in comparative perspective. In K. R. Scherer & P. Ekman (Eds.), *Approaches to emotion* (pp. 397–412). Hillsdale, NJ: Erlbaum.

Lewicki, P. W. (1983). Self-image bias in person perception. *Journal of Personality and Social Psychology, 45*, 384–393.

Lewis-Fernandez, R., & Kleinman, A. (1994). Culture, personality, and psychopathology. *Journal of Abnormal Psychology, 103*(1), 67–71.

Lewis, M. (1997). The self in self-conscious emotions. In J. G. Snodgrass & R. L. Thompson (Eds.), *The self across psychology: Self-recognition, self-awareness, and the self-concept* (pp. 119–142). New York: New York Academy of Sciences Press.

Lewis, P. (2008). Personality development. In S. F. Davis & W. Buskist (Eds.), *21st century psychology: A reference handbook* (Vol. 1, pp. 392–401). Thousand Oaks, CA: Sage.

Lewontin, R. C. (1972). The apportionment of human diversity. *Evolutionary Biology, 6*, 381–398.

Lightfoot-Klein, H. (1989). *Prisoners of ritual: An odyssey into female genital circumcision in Africa.* New York: Harrington Park Press.

Lin, E. J.-L., & Church, A. T. (2004). Are indigenous Chinese personality dimensions culture-specific? *Journal of Cross-Cultural Psychology, 35*, 586–605.

Lin, P., & Schwanenflugel, P. J. (1995). Cultural familiarity and language factors in the structure of category knowledge. *Journal of Cross-Cultural Psychology, 26*(2), 153–168.

Linville, P. W. (1985). Self-complexity and affective extremity: Don't put all your eggs in one cognitive basket. Depression (Special issue). *Social Cognition, 3*, 94–120.

Lipo, C. P., & Madsen, M. E. (2001). Neutrality, 'style,' and drift: Building models for studying cultural transmission in the archaeological record. In T. D. Hurt & C. F. M. Rakita (Eds.), *Style and function: Conceptual issues in evolutionary archaeology* (pp. 91–118). Westport, CT: Bergin and Garvey.

Li-Repac, D. (1980). Cultural influences on clinical perception: A comparison between Caucasian and Chinese-American therapist. *Journal of Cross-Cultural Psychology, 11*, 327–342.

Livingston, R. (1999). Cultural issues in diagnosis and treatment of ADHD. *Journal of American Academy of Child and Adolescent Psychiatry, 38, 1591–1594.*

Locke, K. D. (2003). Status and solidarity inn social comparisons: Agentic and communal values and vertical and horizontal directions. *Journal of Personality and Social Psychology, 84*, 619–631.

Lockwood, P. (2002). Could it happen to you? Predicting the impact of downward social comparisons on the self. *Journal of Personality and Social Psychology, 82*, 343–358.

Lockwood, P., Marshall, T., & Sadler, P. (2005). Promoting success or preventing failure: Cultural differences in motivation by positive and negative role models. *Personality and Social Psychology Bulletin, 31*, 379–392.

Loehlin, J. C. (1992). *Genes and environment in personality development.* Newbury Park, CA: Sage.

Loehlin, J. C., Horn, J. M., Willerman, L. (1989). Modeling IQ change: Evidence from the Texas adoption project. *Child Development, 60*, 993–1004.

Lonner, W. J. (1980). The search for psychological universals. In H. C. Triandis & W. W. Lambert (Eds.), *Handbook of cross-cultural psychology: Perspectives* (Vol. 1, pp. 143–204). Boston, MA: Allyn & Bacon.

Lonner, W. J., & Ibrahim, F. A. (1989). Assessment in cross-cultural counseling. In P. B. Pedersen, J. Draguns, W. Lonner, & J. E. Trimble (Eds.), *Counseling across cultures* (3rd ed., pp. 299–334). Honolulu University of Hawaii Press.

Loranger, A. W., Sartorius, N., Andreoli, A., Berger, P., Buchheim, P., Channabasavanna, S. M., Coid, B., Dahl, A., Diekstra, R., & Ferguson, B., et al. (1994). The international personality disorder examination. The World Health Organization/Alcohol, Drug Abuse, and Mental Health Administration International Pilot Study of Personality Disorders. *Archives of General Psychiatry, 51*(3), 215–224.

Luce, E. (2010, September 10). Unions too weak to upset the apple cart. *Financial times.* Retrieved from: http://www.ft.com/intl/cms/s/0/88906434-bcf6-11df-954b-00144feab49a.html#axzz2AJMva1WN. Last access April 22, 2012.

Lumsden, C. J., & Wilson, E. O. (1981). *Genes, mind and culture: The coevolutionary process.* Cambridge, MA: Harvard University Press.

Luria, A. R. (1976). *Cognitive development: Its cultural and social foundations.* Cambridge, MA: Harvard University Press.

Lycett, S. J. (2009). Are Victoria West cores 'proto-Levallois'? A phylogenetic assessment. *Journal of Human Evolution, 56,* 175–191.

Lykken, D., & Tellegen, A. (1996). Happiness is a stochastic phenomenon. *Psychological Science, 7,* 186–189.

Lynch, J. M. & Kaplan, G. (1997). Understanding how inequality in the distribution of income affects health. *Journal of Health Psychology, 2,* 297–314.

Lyubomirsky, S., King, L. A., & Diener, E. (2005).The benefits of frequent positive affect: Does happiness lead to success.. *Psychological Bulletin, 131,* 803–855.

Ma, H. K. (1988). The Chinese perspective on moral judgment development. *International Journal of Psychology, 23,* 201–227.

Ma, H. K., & Cheung, C. K. (1996). A cross-cultural study of moral stage structure in Hong Kong Chinese, English, and Americans. *Journal of Cross-Cultural Psychology, 27*(6), 700–713.

Maccoby, E. E. (1990). Gender and relationships: A developmental account. *American Psychologist, 45,* 513–520.

Maccoby, E. E., & Jacklin, C. N. (1974). *The psychology of sex differences.* Stanford, CA: Stanford University Press.

Maccoby, E. E., & Martin, J. A. (1983). Socialization in the context of the family: Parent-child interaction. In P. H. Müssen (Series Ed.) & E. M. Hetherington (Vol. Ed.), *Handbook of child psychology: Socialization, personality, and social development* (Vol. 4, pp. 1–101). New York: Wiley.

MacDonald, K. B. (1995). Evolution, the five factor model, and levels of personality. *Journal of Personality, 63,* 525–567.

MacDonald, K. (1998). Evolution, culture, and the five-factor model. *Journal of Cross-Cultural Psychology, 29*(1), 119–149.

Mace, R., & Holden, C. J. (2005). A phylogenetic approach to cultural evolution. *Trends in Ecological Evolution, 20,* 116–121.

Madsen, M. C. (1971). Developmental and cross-cultural differences in the cooperative and competitive behavior of young children. *Journal of Cross-Cultural Psychology, 2,* 365–371.

Magana, S., & Smith, M. J. (2006). Psychological distress and well-being of Latina and non-Latina White mothers of youth and adults with an autism spectrum disorder: Cultural attitudes towards co-residence status. *American Journal of Orthopsychiatry, 76*(3), 346–357.

Malatesta, C. Z. (1990). The role of emotions. I. the development and organization of personality. In R. A. Thompson (Ed.), *Socio-emotional development: Nebraska Symposium on Motivation* (pp. 1–56). Lincoln: University of Nebraska Press.

Malinowski, B. (1960). *A scientific theory of culture and other essays.* New York: Oxford University Press.

Malpass, R. S. (1977). Theory and method in cross-cultural psychology. *American Psychologist, 32,* 1069–1079.

Malpass, R. S. (1993). *Towards understanding cross-racial recognition.* Paper presented at the International Conference on Face Processing, September, Cardiff, Wales

Man, C.D., & Lam, S. S. K. (2003). The effects of job complexity and autonomy on cohesiveness in collectivistic and individualistic work groups: A cross-cultural analysis. *Journal of Organizational Behavior, 24,* 979–1001.

Mange, E. J., & Mange, A. (1999). *Basic human genetics* (2nd ed.). Sunderland, MA: Sinauer.

Manian, N., Strauman, T. J., & Denney, N. (1998). Temperament, recalled parenting styles, and self-regulation: Retrospective tests of the developmental postulates of self-discrepancy theory. *Journal of Personality and Social Psychology, 75,* 1321–1332.

Mann, C. C. (2011). The birth of religion. *National Geographic, 219,* 39–59.

Mann, L., Radford, M., Burnett, P., Ford, S., Bond, M., Leung, K., Nakamura, H., Vaughan, G., & Yang, K. S. (1998). Cross-cultural differences in self-reported decision-making style and confidence. *International Journal of Psychology, 33,* 325–335.

Markus, H. (1977). Self-schemata and processing information about the self. *Journal of Personality and Social Psychology, 35,* 63–78.

Markus, H. R., & Kitayama, S. (1991a). Culture and the self: Implications for cognition, emotion, and motivation. *Psychological Review, 98*(2), 224–253.

Markus, H. R., & Kitayama, S. (1991b). Cultural variation in self-concept. In G. R. Goethals & J. Strauss (Eds.), *Multidisciplinary perspectives on the self* (pp. 18–48). New York: Springer-Verlag.

Markus, H.R., & Kitayama, S. (1994a). The cultural shaping of emotion: A conceptual framework. In S. Kitayama & H. R. Markus (Eds.), *Emotion and culture: Empirical studies of mutual influence* (pp. 339–351). Washington, DC: American Psychological Association.

Markus, H. R., & Kitayama, S. (1994b). A collective fear of the collective: Implications for selves and theories of selves. The self and the collective (Special issue). *Personality and Social Psychology Bulletin, 20,* 568–579.

Markus, H. R., & Nurius, P. S. (1986). Possible selves. *American Psychologist, 41,* 954–969.

Markus, H., & Wurf, E. (1987). The dynamic self-concept: A social-psychological perspective. *Annual Review of Psychology, 38,* 299–337.

Marsella, A. J. (1980). Depressive experience and disorder across cultures. In H.C. Triandis & J. Draguns (Eds.), *Handbook of cross-cultural psychology: Psychopathology* (Vol. 6, pp. 237–289). Boston: Allyn & Bacon.

Marsella, A. J. (2009). Diversity in a global era: The context and consequences of differences. *Counseling Psychology Quarterly, 22,* 119–135.

Marsella, A. J., Kaplan, A., & Suarez, E. (2002). Cultural considerations for understanding, assessment, and treating depressive experience and disorder. In M. Reinecke & M. Davison (Eds.), *Comparative treatments of depression* (pp. 47–78). New York: Springer.

Marsh, H. W., & Parker, J. W. (1984). Determinants of student self-concept: Is it better to be relatively large fish in a small pond if you don't learn to swim so well? *Journal of Personality and Social Psychology, 47,* 213–231.

Marshall, G. N., Schell, T. L., Elliot, M. N., Berthold, S. M., & Chun, C. A. (2005). Mental health of Cambodian refugees 2 decades after resettlement in the United States. *JAMA, 294,* 571–579.

Maslow, A. (1970a). *Religions, values, and peak experience.* New York: Penguin Books.

Maslow, A. H. (1970b). *Motivation and personality* (2nd ed.). New York: Harper & Row.

Masuda, T., & Nisbett, R. E. (2001). Attending holistically vs. analytically : Comparing the context sensitivity of Japanese and Americans. *Journal of Personality and Social Psychology, 81,* 922–934.

Matsumoto, D. (1989). Cultural influences on the perception of emotion. *Journal of Cross-Cultural Psychology, 20,* 92–105.

Matsumoto, D. (1992a). American-Japanese cultural differences in the recognition of universal facial expressions. *Journal of Cross-Cultural Psychology, 23,* 72–84.

Matsumoto, D. (1992b). More evidence for the universality of a contempt expression. *Motivation & Emotion, 16,* 363–368.

Matsumoto, D. (1994). *People: Psychology from a cultural perspective.* Pacific Grove, CA: Brooks/Cole.

Matsumoto, D. (1999). Culture and the self: An empirical assessment of Markus and Kitayama's theory of independent and interdependent self-construals. *Asian Journal of Social Psychology, 2,* 289–310.

Matsumoto, D. (2001). Culture and emotion. In D. Matsumoto (Ed.), *The handbook of culture and psychology* (pp. 171–194). New York: Oxford University Press.

Matsumoto, D. (2002). *The new Japan.* Yarmouth, ME: Intercultural Press.

Matsumoto, D. (2006a). Culture and cultural worldviews: Do verbal descriptions about culture reflect anything other than verbal descriptions of culture? *Culture and Psychology, 12*(1), 33–62.

Matsumoto, D. (2006b). Culture and nonverbal behavior. In V. Manusov & M. L. Patterson (Eds.), *The sage handbook of nonverbal communication* (pp. 219–235). Thousand Oaks, CA: Sage Publications.

Matsumoto, D., & Ekman, P. (1989). American-Japanese cultural differences in intensity ratings of facial expressions of emotion. *Motivation and Emotion, 13*(2), 143–157.

Matsumoto, D., & Ekman, P. (2004). The relationship between expressions, labels, and descriptions of contempt. *Journal of Personality and Social Psychology, 87,* 529–540.

Matsumoto, D., & Fletcher, D. (1996). Cultural influences on disease. *Journal of Gender, Culture, and Health, 1,* 71–82.

Matsumoto, D., Grissom, R., & Dinnel, D. (2001). Do between-culture differences really mean that people are different? A look at some measures of cultural effect size. *Journal of Cross-Cultural Psychology, 32*(4), 478–490.

Matsumoto, D., & Hwang, H. S. (2011). Culture, emotion, and expression. In K. D. Keith (Ed.), *Cross-Cultural Psychology.* Malden, MA: Blackwell-Wiley.

Matsumoto, D., Kasri, F., & Kooken, K. (1999). American-Japanese cultural differences in judgments of expression intensity and subjective experience. *Cognition and Emotion, 13*(2), 201–218.

Matsumoto, D., Keltner, D., Shiota, M. N., Frank, M. G., & O'Sullivan, M. (2008). What's in a face? Facial expressions as signals of discrete emotions. In M. Lewis, J. M. Haviland, & L. Feldman (Eds.), *Handbook of emotions* (pp. 211–234). New York: Guildford Press.

Matsumoto, D., Kudoh, T., Scherer, K., & Wallbott, H. (1988). Antecedents of and reactions to emotions in the United States and Japan. *Journal of Cross-Cultural Psychology, 19*(3), 267–286.

Matsumoto, D., & LeRoux, J. A. (2003). Measuring the psychological engine of intercultural adjustment: the intercultural adjustment potential scale. *Journal of Intercultural Communications, 6,* 27–52.

Matsumoto, D., LeRoux, J. A., Bernhard, R., & Gray, H. (2004). Personality and behavioral correlates of intercultural adjustment potential. *International Journal of Intercultural Relations, 28,* 281–309.

Matsumoto, D., Weissman, M., Preston, K., Brown, B., Kupperbusch, C. (1997). Context-specific measurement of individualism-collectivism on the individual level: The IC Interpersonal Assessment Inventory (ICIAI). *Journal of Cross-Cultural Psychology, 28,* 743–767.

Matsumoto, D., & Willingham, B. (2006). The thrill of victory and the agony of defeat: Spontaneous expressions of medal winners at the 2004 Athens Olympic Games. *Journal of Personality and Social Psychology, 91*(3), 568–581.

Matsumoto, D., & Willingham, B. (2009). Spontaneous facial expressions of emotion of congenitally and non-congenitally blind individuals. *Journal of Personality and Social Psychology, 96*(1), 1–10.

Matsumoto, D., & Yoo, S. (2006). Toward a new generation of cross-cultural research. *Perspectives on Psychological Science, 1*(3), 234–250.

Matsumoto, D., Yoo, S. H., Fontaine, J., Anguas-Wong, A. M., Arriola, M., Ataca, B., Bond, M. H., Boratav, H.B., Breugelmans, S. M., Cabecinhas,R., Chae, J., Chin, W. H., Comunian, A. L., DeGere, D. N., Djunaidi, A., Fok, H. K., Friedlmeier, W., Ghosh, A., Glamcevski, M., Granskaya, J. V., Groenvynck, H., Harb, C., Haron, F., Joshi, R., Kakai, H., Kashima, E., Khan, W., Kurman, J., Kwantes, C. T., Mahmud, S. H., Mandaric, M., Nizharadze, G., Odusanya, J. O. T., Ostrosky-Solis, F., Palaniappan, A. K., Papastylianou, D., Safdar, S., Setiono, K., Shigemasu, E., Singelis, T. M., Polackova Solcova, Iva, Spieß, E., Sterkowicz, S., Sunar, D., Szarota, P., Vishnivetz, B., Vohra, N., Ward, C., Wong, S., Wu, R., Zebian, S., & Zengeya, A. (2008). Mapping expressive differences around the world: The relationship between emotional display rules and individualism vs. collectivism. *Journal of Cross-Cultural Psychology, 39*(1), 55–74.

Matud, M. P. (2005). The psychological impact of domestic violence on Spanish women. *Journal of Applied Social Psychology, 35*(11), 2310–2322.

Mauss, I. B., Levenson, R. W., McCarter, L., Wilhelm, F. L., & Gross, J. J. (2005). The tie that binds? Coherence among emotional experience, behavior, and physiology. *Emotion, 5,* 175–190.

Maxwell, J. A. (1992). Understanding and validity in qualitative research. *Harvard Educational Review, 62*(3), 279–300.

Mazur, A. (1985). A biosocial model of status in face-to-face primate groups. *Social Forces, 64*(2), 377–402.

McClelland, D. C. (1958). The use of measures of human motivation in the study of society. In Atkinson (Ed.), *Motives in fantasy, action, and society* (pp. 518–554). Princeton, NJ: Van Nostrand.

McClelland, D. C. (1987). *Human motivation.* Cambridge: Cambridge University Press.

McCluskey, K., Albas, D., Niemi, R., Cuevas, C., & Ferrer, C. (1975). Cross-cultural differences in the perception of the emotional content of speech. *Developmental Psychology, 11,* 551–555.

McConatha, J. T., Lightner, E., & Deaner, S. L. (1994). Culture, age, and gender as variables in the expression of emotions. *Journal of Social Behavior and Personality, 9*(3), 481–488.

McCracken, L. M., Matthews, A. K., Tang, T. S., & Cuba, S. L. (2001). A comparison of blacks and whites seeking treatment for chronic pain. *Clinical Journal of Pain, 17,* 249–255.

McCrae, R. R. (2001). Trait psychology and culture: Exploring intercultural comparisons. *Journal of Personality, 69*(6), 819–846.

McCrae, R. R. (2002). NEO-PI-R data from 36 cultures: Further intercultural comparisons. In R. R. McCrae & J. Allik (Eds.), *The five-factor model of personality across cultures* (pp. 105–126). New York: Kluwer Academic/Plenum.

McCrae, R. R., & Costa, P. T. (1987). Validation of the Five Factor Model of personality, across instruments and observers. *Journal of Personality and Social Psychology, 52,* 81–90.

McCrae, R. R., & Costa, P. T. (1997, May). Personality trait structure as a human universal. *American Psychologist, 52*(5), 509–51. DOI: 10.1037/0003-066X.52.5.509

McCrae, R. R., & Costa, P. T. (2003). *Personality in adulthood: A five-factor theory perspective* (2nd ed.). New York: Guildford Press.

McCrae, R. R., Costa, P. T., del Pilar, G. H., Rolland, J. P., & Parker, W. D. (1998). Cross-cultural assessment of the five factor model: The revised NEO personality inventory. *Journal of Cross-cultural Psychology, 29*(1), 171–188.

McCrae, R. R., Terracciano, A., Khoury, B., Nansubuga, F., Knezevic, G., Djuric Jocic, D., et al. (2005). Universal features of personality traits from the observer's perspective: Data from 50 cultures. *Journal of Personality and Social Psychology, 88*(3), 547–561.

McCrae, R. R., Terracciano, A., Leibovich, N. B., Schmidt, V., Shakespeare-Finch, J., Neubauer, A., et al. (2005). Personality profiles of cultures: Aggregate personality traits. *Journal of Personality and Social Psychology, 89*(3), 407–425.

McCrea, S. M., & Hirt, E. R. (2011). Limitations on the substitutability of self-protective processes: Self-handicapping is not reduced by related-domain self-affirmations. *Social Psychology, 42*(1), 9–18. doi: 10.1027/1864-9335/a000038.

McGrath, R. G., MacMillan, I. C, Yang, E. A .Y., & Tsai, W. (1992). Does culture endure, or is it malleable? Issues for entrepreneurial economic development. *Journal of Business Venturing, 7,* 441–458.

McGregor, H., Lieberman, J. D. Solomon, S., Greenberg, T., Arndt, J., & Simon, L. (1998). Terror management and aggression: Evidence that mortality salience motivates aggression against world-view threatening others. *Journal of Personality and Social Psychology, 74,* 590–605.

McGurk, H., & Jahoda, G. (1975). Pictorial depth perception by children in Scotland and Ghana. *Journal of Cross-cultural Psychology, 6*(3), 279–296.

McHale, S. M., Crouter, A. C., & Whiteman, S. D. (2003). The family contexts of gender development in childhood and adolescence. *Social Development, 12*(1), 125–148.

Mejía-Arauz, R., Rogoff, B., & Paradise, R. (2005). Cultural variation in children's observations during a demonstration. *International Journal of Behavioral Development, 29,* 283–291.

Merritt, A. (2000). Culture in the cockpit: Do Hofstede's dimensions replicate? *Journal of Cross-cultural Psychology, 31,* 283–301.

Mesoudi, A., & O'Brien, M. J. (2009). Placing archaeology within a unified science of cultural evolution. In S. J. Shennan (Ed.), *Placing archeology within a unified science of cultural evolution* (pp. 21–32). Berkeley, CA: University of California Press.

Mesoudi, A., Whiten, A., & Laland, K. N. (2006). Towards a unified science of cultural evolution. *Behavioral Brain Science, 29,* 329–383.

Mesquita, B. (2001). Emotions in collectivist and individualist contexts. *Journal of Personality and Social Psychology, 80,* 68–74.

Mesquita, B., Frijda, N. H., & Scherer, K. R. (1997). Culture and emotion. In J. W. Berry, P. R. Dasen, & T. S. Saraawathi (Eds.), *Handbook of cross-cultural psychology: Basic processes and human development* (2nd ed., Vol. 2, pp. 255–297). Boston, MA: Allyn & Bacon.

Meyer, J. P., Stanley, D. J., Herscovitch, L., & Topolnytsky, L. (2002). Affective, continuance, and normative commitment to the organization: A meta-analysis of antecedents, correlates, and consequences. *Journal of Vocational Behavior, 61,* 20–52.

Michalon, M. (2001). "Selflessness" in the service of the ego: Contributions, limitations, and dangers of Buddhist psychology for Western psychotherapy. *American Journal of Psychotherapy, 55,* 202–218.

Milgram, S. (1961). Nationality and conformity. *Scientific American, 205,* 45–51.

Milgram, S. (1963). Behavioral study of obedience. *Journal of Abnormal and Social Psychology, 69,* 137–143.

Miller, K., & Rasco, M. (2004). An ecological framework for addressing the mental health needs of refugee communities. In K. Miller & L. Rasco (Eds.), *The mental health of refugees: Ecological approaches to healing and adaptation* (pp. 1–64). Mahwah, NJ: Lawrence Erlbaum Associates.

Miller, P. (2012, January). Twins: Alike but not alike. *National Geographic,* 39–65.

Miller, P. C., Lefcourt, H. M., Holmes, J. G., Ware, E. E., & Saleh, W. E. (1986). Marital locus of control and marital problem solving. *Journal of Personality and Social Psychology, 51,* 161–169.

Minsel, B., Becker, P., & Korchin, S. (1991). A cross-cultural view of positive mental health. *Journal of Cross-cultural Psychology, 22,* 157–181.

Mirin, S. (2002). Testimony of Steven M. Mirin, M.D. Medical Director for the American Psychiatric Association on the HIPAA code set issues/ICD-10-CM implementation before the National Committee on Vital and Health Statistics Standards and Security Subcommittee, May 29.

Mishra, C. (1997). Cognition and cognitive development. In J. W. Berry, P. R. Dasen, & T. S. Saraswathi (Eds.), *Handbook of cross-cultural psychology: Basic processes and human development* (Vol. 2, pp. 143–176). Boston: Allyn & Bacon.

Misumi, J. (1984). Decision-making in Japanese groups and organizations. In B. Wilpert & A. Sorge (Eds.), *International perspectives on organizational democracy* (Vol. 2, pp. 525–539). Chichester: Wiley.

Misumi, J. (1985). *The behavioural science of leadership. An interdisciplinary Japanese research program.* Ann Arbor, MI: University of Michigan Press.

Mitchell, R. W. (2003). Subjectivity and self-recognition in animals. In M. R. Leary & J. P. Tangney (Eds.), *Handbook of self and identity* (pp. 567–593). New York: Guildford Press.

Miyahara, A. (1984). *A need for a study to examine the accuracy of American observers' perceptions of Japanese managers' communication styles.* Paper presented at the Eastern Communication Association Convention, Philadelphia.

Miyawaki, K., Strange, W., Verbrugge, R., Liberman, A. M., Jenkins, J. A., & Fujimura, O. (1975). An effect of linguistic experience: The discrimination of (r) and (l) by native speakers of Japanese and English. *Perception and Psychophysics, 18,* 331–340.

Mohanty, A. (1994). *Bilingualism in a multilingual society: Implications for cultural integration and education.* Keynote address, 23rd International Congress of Applied Psychology, Madrid, July, 1994.

Mor, N., & Winquist, J. (2002). Self-focused attention and negative affect: A meta-analysis. *Psychological Bulletin, 128,* 638–662.

Morelli, G. A., Rogoff, B., Oppenheim, D., & Goldsmith, D. (1992). Cultural variations in infants' sleeping arrangements: Questions of independence. *Developmental Psychology, 28*(4), 604–613.

Moretti, M., & Higgins, E. T. (1990). Relating self-discrepancy to self-esteem: The contribution of discrepancy beyond actual self-ratings. *Journal of Experimental Social Psychology, 26,* 108–123.

Morris, D., Collett, P., & Marsh, P., & O'Shaughnessy, M. (1980). *Gestures: Their origins and distribution.* New York: Scarborough.

Morris, M. W., & Leung, K. (2000). Justice for all? Progress in research on cultural variations in the psychology of distributive and procedural justice. *Applied Psychology: An international research journal. 49,* 100–132.

Mosig, Y. D. (2006). Conceptions of the self in Western and Eastern psychology. *Journal of Theoretical and Philosophical Psychology, 26,* 39–50.

Moskalenko, S., & Heine, S. J. (2002). Watching your troubles away: Television viewing as a stimulus for subjective self-awareness. *Personality and Social Psychology Bulletin, 29,* 76–85.

Mosquera, P. M. R., Manstead, A. S. R., & Fischer, A. (2002). Honour in the Mediterranean and Northern Europe. *Journal of Cross-Cultural Psychology, 33*(1), 16–37.

Mufwene, S.S. (2001). *The ecology of language evolution.* Cambridge MA: Cambridge University Press.

Mulatu, M. S. (2000). Perceptions of mental and physical illness in Northwestern Ethiopia: Causes,treatments and attitudes, *Journal of Health Psychology, 4,* 53–49

Muna, F. A., & Zennie, Z.A. (2010). *Developing multicultural leaders: the journey to leadership success.* Palgrave Macmillan.

Munro, D. (1979). Locus-of-control attribution: Factors among Blacks and Whites in Africa. *Journal of Cross-Cultural Psychology, 10*(2), 157–172.

Murdock, G. P. (1949). *Social structure.* New York: MacMillan.

Murphy-Bernman, V., Levesque, H., & Bernman, J. (1996). U.N. convention of the rights of the child. A cross-cultural view. *American Psychologist, 51,* 1257–1261.

Murphy, J. M. (1976). Psychiatric labeling in cross-cultural perspective. *Science, 191,* 1019–1028.

Murray C., Kulkarni S., Michaud C., Tomijima N., Bulzacchelli M., et al. (2006) Eight Americas: Investigating Mortality Disparities across Races, Counties, and Race-Counties in the United States. *PLoS Medicine 3*(9): e260. doi:10.1371/journal.pmed.0030260

Mussweiler, T., Gabriel, S. & Bodenhausen, G. V. (2000). Shifting social identities as a strategy for deflecting threatening social comparisons. *Journal of Personality and Social Psychology, 79,* 398–409.

Nathan, P. E., & Gorman, J. (2006). *A guide to treatments that work.* New York: Oxford University Press.

National Institute of Mental Health. (2011). *Eating disorders.* Retrieved from: http://www.nimh.nih.gov/health/publications/eating-disorders/index.shtml, Last access April 16, 2012.

Neary, I. (2000). Rights and psychiatric patients in East Asia. *Japan Forum, 12*(2), 157–168.

Neck, C. P., & Manz, C.C. (1994). Fromm groupthink to teamthink: Toward the creation of constructive thought patterns in self-managing work teams. *Human Relations, 47*(8), 929–951.

Neiser, U., Boodoo, G., Bouchard, T., Boykin, W., Brody, N., Ceci, S., Halpern, D., Loehlin, J., Perloff, R., Sternberg, R., & Urbina, S. (1996). Intelligence: Knowns and unknowns. *American Psychologist, 51*(2), 77–101.

Nelson, S. H., McCoy, G. F. Stetter, M., & Vanderwagen, W. C. (1992). An overview of mental health services for American Indians and Alaska Natives in the 1990s. *Hospital and Community Psychiatry, 43,* 257–261.

Nerbonne, J., & Heeringa, W. (2007). Geographic distributions of linguistic variation reflect dynamics of differentiation. In S. Featherstone & W. Sternefeld (Eds.), *Roots: Linguistics in search of its evidential base,*(pp. 267–297). Berlin, Germany: Mouton-De Gruyter.

Nettle, D. (2006). Language: Costs and benefits of a specialized system for social information transmission. In J. K. Wells, S. Strickland, & K. Laland (Eds.), *Social information transmission and human biology.* (pp. 137–152). Boca Raton, FL: CRC Press.

Nezlek, J. B., & Plesko, R. M. (2001). Dao-to-day relationships among self-concept clarity, self-esteem, daily events, and mood. *Personality and Social Psychology Bulletin, 27,* 201–211.

Nguyen, A. M. D., & Benet-Martinez, V. (2007). Biculturalism unpacked: Components, individual differences, measurement, and outcomes. *Social and Personality Psychology Compass, 1,* 101–114.

Niedenthal, P. M., & Kitayama, S. (Eds.). (1994). *The hearts eye: Emotional influences in perception and attention.* San Diego, CA: Academic Press.

Ninio, A. (1979). The naive theory of the infant and other maternal attitudes in two subgroups in Israel. *Child Development, 50,* 076–980.

Nisbett, R. (2003). *The geography of thought: How Asians and Westerners think differently and why.* London: Nicholas Brealey Publishing.

Nisbett, R. E., & Masuda, T. (2003). Culture and point of view. *Proceedings of the National Academy of Science, 100*(19), 11163–11170.

Nisbett, R. E., Peng, K., Choi, I., & Norenzayan, A. (2001). Culture and systems of thought: Holistic versus analytic cognition. *Psychological Review, 108,* 291–310.

Nisbett, R. E., & Wilson, T. D. (1977). Telling more than we can know: Verbal reports on mental processes. *Psychological Review, 84,* 231–259.

Norenzayan, A., & Heine, S. J. (2005). Psychological universals: What are they and how can we know? *Psychological Bulletin, 131*(5), 763–784.

Nsamenang, A. B. (1995). Factors influencing the development of psychology in Sub-Saharan Africa. *International Journal of Psychology, 30,* 729–738.

Nunn, C. L., Mulder, M. B., & Langley, S. (2006). Comparative methods for studying cultural trait evolution: A simulation study. *Cross-Cultural Research, 40,* 177–209.

Nydell, M. K. (1998). *Understanding Arabs: A guide for Westerners.* Yarmouth, ME: Intercultural Press.

O'Brien, M. J., Lyman, R. L., Mesoudi, A., & VanPool, T. L. (2010). Cultural traits as units of analysis. *Philosophical Transactions of the Royal Society, 365,* 3797–3806.

Okello, E. S., & Ekblad, S. (2006). Lay concepts of depression among the Baganda of Uganda: A pilot study. *Transcultural psychiatry, 43*(2), 287–313.

Odling-Smee, F. J., Laland, K. N., & Feldman, M. W. (2003). *Niche construction: The neglected process in evolution: Monographs in Population Biology* (Vol. 37). Princeton: Princeton University Press.

Offermann, L., & Hellmann, P. (1997). Culture's consequences for leadership behavior: National values in action. *Journal of Cross-Cultural Psychology, 28*(3), 342–351.

Ogbu, J. (1994). From cultural differences to differences in cultural frames of reference. In P,. M. Greenfield & R. Cocking (Eds.), *Cross-cultural roots of minority child development* (pp. 365–391). Hillsdale, NJ: Erlbaum.

Oishi, S., & Diener, E. (2001). Goals, culture, and subjective well-being. *Personality and social psychology Bulletin, 27,* 1674–1682.

Oishi, S., & Diener, E. (2003). Culture and well-being: The cycle of action, evaluation, and decision. *Personality and Social Psychology Bulletin, 29*, 939–949.

Okamoto, K. (1993). *Why is a Japanese yes a no?* Tokyo: PHP Research Laboratory.

Olson, S., Kashiwagi, K., & Crystal, D. (2001). Concepts of adaptive and maladaptive child behavior: A comparison of U.S. and Japanese mothers of Preschool-Age Children. *Journal of Cross-Cultural Psychology, 32*(1), 43–57. doi:10.1177/0022022101032001007 SAGE Publications.

Ommundsen, R., Hak, T., Morch, S., Larsen, K. S., & Van der Veer, K. (2002). Attitudes toward illegal immigration: A cross-national methodological comparison. *The Journal of Psychology, 136*(1), 103–110.

Ommundsen, R., & Larsen, K. S. (1997). Attitudes toward illegal immigration: The reliability and validity of a Likert type scale. *The Journal of Social Psychology, 137*, 665–667.

Ommundsen, R., & Larsen, K. S. (1999). Attitudes toward illegal immigration in Scandinavia and the United States. *Psychological Reports, 84*, 1331–1338.

Ommundsen, R., Van der Veer, K., Van Le, H., Krumov, K., & Larsen, K. S. (2007). Developing attitude statements toward illegal immigration: Transcultural reliability and utility. *Psychological Reports, 100*, 901–914.

Organista, P. B., Organista, K. C., & Kurasaki, K. (2003). The relationship between acculturation and ethnic minority health. In K. M. Chun & P. B. Organista (Eds.), *Acculturation: Advances in theory, measurement, and applied research* (pp. 139–161). Washington, DC: American Psychological Association.

Osgood, C. E. (1979). From yang to yin to and or but in cross-cultural perspective. *International Journal of Psychology, 14*, 1–35.

Osgood, C. E. (1980). *Lectures of language performance.* New York: Springer-Verlag.

Osgood, C. E., Suci, G. J., & Tannenbaum, P. H. (1957). *The measurement of meaning.* Urbana, IL: University of Illinois Press.

Oster, H. (2005). The repertoire of infant facial expressions: An ontogenetic perspective. In J. Nadel & D. Muir (Eds.), *Emotional development* (pp. 261–292). New York: Oxford University Press.

Ott, J. (2005a). Book reviews: Well-being manifesto for a flourishing society. Netherlands: New Economics Foundation, Erasmus University, Rotterdam. *Journal of Happiness Studies, 6*(2), 187–193.

Ott, J. (2005b). Level and equality of happiness in nations: Does greater happiness for a greater number imply greater inequality in happiness? *Journal of Happiness Studies, 6*, 397–420.

Ouchi, W. G. (1981). *Theory Z: How American business can meet the Japanese challenge.* Reading, MA: Addison-Wesley.

Ouweneel, P. (2002). Social Security and Well-Being of the Unemployed in 42 Nations. *Journal of Happiness Studies, 3*, 167–192. doi:10.1023/A:1019619324661

Ouweneel, P., & Veenhoven, R. (1990). Cross-national differences in happiness: Cultural bias or societal quality? In N. Bleichrodt & P. J. D. Drenth (Eds.), *Contemporary issues in cross-cultural psychology* (pp. 168–184). Lisse, Netherlands: Swets & Zeitlinger Publishers.

Oyserman, D., Coon, H. M., & Kemmelmeier, M. (2002). Rethinking individualism and collectivism: Evaluation of theoretical assumptions and meta-analyses. *Psychological Bulletin, 128*(1), 3–72.

Oyserman, D., & Lee, S. W. S. (2007). Priming "culture": Culture as situated cognition. In Kitayama & D. Cohen (Eds.), *Handbook of cultural psychology* (pp. 255–285). New York: The Guildford Press.

Oyserman, D., Sorensen, N., Reber, R., & Chen, S. X. (2009). Connecting and separating mind-sets: Culture as situated cognition. *Journal of Personality and Social Psychology, 97*(2), 217–235.

Paabo, S. (2001). Genomics and Society: The human genome and our view of ourselves. *Science, 291*(5507), 1219–1220.

Padilla, A. M. (2006). Bicultural social development. *Hispanic Journal of Behavioral Sciences, 28,* 467–497.

Page, R. (2003). *Tangled trees: Phylogeny, cospeciation, and coevolution.* Chicago, IL: Chicago University Press.

Pagel, M., & Meade, A. & Barker, D. (2004). Bayesian estimation of ancestral character states in phylogenies. *Systematic Biology, 53,* 673–684.

Palthe, J. (2004). The relative importance of antecedents to cross-cultural adjustments: Implications for managing a global workforce. *Journal of Intercultural Relations, 28,* 37–59.

Paniagua, F. A. (2000). Culture-bound syndromes, cultural variations, and psychopathology. In I. Cuellar & F. A. Paniagua (Eds.), *Handbook of multicultural mental health: Assessment and treatment of diverse populations* (pp. 139–169). San Diego: Academic Press.

Parke, R. (2004). Developments in the family. *Annual Review of Psychology, 55,* 365–399.

Parks-Stamm, E. J., Heilman, M. E., & Hearns, K. A. (2008). Motivated to penalize: Women's strategic rejection of successful women. *Personality and Social Psychology Bulletin, 34,* 337–347.

Parr, L., Waller, B. M., Vick, S.-J., & Bard, K. A. (2007). Classifying chimpanzee facial expressions using muscle action. *Emotion, 7*(1), 172–181.

Parra-Cardona, J. R., Cordova, D., Holtrop, K., Villarruel, F. A., & Wieling, E. (2008). Shared ancestry, evolving stories: similar and contrasting life experiences described by foreign born and U.S. born Latino parents. *Family Process, 47,* 157–172.

Parrot, A., & Cummings, N. (2006). *Forsaken females: The global brutalization of women.* Lanham, MD: Rowman & Littlefield.

Parsons, J., & Goff, S. (1978). Achievement motivation: A dual modality. *Educational Psychologist, 13,* 93–96.

Patrick, H., Neighbors, C., & Knee, C. R. (2004). Appearance-related social comparisons: The role of contingent self-esteem and self-perceptions of attractiveness. *Personality and Social Psychology Bulletin, 30,* 501–514.

Paulhus, D. L. (1998). Interpersonal and intrapsychic adaptiveness of trait self-enhancement: A mixed blessing? *Journal of Personality and Social Psychology, 74,* 1197–1208.

Paunonen, S. V. (2003). Big five factors of personality and replicated predictions of behavior. *Journal of Personality and Social Psychology, 84,* 411–422.

Peabody, D. (1985). *National characteristics.* Cambridge: Cambridge University Press.

Pearce, J. L., Bigley, G. A., & Branyiczki, I. (1998). Procedural justice as modernism: Placing industrial/organizational psychology in context. *Applied Psychology: An International Review, 47,* 371–396.

Peat, M. (1997). *Community based rehabilitation.* London: W.B. Saunders.

Pekerti, A. A., & Thomas, D. C. (2003). Communication in intercultural interaction: An empirical investigation of idiocentric and sociocentric communication styles. *Journal of Cross-Cultural Psychology, 34,* 139–154.

Pelto, G., Dickin, K., & Engle, P. (1999). *A critical link: Interventions for physical growth and psychological development: A review.* Geneva: World Health Organization.

Pembrey, M. E., Bygren, L. O., Kaati, G., Edvinsson, S., Northstone, K., Sjostrom, M., Golding, J., & Whitelaw, E. (2006). Sex-specific, male-line transgenerational responses in humans. *European Journal of Human Genetics, 14*(2), 159–166.

Peng, K., & Nisbett, R. (1999). Culture, dialectics, and reasoning about contradictions. *American Psychologist, 54,* 741–754.

Peng, K., Nisbett, R. E., & Wong, N. Y. C. (1997). Validity problems comparing values across cultures and possible solutions. *Psychological Methods, 2,* 329–344.

Pernice, R. E., Van der Veer, K., Ommundsen, R., & Larsen, K. S. (2008). On the use of student samples for scale construction. *Psychological Reports, 102,* 459–464.

Pervin, L. A. (1989a). *Personality: Theory and research* (5th ed.). New York: Wiley.

Pervin, L. A. (1989b). Persons, situations, interactions: the history and a discussion of theoretical models. *Academy of Management Review, 14*(3), 350–360.

Peterson, C., & Barrett, L. C. (1987). Explanatory style and academic performance among university freshmen. *Journal of Personality and Social Psychology, 53,* 603–607.

Peterson, R. (1978). Rorschach. In O. K. Buros (Ed.), *The eight mental measurement yearbook* (Vol. 1, pp. 1042–1045). Highland Park, NJ: Gryphon Press.

Pfeiffer, W. M. (1982). Culture-bound syndromes. In I. Al-Issa (Ed.), *Culture and psychopathology* (pp. 201–218). Baltimore: University Park Press.

Pham, L. B., Taylor, S. E., & Seeman, T. E. (2001). Effects of environmental predictability and personal mastery on self-regulatory and physiological processes. *Personality and Social Psychology Bulletin, 27,* 611–620.

Phillips, M., Yang, G., Li, S., & Li, Y. (2004). Suicide and the unique prevalence pattern of schizophrenia in mainland China: A retrospective observational study. *The Lancet, 364 (9439),* September 18th, 1062–1068.

Phinney, J. S. (1990). Ethnic identity in adolescents and adults: Review of research. *Psychological Bulletin, 108*(3), 499–514.

Phinney, J. S. (1991). Ethnic identity and self-esteem: A review and integration. *Hispanic Journal of Behavioral Sciences, 13,* 193–208.

Phinney, J. S. (1996). When we talk about American ethnic groups, what do we mean? *American Psychologist, 51*(9), 918–927.

Phinney, J. S. (1999). An intercultural approach in psychology: Cultural contact and identity. *Cross-Cultural Psychology Bulletin, 33,* 24–31.

Piaget, J. (1963). *The child's conception of the world.* Paterson, NJ: Littlefield, Adams.

Piaget, J. (1972). *The principles of genetic epistemology.* London: Routledge & Kegan Paul.

Pina, A. A., & Silverman, W. K. (2004). Clinical phenomenology, somatic symptoms, and distress in Hispanic/Latino and Euro-American youths with anxiety disorders. *Journal of Clinical Child and Adolescent Psychology, 33,* 227–236.

Pines, A. M., Lerner, M., & Schwartz, D. (2012) Gender differences among social vs. business entrepreneurs. In Burger-Helmchen, T. (Ed.). *Entrepreneurship—Gender, geographies and social context.* Published by InTech, ISBN 978-953-51-0206-9.

Pinker, S. (1995). *The language instinct: How the mind creates language.* New York: Harper-Collins.

Pinker, S. (2007). The mystery of consciousness. *Time, January 29.* Retrieved from: http://www.time.com/time/magazine/article/0,9171,1580394,00.html, Last access April 17, 2012.

Pinker, S., & Bloom, P. (1990). Natural language and natural selection. *Behavioral and Brain Sciences, 13*(4), 707–784.

Pinker, S., & Bloom, P. (1992). Natural language and natural selection. In Barkow, J. H., Cosmides, L., & Tooby, J. (Eds.), *The adapted mind: Evolutionary psychology and the generation of culture* (pp. 451–493). Oxford: Oxford University Press.

Plomin, R. (1990). *Nature and nurture: An introduction to human behavioral genetics.* Pacific Grove, CA: Brooks/Cole.

Plomin, R. & Caspi, A. (1998). DNA and personality. *European Journal of Personality, 12,* 387–407.

Plomin, R., DeFries, J. C., McClearn, G. E., & Rutter, M. (1997). *Behavioral genetics* (3rd ed.). New York: Freeman.

Ponterotto, J. G., Alexander, C. M., & Hinkston, J. A. (1988). Afro-American preferences for counselor characteristics: A replication and extension. *Journal of Counseling Psychology, 35*(2), 175–182.

Poortinga, Y. H. (1989). Equivalence in cross-cultural data: An overview of basic issues. *International Journal of Psychology, 24*(6), 737–756.

Poortinga, Y. H. (1997). Toward convergence? In J. W.Berry, Y. H. Poortinga, & Pandey (Eds.), *Handbook of cross-cultural psychology: Theory and method* (Vol. 1, pp. 347–387). Boston, MA: Allyn and Bacon.

Poortinga, Y. H. (1999). Do differences in behavior imply a need for different psychologies? *Applied Psychology: An International Review, 48*(4), 419–432.

Poortinga, Y. H., & Van de Vijver, F. J. R. (1987). Explaining cross-cultural differences: Bias analysis and beyond. *Journal of Cross-Cultural Psychology, 18*(3), 259–282.

Povinelli, D. J., Landau, K. R., & Perilloux, H. K. (1996). Self-recognition in young children using delayed versus line feedback: Evidence of a developmental asynchrony. *Child Development, 67,* 1540–1554.

Prasadaro, P. S. D. V. (2009). Culture and mental health: An international perspective. In S. Eshun & R. A. R. Gurung (Eds.), *Culture and mental health: Sociocultural influences, theory, and practice* (pp. 149–178). Malden, MA: Wiley-Blackwell.

Pratt, L. A., & Brody, D. J. (2008). Depression in the United States household population 2005–2006. *National Center for Health Services Data Brief, 7.* Retrieved from http://www.cdc.gov/nchs/data/databriefs/db07.pdf, Last access April 19, 2012.

Premack, D. (2004). Is language the key to human intelligence? *Science, 303*(5656), 318–320.

Price, G. R. (1970). Selection and covariance. *Nature, 227,* 520–521.

Pronin, E., Lin, D. Y., & Ross, L. (2002). The bias blind spot: Perceptions of bias in self versus others. *Personality and Social Psychology Bulletin, 28,* 369–381.

Purnell, L. D., & Paulanka, B. J. (2008). *Transcultural health care: A culturally competent approach* (3rd ed.). F.A. Davis.

Qian, W., Razzaque, M. A., & Keng, K. A. (2007). Chinese cultural values and gift-giving behavior. *Journal of Consumer Marketing, 24,* 214–228.

Qian, M., & Wang, A. (2005). The development of behavioral therapy and cognitive behavioral therapy. In P. R. China. *Japanese Journal of Behavior Therapy, 31,* 111–126.

Rahim, M.A. (1989). Relationships of leader power to compliance and satisfaction with supervision, evidence from a national sample of managers. *Journal of Management. 15,* 545–557.

Rahim, M. A., Antonioni, D., Krumov, K., & Illieva, S. (2000). Power, conflict, and effectiveness: a cross-cultural study in the United States and Bulgaria. *European Psychologist, 5*(10), 28–33.

Rahim, M. A., & Magner, NM. R. (1996). Confirmatory factor analysis of the bases of leader power: First order factor model and its invariance across groups. *Multivariate Behavior Research, 31,* 495–517.

Raven, B., & Rubin, J. (1968). *Social Psychology.* New York: Wiley.

Regan, P. C., Snyder, M., & Kassin, S. M. (1995). Unrealistic optimism: Self-enhancement or person positivity? *Personality and Social Psychology Bulletin, 21,* 1073–1082.

Regier, D. A., Farmer, M. E., Rae, D. S., Myers, J. K., Kramer, M., Robins, L. N., George, L. K., Karno, M., & Locke, B. Z. (1993). One-month prevalence of mental disorders in the United States and sociodemographic characteristics: The Epidemiological Catchment Area study. *Acta Psychiatrica Scandinavia, 88,* 35–47.

Regier, D. A., Narrow, W. E., Rae, D. S., Manderscheid, R. W., Locke, B. Z., & Goodwin, F. K. (1993). The de facto US mental and addictive disorders service system: Epidemiologic Catchment Area prospective 1-year prevalence rates of disorders and services. *Archives of General Psychiatry, 50,* 85–94.

Regier, T., & Kay, P. (2006). Language, thought and color: Recent developments. *Trends in Cognitive Sciences, 10,* 51–54.

Reichers, A. E., & Schneider, B. (1990). Climate and culture: An evolution of constructs. In B. Schneider (Ed.), *Organizational climate and culture* (pp. 5–39). San Francisco: Jossey-Bass.

Reynolds, V., Falger, V., & Vine, I. (Eds.). (1987). *The sociobiology of ethnocentrism.* London: Croom Helm.

Rhee, E., Uleman, J. S., Lee, H. K., & Roman, R. J. (1995). Spontaneous self-descriptions and ethnic identities in individualistic and collectivist cultures. *Journal, of Personality and Social Psychology, 69,* 142–152.

Richerson, P. J., & Boyd, R. (2005). *Not by genes alone: How culture transformed human evolution* (pp. 169–182). Chicago, IL: University of Chicago Press.

Riemann, R., & De Raad, B. (1998). Editorial: Behavior genetics and personality. *European Journal of Personality, 12,* 303–305.

Roberson, L. (1990). Functions of work meanings in organizations: Work meanings and work motivation. In A. Brief & W. Ord (Eds.), *Meanings of occupational work: Collection of essays* (pp. 107–134). Lexington: Lexington Books.

Roberts, B. W., Caspi, A., & Moffitt, T. E. (2003). Work experiences and personality development in young adulthood. *Journal of Personality and Social Psychology, 84*, 582–593.

Roberts, T. A., & Pennebaker, J. W. (1995). Gender differences in perceiving internal state: Toward a his-and-her model of perceptual cue use. In M. Zanna (Ed.), *Advances in experimental social psychology* (Vol. 27, pp. 143–176). New York: Academic Press.

Robins, L. N., Tipp, J., & Przybeck, T. (1991). Antisocial personality. In L. N. Robins & D. A. Regier (Eds), *Psychiatric disorders in America: The epidemiologic catchment area study* (pp. 258–290). New York: Free Press.

Robins, R. W., & Beer, J. S. (2001). Positive illusions about the self: Short-term benefits and long-term costs. *Journal of Personality and Social Psychology, 80*, 340–352.

Roe, R. (1995). Developments in Eastern Europe in work and organizational psychology. In C. L. Cooper & I. T. Robertson (Eds.), *International review of industrial and organizational psychology* (Vol. X, pp. 275–349). Chichester, UK: Wiley.

Rogers, C. (1951). *Client-centered therapy: Its current practice, implications, and theory.* Boston, MA: Houghton Mifflin.

Rogers, D. S., Feldman, M. W., & Ehrlich, P. R. (2009). Inferring population histories using cultural data. *Proceedings of the Royal Society, 276*, 3835–3843.

Rogers, T. B., Kuiper, N. A., & Kirker, W. S. (1977). Self-reference and the encoding of personal information. *Journal of Personality and Social Psychology, 35*, 677–688.

Rogler, L. H., & Cooney, R. S. (1984). *Puerto Rican families in New York City: Intergenerational processes* (Monograph No. 11). Hispanic Research Center. Maplewood, NJ: Waterfront Press.

Rohde, L. A., Szobot, C., Polanczyk, G., Schmitz, M., Martins, S., & Tramontina, S. (2005). Attention-deficit/hyperactivity disorder in a diverse culture: Do research and clinical findings support the notion of a cultural construct for the disorder? *Biological Psychiatry, 57*(11), 1436–1441.

Rokeach, M. (1973). *The nature of human values.* New York: Free Press.

Roseman, I. J., Dhawan, N., Rettek, S. I., Nadidu, R. K., & Thapa, K. (1995). Cultural differences and cross-cultural similarities in appraisals and emotional responses. *Journal of Cross-Cultural Psychology, 26*, 23–48.

Roseman, I. J., & Smith, C. (2001). Appraisal theory: overview, assumptions, varieties, controversies. In K. Scherer, A. Schorr & T. Johnstone (Eds.), *Appraisal processes in emotion: Theory, methods, research* (pp. 3–19). New York: Oxford University Press.

Rosemont, Jr., H., & Ames, R. T. (2009). *The Chinese classic of family reverence: A philosophical translation of the Xiaojing.* Honolulu: University of Hawai'i Press.

Ross, B. M., & Millson, C. (1970). Repeated memory of oral prose in Ghana and New York. *International Journal of Psychology, 5*, 173–181.

Ross, M. (1989). Relation of implicit theories to the construction of personal histories. *Psychological Review, 96*, 341–357.

Ross, M., & Wilson, A. E. (2002). It feels like yesterday: Self-esteem, valence of personal past experiences, and judgments of subjective distance. *Journal of Personality and Social Psychology, 82,* 792–803.

Rotter, J. B. (1966). Generalized expectancies for internal versus external locus of control of reinforcements. *Psychological Monographs, 80*(1, Whole No. 609), 1–28.

Rousseau, D. M. (1989). Psychological and implied contracts in organizations. *Employee Responsibility and Rights Journal, 2,* 121–139.

Rowe, D. C. (1994). *The limits of family influence: Genes, experience, and behavior.* New York: Guilford Press.

Rudmin, F. W. (2003). Critical history of the acculturation psychology of assimilation, separation, integration, and marginalization. *Review of General Psychology, 7,* 3–37.

Rudy, D., & Grusec, J. (2001). Correlates of authoritarian parenting in individualist and collectivist cultures and implications for understanding the transmission of values. *Journal of Cross-Cultural Psychology, 32*(2), 202–212.

Russell, J. A. (1991). Culture and the categorization of emotions. *Psychological Bulletin, 110,* 426–450.

Russell, J. A. (1994). Is there universal recognition of emotion from facial expressions? Review of cross-cultural studies. *Psychological Bulletin, 115,* 102–141.

Russell, J. A., & Barrett, L. F. (1999). Core effect, prototypical emotional episodes, and other things called emotion: Dissecting the elephant. *Journal of Personality and Social Psychology, 76,* 805–819.

Rushton, J. P. (1988). Race differences in behavior: A review and evolutionary analysis. *Journal of Personality and Individual Differences, 9,* 1009–1024.

Rushton, J. P. (1995). *Race, evolution, and behavior.* New Brunswick, NJ: Transaction.

Ruvolo, A. P., & Markus, H. R. (1992). Possible selves and performance: The power of self-relevant imagery. *Social Cognition, 10,* 95–124.

Ryan, R. M., & Deci, E. L. (2000a). Self-determination theory and the facilitation of intrinsic motivation, social development, and well-being. *American Psychologist, 55,* 68–78.

Ryan, R. M., & Deci, E. L. (2000b). Intrinsic and extrinsic motivations: Classic definitions and new directions. *Contemporary Educational Psychology, 25,* 54–67.

Ryder, A. G., Alden, L. E., & Paulhus, D. L. (2000). Is acculturation unidimensional or bidimensional? A head-to-head comparison in the prediction of personality, self-identity, and adjustment. *Journal of Personality and Social Psychology, 79,* 49–65.

Sabini, J., & Maury, S. (2005). Ekman's basic emotions: Why not love and jealousy? *Cognition and emotion, 19*(5), 693–712.

Sagiv, L., & Schwartz, S. H. (2000). A new look at national culture: Illustrative applications to Role Stress and Managerial Behavior Conference presentations. In N. Ashkanasy, M. Peterson, & C. Wilderom (Eds.), *Handbook of organizational culture and climate* (pp. 417–437). Thousand Oaks, CA: Sage.

Sam, D. L. (2000). Psychological adaptation of adolescents with immigrant backgrounds. *Journal of Social Psychology, 140*(1), 5–25.

Sam, D. L., & Berry, J. W. (2006). *Cambridge Handbook of Acculturation Psychology,* Cambridge, UK: Cambridge University Press.

Sama, L. M., & Papamarcos, S. D. (2000). Hofstede's I-C dimension as predictors of allocative behaviors: A meta-analysis. *International Journal of Value-Based Management, 13*, 173–188.

Sanchez-Burks, J., Nisbett, R. E., & Ybarra, O. (2000). Cultural styles, relational schemas and prejudice against outgroups. *Journal of Personality and Social Psychology, 79*(2), 174–189.

Sanday, P. R. (1981). The socio-cultural context of rape: A cross-cultural study. *Journal of Social Issues, 37*, 5–27.

Sandbu, M., Ward, A., & Wigglesworth, R. (2011, July 26th). Terror in Norway: Utopia no more. *Financial Times, 5*.

Sarason, I., & Sarason, B. (1999). *Abnormal psychology*. Toronto: Prentice-Hall.

Sarason, I. G., Sarason, B. R., & Pierce, G. R. (1990). Social support: The search for theory. *Journal of Social and Clinical Psychology, 9*, 397–412.

Sastry, J., & Ross, C.E. (1998). Asian ethnicity and the sense of personal control. *Social Psychology Quarterly, 61*, 101–120.

Savitsky, K., Medvec, V. H., Charlton, A., & Gilovich, T. (1998). "What me worry": Arousal, misattribution, and the effect of temporal distance on confidence. *Personality and Social Psychology Bulletin, 24*, 529–536.

Schachter, S. (1964). The interaction of cognitive and physiological determinants of emotional state. In L. Berkowitz (Ed.), *Advances in experimental social psychology* (Vol. 1, pp. 49–80). New York: Academic Press.

Schachter, S., & Singer, J. E. (1962). Cognitive, social, and physiological determinants of emotional states. *Psychological Review, 69*, 379–399.

Schein, E. H. (1990). Organizational culture. *American Psychologist, 45*, 109–19.

Scheper-Hughes, N. (1992). *Death without weeping: The violence of everyday life in Brazil*. Berkeley: University of California Press.

Scherer, K. R. (1997a). Profiles of emotion-antecedent appraisal: Testing theoretical predictions across cultures. *Cognition & Emotion, 11*, 113–150.

Scherer, K. R. (1997b). The role of culture in emotion-antecedent appraisal. *Journal of Personality and Social Psychology, 73*, 902–922.

Scherer, K.R., Schorr, A., & Johnstone T. (2001). *Appraisal processes in emotion: Theory, methods, research*. New York: Oxford University Press.

Scherer, K. R., & Wallbott, H. (1994). Evidence for universality and cultural variation of differential emotion response patterning. *Journal of Personality and Social Psychology, 66*, 310–328.

Schimmack, U. (1996). Cultural influences on the recognition of emotion by facial expressions. *Journal of Cross-Cultural Psychology, 27*, 37–50.

Schimmel, J. (2009). Development as Happiness: The Subjective Perception of Happiness and UNDP's Analysis of Poverty, Wealth and Development. *Journal of Happiness Studies, 10*, 93–111

Schlenker, B. R. (1980). *Impression management: The self-concept, social identity, and interpersonal relations*. Monterey: Brooks/Cole.

Schlenker, B. R., & Britt, T. W. (1999). Beneficial impression management: Strategically controlling information to help friends. *Journal of Personality and Social Psychology, 76*, 559–573.

Schlenker, B. R., & Pontari, B. A. (2000). The strategic control of information: Impression management and self-presentation in daily life. In A. Tesser, R. Felson, & J. Suls (Eds.), *Perspectives on self and identity* (pp. 199–232). Washington, D.C.: American Psychological Association.

Schliemann, A. D., & Carraher, D. W. (2001). Everyday cognition: Where culture, psychology, and education come together. In D. Matsumoto(Ed.), *Handbook of culture and psychology* (pp. 137–150). New York: Oxford University Press.

Schmidt, J. (1872). *Die Verwandtschaftverhälnisse der Indogermannichen Sprachen.* Weimar, Germany: Böhlau.

Schmitt, D. P., Alcalay, L., Allensworth, M., Allik, J., Ault, L., & Austers, I., et al. (2004). Patterns and universals of adult romantic attachment across 62 cultural regions. Are Models of Self and of Other Pancultural Constructs? *Journal of Cross-Cultural Psychology, 35,* 367–402.

Schmitt, D. P., Allik, J., McCrae, R.R., & Benet-Martinez, V. A. (2007). The geographic distribution of Big Five personality traits. *Journal of Cross-Cultural Psychology, 38,* 173–213.

Schonpflug, U., Silbereisen, R.K., and Schulz, J. (1990). Perceived decision-making influence in Turkish migrant workers' and German workers' families: the impact of social support. *Journal of Cross-Cultural Psychology, 21*(3), 261–282.

Schwanenflugel, P. (1991). Why are abstract concepts hard to understand? In P. J. Schwanenflugel (Ed.), *The psychology of word meanings* (pp. 223–250). Hillsdale, NJ: Lawrence Erlbaum Associates.

Schwanenflugel, P. J. & Rey, M. (1986). The relationship between category typicality and concept familiarity: evidence from Spanish- and English-speaking monolinguals. *Memory & Cognition, 14*(2), 150–163.

Schwartz, S. H. (1999). A theory of cultural values and some implications for work. *Applied Psychology: An International Review, 48*(1), 23–47.

Schwartz, S. H. (2004). Mapping and interpreting cultural differences around the world. In H. Vinken, J. Soeters, & P. Ester (Eds.), *Comparing cultures, dimensions of culture in a comparative perspective* (pp. 43–73). Leiden, The Netherlands: Brill.

Schwartz, S., Melech, G., Lehmann, A., Burgess, S., Harris, M., & Owens, V. (2001). Extending the cross-cultural validity of the theory of basic human values with a different method of measurement. *Journal of Cross-cultural Psychology, 32*(5), 519–542.

Schwartz, S. H., & Ross, M. (1995). Values in the west: A theoretical and empirical challenge to the individualism-collectivism cultural dimension. *World Psychology, 1,* 91–122.

Scribner, S., & Cole, M. (1981). *The psychology of literacy.* Cambridge, MA: Harvard University Press.

Sedikides, C. (1993). Assessment, enhancement, and verification determinants of the self-evaluative process. *Journal of Personality and Social Psychology, 65,* 317–338.

Sedikides, C., Gaertner, L., & Toguchi, Y. (2003). Pancultural self-enhancement. *Journal of Personality and Social Psychology, 84*(1), 60–70.

Sedikides, C., Gaertner, L., & Vevea, J. L. (2005). Pancultural self-enhancement reloaded: A meta-analytic reply to Heine (2005). *Journal of Personality and Social Psychology, 89,* 539–551.

Sedikides, C., & Green, J. D. (2000). On the self-productive nature of inconsistency-negativity management: Using the person memory paradigm to examine self-referent memory. *Journal of Personality and Social Psychology, 65,* 317–338.

Sedikides, C., & Showronski, J. J. (1993). The self in impression formation: Trait centrality and social perception. *Journal of Experimental Social Psychology, 29,* 347–357.

Segall, M. H., Campbell, D. T., & Hersokowitz,, J. (1966). *The influence of culture on visual perception.* Indianapolis: Bobbs-Merrill.

Segall, M. H., Dasen, P. R., Berry, J. W., & Poortinga, Y. H. (1999). *Human behavior in global perspective: An introduction to cross-cultural psychology* (2nd ed.). Boston: Allyn & Bacon.

Segall, M. H., Ember, C. R., & Ember, M. (1997). Aggression, crime, and warfare. In J. W. Berry, M. H. Segall, & C. Kagitçibasi (Eds.), *Handbook of cross-cultural psychology* (2nd ed, Vol. 3, pp. 213–254). Boston: Allyn and Bacon.

Segalowitz, N. S. (1980). Issues in the cross-cultural study of bilingual development. In H. C. Triandis & A. Heron (Eds.), *Handbook of cross-cultural psychology: Vol. 4, Developmental Psychology* (pp. 55–92). Boston, MA: Allyn & Bacon.

Seidl-de-Moura, M. L. (Ed.). (2012). *Human development—Different perspectives.* Published by InTech, ISBN 978-953-51-0610-4.

Seligman, M. E. P. (1991). *Learned optimism.* New York: Knopf.

Seligman, M. E. P., & Csikszentmihalyi, M. (2000). Positive psychology: An introduction. *American Psychologist, 55,* 5–14.

Sellers, R. M., Rowley, S. A., Chavous, N. M., Shelton, J. N., & Smith, M. A. (1997). Multidimensional inventory of Black identity: A preliminary investigation of reliability and construct validity. *Journal of Personality and Social Psychology, 73,* 805–815.

Senko, C., & Harackiewicz, J. M. (2002). Performance goals: The moderating roles of context and achievement orientation. *Journal of Experimental Social Psychology, 38,* 603–610.

Serpell, R. (1993). *The significance of schooling: Life's journey in an African society.* Cambridge: Cambridge University Press.

Serpell, R., & Deregowski, J. B. (1980). The skill of pictorial perception: An interpretation of cross-cultural evidence. *International Journal of Psychology, 15,* 145–180.

Shah, H., & Marks, N. (2004). *A well-being manifesto for a flourishing society.* London: New Economics Foundation.

Shah, J. & Higgins, E.T. (2001). Regulatory concerns and appraisal efficiency: The general impact of promotion and prevention. *Journal of Personality and Social Psychology, 80,* 693–705.

Shane, S., Venkataraman, S., & MacMillan, I. (1995). Cultural differences in innovation championing strategies. *Journal of Management, 21*(5), 931–952.

Shapiro, D. L., Von Glinow, M., & Cheng, J. L. C. (2005). *Managing multinational teams: Global perspectives.* Oxford: Elsevier Science.

Shapiro, J., & Simonsen, D. (1994). Educational/support group for Latino families of children with Down syndrome. *Mental Retardation, 32,* 403–415.

Sharot, T. (2011, June 6). The optimism bias. *Time,* 40–46.

Sharot, T., Guitart-Masip, M., Korn, C. W., Chowdhury, R., & Dolan, R. J. (2012). How dopamine enhances an optimism bias in humans. *Curr. Biol.* 22, 1477–1481.

Sharot, T., Korn, C. W., & Dolan, R. J. (2011). How unrealistic optimism is maintained in the face of reality. *Nat. Neurosci. 14*, 1475–1479.

Sharot, T., Riccardi, A. M., Raio, C. M., & Phelps, E. A. (2007). Neural mechanisms mediating optimism bias. *Nature, 450*, 102–105.

Shayer, M., Demetriou. A., & Pervez, M. (1988). The structure and scaling of concrete operational thought: three studies in four countries. *Genetic, Social and General Psychology Monographs, 114*(3), 307–376.

Shennan S. J. (2008). Canoes and cultural evolution. *Proc. Natl Acad. Sci. USA 105*, 3175–3176. (doi:10.1073/pnas.0800666105)

Shepard, L. A., Camilli, G., & Averill, M. (1981). Comparisons of procedures for detecting test-item bias with both internal and external ability criteria. *Journal of Educational Statistics, 6*, 317–375.

Sherman, D. A. K., Nelson, L. D., & Steele, C. M. (2000). Do messages about health risks threaten the self? Increasing the acceptance of threatening health messages via self-affirmation. *Personality and Social Psychology Bulletin, 26*, 1046–1058.

Shimizi, Y., & Kaplan, B. (1987). Postpartum depression in the United States and Japan. *Journal of Cross-Cultural Psychology, 18*(1), 15–30.

Shin, S.-M., Chow, C., Camacho-Gonsalves, T., Levy, R., Allen, I., & Leff, H. (2005). A meta-analytic review of racial-ethnic matching for African American and Caucasian American clients and clinicians. *Journal of Counseling Psychology, 52*(1), 45–56.

Shiraev, E. (1988). The family is responsible. In A. Svebntsisky (Ed.), *The power of discipline.* Leningrad: Lenizdat

Shiraev, E., & Bastrykin, A. (1988). *Fashion, idols, and the self.* St. Petersburg: Lenizdat.

Shiraev, E., & Boyd. G. (2001). *The Accent of Success.* New York: Prentice Hall.

Shiraev, E., & Sobel, R. (2006). *People and their opinions: Thinking critically about public opinion.* New York: Pearson Longman.

Showers, C. J., & Ryff, C. D. (1996). Self-differentiation and well-being in a life transition. *Personality and Social Psychology Bulletin, 22*, 448–460.

Shrotryia, V. K. (2008). *Shift in the measures of quality of life vis-à-vis happiness: A study of Phongmey Gewog and Trashigang town in Eastern Bhutan.* Paper presented at the 4th international Gross National Happiness Conference, 2008, November. Centre for Bhutan Studies. Thimphu, Bhutan. Retrieved September 12, 2011, Retrieved from: http://www.bhutanstudies.org.bt/pubFiles/27.GNH4.pdf

Shweder, R., & LeVine, R. (1984). *Culture theory: Essays on mind, self, and emotion.* London: Cambridge University Press.

Shweder, R. A., Mahapatra, M, & Miller, J. G. (1990). Culture a moral development. In J. W. Stigler, R. A. Shweder, & G. Herdt (Eds.), *Cultural psychology: Essays on comparative human development* (pp. 130–204). Cambridge, UK: Cambridge University Press.

Shweder, R. A., Minow, M., & Markus, H. R. (Eds.). (2002). *Engaging cultural differences: The multicultural challenge in liberal democracies.* New York: Russell Sage Foundation.

Sigle-Rushton, W., & Waldfogel, J. (2007). Motherhood and women's earnings in Anglo-American, continental European, and Nordic countries. *Feminist Economics, 13*(2), 55–91.

Silverman, D. (1993). *Interpreting qualitative data: Methods for analyzing talk, text, and interaction.* London: Sage.

Silvia, P. J., & Abele, A. E. (2002). Can positive affect induce self-focused attention? Methodological and measurement issues. *Cognition and Emotion, 16,* 845–853.

Simmons, C. H., Vom Kolke, A., & Shimizu, H. (1986). Attitudes toward romantic love among American, German, and Japanese students. *Journal of Social Psychology, 126,* 327–337.

Simon, B., Pantaleo, G., & Mummedy, A. (1995). Unique individual or interchangeable group member? The accentuation of intragroup differences versus similarities as an indicator of the individual self versus the collective self. *Journal of Personality and Social Psychology, 69,* 106–119.

Simons, R., & Hughes, C. (Eds.). (1985). *The culture-bound syndromes: Folk illnesses of psychiatric and anthropological interest.* Dordrecht, The Netherlands: D. Reidel Publishing Company.

Simonton, D. (1987). Developmental antecedents of achieved eminence. *Annals of Child Development, 5,* 131–169.

Sinclair, R. C., Hoffman, C., Mark, M. M., Martin, L. L., & Pickering, T. L. (1994). Construct accessibility and the misattribution of arousal: Schachter and Singer revisited. *Psychological Science, 5,* 15–19.

Singelis, T. M., Triandis, C. H., Bhawuk, S. D., & Gelfand, M. J. (1995). Horizontal and vertical dimensions of individualism and collectivism: A theoretical and measurement refinement. *Cross-Cultural Research, 29*(3), 241–275.

Sinha, D. (1984). Psychology in the context of Third World development. *International Journal of Psychology, 19,* 17–29.

Sinha, D. (1997). Indigenizing psychology. In J. W. Berry, Y. H., Poortinga, & J. Pandey (Eds.). *Handbook of cross-cultural psychology: Theory and Method* (2nd ed., Vol. 1, pp. 129–169). Boston: Allyn and Bacon.

Sistrunk, F., & McDavid, J. W. (1971). Sex variable in conforming behavior. *Journal of Personality and Social Psychology, 17,* 200–207.

Small, M. F. (1998). *Our babies, ourselves: How biology and culture shape the way we parent.* New York: Anchor.

Smedley, A., & Smedley, B. D. (2005). Race as biology is fiction, racism as a social problem is real: Anthropological and historical perspectives on the social construction of race. *American Psychologist, 60*(1), 16–26.

Smith, P. B., Dugan, S., & Trompenaars, F. (1997). Locus of control and affectivity by gender and occupational status: A 14-nation study. *Sex Roles, 36*(1–4), 51–77.

Smith, P. B., Peterson, M. F., & Misumi, J. (1994). Event management and work team effectiveness in Japan, Britain, and USA. *Journal of Occupational and Organizational Psychology, 67,* 33–43.

Smith, P. B., Peterson, M. F., & Schwartz, S. H. (2002). Cultural values, sources of guidance, and their relevance to managerial behaviour: A 47 national study. *Journal of Cross-Cultural Psychology, 33*(2), 188–208.

Smith, S. M., Stinson, F. S., & Dawson, D. A. (2006). Race/ethnic differences in the prevalence and co-occurrence of substance abuse disorder and independent mood and anxiety disorders: Results from the National Epidemiological Survey on Alcohol and Related Conditions. *Psychological Medicine, 36*(7), 987–998.

Snarey, J. (1985). Cross-cultural universality of social-moral development: A critical review of Kohlbergian research. *Psychological Bulletin, 97*(2), 202–232.

Snowden, L., Masland, M., Ma, Y., & Ciemens, E. (2006). Strategies to improve minority access to public mental health services in California: Description and preliminary evaluation. *Journal of Community Psychology. Special Issue: Addressing mental health disparities through culturally competent research and community-based practice, 34*(2), 225–235

Snowden, L., & Yamada, A. M. (2005). Cultural differences in access to care. *Annual Review of Psychology, 1*, 143–166.

Snowdon, C.T. (2003). Expression of emotion in nonhuman animals. In R. J. Davison, K. Scherer, & H. H. Goldsmith (Eds.), *Handbook of affective sciences* (pp. 457–480). New York: Oxford University Press.

Snyder, M. (1974). Self-monitoring of expressive behavior. *Journal of Personality and Social Psychology, 30*, 526–537.

Snyderman, M., & Rothman, S. (1988). *The IQ controversy: The media and public policy.* New Brunswik, NJ: Transaction Books.

Soeng Mu, S. (1991). *Heart sutra: Ancient Buddhist wisdom in the light of quantum reality.* Cumberland, RI: Primary Point.

Sommer, K. L. & Baumeister, R. F. (2002). Self-evaluation, persistence, and performance following implicit rejection: The role of trait self-esteem. *Personality and Social Psychology Bulletin, 28*, 926–938.

Sorkhabi, N. (2005). Applicability of Baumrind's parent typology to collective cultures: Analysis of cultural explanations of parent socialization effects. *International Journal of Behavioral Development, 29*(6), 552–563.

Sow, L. (1978). *The anthropological structure of madness in Black Africa.* Paris: Payot.

Spearman, C. E. (1927). *The abilities of man: their nature and measurement.* New York: Macmillan.

Spector, R. (2004). *Cultural diversity in health and illness.* (6th ed.). Upper Saddle River, NJ: Prentice Hall.

Spencer, S. J., Fein, S., Zanna, M. P., & Olson, J. M. (Eds.). (2003). *Motivated social perception: the Ontario Symposium* (Vol. 9, pp. 117–145). Mahwah, NJ: Lawrence Erlbaum Associates.

Spera, C. (2005). A review of the relationship among parenting practices, parenting styles, and adolescent school achievement. *Educational Psychology Review, 17*(2), 125–146.

Spreitzer, G. M., Perttula, K. H., & Xin, K. (2005). Traditionality matters: An examination of the effectiveness of transformational leadership in the United States. *Journal of Organizational Behavior, 26*, 205–227.

Stahl, G. K., & Caligiuri, P. M. (2005). The effectiveness of expatriate coping strategies: The moderating role of cultural distance, position level and the time on international assignment. *Journal of Applied Psychology, 90*, 603–615.

Stapel, D. A., & Koomen, W. (2000). Distinctiveness of others, mutability of selves: Their impact on self-evaluations. *Journal of Personality and Social Psychology, 79*, 1068–1087.

Stapel, D. A., & Koomen, W. (2001). I, we, and the effects of others on me: Self-construal level moderates social comparison effect. *Journal of Personality and Social Psychology, 80*, 766–781.

Steele, C. M. (1988). The psychology of self-affirmation: Sustaining the integrity of the self. In L. Berkowitz (Ed.), *Advances in Experimental Social Psychology* (Vol. 21, pp. 261–302). New York: Academic Press.

Steele, C. M. (1997). A threat in the air: How stereotypes shape intellectual identity and performance. *American Psychologist, 52*(6), 613–629.

Steger, M. F. (2009). Meaning in life. In S. Lopez (Ed.), *Oxford Handbook of positive psychology* (2nd ed., pp. 679–687). Oxford, UK: Oxford University Press.

Steger, M. F., & Dik, B. J. (2010). Work as meaning. In Linley, P. A., Harrington, S., & Page, N. (Eds.), *Oxford handbook of positive psychology and work* (pp. 131–142). Oxford, UK: Oxford University Press.

Steger, M. F., Frazier, P., Oishi, S., & Kaler, M. (2006). The meaning in life questionnaire: Assessing the presence of and search for meaning in life. *Journal of Counseling Psychology, 53*, 80–93.

Steger, M. F., Kashdan, T. B., Sullivan, B. A., & Lorentz, D. (2008). Understanding the search for meaning in life: Personality, cognitive style, and the dynamics between seeking and experiencing meaning. *Journal of Personality, 76*, 199–228.

Steger, M. F., Kawabata, Y., Shimai, S., & Otake, K. (2008). The meaningful life in Japan and the United States: Levels and correlates of meaning in life. *Journal of Research in Personality, 42*, 660–678.

Steger, M. F., Oishi, S., & Kesebir, S. (2011). Is a life without meaning satisfying? The moderating role of the search for meaning in satisfaction with life judgments. *Journal of Positive Psychology, 6*(3), 173–180.

Stellman, J. M., Stellman, S. D., Christian, R., Weber, T., & Tomasallo, C. (2003). The extent and patterns of usage of agent orange and other herbicides in Vietnam. *Nature, 422*, 681–687.

Stephens, B. (2011). What is Anders Breivik? *The Wall Street Journal*, Tuesday, July 26th, A15.

Sterelny, K. (2012). *The evolved apprentice how evolution made humans unique.* Cambridge, MA: Massachusetts Institute of Technology, A Bradford book,

Sternberg, R. (1997). The concept of intelligence and its role in lifelong learning and success. *American Psychologist, 59*(5), 325–338.

Sternberg, R. J. (2004). Culture and intelligence. *American Psychologist, 59*(5), 325–338.

Sternberg, R. J., Grigorenko, E. L., Kidd, K. K. (2005). Intelligence, race, and genetics. *American Psychologist, 60*(1), 46–59.

Sternberg R. J., & Lubart, T. I. (1996). Investing in creativity, *American Psychologist*, 51, 677–688.

Sternberg, R. J., & Lubart, T. I. (1999). The concept of creativity: Prospects and paradigms. In R. J. Sternberg (Ed.) *Handbook of creativity* (pp. 3–16). London: Cambridge University Press.

Stevenson, B., & Wolfers, J. (2008, August 25). *Economic growth and subjective well-being: Reassessing the Easterlin paradox.* 3rd Annual Conference on Empirical Legal Studies Papers. Retrieved September 12, 2011, Retrieved from: http://ssrn.com/abstract=1121237

Stevenson, H., & Zusho, A. (2002). Adolescence in China and Japan: Adapting to a changing environment. In B. Brown, R. Larson, & T. Saraswathi (Eds.), *The world's youth: Adolescence in eight regions of the globe* (pp. 141–170). New York: Cambridge University Press.

Strelau, J. (1998). *Temperament: A psychological perspective.* New York: Plenum.

Story, D. L. (1998). Self-esteem and memory for favorable and unfavorable personality feedback. *Personality and Social Psychology Bulletin, 24,* 51–64.

Suchman, R. G. (1966). Cultural differences in children's color and form perception. *Journal of Social Psychology, 70,* 3–10.

Sue-Chan, C., & Ong, M. (2002). Goal assignment and performance: Assessing the mediating roles of goal commitment and self-efficacy and the moderating role of power distance. *Organizational Behavior and Human Decision Processes, 89,* 1140–1161.

Sue, D. W., & Sue, D. (2003). *Counseling the culturally diverse* (4th ed.). New York: Wiley.

Sue, D. W., & Sue, D. (2008). *Foundations of counseling and psychotherapy: Evidence based practices for a diverse society.* Hobroken, NJ: John Wiley & Sons.

Sue, S., & Morishima, J. K. (1982). *The mental health of Asian Americans.* San Francisco: Jossey-Bass.

Sugamura, G., Haruki, Y., & Koshikawa, F. (2007). Building more solid bridges between Buddhism and Western Psychology. *American Psychologist, 62,* 1080–1081.

Suh, E. M. (2000). Self, the hyphen between culture and subjective well-being. In E. Diener & E. M. Suh (Eds.), *Culture and subjective well-being* (pp. 63–86). Cambridge, MA: MIT Press.

Suh, E. M., Diener, E., Oishi, S., & Triandis, H. C. (1998). The shifting basis of life satisfaction judgments across cultures: Emotions versus norms. *Journal of Personality and Social Psychology, 74,* 482–493.

Sulloway, F. J. (1996). *Born to rebel: Birth order, family dynamics, and creative lives.* New York: Pantheon Books.

Sulloway, F. J. (2001). Birth order, sibling competition, and human behavior. In H. R. Halcomb III (Ed.), *Conceptual challenges in evolutionary psychology: Innovative research strategies: Studies in cognitive systems* (Vol. 27, pp. 39–83). Dordrecht, The Netherlands: Kluwer Academic Publishers.

Suls, J. M., & Fletcher, B. (1983). Social comparison in the social and physical sciences: An archival study. *Journal of Personality and Social Psychology, 44,* 575–580.

Suls, J. M., Lemos, K., & Stewart, H. L. (2002). Self-esteem, construal and comparisons with the self, friends, and peers. *Journal of Personality and Social Psychology, 82,* 252–261.

Suls, J. M., & Wheeler, L. (2000). *Handbook of social comparisons: Theory and research.* New York: Kluwer Academic/Plenum.

Super, C. M., & Harkness, S. (1994). The developmental niche. In W. Lonner & R. Malpass (Eds.), *Psychology and culture* (pp. 95–99). Boston: Allyn and Bacon.

Super, C. M., & Harkness, S. (2002). Culture structures the environment for development. *Human Development, 45*(4), 270–274.

Super, C. M., Harkness, S., Van Tijen, N., Van der Vlugt, E., Fintelman, M., & Dijkstra, J. (1996). The three Rs of Dutch childrearing and the socialization of infant arousal. In Harkness & C. M. Super (Eds.), *Parent's cultural belief system: Their origins, expressions, and consequences* (pp. 447–465). New York: Guildford Press.

Svoboda, E. (2007). *Faces, faces everywhere.* Mental Health and Behavior. New York Times.

Swann, W. B. Jr. (1983). Self-verification: Bringing social reality into harmony with the self. In J. Suls & A. G. Greenwald (Eds.), *Social Psychology Perspectives* (Vol. 2, pp. 33–66). Hillsdale, NJ.: Erlbaum.

Swann, W. B. Jr., & Read, S. J. (1981). Self-verification processes: How we sustain our self-conceptions. *Journal of Experimental Social Psychology, 17,* 351–370.

Sy, S., & Schulenberg, J. (2005). Parent beliefs and children's achievement trajectories during the transition to school in Asian American and European American families. *International Journal of Behavioral Development, 29*(6), 505–515.

Tafarodi, R. W., Marshall, T. C., & Milne, A. B. (2003). Self-esteem and memory. *Journal of Personality and Social Psychology, 84,* 29–45.

Tajfel, H. (1981). *Human groups and social categories.* Cambridge: Cambridge University Press.

Takano, Y., & Osaka, E. (1999). An unsupported common view: Comparing Japan and the U.S. on individualism/collectivism. *Asian Journal of Social Psychology, 2,* 311–341.

Takeuchi, D. T., Sue, S., & Yeh, M. (1995). Return rates and outcomes from ethnicity-specific mental health programs in Los Angeles. *American Journal of Public Health, 85,* 638–643.

Takeuchi, R., Tesluk, P. E., & Yun, S. (2002). An examination of crossover and spillover effects of spousal and expatriate cross-cultural adjustment on expatriate outcomes. *Journal of Applied Psychology, 87,* 655–666.

Tanaka-Matsumi, J. (2008). Functional approaches to evidence-based practice in multicultural counseling and therapy. In U. P. Gielen, J. G. Draguns, & J. M. Fish (Eds.), *Principles of Multicultural Counseling and Therapy* (pp. 169–198). New York: Routledge.

Tanaka-Matsumi, J., & Draguns, J. (1997). Culture and psychopathology. In J. W. Berry, M. H. Segall, & C. Kagitcibasi (Eds.), *Handbook of cross-cultural psychology: Social behaviors and applications* (Vol. 3, pp. 449–491). Boston, MA: Allyn and Bacon.

Tanaka-Matsumi, J., & Higginbotham, H. N. (1989). Behavioral approaches to counseling across cultures. In P. B. Pedersen, J. G. Draguns, W. J. Lonner, & J. E. Trimble (Eds.), *Counseling across cultures* (3rd ed., pp. 269–298). Honolulu: University of Hawaii Press.

Tanaka-Matsumi, J., & Higginbotham, H. N. (1994). Clinical application of behavior therapy across ethnic and cultural boundaries. *The Behavior Therapist, 17*(6), 123–126.

Tang, S., & Hall, V. C. (1995). The overjustification effect: A meta-analysis. *Applied Cognitive Psychology, 9*, 365–404.

Tareen, A., Hodes, M., & Rangel, L. (2005). Non-fat phobic anorexia nervosa in British South Asian adolescents. *International Journal of Eating Disorders, 37*(2), 161–165.

Taylor, S. E., & Brown, J. (1988). Illusion and well-being: A social-psychological perspective on mental health. *Psychological Bulletin, 103*, 193–210.

Taylor, S. E., & Brown, J. D. (1994). Positive illusions and well-being revisited: separating fact from fiction. *Psychological Bulletin, 116*, 21–27.

Taylor, S. E., Kemeny, M. E., Reed, G. M., Bower, J. E., & Grunewald, T. L. (2000). Psychological resources, positive illusions, and health. *American Psychologist, 55*, 99–109.

Taylor, S. E., Lerner, J. S., Sherman, D. K., Sage, R. M., & McDowell, N. K. (2003). Portrait of the self-enhancer: Well-adjusted and Well-liked or Maladjusted and Friendless? *Journal of Personality and Social Psychology, 84*, 165–176.

Tedeschi, J. T., & Bond, M. H. (2001). Aversive behavior and aggression in cross-cultural perspective. In R. Kowalski (Ed.), *Behaving badly: Aversive behaviors in interpersonal relationships* (pp. 257–293). Washington, DC: American Psychological Association.

Tedeschi, J. T., & Riess, M. (1981). Identities, the phenomenal self, and laboratory research. In J. T. Tedeschi (Ed.), *Impression management theory and social psychological research* (pp. 3–22). New York: Academic Press.

Tehrani, J., & Collard, M. (2009). The evolution of cultural diversity among Iranian tribal populations. In S. Shennan (Ed.), *Pattern and process in cultural evolution.* Berkeley, CA: University of California Press.

Terracciano, A., Abdel-Khalek, A.M., Adam, N., Adamovova, L., Ahn, C.K., Ahn, H.,N., Alansari, B.M., Alcalay, L., Allik, J., Angleitner, A., Avia, M.D., Ayearst, L.E., Barbaranelli, C., Beer, A., et al. (2005). National character does not reflect mean personality trait levels in 49 cultures. *Science,* 310, 96–100.

Tesser, A. (1988). Toward a self-evaluation maintenance model of social behavior. In L. Berkowitz (Ed.), *Advances in experimental socials psychology* (Vol. 21, pp. 181–227). New York: Academic Press.

Tesser, A., Campbell, J., & Smith, M. (1984). Friendship choice and performance: Self-evaluation maintenance in children. *Journal of Personality and Social Psychology, 46*, 561–574.

Thill, E. E., & Curry, F. (2000). Learning to play golf under different goal conditions: Their effects on irrelevant thoughts and subsequent control strategies. *European Journal of Social Psychology, 30*, 101–122.

Thomas, D. C., Au, K., & Ravlin, E.C. (2003). Cultural variations and the psychological contract. *Journal of Organizational Behavior, 24*, 451–471.

Thomas, D. C., & Toyne, D. (1995). Subordinates' responses to cultural adaptation by Japanese expatriate managers. *Journal of Business Research, 32*, 1–10.

Thomas, J. (1988). The role played by metalinguistic awareness in second or third language learning. *Journal of Multilingual and Multicultural Development, 9,* 235–247.

Thoresen, C. (1999). Spirituality and health. *Journal of Health Psychology, 4,* 291–434 (Special Issue).

Thurstone, L. L. (1938). *Primary mental abilities.* Chicago: Chicago University Press.

Timimi, S. (2004). A critique of the international consensus statement on ADHD. *Clinical child and family Psychology Review, 7*(1), 59–63.

Ting-Toomey, S. (1999). *Communicating across cultures.* New York: The Guilford Press.

Tobin, J. J., Wu, D. Y. H., & Davidson, D. H. (1989). *Preschool in three cultures: Japan, China, and the United States.* New Haven, CT: Yale University Press.

Tolson, T. F., & Wilson, M. N. (1990). The impact of two- and three-generational Black family structure on perceived family climate. *Child Development, 61,* 416–428.

Tomasello, M., Kruger, A. C., & Ratner, H. H. (1993). Cultural learning. *Behavioral and Brain Sciences, 16,* 495–552.

Toneatto, T. (2002). Cognitive therapy for problem gambling. Cognitive and Behavioral Practice, 9, 191– 199.

Tracy, J. L., & Robins, R. W. (2004). Show your pride: Evidence for discrete emotion expression. *Psychological Science, 15,* 104–197.

Trafimov, D., Triandis, H. C., & Goto, S. G. (1991). Some tests of the distinction between the private self and the collective self. *Journal of Personality and Social Psychology, 60*(5), 649–655.

Triandis, H. C. (1989). The self and social behavior in differing cultural contexts. *Psychological Review, 96,* 506–520.

Triandis, H. C. (1994). *Culture and Social Behavior.* New York: McGraw-Hill.

Triandis, H. C. (1995). *Individualism and collectivism.* Boulder, CO: Westview Press.

Triandis, H.C. (1996). The psychological measurement of cultural syndromes. *American Psychologist, 51*(4), 407–415.

Triandis, H. C. (2000). Dialectics between cultural and cross-cultural psychology. *Asian Journal of Social Psychology, 3* (3), 185–195.

Triandis, H. C., Bontempo, R., Vllareal, M. J., Asai, M., & Lucca, N. (1988). Individualism and collectivism: Cross-cultural perspectives on self-ingroup relationships. *Journal of Personality and Social Psychology, 54*(2), 323–338.

Triandis, H. C., & Gelfand, M. (1998). Convergent measurement of horizontal and vertical individualism and collectivism. *Journal of Personality and Social Psychology, 74,* 118–128.

Trope, Y. (1983). Self-assessment in achievement behavior. In J. M. Suls & A. G. Creenwald (Eds.), *Psychological Perspectives on the self* (Vol. 2, pp. 93–122). Hillsdale, NJ: Erlbaum.

Trotter, R. T., & Chavira, J. A. (1997). *Curanderismo: Mexican American folk healing.* Athens, GA: The University of Georgia Press.

Trudgill, P. (1974). Linguistic change and diffusion: Description and explanation in sociolinguistic dialect geography. *Language Society, 3,* 215–246.

Trull T. J., & Prinstein, M. J. (2013). *Clinical psychology.* Wadsworth, Cengage Learning.

Tsai, J. L., & Levenson, R. W. (1997). Cultural influences of emotional responding: Chinese American and European American dating couples during interpersonal conflict. *Journal of Cross-Cultural Psychology, 28,* 600–625.

Tseng, W. S. (Ed.). (2001). *Handbook of cultural psychiatry.* San Diego, CA: Academic Press.

Tweed, R. G., & Lehman, D. R. (2002). Learning considered within cultural context: Confucian and Socratic approaches. *American Psychologist, 57,* 89–99.

Twenge, J. M. (2002). Birth cohort, Social change, and personality: The interplay of dysphoria and individualism in the 20th century. In D. Cervone & W. Mischel (Eds.), *Advances in personality science* (pp. 196–218). New York: Guildford Press.

Twenge, J. M., Catanese, K. R., & Baumeister, R. F. (2003). Social exclusion and the deconstructed state: Time perception, meaninglessness, lethargy, lack of emotion, and self-awareness. *Journal of Personality and Social Psychology, 85,* 409–423.

Uchida, Y., Norasakkunkit, V., & Kitayama, S. (2004). Cultural constructions of happiness: Theory and empirical evidence. *Journal of Happiness Studies, 5,* 223–239.

Uehara, E. S., Takeuchi, D. T., & Smukler, M. (1994). Effects of combining disparate groups in the analysis of ethnic differences: Variations among Asian American mental health service consumers in level of community functioning. *American Journal of Community Psychology, 22*(1), 83–99.

Ueno, A., Ueno, Y., & Tomonaga, M. (2004). Facial responses to four basic tastes I newborn rhesus macaques (Macaca mulatta) and Chimpanzees (pan troglodytes). *Behavioral Brain Research, 154,* 261–271.

Ulusahin, A., Basoglu, M., & Paykel, E. S. (1994). A cross-cultural comparative study of depressive symptoms in British and Turkish clinical samples. *Social Psychiatry and Psychiatric Epidemiology, 29,* 31–39.

UNDP. (2007/2008). *Human development report—Fighting climate change: Human solidarity in a divided world.* New York, NY: Palgrave Macmillian for United Nations Development Program.

UNFPA (United Nations Population Fund). (2000). The state of world population 2000. Retrieved from: http://www.unfpa.org/public/cache/offonce/home/publications/pid/3453, Last access April 16, 2012.

UNICEF. (1996). *The state of the world's children.* Oxford: Oxford University Press.

United Nations Statistics Division. (2011). *Statistics and indicators on women and men.* Table 5f: Women legislators and managers. Retrieved from: http://unstats.un.org/unsd/demographic/products/indwm/, Last access April 16, 2012.

United States Census Bureau. (2009). *Latino or Hispanic by race.* Washington, DC

Updegraff, J. A., Gable, S. L., & Taylor, S. E. (2004). What makes experiences satisfying? The interaction of dispositional motivations and emotion in cognitive well-being. *Journal of Personality and Social Psychology, 86,* 496–504.

U.S. Department of State. (2008). *Trafficking in person's report 2008.* Retrieved from: http://www.state.gov/j/tip/rls/tiprpt/2008/, Last access April 16, 2012.

Van Boven, L., & Gilovich, T. (2003). To do or to have? The is the question. *Journal of Personality and Social Psychology, 85,* 1193–1202.

Van Coetsem, F. (2000). *A general and unified theory of the transmission process in language contact.* New York: Carl Winter.

Van de Vijver, F. J. R. (1997). Meta-analysis of cross-cultural comparisons of cognitive test performance. *Journal of Cross-Cultural Psychology, 28,* 678–709.

Van de Vijver, F. J. R., & Hambleton, R.K. (1996). Translating tests: Some practical guidelines. *European Psychologist, 1*(2), 89–99.

Van de Vijver, F. R. J., & Leung, K. (1997a). Methods and data analysis of comparative research. In J. W.Berry, Y. H. Poortinga, & Pandey (Eds.), *Handbook of cross-cultural psychology: Theory and method* (Vol. 1, pp. 257–300). Boston, MA: Allyn and Bacon.

Van de Vijver, F. R. J. & Leung, K. (1997b). *Methods and data analysis for cross-cultural research.* Newbury Park, CA: Sage.

Van de Vijver, F. R. J., & Poortinga, Y. H. (1997). Towards an integrated analysis of bias in cross-cultural assessment. *European Journal of Psychological Assessment, 13,* 21–29.

Van de Vijver, F. J. R., & Tanaka-Matsumi, J. (2008). Cross-cultural research methods. In D. McKay (Ed.), *Handbook of research methods in abnormal and clinical psychology* (pp. 463–481). Thousand Oaks, CA: Sage.

Van de Vijver, F., & Willemsen, M. (1993). Abstract thinking. N J. Altarriba (Ed.), *Cognition and culture: A cross-cultural approach to cognitive psychology* (pp. 31–342). Amsterdam: Elsevier Science.

Van de Vliert, E. (2006). Autocratic leadership around the globe: Do climate and wealth drive leadership culture. *Journal of Cross-Cultural Psychology, 37,* 42–59.

Van de Vliert, E., Kluwer, E. S., & Lynn, R. (2000). Citizens of warmer countries are more competitive and poorer: Culture or chance? *Journal of Economic Psychology, 21,* 143–165.

Van der Veer, K., Ommundsen, R., Krumov, K., Van Le, H., & Larsen, K. S. (2007). Scale development to measure attitudes toward unauthorized migration into a foreign country. In K. Krumov & K. S. Larsen (Eds.), *Migration: Current issues and problems* (pp. 127–139). Sofia, Sofi-R.

Van der Veer, K., Ommundsen, R., Larsen, K. S., Van Le, H., Krumov, K., Pernice. E. & Romans, G. P. (2004). The structure of attitudes toward illegal immigration: the development of cross-national scales. *Psychological Reports, 94,* 897–906.

Van der Werff, J. J. (1985). Heymans' temperamental dimensions in personality research. *Journal of Research in Personality, 19*(3), 279–287.

Van Haaften, E. H., & Van de Vijver, F. J. R. (1999). Dealing with extreme environmental degradation: Stress and marginalization of Sahel dwellers. *Social Psychiatry and Psychiatric Epidemiology, 34,* 376–382.

Van Herk, H., Poortinga, Y., H., & Verhallen, T. M. M. (2004). Response styles in rating scales: Evidence of methods bias in data from six EU countries. *Journal of Cross-Cultural Psychology, 35,* 346–360.

Van Ijzendoorn, M. H., & Kroonenberg, P. M. (1988). Cross-cultural patterns of attachment: A meta-analysis of the strange situation. *Child Development, 59,* 147–156.

Van Muijen, J. J., Koopman, P. L., & De Witte, K. (1996). *Focus on organizational culture.* Schoonhoven: Academic Service.

VanPool T. L., & VanPool C. S. (2003). Agency and evolution: the role of intended and unintended consequences of action. In VanPool T. L., & VanPool C. S. (Eds.). *Essential tensions in archaeological method and theory* (pp. 89–114). Salt Lake City, UT: University of Utah Press.

Van Wyhe, J. (2005). The descent of words: Evolutionary thinking 1780–1880. *Endeavour, 29,* 94–100.

Varela, R. E., Vernberg, E., Sanchez-Sosa, J., Riveros, A., Mitchell, M., & Mashunkashey, J. (2004). Parenting style of Mexican, Mexican American, and Caucasian-Non-Hispanic families: Social context and cultural influences. *Journal of Family Psychology, 18*(4), 651–657.

Veenhoven, R. (1995). The cross-national pattern of happiness. Test of predictions implied in three theories of happiness. *Social Indicators Research, 34,* 33–68.

Veenhoven, R. (2005). Apparent quality of life in nations: How long and happy people live. *Social Indicators Research, 71,* 1, 61–86.

Veenhoven, R. (2011). *World Database of Happiness, Structure of the collections.* Erasmus University, Rotterdam. Retrieved September 12, 2011). Retrieved from: http://worlddatabaseofhappiness.eur.nl Last access April 12, 2012.

Vereijken, C., Riksen-Walraven, J. M., & Van Lieshout, C. (1997). Mother-infant relationships in Japan: Attachment, dependency, and amae. *Journal of Cross-Cultural Psychology, 28*(4), 442–462.

Verkuyten, M. (2005). *The social psychology of ethnic identity.* Hove, UK: Psychology Press.

Verkuyten, M. (2008). Life satisfaction among ethnic minorities: The role of discrimination and group identification. *Social Indicators Research, 89*(3), 391–404. DOI 10.1007/s11205-008-9239-2.

Verkuyten, M., & Pouliasi, K. (2006). Biculturalism and group identification: The mediating role of identification in cultural frame-switching. *Journal of Cross-Cultural Psychology, 37,* 312–326.

Vernon, P. E. (1969). *Intelligence and cultural environment.* Norwood, NJ: Ablex.

Villalba, J. A. (2007). Health disparities among Latina/ o adolescents in urban and rural schools: Educators' perspectives. *Journal of Cultural Diversity, 14,* 169–175.

Vogel, F., & Motulsky, A. G. (1979). *Human genetics: Problems and approaches.* Berlin: Springer-Verlag.

Vohs, K. D., & Heatherton, T. F. (2000), Self-regulatory failure: A resource-depletion approach. *Psychological Science, 11,* 249–254.

Vonk, R. (2002). Self-serving interpretations of flattery: why ingratiation works. *Journal of Personality and Social Psychology, 82,* 515–526.

Vorster, J., & Schuring, G. (1989). Language and thought: Developmental perspectives on counterfactual conditionals. *South Africa Journal of Psychology, 19,* 34–38.

Vygotsky, L. S. (1978). *Mind in Society.* Cambridge MA: Harvard University Press.

Vygotsky, L. S. (1930/1997). *The collected works of L. S. Vygotsky: The history of the development of higher mental functions* (R. W. Rieber, Ed., Vol. 4), New York: Plenum Press.

Waber, D. P., Vuori-Christiansen, L., Ortiz, N., Clement, J. R., Christiansen, N. E., Mora, J. O., Reed, R. B., & Herrera, M. (1981). Nutritional supplementation, maternal education and cognitive development of infants at risk of malnutrition. *American Journal of Clinical Nutrition, 34,* 807–813.

Wagner, D. A. (1977). Ontogeny of the ponzo illusion: Effects of age, schooling and environment. *International Journal of Psychology, 12,* 161–176.

Wagner, D. A. (1978). Memories of Morocco: The influence of age, schooling and environment on memory. *Cognitive Psychology, 10,* 1–28.

Wagner, D. A. (1993). *Literacy, culture and development: Becoming literate in Morocco.* New York: Cambridge University Press.

Wallace, B. A., & Shapiro, S. L. (2006). Mental balance and well-being: Building bridges between Buddhism and Western Psychology. *American Psychologist, 61,* 690–701.

Walumbwa, F. O., & Lawler, J. J. (2003). Building effective organizations: Transformational leadership, collectivist orientation, work-related attitudes and withdrawal behaviors in three emerging economies. *International Journal of Human Resource Management, 14,* 1083–1101.

Wang, X., & Kanungo, R. N. (2004). Nationality, social network and psychological well-being: Expatriates in China. *International Journal of Human Resource Management, 15,* 775–793.

Warneken, F., & Tomasello, M. (2006). Altruistic helping in human infants and young chimpanzees. *Science, 311,* 1301–1303.

Wassmann, J., & Dasen, P. R. (1994). "Hot" and "cold": Classification and sorting among the Yupno of Papua New Guinea. *International Journal of Psychology, 29,* 19–38.

Watson, D. (1989). Stranger's ratings of the five robust personality factors: Evidence for a surprising convergence with self-report. *Journal of Personality and Social Psychology, 57,* 120–128.

Watson, O. M. (1970). *Proxemic behavior: A cross-cultural study.* The Hague, Netherlands: Mouton.

Watson, O. M., & Graves, T. D. (1966). Quantitative research in proxemic behavior. *American Anthropologist, 68,* 971–985.

Weatherly, K. A., & Beach, L. R. (1998). Organizational culture and decision-making. In L. R. Beach (Ed.), *Image theory: Theoretical and empirical foundations* (pp. 211–225). Mahwah, NJ: Erlbaum.

Weber, U., & Hsee, C. K. (2000). Culture and individual decision-making. *Applied Psychology: An International Review, 49,* 32–61.

Wegela, K. (2009). *The courage to be present: Buddhism, psychotherapy, and the awakening of natural wisdom.* Boston: Shambhala.

Wegner, D. M. (2002). *The illusions of conscious will.* Cambridge, MA: MIT Press.

Weisner, T. S., & Gallimore, R. (1977). My brother's keeper: Child and sibling caretaking. *Current Anthropology 18,* 169–190.

Weissman, M. M., Bland, R. C., Canino, G. J., Faravelli, C., Greenwald, S.M, Hwu, H. G., Joyce, P. R., Karam, E. G., Lee, C. K., Lellouch, J., Lepine, J. P., Newman, S. C., Rubin-Stiper, M., Wells, J. E., Wickramaratne, P. J. Wittchen, H., & Yeh, E. K. (1996). Cross-national epidemiology of major depression and bipolar disorder. *Journal of the American Medical Association, 276,* 293–299.

Weissman M., & Olfson M. (1995). Depression in women: Implications for health care research. *Science, 269,* 799–801.

Weisz, J., Suwanlert, S., Chaiyasit, W., Walter, B. (1987). Over- and undercontrolled referral problems among children and adolescents from Thailand and the United States. *Journal of Counsulting and Clinical Psychology, 55,* 719–726.

Welles-Nystrom, B. *(2005)*. Co-sleeping as a window into Swedish culture: Considerations of gender and health care. *Scandinavian Journal of caring Sciences, 19*(4), 354–360.

Wetherick, N. E., & Deregowski, J. B. (1982). Immediate recall: Its structure in three different language communities. *Journal of Cross-Cultural Psychology, 13*(2), 210–216.

Wexley, K. N. & Yukl, G. A. (1984). *Organizational behaviour and personnel psychology.* Homewood, Il.: Irwin.

Wheeler, L., & Kim, Y. (1997). What is beautiful is culturally good: The physical attractiveness stereotype has different content in collectivistic cultures. *Personality and Social Psychology Bulletin, 23*(8), 795–800.

Whitehorn, J., Ayonrinde, O., & Maingay, S. (2002). Female genital mutilation: Cultural and psychological implications. *Sexual and Relationship Therapy, 17*(2), 161–173.

Whiten, A., Horner, V., & De Waal, F. B. M. (2005) Conformity to cultural norms of tool use in chimpanzee. *Nature, 437,* 737–740.

Whiting, J. W. M., & Child, I. (1953). *Child training and personality.* New Haven. CT: Yale University Press.

Whorf, B. L. (1956). *Language, thought, and reality: Selected writing of Benjamin Lee Whorf.* J. Carroll (Ed.), Cambridge, MA: MIT Press.

Widmer, E. D., Treas, J., & Newcomb, R. (1998). Attitudes toward nonmarital sex in 24 countries. *The Journal of Sex Research, 35,* 349–351.

Wierzbicka, A. (1999). *Emotions across languages and cultures: Diversity and universals.* Cambridge: Cambridge University Press.

Wikipedia. (2011). *Sociocultural evolution.* Retrieved from: http://schools-wikipedia. org/wp/s/Sociocultural_evolution.htm Last assess April 22, 2012.

Wilkinson, R. (1996). *Unhealthy societies: The affliction of inequality.* London: Routledge.

Williams, J. E., & Best, D. L. (1990a). *Measuring sex stereotypes: A multination study.* Newbury Park,CA: Sage

Williams, J. E., & Best, D. L. (1990b). *Sex and psyche: Gender and self viewed cross-culturally.* Newbury Park, CA:Sage.

Williams, J. E., Satterwhite, R. C., & Best, D. L. (1999). Pancultural gender stereotypes revisited: The five factor model. *Sex Roles, 40*(7/8), 513–525.

Williams, K. D., Harkins, S. G., & Karau, S. J. (2003). Social performance. In M. A. Hogg & J. Cooper (Eds.), Sage *Handbook of Social Psychology* (pp. 327–346). Thousand Oaks, CA: Sage.

Wilson, A. E., & Ross, M. (2000). The frequency of temporal-self and social comparisons in people's personal appraisals. *Journal of Personality and Social Psychology, 78,* 928–942.

Wilson, E. O. (1975). *Sociobiology: The new synthesis.* Cambridge, MA: Belknap Press of Harvard University Press.

Wilson, S. (2007). "When you have children you are obliged to live": Motherhood, chronic illness and biographical disruption. *Sociology of Health and Illness, 29,* 610–626.

Wilson, T. D. (2002). *Strangers to ourselves: Discovering the adaptive unconscious.* Cambridge, MA.: Harvard University Press.

Winford, D. (2003). *An introduction to contact linguistics.* Oxford: Blackwell.

Winford, D. (2005). Contact-induced changes: Classifications and processes. *Diachronica, 22*(2), 373–427.

Wink, P. (1991). Two faces of narcissism. *Journal of Personality and Social Psychology, 61*, 590–597.

Wintre, M. G., North, C., & Sugar, L. A. (2001). Psychologists' response to criticism about research based on undergraduate participants: A developmental perspective. *Canadian Psychology, 42*, 216–225.

Wisman, A., & Koole, S. L. (2003). Hiding in the crowd: Can mortality salience promote affiliation with others who oppose one's worldviews? *Journal of Personality and Social Psychology, 84*(3), 511–526.

Witkin, H., & Berry, J. W. (1975). Psychological differentiation in cross-cultural perspective. *Journal of Cross-Cultural Psychology, 6*, 4–87.

Witkin, H. A., Dyk, R. B., Patterson, H. F., Goodenough, D. R., & Karp, S. A. (1962). *Psychological differentiation.* New York: John Wiley.

Witkin, H. A., Goodenough, D. R., & Oltman, P. (1979). Psychological differentiation: Current stats. *Journal of Personality and Social Psychology, 37*, 1127–1145.

Woike, B., Gershkovich, I., Piorkowski, R., & Polo, M. (1999). The role of motives in the content and structure of autobiographical memory. *Journal of Personality and Social Psychology, 85*, 566–580.

Wood, J. V. (1989). Theory and research concerning social comparisons of personal attributes. *Psychological Bulletin, 106*, 231–248.

Wood, J. V., Heimpel, S. A., & Michela, J. L. (2003). Savoring versus dampening: Self-esteem differences in regulating positive affect. *Journal of Personality and Social Psychology, 85*, 566–580.

World Health Organization. (1979). *Schizophrenia: An international follow-up study.* New York: John Wiley and Sons.

World Health Organization. (2003). *Diet, nutrition, and the prevention of chronic disease.* Retrieved from: http://www.who.int/dietphysicalactivity/publications/trs916/en/. Last access April 22, 2012.

World Health Organization. (2012). *Gender and women's mental health.* Retrieved from: http://www.who.int/mental_health/prevention/genderwomen/en/. Last access April 22, 2012.

Wright, G. N. (1985). Organizational, group and individual decision making in cross-cultural perspective. In G. N. Wright (Ed.), *Behavioral decision making* (pp. 149–165). New York: Plenum

Wright, G. N., & Phillips, L. D. (1980). Cultural variation in probabilistic thinking: Alternative ways of dealing with uncertainty. *International Journal of Psychology, 15*, 239–257.

Wright, G. N., Philips, L. D., & Wisudha, A. (1983). Cultural comparison on decision making under uncertainty. In J. B. Deregowski, S. Dziurawiec, & R. C. Annis (Eds.), *Expositions in cross-cultural psychology* (pp. 387–402). Lisse, Netherlands: Swets & Zeitlinger.

Wrosch, C., Scheier, M. F., Miller, G. E., Schulz, R., & Carver, C. S. (2003). Adaptive self-regulation of unattainable goals: Goal disengagement, goal reengagement, and subjective well-being. *Personality and Social Psychology Bulletin, 29*, 1494–1508.

Wrzesniewski, A., Dutton, J. F., Debebe, G. (2003). Interpersonal sense making and the meaning of work. *Research in Organizational Behavior, 25*, 93–135.

Wynne-Edwards, V. C. (1962). *Animal dispersion in relation to social behavior.* Edinburgh, UK: Oliver and Boyd.

Xiang, P., Lee, A., & Solomon, M. (1997). Achievement goals, and their correlates among American and Chinese students in physical education: A cross-cultural analysis. *Journal of Cross-Cultural Psychology, 28*(6), 645–660.

Xing, Y., Shi, S., Le, L., Lee, C. A., Silver-Morse, L., & Li, W. X. (2007). Evidence for transgenerational transmission of epigenetic tumor susceptibility in Drosophila. *Public Library of Science Genetics, 3*(9), 151.doi:10.1371/journal.pgen.0030151

Xinyue, Z., Saucier, G., Gao, D. & Liu, J. (2009). The factor structure of Chinese personality terms. *Journal of Personality, 77*, 363–400.

Yamagishi, T. (1986). The provision of a sanctioning system as a public good. *Journal of Personality and Social Psychology, 51*(1), 110–116.

Yamagishi, T. (1988). The provision of a sanctioning system in the United States and Japan. *Social Psychology Quarterly, 51*(3), 265–271.

Yang, K. S. (1999). Towards an indigenous Chinese psychology: A selective review of methodological, theoretical, and empirical accomplishments. *Chinese Journal of Psychology, 41*, 181–211.

Yang, K. S. (2000). Monocultural and cross-cultural indigenous approaches: The royal road to the development of a balanced global psychology. *Asian Journal of Social Psychology, 3*, 241–263.

Yang, K. S., & Bond, M. H. (1990). Exploring implicit personality theories with indigenous or imported constructs: The Chinese case. *Journal of Personality and Social Psychology, 58*, 1087–1095.

Yang, S., & Sternberg, R. J. (1997). Conceptions of intelligence in ancient Chinese philosophy. *Journal of Theoretical and Philosophical Psychology, 17*, 101–119.

Yaroshevski, V. (1996). *A history of psychology.* Moscow: Prosveshenie.

Yates, J. F., Lee, J. W., & Shinotsuka, H. (1996). Beliefs about overconfidence, including its cross national variations. *Organizational Behavior and Human Decision Processes, 65*(2), 138–147.

Yeh, C., Hunter, C. D., Madan-Bahel, A., Chiang, L., & Arora, A. K. (2004). Indigenous and interdependent perspectives of healing: Implications for counseling and research. *Journal of Counseling & Development, 82*(4), 410–419.

Yeh, M., McCabe, K., Hough, R. L., Lau, A., Fakhry, F., & Garland, A. (2005). Why bother with beliefs? Examining relationships between race/ethnicity, parental beliefs about causes of child's problems, and mental health service use. *Journal of Consulting and Clinical Psychology, 73*, 800–807.

Yehuda, R., Bierer, L. M., Schmeidler, J., Aferiat, D. H., Breslau, I., & Dolan, S. (2000). Low cortisol and risk for PTSD in adult offspring of holocaust survivors. *Journal of American Psychiatry, 157*, 1252–1259.

Yehuda, R., Mulherin, E. S., Brand, S. R., Seckl, J., Markus, S. M., & Berkowitz, G. S. (2005). Transgenerational effects of posttraumatic stress disorder in babies of mothers exposed to the World Trade Center attacks during pregnancy. *Journal of Clinical Endocrinology and Metabolism, 90*, 4115–4118.

Yik, M. S., Bond, M. H., & Paulhus, D. L. (1998). Do Chinese self-enhance or self-efface? It's a matter of domain. *Personality and Social Psychology Bulletin, 24,* 399–406.

Ying, Y.-W., Lee, P. A., Tsai, J. L., Yeh, Y-Y, & Huang, J. S. (2000). The conception of depression in Chinese American College students. *Cultural Diversity & Ethnic Minority Psychology, 6*(2), 183–195.

Zakaria, F. (2011). *Transcript of Interview by President Hamid Karzai with CNN*—By CNN, December 18th, Retrieved from: http://www.gmic.gov.af/english/index.php/interviews/252-transcript-of-interview-by-president-hamid-karzai-with-cnn–by-cnn-, Last access April 22, 2012.

Zane, N., & Mak, W. (2003). Major approaches to the measurement of acculturation among ethnic minority populations: A content analysis and an alternative empirical strategy. In K. M. Chun, P.B. Organista, & G. Marín (Eds.), *Acculturation: Advances in theory, measurement, and applied research* (pp. 39–60). Washington, DC: American Psychological Association.

Zhang, Y. (2006). *Zen and psychotherapy.* Victoria, BC (Canada): Trafford.

Zillmann, D. (1978). Attribution and misattribution of excitatory reactions. In J. H. Harvey, W. J. Ickes, & R.F. Kidd (Eds.), *New directions in attribution research* (Vol. 2, pp. 335–368). Hillsdale, NJ.: Lawrence-Erlbaum Associates.

Zuckerman, M. (1990). Some dubious premises in research and theory on racial differences: Scientific, social, and ethical issues. *American Psychologist, 45*(12), 1297–1303. doi:10.1037/0003-066X.45.12.1297

Zuckerman, M. (1996). The psychobiological model for impulsive unsocialized sensation seeking.: A comparative Approach. *Neuropsychobiology, 34,* 125–129.

Zwolinski, J. (2011). Happiness around the world. In K. D. Keith (Ed.), *Cross-Cultural Psychology.* Malden, MA: Blackwell-Wiley.